Parallel Computation: Models And Methods

Selim G. Akl

Queen's University
Kingston, Ontario, Canada

Prentice Hall, Upper Saddle River, New Jersey 07458

Library of Congress Cataloging-in-Publication Data

Akl, Selim G.
  Parallel computation : models and methods / Selim G. Akl.
      p.   cm.
  Includes bibliographical references and index.
  ISBN 0-13-147034-5
  1. Parallel processing (Electronic computers) I. Title.
QA76.58.A48 1997   96-42310
004'.35--dc20   CIP

Publisher: Alan Apt
Acquisitions Editor: Laura Steele
Production Editor: Joseph Scordato
Director Prod. & Mfg.: David Riccardi
Production Manager: Bayani Mendoza DeLeon
Cover Designer: Bruce Kenselaar
Copy Editor: Brian Baker
Buyer: Donna Sullivan
Editorial Assistant: Toni D. Chavez

©1997 by Prentice-Hall, Inc.
Simon & Schuster/A Viacom Company
Upper Saddle River, NJ 07458

The author and publisher of this book have used their best efforts in preparing this book. These efforts include the development, research, and testing of the theories and programs to determine their effectiveness. The author and publisher make no warranty of any kind, expressed or implied, with regard to these programs or the documentation contained in this book. The author and publisher shall not be liable in any event for incidental or consequential damages in connection with, or arising out of, the furnishing, performance, or use of these programs.

Printed in the United States of America

10 9 8 7 6 5 4 3 2 1

ISBN 0-13-147034-5

Prentice-Hall International (UK) Limited, London
Prentice-Hall of Australia Pty. Limited, Sydney
Prentice-Hall Canada Inc., Toronto
Prentice-Hall Hispanoamericana, S.A., Mexico
Prentice-Hall of India Private Limited, New Delhi
Prentice-Hall of Japan, Inc., Tokyo
Simon & Schuster Asia Pte. Ltd., Singapore
Editora Prentice-Hall do Brasil, Ltda., Rio de Janeiro

To Sophia, Theo, and Joseph
Who do all things in parallel

Contents

Preface

Motivation

Two reasons are usually given for studying parallel computation:

1. *Sequential computers*—i.e., computers that perform one operation at a time—
   are quickly reaching a physical limit beyond which the speed at which they
   process data cannot be increased through the use of faster components. This
   limit is imposed by the speed of light in a vacuum. On the other hand, in a
   great many computational problems, the time taken to obtain a solution using
   a sequential computer is unacceptably slow. These problems arise in such
   diverse fields as weather forecasting, biomedical analysis, speech recognition,
   and the management of huge knowledge bases. One way out of this impasse is
   provided by parallel computation. On a *parallel computer*, several processors
   cooperate to solve a problem simultaneously in a fraction of the time required
   by one processor. This idea, of course, is not new; it has been around for
   thousands of years, occurring naturally every time a large job needs to be
   done. But, in computer science, it is an idea whose time has come, thanks to
   the declining cost and size of computers.

2. A second, less often cited, reason for using parallel computers is that they
   sometimes allow problems to be solved that are otherwise impossible to tackle
   sequentially, regardless of how much time one is willing to wait for an answer.
   These problems occur, for example, in applications in which the number of
   data or their values are functions of time, intermediate results affect future
   inputs, the input consists of multiple streams, or the effect of a computation
   cannot be reversed. In these and many other situations, it is not so much
   the speed of a parallel computer that matters. Rather, it is the ability of a
   parallel computer to be "in more than one place at one time," owing to its
   many processors, that guarantees a successful completion of the computation.

These are two perfectly good reasons—and indeed, they provide sufficient jus-
tification, at least from a practical point of view—to investigate the concept of
parallel computation. There is, however, a third, equally compelling, reason for

a computer scientist to be interested in parallel computation: Conceptually, using several processors that work together on a given computation represents a totally new paradigm in computer problem solving. It is a complete departure from the sequential approach that has dominated the field of computer science since its inception. As such, it provides fresh theoretical insights into most computational problems, regardless of their origin or complexity. It offers novel techniques for the design and analysis of algorithms. In fact, its most profound consequence has been to allow a far better understanding of the nature of computation than previously thought possible.

All these considerations provided the motivation for writing this book.

Parallel Computation

Among the key ingredients necessary for parallel computation are the architecture (or hardware) and the operating system, language, and compiler (or software). Most important of all, however, are the *parallel algorithms* (or parallel solution methods), without which no problem can be solved in parallel. In the same way that algorithms occupy a central place in computer science, parallel algorithms are at the heart of parallel computation. Given a problem to be solved in parallel, a parallel algorithm defines how the problem can be solved on the given parallel computer—that is, how the problem is divided into subproblems, how the processors communicate, and how the partial solutions are combined to produce the final answer. An understanding of the role of parallel algorithms and a good knowledge of the techniques of designing and analyzing them are essential to anyone entering the field of parallel computation. They provide a firm foundation for all subareas of the field.

One cannot speak meaningfully of a parallel algorithm without mentioning the associated *model of parallel computation* for which the algorithm was designed. This is because, unlike the case in sequential computation, where the overwhelming majority of computers belong to one model of computation, a wide variety of models has been proposed and used to study parallel computation in theory and to build parallel computers in practice. These models differ according to whether the processors communicate among themselves through a shared memory or an interconnection network, whether the interconnection is in the form of an array, a tree, or a hypercube, whether the processors execute the same or different algorithms, whether the processors operate synchronously or asynchronously, and so on. The obvious reason for this diversity is that no single model has established itself as the preferred model for designing parallel computers. A more subtle reason is that no universal parallel computer is likely or even desirable: For each application, there is a preferred parallel computer that best fits its needs. Whatever the reason, the diversity sets parallel computation apart as a rich and exciting field for practitioners and researchers alike. As a result of their activity, a large body of knowledge has been developed which has undoubtedly improved our appreciation of parallel computation in general and parallel algorithms in particular.

Models and Methods

The literature on parallel computation generally uses one of the following two main approaches to classify parallel algorithms:

1. *The model approach:* The existence of many models of parallel computation has naturally prompted parallel algorithms to be proposed for each of these models. Each algorithm solves a particular problem on one particular model. In the *model approach*, parallel algorithms are classified and presented according to the model for which they were designed.

2. *The problem approach:* Parallel algorithms have been proposed and implemented to solve a host of computational problems. Some of these problems are fundamental to computer science (e.g., sorting and searching), while others arise in many different application areas (from operations research to artificial intelligence). Some problems are numerical (e.g., computing matrices and solving partial differential equations), while others are nonnumerical (e.g., graph-theoretic and combinatorial problems). In the *problem approach*, parallel algorithms are grouped and described according to the problem or family of problems they are destined to solve.

A third alternative is chosen in this book, namely, the *models-and-methods approach*. Here, the various *models* that characterize and distinguish parallel computation are presented as subjects worthy of study in their own right. These include combinational circuits, interconnection networks, and shared memory machines, as well as models that use buses. The multitude of different algorithms that these models generate attest to their great potential as sources of ideas for problem solving. At the same time, there is an explicit emphasis on general *methods* for designing parallel algorithms. These methods include prefix computation, list ranking, divide and conquer, split and plan, matrix multiplication, and broadcasting with selective reduction, among many others. A wide variety of computational problems is used to illustrate and contrast the models and methods. Examples of such problems are sorting, searching, numerical problems, and combinatorial problems, as well as problems in graph theory and computational geometry.

Audience

It is predicted that before long, parallel computers of different sizes and forms will be pervasive in our society. A new breed of computer architects, programmers, and algorithm designers will be needed to conceive, build, program, operate, and, above all, develop algorithms for these computers. In universities, most departments of computer science will soon have undergraduate and graduate courses on parallel computation in their curricula.

This book is aimed at the senior undergraduate and first-year graduate levels. It should also be useful to practicing computer scientists and engineers, as well as researchers in the field. Some knowledge of design and analysis techniques for sequential algorithms is helpful, but not necessary. The text provides many references in which such background is amply covered. Relatively advanced material is contained in sections whose headings are identified with a ($\star$). This material can be skipped on a first reading or in an undergraduate course.

Acknowledgments

The contributions of two people to this book deserve special mention. Sandy Pavel prepared the electronic version for all the figures, skillfully and enthusiastically. I am grateful to him for giving his time and talent so generously. I am also indebted to Tanya Wolff for her careful reading of an early draft. Her numerous comments helped improve the quality of the work.

The book has benefited substantially from the extensive and detailed suggestions provided by Professor Johnnie W. Baker of Kent State University (Ohio) and Professor Ivan Stojmenović of the University of Ottawa (Ontario). It is a privilege to have had them as my reviewers.

John Jorgensen and Peter Taillon offered technical advice that is greatly appreciated. Credit is also due to my publisher, Prentice Hall, for creating the opportunity to write this book and to the staff at Prentice Hall, which, as always, was helpful and supportive at every stage.

Finally, I wish to thank the members of my family—my wife Karolina and my children Sophia, Theo, and Joseph—for their reliable and unconditional love and understanding, without which this book would still be a project.

Selim G. Akl
Kingston, Ontario

Chapter 1

Introduction

Among all the ideas spawned by computer science over the last 20 years, none has transformed the field so profoundly as has parallel computation. Virtually all aspects of computing were affected, and a wealth of new concepts was generated. From computer architecture to operating systems, from programming languages and compilers to databases and artificial intelligence, and from numerical to combinatorial computing, every branch of the discipline is undergoing a revival. In theoretical as well as in practical circles, a degree of activity and excitement is being experienced not witnessed since the dawn of the computing era. Understandably, the most dramatic effect was felt at the foundation of computer science, namely, *the design and analysis of algorithms*. Just when the traditional study of algorithms was reaching a certain degree of maturity and stability, with significant results few and far between, the parallel computation revolution took place. This rejuvenating jolt led to a renaissance of the field that is expected to continue unabated for a long time to come.

This book is about *parallel algorithms*. It shows how a parallel algorithm can be *designed* for a given computational problem to run on a *parallel computer* and then how it can be *analyzed* to determine its "goodness." In the process, it is hoped that the reader will develop and master a new way to think about and solve problems, and come to appreciate the beauty and effectiveness of parallel algorithms. In this first chapter, the basic notions of a parallel computer and a parallel algorithm are introduced. The main criteria used in evaluating parallel algorithms are also presented.

1.1 WHAT IS A PARALLEL COMPUTER?

In the late 1940s, a group of researchers at Princeton University proposed a design that ushered the modern computer era. Today, 50 years later, the overwhelming majority of computers in use follow, more or less faithfully, this original design in

1

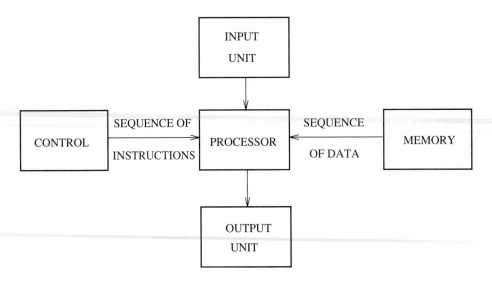

Figure 1.1: A sequential computer.

which a computer consists essentially of a single processing unit, or *processor*, that executes a single sequence of instructions on a single sequence of data, as shown in Fig. 1.1.

The sequence of instructions is the *program*, which tells the processor how to solve a certain *problem*. The sequence of data is an *instance* of that problem. At each step during the computation, the control unit emits one instruction that operates on a datum (such as a pair of numbers) obtained from the memory unit. For example, such an instruction may direct the processor to perform some arithmetic or logical operation on the datum and then put the result back into memory. Note that the processor has a small local memory, consisting of a constant number of fixed-size registers, to perform its computations. It is also connected to an input unit and an output unit in order to communicate with the outside world. Usually, other connections exist among the different units; they are not shown in Fig. 1.1, for simplicity. This model of computation is known as a *sequential* (or *serial*, or *conventional*) computer.

In a *parallel computer*, by contrast, there are several processors (two or more). Given a problem to be solved, it is broken into a number of subproblems. All of these subproblems are solved simultaneously, each on a different processor. In doing so, the processors may communicate with one another to exchange partial results. Finally, the results are combined to produce an answer to the original problem. This is a radical departure from the way the process of computation has been conducted over the past half century.

But how is a parallel computer organized? How are the processors to com-

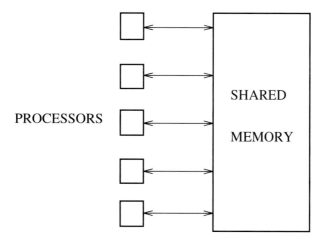

Figure 1.2: A shared-memory parallel computer.

municate? Do they execute the same or different programs? Are they to operate synchronously (i.e., in *lockstep* fashion) or asynchronously? Are their data the same or different? These (and many other) questions and their answers define the field of parallel computation. Unlike sequential computers, for which the questions have a unique answer by default, parallel computers admit a wide range of possible designs. Let us look at a few models of parallel computation.

Example 1.1 In Fig. 1.2, there are five processors connected to a single shared memory. The processors use this memory for their communication. Any pair of processors wishing to exchange data can do so through the shared memory: One processor writes its datum in a given memory location, which is then read by the other processor. When solving a computational problem, the program is the same for all processors, and each processor has enough local memory to store its own copy of the program. The processors operate synchronously, all executing the same instruction of the program simultaneously, each on a different datum. Every processor has an input and an output unit (not shown in the figure) to communicate with the outside world. This parallel computer is an example of a large class of computers whose processors share a common memory. In this chapter, we refer to the parallel computer described in this example (with an arbitrary number of processors larger than 1) as a *shared-memory parallel computer.* □

Example 1.2 In Fig. 1.3, there are seven processors connected in the shape of a complete binary tree. In such a tree, each processor has one parent and two children (except the root, which has no parent, and the leaves, which have no children). There is no shared memory. Instead, the memory is distributed among the processors, each getting an equal portion. The processors communicate through

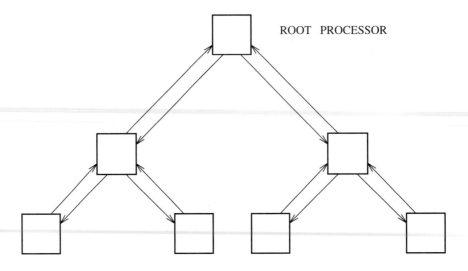

Figure 1.3: A binary tree of processors.

an interconnection network formed by the pair of oriented links connecting each child and its parent. Each processor stores its own copy of the same program. However, not all processors execute the same instruction at the same time: A processor is *active* only when it receives a datum from one or more of the other processors. Only the leaves and the root can communicate with the outside world. This parallel computer is an example of a larger class of computers whose processors are connected by an interconnection network. In this chapter, we refer to the parallel computer described in this example (with an arbitrary number of processors larger than 1) as a *binary tree of processors.* □

Example 1.3 In Fig. 1.4, there are 32 processors organized in four columns. There is no shared memory, and each processor has a very small local memory consisting of a constant number of fixed-size registers. The processors are connected by unidirectional links. Each processor receives input from a processor in the previous column and delivers its output to a processor in the next column. There is effectively no program to run the processors. In fact, all of the processors are hardwired to execute one of a small set of operations (such as comparison, addition, propagation, and so on) on their input (one or two values) and produce their output (one or two values). Exactly which operation is to be performed is determined by the computational problem to be solved. The processors in the leftmost column receive input from the outside world, while those in the rightmost column produce

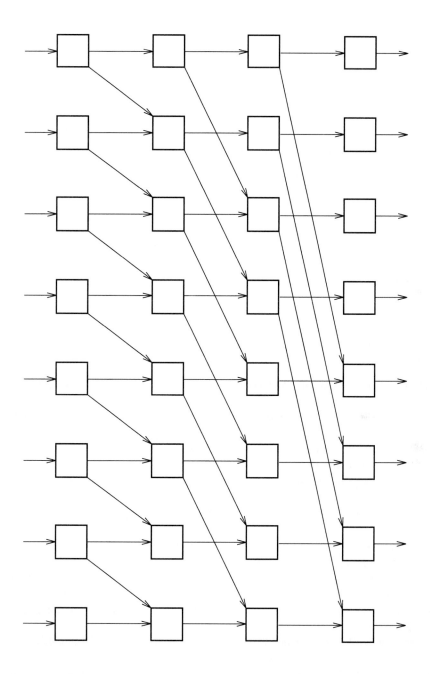

Figure 1.4: A combinational circuit.

the output. Data thus flow from left to right, and a processor is active only when it receives two inputs. While performing the computations required to solve a problem, no processor is used more than once. This parallel computer is representative of a large class of computers known as *combinational circuits.* □

We now turn to the question of how to use a parallel computer to solve a computational problem.

1.2 WHAT IS A PARALLEL ALGORITHM?

Designing algorithms is a fundamental aspect of computer science. Every branch of the field is concerned at some point or another with designing a method—that is, an *algorithm*, later translated into a *program*—to solve a problem. Algorithms for conventional computers are known as *sequential* or *serial* algorithms. They are familiar to anyone who has taken a first course in computing. Algorithms for parallel computers, or *parallel algorithms* (i.e., methods for solving computational problems on parallel computers) are perhaps less familiar. As in the previous section, some simple examples are helpful in introducing the concept.

First, in order to develop some intuition as to the nature of parallel algorithms, the reader may wish to pause at this point and consider the following computational problems. Suppose that a binary tree of processors is given. The tree has n leaves and hence $n-1$ nonleaves, for a total of $2n-1$ processors.

1. How can the sum of n numbers, stored one per leaf, be computed?

2. How can the smallest of n numbers, stored one per processor, be computed?

3. How can a number stored at the root be made known to all leaves?

4. Let $n-1$ of the leaves, chosen arbitrarily, contain one number each. How can these $n-1$ numbers be moved to the $n-1$ nonleaf processors, one number per processor?

5. If the leftmost $n/2$ leaves contain one number each, how can these numbers be moved to the rightmost $n/2$ leaves?

6. How many steps does each of the above computations require?

Having given these questions some thought, we are now ready to proceed with examples illustrating several basic ideas in the design and analysis of parallel algorithms. We use the notation $\{a_1, a_2, \ldots, a_n\}$, here and throughout the book, to represent a sequence of elements on which some order is defined such that a_1 is the first element of the sequence, a_2 the second, and a_n the last. This notation is also used to represent an array of data stored in memory. Occasionally, we use $a(1), a(2), \ldots, a(n)$ to represent an array when this notation is more convenient. Indexing begins at 0 instead of 1 wherever appropriate.

Example 1.4 A sequence of pairs $\{(x_1, d_1), (x_2, d_2), \ldots, (x_n, d_n)\}$ is given, where each x_i is an integer satisfying $0 \leq x_i \leq m-1$, each d_i is an arbitrary datum of fixed size, and $m < n$. Because of the last condition, several of the x_i will be equal. It is required to group all the pairs (x_i, d_i) whose x_i are equal into contiguous locations in memory. For instance, this computation may be the first step of an algorithm that sorts the sequence of pairs in nondecreasing order of the x_i. Since $0 \leq x_i < m$ for all i, we expect at most m groups to be formed. On a sequential computer, this problem requires at least n elementary steps to be solved, since that many steps are needed just to read the input.

Now consider a shared-memory parallel computer with n processors P_1, P_2, $\ldots$, P_n. A simple parallel algorithm proceeds as follows. The processors use $m \times (2n-1)$ memory locations of the shared memory. These are viewed (conceptually) as m complete binary trees T_0, T_1, $\ldots$, T_{m-1}, associated logically with the integers 0, 1, $\ldots$, $m - 1$, one tree per integer. Each virtual tree has n leaves, numbered 1 to n, and hence a total of $2n - 1$ nodes. Further, leaf i of tree T_j is associated with processor P_i for $j = 0, 1, \ldots, m - 1$. This is illustrated in Fig. 1.5, where each tree is shown lying on its side. The algorithm consists of two phases.

In the first phase, processor P_i reads (x_i, d_i) and writes it in leaf i of tree T_k, where $k = x_i$. In the second phase, processor P_i moves the pair (x_i, d_i) up the tree in which it was stored, until it can go no higher. This is done according to the following rule: If a node v is unoccupied, then the pair (if any) in v's right child takes precedence in moving to v over the pair (if any) in v's left child. The first phase of the algorithm requires one elementary step, the second $\log n$ elementary steps, since the distance from leaf to root in each of the binary trees is $\log n$. The algorithm therefore requires on the order of $\log n$ steps, which is significantly faster than any sequential solution. □

Note that in the above example the logarithm used is to the base 2. This is the case for all logarithms in this book, unless otherwise indicated. If it so happens that n is not a power of 2, then $\log n$ is always rounded to the next higher integer. The same is also true of all real quantities (such as those arising from computing ratios and square roots), which we will assume are rounded appropriately, unless otherwise stated. The following notation is used when we need to be specific about the direction of rounding: For a real number x, $\lfloor x \rfloor$ denotes the largest integer smaller than or equal to x (the "floor" of x), while $\lceil x \rceil$ denotes the smallest integer larger than or equal to x (the "ceiling" of x). Thus, $\lfloor 4.8 \rfloor = 4$, $\lceil 4.1 \rceil = 5$, and $\lfloor 4.0 \rfloor = \lceil 4.0 \rceil = 4$.

Example 1.5 Suppose that a database consisting of n records is stored in the leaves of a binary tree of processors. In this case the tree has n leaves, each holding one record of the form (k, d), where k is a *key* identifying the record and d is the *datum* held by the record. We assume that all the keys are distinct and that the records are stored in the leaves in no particular order.

A simple query of this database may take the following form: Retrieve the record

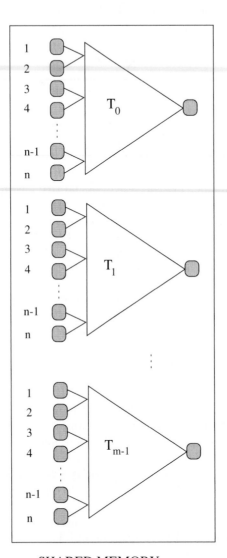

SHARED MEMORY

Figure 1.5: Binary trees of memory locations.

whose key equals K, if one such record exists. An answer to the query is obtained as follows: The root processor reads K and sends it to its two children. The latter send K to their children, and this continues until K reaches the leaves. Each leaf now compares K to the key it holds. If they are equal, the datum d held by the leaf is sent to the leaf's parent; otherwise, the leaf sends a *null* datum to its parent. A node thus receives two data from its children. If one of the two data is not *null,* the node sends it to its parent; otherwise *null* is sent. This continues upwards until either d or *null* emerges from the root. The answer to the query is thus obtained in $2 \log n$ elementary steps: It takes $\log n$ steps for K to go down from the root to the leaves and another $\log n$ steps for the answer to go back from the leaves to the root.

Suppose now that there are m such queries to be processed for keys K_1, K_2, ..., K_m. Once the root has sent K_1 to its two children, it can read K_2 and send it down. Meanwhile, the root's children, having sent K_1 down to their children, are now ready to receive K_2. This process, known as *pipelining,* continues all the way to the leaves. Once K_1 reaches the leaves, it is compared to the k held by each leaf, and a d or *null* is sent up. The leaves are now ready to receive K_2, which arrives in the next step. The answer to the first query reaches the root in $2 \log n$ steps, followed by the answer to K_2 in the next step, the answer to K_3 in the next step, and so on. All m queries are therefore answered in $2 \log n + (m - 1)$ elementary steps.

How many steps does the same problem require on a conventional computer? For a database of n records in no particular order, n steps are required to answer a query in the worst case. The number of elementary steps needed to process m queries is therefore $m \times n$ in the worst case, considerably more than on the parallel computer. $\square$

Example 1.6 We are given n numbers $x_0, x_1, \ldots, x_{n-1}$, where n is a power of 2. It is required to compute the following sums, known as the *initial* or *prefix* sums: $s_0 = x_0$, $s_1 = x_0 + x_1$, $s_2 = x_0 + x_1 + x_2$, ..., $s_{n-1} = x_0 + x_1 + \cdots + x_{n-1}$. A sequential algorithm to solve this problem reads one number at a time and executes $n - 1$ additions in sequence. The number of elementary steps required by the algorithm is therefore on the order of n.

In parallel, the problem can be solved much faster. The parallel algorithm consists of $\log n$ steps. Initially, $s_i = x_i$ for $i = 0, 1, \ldots, n - 1$. During the jth step, where $j = 0, 1, \ldots, (\log n) - 1$, the following operation is performed simultaneously for all i, $2^j \le i \le n - 1$:

$$s_i \leftarrow s_{i-2^j} + s_i.$$

In other words, during each step, two numbers are added whose indices are twice the distance in the previous step. For example, if $n = 8$, the sums computed during each step are as follows:

Sum	Step 0	Step 1	Step 2
s_0	x_0	x_0	x_0
s_1	$x_0 + x_1$	$x_0 + x_1$	$x_0 + x_1$
s_2	$x_1 + x_2$	$x_0 + x_1 + x_2$	$x_0 + x_1 + x_2$
s_3	$x_2 + x_3$	$x_0 + x_1 + x_2 + x_3$	$x_0 + x_1 + x_2 + x_3$
s_4	$x_3 + x_4$	$x_1 + x_2 + x_3 + x_4$	$x_0 + x_1 + x_2 + x_3 + x_4$
s_5	$x_4 + x_5$	$x_2 + x_3 + x_4 + x_5$	$x_0 + x_1 + x_2 + x_3 + x_4 + x_5$
s_6	$x_5 + x_6$	$x_3 + x_4 + x_5 + x_6$	$x_0 + x_1 + x_2 + x_3 + x_4 + x_5 + x_6$
s_7	$x_6 + x_7$	$x_4 + x_5 + x_6 + x_7$	$x_0 + x_1 + x_2 + x_3 + x_4 + x_5 + x_6 + x_7$

It is clear that after each step the number of final sums is twice that in the previous step. Now consider the combinational circuit of Example 1.3, with $1 + \log n$ columns of n processors each. Each processor in the first (i.e., leftmost) column receives one of the x_i as input and sends it to the processors in the second column to which it is connected. A processor in the second and subsequent columns either adds its two inputs and sends the result to the next column or propagates its single input. The last (i.e., rightmost) column produces the required sums. The parallel solution therefore takes $1 + \log n$ elementary steps, which is significantly fewer than the sequential one. $\square$

1.3   WHY PARALLEL COMPUTATION?

Parallel computers are used primarily to speed up computations. As illustrated by the examples in the previous section, a parallel algorithm can be significantly faster than the best possible sequential solution. This is true in the majority of computational problems. But are such fast solutions truly needed? Indeed, they are. There is a growing number of applications—for example, in science, engineering, business, and medicine—requiring computing speeds that cannot be delivered by any current or future conventional computer. These applications involve processing huge amounts of data, or performing a large number of iterations, or both, thus leading to inordinate running times. Parallel computation is the only approach known today that would make these computations feasible.

There is, however, a second, less well understood, reason for using parallel computers whose importance has been recently recognized. Consider the following situation:

Example 1.7 In a real-time application, a computer needs certain data from the outside world in order to solve a computational problem. It receives s independent data streams at the same time (sent by s sources). The data within each stream arrive at a rate that makes it impossible for a sequential computer (even one which operates at the speed of light!) to process more than one stream at a time. Furthermore, it is not feasible to store data arriving from the other $s - 1$ streams for later processing, as the data become meaningless if not used immediately. Suppose that precisely one stream contains data useful in solving the current instance of the computational problem, all other streams containing spurious data. The "good" stream is not known in advance and can only be recognized at the end of the computation—that is, when the data it contains leads to a solution.

Clearly, a sequential computer has a probability of $1/s$ of choosing the good data stream and hence succeeding in solving the problem. On the other hand, a parallel computer with s processors, each dedicated to monitoring one stream, always succeeds. □

The foregoing example is representative of a host of situations in which the probability of success in performing a computational task is increased through the use of a parallel computer. In some extreme cases, a parallel approach can make the difference between guaranteed success and guaranteed failure. In these situations, tackling a problem through parallel computation is not simply the *best* approach, but rather the *only* way to obtain a solution.

We have presented two principal motivations for computing in parallel. An exploration of their many aspects and implications for computing in general is the main theme of this book.

1.4 ANALYSIS OF PARALLEL ALGORITHMS

A number of criteria are commonly used in evaluating the goodness of an algorithm. The most important of these are the algorithm's running time, how many processors it uses, and the total number of steps it performs. A less widely used, but no less important, criterion is the algorithm's probability of success in completing the task, in those situations where such a criterion is meaningful. These four criteria and the techniques employed in measuring them and interpreting the results of such evaluations are referred to collectively as *algorithm analysis*.

A Bit of Notation. Deriving and expressing measures of an algorithm's behavior are greatly simplified if certain notations are used. We define two such notations: Let $f(n)$ and $g(n)$ be functions from the positive integers to the positive reals. Then

1. The function $g(n)$ is said to be *of order at least* $f(n)$, denoted $\Omega(f(n))$, if there are positive constants k and n_0 such that $g(n) \geq kf(n)$ for all $n \geq n_0$.

2. The function $g(n)$ is said to be *of order at most* $f(n)$, denoted $O(f(n))$, if there are positive constants k and n_0 such that $g(n) \leq kf(n)$ for all $n \geq n_0$.

Example 1.8 In Example 1.4, the number of elementary steps required by a sequential computer to solve the problem presented there is $\Omega(n)$—that is, at least $k_1 n$ for some positive constant k_1. On the other hand, it takes the parallel algorithm $O(\log n)$ elementary steps to obtain the solution—that is, at most $k_2 \log n$ for some positive constant k_2. □

The O and Ω notations simplify our analyses, as they allow us to focus primarily on the *order of growth* of the function under consideration. Thus, for example, if $g(n) = 7n^3 + 2n^2 + 5$, we write $g(n) = O(n^3)$, ignoring constants and lower order terms. In other words, we are mainly concerned with the behavior of a function $g(n)$ *in the limit*, as n grows without bound. This type of analysis is referred to as *asymptotic analysis*. We say that an algorithm which performs $O(n^2)$ elementary steps in solving a problem is *asymptotically* better than one which performs $O(n^3)$ such steps. In the special case where $g(n)$ is itself a constant, we write $g(n) = O(1)$.

What Is an Elementary Step?   In some of the preceding examples, we have used the total number of *elementary steps* performed by an algorithm (in the worst case) as a measure of the algorithm's speed. It is now appropriate to define this term. A parallel algorithm typically uses two kinds of elementary steps:

1. *Computational steps*: A computational step is a basic arithmetic or logical operation performed on one or two data within a processor. Examples include adding, comparing, and swapping two numbers.

2. *Routing steps*: A routing step is used by an algorithm to move a datum of constant size from one processor to another, via the shared memory or through the links connecting the processors.

In general, a computational step requires a constant number of *time units*, whereas a routing step depends on the distance between the processors. Exactly how long does a routing step take? The answer depends on whether the processors share a common memory (as in Example 1.4) or communicate via direct links (as in Examples 1.5 and 1.6).

We first consider the case where the processors communicate through a shared memory. If processor P_i wishes to send a datum d to processor P_j, it writes d in some memory location, which is then read by P_j. This involves two memory accesses. In *uniform analysis*, a memory access is assumed to require a constant number of time units, and consequently, so does a routing step. This assumption, though unrealistic, often simplifies the analysis and is most widely used. In *nonuniform* or *discriminating analysis*, by contrast, a memory access is assumed to require $O(\log M)$ time units, where M is the number of memory locations in the shared memory. This assumption is justified by the way memory access mechanisms are actually built, as explained in the next chapter. We use both assumptions in this book, each when appropriate. Thus, when discriminating between computational and routing steps does not affect the result, we use uniform analysis for the sake of simplicity. On the other hand, when such discrimination makes a difference, we opt for nonuniform analysis. Therefore, uniform analysis is assumed, unless otherwise stated.

Let us now turn to the case where processors communicate by sending data across the links joining them. If two processors P_i and P_j are directly connected by a link, then a routing step from P_i to P_j is assumed to take a constant number of time units. If, on the other hand, the two processors are not directly connected, then routing a datum from P_i to P_j requires a number of time units linear in the number of links on the shortest path from P_i to P_j. Thus, in Example 1.5, it takes a datum $O(\log n)$ time units to go from the root processor of the tree to a leaf processor.

1.4.1 Running Time

The *running time* of a parallel algorithm is defined as the time required by the algorithm to solve a computational problem. More precisely, it is the time elapsed between the moment the first processor on the parallel computer to begin operating on the input starts and the moment the last processor to end producing the output terminates. We are interested in the *worst case* running time—that is, the time needed by the algorithm when applied to the most difficult instance of the problem (the one which takes the most time to solve).

Running time is measured by counting the number of consecutive elementary steps performed by the algorithm (in the worst case), from the beginning to the end of the computation.

Example 1.9 Suppose that a parallel algorithm uses three processors P_1, P_2, and P_3 to perform a certain computation. The processors behave as follows: P_1 executes 10 steps, is then idle for 3 steps, and finally executes 5 more steps; P_2 executes 12 steps without interruption; P_3 executes 14 steps, is then idle for 4 steps, and finally executes 2 more steps. This algorithm therefore is said to have executed 20 steps. □

Since each step (computational or routing) is assumed to take a constant number of time units, the number of steps is a good theoretical estimate of the actual amount of time that the algorithm will take to solve the problem on a real parallel computer. The number of steps, and hence the running time, of a parallel algorithm is a function of the size of the input and the number of processors used. Moreover, the number of processors is often itself a function of the size of the input. Therefore, for a problem of size n, the worst case running time of a parallel algorithm is denoted by $t(n)$. Henceforth, when we say that an algorithm has a running time of $t(n)$, or takes $t(n)$ time, we mean that $t(n)$ is the number of time units required by the algorithm.

Example 1.10 In Example 1.4, $t(n) = O(\log n)$. □

In some cases, we denote by t_p the running time of an algorithm that uses p processors. This is particularly useful when comparing algorithms that solve the same problem with different numbers of processors. In these cases, the size n of the problem is usually omitted to simplify the notation.

Once the running time of an algorithm for a given problem has been derived, it is instructive to compare it to existing lower and upper bounds for the problem.

A *lower bound* on a certain problem gives the minimum number of steps required by an algorithm to solve the problem in the worst case. In parallel computation, a lower bound usually depends on the size and nature of the problem, the type of parallel computer used, and the number of processors involved.

Example 1.11 In Example 1.5, queries are received by the root of a binary tree of processors whose n leaves store the records of a database. Since there are $\log n$ links separating the root from the leaves, a lower bound on the running time required to process a query is $\Omega(\log n)$. □

An *upper bound*, on the other hand, is established by the best algorithm known to solve the problem—that is, the algorithm using the fewest number of steps in the worst case.

Example 1.12 No algorithm is known for processing queries on a binary tree of processors faster than the algorithm in Example 1.5. This algorithm therefore sets an upper bound of $O(\log n)$ for the database query problem on a binary tree of processors. □

When the upper and lower bounds for a problem coincide (up to a constant multiplicative factor), the algorithm setting the upper bound is said to be asymptotically *time optimal* for the problem, on that particular parallel computer. Otherwise, a faster algorithm may have to be found, or a lower bound of higher value needs to be derived.

Example 1.13 In light of the analysis in Examples 1.11 and 1.12, the algorithm in Example 1.5 is time optimal for the database query problem on a binary tree of processors. □

Speedup.   The primary reason for using parallel algorithms is to speed up sequential computations. It is therefore quite natural, as we did in Examples 1.4, 1.5, and 1.6, to compare the running time of a parallel algorithm designed for a certain problem to that of the best available sequential algorithm for the same problem. This is usually done by computing a ratio known as the *speedup*, defined as follows: Let t_1 denote the worst case running time of the fastest known sequential algorithm for the problem, and let t_p denote the worst case running time of the parallel algorithm using p processors. Then the speedup provided by the parallel algorithm is

$$S(1, p) = \frac{t_1}{t_p}.$$

A good parallel algorithm is one for which this ratio is large.

Example 1.14 Suppose that we wish to add n numbers stored in memory. On a sequential computer, a number can be read from memory and added to a running sum in one time unit. Therefore, the sum of the n numbers can be computed in n time units. This is optimal, since n accesses to memory and $n - 1$ additions are required.

On a binary tree of processors with $n/\log n$ leaves, and hence a total number of processors equal to $2(n/\log n) - 1$, the parallel algorithm consists of two phases. In the first phase, with all leaves operating in parallel, each leaf sequentially reads $\log n$ numbers from the input and computes their sum. This takes $\log n$ time units. In the second phase, partial results are sent up the tree: Each node receives two sums from its children, adds them, and sends the result to its parent. This continues until the final sum emerges from the root. The second phase takes $\log(n/\log n)$ time units. The time required by the algorithm is therefore $k_1 \log n$, for some constant k_1, where $1 < k_1 < 2$. A speedup of $k_2 n/\log n$ is therefore achieved by the algorithm, for some constant k_2, where $1/2 < k_2 < 1$. $\square$

In the preceding example, the speedup equals (up to a constant factor) the number of processors used. For many computational problems, this is the largest speedup possible; that is, the speedup is at most equal to the number of processors used by the parallel computer. Because this condition is satisfied by so many traditional problems, it has become part of the folklore of parallel computation and is usually formulated as a theorem:

> **Speedup Folklore Theorem:** For a given computational problem, the speedup provided by a parallel algorithm using p processors, over the fastest possible sequential algorithm for the problem, is at most equal to p; that is, $S(1, p) \leq p$. $\square$

The "proof" of this folklore theorem goes as follows: Let the fastest sequential algorithm for the problem require time t_1, and let the parallel algorithm require time t_p. Proceeding by contradiction, assume that $t_1/t_p > p$. Since any parallel algorithm can be simulated on a sequential computer by having the single processor execute the parallel steps serially, the simulation requires $p \times t_p$ time. Because $p \times t_p < t_1$ by assumption, the simulation yields a faster sequential algorithm, thus leading to a contradiction.

The speedup folklore theorem is true, and its "proof" holds, for the majority of *standard* problems in computer science. These problems typically obey very restrictive constraints on input, computation, and output. Examples of such problems are provided by operations on a list of numbers stored in memory, such as adding the numbers, searching for a particular number, sorting the numbers, and so on. In fact, for many of these problems, the speedup provided by a parallel algorithm using p processors is much smaller than p either

1. because the problem cannot be decomposed into an appropriate number of independent computations to be executed simultaneously, while keeping all processors sufficiently busy, or

2. because the structure of the parallel computer used imposes restrictions that render the desired running time unattainable. Specifically, the communications required among the processors within a given model of computation may unduly delay the completion of the task.

Example 1.15 Given a sequence of n distinct numbers $\{s_1, s_2, \ldots, s_n\}$, sorted in increasing order, it is required to search the list for a particular number x. Sequentially, this problem can be solved using a binary search in $k \log n$ time, for some positive constant k, and this is optimal.

A parallel algorithm using n processors $P_1, P_2, \ldots, P_n$ solves this problem on a shared-memory parallel computer as follows: First, a special memory location, *answer*, is initialized to 0; this can be done by one processor—for instance, P_1. Then, all processors read x simultaneously. Now P_i compares x to s_i, in parallel for all i, $1 \leq i \leq n$. At most one processor—for instance, P_k—finds a match and writes its index k in *answer*, thus indicating that $s_k = x$. If *answer* is still equal to 0 at the end of the execution of the algorithm, then the search was unsuccessful. Each step takes a constant amount of time, leading to an $O(1)$ overall running time for the parallel solution.

The speedup here is $O(\log n)$, which is significantly smaller than n, the number of processors used by the parallel algorithm. In fact, it is clear in this case that, in order to achieve a speedup equal to the number of processors, a parallel algorithm is needed whose running time multiplied by the number of processors it uses is $k \log n$. Here, k is the positive constant appearing in the running time of a binary search. For instance, if $\log n$ processors could solve the problem in k time units, then the speedup would be $\log n$. In reality, no such algorithm exists. □

Example 1.16 Suppose that the search problem of Example 1.15 is to be solved on a binary tree of processors with n leaves $P_1, P_2, \ldots, P_n$, where P_i holds s_i, for $1 \leq i \leq n$. The number x for which the search is to be conducted is received by the root, and the result of the search for x among $s_1, s_2, \ldots, s_n$ is also to be returned by the root. These conditions impose a lower bound of $\Omega(\log n)$ on any parallel algorithm for solving the search problem on this model. Indeed, there are $\log n$ links separating the root from each leaf, and these links must somehow be traversed. Therefore, the speedup here is at best $O(1)$, which is asymptotically smaller than the number of processors used, namely, $2n - 1$. □

For many nontraditional problems, however, the speedup folklore theorem does not hold. In other words, there are situations in which a speedup larger than the number of processors used can be obtained. In order to see this, we must look beyond the narrow perspective provided by conventional computations. There is evidence today that the *nature of computing* is changing and must be viewed in a context much broader than before. With increasing frequency, computers are being asked to process data in applications not conceived of until recently, wherein they interact with their environment, affect it, and often move about it freely and autonomously. In these situations, computation can no longer be regarded solely as the process of evaluating a function of a given input, the traditional definition. For example, it may be the case that each input arrives in real time or varies with time, or it may be that each output affects the next input or has to meet a certain deadline. In these conditions, it is obvious that the speedup folklore theorem fails simply because it no longer makes sense. The following example is representative of many real-time applications in which a parallel algorithm using p processors is more than p times faster than the best possible sequential algorithm.

Example 1.17 Consider n independent streams of data arriving as input at a computer. Each stream contains a distinct cyclic permutation of the values in a sequence $S = \{s_1, s_2, \ldots, s_n\}$. Thus, for $n = 3$, the three input streams may be $< s_1, s_2, s_3 >$, $< s_2, s_3, s_1 >$, and $< s_3, s_1, s_2 >$. In addition, each two consecutive values in a stream are separated by n time units. A single processor can monitor the values in only one stream: By the time the processor reads and stores the first value of a selected stream, it is too late to turn and process the remaining $n - 1$ values from the other streams, which arrived at the same time. Furthermore, a stream remains active if and only if its first value has been read and stored by a processor.

This situation can occur when n sensors are used to make certain measurements from an environment. Each s_i is measured in turn by a different sensor and relayed to the computer. It takes n time units to make a measurement. There are at least two reasons why several sensors are used to make the same set of measurements (in different orders):

1. To increase the chances that the measurements will be made, even if some sensors break down.

2. To exploit parallelism, as explained next.

Suppose that we need to compute the smallest value in S. If the computer is a conventional one, its single processor selects a stream and reads the consecutive values it receives, keeping track of the smallest encountered so far. Assume that in one time unit a processor can read a value, compare it to the smallest so far, and update the latter if necessary. It therefore takes n time units to process the n inputs, plus $n(n - 1)$ time units of waiting time in between consecutive inputs. Therefore, after exactly n^2 time units, the minimum value is known.

On the other hand, suppose that the computer is a binary tree of processors with n leaves, each connected to a stream. As soon as the first n values arrive at the leaves, with each leaf receiving one value from a different stream, computation of the minimum can commence. Each leaf reads its input value and sends it to its parent. The latter finds the smaller of the two values received from its children and sends it to its parent. This continues up the tree, and after $\log n$ time units, the minimum emerges from the root. (Once the computation is completed successfully, the root can send a message to the leaves, if so required, to stop reading the input.

The message reaches the leaves in another $\log n$ steps—that is, before the next set of inputs arrives.) The speedup is therefore $n^2/\log n$, which is asymptotically larger than $2n - 1$, the number of processors used on the parallel computer. $\square$

It should be noted here that the choice of the binary tree of processors in the foregoing example is strictly for the purpose of illustration: The structure of the tree plays no role whatsoever in contradicting the speedup folklore theorem. The same (or even a larger) speedup could be obtained using other parallel computers (e.g., a shared-memory parallel computer).

Slowdown.   Another concept that is useful in studying the running time of parallel algorithms is what we call *slowdown* (by contrast with speedup). Slowdown measures the effect on running time of reducing the number of processors on a parallel computer. Naturally, one would expect the running time of an algorithm to increase as the number of processors decreases. The question is, how much slower is a parallel algorithm solving a problem with fewer processors? The traditional answer to this question has given rise to a second folklore theorem:

> **Slowdown Folklore Theorem:** If a certain computation can be performed with p processors in time t_p and with q processors in time t_q, where $q < p$, then $t_p \leq t_q \leq t_p + pt_p/q$. $\square$

The slowdown folklore theorem essentially puts an upper bound on the running time of the machine with fewer processors. It says that the running time of the machine with p processors increases at worst by a factor of $1+p/q$ when the number of processors is reduced to q. The "proof" of this theorem is as follows: Let W_i denote the number of elementary steps performed simultaneously during the ith time unit by the p-processor algorithm such that

$$\sum_{i=1}^{t_p} W_i = W.$$

In other words, W is the total number of elementary steps performed collectively by the p processors to complete the computation in time t_p. Since not all p processors are necessarily busy all the time, it follows that $W \leq pt_p$. On a smaller computer with only q processors, we can simulate the ith time unit of the p-processor algorithm by distributing the W_i elementary steps among the q processors, so that each executes $\lceil W_i/q \rceil$ such steps. The simulation of the entire algorithm requires t_q time units, where

$$t_q \leq \sum_{i=1}^{t_p} \lceil \frac{W_i}{q} \rceil = \sum_{i=1}^{t_p} \left(\lfloor \frac{W_i}{q} \rfloor + 1 \right) \leq t_p + \lfloor \frac{W}{q} \rfloor \leq t_p + \frac{pt_p}{q}.$$

This completes the "proof."

As with the speedup folklore theorem, evidence from standard computations supports the slowdown folklore theorem: For most conventional problems, the theorem holds.

Example 1.18 Assume that p processors on a shared-memory parallel computer are given the task of adding two $n \times n$ matrices $\boldsymbol{A}$ and $\boldsymbol{B}$, stored in the shared memory. The result is to be placed in a third $n \times n$ matrix $\boldsymbol{C}$, also in shared memory. Each processor can be assigned to adding two corresponding submatrices of size n^2/p each. The job is completed in $O(n^2/p)$ time.

Suppose now that only $p^{2/3}$ processors are available. Then the same algorithm can be used, except that in this case each of the $p^{2/3}$ processors present does the job of $p^{1/3}$ of the previous processors. The computation now requires a factor of $p^{1/3}$ longer—that is, $O(n^2/p^{2/3})$ time—as predicted by the slowdown folklore theorem. $\square$

On the other hand, there are situations in which the slowdown folklore theorem does not apply. In other words, there are problems for which t_q is considerably larger than $t_p + pt_p/q$. For example, when the distribution of the input data or the communication of partial results among the processors in the smaller machine imposes a significant overhead on the running time, clearly, the upper bound on t_q is violated.

There are, however, situations in which the theorem does not hold due to the *inherently parallel* nature of the problem itself, regardless of implementation considerations. If fewer than a certain number of processors are present, then the algorithm's running time can be arbitrarily bad. Thus, for these problems, t_q is larger than any constant multiple of pt_p/q. The following example illustrates some characteristics of such problems.

Example 1.19 In Example 1.17, a binary tree of processors with n leaves solved the problem in $\log n$ time. Let a tree with $n^{1/2}$ leaves (and hence a total of $2n^{1/2} - 1$ processors) be available instead. By the slowdown folklore theorem, they should be able to complete the computation in at most $\log n + (2n - 1)\log n/(2n^{1/2} - 1)$—that is, $O(n^{1/2} \log n)$—time. As can be easily seen, there is no way for this to be achieved. At best, assuming that the order of arrival of data on each stream is known ahead of time, we can assign the $n^{1/2}$ processors to monitor $n^{1/2}$ streams whose first $n^{1/2}$ values are distinct from one another. As before, the algorithm consists of two phases. Since consecutive data in each stream are separated by n time units, it takes each processor $(n^{1/2} - 1)n$ time in the first phase to see the first $n^{1/2}$ values in its stream and determine their minimum. During the second phase, the minima climb the tree, and the result is obtained in $\log n^{1/2}$—that is, $O(\log n)$—time. Clearly, the time required by the first phase alone suffices to contradict the slowdown folklore theorem, since $(n^{1/2} - 1)n$ is asymptotically larger than $n^{1/2} \log n$. $\square$

As stated earlier, the binary tree of processors was selected simply to make the point; the specific structure of this parallel computer is immaterial in the failure of the theorem. Any other parallel computer would have the same first phase (as in Example 1.19), during which the theorem is violated.

1.4.2   Number of Processors

Another criterion for measuring the performance of a parallel algorithm is the number of processors it uses. There are several reasons for our interest in including this number in our analysis. Some of these are outlined as follows:

1. Given two parallel algorithms for solving a problem with different processor requirements, the one using fewer processors (and hence, the less expensive one) is preferred, everything else—in particular, the running time and the type of parallel computer used—being equal.

2. If an analysis reveals that two parallel algorithms for solving a problem require the same number of processors, then this suggests that another criterion (such as running time, type of computer used, and so on) needs to be found in order to distinguish between the algorithms.

3. In some cases, an optimal time, or a certain speedup, may be achieved only with a given number of processors.

4. It may be that the slowdown of a parallel algorithm is too severe if the number of processors drops below a certain value.

5. If a lower bound exists on the total number of steps required to solve a problem, then choosing a certain number of processors puts a lower bound on the running time of any parallel algorithm for the problem.

6. A minimum number of processors may be required to guarantee the success of a computation.

7. By trying to keep all of its processors continuously busy while solving a problem, a parallel computer may require a longer running time (and hence execute more steps) than if it had used fewer processors.

8. An analysis may reveal that a number of the processors used by an algorithm are idle most of the time and can be discarded, while maintaining the same performance.

9. The structure of the parallel computer for which an algorithm is destined may not accommodate the number of processors required by the algorithm (e.g., if the parallel computer always consists of a number of processors that is a perfect square or a power of 2).

10. In a combinational circuit, each processor is used at most once. The number of processors is therefore an upper bound on the total number of operations performed by the circuit.

For a problem of size n, if the number of processors required by an algorithm is a function of n, then it is denoted by $p(n)$. We use p to indicate a number of processors independent of n, the size of the input.

Example 1.20 In Example 1.4 $p(n) = n$, while in Example 1.5 $p(n) = 2n - 1$, and in Example 1.6 $p(n) = n(1 + \log n)$. Note that in Example 1.18, the number of processors p is not directly a function of the size of the input, except for the fact that $p \leq n^2$. $\square$

1.4.3 Cost

Suppose that a parallel algorithm runs in time $t(n)$ in the worst case and uses $p(n)$ processors to solve a problem of size n. An upper bound on the total number of elementary steps executed by this algorithm is given by its cost $c(n)$, which is defined as $c(n) = p(n) \times t(n)$. In other words, the cost of a parallel algorithm is equal to the product of its running time and the number of processors it uses. We say that the cost is an upper bound on the number of steps, since it may be the case that not all $p(n)$ processors are active throughout the $t(n)$ time units (as observed in Section 1.4.1). If they are, then of course, $c(n)$ equals the total number of steps executed.

Sometimes the total number of steps performed by the processors of a parallel algorithm can be obtained exactly. This is known as the *work* of the parallel algorithm and is equal to the sum of the steps executed individually by the various processors.

Example 1.21 In Fig. 1.6, the work is shown as the shaded area and is equal to 33 steps. The cost, on the other hand, is the area of the rectangle $ABCD$ and is equal to 48 steps. $\square$

Note that in the special case of combinational circuits, an alternative definition of cost may be employed. Since each processor is used at most once, an upper bound on the number of steps—that is, the cost—is the number of processors in the circuit.

Cost Optimality. We now show how the cost of a parallel algorithm can be used to assess the performance of the algorithm. Consider first those problems to which the speedup folklore theorem applies. In other words, we restrict our attention to those problems for which a p-processor parallel algorithm running in time t_p can be simulated on a sequential computer in time $p \times t_p$.

1. Assume that a lower bound of $\Omega(f(n))$ is known on the number of steps required in the worst case to solve one such problem of size n. If the cost of

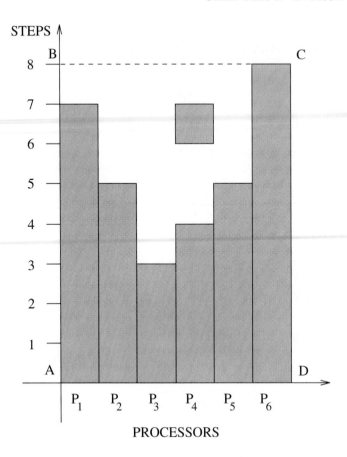

Figure 1.6: Work versus cost.

a parallel algorithm for that problem is $O(f(n))$, then the algorithm is said to be asymptotically *cost optimal.* This is due to the fact that the parallel algorithm can be simulated on a sequential computer. If the total number of steps executed during the simulation matches the lower bound (to within a constant multiplicative factor), then when it comes to *cost*, this parallel algorithm cannot be improved upon: It executes the minimum number of steps possible. One can, of course, *use more processors* in order to *reduce the running time* of a cost-optimal parallel algorithm. Alternatively, one can use *fewer processors*, while retaining cost optimality, if the resulting *higher running time* is acceptable.

Example 1.22 In Example 1.14, a binary tree of processors is used to add n numbers. We have $p(n) = O(n/\log n)$, $t(n) = O(\log n)$, and hence, $c(n) =$

$O(n)$. Since $\Omega(n)$ is a lower bound on the number of steps required to solve this problem, the algorithm is cost optimal. $\square$

The foregoing discussion leads to an approach for deriving general lower bounds on parallel algorithms—that is, lower bounds which are independent of the type of parallel computer used. Let $\Omega(f(n))$ be a lower bound on the number of steps required to solve a problem of size n. Then $\Omega(f(n)/p)$ is a lower bound on the running time of any parallel algorithm which uses p processors to solve that problem.

Example 1.23 Since $\Omega(n \log n)$ comparisons are needed to sort n numbers in the worst case, any comparison-based parallel algorithm that uses n processors for sorting must require $\Omega(\log n)$ time. $\square$

2. A parallel algorithm is *not cost optimal* if a sequential algorithm exists for solving the same problem, whose worst case running time is smaller than the parallel algorithm's cost. (Note that this is true regardless of whether the speedup folklore theorem holds or not.)

Example 1.24 In Example 1.4, n processors are used to distribute n integers into m groups in $O(\log n)$ time, for a cost of $O(n \log n)$. The algorithm presented there is therefore not cost optimal, since the same problem can be solved by a sequential algorithm in $O(n)$ time. Such an algorithm uses m linked lists, one for each group, and completes its job in one pass over the input. Note that the sequential algorithm uses a total of n memory locations for the linked lists, as opposed to the $O(nm)$ memory locations used by the parallel algorithm. $\square$

3. Sometimes it is not known whether a parallel algorithm is cost optimal. Let the cost of a parallel algorithm for a given problem match the running time of the fastest existing sequential algorithm for the same problem. Furthermore, assume that it is not known whether the sequential algorithm is time optimal. In this case, the status of the parallel algorithm with respect to cost optimality is unknown.

Example 1.25 A lower bound on the number of steps required to multiply two $n \times n$ matrices is $\Omega(n^2)$. This is easy to see, since that many steps are needed simply to produce the result matrix as output. The best available sequential algorithm for multiplying two $n \times n$ matrices runs in $O(n^\epsilon)$ time, where $2 < \epsilon < 2.38$. It is not known whether this algorithm is optimal. Suppose now that a parallel algorithm for the same problem exists whose cost is $O(n^\epsilon)$. Then this algorithm's cost optimality would be an open question. $\square$

Efficiency.   A simple way to measure the goodness of a parallel algorithm's cost is to compute a quantity called the *efficiency*. Let t_1 be the worst case running time of the fastest known sequential algorithm for a given problem. Similarly, let t_p be the worst case running time of a p-processor parallel algorithm for the same problem. Then the latter algorithm has a cost of pt_p, and its efficiency is

$$E(1, p) = \frac{t_1}{pt_p}.$$

For the problems under consideration—that is, those for which the speedup folklore theorem holds—efficiency is usually at most equal to 1:

1. If $E(1, p) < 1$, then the parallel algorithm is not cost optimal.

2. If $E(1, p) = 1$, then the parallel algorithm is cost optimal, provided that the sequential algorithm is time optimal.

3. If $E(1, p) > 1$, then a faster sequential algorithm can be obtained by simulating the parallel one.

Note that if a sequential algorithm is discovered which is faster than the one used to compute $E(1, p)$, then this quantity must be recomputed for all parallel algorithms for the same problem. Suppose that this faster sequential algorithm is obtained by simulating a parallel algorithm. In this special case, the recomputed $E(1, p)$ is 1 for the parallel algorithm that was simulated. However, the latter is cost optimal only if the sequential algorithm that it yields is time optimal. When $t_1/pt_p = O(1)$, we take $E(1, p)$ as equal to 1, for simplicity.

Example 1.26 Each of the three situations just described is now illustrated.

1. Suppose that a parallel algorithm searches a sorted list of n numbers for a given number, using p processors, where $p < n$, and has a running time of $O(\log n/\log p)$. Sequentially, the problem can be solved in $O(\log n)$ time. The parallel algorithm's efficiency is $O(\log n)/(p \times O(\log n/\log p))$, which is smaller than 1. This parallel algorithm is therefore not cost optimal.

2. Let a parallel algorithm sort n numbers using n processors in $O(\log n)$ time. This algorithm has a cost of $O(n \log n)$. Since the same problem is solved optimally on a sequential computer in $O(n \log n)$ time, the parallel algorithm has an efficiency of 1 and is hence cost optimal.

3. A parallel algorithm for multiplying two $n \times n$ matrices using n processors in $O(n)$ time would have a cost of $O(n^2)$. As mentioned in Example 1.25, the best existing sequential algorithm for the problem has a running time of $O(n^\epsilon)$, where $2 < \epsilon < 2.38$. Consequently, the parallel algorithm would have an efficiency larger than 1 and would hence lead to a faster (in fact, optimal) sequential algorithm. □

Let us now turn to those problems to which the speedup folklore theorem does not apply. For such problems, a parallel algorithm using p processors and running in time t_p yields a speedup larger than p over the best possible sequential algorithm running in time t_1; that is, $t_1/t_p > p$. The cost of a parallel algorithm for these problems is pt_p, and its efficiency equals t_1/pt_p, which is larger than 1. However, by contrast with the previous class of problems, here an efficiency greater than 1 does not lead to a faster sequential algorithm. This is because simulation of the parallel algorithm on a sequential computer is either meaningless or impossible (let alone the fact that the sequential algorithm whose running time is used to compute the efficiency is already the best possible!).

Example 1.27 The parallel algorithm of Example 1.17 runs in $\log n$ time and uses $2n - 1$ processors. The best possible sequential algorithm requires n^2 time. The efficiency of the parallel algorithm is $n^2/((2n - 1) \log n)$, which is larger than 1. There is, however, no way for a sequential computer to simulate the parallel algorithm. $\square$

1.4.4 Success Ratio

Our final criterion for evaluating a parallel algorithm pertains to those circumstances in which an algorithm succeeds in solving a problem with a certain probability. Let $Pr(1)$ and $Pr(p)$ be the probabilities of success of two algorithms using one processor and p processors, respectively. The *success ratio* is defined as

$$sr(1, p) = \frac{Pr(p)}{Pr(1)}.$$

We can also define a *scaled success ratio* as

$$ssr(1, p) = \frac{Pr(p)}{Pr(1)} \times \frac{1}{p}.$$

For standard problems involving an aspect of success or failure, the success ratio is at most p, and the scaled success ratio is at most 1. (These bounds are reminiscent of the same bounds placed on speedup and efficiency for problems obeying the speedup folklore theorem.)

Example 1.28 In Example 1.7, $Pr(1) = 1/s$ and $Pr(s) = 1$. Thus, $sr(1, s) = s$ and $ssr(1, s) = 1$. $\square$

There are numerous situations, however, in which the foregoing bounds do not hold. In those cases, a success ratio larger than p (and hence, a scaled success ratio larger than 1) can be obtained. The following simple example is representative:

Example 1.29 A certain job has a deadline of D. One processor finishes the job at time $D' > D$ and hence fails to meet the deadline. By contrast, p processors complete the job at time $D'/p < D$ and therefore succeed. In this case, $sr(1, p) = Pr(p)/Pr(1) = 1/0 = \infty$. $\square$

The notion of success or failure is relevant to some of the most important computational tasks, namely, those which are called upon to respond to their environment in a timely manner. As it seems certain that parallel computation will be increasingly called upon to perform such tasks, the metric of success ratio will likewise grow in importance.

1.5   ORGANIZATION OF THE BOOK

The remainder of the book is divided into 11 chapters. Our guiding philosophy in organizing the material throughout is based on the twin themes of *models of computation* and *methods of problem solving.* We begin in Chapter 2 by presenting the most widely used models of parallel computation, emphasizing the shared-memory, interconnection network, and combinational circuit models. Algorithms for solving problems in parallel on most of these models are described in subsequent chapters. Chapter 3 is devoted to a study of the combinational circuit model. Circuits that perform such diverse computations as sorting, taking Fourier transforms, permuting data, and computing prefix sums are presented.

The next three chapters expose fundamental methods for designing algorithms for a shared-memory model of parallel computation known as the *parallel random access machine* (PRAM). Thus, Chapter 4 demonstrates the importance to parallel algorithms of efficient computation of prefixes. Applications ranging from operations on arrays and sequences to the solution of combinatorial and geometric problems are illustrated. In Chapter 5, the well-known method of divide and conquer is applied to the parallel solution of various computational problems, including searching, merging, selection, and computing convex hulls. Parallel algorithms for problems defined on pointer-based data structures, from linked lists and trees to graphs in general, are developed in Chapter 6.

Our focus in the next three chapters is on interconnection network parallel computers, such as the *linear array*, the *mesh*, and the *hypercube.* It is shown how certain fundamental computational problems are solved on these models. The problems include convolution on a linear array (Chapter 7), sorting on a mesh (Chapter 8), and matrix multiplication on a hypercube (Chapter 9).

The final three chapters explore advanced models, methods, and paradigms. In Chapter 10, we examine the possibility of extending certain interconnection network parallel computers (particularly, the linear array and the mesh) with a new communication medium known as a *bus.* Different forms of buses and two environments for implementing them (namely, electronic and optical) are studied. Chapter 11 offers effective ways for exploiting the network connecting processors to memory locations in shared-memory machines. What results is a model, called *broadcasting with selective reduction* (BSR), that combines computational power and mathematical elegance. The BSR model, while more powerful than the PRAM, requires no more basic components asymptotically than the latter. In Chapter 12, new paradigms for parallel computation are described for which the folklore theorems do not hold.

Specifically, examples of computations are presented achieving a speedup that is larger than the number of processors used. Each chapter concludes with a set of problems and a number of bibliographical remarks. Sections whose headings are labeled with a $(\star)$ contain relatively advanced material and can be skipped on a first reading.

1.6 PROBLEMS

1.1 Two sequences of numbers $X = \{x_1, x_2, \ldots, x_n\}$ and $Y = \{y_1, y_2, \ldots, y_n\}$ are given. It is required to construct a third sequence $Z = \{z_1, z_2, \ldots, z_n\}$, where $z_i = x_i + y_i$ for $1 \leq i \leq n$.

(a) Assume that X and Y are initially stored in the memory of a sequential computer. Design a sequential algorithm for computing Z and storing it in memory. Analyze the running time of your algorithm.

(b) Design a parallel algorithm for computing Z on a shared-memory parallel computer, assuming that X and Y are initially stored in the shared memory. When the algorithm terminates, Z is to be found in the shared memory.

(c) Analyze the running time, number of processors, and cost of the parallel algorithm obtained in (b).

(d) Derive the speedup of the parallel algorithm in (b) and its efficiency with respect to the sequential algorithm in (a).

1.2 It is required to *reverse* the elements of a sequence $X = \{x_1, x_2, \ldots, x_n\}$ such that after the reversal, element x_{n-i+1} occupies the ith position of the sequence for $1 \leq i \leq n$.

(a) Assume that X is initially stored in the memory of a sequential computer. Design a sequential algorithm to reverse X, and analyze the running time of the algorithm.

(b) Design a parallel algorithm for solving the same problem on a shared-memory parallel computer, assuming that X is initially stored in the shared memory.

(c) Analyze the running time, number of processors, and cost of the parallel algorithm obtained in (b).

(d) Derive the speedup of the parallel algorithm in (b) and its efficiency with respect to the sequential algorithm in (a).

1.3 The parallel algorithm of Example 1.4 uses n processors and runs in $O(\log n)$ time, for a cost of $O(n \log n)$. This cost is not optimal in view of the sequential algorithm that performs the same computation in $O(n)$ time. Design a cost-optimal parallel algorithm for solving this problem on a shared-memory parallel computer.

1.4 A sequence of pairs $\{(x_1, d_1),\ (x_2, d_2),\ \ldots,\ (x_n, d_n)\}$ is given, where each x_i is an integer satisfying $0 \leq x_i \leq m - 1$, each d_i is an arbitrary datum of fixed size, and $m < n$. Design a parallel algorithm to sort the pairs in nondecreasing order of the x_i on a shared-memory parallel computer. Analyze your algorithm's running time, the number of processors it uses, and its cost.

1.5 Sorting is the quintessential problem of computer science. Like few other problems, its origins, its applications, and the algorithms for its solution, as well as their analyses, are all found within the field. Simply stated, the problem calls for arranging, in nondecreasing order, a sequence of arbitrary numbers $\{x_1,\ x_2,\ \ldots,\ x_n\}$ given in random order. Design and analyze a parallel sorting algorithm for a shared-memory parallel computer.

1.6 A file of n records is stored in the memory of a shared-memory parallel computer. The records are stored in contiguous locations, but are not arranged in any particular order. Each record is of the form (x, d), where x is a key and d is a datum. Two or more records may have the same key. It is required to determine whether at least one record exists in the file whose key is equal to a given k. Discuss a parallel solution to this problem that uses p processors, where $p < n$.

1.7 Show how the problem of computing the prefix sums of n numbers (discussed in Example 1.6) can be solved on a shared-memory parallel computer with p processors, where $p < n$.

1.8 Consider a shared-memory parallel computer with n processors and the following constraint: No two processors can read from or write into the same memory location simultaneously. Show how the sum of n numbers stored in memory can be computed. (*Hint*: By adding pairs of numbers simultaneously, the size of the problem can be *halved* in one step.) How many processors did you use? Is your algorithm cost optimal? If not, how can you make it cost optimal?

1.9 A shared-memory parallel computer with n processors and the same constraint as in Problem 1.8 is given. One of the processors possesses a datum that it wishes to communicate to all the other processors. This problem is known as *broadcasting*. Show how it can be solved in $O(\log n)$ time. (*Hint*: The number of processors holding the datum can be *doubled* in one step by having each processor that possesses the datum communicate it to another processor that does not.)

1.10 Once again, consider the parallel computer of Problem 1.8. The set of processors is divided into m subsets, $m < n$, such that all processors in a given subset wish to read from the same distinct memory location. This problem, known as *multiple broadcasting*, can be solved through m applications of the algorithm developed in Problem 1.9, leading to a running time of $O(m \log n)$. Can the problem be solved in $O(\log n)$ time?

1.11 A set of equilateral triangles in the plane is given. All the triangles are of the same size, and each has one edge parallel to the x-axis. Design a parallel algorithm, for a parallel computer of your choice, that computes all intersections among the triangles.

1.12 Design a parallel algorithm for solving the following problem: A collection U of points in the plane is given, together with two integers C and R. The elements of U represent the users of a set F of facilities to be located in the plane. Each facility can serve up to C users, and each user should be at most at a distance R from a facility. It is required to find a set F of points in the plane such that each user can be assigned to some facility satisfying the two stated conditions.

1.13 Repeat parts **(b)**–**(d)** of Problem 1.1 for the case where the sequence Z is to be computed on a binary tree of processors in which the input is received at the leaves and the output is produced by the root.

1.14 Given two sequences of numbers $X = \{x_1, x_2, \ldots, x_n\}$ and $Y = \{y_1, y_2, \ldots, y_n\}$, it is required to compute the quantity

$$v = (x_1 \times y_1) + (x_2 \times y_2) + \cdots + (x_n \times y_n).$$

(a) Assume that X and Y are initially stored in the memory of a sequential computer. Design a sequential algorithm to compute v, and analyze the running time of the algorithm.

(b) Design a parallel algorithm to solve this problem on a binary tree of processors. Make appropriate assumptions about input and output.

(c) Analyze the running time, number of processors, and cost of the parallel algorithm obtained in **(b)**.

(d) Derive the speedup of the parallel algorithm in **(b)** and its efficiency with respect to the sequential algorithm in **(a)**.

1.15 Repeat parts **(b)**–**(d)** of Problem 1.2 for the case where the sequence X to be reversed is stored in the n leaves $P_1, P_2, \ldots, P_n$ of a binary tree of processors. Initially, P_i holds x_i. After the reversal, P_i should hold x_{n-i+1} for $1 \leq i \leq n$.

1.16 It is required to find the two smallest numbers in a sequence $\{x_1, x_2, \ldots, x_n\}$.

(a) Assume that the sequence is initially stored in the memory of a sequential computer. Design a sequential algorithm to solve this problem, and analyze the running time of the algorithm.

(b) Design a parallel algorithm to solve the problem on a binary tree of processors. Make appropriate assumptions about input and output.

(c) Analyze the running time, number of processors, and cost of the parallel algorithm obtained in (b).

(d) Derive the speedup of the parallel algorithm in (b) and its efficiency with respect to the sequential algorithm in (a).

1.17 Given a set S of points in the plane, design algorithms for solving the following problems on a binary tree of processors:

(a) For each point in S, determine its closest neighbor in S.

(b) Determine which point of S is closest to a query point q.

(c) Determine the closest pair of points in S.

1.18 Describe a parallel algorithm for multiplying an $m \times n$ matrix A by an $n \times 1$ vector v to produce an $m \times 1$ vector w. Your algorithm should be designed to run on a binary tree of processors.

1.19 Show how the problem of computing the prefix sums of n numbers (discussed in Example 1.6) can be solved on a binary tree of processors with p leaves, where $p < n$.

1.20 Design a combinational circuit to solve the following problem: The leftmost column of processors receives as input the sequence of numbers $\{x_1, x_2, \ldots, x_n\}$, one number per processor. The rightmost column of processors produces the sequence of numbers $\{y_1, y_2, \ldots, y_n\}$, one number per processor, where, for each i, $1 \leq i \leq n$, y_i is equal to the largest number in the sequence $\{x_i, x_{i+1}, \ldots, x_n\}$. How many columns of processors does your circuit have? What is the total number of processors used by the circuit?

1.21 It is required to maximize the function

$$h(x_1, x_2, \ldots, x_n) = \sum_{i=1}^{n} g_i(x_i),$$

where $g_i(0) = 0$ and $g_i(x_i) \geq 0$, subject to the conditions

$$\sum_{i=1}^{n} x_i = x \quad \text{and} \quad x_i \geq 0 \quad \text{for all } i.$$

One method for solving this problem is *dynamic programming*. According to that method, the sequence $\{f_1(x), f_2(x), \ldots, f_n(x)\}$ is constructed from

$$f_i(x) = \max_{0 \leq x_i \leq x} (g_i(x_i) + f_{i-1}(x - x_i)),$$

where $f_0(x) = 0$. The sequence $\{x_1(x), x_2(x), \ldots, x_n(x)\}$ is obtained in this way, where $x_i(x)$ is the value that maximized $g_i(x_i) + f_{i-1}(x - x_i)$. Computationally, $x_i(x)$ is found by probing the range $[0, x]$ at equal subintervals. Derive a parallel version of this algorithm.

1.22 Let G be a directed and weighted graph where each edge weight is positive. Two vertices of G are distinguished as the *source* and the *sink*. Each edge may be thought of as a conduit for fluid, and the edge's weight determines how much fluid it can carry. The *network flow problem* asks for the maximum quantity of fluid that could flow from source to sink. Design a parallel algorithm for this problem.

1.23 Numerical integration is the computation of an approximation to the definite integral

$$D = \int_a^b f(x)dx.$$

One very simple formula for approximating D is the *trapezoidal rule*. The interval $[a, b]$ is divided into N subintervals of equal size $h = (b - a)/N$. With $x_0 = a$, $x_1 = a + h$, ..., $x_N = b$, and $f_i = f(x_i)$, the approximate value of D is given by

$$\frac{h}{2}(f_0 + 2f_1 + 2f_2 + \cdots + 2f_{N-1} + f_N).$$

Discuss a parallel implementation of this rule.

1.24 Show that for the special case of $q = 1$, the slowdown folklore theorem is essentially the speedup folklore theorem, but with a less sharp upper bound on $S(1, p)$.

1.25 Modify Example 1.7 so that the number of processors on the parallel computer is $s - 1$ (instead of s).

(a) Compute $Pr(s - 1)$, that is, the probability with which the parallel computer solves the problem successfully.

(b) Compute $sr(1, s - 1)$, that is, the success ratio achieved in this case.

(*Hint*: Refer to Example 1.28.)

1.26 As mentioned in Section 1.4.2, there are circumstances in which a parallel
computer that tries to keep all of its processors as busy as possible may require a longer running time while solving a problem than if it had used fewer
processors. Consider, for example, the situation in which 10 computational
jobs $J_1, J_2, \ldots, J_{10}$ are to be executed on a shared-memory parallel computer
with three processors P_1, P_2, and P_3 according to the following conditions:

(a) The jobs have running times of 3, 2, 2, 2, 4, 6, 4, 5, 1, and 10 time units,
respectively.

(b) Initially, only jobs J_1, J_2, J_3, and J_4 are ready to be executed. Jobs J_5,
J_6, J_7, J_8, and J_9 are ready only after J_4 is completed. Similarly, J_1
must be completed before J_{10} becomes ready.

(c) If P_i is assigned a job J_k, it executes it without interruption until the job
is completed.

(d) Among all jobs ready to be executed, the one that became ready first is
assigned to the free processor with the smallest index.

Under these conditions, the jobs are executed as follows: First, J_1, J_2, and
J_3 are assigned to P_1, P_2, and P_3, respectively. After 2 time units, P_2 and P_3
are free; P_2 is assigned J_4, while P_3 must remain idle, since no other job is
ready. Meanwhile, P_1 completes J_1 in 3 time units and begins executing J_{10}.
When P_2 finishes executing J_4 after a total of 4 time units, it is assigned J_5,
and P_3 is assigned J_6. These two jobs are completed simultaneously when 8
time units have elapsed from the beginning of the computation. Processors
P_2 and P_3 are then assigned J_7 and J_8, respectively. Finally, P_2 executes J_9.
All processors terminate 13 time units after the start.

Suppose now that four processors P_1, P_2, P_3, and P_4 are available on the
shared-memory parallel computer to execute the 10 jobs and that no processor
is to be left idle if a task is ready for execution. Show that in this case the
running time (i.e., the time elapsed from the beginning to the end of the
computation) is 16 time units. In other words, show that four processors
require *more* time to solve the problem than three processors do. (*Hint*: A
diagram similar to the one used in Fig. 1.6 is useful.)

1.7   BIBLIOGRAPHICAL REMARKS

The design and analysis of parallel algorithms have been treated in a number
of books, including Akl [18, 21], Akl and Lyons [42], Bertsekas and Tsitsiklis [99],
Freeman and Phillips [251], JáJá [310], Kumar et al. [343], Lakshmivarahan and
Dhall [355, 356], Leighton [367], Modi [431], Quinn [515], Ranka and Sahni [526],
Reif [533], Robert [537], and Smith [575]. While some of these works, such as

Akl [21], JáJá [310], and Reif [533] present a broad perspective of the field, others are devoted to an in-depth coverage of a particular topic, including sorting in Akl [18], computational geometry in Akl and Lyons [42], and numerical computation in Bertsekas and Tsitsiklis [99], Freeman and Phillips [251], Lakshmivarahan and Dhall [355], Modi [431], and Robert [537]. Similarly, some of the books describe algorithms for a variety of different parallel computers, such as Akl [18, 21], Akl and Lyons [42], and Smith [575], while others focus on a particular architecture, such as shared-memory parallel computers in JáJá [310] and Reif [533] and interconnection networks in Leighton [367] and Ranka and Sahni [526].

Interconnection network parallel computers and combinational circuits are usually viewed as *graphs* in which processors are the *nodes* (or *vertices*) and the links connecting them are the *edges* (or *lines*). A graph whose edges are *oriented* is said to be *directed*; otherwise, a graph whose edges have no orientation is said to be *undirected*. For a definition of the terminology and notation of graph theory, see Behzad et al. [93] and Liu [391]. A comprehensive study of the fundamental problem of computing prefix sums in parallel and its numerous applications in parallel computation is the focus of Lakshmivarahan and Dhall [356].

The search problem of Example 1.15 is investigated in Snir [576]. It is shown therein that no parallel algorithm for solving this problem on a shared-memory parallel computer can achieve a speedup equal to the number of processors used. A detailed treatment of the search problem is provided in Chapter 5. The speedup and slowdown folklore theorems are known in the literature, respectively, as the *speedup theorem* and *Brent's theorem* (after Brent [124]); see, for example, Akl [21], Gibbons and Rytter [258], JáJá [310], Karp and Ramachandran [323], Leighton [367], Reif [533], and Smith [575]. Several examples of computations for which these folklore theorems do not hold are provided in Akl and Fava Lindon [35], Bilardi and Preparata [107], Fava Lindon [225], Luccio and Pagli [395, 396], and Luccio et al. [397]. Certain anomalous situations in which the slowdown folklore theorem is violated due to the fact that q processors actually require *less* time than p processors in solving a problem, where $q < p$, are described in Graham [265, 266, 267]. These anomalous situations arise when one *schedules* or *sequences* computational jobs for execution on a parallel computer with a given number of processors; for a review of such problems, see Garey and Johnson [255]. A more detailed study of the speedup and slowdown folklore theorems and the circumstances in which they fail is provided in Chapter 12 and the references therein. The use of discriminating analysis in connection with parallel algorithms is illustrated in Fava Lindon [224]. The success ratio, as a criterion for evaluating parallel algorithms, was first defined formally in Akl and Fava Lindon [35].

Besides the study of parallel algorithms, other aspects of parallel computation are also well documented in books, including parallel architectures in Dongarra [207], Hillis [294], Hulle et al. [306], Hwang and Briggs [307], Potter [495], Sabot [543], Shiva [566], Stone [594], and Trew and Wilson [614], parallel computer organization in Almasi and Gottlieb [60], Blelloch [112], El-Rewini et al. [218],

Flynn [235], Lewis and El-Rewini [375], Pfister [491], Schröder-Preikschat [555], Sharp [562], and Wilkinson [640], and parallel programming in Babb [79], Brawer [121], Brinch Hansen [126], Carriero and Gelernter [131], Chandy and Misra [138], Hatcher and Quinn [289], Lester [372], Perrott [489], and Wilson [641]. General issues pertaining to parallel computation are discussed in Codenotti and Leoncini [164], Cosnard and Trystram [189], Foster [237], Fountain [239], Krishnamurthy [331], Leiss [369], Moldovan [432], Morse [433], and Zomaya [649, 650]. A list of certain computational problems believed by some researchers not to have efficient parallel solutions is given in Greenlaw et al. [269].

We shall refer to sequential algorithms on various occasions for the purpose of comparison. While knowledge of these algorithms is not essential, it is helpful in appreciating the parallel algorithms. A good coverage of sequential algorithms is provided in Cormen et al. [185] and Rawlins [529]. A fast algorithm for multiplying two matrices is described in Coppersmith and Winograd [184].

Chapter 2

Models of Computation

In science, a *model* is a physical, mathematical, or logical representation of a real-world entity. Its purpose is to simulate a certain phenomenon, thereby allowing a systematic study of the properties of that phenomenon. Models can also be used to describe certain conceptual systems. In this capacity, a model provides a concrete manifestation of the process it is meant to represent.

In computer science, *models of computation* serve both of these purposes. First, they are used to describe real entities, namely, *computers*. As such, a model of computation is a stylized version of an existing or contemplated piece of machinery. It attempts to capture the essential features of the machine, while ignoring unimportant details of implementation. The model, therefore, affords an abstracted description that is simpler to understand theoretically and easier to manipulate mathematically. Second, models of computation are used as tools for thinking about problems and expressing algorithms. Here, a model is not necessarily linked to any (existing or contemplated) real computer. Instead, its main reason for being is to lead to an understanding of *computation*. A model provides a framework for studying computational problems, obtaining an insight into their different structures, and developing solutions to them. Once an algorithm has been designed to solve a problem within a certain model, the model permits a meaningful description of the algorithm to be given and a precise analysis of it to be derived.

Models have been used since the early days of computer science, before the field was even named. Examples of early models are *automata*, *Turing machines*, *formal grammars*, and *recursive functions*. More recent models include *random access machines* and *parallel random access machines*. Four models of computation were described in Chapter 1, namely, a sequential computer, a shared-memory parallel computer, a binary tree of processors, and a combinational circuit for computing prefix sums. The purpose of the present chapter is to provide a complete definition of the various models of computation to be used in this book. Essentially, we expand on our definition of the four models of Chapter 1.

We begin in Section 2.1 with the random access machine, a theoretical sequential computer. This is followed in Section 2.2 by the parallel random access machine, a theoretical shared-memory parallel computer. In Section 2.3, we describe several members of the family of interconnection network parallel computers. General properties of combinational circuits are presented in Section 2.4, along with some examples and applications.

Our description of each model attempts to be as precise and as complete as possible. While irrelevant details of implementation may (in fact, ought to) be omitted, no important component of the model should be missing. There are two reasons for this:

1. From the theoretical point of view, algorithms should be designed with all features of the model accounted for, including its strengths and weaknesses. Analyses of algorithms designed for the model are meaningful only if all integral parts of the model are taken into consideration.

2. From the practical point of view, if the model is to be implemented, there should be no essential building block left unspecified by the theoretical description. This allows the implementation to be faithful to the model. It also allows the algorithms to be translated into programs with little or no change, and their analyses to apply without qualification.

2.1 THE RANDOM ACCESS MACHINE

Our sequential model of computation is the random access machine (RAM), shown in Fig. 2.1. It consists of:

1. A memory with M locations. In principle, M can be unbounded. For our purposes, M is an arbitrarily large, but finite, number. Each memory location stores a datum and can be accessed at random using a unique address.

2. A processor operating under the control of a sequential algorithm. The processor is capable of loading and storing data from and into the memory, and executing basic arithmetic and logical operations. It possesses a constant number of internal (or local) registers to perform computations on data.

3. A memory access unit (MAU) whose purpose is to create a path from the processor to an arbitrary location in memory. Every time the processor wishes to read from or write into a location in memory, it provides the MAU with the address of that location. Using this address, a direct connection is established between the processor and the memory location. (The MAU was not shown in Fig. 1.1, for simplicity.)

Each step of the algorithm consists of (up to) three phases:

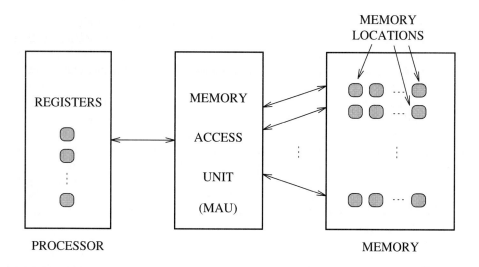

Figure 2.1: The random access machine.

1. A READ phase, in which the processor reads a datum from an arbitrary location in memory into one of its internal registers,

2. A COMPUTE phase, in which the processor performs a basic operation on the contents of one or two of its registers, and

3. A WRITE phase, in which the processor writes the contents of one register into an arbitrary memory location.

How Long Does a Step Take on the RAM?   We now determine the time required by each of the three phases of an algorithm's step on the RAM. Assume that memory locations are each of size w bits, where w is arbitrarily large. Therefore, each memory location is capable of storing 2^w distinct values. If $M < 2^w$, then the M memory locations are not capable of representing all of the distinct values at any given time. Alternatively, if $M > 2^w$, then some values are duplicated, as the memory locations are not sufficiently large to accommodate M distinct values. We avoid these complications by assuming that $M = 2^w$. Therefore, the maximum size of a memory location is $\log M$. It follows that the maximum size of a processor's register is $\log M$.

1. Let us first consider the COMPUTE phase. As a consequence of our choice of $w = \log M$, the time required by the processor to perform a unary or binary operation (such as complementation, addition, multiplication, comparison, and so on) is a function of $\log M$. Let us denote this time by $\tau_c(1, M)$, where

the 1 represents the fact that the RAM has one processor. Usually, a binary operation (e.g., addition) on two numbers of size s takes time $O(\log s)$. Since in our case $s = \log M$, it follows that $\tau_c(1, M) = O(\log \log M)$. The latter is a very small number for all practical purposes, even for large values of M. For example, if $w = 2^{10}$, then $M = 2^{2^{10}}$, and $\log \log M = 10$. (Of course, M cannot be *that* big, since the number of atoms in the known universe is estimated to be less than 2^{2^9}! In fact, such a memory would have $B = w2^w = 2^{10} \times 2^{2^{10}}$ bits, and hence 2^B states, which by far exceeds the number of *possible universes*. Our point is to show that even if M is excessively large, $\tau_c(1, M)$ is small.) We therefore take $\tau_c(1, M) = O(1)$. One should note here that the function chosen for the time of a basic operation (i.e., $O(\log \log M)$ or $O(1)$) does not affect the result of comparing the running time of a RAM algorithm to that of a parallel algorithm, provided that the latter uses the same function.

2. Similarly, since the memory is of size M, the size of a location's address is $\log M$. It follows that the MAU requires an amount of time that is a function of $\log M$, in order to create a path from the processor to a memory location, for each memory access (i.e., for each READ phase and for each WRITE phase). Let us denote this time by $\tau_a(1, M)$. We show in Section 2.4 that if the MAU is implemented as a combinational circuit, then $\tau_a(1, M) = \Omega(\log M)$. Moreover, an implementation of the RAM's MAU that can connect the processor to an arbitrary memory location in $O(\log M)$ steps is described in Section 2.4. It is therefore appropriate to take $\tau_a(1, M) = O(\log M)$. Through pipelining, however, this implementation often allows k memory accesses to be completed in $O(k + \log M)$ time, and not the obvious $O(k \times \log M)$.

There are many circumstances in which choosing $\tau_a(1, M)$ to be of the same order as $\tau_c(1, M)$ does not affect the result of a RAM algorithm's running-time analysis, either in absolute terms, or relative to a parallel algorithm. It is therefore appropriate in those cases to take $\tau_a(1, M) = \tau_c(1, M) = O(1)$. As a result, a step takes $O(1)$ time, thus simplifying the analysis. In Chapter 1, we referred to this as *uniform analysis*.

On the other hand, when choosing $\tau_a(1, M) = O(\log M)$ makes a difference in the running-time analysis of the RAM algorithm, particularly as compared to a parallel algorithm, this choice is made. In that case, a RAM step takes $\tau_c(1, M) + 2\tau_a(1, M) = O(\log M)$. In Chapter 1, we referred to this as *nonuniform*, or *discriminating, analysis*.

In this book, the RAM (and its algorithms) will serve as the sequential computational model against which parallel computational models (and their algorithms) are compared. The following example illustrates a RAM algorithm:

Example 2.1 An algorithm for computing the prefix sums of a sequence of n numbers $\{x_0, x_1, \ldots, x_{n-1}\}$ stored in the memory of a RAM is as follows:

Algorithm RAM PREFIX SUMS

> **Step 1:** $s_0 \leftarrow x_0$
> **Step 2: for** $i = 1$ **to** $n - 1$ **do**
> $$s_i \leftarrow s_{i-1} + x_i$$
> **end for.** ∎

The algorithm consists of $n - 1$ elementary steps: n READ phases to read x_0, x_1, $\ldots$, x_{n-1} from memory, $n - 1$ COMPUTE phases to obtain s_1, s_2, $\ldots$, s_{n-1}, and n WRITE phases to write s_0, s_1, $\ldots$, s_{n-1} into memory. Therefore, under uniform analysis, the algorithm runs in $t(n) = O(n)$ time. Assuming that $M = O(n)$, discriminating analysis leads to the same running time, since in this particular computation pipelining of the memory accesses is possible. Indeed, the READ requests are pipelined so that x_0 arrives to the processor $O(\log n)$ time units after the beginning of the algorithm and a new x_i is received every time unit thereafter. Similarly, the WRITE operations are pipelined so that s_0 is sent out to memory immediately after x_0 is received and a new s_i is issued every time unit thereafter. Since the algorithm performs $n - 1$ additions sequentially, the overall running time is $O(n + \log n)$, which is $O(n)$. □

As mentioned in Chapter 1, we use uniform analysis for RAM algorithms throughout this book, unless otherwise stated.

2.2 THE PARALLEL RANDOM ACCESS MACHINE

Our first model of parallel computation is the parallel random access machine (PRAM), shown in Fig. 2.2. It consists of:

1. A number of identical processors P_1, P_2, $\ldots$, P_N (of the type used in the RAM). In principle, N is unlimited. For our purposes, however, N is an arbitrarily large, but finite, number.

2. A common memory (also of the type used in the RAM) with M locations. Again, M is unbounded in principle; however, for our purposes, it will be an arbitrarily large, but finite, number such that $M \geq N$. The common memory is shared by the N processors.

3. A memory access unit (MAU) that allows the processors to gain access to memory. (The MAU was not shown in Fig. 1.2, for simplicity.)

The shared memory stores data and serves as the communication medium for the processors. Two processors P_i and P_j wishing to communicate can use the shared memory as a bulletin board: P_i, for example, writes a datum to memory (i.e., posts it on the bulletin board); the datum is then read by P_j. The model allows each processor to have its own algorithm and the processors to operate in a totally asynchronous fashion.

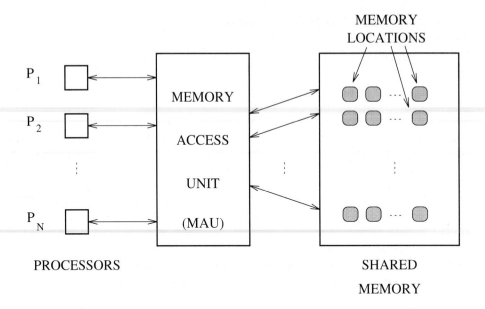

Figure 2.2: The parallel random access machine.

An interesting and useful application of the PRAM occurs when all the processors execute the same algorithm in a synchronous fashion. This mode of operation is amenable to the design and analysis of efficient algorithms for a host of problems. We now consider it in more detail.

Each step of an algorithm for the PRAM consists of (up to) three phases:

1. A READ phase, in which (up to N) processors read simultaneously from (up to N) memory locations. Each processor reads from at most one memory location and stores the value obtained in a local register,

2. A COMPUTE phase, in which (up to N) processors perform basic arithmetic or logical operations on their local data, and

3. A WRITE phase, in which (up to N) processors write simultaneously into (up to N) memory locations. Each processor writes the value contained in a local register into at most one memory location.

In the preceding description, the phrase "up to N processors" means that through algorithmic control, some processors may be prevented (if so desired) from executing a given step. Indeed, since the processors are indexed, the algorithm can explicitly state which of them are to be active. For example, the algorithm can specify that a given step is to be executed only by the even-numbered processors.

By comparing its index with this specification, an odd-numbered processor determines that it is to wait until the end of the current step. The phrase "up to N memory locations," on the other hand, has a broader meaning, to which we now turn.

2.2.1 Memory Access

There are a number of different ways for the processors to gain access to memory, which are made possible by the PRAM's repertoire of instructions. These instructions, for reading and for writing, are as follows:

Exclusive Read (ER). In this form of memory access, processors gain access to memory locations for the purpose of reading in a one-to-one fashion, as shown, for example, in Fig. 2.3(a). Thus, when this instruction is executed, p processors can simultaneously read the contents of p distinct memory locations, where $p \le N$, such that each of the p processors involved reads from exactly one memory location and each of the p memory locations involved is read by exactly one processor.

Concurrent Read (CR). In this form of memory access, two or more processors can read from the same memory location at the same time, as shown, for example, in Fig. 2.3(b). Thus, when this instruction is executed, p processors can simultaneously read the contents of p' distinct memory locations, where $p \le N$ and $p' \le p$, such that each of the p processors involved reads from exactly one memory location, whereas each of the p' memory locations involved can be read by more than one processor. Obviously, **CR** includes **ER** as a special case.

Exclusive Write (EW). In this form of memory access, processors gain access to memory locations for the purpose of writing in a one-to-one fashion, as shown, for example, in Fig. 2.4(a). Thus, when this instruction is executed, p processors can simultaneously write into p distinct memory locations, where $p \le N$, such that each of the p processors involved writes into exactly one memory location and each of the p memory locations involved is written into by exactly one processor.

Concurrent Write (CW). In this form of memory access, two or more processors can write into the same memory location at the same time, as shown, for example, in Fig. 2.4(b). Thus, when this instruction is executed, p processors can simultaneously write into p' distinct memory locations, where $p \le N$ and $p' \le p$, such that each of the p processors involved writes in exactly one memory location, whereas each of the p' memory locations involved can be written into by more than one processor. Again, note that **EW** is a special case of **CW**.

The **CW** instruction is further defined by specifying what ends up stored in a given memory location when several processors attempt to write in it simultaneously. Several extensions are therefore available to be used with **CW**. This gives rise to the following variants of the instruction:

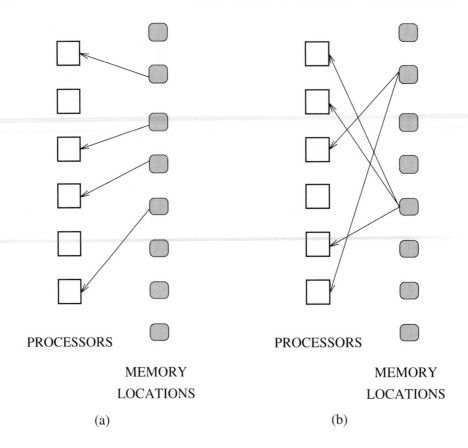

PROCESSORS

MEMORY
LOCATIONS

(a)

PROCESSORS

MEMORY
LOCATIONS

(b)

Figure 2.3: Read access to memory in the PRAM: (a) Exclusive; (b) Concurrent.

1. **PRIORITY CW**: Here the processors are assigned certain priorities. Of
   all the processors attempting to write in a given memory location, only the
   one with the highest priority is allowed to do so. The algorithm determines
   whether the priorities are fixed (for example, the priority of each processor
   may be equal to its index), or vary according to a certain rule during the
   execution of the algorithm.

2. **COMMON CW**: Here the processors wishing to write in a memory location
   are allowed to do so only if they are attempting to write the *same* value. In
   this case, one processor that is selected arbitrarily succeeds. The instruction
   is further specified as follows:

   (a) **FAIL COMMON**: If the values to be written by the processors into
       a memory location are not all equal, then the contents of the memory
       location are unchanged.

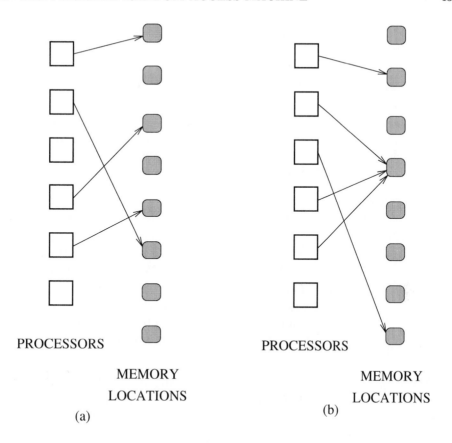

PROCESSORS

MEMORY
LOCATIONS

(a)

PROCESSORS

MEMORY
LOCATIONS

(b)

Figure 2.4: Write access to memory in the PRAM: (a) Exclusive; (b) Concurrent.

(b) **COLLISION COMMON**: This instruction requires a "failure" label to be stored in the memory location in case the **CW** does not succeed, due to two or more processors attempting to write unequal values.

(c) **FAIL-SAFE COMMON**: Here failure is not tolerated. The algorithm must be designed in such a way that whenever more than one processor wishes to write into the same memory location, they must be trying to write the same value. (Otherwise, execution of the algorithm is aborted.)

3. **ARBITRARY CW**: Of all the processors attempting to write simultaneously in a memory location, *any one* can succeed without affecting the correctness of the algorithm. However, the algorithm must specify exactly how the successful processor is to be selected.

4. **RANDOM CW**: Here the processor that succeeds in writing is chosen by
   a random process. This instruction may be used by algorithms that include
   an element of randomness in their execution.

5. **COMBINING CW**: In this mode of concurrent writing, *all* the values that
   a set of processors wishes to write simultaneously into a memory location
   are combined into a single value, which is then stored in that location. This
   instruction takes several forms, depending on which function the algorithm
   needs to use to combine the values (written by several processors) before storing the result (in the memory location). The following variants are available:

   (a) *Arithmetic functions*: The values to be written are either added up (using
       SUM) or multiplied (using **PRODUCT**).

   (b) *Logical functions*: A set of Boolean values can be combined using **AND**,
       OR, or **EXCLUSIVE-OR**. The negations of these functions are also
       available, namely, **NAND**, **NOR**, and **NXOR**, respectively.

   (c) *Selection functions*: The largest or smallest of the values to be written is
       selected using **MAX** and **MIN**, respectively. If several processors hold
       the largest or smallest, then one is chosen by further specifying whether
       the **PRIORITY**, **ARBITRARY**, or **RANDOM** instructions should
       be used.

It is important to stress again that all of the preceding forms of memory access
belong to the repertoire of instructions of the PRAM. The model allows an algorithm to use any one it wishes when solving a problem. In fact, several different
instructions may be invoked by the same algorithm according to its needs.

Example 2.2 A sequence of values $S = \{x_1, x_2, \ldots, x_n\}$, where $n \geq 2$, as well as
a datum x, is stored in the shared memory of the PRAM. It is known that $x \neq x_i$
for all i, $1 \leq i \leq n$. If $x_i < x$ for all i, $1 \leq i \leq n$, then the largest of the x_i is to
be computed. Otherwise, if $x_i > x$ for all i, $1 \leq i \leq n$, then the smallest of the x_i
is to be computed. Finally, if some x_i are smaller than x and some are larger, then
the average value of those smaller and the average value of those larger are to be
computed.

  The problem can be solved on the PRAM with n processors P_1, P_2, $\ldots$, P_n.
Using **ER**, P_i reads x_i for all i, $1 \leq i \leq n$. Then using **CR**, all processors read x.
Now P_i compares x_i to x for all i, $1 \leq i \leq n$. Using **NXOR CW**, P_i writes 1 in
a location A of memory if $x_i < x$; otherwise it writes 0, $1 \leq i \leq n$. All processors
now read A using **CR**. If it is 1, then this implies either that all x_i are smaller than
x or that all x_i are larger than x. In this case, all processors use either **MAX CW**
(if $x_i < x$) or **MIN CW** (if $x_i > x$) to write the largest or the smallest value of
the sequence S in a location B in memory. On the other hand, if A contains a 0,
then some x_i are smaller than x, while some are larger. Those processors for which
$x_i < x$ $(x_i > x)$ use **SUM CW** to write their x_i in a location C_1 (C_2) of memory

and a 1 in location D_1 (D_2). The desired averages are then found by processors P_1 and P_2, which compute $G_1 = C_1/D_1$ and $G_2 = C_2/D_2$, respectively.

The algorithm can be expressed as follows: All steps are done by processors P_1, $P_2, \ldots, P_n$, except for Steps 5 and 6, which are done by processors P_1 and P_2 only. Each step is implemented using a number of *elementary steps*.

Step 1:

> READ: P_i uses **ER** to read x_i
> COMPUTE and WRITE phases not used.

Step 2:

> READ: P_i uses **CR** to read x
> COMPUTE: **if** $x_i < x$
>   **then** $a_i \leftarrow 1$
>   **else** $a_i \leftarrow 0$
>   **end if**
> WRITE: P_i uses **NXOR CW** to write a_i in A.

Step 3:

> READ: P_i uses **CR** to read A
> COMPUTE: **if** $A = 1$
>   **then if** $x_i < x$
>   **then** do (3.1)
>   **else** do (3.2)
>   **end if**
>   **else** **if** $x_i < x$
>   **then** do (3.3) and (4.1)
>   **else** do (3.4) and (4.2)
>   **end if**
>   **end if**
> WRITE: (3.1) P_i uses **MAX CW** to write x_i in B
>   (3.2) P_i uses **MIN CW** to write x_i in B
>   (3.3) P_i uses **SUM CW** to write x_i in C_1
>   (3.4) P_i uses **SUM CW** to write x_i in C_2.

Step 4:

> READ and COMPUTE phases not used
> WRITE: (4.1) P_i uses **SUM CW** to write 1 in D_1
>   (4.2) P_i uses **SUM CW** to write 1 in D_2.

Step 5:

> READ: P_i uses **ER** to read C_i
> COMPUTE and WRITE phases not used.

Step 6:

READ: P_i uses **ER** to read D_i
COMPUTE: $g_i \leftarrow C_i/D_i$
WRITE: P_i uses **EW** to write g_i in G_i. ∎

A more succinct formulation of the algorithm is given next as algorithm PRAM BOUNDS. In it, many details set forth in the previous description (in particular, a separate specification of each phase of a step and an identification of each form of memory access used) are now omitted. These details can easily be inferred from context.

Algorithm PRAM BOUNDS

Step 1: **for** $i = 1$ **to** n **do in parallel**
    (1.1) **if** $x_i < x$
        then $A \xleftarrow{\text{NXOR}} 1$
        else $A \xleftarrow{\text{NXOR}} 0$
        end if
    (1.2) **if** $A = 1$
        then if $x_i < x$
            then $B \xleftarrow{\text{MAX}} x_i$
            else $B \xleftarrow{\text{MIN}} x_i$
            end if
        else if $x_i < x$
            then (i) $C_1 \xleftarrow{\text{SUM}} x_i$
                  (ii) $D_1 \xleftarrow{\text{SUM}} 1$
            else (i) $C_2 \xleftarrow{\text{SUM}} x_i$
                  (ii) $D_2 \xleftarrow{\text{SUM}} 1$
            end if
        end if
    end for
Step 2: **for** $i = 1,\ 2$ **do in parallel**
        $G_i \leftarrow C_i/D_i$
    end for. ∎

In algorithm PRAM BOUNDS, the statement

for $i = 1$ **to** n **do in parallel**

means that *all* processors P_i, $1 \leq i \leq n$, perform Step 1 simultaneously: Each processor P_i executes first Step (1.1) and *then* Step (1.2). Similarly, the statement

for $i = 1,\ 2$ **do in parallel**

means that Step 2 is executed *only* by P_1 and P_2. We use this high-level form of algorithmic description in the remainder of the book. □

The memory access instructions of the PRAM obey the following two properties:

1. Each of them can be simulated on a RAM in a time proportional to the number of processors involved. Suppose, for example, that the N processors on a PRAM wish to write the sum of values they hold, one per processor, into a location in shared memory using **SUM CW**. Assuming that $\tau_c(1, M)$ and $\tau_a(1, M)$, the binary operation and memory access times, respectively, on a RAM are both $O(1)$, the sum can be computed sequentially in $O(N)$ time.

2. All of them can be executed on the PRAM in the same amount of time and using the same resources. Thus, an **ER** instruction, for example, requires no fewer resources and no less time than a **CW** instruction. Specifically, the same MAU can execute all READ and WRITE instructions in the same amount of time. We elaborate on this point in the next section.

2.2.2 How Long Does a Step Take on the PRAM?

As we saw in the previous section, each step of a PRAM algorithm consists of three phases: A READ phase, a COMPUTE phase, and a WRITE phase. In order to define the time required to execute a step on the PRAM, we must determine how much time each of the three phases needs. Recall that the PRAM has N processors and M memory locations.

1. Let the time taken by the COMPUTE phase on a PRAM be $\tau_c(N, M)$. We can use the same reasoning here as used previously for the RAM, since:

    (a) Each processor on the PRAM is the same as a RAM processor,

    (b) All operations executed during the COMPUTE phase are the same for both models, and

    (c) A memory of size M is assumed in both cases.

    It follows, therefore, that $\tau_c(N, M) = O(\log \log M)$. Since the latter is a very small number, for convenience we take $\tau_c(N, M) = O(1)$, as we did for the RAM. It is worth noting here that the choice of the function to describe $\tau_c(N, M)$ (i.e., $O(\log \log M)$ or $O(1)$) does not affect the result of comparing the running time of a PRAM algorithm to that of an algorithm for another model, as long as the latter uses the same function to describe the time taken by a basic operation.

2. Let the time taken by each of the READ and WRITE phases be $\tau_a(N, M)$. Again, the same argument as in Section 2.1 applies. It follows that $\tau_a(N, M)$ is a function of $\log M$, assuming that $N = O(M)$. We show in Section 2.4 that if the MAU of the PRAM is implemented as a combinational circuit, then $\tau_a(N, M) = \Omega(\log M)$. Further, as discussed in Section 2.4, an implementation can be obtained that connects $N = O(M)$ processors to M memory locations in $O(\log M)$ time. It is therefore appropriate to take $\tau_a(N, M) = O(\log M)$. Interestingly, however, this implementation often allows k accesses to memory to be completed in $O(k + \log M)$ through pipelining, instead of the obvious $O(k \times \log M)$.

There are many problems for which choosing $\tau_c(N, M)$ and $\tau_a(N, M)$ to be of the same order does not affect the result of a PRAM algorithm's running-time analysis, either in absolute terms or relative to an algorithm for another model. In those cases, it is sensible and convenient to take $\tau_a(N, M) = \tau_c(N, M) = O(1)$. Therefore, a PRAM step takes $O(1)$ time, thus simplifying the analysis. In Chapter 1, we referred to this as *uniform analysis*.

Example 2.3 Consider algorithm PRAM BOUNDS of Example 2.2. It consists of two steps. In Step 1, executed in parallel by processors P_1, P_2, ..., P_n, a processor performs a constant number of elementary operations. The same is true of Step 2, executed in parallel by P_1 and P_2. Under uniform analysis, each computation and each memory access (READ or WRITE) takes constant time. Therefore, the running time of algorithm PRAM BOUNDS is $t(n) = O(1)$.

By contrast, assuming that $N = M = O(n)$ and taking $\tau_a(N, M) = O(\log n)$ leads to the obvious running time of $t(n) = O(\log n)$ for algorithm PRAM BOUNDS. In this case, the increase in the running time by a factor of $O(\log n)$ is expected and not particularly revealing. $\square$

On the other hand, there are cases where taking $\tau_a(N, M) = O(\log M)$ makes a significant difference when analyzing the running time of a PRAM algorithm. This is true regardless of whether $\tau_c(N, M)$ is $O(\log \log M)$ or $O(1)$. In these cases, this (more realistic) function is chosen to describe $\tau_a(N, M)$ in order for the results of the analysis to be meaningful. A PRAM step now takes at most $\tau_c(N, M) + 2\tau_a(N, M) = O(\log M)$ time. In Chapter 1, we referred to this as *nonuniform*, or *discriminating*, *analysis*.

Example 2.4 Let x, y, and z be arrays of numbers stored in the shared memory of a PRAM, where x is a one-dimensional array of size n, while y and z are two-dimensional arrays, each with n rows and n columns for $n \geq 2$. Further, assume that the number of processors and the number of memory locations are both linear functions of n; that is, $N = M = O(n)$. Now consider the following PRAM algorithm:

Algorithm PRAM MULTIPLY_1

    for $i = 1$ **to** n **do in parallel**
      for $j = 1$ **to** n **do**
        $x(i) \leftarrow x(i) \times x(i)$
      end for
    end for. ∎

Here each P_i reads a distinct value $x(i)$ from shared memory, performs n operations on it, and then writes the resulting $x(i)$ back into memory. In all, P_i performs n local computations (whereby $x(i)$ is multiplied by itself n times in the processor's local registers) and two memory accesses (one READ—specifically, an **ER**—to obtain the initial value of $x(i)$ from memory, and one WRITE—specifically, an **EW**—to write the final value of $x(i)$, namely, $(x(i))^{n+1}$, back into memory). Therefore, taking $\tau_a(N, M)$ to equal $O(1)$ or $O(\log n)$ makes no difference in the analysis. Indeed,

$$
\begin{aligned}
t(n) &= n \times \tau_c(N, M) + 2 \times \tau_a(N, M) \\
&= O(n).
\end{aligned}
$$

Let us now modify algorithm PRAM MULTIPLY_1 to read as follows:

Algorithm PRAM MULTIPLY_2

    for $i = 1$ **to** n **do in parallel**
      for $j = 1$ **to** n **do**
        $z(i, j) \leftarrow y(i, j) \times y(i, j)$
      end for
    end for. ∎

In this case, during the jth iteration, $1 \leq j \leq n$, processor P_i, $1 \leq i \leq n$, reads a distinct value $y(i, j)$ from memory, squares it, and writes the result back into memory in $z(i, j)$. In all, P_i executes n READ operations (specifically, one **ER** to obtain each of $y(i, 1)$, $y(i, 2)$, $\ldots$, $y(i, n)$), n multiplications (to compute $z(i, 1)$, $z(i, 2)$, $\ldots$, $z(i, n)$), and n WRITE operations (specifically, **EW**, to store the latter in memory). The multiplications require $O(n)$ time. How long do the READ and WRITE operations take? Assuming that $\tau_a(N, M) = O(1)$, they all require $O(n)$ time. On the other hand, assuming that $\tau_a(N, M) = O(\log n)$ may lead one to believe that n memory accesses will take $O(n \log n)$ time. It turns out, however, that the READ and WRITE operations can be pipelined: P_i "knows" ahead of time the memory locations where reading will take place. Therefore, it can issue the READ requests one after the other without waiting for the values to be returned. After $O(\log n)$ time $y(i, 1)$ will be received, and every time unit after that a new $y(i, j)$ will arrive. Thus, all n READ operations can be completed in

$O(n + \log n)$ time, which is $O(n)$. The same can be done for WRITE operations: As soon as $z(i, 1)$ has been computed, it is written in memory. Each step after that, a new $z(i, j)$ will be sent to memory. All WRITE operations therefore take $O(n + \log n)$ time, which is $O(n)$. Hence, $t(n) = O(n)$, and as in the previous case, taking $\tau_a(N, M) = O(1)$ or $O(\log n)$ made no difference in the analysis.

Finally, consider the following modification:

Algorithm PRAM MULTIPLY_3

> **for** $i = 1$ **to** n **do in parallel**
>> **for** $j = 1$ **to** n **do**
>>> $z(a, b) \leftarrow y(h, d) \times y(e, f)$
>> **end for**
> **end for.** ∎

Here the indices $a, b, h, d, e,$ and f are functions of the result of the computation in the previous iteration. Thus, for example, the new value of h for this iteration is obtained from the value of $z(a, b)$ computed during the previous iteration: $h = g(z(a, b))$ for some function g. Initially, $a = b = h = d = e = f = 1$. The main difference between this algorithm and the previous one is that neither the READ nor the WRITE requests can be pipelined: Until the current computation is completed, P_i does not "know" where next to read from or write into. It follows, therefore, that the n READ and WRITE operations take $O(n)$ time with $\tau_a(N, M) = O(1)$ and $O(n \log n)$ time with $\tau_a(N, M) = O(\log n)$. Hence, $t(n) = O(n)$ in the first case and $O(n \log n)$ in the second. □

As mentioned in Chapter 1, we use uniform analysis for PRAM algorithms throughout this book, unless otherwise stated. In particular, if a PRAM algorithm (involving memory access) is claimed to run in constant time, then, obviously, uniform analysis is used to derive the running time.

2.3 INTERCONNECTION NETWORKS

In the PRAM, all exchanges of data among processors take place through the shared memory. Another way for processors to communicate is via direct links connecting them. There is no longer a shared memory; instead, the M locations of memory are distributed among the N processors. The local memory of each processor now consists of M/N locations. The arrangement is shown in Fig. 2.5 for $N = 16$. When processor P_i wishes to send a datum to processor P_j, it uses the network to route the datum from its memory to that of P_j. The analogy here is a network of roads connecting cities: A datum sent from one processor to another follows a path through the network in the same way that a car travels from one city to another.

Two processors directly connected by a link are said to be *neighbors*. In Fig. 2.6, the neighbors of P_1 are P_2, P_3, and P_4, while the neighbors of P_2 are P_1 and

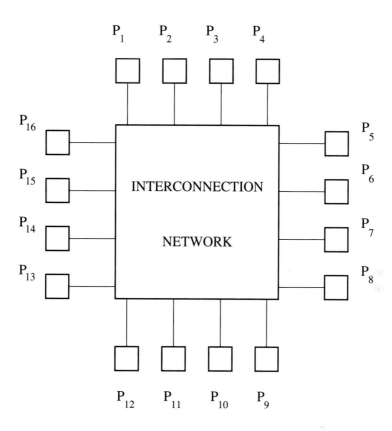

Figure 2.5: Interconnection network parallel computer.

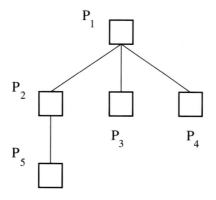

Figure 2.6: The neighbors of a processor.

P_5. Note that P_1 and P_5 are not neighbors. The links used in Fig. 2.6 are *two-way* communication lines: Two processors connected by a link can exchange data simultaneously. In other words, in reality, the link between P_i and P_j represents two links, namely, one from P_i to P_j and one from P_j to P_i. Recall that in Fig. 1.3 *two* such oriented links were used for each pair of neighbors. The representation used in Fig. 2.6, wherein a single unoriented link indicates two-way communication, is adopted henceforth for simplicity. However, in those cases where a link is meant to represent a one-way communication line (either from P_i to P_j or from P_j to P_i), a single oriented link is used.

There are a number of questions that we need to answer when designing a model of computation of this kind:

1. What shape should the network have? In other words, how many neighbors should each processor have, how are these neighbors selected, and should all processors have the same number of neighbors?

2. Can a processor communicate with all of its neighbors at once? In other words, can a processor send data to all of its neighbors and receive data from all of its neighbors in one time unit?

3. What is the size of a message that a processor can transmit at a time? In other words, if a datum is considered to have constant size, how many data can be sent in one transmission?

4. How long does it take for a processor to initiate a transmission? In other words, is the time required by a processor to start up a communication significant?

5. How long does it take for a datum to travel between two neighboring processors? In other words, is the time required by a datum to go from P_i to its neighbor P_j a function of the length of the link connecting P_i to P_j?

6. How long does it take a processor to receive a datum? In other words, is the time required by a datum sent by P_i to gain access to processor P_j significant?

7. How long does it take a processor to read or write a datum in its local memory? In other words, if the memory of a processor is of size M/N, is the time to gain access to that memory a function of M/N?

8. How does a datum actually travel from P_i to P_j? In other words, is the datum sent from P_i to a neighbor P_k, which stores it and then forwards it to a neighbor P_l, and so on, until the datum reaches P_j? Or is a path established first, and then the datum travels directly from P_i to P_j?

9. Are the paths static or dynamic? In other words, are the paths established by the algorithm designer, or does the algorithm allow for flexibility in choosing the paths?

10. Is a *handshake* required between the sending and receiving processors? In other words, should a destination processor acknowledge receipt of a datum to the source processor? Or, in the case where a path is first established and then the data sent, do the sender and receiver need to agree that a path has been set before data actually start flowing?

11. Do the processors operate synchronously or asynchronously? In other words, do all processors execute the same step of the same algorithm at the same time?

12. What kind of processor is used by an interconnection network? In other words, what are the operations that can be performed by a processor?

All of these questions are useful, and each, of course, has many answers. Some, however, are far more important than others and serve to clearly distinguish among different submodels in this general family of interconnection network parallel computers. On the other hand, some of the questions concern details that, when incorporated into the model, provide no new insight and only cause the algorithms to be unnecessarily complicated. We now provide answers to all of the questions.

Network Topology. The most obvious, and most general, way to connect N processors is to connect each pair by a two-way link, as shown in Fig. 2.7 for $N = 5$. Each processor has $N - 1$ neighbors and can send a datum directly to, or receive a datum directly from, any of its neighbors. This is known as a *complete network*. While convenient, such a network is costly and unrealistic for all but the smallest values of N. Indeed, there are $N(N - 1)/2$ links in the network, rendering it infeasible in practice for two reasons, namely, the expense associated with the total number of links and the limit on the number of links that can be physically connected to a processor. As a consequence, more reasonable networks are sought. Fortunately, a small subset of all pairwise connections usually suffices to obtain efficient algorithms in most applications. In some models the number of a processor's neighbors is constant, while in others it is a function of N. We describe examples of these networks in Sections 2.3.1–2.3.10.

Constant Number of Neighbors per Communication. Whether the number of neighbors of a processor is constant or a function of N, we assume that a processor can send and/or receive data to and from a constant number of neighbors in one time unit.

Constant-Size Message per Transmission. Every message that a processor wishes to transmit is considered a datum of fixed size. If m data are to be sent from one processor to another, then m transmissions are required.

Constant Initiation Time per Communication. Suppose that a processor has x neighbors (where x is either a constant or a function of N). In order to select one of its neighbors for a transmission, the processor needs time that is a function

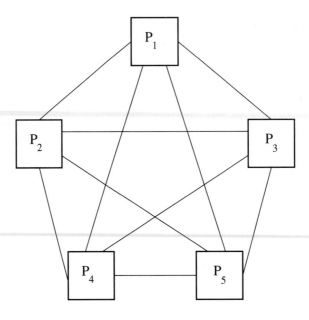

Figure 2.7: A complete network.

of x. For example, an address of $\log x$ bits requires $O(\log x)$ time to be decoded. In what follows, we take this time to be a constant for simplicity.

Constant Time per Link. If the link connecting two processors has length l, then the time to traverse the link is a function of l. Again, for simplicity, we assume that a datum can travel from one processor to any of its neighbors in constant time.

Constant Time to Receive a Datum. If a processor has x neighbors (where x is either a constant or a function of N), then it needs time that is a function of x to select a neighbor from which to receive data. We take this time to be constant.

Constant Time per Memory Access. Each processor has a memory of size M/N. If a processor is the source (the destination) of a datum, it must read the datum from (write the datum into) its memory. This takes time that is a function of M/N. We assume this time to be constant.

Store-and-Forward Communication. When processor P_i wishes to send a datum d to processor P_j, to which it is not directly connected, the following scheme is used: First P_i sends d to one of its neighbors—for example, P_k. Now P_k receives and stores d and then relays it to one of its own neighbors—for example, P_l. This continues until d reaches P_j. Since each datum is of constant size, it makes no difference whether this scheme is used or another whereby a path is first established from P_i to P_j and *then* d is sent.

Static Communication.   Unless otherwise stated, we assume that paths are predefined. In other words, the address of the destination processor is used to find a shortest path from the source processor. This is the responsibility of the algorithm designer. Specifically, the algorithm defines the required path when a processor P_i is to send a datum to another processor P_j at any given step. Thus, a path from P_i to P_j is fully specified from beginning to end, prior to that step. When the step is executed, each processor on the path from P_i to P_j, upon receipt of a datum d, simply forwards d to that specific neighbor indicated by the algorithm. All processors are assumed to "know" N, the total number of processors, as well as the topology of the network. Furthermore, no processor is isolated: There is always at least one path from a source processor to a destination processor.

Implicit Handshaking.   While handshaking may be a useful feature in practice, it serves no purpose to explicitly include it in the model and allow time for it. We assume that handshaking is done implicitly as part of the communication between P_i and P_j. In fact, the messages involved in a handshake can themselves be viewed as data, and communicating them involves the same routing mechanisms and requires the same amount of time as sending a regular datum.

Synchronous Operation.   We assume that all the processors operate synchronously. In one step, requiring constant time, a processor can receive data from a constant number of neighbors, perform a computation, and send data to a constant number of neighbors. Each processor holds a copy of the common algorithm, and all processors execute this algorithm in lockstep fashion. The algorithm may indicate that only a subset of the processors is active, using the indices of the processors. Active processors execute the same step at the same time.

Processors.   Each processor in the network may be viewed as a RAM: It can perform a number of basic arithmetic or logical operations and has access to a random access memory. Each basic operation requires constant time to be performed. In addition to a RAM, however, each processor has a number of special registers (called *ports*) that allow it to communicate with its neighbors. Each port is physically connected by a link to a port in another processor.

The preceding choices define our model. Of particular relevance at this point are the assumptions made regarding communication. We can summarize these as follows: If P_i wishes to send a datum to P_j, and if the shortest distance from P_i to P_j is s links, then the time taken to complete the transmission is $O(s)$. Thus, when analyzing the running time of an algorithm for an interconnection network parallel computer, we take into consideration both types of elementary steps performed by the algorithm, namely, *computational* steps and *routing* steps (as defined in Chapter 1).

It should be noted that other choices lead to different models. For example,

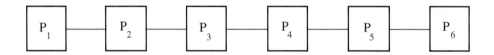

Figure 2.8: A linear array interconnection network.

allowing the paths to be dynamic (i.e., defined on the fly during the execution of an algorithm) may be useful when asynchronous operation is assumed, when congestion of messages at a node may be a problem, or when the algorithm must tolerate faults (i.e., continue to operate correctly despite the failure of some nodes and/or links). Similarly, it may sometimes be convenient to use a *header* to establish a path from P_i to P_j and then send a message of arbitrary size along this path.

We now turn to a description of the various network topologies used in this book. As mentioned before, a network topology defines the neighbors of each processor— that is, all the processors to which a processor is connected directly by a two-way link.

2.3.1   Linear Array

A linear array is the simplest and perhaps most fundamental topology. In this model, the N processors P_1, P_2, $\ldots$, P_N are interconnected in the form of a one-dimensional array. Here processor P_i is linked to its two neighbors P_{i-1} and P_{i+1}. Each of the end processors, namely, P_1 and P_N, has only one neighbor. A linear array of processors is shown in Fig. 2.8 for $N = 6$. In a variant of this model, P_1 and P_N are connected to each other, thus yielding a *ring* of processors.

2.3.2   Mesh

A two-dimensional network is obtained by arranging the N processors P_0, P_1, $\ldots$, P_{N-1} into an $m \times m$ array, where $m = N^{1/2}$, as shown in Fig. 2.9 for $m = 4$. The processor in row j and column k is denoted by $P(j, k)$, where $0 \leq j \leq m - 1$ and $0 \leq k \leq m - 1$. A two-way communication line links $P(j, k)$ to its neighbors $P(j + 1, k)$, $P(j - 1, k)$, $P(j, k + 1)$, and $P(j, k - 1)$. Processors on the boundary rows and columns have fewer than four neighbors and, hence, fewer connections.

A number of indexing schemes are used for the processors in a mesh. For example, in *row-major* order, processor P_i is placed in row j and column k of the two-dimensional array, where $i = jm + k$ for $0 \leq i \leq N - 1$, $0 \leq j \leq m - 1$, and $0 \leq k \leq m - 1$. In *snakelike row-major* order, processor P_i is placed in row j and column k of the processor array such that $i = jm + k$ when j is even, and $i = jm + m - k - 1$ when j is odd, where i, j, and k are as before. Finally, *shuffled row-major* order is defined as follows: Let $b_1 b_2 \ldots b_q$ and $b_1 b_{(q/2)+1} b_2 b_{(q/2)+2} b_3 b_{(q/2)+3} \ldots b_{q/2} b_q$ be the binary representations of two indices

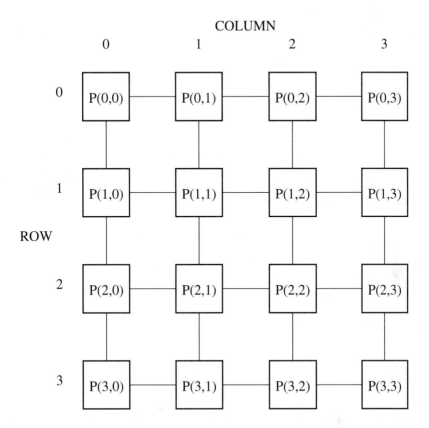

Figure 2.9: A mesh interconnection network.

i and i_s, respectively, where $0 \leq i, i_s \leq N - 1$. Then processor P_{i_s} occupies in shuffled row-major order the position that would be occupied by processor P_i in row-major order.

The mesh model can be generalized to dimensions higher than two. In a $d-$dimensional mesh, each processor is connected to two neighbors in each dimension, with processors on the boundary having fewer connections. Several other extensions to the mesh are possible. For example, a two-dimensional mesh can have m rows and n columns, where $m \neq n$ and $mn = N$. Another possibility is to allow each row and/or each column of processors to form a ring. Alternatively, the rightmost (bottommost) processor in each row (column) can be connected to the leftmost (topmost) processor of the next row (column), if any. Other extensions are described in Sections 2.3.4 and 2.3.5.

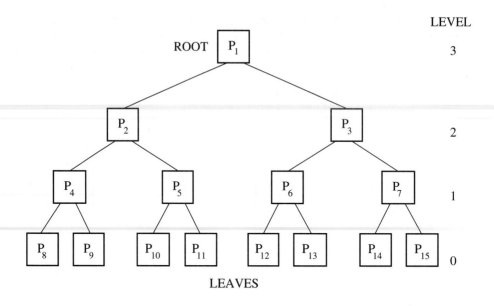

Figure 2.10: A tree interconnection network.

2.3.3   Tree

In a tree network, the processors form a *complete binary tree*. Such a tree has d levels, numbered 0 to $d - 1$, and $N = 2^d - 1$ nodes, each of which is a processor, as shown in Fig. 2.10 for $d = 4$. Each processor at level i is connected by a two-way communication line to its parent at level $i + 1$ and to its two children at level $i - 1$. The *root* processor (at level $d - 1$) has no parent, and the *leaves* (all of which are at level 0) have no children.

Two variants of the tree, which combine the tree, linear array, and mesh connections, are described next.

2.3.4   Mesh of Trees

In a mesh-of-trees network, N processors are placed in a square array with $N^{1/2}$ rows and $N^{1/2}$ columns. The processors in each row are interconnected to form a binary tree, as are the processors in each column. The roots of these binary trees are the processors in the leftmost column and topmost row. The tree interconnections are the only links among the processors. A mesh of trees is shown in Fig. 2.11 for $N = 16$.

It is sometimes more convenient to use a slightly different model. Here, N processors form an $N^{1/2} \times N^{1/2}$ *base* such that each base processor is a leaf of a column binary tree and a row binary tree. These column binary trees and row

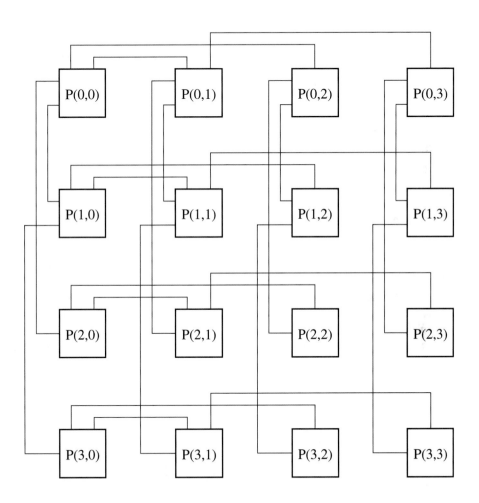

Figure 2.11: A mesh-of-trees interconnection network.

binary trees are formed by a set of additional processors. Each base processor is
connected to its parent processor in its column binary tree and its parent processor
in its row binary tree. The total number of processors is $O(N)$. This variant is
illustrated in Fig. 2.12, again for $N = 16$; the additional processors are shown as
small circles.

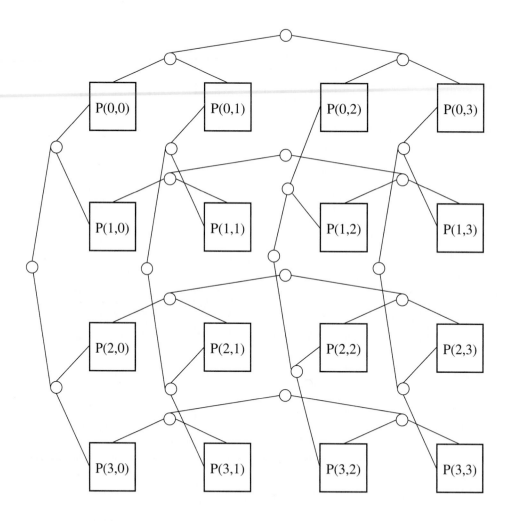

Figure 2.12: A different mesh of trees.

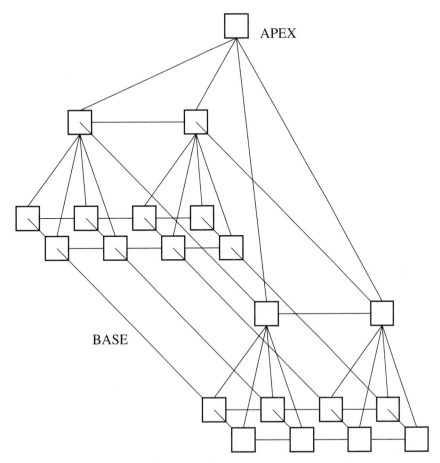

Figure 2.13: A pyramid interconnection network.

2.3.5 Pyramid

A *one-dimensional pyramid* parallel computer is obtained by adding two-way links connecting processors at the same level in a binary tree, thus forming a linear array at each level. This concept can be extended to higher dimensions.

For example, a *two-dimensional pyramid* consists of $(4^{d+1} - 1)/3$ processors distributed among $d + 1$ levels. All processors at the same level are connected to form a mesh. There are 4^d processors at level 0 (also called the *base*), arranged in a $2^d \times 2^d$ mesh. There is only one processor at level d (also called the *apex*). In general, a processor at level i, in addition to being connected to its four neighbors at the same level, has connections to four children at level $i - 1$ (provided that $i \geq 1$) and to one parent at level $i + 1$ (provided that $i \leq d - 1$). A pyramid is shown in Fig. 2.13 for $d = 2$.

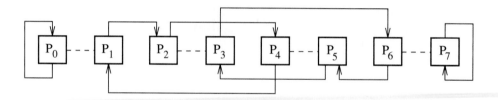

Figure 2.14: A perfect-shuffle interconnection network.

2.3.6 Shuffle Exchange

Let N processors P_0, P_1, ..., P_{N-1} be available, where N is a power of 2. In the *perfect-shuffle* interconnection, a one-way communication line links P_i to P_j, where

$$j = \begin{cases} 2i & \text{for } 0 \le i \le N/2 - 1, \\ 2i + 1 - N & \text{for } N/2 \le i \le N - 1, \end{cases}$$

as shown in Fig. 2.14 for $N = 8$.

Equivalently, the binary representation of j is obtained by cyclically shifting that of i one position to the left. This is illustrated in Fig. 2.15, in which an alternative representation of the perfect-shuffle interconnection is given as a mapping from the set of processors to itself. This representation explains the origin of the network's name: When a deck of playing cards is split into two piles of equal size, a "perfect shuffle" is obtained by interleaving the cards in the two piles.

If the directions on the one-way links are reversed, we obtain the *perfect-unshuffle* connection. A network as in Fig. 2.14, in which the links are undirected (i.e., are two-way communication lines), is known as the *shuffle-unshuffle network*. Finally, two-way lines connecting every even-numbered processor to its successor are added to the network. These connections, called *exchange* links, are shown as broken lines in Fig. 2.14. A network with the shuffle, unshuffle, and exchange links is called a *shuffle-exchange network*.

2.3.7 Hypercube

Assume that $N = 2^q$ for some $q \ge 0$, and let N processors P_0, P_1, ..., P_{N-1} be available. A *q-dimensional hypercube* is obtained by connecting each processor to exactly q neighbors. The q neighbors of P_i are those processors P_j such that the binary representations of the indices i and j differ in exactly one bit. This is illustrated in Fig. 2.16 for $q = 0$, 1, 2, 3, and 4. The indices of the processors are given in binary notation. Note that the hypercube in dimension q is obtained by connecting corresponding processors in two $q/2$-dimensional hypercubes.

An alternative representation, which may be used to implement a hypercube in a two-dimensional plane, is shown in Fig. 2.17 for $N = 8$.

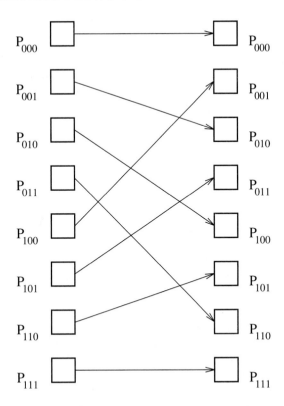

Figure 2.15: Alternative representation of the perfect shuffle.

2.3.8 Cube-Connected Cycles

To obtain a cube-connected cycles network, we begin with a q-dimensional hypercube and then replace each of its 2^q corners with a ring of q processors. Each processor in a ring is connected to a processor in a neighboring ring in the same dimension. The number of processors is $N = 2^q \times q$. A cube-connected cycles network is shown in Fig. 2.18, where $q = 3$ and $N = 24$. In the figure, each processor has two indices i and j, where i is the processor order in ring j.

2.3.9 De Bruijn

An undirected de Bruijn network has $N = d^k$ processors, each represented with a k-digit word $b_{k-1}b_{k-2}\ldots b_1b_0$, where $b_j \in \{0, 1, \ldots, d-1\}$ for $j = 0, 1, \ldots, k-1$. The neighbors of $b_{k-1}b_{k-2}\ldots b_1b_0$ are $b_{k-2}b_{k-3}\ldots b_0q$ and $qb_{k-1}b_{k-2}\ldots b_2b_1$, where $q = 0, 1, \ldots, d-1$. A de Bruijn network with $d = 2$ and $k = 3$ is shown in Fig. 2.19.

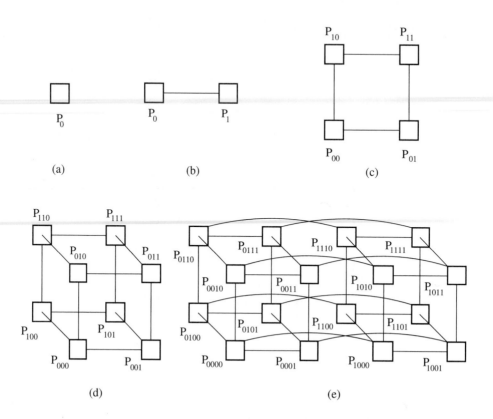

Figure 2.16: A hypercube interconnection network: (a) $q = 0$; (b) $q = 1$; (c) $q = 2$; (d) $q = 3$; (e) $q = 4$.

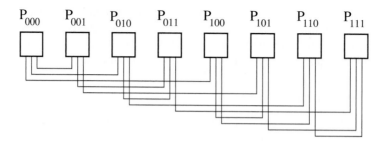

Figure 2.17: Alternative representation of the hypercube.

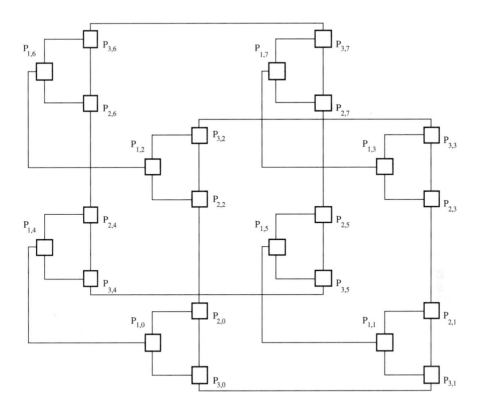

Figure 2.18: A cube-connected cycles interconnection network.

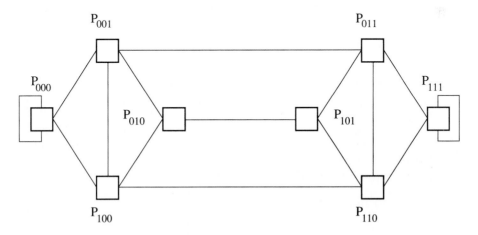

Figure 2.19: A de Bruijn interconnection network.

2.3.10   Star

A star is an interconnection network with the property that for a given integer m, each processor corresponds to a distinct permutation of m symbols—for example, $\{1, 2, \ldots, m\}$. In other words, the network connects $N = m!$ processors, where $m! = m \times (m - 1) \times (m - 2) \times \cdots \times 3 \times 2 \times 1$. Each processor is labeled with the permutation to which it corresponds. Thus, for $m = 4$, a processor may have the label 2134. In this network, denoted by $\mathcal{S}_m$, a processor P_v is connected to a processor P_u if and only if the index u can be obtained from v by exchanging the first symbol with the ith symbol, where $2 \leq i \leq m$. Thus, for $m = 4$, if $v = 2134$ and $u = 3124$, then P_u and P_v are connected by a two-way link in $\mathcal{S}_4$, since 3124 and 2134 can be obtained from one another by exchanging the first and third symbols. The star network is illustrated in Fig. 2.20 for $m = 4$.

Comparing Topologies. How do the several network topologies just described compare to one another? A number of criteria are usually used to help determine which topology is best suited for a certain application. We now introduce some of these criteria:

1. **Degree.** The *degree* of a processor in a given network topology is defined as the number of neighbors of that processor. The degree of the network is the maximum of all processor degrees in that network. For example, the degree of a binary tree of processors is 3, while that of a q-dimensional hypercube is q. Degree is an important criterion for assessing a topology and must be considered carefully. On the one hand, a large degree is interesting from a theoretical point of view, since many processors are one step away from any given processor. On the other hand, a small degree is preferable to a large one from a practical point of view, for the reasons given earlier: Having many neighbors is not only expensive, but may also be infeasible.

2. **Diameter.** The *distance* between two processors P_i and P_j in a given network topology is the number of links on the shortest path from P_i to P_j. The *diameter* of the network is the length of the longest distance among all distances between pairs of processors in that network. For example, the diameter of a linear array with N processors is $N - 1$, while that of a mesh with N processors is $2N^{1/2} - 2$. Since processors need to communicate among themselves, and since the time for a message to go from one processor to another depends on the distance separating them, a network with a small diameter is better than one with a large diameter.

3. **Length of links.** Although the models that we study are abstract objects, some of them may represent parallel computers to be implemented. In this light, one network topology is more desirable than another if it is more efficient, more convenient, and more extendable than the other. One particular criterion is the length of the longest link in the network. For example, in

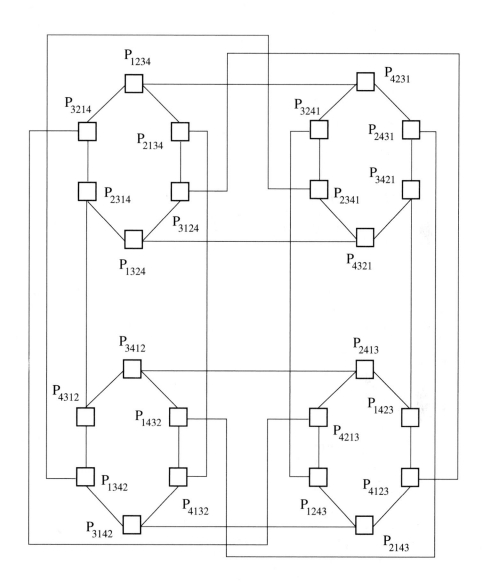

Figure 2.20: A star interconnection network.

Table 2.1: Comparing topologies with respect to degree and diameter.

Topology	Degree	Diameter
Linear Array	2	$O(N)$
Mesh	4	$O(N^{1/2})$
Tree	3	$O(\log N)$
Mesh of Trees	6	$O(\log N)$
Pyramid	9	$O(\log N)$
Shuffle-Exchange	3	$O(\log N)$
Hypercube	$O(\log N)$	$O(\log N)$
Cube-Connected Cycles	3	$O(\log N)$
De Bruijn	$2d$	k
Star	$m - 1$	$O(m)$

the linear array and the mesh, all links have constant length regardless of the number of processors, whereas all of the other networks described in Sections 2.3.3–2.3.10 have links whose length depends on the number of processors they have. A network whose links have constant length is usually easier and more efficient to implement.

Let us now examine how the topologies of Sections 2.3.1–2.3.10 compare with respect to the first two criteria, namely, degree and diameter. We assume $O(N)$ processors per network, where N is sufficiently large. We also take $N = d^k$ for the de Bruijn network and $N = m!$ for the star.

As Table 2.1 shows, it is difficult to find a winner. For example, the mesh is superior to the hypercube, since it has a constant degree. On the other hand, the hypercube has a smaller diameter than the mesh. The tree would appear to be better than both the mesh and the hypercube, until one realizes that its link length is a function of N. The star is also superior to the hypercube, since both its degree and diameter are $O(m)$. This can be seen more readily as follows: Since $N = m!$ and $\log m! = O(m \log m)$, the star's diameter is $O(\log N / \log m)$, which is smaller than the corresponding value of $O(\log N)$ for the hypercube.

Beside the three criteria listed, there are sometimes other features to take into consideration. For example, the tree has a particular weakness in that the root is a potential bottleneck: All communications between its left and right subtrees must go through the root. On the other hand, the strength of the mesh lies in its regularity and modularity: With its constant degree and link length, it consists of the same repeated pattern, making it easy to implement and extend by a row or a column if required.

The applications to which a parallel computer is destined also play an important role in selecting an interconnection network. Thus, one may want a network that is best suited for a particular problem to be solved. For example, a mesh is appropriate for problems involving matrices, while a tree is better equipped to handle database search problems. Alternatively, one may want a network that is capable of solving a wide variety of problems efficiently. One such network is the hypercube. We conclude this section with an algorithm illustrating the use of interconnection network parallel computers.

Example 2.5 We are given a hypercube model of parallel computation with n processors P_0, P_1, ..., P_{n-1} and a number x_i in each processor P_i, $0 \leq i \leq n - 1$. It is required to compute the prefix sums of the sequence $\{x_0,\ x_1,\ ...,\ x_{n-1}\}$. Specifically, we want to replace x_i with $x_0 + x_1 + \cdots + x_i$ in each P_i, $0 \leq i \leq n - 1$.

The following algorithm solves the problem using the technique presented in Example 1.6 for computing prefix sums. This technique is sometimes referred to as *recursive doubling*. Each hypercube processor P_i has two registers A_i and B_i. Initially, both A_i and B_i contain x_i, $0 \leq i \leq n - 1$. When the algorithm terminates, A_i contains $x_0 + x_1 + \cdots + x_i$. Let i and $i^{(j)}$ be two integers of $\log n$ bits each that differ in the jth bit, where $0 \leq j \leq (\log n) - 1$, the 0th bit being the rightmost, or least significant, bit. The algorithm consists of $\log n$ iterations, as follows:

Algorithm HYPERCUBE PREFIX SUMS

> **for** $j = 0$ **to** $(\log n) - 1$ **do**
> > **for all** $i < i^{(j)}$ **do in parallel**
> > > (1) $A_{i^{(j)}} \leftarrow A_{i^{(j)}} + B_i$
> > > (2) $B_{i^{(j)}} \leftarrow B_{i^{(j)}} + B_i$
> > > (3) $B_i \leftarrow B_{i^{(j)}}$
> > **end for**
> **end for.** ∎

This algorithm is illustrated in Fig. 2.21 for $n = 8$, where A_i and B_i are represented as the top and bottom registers of P_i, respectively, and X_{ij} is used to denote $x_i + x_{i+1} + \cdots + x_j$. The arrowheads on the links indicate the direction in which B_i travels at each step. Note that when the algorithm terminates, $A_i = X_{0i}$, while $B_i = X_{0n-1}$, for $0 \leq i \leq n - 1$. The algorithm runs in $t(n) = O(\log n)$ time and uses $p(n) = n$ processors, for a cost of $c(n) = O(n \log n)$. This cost, however, is not optimal in view of the $O(n)$ time sufficient to solve the prefix sums problem on the RAM, as described in Example 2.1. □

2.4 COMBINATIONAL CIRCUITS

As with the interconnection network parallel computers studied in the previous section, the term *combinational circuit* refers to a family of models of computation. In general terms, we define a combinational circuit as a device taking a number of inputs at one end and producing a number of outputs at the other end. Such a circuit is made up of a number of interconnected *components* arranged in columns

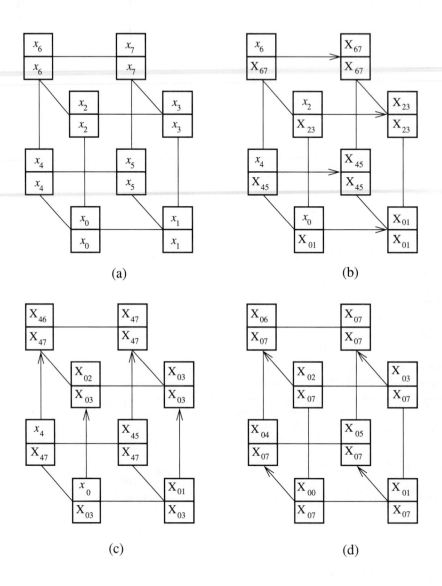

Figure 2.21: Computing the prefix sums on a hypercube: (a) Initially; (b) $j = 0$; (c) $j = 1$; (d) $j = 2$.

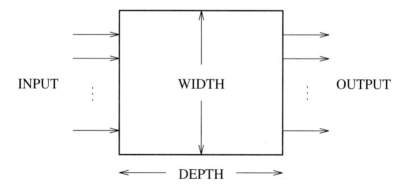

Figure 2.22: Depth and width of a combinational circuit.

called *stages*. Each component can be viewed as a simple processor. It has a constant *fan-in*—that is, a constant number of input lines. These lines carry data from the outside world or from (a constant number of) components in a previous stage. Each component also has a constant *fan-out*—that is, a constant number of output lines. These lines carry data to the outside world or to (a constant number of) components in a subsequent stage. Because each component has a constant number of neighbors, the circuit is said to have *fixed degree*.

Each component, having received its inputs, computes a certain function of these inputs in *one time unit* and produces the result as output. This function is essentially a simple arithmetic or logical operation such as comparison, addition, or logical **and**. A component is active only when it receives all the inputs necessary for its computation. An example of a combinational circuit is the circuit for computing prefix sums described in Example 1.3.

An important feature of a combinational circuit is that it has no feedback: No component can be used more than once while computing the circuit's output for a given input. One can imagine that data traverse the circuit in the same way that water flows from high altitudes to low ones or in the way that electricity travels from high to low voltage.

The *size* of a combinational circuit is defined as the number of components it uses. In Fig. 2.22, a circuit is represented by a rectangular box. The figure shows what is meant by the *depth* and *width* of a combinational circuit. The depth is the number of stages in the circuit—that is, the maximum number of components on a path from input to output. Depth, therefore, represents the worst case running time in solving a problem, assuming that all inputs arrive at the same time and all outputs exit at the same time. The width of a circuit is the maximum number of components in a stage. Note that the product of the depth and width provides an upper bound on the size of the circuit. We illustrate these definitions with the following examples:

COLUMN

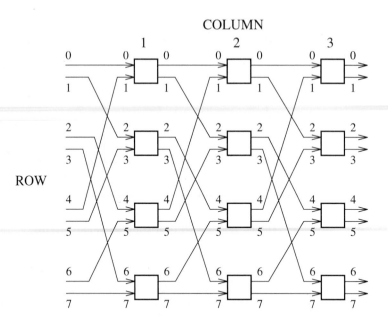

Figure 2.23: An omega circuit.

Example 2.6 The circuit of Fig. 2.23, known as an *omega circuit*, has n inputs and n outputs. It consists of $\log n$ columns (stages), numbered $1, 2, \ldots, \log n$ from left to right, with n rows (input or output lines) per column, numbered $0, 1, \ldots,$ $n-1$ from top to bottom. There are $n/2$ processors per stage, each with two input and two output lines. The processors in stage j are connected to those in stage $j+1$, $j = 1, 2, \ldots, (\log n) - 1$, by a perfect-shuffle interconnection. Thus, output line i in stage j is connected to input line $2i$ in stage $j + 1$, for $0 \leq i \leq (n/2) - 1$, and to input line $2i + 1 - n$ in stage $j + 1$, for $(n/2) \leq i \leq n - 1$. The circuit has a depth of $\log n$, a width of $n/2$, and a size of $(n/2) \log n$. In Fig. 2.23, $n = 8$. $\square$

Example 2.7 The circuit of Fig. 2.24, known as a *butterfly circuit*, has n inputs and n outputs. It consists of $1 + \log n$ columns, numbered $0, 1, \ldots, \log n$, with n rows per column, numbered $0, 1, \ldots, n - 1$. Let $P(i, j)$ represent the processor in row i and column j. For $0 \leq j < \log n$, $P(i, j)$ is connected to $P(i, j + 1)$ and $P(k, j + 1)$, where the binary representations of i and k differ only in their jth least significant bit. The circuit has a depth of $1 + \log n$, a width of n, and a size of $n + n \log n$. In Fig. 2.24, $n = 8$. $\square$

Example 2.8 A *merging circuit* receives as input two sequences of data, each consisting of $n/2$ values sorted in nondecreasing order. It produces as output these two sequences combined into a single sequence of n data values sorted in nondecreasing order. One such circuit, known as the *odd-even merging circuit*, is shown

COLUMN

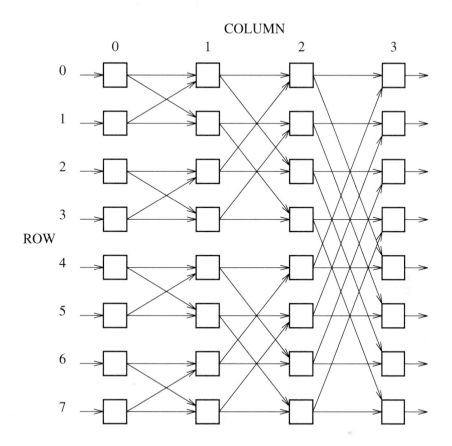

Figure 2.24: A butterfly circuit.

in Fig. 2.25 for $n = 8$. It consists of $\log n$ stages, with at most $n/2$ processors per stage. Each processor is a *comparator*: It receives two values as input and produces the smaller of the two on its top output line and the larger on the bottom line. (If the two inputs are equal, their order is unchanged.) The circuit has a depth of $\log n$, a width of $n/2$, and a size of $1 + (n/2) \times ((\log n) - 1)$. □

Example 2.9 A *sorting circuit* receives as input a sequence of n data values and produces as output these same data values arranged in nondecreasing order. One such circuit, known as the *odd-even-merge sorting circuit* is shown in Fig. 2.26 for $n = 8$. It consists of $O(\log^2 n)$ stages, with at most $n/2$ processors per stage. Each processor is a comparator (as defined in Example 2.8). The circuit has a depth of $O(\log^2 n)$, a width of $O(n)$, and a size of $O(n \log^2 n)$. □

Example 2.10 A (theoretically) more efficient sorting circuit is shown in Fig. 2.27. It consists of a complete binary tree with n leaves, $1 + \log n$ levels, and a total of

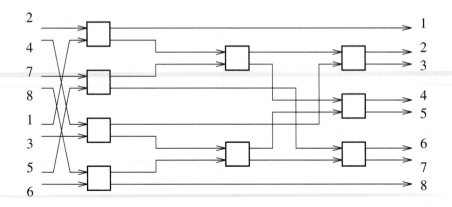

Figure 2.25: A merging circuit.

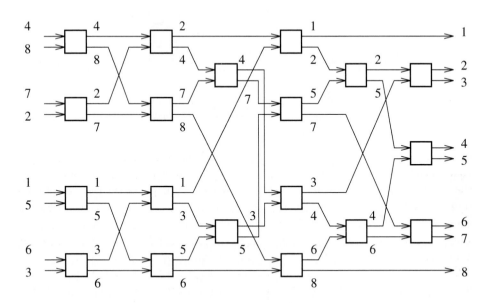

Figure 2.26: An odd-even-merge sorting circuit.

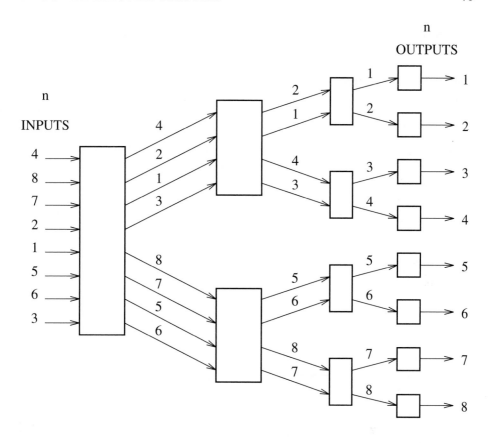

Figure 2.27: A (theoretically) efficient sorting circuit.

$2n - 1$ nodes. Each nonleaf node is a circuit made of comparators (as defined in Example 2.8). The circuit in a node is capable of receiving a set of m numbers, $2 \leq m \leq n$, and splitting it into two sets: The node's top child receives a set of $m/2$ numbers, each of which is smaller than or equal to the $m/2$ numbers sent to the node's bottom child. In this way, if n numbers in arbitrary order are fed to the root as input, they emerge from the leaves sorted in nondecreasing order from top to bottom. This circuit, referred to as the *sorting-by-splitting circuit*, has a depth of $O(\log n)$, a width of $O(n)$, and a size of $O(n \log n)$. It is therefore optimal in view of the $\Omega(n \log n)$ comparisons required in the worst case to sort a set of n numbers and the fact that each comparator is used exactly once. However, the circuit is far less practical than the odd-even-merge sorting circuit of Example 2.9, since the order notation used to express the circuit's depth (i.e., $O(\log n)$) hides a very large constant.

While sufficient for our purposes in this chapter, the foregoing description is necessarily greatly simplified. Indeed, the circuit inside a node receiving m inputs must have a depth of $\Omega(\log m)$ in order to perform correctly its job of splitting the input into two disjoint outputs. This would lead to an overall depth of $\Omega(\log^2 n)$ for the sorting circuit, thus contradicting the $O(\log n)$ bound claimed in the previous paragraph. Therefore, there is a lot more to the sorting-by-splitting circuit than meets the eye in Fig. 2.27. A complete description of this circuit is provided in Chapter 3. $\square$

Combinational circuits may be *special purpose* or *multipurpose*. A special-purpose circuit is designed to solve a particular problem. For example, the prefix sums, merging, and sorting circuits of Examples 1.3, 2.8, and 2.9, respectively, are special-purpose circuits. On the other hand, a multipurpose circuit may be used for many different kinds of applications. The omega and butterfly circuits are examples of multipurpose circuits. In Chapter 3, we revisit the merging and sorting circuits and study them in detail. We also give examples of problems that are solved using multipurpose circuits.

We conclude this section by noting that in many applications, a combinational circuit is used as a *two-way* device. Specifically, for some computations, the input and output ends of the circuit switch roles. Consider Fig. 2.22. In it, the data travel from the input (on the left) to the output (on the right). When the input and output ends switch roles, data travel from right to left. This variant is particularly useful in those applications where the circuit serves as a communication mechanism between two entities. Such an application is illustrated in the next two sections. Recall that in our description of the RAM and PRAM, an important part of the two models was left unspecified, namely, the memory access unit connecting processors to memory locations. We now show how combinational circuits can be used to implement the memory access units of the RAM and PRAM, thus completing our definition of these two models.

2.4.1　A Memory Access Unit for the RAM

In the RAM, there is one processor and a memory consisting of M locations. The model allows the processor to specify an arbitrary memory location from which it wishes to read or to which it wishes to write. The job of the MAU is to set up a path from the processor to the chosen memory location.

Lower Bounds. Since the MAU is to be implemented as a combinational circuit, we begin by deriving lower bounds on the width, size, and depth of such a circuit. Because there are M memory locations, the circuit must have M output lines, each leading to a distinct location. It follows that $\Omega(M)$ is a lower bound on the circuit's width and size. Also, in a combinational circuit, components have a constant fan-out. Let this fan-out be d. Then, starting at a component in the first stage and traversing s subsequent stages, a processor can reach one of at most d^s locations. Thus, the number of stages is at least $1 + \log_d M$, leading to a lower bound of $\Omega(\log M)$ on the circuit's depth.

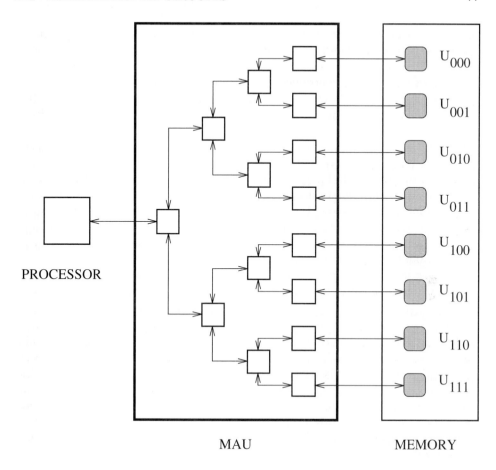

Figure 2.28: A memory access unit for the RAM.

A Binary Tree Implementation. A MAU for the RAM can be implemented as a binary tree of *switches*. As illustrated in Fig. 2.28 for $M = 8$, the tree's root is connected to the processor, and each of its leaves to a distinct memory location. The tree has $1 + \log M$ stages, numbered $1, 2, \ldots, 1 + \log M$, with the root at stage 1.

The tree links are assumed to be two-way communication lines. A switch can therefore send or receive a datum to or from one of its children. This way, a datum can travel from root to leaf and back if necessary. In fact, it is possible for two or more data to be traveling in the same or opposite directions at the same time: Each switch can receive a datum from its child and send the datum to its parent and at the same time receive a datum from its parent and send the datum to its child. It is important, however, to stress that the MAU is a combinational circuit, and therefore, a datum never backtracks: It goes either from root to leaf or from leaf to root.

In order to gain access to a memory location U_a, the processor sends an address a of $\log M$ bits to the root of the tree. The MAU decodes this address bit by bit. When it receives a, a switch at stage i, $1 \leq i \leq \log M$, examines its ith most significant bit: If this bit is 0, the switch sends a to its top subtree; otherwise it sends it to its bottom subtree. This way a path is created from the root to the leaf connected to U_a. A variable v travels along with the address a. If the processor wishes to write the value of v into U_a, then this is done by the leaf connected to that location, and the access is complete. Otherwise, if the processor wishes to read into v the value stored in U_a, then this value is read by the leaf connected to U_a and sent back to the processor (through the MAU), thus completing this memory access. Note that the path established by the MAU from the root to a leaf while decoding a need not be maintained for v's return trip during a READ access: In order to go from a leaf to the root, v follows a unique path.

Analysis.   Clearly, this MAU has depth $O(\log M)$ and width $O(M)$. Since the tree has $2M - 1$ switches, its size is $O(M)$. In view of the lower bounds derived earlier, the circuit is optimal. Another interesting property of this implementation is that it allows memory access requests (when known ahead of time) to be pipelined: The processor can issue a sequence of k such requests, each separated from the previous one by one time unit. The requests traverse the tree one after the other, and in $O(k + \log M)$ time they are all complete.

2.4.2   A Memory Access Unit for the PRAM

In a PRAM, there are N processors and M memory locations. The model allows each processor to specify an arbitrary memory location to which it wishes to gain access. Several processors are allowed to read from or write into the same memory location, and in the latter case a number of instructions are available to determine what ends up stored in that memory location. A MAU for the PRAM creates paths from the processors to the memory locations. It should be capable of handling exclusive accesses to memory (namely, **ER** and **EW**), as well as concurrent accesses (namely, **CR** and all forms of **CW**). We assume in what follows that $N = O(M)$.

A Naive Approach.   One simple way to construct a MAU for the PRAM using combinational circuits is to base it on the MAU for the RAM. Each processor P_i is connected to the root of a binary tree with M leaves numbered 1 to M. Similarly, each memory location U_j is connected to a binary tree with N leaves numbered 1 to N. This is illustrated in Fig. 2.29 for $N = 3$ and $M = 4$. Leaf j of P_i is directly connected to leaf i of U_j.

This circuit allows each processor to gain access to any of the memory locations.

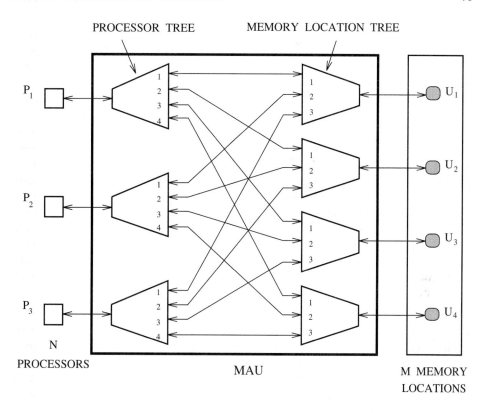

Figure 2.29: A naive MAU for the PRAM.

In order to do so, a processor P_i submits to its associated tree the address a of a given location. The tree associated with P_i now creates a path to the tree associated with U_a. The circuit also allows each memory location to receive either several READ or several WRITE requests simultaneously. Since all such requests arrive at the leaves of the tree associated with that location, the tree is used to reduce all these requests into one. Suppose that several READ requests are received by the leaves of the tree associated with memory location U_a. These requests now traverse the tree (in the manner described in Example 1.4) until one request makes it to the root. The value stored in U_a is read, sent back to the leaves, and, from there, sent to the processors that made the request. The case of several WRITE requests is handled similarly, with two differences:

1. As the requests traverse U_a's tree, the switches of the latter combine each pair of requests according to the **CW** instruction being used (e.g., checking whether two values to be written are the same in the case of **COMMON CW**, adding the two values in the case of **SUM CW**, and so on), until one value reaches U_a and is stored in it.
2. There is no return trip for the data.

It is easy to see that this MAU has a width of $O(N \times M)$, a depth of $O(\log M + \log N)$, and a size of $O(N \times M)$. When $N = O(M)$, the size of the MAU grows as the square of the number of memory locations. This is excessive, and we therefore seek to obtain a better design.

Lower Bounds. Let us begin by deriving lower bounds on the width, depth, and size of a MAU for the PRAM. Since there are M memory locations to be reached by the processors, $\Omega(M)$ is an obvious lower bound on the width of a MAU. As mentioned earlier, due to the fixed degree of the circuit's components, $\Omega(\log M)$ is a lower bound on the circuit's depth. Finally, a lower bound on the size of the circuit can be derived as follows: If M processors wish to gain access to M memory locations, there are $M!$ possibilities (assuming the simplest form of memory access, i.e., the one-to-one mapping that occurs in **ER** or **EW**). Suppose that the circuit uses x switches, each of which is capable of being in one of b states, where b is fixed. (For example, the switches could be binary, as in the MAU for the RAM, directing a datum they receive one way or the other.) The total number of states (or configurations) in which the entire circuit can be is b^x. In order to accomplish all $M!$ possible memory accesses, the circuit must be such that $b^x \geq M!$. Consequently, $x = \Omega(M \log_b M)$, thus placing an $\Omega(M \log M)$ lower bound on the circuit's size.

The preceding three lower bounds indicate that the naive approach to building a MAU for the PRAM, while optimal with regard to depth, may not be so with regard to width and size. Another point worth stressing again is that these bounds are derived for the weakest (i.e., exclusive) forms of memory access and hence apply automatically to the more powerful (i.e., concurrent) ones. If we could build a combinational circuit capable of executing all the different kinds of READ and WRITE instructions on the PRAM, and whose width, depth, and size match these lower bounds, then this circuit would be optimal for each form of memory access. We now describe such a circuit.

An Efficient MAU Implementation. Consider the MAU of Fig. 2.30. It allows N processors $P_1, P_2, \ldots, P_N$ to gain access to M shared-memory locations $U_1, U_2, \ldots, U_M$ on a PRAM. The MAU consists of a sorting circuit and a merging circuit. The sorting circuit receives its input from the processors and delivers its output to the merging circuit. The latter receives two sorted lists to be merged: One is the output of the sorting circuit, and the second is received from the shared memory. As can be seen from Fig. 2.30, the merging circuit has no output; rather, the circuit is useful for the data exchanges that take place *inside* it.

Upon execution of a READ or WRITE instruction, each processor P_i produces a record (INSTRUCTION, a_i, d_i, i), where:

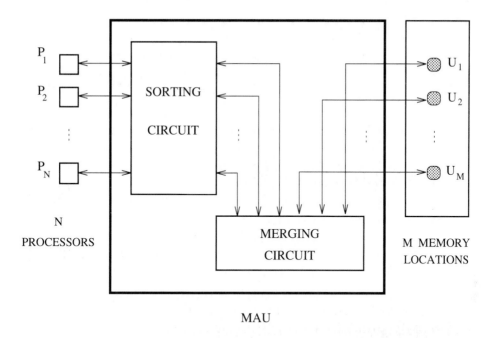

MAU

Figure 2.30: An efficient MAU for the PRAM.

1. INSTRUCTION is a field containing the name of the instruction (i.e., **ER**, **EW**, **CR**, **PRIORITY CW**, **SUM CW**, and so on) and the processor's priority in case of a **PRIORITY CW**;

2. a_i is the address of the memory location U_{a_i} to which P_i is requesting access;

3. d_i is a variable whose value is to be read from or written into the memory location U_{a_i};

4. i is P_i's unique index.

These processor records are input into the sorting circuit, where they are sorted in nondecreasing order on the address fields a_i. Here (INSTRUCTION, a_i, d_i, i) precedes (INSTRUCTION, a_k, d_k, k) if $a_i < a_k$, or if $a_i = a_k$ and $i < k$. Note that if P_i is requesting to write into U_{a_i}, then d_i holds the value to be written, whereas if P_i is requesting to read, then d_i will receive its value from U_{a_i}.

At the same time, a record (INSTRUCTION, j, h_j) is produced by each memory location U_j, where:

1. INSTRUCTION is an empty field to be filled later if required;

2. j is the unique address of U_j;

3. h_j carries the contents of U_j.

These memory records are already sorted in increasing order on their address fields j.

The two sorted lists of records are now provided as input to the merging circuit, where they are merged on the address fields. Here processor record (INSTRUC-TION, a_i, d_i, i) precedes memory record (INSTRUCTION, j, h_j) if and only if $a_i \leq j$. All necessary transfers of information between processor records and memory records occur at the comparators within the merging circuit, since records with identical values in their address fields are brought together. These transfers of information are as follows:

1. The INSTRUCTION field in a memory record receives its value from the INSTRUCTION field in a processor record.

2. In the case of a WRITE, d_i gives its value to h_j.

3. In the case of a READ, h_j gives its value to d_i.

4. Binary arithmetic or logical operations required in the case of a **CW** take place. (These include, for example, comparing values or priorities for a **COM-MON CW** or a **PRIORITY CW**, respectively, adding or computing the **and** of values for a **SUM CW** or an **AND CW**, respectively, and so on.)

In addition, the comparators store, for each record, the line on which it was input, so that processor records can be routed back to their source processors in order to complete a READ step or memory records can be routed back to their source memory locations in order to complete a WRITE step. Note that the comparators used here are slightly more sophisticated than those described in Example 2.8, since, in addition to their basic task of comparing two values, they must perform the (arithmetic or logical) operation specified in a **CW** and accommodate the information transfer and back routing just mentioned.

We now describe in more detail how the transfers of information take place inside the merging circuit for each form of memory access:

1. **Exclusive Read.** When processor record (**ER**, j, d_i, i) meets memory record (INSTRUCTION, j, h_j) in a comparator, the value of h_j is assigned to d_i.

2. **Exclusive Write.** When processor record (**EW**, j, d_i, i) meets memory record (INSTRUCTION, j, h_j) in a comparator, the value of d_i is assigned to h_j.

3. **Concurrent Read.** When processor record (**CR**, j, d_i, i) meets memory record (INSTRUCTION, j, h_j) in a comparator, the value of h_j is assigned to d_i. In addition, when two processor records (**CR**, j, d_i, i) and (**CR**, j, d_k, k) meet in a comparator, then if one of the two variables (for instance, d_i) has already received the value of h_j, it assigns its value to the other variable (in this case, d_k).

4. **Concurrent Write.** For definiteness, suppose that the processors are performing a **SUM CW**. (Other forms of **CW** are executed in the same way.) The processor and memory records first traverse the merging circuit in the forward direction (i.e., downwards in Fig. 2.30). As they do so, they remain unmodified (except for their relative order, which is altered by the merging process). Now consider the output of the last stage of comparators in the merging circuit. It is a sequence of processor records merged with memory records. In this sequence, the records of all processors P_k, P_l, ..., P_m wishing to write to the same memory location U_j are contiguous and are followed by the record of U_j. The records of P_k, P_l, ..., P_m, U_j are the leaves of a binary tree whose root is U_j and whose remaining nodes are comparators. These records now climb this tree by traversing the merging circuit in the opposite direction (i.e., upwards in Fig. 2.30), each record retracing its own path to its source. The values in their d_i and h_j fields are modified as follows:

(a) When two processor records meet—for example, (**SUM CW**, j, d_k, k) and (**SUM CW**, j, d_l, l)—the values of d_k and d_l become $d_k + d_l$.

(b) When a processor record and a memory record meet—for example, (**SUM CW**, j, d_i, i) and (INSTRUCTION, j, h_j)—the value of h_j (initially set to 0) becomes $h_j + d_i$.

When the record of U_j reaches U_j, it contains the correct value to be stored in U_j.

Example 2.11 Suppose, for illustration purposes, that $N = M = 4$, and let the four records produced by P_1, P_2, P_3, and P_4 be (**SUM CW**, 3, 6, 1), (**SUM CW**, 3, 5, 2), (**SUM CW**, 2, 8, 3), and (**SUM CW**, 2, 7, 4), respectively. In other words, processors P_3 and P_4 wish to write the values 8 and 7, respectively, into U_2, while processors P_1 and P_2 wish to write the values 6 and 5, respectively, into U_3. The four records produced by U_1, U_2, U_3, and U_4 are (INSTRUCTION, 1, h_1), (INSTRUCTION, 2, h_2), (INSTRUCTION, 3, h_3), and (INSTRUCTION, 4, h_4), respectively. The processor records are given as input to the sorting circuit, and they exit in the following order: (**SUM CW**, 2, 8, 3), (**SUM CW**, 2, 7, 4), (**SUM CW**, 3, 6, 1), (**SUM CW**, 3, 5, 2). These and the memory records are now fed to the merging circuit, where they are merged on their second fields. The two memory records (INSTRUCTION, 1, h_1) and (INSTRUCTION, 4, h_4) meet no processor record with the same second field and therefore remain unchanged. On the other hand, there are two processor records, namely, (**SUM CW**, 2, 8, 3) and (**SUM CW**, 2, 7, 4), with the same second field as the memory record (INSTRUCTION, 2, h_2), and, as a result, the latter becomes (**SUM CW**, 2, 15). Similarly, the memory record (INSTRUCTION, 3, h_3) becomes (**SUM CW**, 3, 11) due to the presence of the two processor records (**SUM CW**, 3, 6, 1) and (**SUM CW**, 3, 5, 2). □

Analysis. The width, depth, and size of the MAU described here depend on the choice of merging and sorting circuits. Suppose that the circuits of Examples 2.8

and 2.9 are used. This gives a MAU of width $O(M + N)$, depth $O(\log^2 N) + O(\log(M + N))$, and size $O(N \log^2 N) + O((M + N) \log(M + N))$. Taking $N = O(M)$, we find that these values become $O(M)$, $O(\log^2 M)$, and $O(M \log^2 M)$, respectively. With the exception of width, the values are not optimal.

A far less practical, but theoretically optimal, MAU can be obtained by replacing the sorting circuit used with that in Example 2.10. The MAU now has a width of $O(M + N)$, a depth of $O(\log N) + O(\log(M + N))$, and a size of $O(N \log N) + O((M + N) \log(M + N))$. Again, taking $N = O(M)$, these values become $O(M)$, $O(\log M)$, and $O(M \log M)$, respectively, all of which match the lower bounds, up to a constant multiplicative factor. An alternative MAU for the PRAM whose width, depth, and size are also optimal is described in Problem 11.28.

Two final comments are in order:

1. Implementing the PRAM's MAU as a combinational circuit often allows memory access requests to be pipelined. As illustrated in Example 2.4, k requests can be completed in $O(k + \log M)$ time. One important detail here is that each comparator needs to "remember" which of its two input lines was used by a record, in order to be able to route the record back to its origin (processor or memory location). One bit suffices for this purpose. However, during pipelining, $O(\log M)$ different memory requests may coexist in the MAU at the same time (since the MAU has a depth of $O(\log M)$). This means that a comparator needs to remember the return path for $O(\log M)$ records at a time, and thus, $O(\log M)$ bits are required. This is not unreasonable, since the comparator must have registers of that size to handle the values and addresses associated with a memory of size M.

2. The MAU described in this section executes the most powerful forms of memory access, while requiring no more resources asymptotically (i.e., up to a constant multiplicative factor for large M) than are necessary to execute the weakest ones. Thus, a **SUM CW** is executed in the same amount of time as an **ER**, while using no more resources than are required by an **ER**.

2.5   PROBLEMS

2.1 Show how the prefix sums of a sequence of numbers $\{x_0, x_1, \ldots, x_{n-1}\}$ can be computed in constant time on the PRAM. How many processors did you use?

2.2 In algorithm PRAM MULTIPLY_2 of Example 2.4, it is possible to pipeline READ requests. Modify the algorithm such that the statement

$$z(i, j) \leftarrow y(i, j) \times y(i, j)$$

is replaced with the statement

$$y(i, j) \leftarrow y(i, j) \times y(i, j).$$

Is pipelining of READ requests still possible?

2.3 In algorithm PRAM MULTIPLY_3 of Example 2.4, it is not possible to pipeline READ requests. Modify the algorithm such that the statement

$$z(a, b) \leftarrow y(h, d) \times y(e, f)$$

is replaced with the two statements

$$k \leftarrow (\lceil y(i, j) \rceil \bmod n) + 1, \quad y(i, j) \leftarrow y(i, k) \times y(k, j).$$

Is pipelining of READ requests now possible?

2.4 In algorithm PRAM MULTIPLY_3 of Example 2.4, it is not possible to pipeline READ requests, since the *address* of the value to be read during the ith iteration depends on the value computed during the $(i-1)$st iteration. Sometimes pipelining is not possible even if all the addresses from which reading is to take place are known in advance. This occurs when the *value* stored in a certain memory location may change after it has been requested by a processor and before it is received by that processor. Suppose that location U_i contains a value V and that a processor P_j issues a request to read from U_i, several time units before that value is actually needed. Now, as the value V travels through the MAU towards the processor, the algorithm causes a new value W to be stored in U_i. As a result, when V reaches P_j, it is the *old* value of U_i, and not necessarily the one needed by P_j at that moment. Describe a computation that fits this description.

2.5 Modify algorithm PRAM MULTIPLY_3 of Example 2.4 such that the statement

$$z(a, b) \leftarrow y(h, d) \times y(e, f)$$

is replaced with the statement

$$y(i, j) \leftarrow y(i, i) \times y(j, j).$$

Is pipelining of READ requests possible in this case?

2.6 A sequence $X = \{x_1, x_2, \ldots, x_n\}$ of n distinct integers is stored in the shared memory of a PRAM. It is required to find the smallest integer in X and place it in location *smallest* of the shared memory.

(a) Design an $(n/2)$-processor PRAM algorithm for this problem that uses no **CW** instruction.

(b) Analyze the running time of your algorithm. Is it cost optimal?

(*Hint*: A lower bound on the number of operations required to find the smallest element of X is $\Omega(n)$, since each integer must be examined at least once.)

2.7 Repeat Problem 2.6 for the case where $O(n/\log n)$ processors are available and no **CW** instruction is allowed. (*Hint*: Each processor finds the smallest of $O(\log n)$ integers sequentially; then the algorithm developed to solve Problem 2.6 is applied.) What is the cost of your algorithm?

2.8 Repeat Problem 2.6 for the case where $O(n^2)$ processors are available and the **COMMON CW** (but no other **CW**) instruction is allowed. Can the smallest integer in X be found in constant time? (*Hint*: All pairs (x_i, x_j) can be compared simultaneously. If, for some k, no integer in X is found to be smaller than x_k, then x_k is the smallest.)

2.9 Repeat Problem 2.6 for the case where $O(n)$ processors are available and the **COMMON CW** (but no other **CW**) instruction is allowed. Show that the smallest integer in X can be found in $O(\log \log n)$ time. (*Hint*: The algorithm is modeled using a logical tree T with n leaves. Each leaf holds one of the integers x_i. Each nonleaf vertex v has $n_v^{1/2}$ children, where n_v is the number of leaves of the subtree T_v of T whose root is v. Thus, for example, the root of T has $n^{1/2}$ children. It follows that T has $O(\log \log n)$ levels. Each nonleaf vertex v is in charge of finding the minimum of the integers stored in the leaves of T_v. It does so with $O(n_v)$ processors using the algorithm of Problem 2.8.)

2.10 Show how a cost-optimal parallel algorithm (i.e., one whose cost is $O(n)$) can be obtained for solving Problem 2.6 in $O(\log \log n)$ time using $O(n/\log \log n)$ processors when the **COMMON CW** (but no other **CW**) instruction is allowed. (*Hint*: Combine the approaches applied in Problems 2.7 and 2.9.)

2.11 Two points q and s in a simple polygon R are said to be *visible* from one another if the line segment with endpoints q and s does not intersect any edge of R. The *visibility polygon* from a point q contained inside a polygon R is that region of R that is visible from q. Show how the visibility polygon can be computed in parallel on a PRAM model of computation.

2.12 Let $G = (V, E)$ be a connected undirected graph, where V is the set of vertices and E is the set of edges of G. Further, let $H = (V_H, E_H)$ and $K = (V_K, E_K)$ be two subgraphs of G. The *symmetric difference* of H and K, denoted by $H \oplus K$, is the subgraph $G' = (V', E')$ of G, where E' is the set of edges in $E_H \cup E_K$, but not in $E_H \cap E_K$, and V' is the set of vertices connected by edges in E'. A *cycle* in G is a sequence of edges $\{(v_i, v_j), (v_j, v_k), \ldots, (v_l, v_m), (v_m, v_i)\}$ from E. A set of *fundamental cycles* of G is a collection F of cycles of G with the property that any cycle C of G can be written as $C = C_1 \oplus C_2 \oplus \cdots \oplus C_m$ for some collection of cycles $C_1, C_2, \ldots, C_m$ of F. Design a PRAM algorithm for determining the set of fundamental cycles of an n-vertex graph. Analyze your algorithm's running time, number of processors used, and cost.

2.13 In Section 2.2, we defined the PRAM as a model of parallel computation in which the processors do not necessarily operate in lockstep fashion and/or the program to be executed is not necessarily the same for all processors. Let us refer to this general model as the *asynchronous* PRAM. Our focus in Section 2.2, however, was on a special case of the general model, namely, the *synchronous* PRAM. As it turns out, there are many problems that lack the structure to be effectively solved by the synchronous PRAM. Describe a problem for which the asynchronous PRAM is particularly suitable, and design an algorithm for the solution to the problem on this model. (*Hint:* Consider the following example: When a computer plays a game of strategy (such as chess or checkers), it typically searches a tree data structure in order to choose a move. In this tree, each node is a board position and each edge is a move. Associated with each node is a value indicating the goodness to the computer of the board position the node represents. The move from the root, on the path leading to the position deemed best among all positions examined to a certain depth, is then chosen by the computer. A parallel computer may search such a tree by exploring several move sequences simultaneously. There are many reasons why an asynchronous PRAM may be useful, including, for example, the fact that the tree is not necessarily uniform (since not all nodes have the same number of children), the need to abandon certain unpromising paths, and so on.)

2.14 *Branch and bound* is the name of a well-known algorithm for solving combinatorial optimization problems. Suppose that we are given one such problem for which it is desired to find a *least cost* solution from among N *feasible* solutions. The number N is assumed to be so large as to preclude exhaustive enumeration. In branch and bound, we think of the N feasible solutions as the leaves of a giant tree. Each node on a path from root to leaf represents a partial solution, obtained by extending the partial solution represented by its parent. Starting with the empty solution at the root, the algorithm generates all of the root's descendants. Expansion then continues from the node with least cost, and the process is repeated. When the cost of a partial solution exceeds a certain bound, the associated node is no longer a candidate for expansion. The search continues until a leaf is reached and there are no more nodes to be expanded. This leaf represents a least cost solution. Show how the branch-and-bound algorithm can be implemented naturally on an asynchronous PRAM.

2.15 It is sometimes computationally infeasible (even with a parallel computer) to obtain exact answers to some combinatorial optimization problems. Instead, a *near-optimal* solution is computed using an approximation method. One such method is known as *local neighborhood search*. For example, let f be a combinatorial function that is to be minimized. We begin by computing the value of f at a randomly chosen point. Points in the vicinity of that point are then examined and the value of f computed for each new point. Each time a point reduces the value of the function, we move to that point. This continues until no further improvement can be obtained. The point reached is labeled a *local minimum*. The entire process is repeated several times, each time from a new random point. Finally, a *global minimum* is computed from all local minima thus obtained. This is the approximate answer. The asynchronous PRAM appears to be particularly appropriate for obtaining parallel versions of this method. Describe at least two different versions of local neighborhood search for the asynchronous PRAM.

2.16 The PRAM has a repertoire of instructions for memory access consisting of **ER**, **CR**, **EW**, and (several variants of) **CW**. What other instructions would you add to this repertoire? In particular, what other forms of **CW** would be useful? Would these other forms be implementable on the MAU of Fig. 2.30? If the answer is yes, what mathematical properties do they share with the forms of **CW** in Section 2.2 (e.g., do they need to be associative and/or commutative)? Alternatively, how should the MAU be modified to accommodate these new variants?

2.17 Consider the following variant of the PRAM. The shared memory is divided into B blocks of M/B memory locations each. Only one of the N processors can gain access to any given block at any given time. In case two or more processors wish to read from or write into the same block simultaneously, a *collision* is said to have occurred: The requests are queued up and then serviced sequentially, one request at a time.

   (a) Discuss the advantages and disadvantages of this variant.

   (b) Suggest ways to organize the data in the memory blocks so that the number of collisions is minimized.

2.18 It is required to prove that the PRAM can simulate any interconnection network parallel computer, as well as any combinational circuit, with no degradation in performance. Specifically, show that:

   (a) If a network with n processors solves a problem of size n in time $t(n)$, then a PRAM with n processors and $O(n)$ shared-memory locations solves the same problem in time $O(t(n))$.

   (b) If a combinational circuit with n inputs and n outputs has width $w(n)$, depth $d(n)$, and size $s(n)$, then a PRAM with $O(w(n))$ processors and $O(w(n))$ shared-memory locations takes the same n inputs and produces the same n outputs in $O(d(n))$ time with $O(s(n))$ work.

   (*Hint*: Any computation (e.g., addition, comparison, and so on) performed by a network or circuit processor can be executed in the same amount of time by a PRAM processor. Where the PRAM differs from a network or a circuit is in the way processors exchange data. Suppose that in the network, or circuit, solution, processor P_i sends a datum d_i to processor P_j using the direct link connecting them. The same step can be performed on the PRAM by having P_i write d_i in some location of shared memory and then having P_j read d_i from that location.)

2.19 Consider the following two models of computation:

(a) A PRAM with N processors and $M = kN$ shared-memory locations, where k is some constant positive integer.

(b) A complete network with N processors and k memory locations per processor.

Which of the various forms of memory access allowed on the PRAM (i.e., **ER**, **EW**, **CR**, and **CW**) can be executed in constant time on the complete network?

2.20 Consider a PRAM with N processors and M shared-memory locations, where $M \geq N$. Describe an algorithm for simulating this machine on a complete network of N processors, each with M/N locations in its local memory. Note that, since computations performed locally by the processors take the same amount of time on both models, we are mainly concerned with simulating on the network all forms of memory access available on the PRAM. Also, unlike the case in Problem 2.19, the number of memory locations per processor on the complete network is not necessarily constant. For example, if $M = N^2$, then each processor has N memory locations. Finally, recall that on the PRAM, N processors can gain access to (at most) N memory locations in constant time. The simulation, therefore, should be able to accommodate the situation in which all memory locations to which the N processors wish to gain access (simultaneously) are held by one processor.

2.21 It is required to determine the smallest of a set of n numbers $x_0, x_1, \ldots, x_{n-1}$. Describe an algorithm for solving this problem on each of the following models, and express the running time of each solution as a function of n:

(a) Linear array

(b) Tree

(c) Shuffle exchange

(d) Hypercube

(e) Star.

2.22 For each of the following interconnection networks, describe a problem which can be solved efficiently on that network, give an algorithm for each problem, and derive the running time and cost of the algorithm:

(a) Mesh

(b) Mesh of trees

(c) Pyramid

(d) Cube-connected cycles

(e) De Bruijn.

2.23 Suppose that an algorithm is available for sorting the n numbers of a sequence S on an interconnection network with n processors such that when the algorithm terminates, processor P_i contains element x_i of S, where $x_1 \leq x_2 \leq \cdots \leq x_n$. Let the running time of this algorithm be $t(n)$. The network can be any one of the networks described in Sections 2.3.1–2.3.10, but for definiteness, we take it to be the hypercube. Show that a complete network of n processors can be simulated on a hypercube with the same number of processors such that each step of a computation on the first network requires $O(t(n))$ steps on the second. (*Hint*: The processors used by the hypercube are exactly the same as the processors used by the complete network. Therefore, computational steps performed by an algorithm on a complete network require precisely the same amount of time when executed on the hypercube. The difference between the two models is in the way routing steps are handled. Processors P_1, P_2, ..., P_n on the complete network can execute an arbitrary permutation on their respective data d_1, d_2, ..., d_n in one step such that each processor ends up with a datum initially held by another processor. Since not all pairs of processors are directly connected on the hypercube, a permutation is performed by sorting the data using the indices of their destination processors.)

2.24 Prove that an algorithm requiring $t(n)$ time to solve a problem of size n on a hypercube with N processors can be simulated on a shuffle-exchange network with the same number of processors in $O(\log N) \times t(n)$ time. (*Hint*: Computational steps require the same amount of time on both models, since the processors used by the hypercube are identical to the ones used by the shuffle-exchange network. Two processors P_i and P_j directly connected on the hypercube are not necessarily so connected on the shuffle exchange. The latter network must therefore use its existing links to simulate any nonexisting ones used by the hypercube algorithm.)

2.25 Show how the prefix sums of a sequence of numbers $\{x_0, x_1, \ldots, x_{n-1}\}$ can be computed on a hypercube network so that the cost of the computation is $O(n)$.

2.26 A sequence of numbers $\{x_1, x_2, \ldots, x_n\}$ is stored in the processors of a de Bruijn network such that P_i contains x_i for $1 \leq i \leq n$. Describe an algorithm for sorting the sequence on the network such that when the algorithm terminates, P_i stores the ith smallest number.

2.27 Show how a shuffle-exchange network can be transformed into a de Bruijn network (with $d = 2$).

2.28 In the *pancake* interconnection network, denoted by $\mathcal{P}_m$, each processor corresponds to a distinct permutation of m symbols—for example, $\{1, 2, \ldots, m\}$—for some integer m. Thus, $\mathcal{P}_m$ consists of $m!$ processors, and each processor is labeled with the permutation to which it corresponds. Accordingly, for $m = 4$, a processor may have the label 2134. A processor P_v is connected to a processor P_u if and only if u can be obtained from v by flipping the first i symbols, where $2 \leq i \leq m$. Hence, for $m = 4$, if $v = 2134$ and $u = 4312$, then P_u and P_v are connected by a two-way link in $\mathcal{P}_4$, since 4312 can be obtained from 2134 by flipping the four symbols and vice versa. A pancake network is shown in Fig. 2.31 for $m = 4$. Suppose that one processor in $\mathcal{P}_m$—for example, P_{1234}—holds a datum d that it must "make known" to all remaining $m! - 1$ processors. Describe an algorithm for completing this task in $O(m \log m)$ time. Is that time optimal?

2.29 The *plus-minus* 2^i (PM2I) interconnection network for an N-processor parallel computer is defined as follows: P_j is connected to P_r and P_s, where $r = j + 2^i \bmod N$ and $s = j - 2^i \bmod N$, for $0 \leq i < \log N$, and $2^i \bmod N$ is the remainder when 2^i is divided by N.

   (a) Let A be an algorithm that requires S steps to run on a hypercube network. Prove that a PM2I network with the same number of processors can execute A in at most $2S$ steps.

   (b) Let A be an algorithm that requires S steps to run on a PM2I network with N processors. Prove that a hypercube network with the same number of processors can execute A in at most $S \log N$ steps.

2.30 Consider the following variant to the approach used in Section 2.3 for routing messages on an interconnection network: Let each message be of size L bits, where L is not fixed. Each message has a *header* specifying its destination processor. The header first travels from source to destination, establishing a path. Once the path has been created, it is reserved for the transmission of the message. The latter is divided into *packets* of fixed size, each of which follows the path set up by the header. The packets are transmitted one after the other in a pipeline fashion. The path remains reserved for this communication until the last packet reaches its destination. The time required by the communication is given by

$$a + (k \times d) + (L \times r),$$

where a is the start-up time (to initiate the transmission), k is the time taken to traverse a link between two processors, d is the diameter of the network, and r is the rate of transmission (in bits per unit time). Discuss the merits, if

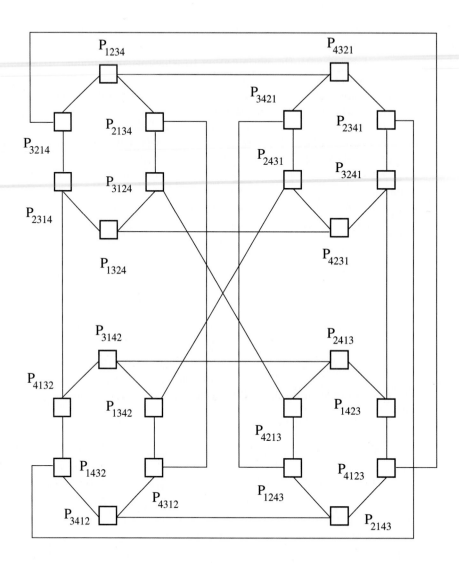

Figure 2.31: A pancake interconnection network.

any, of this approach, known as *circuit-switched communication* or *cut-through routing*. Give an example illustrating the difference between this scheme and that adopted in Section 2.3.

2.31 In a variant of circuit-switched communication known as *wormhole routing*, the message packets are sent as the path is being established by the header. Thus, the header may be viewed as a worm's head, with the packets forming the worm's body. The path itself is the *wormhole*, each one of its links becoming free immediately after it has been traversed by the last packet in the message. Discuss the advantages and disadvantages of this approach.

2.32 Relate the butterfly circuit to the hypercube network and the cube-connected cycles network. Specifically, establish a correspondence between the processors of the butterfly and those of the hypercube and cube-connected cycles. Then show that any problem solved on the butterfly in S steps can be solved on the hypercube and cube-connected cycles networks (with an appropriate number of processors) in $O(S)$ steps.

2.33 Use the sorting circuit of Example 2.9 and the merging circuit of Example 2.8 to trace the progress of the processor and memory records of Example 2.11 through the PRAM's MAU shown in Fig. 2.30, and show all transfers of information among records.

2.34 A sequence of variables $\{x_0, x_1, \ldots, x_{n-1}\}$ is given. Some of the variables are *leaders*. It is required to assign the value of each leader to all the variables that follow it in the sequence up to, but not including, the next leader. Design a combinational circuit for solving this problem. The circuit takes the sequence $\{x_0, x_1, \ldots, x_{n-1}\}$ as input and produces the same sequence as output with all the values assigned properly.

2.35 A *Beneš circuit* consists of two back-to-back butterfly circuits, as shown in Fig. 2.32. An s-dimensional Beneš circuit consists of $2s + 1$ stages, each with 2^s components. In the figure, $s = 2$. Beneš circuits belong to the family of *rearrangeable* or *permutation* circuits, due to their ability to produce as output any permutation of the input. In the figure, the input 1 2 3 4 5 6 7 8 is permuted into 5 4 3 1 8 7 6 2. Note that each component can be set in one of two states as shown in the figure, either to swap its two inputs or to pass them through unchanged. Prove that a Beneš circuit can permute any input to any output, using disjoint paths.

2.36 Three models of parallel computation were described in this chapter, namely, the PRAM and the two families of interconnection networks and combinational circuits. Can you think of other models? For every model you propose, explain how it differs from the three models described.

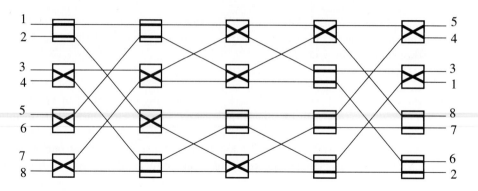

Figure 2.32: A Beneš circuit.

2.37 Of all models of computation described in this chapter, the most powerful
is the asynchronous PRAM of Problem 2.13. In theory, any parallel algorithm can be efficiently executed on it. The asynchronous PRAM is therefore
said to be a *general-purpose parallel computer*. The interconnection networks,
because of their rigid hardware architecture, are less powerful: While many
problems can be solved efficiently on them, these problems have a special
structure. Further specialized are the combinational circuits, with their constraints on data flow: The class of problems they can solve efficiently is even
more limited. At the extreme end of this spectrum, we can identify a family of
models known as *special-purpose parallel computers*. Here several processors
are assembled (e.g., as an interconnection network or a combinational circuit)
in a configuration specifically designed for the problem at hand. The result
is a parallel computer well suited for solving that problem very quickly, but
which cannot in general be used for any other purpose. Describe a specialized parallel computer for solving the following problem: A black-and-white
picture is stored in a computer in the form of a two-dimensional array. Each
array entry represents a *picture element* or *pixel*. A 0 entry represents a white
pixel, a 1 entry a black pixel. It is desired to execute a noise removal operation
that gets rid of sparse white dots on a black background and sparse black dots
on a white background.

2.38 A satellite picture is represented as an $n \times n$ array of pixels, each taking an
integer value between 0 and 9, thus providing various *gray levels*. It is required
to smooth the picture; that is, the value of pixel (i, j) is to be replaced by the
average of its value and those of its eight neighbors $(i - 1, j)$, $(i - 1, j - 1)$,
$(i, j - 1)$, $(i + 1, j - 1)$, $(i + 1, j)$, $(i + 1, j + 1)$, $(i, j + 1)$, and $(i - 1, j + 1)$,
with appropriate rounding. Describe a special-purpose parallel computer that
will solve this problem. Assume that N, the number of processors available,
is less than n^2, the number of pixels. Give two different implementations of

the smoothing process, and analyze their running times.

2.39 Let A and B be two $n \times n$ matrices with elements a_{ij} and b_{ij}, respectively, for $i, j = 1, 2, \ldots, n$. It is required to compute the matrix $D = A \times B$, whose elements d_{ij} are given by

$$d_{ij} = \sum_{k=1}^{n} a_{ik} \times b_{kj} \qquad \text{for} \quad i, j = 1, 2, \ldots, n.$$

Design a parallel algorithm for computing the product matrix D on the following model of computation, and analyze the algorithm's running time, the number of processors required, and the cost of running the algorithm. The model consists of n^2 processors arranged in an $n \times n$ array (n rows and n columns). The processors are interconnected as follows:

(a) The processors of each column are connected to form a ring.

(b) The processors of each row are connected to form a binary tree; that is, if the processors in the row are numbered $1, 2, \ldots, n$, then processor i is connected to processors $2i$ and $2i + 1$, if they exist.

The local memory of each processor consists of a constant number of registers.

2.40 Given the values of a_{ij} and b_i, for $i, j = 1, 2, \ldots, n$, design a special-purpose architecture to solve the following system of linear equations for the unknowns $x_1, x_2, \ldots, x_n$:

$$
\begin{aligned}
a_{11}x_1 &+ a_{12}x_2 + \cdots + a_{1n}x_n = b_1, \\
a_{21}x_1 &+ a_{22}x_2 + \cdots + a_{2n}x_n = b_2, \\
&\vdots \\
a_{n1}x_1 &+ a_{n2}x_2 + \cdots + a_{nn}x_n = b_n.
\end{aligned}
$$

2.6 BIBLIOGRAPHICAL REMARKS

The study of models occupies a central place in the theory of computation. For descriptions of various sequential models of computation, see, for example, Davis and Weyuker [195], Hopcroft and Ullman [301], Mandrioli and Ghezzi [403], McNaughton [411], and Wood [643]. A definition of the RAM is given in Aho et al. [7] that uses a read-only input tape, a write-only output tape, a program, and a set of registers. We use a more modern interpretation of the model in Section 2.1, as given in Akl et al. [29], Cormen et al. [185], and JáJá [310]. The MAU for the RAM, presented in Section 2.4.1, is from Akl [24] and is essentially the mechanism used for memory access in digital computers. (See, for example, Kuck [341].) For circuits that implement binary operations such as addition and multiplication, see

Cormen et al. [185]. The estimate of the number of atoms in the universe is from Gamow [254]. The number of different ways our universe might have started off—that is, the number of possible universes—is estimated in Penrose [486] to be $10^{10^{123}}$.

Early models of parallel computation (which predate today's more popular ones developed mostly since the late 1970s) include perceptrons and cellular automata. The *perceptron*, proposed in the late 1950s and described in Rosenblatt [538], was intended to model visual pattern recognition in animals. The device consists of a rectangular array of photocells that receives a binary pattern as input and uses a thresholding scheme to assign the pattern to one of two classes. A number of limitations of the perceptron model are uncovered in Minsky and Papert [429]. A *cellular automaton* consists of a collection of simple processors, all of which are identical. Each processor has a fixed amount of local memory and is connected to a finite set of neighboring processors. At each step of a computation, all of the processors operate simultaneously on data received from neighbors or the outside world and send the results to their neighbors and the outside world. Developed in the early to mid-1960s (see, for example, Codd [163]), this model enjoyed a purely theoretical appeal. Interestingly, the salient features of perceptrons and cellular automata were later rediscovered, and new names are now used for them. For example, many of the ideas underlying today's *neural net* model of computation, described in Diedrick et al. [204], owe their origins to perceptrons. Similarly, the dramatic reduction in the size of processors brought about by very large-scale integration (VLSI) has rendered the cellular automaton a feasible model for real computers. Today's *systolic arrays*, first described by Foster and Kung [238], are essentially finite cellular automata often restricted to two-dimensional regular interconnection patterns, with various input and output limitations. An in-depth study of systolic arrays is provided in Quinton and Robert [517].

The PRAM was originally proposed in Fortune and Wyllie [236] and later refined by Kučera [340] and Snir [576], among others. In the literature, the model is usually divided into the following four submodels, according to the way in which processors gain access to the shared memory:

1. the exclusive-read, exclusive-write (EREW) PRAM, in which no two processors can gain access to the same memory location at the same time.

2. The concurrent-read, exclusive-write (CREW) PRAM, in which two or more processors are allowed to read from, but not write into, the same memory location simultaneously.

3. The concurrent-read, concurrent-write (CRCW) PRAM, in which two or more processors are allowed to read from or write into the same memory location simultaneously.

4. The exclusive-read, concurrent-write (ERCW) PRAM, in which two or more processors are allowed to write into, but not read from, the same memory location simultaneously.

The ERCW is defined for completeness, but is not usually studied. (It is argued that a model which allows concurrent writing should be able to handle concurrent reading as well.) On the other hand, the CRCW PRAM is further divided into a number of submodels, according to the rule used to resolve so-called *memory write conflicts*, which occur when two or more processors attempt to write into the same memory location simultaneously. This gives rise to submodels such as the COMMON CRCW PRAM, the PRIORITY CRCW PRAM, and so on. A considerable amount of effort has been expounded to separate these models and place them in some hierarchy with respect to their power. For example, the CREW PRAM is shown in Snir [576] to be more powerful than the EREW PRAM and in Cook et al. [180] to be less powerful than the COMMON CRCW PRAM. Several papers were published to show how one model can simulate the other; see, for example, Vishkin [622] and Wah and Akl [632]. In fact, a large body of work exists whose aim is to distinguish among the variants of the CRCW PRAM with respect to power; see, for example, Boppana [116], Chlebus et al. [154], and Fich et al. [229]. Studies of the various PRAM submodels and their algorithms appear in Akl [21], Akl and Fava Lindon [34], JáJá [310], Karp and Ramachandran [323], Reif [533], and Smith [575]. In Section 2.2, we combined all of these models (i.e., the EREW PRAM, the CREW PRAM, the ERCW PRAM, and all variants of the CRCW PRAM) into *one* model, and we showed in Section 2.4.2 how one MAU can execute *all* forms of memory access. This is based on work appearing in Akl [22, 23, 24], Akl et al. [36], and Fava Lindon and Akl [226]. In particular, it is shown in Akl [22] that the distinctions among the various PRAM submodels are artificial and that all the variants are equivalent once the model is defined precisely—that is, so as to include a most important component, namely, the MAU. Curiously, the MAU is seldom mentioned in descriptions of the PRAM. Some of the rare works (besides the ones just mentioned) in which the MAU is included as part of the PRAM are Baase [80], Cormen et al. [185], and Quinn [515]. Its implementation as a combinational circuit in Section 2.4.2 is based on the work of Vishkin [623]. A number of experimental and commercial parallel computers were developed whose architecture implements the PRAM to some extent—in particular the CRCW PRAM; see, for example, Dongarra [207], Hillis [294], and Trew and Wilson [614]. Algorithms for the asynchronous PRAM are described in Akl et al. [25], Akl and Doran [31], Cole and Zajicek [175, 176], Gibbons [259], Martel and Subramonian [408], Martel et al. [409], Nishimura [444], and Ragde [519].

Interconnection network parallel computers were among the first models to be studied in some detail; see, for example, Hwang and Briggs [307], Reed and Fujimoto [530], Stone [593, 594], Varma and Raghavendra [621], and Wu and Feng [644]. Algorithms for arrays, trees, and hypercubes are presented in Leighton [367], while Fox et al. [240] and Ranka and Sahni [526] focus on hypercube algorithms. A tutorial overview of interconnection networks, particularly their graph-theoretic properties and routing and broadcasting algorithms, is provided in Stojmenović [589]. Star graphs were first proposed in Akers et al. [11]. Issues pertaining to the implementation of interconnection network parallel computers in a specific technology, namely, VLSI, are presented in Leighton [365], Leiserson [368], Mead and Conway [412], and Ullman [615]. The various forms of communication known as store and forward, circuit switched, and wormhole are studied in Kumar et al. [343]. Networks are also used to simulate the PRAM; an excellent survey of results on this subject is provided in Harris [288].

One can view combinational circuits as a special case of interconnection network parallel computers. However, because of their one-way data flow and their resulting ability to handle pipelining, it is far more useful to study them separately. For several examples, see Parberry [466] and Siegel [571]. The merging and sorting circuits of Examples 2.8 and 2.9 are due to Batcher [89]. The sorting circuit of Example 2.10 is a thoroughly simplified representation of one due to Ajtai et al. [9], widely known as the AKS sorting circuit. Other descriptions of the AKS circuit appear in Gibbons and Rytter [258] and Paterson [471].

Parallel computers can be classified in many different ways besides the one used in this chapter, as discussed in Hockney and Jesshope [298]. One particularly popular classification due to Flynn [234] groups parallel computers into two classes:

1. Single-instruction stream, multiple-data stream (SIMD) machines, in which a control unit issues an instruction to be executed simultaneously by all processors on their respective data.

2. Multiple-instruction stream, multiple-data stream (MIMD) machines, in which each processor has its own control unit and, hence, its own program, which it executes on its own data independently of all other processors.

SIMD and MIMD machines can belong either to the shared-memory family or to the interconnection network family; see, for example, Akl [21]. Examples of special-purpose parallel computers are provided in Mikloško et al. [424] and Snyder et al. [580].

Chapter 3

Combinational Circuits

This chapter is devoted to an in-depth study of parallel algorithms for the combinational circuit model of computation. There are at least three reasons for beginning our exposition of parallel algorithms with a description of algorithms for combinational circuits:

1. The first reason is a historic one: Algorithms for combinational circuits were among the earliest to be developed in the context of a systematic study of parallel algorithms. Algorithms for combinational circuits have withstood the test of time, and their importance is well appreciated.

2. The second reason is a pedagogic one: Because of its inherent simplicity, the combinational circuit model is a natural place to start for a good understanding of parallel algorithms.

3. The third reason is a practical one: Many algorithms for combinational circuits provide the basis for algorithms for other models or are often used as components of such algorithms. Again, owing to their simple structure in most cases, combinational circuits are considered the most amenable to direct implementation and can be used as building blocks for other models.

Several examples of combinational circuits were presented in Chapters 1 and 2. Also, it was shown in Chapter 2 how combinational circuits could be used to implement the memory access units of the RAM and PRAM models of computation. In this chapter, we provide the theory behind these and other circuits and show how combinational circuits for solving certain computational problems can be designed and analyzed. Section 3.1 introduces two circuits for sorting a sequence of numbers into nondecreasing order. The first circuit is based on the idea of sorting by merging and is simple to describe. However, its depth and size are not optimal. The second circuit uses sorting by splitting. While optimal in both depth and size, this circuit is significantly more involved, and consequently, its details are postponed until the

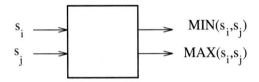

Figure 3.1: A comparator.

end of the chapter. A circuit for computing the fast Fourier transform is derived in Section 3.2. It is shown in Section 3.3 how a circuit can be used to perform an arbitrary permutation. This problem is related to the previous two, namely, sorting and computing the fast Fourier transform. In Section 3.4, we study circuits for computing prefix sums. Finally, Section 3.5 provides a more complete presentation of the circuit for sorting by splitting.

3.1   SORTING CIRCUITS

In this section, we describe two circuits for solving the following problem: Given a sequence of n numbers $S = \{s_1, s_2, \ldots, s_n\}$, where the elements of S are listed in arbitrary order, rearrange the numbers so that the resulting sequence is in nondecreasing order. For example, if the input is $\{30, 6, 2, 17, 3, 4, 18, 4\}$, then the output should be $\{2, 3, 4, 4, 6, 17, 18, 30\}$. A combinational circuit for solving this problem is called a *sorting circuit*.

All sorting circuits discussed in this chapter are built using one basic processor known as a *comparator*. Each comparator has two input lines and two output lines, as shown in Fig. 3.1. Given two inputs s_i and s_j, each arriving on one of its input lines, a comparator produces the smaller of s_i and s_j on its top output line and the larger on its bottom output line. If $s_i = s_j$, then s_i emerges on the top output line and s_j on the bottom one, provided that $i < j$; otherwise s_i and s_j are swapped. A comparator, therefore, is only capable of performing simple operations on its two inputs, namely, a comparison between s_i and s_j (and, if necessary, a comparison between i and j), followed (if necessary) by a swap. It takes one time unit for the comparator to read its inputs, compare them, and produce its outputs.

Each circuit is designed using one of the following two approaches to sorting:

1. **Sorting by merging.** Here the sequence to be sorted is divided into two subsequences of equal length. Each of the two subsequences is now sorted recursively. Finally, the two sorted subsequences are merged into one sorted sequence, thus providing the answer to the original problem. A circuit based on this approach was illustrated in Example 2.9.

2. **Sorting by splitting.** Here the sequence to be sorted is divided into two subsequences of equal length such that each element of the first subsequence is

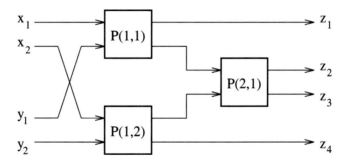

Figure 3.2: A merging circuit for two sequences of two elements each.

smaller than or equal to each element of the second subsequence. This splitting operation is then applied to each of the two subsequences recursively. When the recursion terminates, the sequence is in sorted order. A circuit based on this approach was illustrated in Example 2.10.

One important characteristic common to the circuits presented is that they are *oblivious* to their input: The sequence of comparisons they perform is fixed in advance. Regardless of the input, each circuit performs the same number of comparisons in a predetermined order. This is to be contrasted with sorting algorithms for the RAM, such as Heapsort and Quicksort, where the sequence of comparisons depends on the input. In what follows, two circuits are described, each based on one of the above approaches. The presentation is greatly simplified by assuming that n, the length of the sequence to be sorted, is a power of 2.

3.1.1 Sorting by Merging

Our first sorting circuit is based on the idea of sorting by successively merging sorted subsequences. We begin by describing the merging circuit used as a building block in the sorting circuit.

The Odd-Even Merging Circuit. Assume that it is required to merge two sorted sequences $\{x_1, x_2, \ldots, x_m\}$ and $\{y_1, y_2, \ldots, y_m\}$, to form a single sorted sequence $\{z_1, z_2, \ldots, z_{2m}\}$, where m is a power of 2. If $m = 1$, then we can use one comparator to produce x_1 and y_1 in sorted order. If $m = 2$, then it is easy to verify that the two sorted sequences $\{x_1, x_2\}$ and $\{y_1, y_2\}$ are merged correctly by the circuit of Fig. 3.2. By comparing the smallest two inputs, namely, x_1 and y_1, comparator $P(1, 1)$ determines the overall smallest number, namely, z_1. Similarly, $P(1, 2)$ determines the overall largest number, namely, z_4, by comparing the largest two inputs. The remaining two numbers are produced in sorted order by $P(2, 1)$.

If $m = 4$, then it is possible to prove (with some effort!) that the circuit of Fig. 2.25 (consisting of two copies of the circuit of Fig. 3.2, followed by three

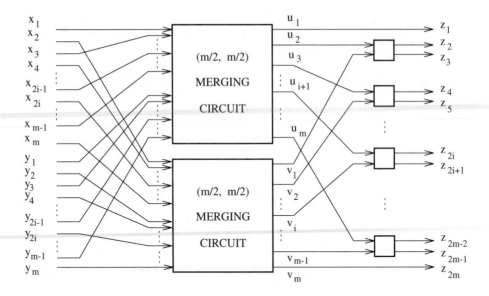

Figure 3.3: Odd-even merging circuit.

comparators) always merges two sorted sequences $\{x_1, x_2, x_3, x_4\}$ and $\{y_1, y_2, y_3, y_4\}$ correctly.

In general, a circuit for merging $\{x_1, x_2, \ldots, x_m\}$ and $\{y_1, y_2, \ldots, y_m\}$ is obtained as follows:

1. The odd-indexed elements of the two sequences—that is, $\{x_1, x_3, \ldots, x_{m-1}\}$ and $\{y_1, y_3, \ldots, y_{m-1}\}$—are merged to produce a sorted sequence $\{u_1, u_2, \ldots, u_m\}$.

2. Simultaneously, the even-indexed elements of the two sequences—that is, $\{x_2, x_4, \ldots, x_m\}$ and $\{y_2, y_4, \ldots, y_m\}$—are also merged to produce a sorted sequence $\{v_1, v_2, \ldots, v_m\}$.

3. Finally, the output sequence $\{z_1, z_2, \ldots, z_{2m}\}$ is obtained from $z_1 = u_1$, $z_{2m} = v_m$, $z_{2i} = \min(u_{i+1}, v_i)$, and $z_{2i+1} = \max(u_{i+1}, v_i)$, for $i = 1, 2, \ldots, m - 1$.

This construction is illustrated in Fig. 3.3. Let us refer to a circuit for merging two sorted sequences of length m each as an (m, m) *odd-even merging circuit*. As the figure shows, an (m, m) odd-even merging circuit consists of two $(m/2, m/2)$ odd-even merging circuits, followed by a column of $m - 1$ comparators. The two $(m/2, m/2)$ merging circuits are obtained by applying the same construction recursively; that is:

1. Each $(m/2, m/2)$ merging circuit views its input as two sequences, each indexed from 1 to $m/2$.

2. Each $(m/2, m/2)$ merging circuit uses two $(m/4, m/4)$ merging circuits, followed by a column of $(m/2) - 1$ comparators.

We establish that an (m, m) merging circuit correctly merges two sorted sequences $\{x_1, x_2, \ldots, x_m\}$ and $\{y_1, y_2, \ldots, y_m\}$ into a single sorted sequence $\{z_1, z_2, \ldots, z_{2m}\}$ using the following observations:

1. Since $u_1 = \min(x_1, y_1)$ and $v_m = \max(x_m, y_m)$, it follows that z_1 and z_{2m} are computed correctly as the smallest and largest numbers of the output sequence.

2. Each element of the sequence $\{u_1, u_2, \ldots, u_m\}$ is an odd-indexed element of either $\{x_1, x_2, \ldots, x_m\}$ or $\{y_1, y_2, \ldots, y_m\}$. Now in the latter two sequences, each odd-indexed element (except for x_1 and y_1) is larger than or equal to the preceding even-indexed element. It follows that $2i$ elements of the input are smaller than or equal to u_{i+1}; that is, $u_{i+1} \geq z_{2i}$. Similarly, $v_i \geq z_{2i}$.

3. In the sequence $\{z_1, z_2, \ldots, z_{2i+1}\}$, let k elements come from $\{x_1, x_2, \ldots, x_m\}$ and $2i + 1 - k$ come from $\{y_1, y_2, \ldots, y_m\}$, where k may be even or odd. Thus, z_{2i+1} is larger than or equal to k elements of $\{x_1, x_2, \ldots, x_m\}$ and $\lfloor (k+1)/2 \rfloor$ elements of $\{x_1, x_3, \ldots, x_{m-1}\}$. Also, z_{2i+1} is larger than or equal to $2i + 1 - k$ elements of $\{y_1, y_2, \ldots, y_m\}$ and $(i+1) - \lfloor (k+1)/2 \rfloor$ elements of $\{y_1, y_3, \ldots, y_{m-1}\}$. This means that z_{2i+1} is larger than or equal to $(i + 1)$ elements belonging to either $\{x_1, x_3, \ldots, x_{m-1}\}$ or $\{y_1, y_3, \ldots, y_{m-1}\}$. In other words, $z_{2i+1} \geq u_{i+1}$. Similarly, $z_{2i+1} \geq v_i$.

4. Since $z_{2i} \leq z_{2i+1}$, it follows that $z_{2i} = \min(u_{i+1}, v_i)$ and $z_{2i+1} = \max(u_{i+1}, v_i)$, as computed by the circuit.

Analysis. We now derive expressions for the width, depth, and size of the (m, m) odd-even merging circuit.

1. **Width.** Each comparator has exactly two inputs and two outputs. The circuit takes $2m$ inputs and produces $2m$ outputs. It therefore has a width of m.

2. **Depth.** Let $d(2m)$ denote the circuit's depth. We can write

$$
\begin{aligned}
d(2) &= 1 & \text{for } m = 1, \\
d(2m) &= d(m) + 1 & \text{for } m > 1,
\end{aligned}
$$

as illustrated by Fig. 3.1 and Fig. 3.3, respectively. Therefore, $d(2m) = 1 + \log m$. For $2m = 2^i$, $d(2^i) = i$.

3. **Size.** Let $p(2m)$ denote the number of comparators in the circuit. Again, we can write

$$\begin{aligned} p(2) &= 1 & \text{for } m = 1, \\ p(2m) &= 2p(m) + (m-1) & \text{for } m > 1. \end{aligned}$$

It follows that $p(2m) = 1 + m \log m$. Again, for $2m = 2^i$, $p(2^i) = 1 + 2^{i-1}(i-1)$.

The time taken by the circuit to merge two sequences is the circuit's depth—that is, $O(\log m)$. This time is quite fast, compared to the obvious lower bound of $\Omega(m)$ on the time required by the RAM to merge two sorted sequences of length m each. On the other hand, the number of comparisons performed by the circuit is the circuit's size—that is, $O(m \log m)$. The latter is not optimal in view of the $O(m)$ comparisons sufficient for merging on the RAM in the worst case.

The Odd-Even-Merge Sorting Circuit.   We now develop a circuit for sorting the sequence $S = \{s_1, s_2, \ldots, s_n\}$, based on the odd-even merging circuit. The circuit consists of a number of phases. In the first phase, $n/2$ sorted sequences of two elements each are obtained using a column of $n/2$ comparators. In the second phase, (2,2) odd-even merging circuits are used; a column of $n/4$ such circuits produces sorted sequences of length 4. Pairs of these are now merged into sequences of eight elements in the third phase, using (4,4) odd-even merging circuits. This continues until the final phase, in which two sequences of length $n/2$ each are merged by an $(n/2, n/2)$ odd-even merging circuit into a single sorted sequence of length n. The general structure of this circuit, called the *odd-even-merge sorting circuit*, is shown in Fig. 3.4. The operation of the circuit is illustrated in Fig. 2.26 for $n = 8$.

Analysis.   We analyze the circuit's width, depth, and size. Note that because the length of the merged sequences doubles after every phase, there are $\log n$ phases in all. The ith phase consists of $n/2^i$ circuits, each a $(2^{i-1}, 2^{i-1})$ odd-even merging circuit, for $i = 1, 2, \ldots, \log n$.

1. **Width.** Since the input and output are of size n, and since each comparator has two inputs and two outputs, the circuit's width is $n/2$.

2. **Depth.** Let $d(2^i)$ be the depth of a $(2^{i-1}, 2^{i-1})$ odd-even merging circuit used in the ith phase. We established earlier that $d(2^i) = i$. Therefore, the depth of an odd-even-merge sorting circuit for a sequence of length n is given by

$$\sum_{i=1}^{\log n} i = (\log n)(1 + \log n)/2.$$

This means that the time required for sorting is $O(\log^2 n)$.

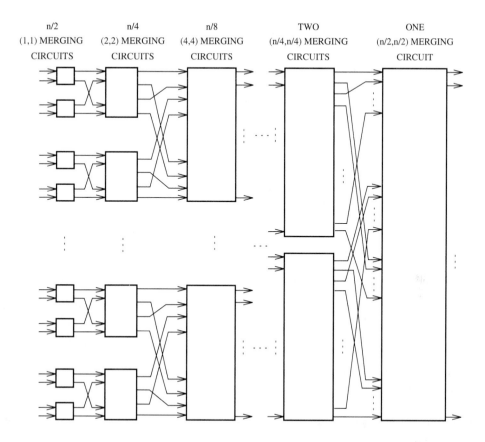

n/2	n/4	n/8	TWO	ONE
(1,1) MERGING	(2,2) MERGING	(4,4) MERGING	(n/4,n/4) MERGING	(n/2,n/2) MERGING
CIRCUITS	CIRCUITS	CIRCUITS	CIRCUITS	CIRCUIT

Figure 3.4: Odd-even-merge sorting circuit.

3. **Size.** Let $p(2^i)$ be the number of comparators required by a $(2^{i-1}, 2^{i-1})$ odd-even merging circuit in the ith phase. Earlier, we established that $p(2^i) = 1 + 2^{i-1}(i-1)$. Since the ith phase uses $n/2^i$ such merging circuits, the total number of comparators in the sorting circuit is

$$\sum_{i=1}^{\log n} (n/2^i)\left(1 + 2^{i-1}(i-1)\right) = (n/4)(\log^2 n - \log n + 4) - 1.$$

In other words, the circuit performs $O(n \log^2 n)$ comparisons.

In view of the $\Omega(n \log n)$ comparisons required in the worst case for sorting a sequence of length n on the RAM, the circuit's depth of $O(\log^2 n)$ is indeed quite small. By contrast, the circuit's size is not optimal, in view of the $O(n \log n)$ worst case time sufficient for sorting on the RAM (using, for example, algorithm Mergesort).

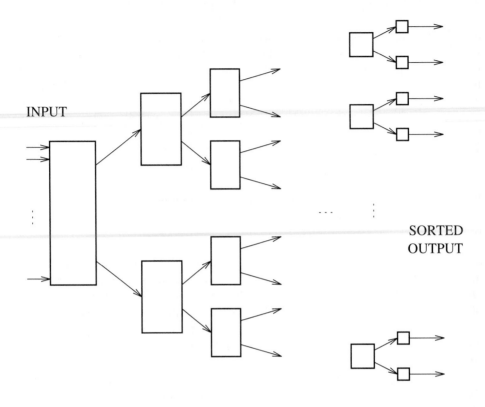

Figure 3.5: A tree for sorting by splitting.

3.1.2   Sorting by Splitting

Assume (hypothetically) that a complete binary tree with n leaves, and hence a total of $2n - 1$ nodes, is available. Each nonleaf node is itself a circuit of comparators capable of splitting its input into two halves, with all the elements in the first half (sent to the node's top child) smaller than or equal to all the elements in the second half (sent to the node's bottom child). The circuit inside a node with m inputs consists of $O(m)$ comparators, where $2 \leq m \leq n$. If we feed n numbers to the root, then after going through the $1 + \log n$ levels of the tree, the numbers reach the leaves, one number per leaf, sorted from smallest (at the top) to largest (at the bottom). This arrangement is depicted in Fig. 3.5. Since there are $O(n)$ comparators in each level of the tree, the size of the circuit is $O(n \log n)$.

What would the depth of this circuit be? Let us look at the circuit *inside* each node. If the node receives m numbers as input, then the circuit inside it is supposed to split this input into two subsets, the "smaller" with $m/2$ elements and the "larger" with $m/2$ elements. Now the first of these two subsets necessarily contains the overall smallest number among the m inputs. However, a circuit of comparators which identifies *that* number (even implicitly) and routes it appropriately to the node's top child must have a depth of $\Omega(\log m)$. (To see this, note that the smallest number emerges from a comparator that must have received its two inputs from two other comparators. The latter must have received their inputs from four others, and so on, until we have $m/2$ comparators that must have operated directly on the m input numbers.) This leads to a depth of $\Omega(\log^2 n)$ for the entire sorting circuit. With $O(n)$ comparators per stage, the circuit's size would be $\Omega(n \log^2 n)$, thus contradicting the $O(n \log n)$ upper bound claimed in the previous paragraph.

A modification of the hypothetical tree allows this contradiction to be resolved. It is possible to reduce the circuit's total depth to $O(\log n)$ by not insisting that the split performed at each node be exact. A number of *strangers* are allowed to propagate in each of the two subsets created by a node from its input—that is, numbers placed in one subset that should have been placed in the other. Most of these strangers are caught and reprocessed. The number of strangers grows increasingly small, so as to guarantee that the circuit's total depth and size are $O(\log n)$ and $O(n \log n)$, respectively. What remains to be shown is how the nodes of the tree in Fig. 3.5 are actually designed so as to satisfy the required bounds on the depth and size. This will demonstrate that the tree is no longer hypothetical and can indeed be built (at least in principle). We call the resulting circuit the *sorting-by-splitting circuit*.

Because of the optimality of its depth and size, this circuit is important from the theoretical point of view. However, its design is fairly complex by comparison with other circuits presented in this chapter. Therefore, we defer a detailed description of the sorting-by-splitting circuit until Section 3.5.

Also, it must be noted here that the asymptotic expression for the depth of the sorting-by-splitting circuit, namely, $O(\log n)$, hides a very large constant. Consequently, this circuit is not as useful in practice as the odd-even-merge sorting circuit.

3.2 A CIRCUIT FOR THE FAST FOURIER TRANSFORM

This section is concerned with designing a combinational circuit for the efficient computation of the fast Fourier transform (FFT). Such a circuit would be very useful, due to the many applications of the Fourier transform in science and engineering. The importance of the FFT stems from the fact that it reduces the complexity of a host of computations on problems of size n from $O(n^2)$ to $O(n \log n)$, thus making the computations feasible. We begin with some background in Section 3.2.1 and then define the FFT and present some algorithms for computing it in Section 3.2.2. The FFT circuit is described and analyzed in Section 3.2.3. Finally, in Section 3.2.4, the FFT circuit is related to the butterfly circuit.

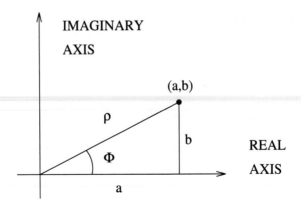

Figure 3.6: Polar form of complex numbers.

3.2.1   Complex Numbers and Roots of Unity

Understanding the FFT requires knowledge of complex roots of unity, and hence of complex numbers, both of which will now be briefly introduced.

Complex Numbers.   Since there is no real number x that satisfies the polynomial equation $x^2 + 1 = 0$ or similar equations, the set of complex numbers is introduced. For example, $x^2 + 4x + 6 = 0$ has the solutions

$$x = -2 + \sqrt{-2} \quad \text{and} \quad x = -2 - \sqrt{-2}.$$

If the number system is extended to include

$$i = \sqrt{-1},$$

all algebraic equations could be solved. In the preceding example, the solutions are

$$x = -2 + i\sqrt{2} \quad \text{and} \quad x = -2 - i\sqrt{2}.$$

Thus, complex numbers have the form $a + ib$, where a and b are real numbers. For historical reasons, a is called the *real part* and ib the *imaginary part* of the complex number.

It is often convenient to express complex numbers using the *polar form*, as shown in Fig. 3.6. A point (a, b) in the complex polar plane is represented using a *modulus* ρ and an *angle* ϕ. Hence,

$$a = \rho \cos \phi \quad \text{and} \quad b = \rho \sin \phi,$$

where $\rho = \left(a^2 + b^2\right)^{1/2}$ and sin and cos are the *sine* and *cosine* functions, respectively. It follows that

$$z = a + ib = \rho(\cos \phi + i \sin \phi).$$

The product of two complex numbers,

$$z_1 = \rho_1(\cos\phi_1 + i\sin\phi_1) \quad \text{and} \quad z_2 = \rho_2(\cos\phi_2 + i\sin\phi_2),$$

is expressed as

$$z_1 z_2 = \rho_1 \rho_2 \left(\cos(\phi_1 + \phi_2) + i\sin(\phi_1 + \phi_2) \right).$$

Therefore, for $z = \rho\cos\phi + i\sin\phi$ and a real number n, we have

$$
\begin{aligned}
z^n &= (\rho(\cos\phi + i\sin\phi))^n \\
&= \rho^n(\cos n\phi + i\sin n\phi).
\end{aligned}
$$

If n is a positive integer, then an nth root of z is

$$
\begin{aligned}
z^{1/n} &= (\rho(\cos\phi + i\sin\phi))^{1/n} \\
&= \rho^{1/n}\left(\cos\tfrac{\phi + 2k\pi}{n} + i\sin\tfrac{\phi + 2k\pi}{n} \right)
\end{aligned}
$$

for $k = 0, 1, \ldots, n-1$, which means that there are n different values for $z^{1/n}$, called the nth *roots* of z. Note that $\cos(\phi + 2k\pi) = \cos\phi$ and $\sin(\phi + 2k\pi) = \sin\phi$.

Finally, let e denote the base of the natural logarithm. Using Taylor's infinite series for e^x, $\cos x$, and $\sin x$, we can write

$$e^{i\phi} = \cos\phi + i\sin\phi,$$

and hence,

$$z^{1/n} = \rho^{1/n} e^{i(\frac{\phi + 2k\pi}{n})}, \quad \text{for} \quad k = 0, 1, \ldots, n-1.$$

Complex Roots of Unity. A complex nth root of unity is a complex number ω_n such that $(\omega_n)^n = 1$. Since

$$
\begin{aligned}
1^{1/n} &= (1(\cos 0 + i\sin 0))^{1/n} \\
&= \cos\tfrac{2k\pi}{n} + i\sin\tfrac{2k\pi}{n} \\
&= e^{i\frac{2k\pi}{n}}, \quad \text{for} \quad k = 0, 1, \ldots, n-1,
\end{aligned}
$$

it follows that there are exactly n complex nth roots of unity. Of particular importance is the root obtained when $k = 1$, namely,

$$\omega_n = e^{i\frac{2\pi}{n}}.$$

This is called the *primitive* or *principal* complex nth root of unity. The remaining $n-1$ complex nth roots of unity are powers of ω_n:

$$(\omega_n)^0, (\omega_n)^2, \ldots, (\omega_n)^{n-1}.$$

Henceforth, we write ω_n^k instead of $(\omega_n)^k$, for simplicity.

The roots of unity have a property that will prove very useful in computing the Fourier transform. Suppose that n is even. If the n complex nth roots of unity, namely, $\omega_n^0, \omega_n^1, \ldots, \omega_n^{n-1}$, are *squared*, then the resulting set of n values represents the $n/2$ complex $(n/2)$nd roots of unity, namely,

$$\omega_{n/2}^0, \omega_{n/2}^1, \ldots, \omega_{n/2}^{n/2-1},$$

each appearing twice. To see this, note that

$$
\begin{aligned}
\omega_n^{n/2} &= \left(e^{i\frac{2\pi}{n}} \right)^{n/2} \\
&= e^{i\pi} \\
&= \cos\pi + i\sin\pi \\
&= -1.
\end{aligned}
$$

Consequently, $\omega_n^{k+\frac{n}{2}} = -\omega_n^k$, and thus,

$$\left(\omega_n^{k+\frac{n}{2}} \right)^2 = \left(\omega_n^k \right)^2.$$

This shows that pairs of nth roots have the same square. Also,

$$
\begin{aligned}
\left(\omega_n^k \right)^2 &= \left(e^{i\frac{2\pi}{n}} \right)^{2k} \\
&= \left(e^{i\frac{2\pi}{n/2}} \right)^k \\
&= \omega_{n/2}^k,
\end{aligned}
$$

indicating that each nth root, when squared, gives an $(n/2)$nd root.

3.2.2   The Fast Fourier Transform

We are now ready to define the Fourier transform and its algorithms. Given a sequence of numbers $\{a_0, a_1, \ldots, a_{n-1}\}$, its discrete Fourier transform (DFT) is the sequence $\{b_0, b_1, \ldots, b_{n-1}\}$, where

$$b_j = \sum_{k=0}^{n-1} a_k \times \omega_n^{kj}, \quad \text{for} \quad j = 0, 1, \ldots, n-1,$$

and ω_n is a primitive nth root of unity. Computing b_j can be viewed as evaluating the polynomial

$$a_0 + a_1 x + a_2 x^2 + \cdots + a_{n-1} x^{n-1}$$

at $x = \omega_n^j$.

A Recursive RAM Algorithm.   On the RAM, a straightforward computation of b_j from its definition would require n multiplications and $n - 1$ additions of complex numbers. Therefore, $O(n^2)$ computation time would be needed to obtain the entire sequence $\{b_0, b_1, \ldots, b_{n-1}\}$. This approach would not be practical in applications where n is large or where several such sequences must be computed in succession. Accordingly, we now describe a faster algorithm. Let $n = 2^s$ for some positive integer s. The expression for b_j can be rewritten as

$$b_j = \sum_{m=0}^{2^{s-1}-1} a_{2m}\omega_n^{2mj} + \omega_n^j \sum_{m=0}^{2^{s-1}-1} a_{2m+1}\omega_n^{2mj}$$

for $j = 0, 1, \ldots, n-1$. In other words, the sum in the expression for b_j is broken into two sums, one for the even indices in the input sequence and one for the odd ones.

Now consider the two sums in the foregoing expression:

$$u_j = \sum_{m=0}^{2^{s-1}-1} a_{2m}\omega_n^{2mj} = a_0 + a_2\omega_n^{2j} + a_4\omega_n^{4j} + \cdots + a_{n-2}\omega_n^{(n-2)j}$$

and

$$v_j = \sum_{m=0}^{2^{s-1}-1} a_{2m+1}\omega_n^{2mj} = a_1 + a_3\omega_n^{2j} + a_5\omega_n^{4j} + \cdots + a_{n-1}\omega_n^{(n-2)j}.$$

They suggest that the problem of evaluating the polynomial

$$a_0 + a_1 x + a_2 x^2 + \cdots + a_{n-1}x^{n-1}$$

at $\omega_n^0, \omega_n^1, \ldots, \omega_n^{n-1}$—that is, the problem of computing $b_0, b_1, \ldots, b_{n-1}$—can be solved by:

1. Evaluating the two polynomials

$$a_0 + a_2 x + a_4 x^2 + \cdots + a_{n-2}x^{\frac{n}{2}-1}$$

and

$$a_1 + a_3 x + a_5 x^2 + \cdots + a_{n-1}x^{\frac{n}{2}-1}$$

at $\left(\omega_n^0\right)^2, \left(\omega_n^1\right)^2, \ldots, \left(\omega_n^{n-1}\right)^2$, and

2. Computing b_j from

$$b_j = u_j + \omega_n^j v_j$$

for $j = 0, 1, \ldots, n-1$.

However, as we saw earlier, the sequence

$$\left\{\left(\omega_n^0\right)^2, \left(\omega_n^1\right)^2, \ldots, \left(\omega_n^{n-1}\right)^2\right\}$$

represents the $n/2$ complex $(n/2)$nd roots of unity, and in this sequence each $(n/2)$nd root appears twice. As a result, the original problem of size n has been reduced to two problems of size $n/2$. Continuing in this manner recursively leads to an algorithm known as the fast Fourier transform. This algorithm is given next as algorithm RAM FFT. It receives $A = \{a_0, a_1, \ldots, a_{n-1}\}$ as input and returns $B = \{b_0, b_1, \ldots, b_{n-1}\}$ as output.

Algorithm RAM FFT (A, B)

> **if** $n = 1$
> **then** $b_0 \leftarrow a_0$
> **else** (1) RAM FFT $(a_0, a_2, \ldots, a_{n-2}, u_0, u_1, \ldots, u_{(n/2)-1})$
>   (2) RAM FFT $(a_1, a_3, \ldots, a_{n-1}, v_0, v_1, \ldots, v_{(n/2)-1})$
>   (3) $z \leftarrow 1$
>   (4) **for** $j = 0$ **to** $n - 1$ **do**
>   (4.1) $b_j \leftarrow u_{j \bmod (n/2)} + z v_{j \bmod (n/2)}$
>   (4.2) $z \leftarrow z \times \omega_n$
>   **end for**
> **end if.** ■

Let $t(n)$ be the running time of algorithm RAM FFT. Steps (1) and (2) require $t(n/2)$ time each, step (4) runs in time linear in n, and the remaining steps take constant time. Therefore,

$$t(n) = dn + 2t(n/2)$$

for some positive constant d. It follows that $t(n) = O(n \log n)$, which is a significant improvement over the $O(n^2)$ running time of the straightforward computation.

3.2.3 A Recursive FFT Circuit

Algorithm RAM FFT directly leads to a combinational circuit for computing the FFT. First note that steps (1) and (2) are totally independent of one another and can be performed simultaneously. Second, each iteration of the loop in step (4) is executed on a different pair (u_j, v_j), and therefore, all b_j's can be computed simultaneously (provided that the appropriate $z = \omega_n^j$ is available). The resulting recursive structure is illustrated in Fig. 3.7. The figure shows how an FFT circuit for n inputs can be built out of two FFT circuits for $n/2$ inputs, followed by a column of $n - 1$ processors that compute

$$b_j = u_{j \bmod (n/2)} + \omega_n^j v_{j \bmod (n/2)}$$

for $j = 0, 1, \ldots, n - 1$.

Analysis. The circuit's width is $O(n)$; this is easy to see, since there are n inputs and n outputs to the circuit, and each processor has no more outputs than it has inputs. Let $d(n)$ denote the circuit's depth. Since $b_0 = a_0$ when $n = 1$, we have $d(1) = 0$. For $n \geq 2$,

$$d(n) = d(n/2) + 1,$$

the solution of which is $d(n) = O(\log n)$. Finally, let $p(n)$ be the circuit's size. Again, $p(1) = 0$, and for $n \geq 2$, we have

$$p(n) = 2p(n/2) + n.$$

It follows that $p(n) = O(n \log n)$.

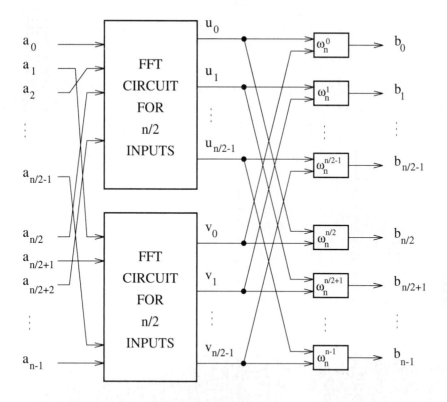

Figure 3.7: A recursive circuit for computing the FFT.

3.2.4 The Butterfly Operation

This section is devoted to a better understanding of the FFT circuit. We essentially show that this combinational circuit is precisely the butterfly circuit of Example 2.7. Let us consider again algorithm RAM FFT for a moment. The loop in Step (4) can be rewritten as follows:

> **for** $j = 0$ **to** $(n/2) - 1$ **do**
>   (1) $b_j \leftarrow u_j + zv_j$
>   (2) $b_{j+(n/2)} \leftarrow u_j - zv_j$
>   (3) $z \leftarrow z \times \omega_n$
> **end for.** ∎

This is because the indices of the sequences $\{u_0, u_1, \ldots, u_{(n/2)-1}\}$ and $\{v_0, v_1, \ldots, v_{(n/2)-1}\}$ run only from 0 to $(n/2) - 1$, as well as the fact that $\omega_n^{k+(n/2)} = -\omega_n^k$.

In the new loop, the two computations

$$u_j + zv_j \qquad \text{and} \qquad u_j - zv_j$$

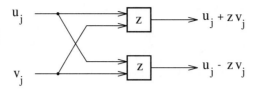

Figure 3.8: The butterfly operation.

are referred to as a *butterfly operation*. This operation is illustrated in Fig. 3.8, where $z = \omega_n^j$.

The butterfly operation generalizes as follows: If the butterfly of Fig. 3.8 is called a *2-butterfly*, then for m inputs u_0, u_1, ..., $u_{(m/2)-1}$, v_0, v_1, ..., $v_{(m/2)-1}$, an *m-butterfly* consists of $m/2$ 2-butterflies performed simultaneously on the pairs (u_0, v_0), (u_1, v_1), ..., $(u_{(m/2)-1}, v_{(m/2)-1})$.

Now consider the circuit of Fig. 3.7, and let $n = 16$ for purposes of illustration. The circuit receives $a_0, a_1, \ldots, a_{15}$ as input. It splits this sequence into two, namely, those elements with even indices—that is, $\{a_0, a_2, \ldots, a_{14}\}$—and those with odd indices—that is, $\{a_1, a_3, \ldots, a_{15}\}$. Each sequence is then fed to a separate circuit. Each of these circuits views its input sequence as being indexed from 0 to $(n/2) - 1$ and splits it into two subsequences, using the same rule. This continues until a circuit receives a sequence of size 2, at which point the splitting stops and the circuit performs a 2-butterfly operation on its two inputs and produces two outputs. The splitting process is illustrated in Fig. 3.9 for $n = 16$.

A combinational circuit for the FFT of n elements can now be designed on the basis of Fig. 3.9: In the ith stage, data received from the $(i-1)$st stage are divided into $n/2^i$ groups of 2^i adjacent data each, and a 2^i-butterfly operation is performed on each such group, where $i = 1, 2, \ldots, \log n$. Thus:

1. In the first stage, the inputs are divided into $n/2$ adjacent pairs, and a 2-butterfly operation is performed on each pair.

2. In the second stage, data received from the first stage are divided into $n/4$ adjacent quadruples, and a 4-butterfly operation is performed on each quadruple.

3. In the final, stage, an n-butterfly operation is performed on the n data received from the previous stage.

The question is, how do we organize the elements of the input for an easy pairing in the first stage? In other words, is there a simple way to recognize on which two elements each of the $n/2$ 2-butterflies in the first stage is performed? A glance at Fig. 3.9 gives us a hint. Let us rewrite the indices of the elements in the leftmost column (representing the first stage of computation) in decimal and binary notations as follows:

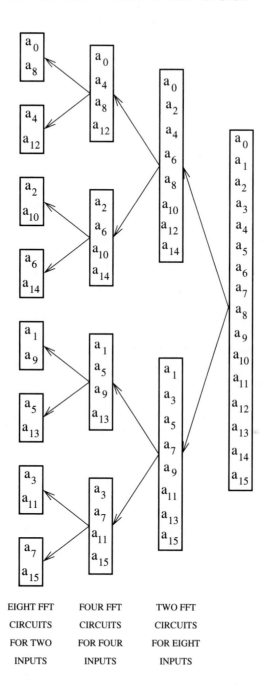

Figure 3.9: Recursive splitting by the FFT circuit.

| 0 | 8 | 4 | 12 | 2 | 10 | ... | 13 | 3 | 11 | 7 | 15 |
| 0000 | 1000 | 0100 | 1100 | 0010 | 1010 | ... | 1101 | 0011 | 1011 | 0111 | 1111 |

Now let us write the indices of the input elements in decimal and binary notation:

| 0 | 1 | 2 | 3 | 4 | 5 | ... | 11 | 12 | 13 | 14 | 15 |
| 0000 | 0001 | 0010 | 0011 | 0100 | 0101 | ... | 1011 | 1100 | 1101 | 1110 | 1111 |

What we observe is that each binary string in the first list is a mirror image (or the *reverse*) of the corresponding string in the second case. That this is true in general can be seen from the fact that the first split separates indices with a 0 in their rightmost bit from those with a 1. By putting those strings whose least significant bit is equal to 0 at the top of the list and those whose least significant bit is equal to 1 at the bottom, the least significant bit is treated as though it were the most significant bit. The second split separates indices with a 0 in their second rightmost bit from those with a 1. Continuing in this fashion, we complete the bit reversal when the splitting terminates.

A complete circuit for computing the FFT of a sequence of length 16 is presented in Fig. 3.10. As the figure shows, the input sequence $\{a_0, a_1, \ldots, a_{n-1}\}$ is first permuted according to the bit-reversal permutation. In stage 1, one 2-butterfly operation is performed on each pair of adjacent inputs. In stage 2, a 4-butterfly operation is performed on each four adjacent values resulting from stage 1. This continues until stage $\log n$, at which point one n-butterfly operation is performed on the n values obtained from stage $(\log n) - 1$, thus yielding the output sequence $\{b_0, b_1, \ldots, b_{n-1}\}$.

Finally, using the definition of the butterfly circuit given in Example 2.7, we can easily verify that this combinational circuit for the computation of the FFT is a butterfly circuit.

3.3   PERMUTATION CIRCUITS

A *permutation circuit* is a combinational circuit capable of applying an arbitrary permutation Ψ_n to its input $x_1, x_2, \ldots, x_n$, so that its output is

$$y_1, y_2, \ldots, y_n = \Psi_n(x_1, x_2, \ldots, x_n).$$

The permutation Ψ_n is usually defined by specifying, for each input x_i, on which output line it should exit the circuit. For example, a permutation of 1 2 3 4 5 6 7 8 may be given as

$$\Psi_8 = \begin{pmatrix} 1 & 2 & 3 & 4 & 5 & 6 & 7 & 8 \\ 4 & 8 & 3 & 2 & 1 & 7 & 6 & 5 \end{pmatrix},$$

indicating that 1 exits the circuit on line 4 (i.e., $y_4 = 1$), 2 exits on line 8 (i.e., $y_8 = 2$), and so on; thus, $y_1 = 5$, $y_2 = 4$, $y_3 = 3$, $y_4 = 1$, $y_5 = 8$, $y_6 = 7$, $y_7 = 6$, and $y_8 = 2$.

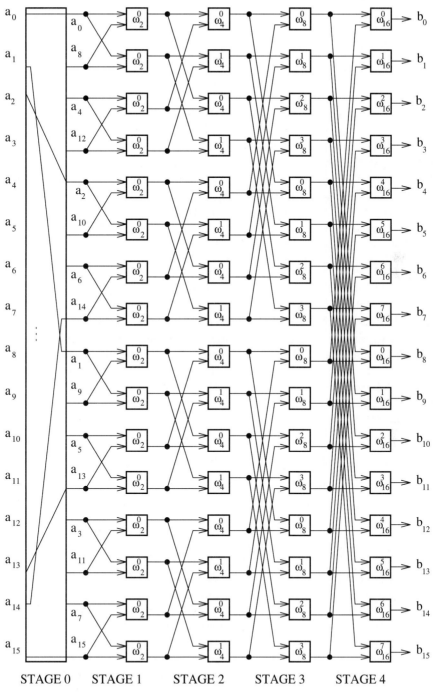

Figure 3.10: A complete FFT circuit for $n = 16$.

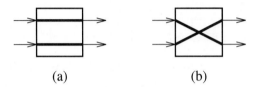

(a)   (b)

Figure 3.11: A switch: (a) OFF position; (b) ON position.

A permutation circuit is built of simple processors called *switches*. Each switch has two inputs and two outputs. As shown in Fig. 3.11, a switch can be in one of two positions: The switch in Fig. 3.11(a) is in the OFF position, in which its two inputs are propagated to the output with their order unchanged, while the switch in Fig. 3.11(b) is in the ON position, where the two inputs are swapped before exiting the switch.

Given a certain permutation Ψ_n, the switches of a permutation circuit can be set to realize that permutation on a given input. An example of a permutation circuit is the Beneš circuit of Fig. 2.32, with its switches set to perform the preceding permutation Ψ_8.

On the surface the permutation problem seems simpler than the sorting problem, since the destination of each element—that is, the output line on which the element exits the circuit—is known at the outset. It turns out, however, that the same lower bounds apply to the two problems.

Lower Bounds.   Suppose that a permutation circuit for an input of size n consists of s switches. Since each switch can be in either the ON or the OFF position, the circuit can be in one of 2^s configurations. In order for the circuit to be capable of executing *any* permutation of its inputs, it must be the case that

$$2^s \geq n!$$

This implies that $s \geq n \log n$, thus putting an $\Omega(n \log n)$ lower bound on the size of a permutation circuit. An obvious lower bound on the width is $\Omega(n)$, since there are n inputs and n outputs. Similarly, since each input line must have a path to each output line, and each switch has only two inputs and two outputs, a lower bound on the depth of a permutation circuit is $\Omega(\log n)$. These lower bounds are essentially the same as the ones derived for the MAU of the PRAM in Section 2.4.2. The reason for this similarity should be clear: A MAU for the PRAM must be (at least) capable of connecting each processor to a distinct memory location; if there are as many processors as there are memory locations, then the MAU needs to be able to perform a *permutation*.

3.3.1 Switches and Comparators

The behavior of a switch resembles that of a comparator in that the two inputs are either swapped or not. However, the similarity ends there: A comparator's decision as to whether to swap depends on the *values* of its inputs (the smaller exiting on the top output line, the larger on the bottom one); a switch, on the other hand, is preset to the ON or OFF position and behaves independently of the values of its two inputs.

Having said that, it is clear that a sorting circuit could be used as a permutation circuit. Suppose that the inputs to the circuit are pairs of the form (x_i, j), indicating that the input value x_i is to exit on the jth line of the output; that is, $y_j = x_i$. A sorting circuit can sort the pairs on their destinations (i.e., the j's), correctly completing the permutation. Either of the two sorting circuits of Section 3.1 could be used. Each, however, has a drawback:

1. The circuit of Section 3.1.2, while matching the aforementioned lower bounds on width, depth, and size, is only of theoretical interest due to its complicated nature and the large constant involved in its depth for all practical values of n.

2. The circuit of Section 3.1.1, on the other hand, is fairly simple and practical; however, it does not meet the depth and size lower bounds.

We therefore endeavor to find more efficient circuits for the permutation problem. Before leaving this discussion of the relative merits of sorting circuits versus specialized permutation circuits, we need to emphasize one important point: Sorting circuits are *self-routing*. As mentioned earlier, each comparator makes its decision as to which way the data it receives are to be directed; this decision is made when the two data reach the comparator and is based on their values. In permutation circuits, by contrast, switches are to be set ahead of time, thus adding a level of complexity not present in sorting circuits. Any attempt to introduce the self-routing property into permutation circuits usually results in either a reduction in the number of realizable permutations or an increase in the circuit's size.

3.3.2 An Optimal Permutation Circuit

As with the merging circuit of Section 3.1.1 and the FFT circuit of Section 3.2.3, a recursive construction will prove useful in deriving a permutation circuit. We assume that n is a power of 2. If $n = 1$, then no switches are needed: The circuit consists of a direct connection from the input x_1 to the output y_1. Also, when $n = 2$, it is clear that one switch suffices to produce the two permutations of the input. If $n > 2$, the input is fed into a column of $n/2$ (input) switches, labeled $I_1, I_2, \ldots, I_{n/2}$, where I_i receives x_{2i-1} and x_{2i} for $i = 1, 2, \ldots, n/2$. The top outputs of the switches, and simultaneously the bottom outputs, are fed into two permutation circuits for sequences of size $n/2$, as shown in Fig. 3.12. There, they

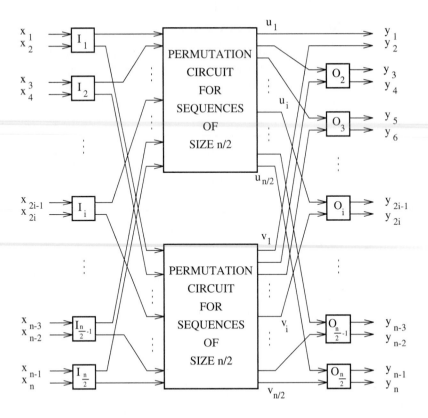

Figure 3.12: A recursive permutation circuit.

are recursively permuted. Let the output sequences thus obtained from the top and bottom circuits be $\{u_1, u_2, \ldots, u_{n/2}\}$ and $\{v_1, v_2, \ldots, v_{n/2}\}$, respectively. We take $y_1 = u_1$ and $y_2 = v_1$, and feed u_i and v_i into an output switch O_i to obtain y_{2i-1} and y_{2i}, for $i = 2, 3, \ldots, n/2$.

It remains to show how the switches are set to produce as output *any* permutation of the input. To explain the procedure, we work alternately backward and then forward, setting a path from one of the outputs $y_1, y_2, \ldots, y_n$ to the corresponding input among $x_1, x_2, \ldots, x_n$ and vice versa. Consider y_1, and suppose that $y_1 = x_{2i}$. The switches of the top permutation circuit are set to route y_1 to the appropriate input switch, namely, I_i. Then I_i is set to route y_1 to x_{2i}. Inevitably, x_{2i-1} must now be routed to the bottom permutation circuit. Suppose that $y_{2j} = x_{2i-1}$. The switches of the bottom permutation circuit are set to route x_{2i-1} to the appropriate output switch, namely, O_j. Now O_j is set to output x_{2i-1} correctly as y_{2j}. We start at y_{2j-1} and work our way back to the input. The algorithm for setting the switches can therefore be summarized as follows:

1. If, beginning from some output y_l, input x_{2k} (alternatively, x_{2k-1}) is reached, then select its neighbor in switch I_k, namely, x_{2k-1} (alternatively, x_{2k}), and begin setting the switches from there to reach the correct output. If the neighbor has already been selected, start with any other unselected input.

2. If, beginning from some input x_l, output y_{2k} (alternatively, y_{2k-1}) is reached, then select its neighbor in switch O_k, namely, y_{2k-1} (alternatively, y_{2k}), and begin setting the switches from there to reach the correct input. If the neighbor has already been selected, or if y_2 is reached from x_l, start with any other unselected output.

The algorithm terminates when all required paths from inputs to outputs have been established. Owing to the recursive nature of the construction, the switches of the top and bottom permutation circuits (for sequences of size $n/2$) can be set correctly using the same algorithm. It may be helpful to note that the ability of this algorithm to map each input to the correct output depends upon the fact that each switch I_i (O_j) in Fig. 3.12 has exactly one output to (input from) each of the two permutation circuits for sequences of size $n/2$. Thus, regardless of which of the latter two circuits an input is sent to, that input can always be routed to the proper output line.

Example 3.1 A permutation circuit using the foregoing recursive construction is shown in Fig. 3.13 for $n = 8$. The switches are set to perform the permutation Ψ_8 given earlier. It is interesting to compare this circuit with that of Fig. 2.32. Because no switch is used to produce y_1 and y_2, the circuit of Fig. 3.13 uses three fewer switches than that of Fig. 2.32. We show next that the difference in size between the two circuits is, in general, $(n/2) - 1$ comparators. □

   Analysis. Let the depth of the permutation circuit of Fig. 3.12 be $d(n)$, where $d(1) = 0$, $d(2) = 1$, and for $n > 2$, $d(n) = d(n/2) + 2$. It follows that $d(n) = 2 \log n - 1$. The circuit has width $n/2$, since it takes n inputs and produces n outputs, and each switch has exactly two inputs and two outputs. Finally, let $p(n)$ be the circuit's size, with $p(1) = 0$, $p(2) = 1$, and for $n > 2$, $p(n) = 2p(n/2) + n - 1$. Hence, $p(n) = n \log n - n + 1$. The circuit is therefore optimal to within a constant factor with respect to depth, width, and size. It should be noted that the circuit of Fig. 2.32 (which is based on the same recursive construction, except for the extra switch to produce y_1 and y_2) consists of $2 \log n - 1$ stages, each with $n/2$ switches and, as a result, has a size of $n \log n - n/2$.

3.4 CIRCUITS FOR COMPUTING PREFIX SUMS

Our study of combinational circuits concludes with the derivation of circuits for solving the problem of computing the prefix sums of an input sequence $\{x_0, x_1, \ldots, x_{n-1}\}$. As we saw in Examples 1.6 and 2.5, this problem calls for computing the

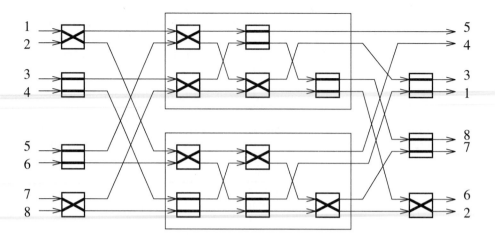

Figure 3.13: A permutation circuit for $n = 8$.

values $s_0 = x_0$, $s_1 = x_0 + x_1$, $s_2 = x_0 + x_1 + x_2$, $\ldots$, $s_{n-1} = x_0 + x_1 + \cdots + x_{n-1}$. In a combinational circuit for solving the problem, the building block is an *adder* capable of adding its two inputs or simply propagating its single input; in either case, the result is sent to at most two other adders in the next stage or to the output.

Lower Bounds.   A circuit for computing s_{n-1} using adders must have a depth of $\Omega(\log n)$. (This is seen using the same argument presented in Section 3.1.2 to derive a lower bound on the depth of a circuit that finds the smallest number in a sequence of numbers.) It follows that $\Omega(\log n)$ is a lower bound on the depth of a circuit for computing s_0, s_1, $\ldots$, s_{n-1}. Further, it is evident that $\Omega(n)$ is a lower bound on such a circuit's width. Since $n - 1$ additions are required (just to compute s_{n-1}), it follows that $\Omega(n)$ is also a lower bound on the circuit's size.

3.4.1   A Recursive Circuit

Assume that n is a power of 2. In Sections 3.1.1, 3.2.3, and 3.3.2, we saw how a recursive construction can be used to obtain combinational circuits for merging, computing the FFT, and performing a permutation, respectively. In each case, a problem of size n is broken into two identical problems of size $n/2$ each, of the same form as the original problem. These two problems are solved recursively, and their solutions are combined to obtain a solution to the original problem. We use the same idea to address the problem in this section. The idea is illustrated in Fig. 3.14 for $n = 8$. In general, the even-indexed elements $\{x_0, x_2, \ldots, x_{n-2}\}$ and the odd-indexed elements $\{x_1, x_3, \ldots, x_{n-1}\}$ of the input are fed separately and simultaneously into two circuits for computing the prefix sums of a

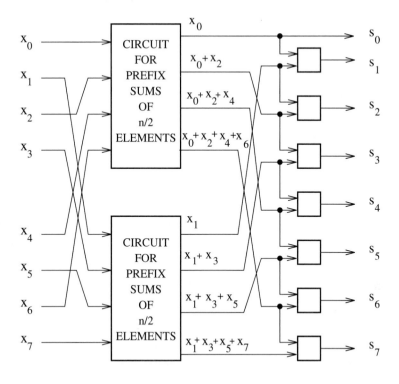

Figure 3.14: Recursive computation of prefix sums.

sequence of $n/2$ elements. The first circuit recursively computes the prefix sums x_0, $x_0 + x_2$, ..., $x_0 + x_2 + \cdots + x_{n-2}$, while the second circuit recursively computes the prefix sums x_1, $x_1 + x_3$, ..., $x_1 + x_3 + \cdots + x_{n-1}$. A column of $n - 1$ adders now completes the computation by combining these prefix sums: A sum from the first circuit is paired with one from the second and fed into an adder. Specifically, the sum $x_0 + x_2 + \cdots + x_{2i}$ is added to $x_1 + x_3 + \cdots + x_{2i-1}$ to produce s_{2i}, and to $x_1 + x_3 + \cdots + x_{2i+1}$ to produce s_{2i+1}, for $i = 1, 2, \ldots, (n/2) - 1$. Each recursively computed sum is thus used twice, except for x_0 and $x_1 + x_3 + \cdots + x_{n-1}$, each of which is used in one adder (to compute s_1 and s_{n-1}, respectively). Note also that $s_0 = x_0$.

Analysis. It is easy to see that the circuit has a width of $O(n)$. Let $d(n)$ be the circuit's depth, with $d(1) = 0$, and for $n \geq 2$, $d(n) = d(n/2) + 1$. Thus, $d(n) = O(\log n)$. Now let $p(n)$ be the circuit's size, with $p(1) = 0$, and for $n \geq 2$, $p(n) = 2p(n/2) + n - 1$. Therefore, $p(n) = O(n \log n)$. It follows that the circuit is optimal with respect to depth and width. Its size, however, is not optimal, in view of the $n - 1$ additions sufficient for computing the prefix sums on the RAM (using algorithm RAM PREFIX SUMS of Section 2.1).

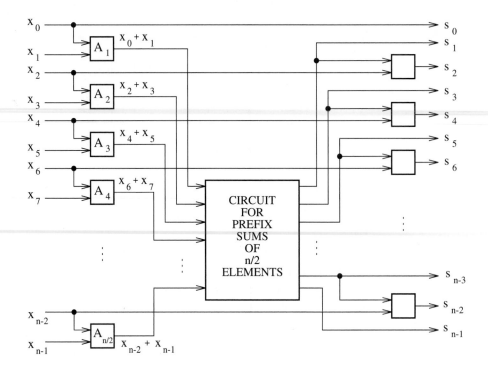

Figure 3.15: An optimal circuit for computing prefix sums.

3.4.2   An Optimal Circuit

As the preceding analysis shows, the circuit of Fig. 3.14 uses too many adders. This problem can be remedied, while retaining the circuit's simplicity. The idea is to:

1. First reduce the size of the problem from n elements to $n/2$,

2. Then solve the new problem recursively (using a circuit for sequences of size $n/2$),

3. And finally, combine the sums to obtain the sequence $\{s_0, s_1, \ldots, s_{n-1}\}$.

This new design is shown in Fig. 3.15. The circuit begins with a column of $n/2$ adders $A_1, A_2, \ldots, A_{n/2}$, where A_i adds x_{2i-2} and x_{2i-1}. These sums are fed into a circuit for computing prefix sums of $n/2$ elements. This circuit recursively computes the odd-indexed sums $s_1 = x_0 + x_1$, $s_3 = x_0 + x_1 + x_2 + x_3$, $\ldots$, $s_{n-1} = x_0 + x_1 + \cdots + x_{n-1}$. To the sum $s_i = x_0 + x_1 + \cdots + x_i$ is now added x_{i+1}, for $i = 1$, $3, \ldots, n-3$. This requires $(n/2) - 1$ adders and yields the even-indexed sums s_2, $s_4, \ldots, s_{n-2}$. Note that $s_0 = x_0$. The circuit is illustrated in Fig. 3.16 for $n = 8$.

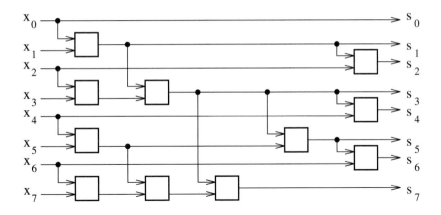

Figure 3.16: Optimal prefix sums circuit for 8 inputs.

Analysis. The circuit's width is $O(n)$. Its depth is given by $d(n) = d(n/2) + 2$ for $n > 2$, with $d(1) = 0$ and $d(2) = 1$. Therefore, $d(n) = 2\log n - 1$. Let $p(n)$ denote the circuit's size, with $p(1) = 0$, $p(2) = 1$, and for $n > 2$, $p(n) = p(n/2) + n - 1$. It follows that $p(n) = 2n - 2 - \log n$. The circuit's width, depth, and size are therefore all optimal.

3.5   AN OPTIMAL SORTING CIRCUIT (⋆)

In this section, we revisit the sorting-by-splitting circuit, briefly introduced in Section 3.1.2, and present its details in full. Let us reconsider the tree of Fig. 3.5. Each node of the tree is made up of a circuit, called an *expander*, capable of splitting the node's input into two subsets in constant time. We now define this circuit by presenting some background from *graph theory*. References to the literature in which proofs of the graph-theoretic results presented next can be found are given in Section 3.7.

3.5.1   Expanders

A graph $G = (V, E)$ is a set of vertices V joined by a set of edges E. Such a graph is said to be *bipartite* if it is possible to partition its set of vertices into two subsets V_1 and V_2, such that each edge in E has one endpoint in V_1 and the other in V_2. Let $\Gamma(U)$ denote the set of all neighbors of vertices in a set U—that is, all vertices to which the vertices in U are connected. Also, let $|A|$ denote the number of elements of a set A.

A bipartite graph G with n vertices s_1, s_2, ..., s_n is a (d, ε)-*expander* if and only if it satisfies the following three conditions:

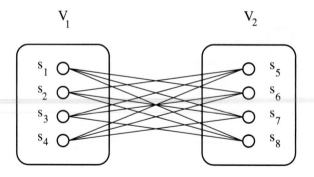

Figure 3.17: A (3,1/4)-expander.

1. The sets V_1 and V_2 have the same number of vertices, namely, $n/2$.

2. Every vertex in V_1 and every vertex in V_2 has exactly d neighbors.

3. For every nonempty set of vertices U such that $U \subseteq V_1$ or $U \subseteq V_2$,

$$\frac{|\Gamma(U)|}{\min(\varepsilon n/2, |U|)} \geq \frac{1-\varepsilon}{\varepsilon},$$

where $0 < \varepsilon < 1/2$.

Example 3.2 Let $|V_1| = |V_2| = 4$, $d = 3$, and $\varepsilon = 1/4$. A (3,1/4)-expander is shown in Fig. 3.17. Here

$$\frac{1-\varepsilon}{\varepsilon} = 3,$$

and $\min(\varepsilon n/2, |U|) = 1$ for all nonempty $U \subseteq V_1, V_2$.

It can be verified that $|\Gamma(U)| \geq 3$ for all such U. $\square$

Example 3.3 Let $|V_1| = |V_2| = 5$, $d = 3$, and $\varepsilon = 3/10$. A (3,3/10)-expander is shown in Fig. 3.18. Here $(1-\varepsilon)/\varepsilon = 7/3$, and for all nonempty $U \subseteq V_1, V_2$,

$$\min(\varepsilon n/2, |U|) = \begin{cases} 1 & \text{when } |U| = 1, \\ 3/2 & \text{when } |U| \geq 2. \end{cases}$$

Therefore,

$$\frac{|\Gamma(U)|}{\min(\varepsilon n/2, |U|)} \geq 7/3$$

for all such U. $\square$

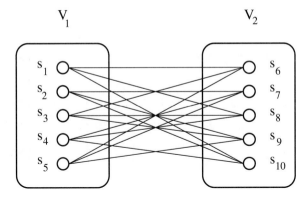

Figure 3.18: A (3,3/10)-expander.

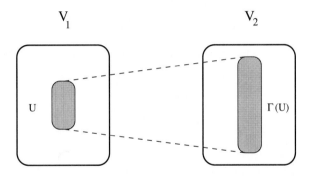

Figure 3.19: Expansion of a small subset of V_1 to a larger subset of V_2.

It is possible to show that for every $0 < \varepsilon < 1/2$, there exists some large constant d such that for sufficiently large n, (d, ε)-expanders can be found. For our purposes, the important characteristic of expander graphs is the following: Since $0 < \varepsilon < 1/2$ (i.e., $(1 - \varepsilon)/\varepsilon > 1$), every sufficiently small subset U of V_1 is mapped (or *expanded*) to a subset $\Gamma(U)$ of V_2 that is $(1 - \varepsilon)/\varepsilon$ times larger. This is illustrated in Fig. 3.19. Similarly, every sufficiently small subset of V_2 is expanded to a subset $\Gamma(U)$ of V_1 that is $(1 - \varepsilon)/\varepsilon$ times larger. By "sufficiently small," we mean that $|U| \le \varepsilon n/2$, where $|V_1| = |V_2| = n/2$.

We need two further results from graph theory before proceeding. A graph is said to have a *d-edge coloring* if d colors can be assigned to its edges, one color per edge, such that no two edges adjacent to the same vertex receive the same color. It is easy to see that every bipartite graph with maximum vertex degree d has a d-edge coloring. It follows that every (d, ε)-expander has a d-edge coloring.

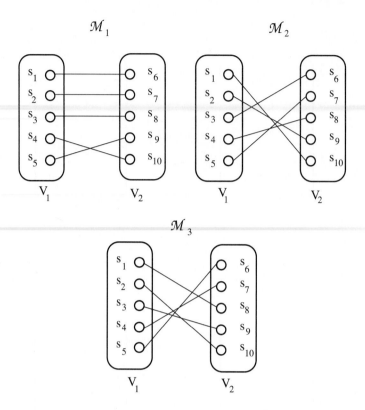

Figure 3.20: Partitioning an expander into disjoint matchings.

A *perfect matching* of a graph G is a subset $\mathcal{M}$ of the edges of G such that every vertex of G is an endpoint of some edge in $\mathcal{M}$, and no two edges in $\mathcal{M}$ are adjacent to the same vertex. Every (d, ε)-expander can be partitioned into d disjoint perfect matchings $\mathcal{M}_1$, $\mathcal{M}_2$, ..., $\mathcal{M}_d$. These matchings are obtained by first coloring the edges with d colors; each color then defines a matching.

Example 3.4 The $(3,3/10)$-expander of Fig. 3.18 is partitioned into three matchings as shown in Fig. 3.20. $\square$

This concludes our presentation of definitions and results from graph theory. We next turn to our description of the sorting circuit. Each node of the tree in Fig. 3.5 will be a circuit called a *separator*, which is itself constructed using another circuit called a *halver*. The latter is essentially an expander graph. We now describe these two circuits.

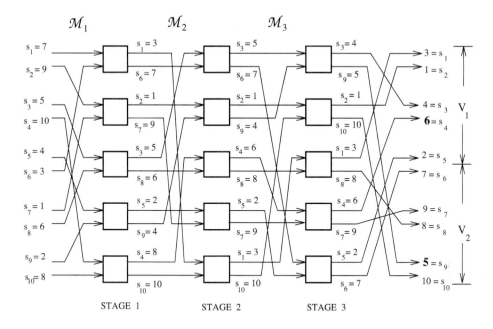

Figure 3.21: An ε-halver.

3.5.2 The Halver Circuit

Recall that $S = \{s_1, s_2, \ldots, s_n\}$ is the sequence to be sorted. We can think of the s_i as the vertices of a (d, ε)-expander graph with $V_1 = \{s_1, s_2, \ldots, s_{n/2}\}$ and $V_2 = \{s_{n/2+1}, s_{n/2+2}, \ldots, s_n\}$. Suppose that we have partitioned the expander graph into d disjoint perfect matchings $\mathcal{M}_1, \mathcal{M}_2, \ldots, \mathcal{M}_d$. We now construct a splitting circuit for S, consisting of d stages. In any stage i, two elements of S joined by an edge in $\mathcal{M}_i$ are fed into the same comparator, for $i = 1, 2, \ldots, d$. This circuit is also known as an ε-halver.

Example 3.5 Let $S = \{7, 9, 5, 10, 4, 3, 1, 6, 2, 8\}$. The splitting circuit for the matchings in Fig. 3.20 is shown in Fig. 3.21. □

The ε-halver splits the input into two sets V_1 and V_2. If every element in V_1 is smaller than or equal to every element in V_2, then the splitting has been performed correctly. This is not the case, however, for the example in Fig. 3.21, since elements 6 in V_1 and 5 in V_2 do not satisfy the condition. Therefore, the ε-halver does not always produce a correct split, and any element it places in the wrong set is said to be a *stranger*. As it turns out, however, the total number of strangers never exceeds εn. We prove this as follows: Without loss of generality, let $S = \{1, 2, \ldots, n\}$; that is, $V_1 = \{1, 2, \ldots, n/2\}$ and $V_2 = \{(n/2) + 1, (n/2) + 2, \ldots, n\}$. Also, denote by

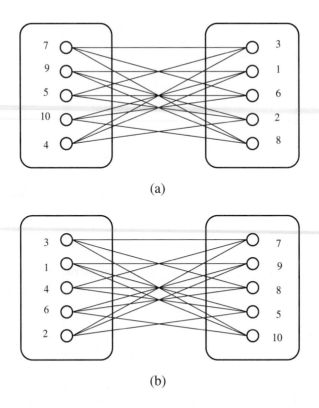

(a)

(b)

Figure 3.22: Effect of splitting on neighbors: (a) Before the splitting; (b) After the splitting.

X_1 and X_2 the subsets of elements of V_1 and V_2, respectively, that are strangers. Since $|X_1| = |X_2|$, it suffices to show that $|X_1| \leq \varepsilon n/2$. Assume, to the contrary, that $|X_1| \geq \varepsilon n/2$. Clearly, every $x \in X_1$ satisfies

$$\frac{n}{2} + 1 \leq x \leq n.$$

Now let $\Gamma(X_1)$ be the set of neighbors of the elements of X_1 *after the splitting*. This is illustrated in Fig. 3.22 for the sets V_1 and V_2 of Example 3.5. Here $X_1 = \{6\}$ and $\Gamma(X_1) = \{8, 9, 10\}$.

We now show that for every $y \in \Gamma(X_1)$, we also have

$$\frac{n}{2} + 1 \leq y \leq n.$$

This is true because each $x \in X_1$ and its neighbor $y \in \Gamma(X_1)$ satisfy $x < y$. In order to see this, consider the vertex $v_1 \in V_1$ containing x and the vertex $v_2 \in V_2$

containing y. By the definition of the ε-halver, the element in v_1 was compared at some point to the element in v_2 and the larger of the two placed in v_2. Subsequently, the element in v_2 can only increase, and the one in v_1 can only decrease. It follows that

$$|X_1| + |\Gamma(X_1)| \leq \frac{n}{2}.$$

Finally, by the definition of a (d, ε)-expander and our assumption that $|X_1| \geq \varepsilon n/2$, we have

$$|\Gamma(X_1)| \geq (1 - \varepsilon)\frac{n}{2}.$$

The last two inequalities involving $\Gamma(X_1)$ imply that $|X_1| \leq \varepsilon n/2$. This, coupled with our assumption, suggests that $|X_1| = \varepsilon n/2$. It follows that $|X_1| \leq \varepsilon n/2$ is always true.

3.5.3 The Separator Circuit

We now use the splitting circuit just described to construct a slightly more involved circuit. This new circuit, called a $(\lambda, \sigma, \varepsilon)$-*separator*, is built of ε-halvers. Specifically, $\lambda = 2^{1-q}$ and $\sigma = q\varepsilon$, where q is the number of levels in the separator. Thus, a $(2^{1-q}, q\varepsilon, \varepsilon)$-separator uses q levels of ε-halvers as explained in the next paragraph.

Given an input consisting of m numbers to be sorted in nondecreasing order, the $(\lambda, \sigma, \varepsilon)$-separator produces a partition of the input into four sequences A_1, A_2, A_3, and A_4 as follows: The m input elements are fed into an ε-halver. This yields two sequences of size $m/2$ each, to which two ε-halvers are applied. Now two ε-halvers are applied to each extreme sequence of size $m/4$, and so on. This continues through q levels and results in $2q$ blocks. The extreme blocks are taken as A_1 and A_4, while the remaining elements of the top and bottom halves are combined to form A_2 and A_3, respectively.

The concatenation of the four sequences A_1, A_2, A_3, and A_4 represents an *approximation* of the sorted output. Thus, some elements appear in the wrong sequence and are called *strangers* (the same term that was used to refer to the incorrectly placed elements in the output of an ε-halver). It is easy to verify that:

1. $|A_1| = |A_4| = \lambda m/2$, $|A_2| = |A_3| = (1 - \lambda)m/2$.

2. The number of strangers in A_1 or in A_4 is at most $\sigma\lambda m/2$.

Example 3.6 Taking $\varepsilon = 1/72$ and $q = 4$, we have $\lambda = 2^{1-q} = 1/8$ and $\sigma = q\varepsilon = 1/18$. A $(\lambda, \sigma, \varepsilon)$-separator is shown in Fig. 3.23 for $q = 4$. $\square$

It should be stressed here that the $(\lambda, \sigma, \varepsilon)$-separator consists of q levels of ε-halvers, where q is a constant. Each ε-halver is obtained from a (d, ε)-expander. Here d is the degree of the expander and is also the number of stages in the ε-halver. Since d is a (large) constant, the ε-halver has constant depth, and consequently, so does the $(\lambda, \sigma, \varepsilon)$-separator.

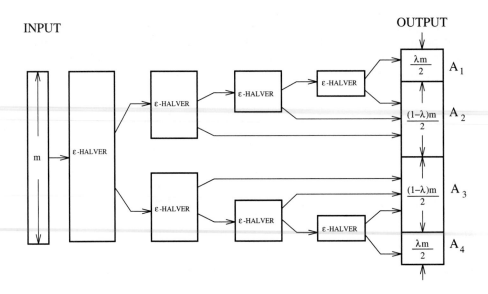

Figure 3.23: A $(\lambda, \sigma, \varepsilon)$-separator.

3.5.4   The Sorting-by-Splitting Circuit

Having constructed the separator circuit using the halver circuit, we now place a separator inside each node of the tree in Fig. 3.5. The sequence to be sorted is fed to the root and propagates from left to right, until it reaches the leaves in sorted order from top to bottom. A node receiving input is *active*, and active nodes operate in parallel. A node is active at every other step. Every active node (excluding the root and leaves) performs the following operations on its input:

1. The elements of the input are partitioned into four sequences A_1, A_2, A_3, and A_4.

2. The sequences A_2 and A_3 are sent to the node's two children, one sequence per child.

3. The sequences A_1 and A_4 are sent to the node's parents.

Operation 3 above would seem to violate the property of combinational circuits that no feedback is allowed. Indeed, we use this formulation only for descriptive purposes; it helps in explaining the circuit's behavior at a conceptual level. In reality, the circuit consists of several "layers," each of which is a copy of the tree in Fig. 3.5. Each time a node wishes to send A_1 and A_4 to its parent, it sends them to a fresh node that has not been used before. We will see shortly that no more than $O(\log n)$ layers (i.e., stacked copies of the tree) are needed.

What about the root and the leaves? The root applies steps 1, 2, and 3 as any other node, except that during step 3 it sends A_1 and A_4 to a fresh root (i.e., one in a new layer). By the time an element reaches a leaf, it is in its final position. The leaf simply produces it as output. This description is illustrated in Fig. 3.24. Note that the circuit's input sequence is received by the root in the first layer, while the circuit's sorted output is produced by the leaves in the last layer.

As shown in the figure, there are $2n - 1$ nodes per tree and $O(\log n)$ copies of each node, one per layer. In what follows, when we speak of "a" node (or "the" root), we mean that copy which is currently being used. Note, however, that not all copies of a node are of the same size: We show in what follows that at each step the number of elements of S to be processed by a node decreases. Therefore, the copy of a node on the $(i + 1)$st layer is smaller (i.e., uses a separator of smaller width) than the copy on the ith layer. It is important to note that, since each layer has $2n - 1$ nodes, it can hold all n elements of the input simultaneously if so required.

Analysis. Let $r(i)$ denote an upper bound on the number of elements to be processed by the root node during the ith step. Initially, $r(0) = n$, since the input sequence to be sorted is of size n. For each active node (above the leaves), we have the following:

1. An upper bound on the number of elements to be processed by a node at level L during the ith step is $n(i) = r(i)a^L$, for some constant $a > 1$ and $L \geq 1$.

2. An upper bound on the number of elements to be processed by the root at level $L = 0$ during step $i + 1$ is given by $r(i + 1) = br(i)$, for some constant $b < 1$.

These can be seen from Fig 3.25. Note that during step $i + 1$, a node at level L receives the following number of elements to process:

$$
\begin{aligned}
n(i + 1) &= \tfrac{1-\lambda}{2}r(i)a^{L-1} + 2\lambda r(i)a^{L+1} \\
&= br(i)a^L \\
&= r(i + 1)a^L,
\end{aligned}
$$

where $b = 2\lambda a + (1 - \lambda)/2a$. Taking, for example, $\lambda = 1/8$ and $a = 3$, we get $b = 43/48$.

Now let α be a constant representing the number of elements at the root when the number of elements in the wrong half of the tree drops below 1. This constant depends, of course, on the choices of the three other constants characterizing the circuit, namely, λ, σ, and ε. Suppose that the number of elements at the root is α after s steps. Since $r(0) = n$, we have

$$
r(s) = b^s n = \alpha,
$$

implying that $s = O(\log n)$. At this point, the root can split its elements correctly into two disjoint halves, with *all* elements in the top half smaller than or equal

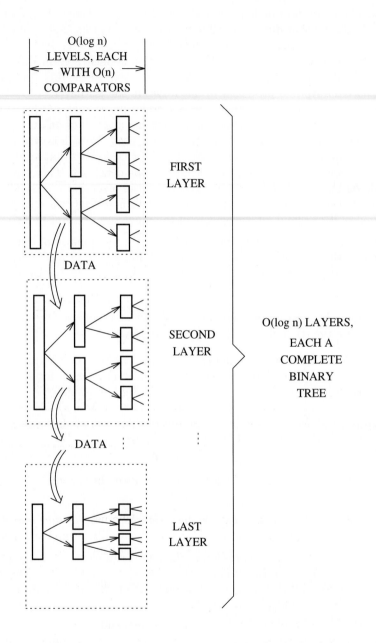

Figure 3.24: The complete sorting-by-splitting circuit: Each tree node is a $(\lambda, \sigma, \varepsilon)$-separator.

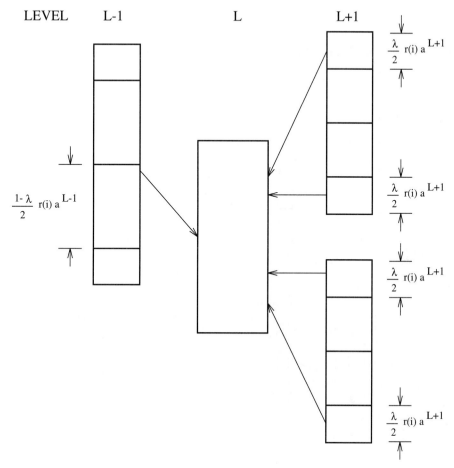

Figure 3.25: Number of elements to be processed by a node at level L.

to *all* elements in the bottom half. This can be done using, for example, an odd-even-merge sorting circuit. (See Section 3.1.1.) Since α is a constant, this circuit's width, depth, and size are all constants. Now the $\alpha/2$ smaller elements are sent to the top child of the root and the $\alpha/2$ larger elements to the bottom child. These two children become the roots of two disjoint trees, and they operate henceforth completely independently of one another.

Each new root now contains at most $a\alpha$ elements, and after a constant number of steps, this number drops below α. As was done previously, the subtrees of this root are separated in constant time into two disjoint subtrees. Thus, a new separation of subtrees is executed at intervals bounded by a constant number of steps. After $O(\log n)$ steps, the process terminates and the sequence is sorted. The circuit's width, depth, and size are as follows:

1. **Width.** The root node receives n elements, and the leaves produce these elements in sorted order from top to bottom. There are 2^L nodes at level L, each receiving at most $n/2^L$ elements as input and producing the same number of elements as output. The circuit therefore has a width of $O(n)$. This is clearly optimal in view of the $\Omega(n)$ lower bound on the width of any combinational circuit taking n inputs and producing n outputs.

2. **Depth.** The tree consists of $1 + \log n$ levels (the root being at level 0 and the leaves at level $\log n$). The nodes in each level consist of a separator circuit of constant depth. There are $O(\log n)$ layers (i.e., copies of the tree). It takes $O(\log n)$ steps to go from the first to the last layer and then another $O(\log n)$ steps to traverse the final layer from left to right. Therefore, the circuit has a depth of $O(\log n)$. Recall that $\Omega(\log n)$ is a lower bound on the depth of a circuit of comparators which simply finds the smallest of its n inputs. This lower bound also applies to sorting circuits, since the latter necessarily find the smallest of their n inputs. It follows that the circuit's depth is optimal.

3. **Size.** Level L of the tree consists of 2^L nodes. In layer 0, each node is a separator circuit of constant depth, with width at most $n/2^L$ (since there are only n elements to be sorted). Therefore, each level of the tree consists of $O(n)$ comparators. This leads to a total of $O(n \log n)$ comparators for the tree in layer 0. Each subsequent layer contains fewer comparators; however, the total number of comparators, over all layers, remains $O(n \log n)$. For example, the root of the tree in layer i uses a separator of width at most $b^i n$ (and constant depth). Therefore, the total number of comparators required by all roots is

$$\sum_{i=0}^{O(\log n)} b^i n = O(n).$$

Similarly, a node at level L, $L \geq 1$, in layer i uses a separator of constant depth and width at most $n(i)$, where $n(i) = bn(i-1)$. Since $n(0) = n/2^L$,

$$n(i) = b^i n/2^L.$$

It follows that the total number of comparators required by the 2^L nodes at level L, over all layers, is

$$\sum_{i=0}^{O(\log n)} b^i n = O(n).$$

Hence, the overall size of the circuit is $O(n \log n)$. This size is optimal in view of the $\Omega(n \log n)$ comparisons required to sort a sequence of n elements in the worst case.

The sorting-by-splitting circuit is therefore theoretically optimal with respect to all three criteria. Unfortunately, the circuit is only of academic interest, for three reasons:

1. Conceptually, the circuit is quite complex.

2. It is very intricate and therefore difficult to build in practice.

3. The circuit's depth is unreasonably large due to the large constant hidden by the O-notation. This constant is approximately 6,000; in other words, the depth is $6{,}000 \times \log n$. Thus, n must be astronomically large for this circuit's depth to be smaller than the $(\log n)(1 + \log n)/2$ depth of the odd-even-merge sorting circuit of Section 3.1.1.

It is therefore an interesting and challenging open problem to discover a sorting circuit for n elements that is conceptually simple and easy to construct, and whose width, depth, and size are $\delta_1 n$, $\delta_2 \log n$, and $\delta_3 n \log n$, respectively, for small constants δ_1, δ_2, and δ_3.

3.6 PROBLEMS

3.1 Consider a combinational circuit $\mathcal{C}$ whose processors are comparators. (Such a circuit is called a *comparison circuit*.) The circuit takes a sequence of numbers $\{x_1, x_2, \ldots, x_n\}$ as input and produces these same numbers as output in some order. Let the sequence $\{y_1, y_2, \ldots, y_n\}$ denote the circuit's output. Now suppose that F is a monotonically increasing function; that is, if $a \leq b$ for two numbers a and b, then $F(a) \leq F(b)$. Show that if $\mathcal{C}$ is given the sequence $\{F(x_1), F(x_2), \ldots, F(x_n)\}$ as input, it produces $\{F(y_1), F(y_2), \ldots, F(y_n)\}$ as output.

3.2 Let $\mathcal{C}$ be a comparison circuit, as defined in Problem 3.1. When given an input sequence of n binary digits (in random order), $\mathcal{C}$ produces an output sequence of 0's followed by 1's. (In other words, the circuit correctly *sorts* all 2^n possible sequences of n 0's and 1's.) Show that such a circuit can sort correctly any sequence of arbitrary numbers (i.e., not necessarily 0's and 1's). This is known as the *0–1 principle*. (*Hint*: Use the result in Problem 3.1.)

3.3 Use the 0–1 principle, derived in Problem 3.2, to show that the odd-even merging circuit of Section 3.1.1 works correctly. (*Hint*: First show that the circuit works correctly for sequences of 0's and 1's.)

3.4 Suppose that two sequences $A = \{a_0, a_1, \ldots, a_{n-1}\}$ and $B = \{b_0, b_1, \ldots, b_{n-1}\}$ are sorted in nondecreasing order. Show that the two sequences can be merged to form a single sequence W sorted in nondecreasing order as follows:

(a) The odd-indexed elements of A—that is, $\{a_1, a_3, \ldots, a_{n-1}\}$—and the even-indexed elements of B—that is, $\{b_0, b_2, \ldots, b_{n-2}\}$—(both of which are sorted subsequences) are merged recursively to produce $E = \{e_0, e_1, \ldots, e_{n-1}\}$.

(b) The even-indexed elements of A—that is $\{a_0, a_2, \ldots, a_{n-2}\}$—and the odd-indexed elements of B—that is, $\{b_1, b_3, \ldots, b_{n-1}\}$—(both of which are sorted subsequences) are merged recursively to produce $D = \{d_0, d_1, \ldots, d_{n-1}\}$.

(c) The sequence W is obtained by interleaving the elements of E and D to obtain

$$\{e_0, d_0, e_1, d_1, \ldots, e_{n-1}, d_{n-1}\}$$

and then comparing (and, if necessary, exchanging) pairs (e_i, d_i) for $i = 0, 1, \ldots, n-1$.

3.5 Implement the algorithm in Problem 3.4 on a butterfly circuit.

3.6 A sequence $\{a_1, a_2, \ldots, a_{2m}\}$ is said to be *bitonic* if and only if:

(a) Either there is an integer j, $1 \le j \le 2m$, such that

$$a_1 \le a_2 \le \cdots \le a_j \ge a_{j+1} \ge a_{j+2} \ge \cdots \ge a_{2m}$$

(b) Or the sequence does not initially satisfy the condition in (a), but can be shifted cyclically until the condition *is* satisfied.

For example, the sequence $\{5, 7, 8, 9, 4, 3, 1\}$ is bitonic, as it satisfies condition (a). Similarly, the sequence $\{7, 9, 5, 4, 2, 3, 6\}$, which does not satisfy condition (a), is also bitonic, as it can be shifted cyclically to obtain $\{3, 6, 7, 9, 5, 4, 2\}$. Let $\{a_1, a_2, \ldots, a_{2m}\}$ be a bitonic sequence, and let $d_i = \min(a_i, a_{m+i})$ and $e_i = \max(a_i, a_{m+i})$ for $i = 1, 2, \ldots, m$. Show that:

(a) The sequences $\{d_1, d_2, \ldots, d_m\}$ and $\{e_1, e_2, \ldots, e_m\}$ are both bitonic.

(b) $\max(d_1, d_2, \ldots, d_m) \le \min(e_1, e_2, \ldots, e_m)$.

3.7 When concatenated, two given sequences $A = \{a_1, a_2, \ldots, a_m\}$ and $B = \{a_{m+1}, a_{m+2}, \ldots, a_{2m}\}$ form a bitonic sequence $\{a_1, a_2, \ldots, a_{2m}\}$. Use the two properties of bitonic sequences derived in Problem 3.6 to design an (m, m) *bitonic merging circuit* for merging A and B, to produce a sequence C, sorted in nondecreasing order. Analyze the width, depth, and size of the circuit.

3.8 Use the (m, m) bitonic merging circuit obtained in Problem 3.7 to design and analyze a circuit for sorting arbitrary (i.e., not necessarily bitonic) input sequences.

3.9 Relate the circuit obtained in Problem 3.7 to the butterfly circuit.

3.10 Relate the circuit obtained in Problem 3.8 to the omega circuit.

3.11 Consider a sequence $S = \{s_0, s_1, \ldots, s_{n-1}\}$, where $n = 2^k$. The *even chain* of S is the subsequence of S that contains all the elements of S with even indices, in the same order as they appear in S. Similarly, the *odd chain* of S contains all the elements of S with odd indices, in the same order as they appear in S. The set of level i chains of S, where $1 \leq i \leq k$, contains 2^i subsequences of S whose indices are equal modulo 2^i. For instance, the even and odd chains are the level 1 chains. A sequence S is said to be *modulo balanced* if the following condition holds: When the elements of S are arranged in nondecreasing order in pairs, one element from each pair lies in the even chain of S and the other in the odd chain. The sequence S is *recursively modulo balanced* if it is modulo balanced and both its even and odd chains are recursively modulo balanced. (Any sequence of two elements is recursively modulo balanced.)

Consider, for example, the sequence $S = \{0, 5, 4, 1, 7, 2, 3, 6\}$ with even chain $\{0,4,7,3\}$ and odd chain $\{5,1,2,6\}$. This sequence is recursively modulo balanced. Note first that S is modulo balanced, because when its elements are arranged in nondecreasing order in pairs—that is, $(0,1)$, $(2,3)$, $(4,5)$, $(6,7)$—one element from each pair belongs to the even chain and the other to the odd chain. Second, both the even and odd chains of S are recursively modulo balanced. Show that:

(a) The number of sequences S that are recursively modulo balanced is considerably larger than the number of bitonic sequences of the same length.

(b) The (m, m) bitonic merging circuit of Problem 3.7 sorts a sequence S of $n = 2m$ elements if and only if S is recursively modulo balanced.

3.12 A sorting circuit for arbitrary sequences of length $n = 2^k$ may be obtained as follows:

(a) First the arbitrary sequence is made into a recursively modulo balanced sequence (as defined in Problem 3.11).

(b) Then the circuit of Problem 3.7 is used to sort the sequence obtained in **(a)**.

If step **(a)** can be done efficiently, then the entire sorting circuit will be very efficient. Can you construct a circuit of depth $O(\log n)$ and size $O(n \log n)$ to perform step **(a)**?

3.13 A sequence $S = \{s_0, s_1, \ldots, s_{n-1}\}$, where $n = 2^k$, is said to satisfy the *dominance* property if the level $k - 1$ chains (as defined in Problem 3.11) are sorted—that is, if $s_i \leq s_{i+(n/2)}$ for $0 \leq i \leq n/2$. The sequence is *recursively dominant* if it satisfies the dominance property and its lower and upper halves are recursively dominant. (A sequence of two elements that satisfies the dominance property is recursively dominant.)

For example, $S = \{1, 4, 3, 7, 2, 6, 5, 8\}$ is recursively dominant. Note first that S satisfies the dominance property because $1 \leq 2$, $4 \leq 6$, $3 \leq 5$, and $7 \leq 8$. Second, the upper half $\{1, 4, 3, 7\}$ and the lower half $\{2, 6, 5, 8\}$ of S are both recursively dominant. Show that if an arbitrary sequence (i.e., one that is not necessarily bitonic) is fed into the merging circuit of Problem 3.7, then the output is a recursively dominant sequence.

3.14 A sorting circuit for arbitrary sequences of length $n = 2^k$ may be obtained as follows:

(a) First the sequence is fed into the circuit of Problem 3.7.

(b) Then the sequence obtained in **(a)**, which is recursively dominant (as defined in Problem 3.13), is sorted.

If step **(b)** can be done efficiently, then the entire sorting circuit will be very efficient. Can you construct a circuit of depth $O(\log n)$ and size $O(n \log n)$ to perform step **(b)**?

3.15 A sequence $S = \{s_0, s_1, \ldots, s_{n-1}\}$, where $n = 2^k$, is said to be *shift balanced* if its smallest element belongs to its even chain, its largest element belongs to its odd chain, and when the rest of its elements are sorted and paired, one element from each pair lies in the even chain and the other element lies in the odd chain (as defined in Problem 3.11). The sequence is *recursively shift balanced* if it is shift balanced and both its even and odd chains are recursively shift balanced. (Any sequence of two elements that is shift balanced is recursively shift balanced.)

For example, $S = \{4, 1, 5, 7, 0, 6, 2, 3\}$ is recursively shift balanced. Note first that S is shift balanced, because its smallest element belongs to the even chain $\{4, 5, 0, 2\}$, its largest element belongs to the odd chain $\{1, 7, 6\ 3\}$, and when the remaining elements are sorted and paired—that is, $(1,2)$, $(3,4)$, $(5,6)$—the elements of each pair belong to different chains. Second, the even and odd chains are recursively shift balanced. Show that:

(a) The number of sequences S that are recursively shift balanced is larger than the number of sequences consisting of two sorted subsequences $\{s_0, s_1, \ldots, s_{(n/2)-1}\}$ and $\{s_{n/2}, s_{(n/2)+1}, \ldots, s_{n-1}\}$.

(b) The (m, m) odd-even merging circuit of Section 3.1.1 sorts an input sequence S of $n = 2m$ elements (i.e., merges $\{s_0, s_1, \ldots, s_{(n/2)-1}\}$ and $\{s_{n/2}, s_{(n/2)+1}, \ldots, s_{n-1}\}$) if and only if S is recursively shift balanced.

3.16 A sorting circuit for arbitrary sequences of length $n = 2^k$ can be obtained as follows:

(a) First the arbitrary sequence is made into a recursively shift-balanced sequence (as defined in Problem 3.15).

(b) Then an $(n/2, n/2)$ odd-even merging circuit is used to sort the sequence obtained in (a).

If step (a) can be done efficiently, then the entire sorting circuit will be very efficient. Can you construct a circuit of depth $O(\log n)$ and size $O(n \log n)$ to perform step (a)?

3.17 A sequence $S = \{s_0, s_1, \ldots, s_{n-1}\}$ is said to satisfy *double dominance* if it satisfies *pair dominance*, whereby $s_{2i-1} \leq s_{2i}$ for $1 \leq i < n/2$, and *dominance* (as defined in Problem 3.13). The sequence S satisfies *recursively reachable double dominance* if it can be turned into a sequence S' by performing exchanges of s_{2i-1} and s_{2i} for some indices i, $1 \leq i < n/2$, such that both the even and odd chains of S' satisfy double dominance and recursively reachable double dominance. (Any sequence of two elements satisfies recursively reachable double dominance.)

For example, $S = \{1, 3, 5, 0, 4, 6, 7, 2\}$ exhibits double dominance, since both pair dominance (i.e., $3 \leq 5$, $0 \leq 4$, and $6 \leq 7$) and dominance (i.e., $1 \leq 4$, $3 \leq 6$, $5 \leq 7$, and $0 \leq 2$) are satisfied. The sequence also satisfies recursively reachable double dominance: If $s_1 = 3$ and $s_2 = 5$ are exchanged, the resulting even chain $\{1, 3, 4, 7\}$ and odd chain $\{5, 0, 6, 2\}$ of the new sequence satisfy double dominance and recursively reachable double dominance. Show that if an arbitrary sequence S (i.e., one in which $\{s_0, s_1, \ldots, s_{n-1}\}$ and $\{s_{n/2}, s_{(n/2)+1}, \ldots, s_{n-1}\}$ are not necessarily sorted) is fed into an $(n/2, n/2)$ odd-even merging circuit, then the output is a sequence that satisfies both double dominance and recursively reachable double dominance.

3.18 A sorting circuit for arbitrary sequences of length $n = 2^k$ may be obtained as follows:

(a) First the sequence is fed into an $(n/2, n/2)$ odd-even merging circuit,

(b) Then the sequence obtained in (a), which satisfies double dominance and recursively reachable double dominance (as defined in Problem 3.17), is sorted.

If step (b) can be done efficiently, then the entire sorting circuit will be very efficient. Can you construct a circuit of depth $O(\log n)$ and size $O(n \log n)$ to perform step (b)?

3.19 A sequence of numbers $\{x_1, x_2, \ldots, x_{n-1}\}$ sorted in nondecreasing order is given along with an arbitrary number x_0. Design a combinational circuit for inserting x_0 into its correct position in the sequence. (In other words, x_0 is to be inserted between two consecutive elements of the sequence x_i and x_{i+1}

such that $x_i \leq x_0 \leq x_{i+1}$ if two such elements exist; otherwise, x_0 is placed in the first position if $x_0 \leq x_1$ or in the last position if $x_{n-1} \leq x_0$.)

3.20 In Section 3.2.2, the DFT was defined as the computation of the sequence $\{b_0, b_1, \ldots, b_{n-1}\}$ from the sequence $\{a_0, a_1, \ldots, a_{n-1}\}$, where

$$b_j = \sum_{k=0}^{n-1} a_k \times \omega_n^{kj}.$$

This computation can be rewritten as a matrix-by-vector product—that is, $\boldsymbol{b} = \boldsymbol{W}\boldsymbol{a}$, where $\boldsymbol{a}$ and $\boldsymbol{b}$ are $n \times 1$ vectors (equal to the input and output sequences, respectively) and $\boldsymbol{W}$ is an $n \times n$ matrix whose entry in row j and column k is ω_n^{kj} for $k, j = 0, 1, \ldots, n - 1$. Using this representation, design and analyze a circuit for computing the DFT directly from its definition.

3.21 Suppose that the DFT of *several* sequences of the form $\{a_0, a_1, \ldots, a_{n-1}\}$ is to be computed directly from the definition, as in Problem 3.20. Suggest ways to extend your solution to handle this situation.

3.22 Consider the following iterative RAM algorithm for computing the FFT of a sequence $\{a_0, a_1, \ldots, a_{n-1}\}$:

> **Algorithm RAM ITERATIVE FFT (A, B)**
> **Step 1: for** $k = 0$ to $n - 1$ **do**
> $\qquad d_k \leftarrow a_k$
> **end for**
> **Step 2: for** $h = (\log n) - 1$ **downto** 0 **do**
> $\qquad$ (2.1) $g \leftarrow 2^h$
> $\qquad$ (2.2) $q \leftarrow n/g$
> $\qquad$ (2.3) $z \leftarrow \omega_n^{q/2}$
> $\qquad$ (2.4) **for** $k = 0$ to $n - 1$ **do**
> $\qquad\qquad$ **if** $k \bmod g = k \bmod 2g$
> $\qquad\qquad$ **then** (i) $r \leftarrow d_k$
> $\qquad\qquad\qquad$ (ii) $d_k \leftarrow r + d_{k+g}$
> $\qquad\qquad\qquad$ (iii) $d_{k+g} \leftarrow (r - d_{k+g})z^{k \bmod g}$
> $\qquad\qquad$ **end if**
> $\qquad$ **end for**
> **end for**
> **Step 3: for** $k = 0$ to $n - 1$ **do**
> $\qquad b_{\text{rev}(k)} \leftarrow d_k$
> **end for.** ∎

Note that in Step 3, $\text{rev}(k)$ is the binary string obtained by reversing the binary representation of k. Show how to implement this algorithm on an omega circuit.

3.23 It is often required to generate a *random* permutation of a given sequence. This occurs, for example, in certain experiments in which not all permutations can be tested. Suggest a way for using a permutation circuit to generate random permutations according to a certain probability distribution (e.g., the resulting permutations may be *uniformly* distributed).

3.24 In Section 3.2.4, the input sequence $\{a_0, a_1, \ldots, a_{n-1}\}$ needed to be permuted before being fed to the FFT circuit. The permutation used was the *bit reversal* of the indices of the input elements. Since these indices always appeared in sorted order—that is, in the order $0, 1, \ldots, n-1$—the permutation was performed in a straightforward way by *hardwiring* a_i to line $\text{rev}(i)$, where $\text{rev}(i)$ is the reverse of the binary representation of i. Suggest a permutation circuit capable of performing the bit-reversal permutation for any order of the indices of the input elements. In other words, if the ith input line carries a_j, then a_j exits the circuit on the $\text{rev}(j)$th output line.

3.25 A method is described in Section 3.3.2 for setting the switches of a permutation circuit, in order to perform a permutation of the input. Develop a parallel algorithm to determine the circuit's switch settings needed for a given permutation. The algorithm should be designed to run on the PRAM. Analyze the running time of your algorithm and the number of processors it requires.

3.26 In the permutation circuit of Section 3.3.2, the switches need to be set ahead of time for every permutation of the input. Suggest ways to allow the circuit to set its own switches *on the fly*—that is, as the permutation is being performed on the input. Analyze the resulting circuit's width, depth, and size in each case, and determine whether the circuit is capable of executing *all* permutations of the input.

3.27 It is sometimes known which permutations are needed in a particular application. A customized permutation circuit can then be built that executes these permutations. Define some nontrivial classes of permutations, and for each class, propose a permutation circuit to perform the permutations in that class. What are the width, depth, and size of each circuit?

3.28 Suppose that the omega circuit with n inputs and n outputs is used as a permutation circuit. Can it perform *all* $n!$ permutations of the input? If not, which permutations is it capable of performing?

3.29 The circuit shown in Fig. 3.26 is known as a *Clos permutation circuit* and is a forerunner of the circuit studied in Section 3.3.2. Let $n = rs$. The circuit consists of three levels. In the first and third levels, s circuits $C(r)$ are used, each capable of performing all permutations of r inputs. In the middle level, r circuits are used, each capable of performing all permutations of s inputs. Show that this general construction can perform all $n!$ permutations of its input.

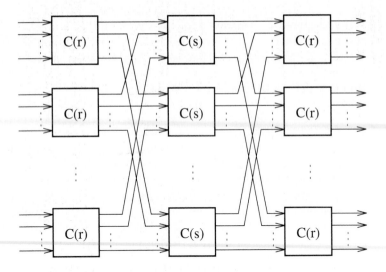

Figure 3.26: A Clos permutation circuit.

3.30 A circuit for computing prefix sums is described in Example 1.6 and Fig. 1.4. Compare this circuit to those in Section 3.4.

3.31 Consider the construction in Fig. 3.27 for computing the prefix sums of n input elements. It consists of two circuits for computing prefix sums of $n/2$ elements, followed by a column of $n/2$ adders. What property of combinational circuits, as defined in Section 2.4, does this construction violate?

3.32 The circuits studied in Section 3.4 use adders and therefore compute prefix *sums* of their inputs. If adders were replaced by different kinds of processors, what other operations could these circuits perform? What mathematical properties should all of these operations share with addition?

3.33 For the sorting-by-splitting circuit of Section 3.5, show that when the number of elements to be processed by the root drops to a certain constant α, there are no strangers in either of the root's two subtrees. Give an expression for α as a function of λ, σ, and ε, the parameters of the circuit.

3.34 The main reason for the large constant in the depth of the sorting-by-splitting circuit is the ε-halver. The latter uses a (d, ε)-expander, where d is very large. Suggest another way of implementing the ε-halver that is not based on expander graphs.

3.35 The sorting circuit of Section 3.1.1 is unsatisfactory from the *theoretical* point of view, as it is a factor of $O(\log n)$ away from the optimal in both its depth

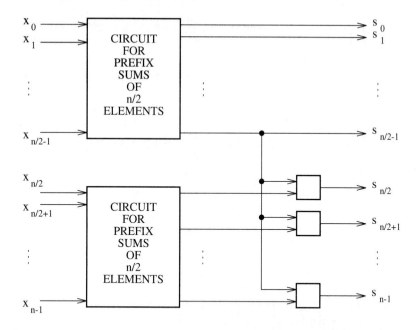

Figure 3.27: A construction for computing prefix sums.

and size. On the other hand, the circuit of Section 3.5, which is optimal theoretically, is infeasible *in practice*: There is a large constant hidden by the O-notation, not to mention the circuit's involved design. Design a sorting circuit that is asymptotically faster and more efficient than the first circuit, while being more appealing than the second from the practical point of view. For example, a circuit that sorts n numbers in $k_1 \log^{3/2} n$ time using $k_2 n \log^{3/2} n$ comparators, where k_1 and k_2 are small constants, would fit the requirements.

3.36 Design a sorting circuit which combines the idea of sorting by merging with that of sorting by splitting.

3.37 Establish a correspondence between the butterfly and omega circuits.

3.7 BIBLIOGRAPHICAL REMARKS

Interest in sorting circuits has both theoretical and practical origins. Some researchers were attracted by the intrinsic importance of sorting as a fundamental task in information processing, while others were motivated by the potential use of these circuits in connecting processors and memories in parallel computers. The odd-even and bitonic merging circuits and the resulting sorting circuits are due to

Batcher [89]. Batcher's ingenious constructions have no rival to this day in simplicity and (practical) efficiency. A number of attempts have been made to provide new statements or new proofs of correctness of these two circuits; however, Batcher's original formulation remains the most elegant, most lucid, and most convincing. Several authors have proposed implementations of Batcher's circuits on a variety of interconnection network parallel computers, including the linear array, the mesh, the perfect shuffle, and the hypercube; see, for example, Kumar and Hirschberg [342], Leighton [367], Nassimi and Sahni [437], Stone [590], and Thompson and Kung [612]. Related results appear in Batcher [91], Knuth [325], Paul [475], and Perl [488]. In particular, it is shown in Perl [488] that the odd-even and bitonic merging circuits can each merge a class of sequences larger than the class for which it was designed. Note that some authors refer to sorting circuits (and to other circuits as well, such as permutation circuits) as *networks*.

Although a gap of $O(\log n)$ separates the depth and size of Batcher's circuits for sorting a sequence of size n from the lower bounds of $\Omega(n)$ and $\Omega(n \log n)$, respectively, it was believed for a long time that these circuits were optimal (i.e., that the lower bounds needed to be improved upon). In 1983, Ajtai et al. [9, 10] proposed the sorting-by-splitting circuit, which meets the above lower bounds on depth and size and is therefore optimal. This circuit is known as the AKS sorting circuit, after its inventors. As mentioned in the text, the circuit is based on expander graphs, and while it represents a remarkable theoretical achievement, it is of little practical value due to the large constant in the function describing its depth. A somewhat smaller constant, but still on the order of several thousands, is achieved in the formulation of the AKS circuit due to Paterson [471]. Other descriptions, based on Paterson's, appear in Gibbons and Rytter [258], Parberry [466], and Smith [575]. Expander graphs are studied in Alon [63], Chung [157], Gabber and Galil [253], Jimbo and Maruoka [315], Klawe [324], Lubotzky et al. [394], and some references therein. Other definitions and results from graph theory may be found in Behzad et al. [93], Christofides [156], Deo [199], Even [221], and Papadimitriou and Steiglitz [465].

Work related to sorting circuits continues unabated, despite (perhaps because of) the preceding results. For example, Leighton [366] derives a *network* (based on the AKS circuit) that sorts n items in $O(\log n)$ time using $O(n)$ processors. There are also circuits that approach the theoretical performance of the AKS circuit in a variety of ways, while being more practical. For example, a circuit of depth $7.45 \log n$ that sorts a sequence of length n *with high probability* is described in Leighton [367]. Similarly, an algorithm for sorting on an $O(n)$-processor cube-connected cycles network that terminates in $O(\log n)$ time with high probability is given in Reif and Valiant [534]; this can be transformed into a circuit with depth $O(\log n)$ that sorts with high probability. An algorithm for sorting in $O(\log n (\log \log n)^2)$ time on an $O(n)$-processor hypercube is derived in Leighton [367]; this can be transformed into a circuit of depth $O(\log n (\log \log n)^2)$ and size $O(n \log n (\log \log n)^2)$. Each stage of the circuit is a hypercube of n processors: Processor P_i in stage k is connected to processor P_j in stage $k + 1$ if the kth step of the algorithm requires P_i to send its contents to P_j. Finally, an algorithm due to Cole [166] sorts a sequence of length n on an n-processor PRAM in $O(\log n)$ time; it is not clear, however, how this algorithm can be transformed into an optimal circuit. Other references include Dowd et al. [208], Hong and Sedgewick [300], Parberry [467], Parker and Parberry [469], Rudolph [541], and Yao and Yao [646]. Descriptions of sequential sorting algorithms such as Heapsort, Mergesort, and Quicksort can be found in Brassard and Bratley [120], Manber [402], and Reingold et al. [535]. The merge procedure on which Mergesort is based is given in Chapter 5 as algorithm RAM MERGE. Lower bounds on the number of operations required to sort are derived in Ben-Or [97], Friedman [252], Horowitz and Sahni [303], Knuth [325], and Smith [574].

The fast Fourier transform is without doubt one of the most important computations arising in engineering and scientific applications, such as digital signal processing, coding theory, computerized axial tomography scanning, speech transmission, weather prediction, statistics, image processing, multiplication of very large integers, and multiplication of polynomials; see, for example, Burrus and Parks [127], Cochran et al. [162], Cooley et al. [182], and Oppenheim and Willsky [453]. Historical accounts of the development of the FFT can be found in Cooley [181] and Press et al. [503]. The butterfly circuit was originally conceived to compute the FFT (in fact, it is sometimes referred to as the FFT circuit); see, for example, Hwang and Briggs [307], Kronsjö [334, 335], Leighton [367], and Ullman [615]. Other parallel implementations of the FFT include implementations on the linear array (Thompson [611]), the mesh (Thompson [610]), the perfect shuffle (Heller [291], Pease [484], Stone [590]), the hypercube (Pease [485]), the tree (Ahmed et al. [6]), the cube-connected cycles (Preparata and Vuillemin [502]), and the mesh of trees (Akl [21]). A definition of the Taylor's series is provided in Rees and Sparks [531].

Permutation circuits have their origins in the design of telephone exchanges; see Beneš [96], Clos [161], Joel [316], and Shannon [561]. A circuit is defined in Clos [161] for permuting $n = s \times r$ elements, using smaller circuits for permuting s elements and r elements. In Clos's design, a circuit for permuting s elements is defined as a *cross-bar* switch—that is, an $s \times s$ grid of s horizontal and s vertical lines. There are s^2 cross-points, which let a datum traveling on a horizontal line either go through or switch to a vertical line. The inputs are fed in on the horizontal lines (from the left side of the grid), and if datum i is to be permuted to position j, it switches to the jth vertical line once it reaches the jth cross-point. Outputs thus exit permuted on the top side of the grid. A circuit was described by Beneš [96] based on the design of Clos, which uses switches with two inputs and two outputs. This design was improved by Waksman [633], who reduced the number of switches used in the Beneš circuit. The circuit proposed by Waksman [633] is described in Section 3.3.2. Since then, there has been a flurry of research on permutation circuits. Some work, as in Lee [363], Lev et al. [373], and Nassimi and Sahni [440], is directed at developing fast algorithms for setting the switches of a permutation circuit. Other efforts are aimed at designing circuits that are self-routing; see, for example, Boppana and Raghevandra [117], Koppelman and Oruç [328], Lenfant [370], and Nassimi and Sahni [439]. Finally, circuits are obtained in Lawrie [360], Lenfant [370], and Lenfant and Tahé [371] that can execute only a subset of all possible permutations.

The problem of computing prefix sums has received considerable attention since the early days of parallel computation. This is due to its inherent parallelism and to its many applications. Circuits for computing prefix sums are given in Brent and Kung [125] and Ladner and Fischer [352]. The circuit of Section 3.4.2 was first proposed by Ladner and Fischer [352]. In Reif [532], *probabilistic* circuits are described for the same problem: For a sequence of size n, these circuits have a depth of $O(\log \log n)$ and a probability of n^{-x}, $x > 0$, that the output will contain an error. A comprehensive study of prefix sum circuits is provided in Lakshmivarahan and Dhall [356].

The study of combinational circuits is at the heart of parallel computation. In some sense, these circuits represent the purest and most fundamental model. Although they were historically the first to be studied, and are fairly well understood, they continue to attract a good deal of research. Several circuits are described in Leighton [367], Moldovan [432], Siegel [571], and Wu and Feng [644]. They include the *baseline*, the *delta* (or *banyan*), and *flip* circuits, which are essentially various forms of the butterfly circuit. See also Parberry [468] for a study of circuits as models for neural networks.

Chapter 4

Parallel Prefix Computation

In previous chapters, we had the opportunity to define and solve the problem of computing the *prefix sums* of a sequence of numbers. Combinational circuits for this computation are described in Chapters 1 and 3, while an algorithm is developed in Chapter 2 for obtaining prefix sums on a hypercube interconnection network. Our earlier treatment also mentioned the importance of the problem in parallel computation. The purpose of this chapter is to illustrate that importance through a number of examples. We will see that in many applications, the problem to be solved can be reduced to a prefix sums computation. In others, this computation is a main step in the algorithm for solving the problem at hand. Therefore, efficient algorithms for computing prefix sums play a key role in these applications. For definiteness, the PRAM model is assumed throughout. Also, we focus in this chapter on the problem of computing prefix sums when the inputs are presented in contiguous positions of an array in shared memory. The case where this computation is to be performed on a linked list is studied in Chapter 6.

We begin in Section 4.1 by casting the problem of computing prefix sums in slightly more general terms, referring to it as *prefix computation*. We then explain briefly the reasons behind the wide applicability of this problem in parallel computation. In Section 4.2, an algorithm for prefix computation on the PRAM is derived and analyzed. The next six sections are devoted to descriptions of applications of parallel prefix computation. These applications originate in such diverse areas as the study of sequences, computational geometry, and numerical analysis. A further generalization of prefix computation called *general prefix computation* is obtained in Section 4.9. Applications of general prefix computation in computational geometry, graph theory, and combinatorial computing are the subject of Section 4.10. As usual, uniform analysis is used to derive the running time of algorithms, unless otherwise stated.

4.1　PREFIX COMPUTATION

A set $\mathcal{X}$ is given, together with an operation $\circ$ defined on the elements of $\mathcal{X}$ such that:

1. The operation $\circ$ is *binary*; that is, $\circ$ applies to pairs of elements of $\mathcal{X}$.

2. The set $\mathcal{X}$ is *closed* under the operation $\circ$; that is, if x_i and x_j are elements of $\mathcal{X}$, then so is $x_i \circ x_j$.

3. The operation $\circ$ is *associative*; that is, if x_i, x_j, and x_k are elements of $\mathcal{X}$, then

$$
\begin{aligned}
(x_i \circ x_j) \circ x_k &= x_i \circ (x_j \circ x_k) \\
&= x_i \circ x_j \circ x_k.
\end{aligned}
$$

Example 4.1 The set $\mathcal{X}$ is a set of numbers (such as the *integers* or the *reals*), and $\circ$ is a binary associative operation on numbers (such as *addition, multiplication, max,* or *min*). $\square$

Example 4.2 The set $\mathcal{X}$ is a set of *strings* over a finite alphabet of symbols, and $\circ$ is *concatenation*. $\square$

Example 4.3 The set $\mathcal{X}$ consists of the two Boolean values **true** and **false**, and $\circ$ is a logical operation such as **and, or,** or **exclusive-or.** $\square$

Note that the operations in Examples 4.1 and 4.3 are *commutative*; that is, for two elements x_i and x_j of $\mathcal{X}$, $x_i \circ x_j = x_j \circ x_i$. On the other hand, the operation in Example 4.2 is not commutative.

Now consider the sequence $X = \{x_0, x_1, \ldots, x_{n-1}\}$ where $x_i \in \mathcal{X}$ for $i = 0$, $1, \ldots, n - 1$. It is required to compute the following quantities:

$$
\begin{aligned}
s_0 &= x_0 \\
s_1 &= x_0 \circ x_1 \\
s_2 &= x_0 \circ x_1 \circ x_2 \\
&\;\;\vdots \\
s_{n-1} &= x_0 \circ x_1 \circ \cdots \circ x_{n-1}.
\end{aligned}
$$

In other words, $s_i = s_{i-1} \circ x_i$, for $i = 1, 2, \ldots, n - 1$, with $s_0 = x_0$. The process of obtaining $S = \{s_0, s_1, \ldots, s_{n-1}\}$ from $X = \{x_0, x_1, \ldots, x_{n-1}\}$ is known as *prefix computation*. To see the reason for this name, note that the indices of the elements used to compute s_i form a string $012\ldots i$, which is a *prefix* of the string $012\ldots n-1$.

A computation symmetric to prefix computation and referred to as *suffix computation* is defined similarly. Here, a sequence $\{a_0, a_1, \ldots, a_{n-1}\}$, is computed, where $a_{n-1} = x_{n-1}$, $a_{n-2} = x_{n-2} \circ x_{n-1}$, $\ldots$, $a_0 = x_0 \circ x_1 \circ \cdots \circ x_{n-1}$.

Unless otherwise stated, we assume in what follows that ∘ takes constant time to be executed. Since computing s_{n-1} involves combining *all* the x_i, a lower bound on the number of operations required for prefix computation is $\Omega(n)$. In Chapters 1–3, prefix computation was studied for the case where $\{x_0, x_1, \ldots, x_{n-1}\}$ is a sequence of numbers and ∘ is addition. It should be clear that the algorithms developed therein for computing prefix sums (i.e., the RAM algorithm in Chapter 2, the combinational circuits in Chapters 1 and 3, and the hypercube algorithm in Chapter 2) can all be used to solve the general problem by replacing + with ∘. (Note, however, that the recursive circuit of Section 3.4.1 exploits the commutativity of addition—that is, $x_i + x_j = x_j + x_i$—and hence can be used for prefix computation only if ∘ is commutative.)

Why Prefix Computation?   It may be useful to examine the definition of prefix computation, in order to get an appreciation of its importance in parallel computation. First, consider a sequential algorithm $\mathcal{A}_1$ for prefix computation (e.g., algorithm RAM PREFIX SUMS of Section 2.1). The algorithm traverses the input sequence $X = \{x_0, x_1, \ldots, x_{n-1}\}$, computing the different s_i one after the other. This traversal can be seen as a *sweep* (or *scan*) of the sequence. Depending on the application, this sweep:

1. Either collects information about the different x_i,

2. Or computes partial results involving the x_i.

Algorithm $\mathcal{A}_1$ runs in $O(n)$ time. Suppose now that $\mathcal{A}_1$ is a step in another algorithm $\mathcal{B}_1$. The latter solves a larger problem that requires computations involving every element of the sequence X. One can readily see that, although the computations performed by $\mathcal{A}_1$ may be useful to $\mathcal{B}_1$, their running time is not crucial to the efficiency of $\mathcal{B}_1$. Indeed, $\mathcal{A}_1$ is a straightforward traversal of $\{x_0, x_1, \ldots, x_{n-1}\}$ which can be done while these input data are being read (a necessary operation, itself requiring $\Omega(n)$ time).

On a parallel computer, however, the situation is quite different. Global operations such as reading, updating, or writing the elements of a sequence can be done in *constant time*. Computing partial functions of the x_i, on the other hand, requires more time. The information obtained by a sweep of the sequence X reveals relationships among the x_i that may be the key to the efficiency of subsequent steps of an algorithm $\mathcal{A}_p$. Therefore, an *efficient* computation of $s_0, s_1, \ldots, s_{n-1}$ is doubly important in the situations where it is applicable, since it:

1. Does not appreciably increase the running time of $\mathcal{A}_p$ and

2. Helps make subsequent steps run faster.

4.2   PREFIX COMPUTATION ON THE PRAM

We now describe an algorithm for computing $S = \{s_0, s_1, \ldots, s_{n-1}\}$ from $X = \{x_0, x_1, \ldots, x_{n-1}\}$ on the PRAM. Note first that the efficient solutions developed for this problem in earlier chapters can be directly implemented on the PRAM without any loss of efficiency. Thus, the hypercube algorithm of Example 2.5 can be simulated on a PRAM with n processors: Whenever two processors on the hypercube use the direct link connecting them to exchange data, the two corresponding processors on the PRAM execute the same communication through shared memory. The PRAM algorithm therefore runs in $O(\log n)$ time. Similarly, the combinational circuit of Section 3.4.2 can be simulated on a PRAM with n processors to run in $O(\log n)$ time.

Our motivation for presenting an algorithm specifically designed for the PRAM is twofold:

1. The algorithm is simple and exploits the convenience of the shared memory for communication between arbitrary pairs of processors.

2. The algorithm allows us to present a technique for obtaining a cost-optimal algorithm from one that is not.

4.2.1   A First Attempt at Prefix Computation

Let n processors $P_0, P_1, \ldots, P_{n-1}$ be available on the PRAM, where n is a power of 2. Initially, the sequence X is stored in shared memory by having P_i read x_i from the input, for $0 \le i \le n - 1$, and store it in memory. Processor P_i also sets s_i equal to x_i for $i = 0, 1, \ldots, n - 1$. This takes constant time. The algorithm consists of $\log n$ iterations; during each step, the binary operation $\circ$ is performed by pairs of processors whose indices are separated by a distance twice that in the previous iteration.

Thus, in the first iteration we compute

$$s_1 \leftarrow s_0 \circ s_1, \ s_2 \leftarrow s_1 \circ s_2, \ \ldots, \ s_{n-1} \leftarrow s_{n-2} \circ s_{n-1}.$$

In the second iteration we compute

$$s_2 \leftarrow s_0 \circ s_2, \ s_3 \leftarrow s_1 \circ s_3, \ \ldots, \ s_{n-1} \leftarrow s_{n-3} \circ s_{n-1}.$$

In the final iteration we compute

$$s_{n/2} \leftarrow s_0 \circ s_{n/2}, \ s_{n/2+1} \leftarrow s_1 \circ s_{n/2+1}, \ \ldots, \ s_{n-1} \leftarrow s_{n/2-1} \circ s_{n-1}.$$

This computation, illustrated graphically in Fig. 4.1 for $n = 8$, is expressed as follows:

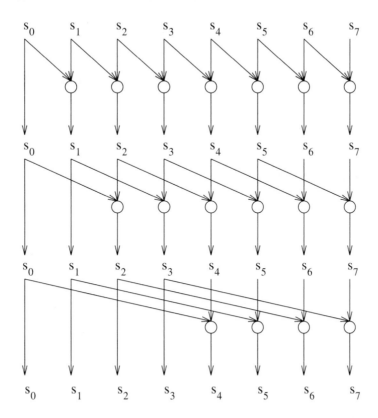

Figure 4.1: Prefix computation on the PRAM.

for $j = 0$ **to** $(\log n) - 1$ **do**
  for $i = 2^j$ **to** $n - 1$ **do in parallel**
    $s_i \leftarrow s_{i-2^j} \circ s_i$
  end for
end for. ∎

It is easy to see that each iteration yields twice as many final values s_i as the previous one. The algorithm therefore runs in $O(\log n)$ time. Since $p(n) = n$, the algorithm's cost is

$$
\begin{aligned}
c(n) &= p(n) \times t(n) \\
&= n \times O(\log n) \\
&= O(n \log n).
\end{aligned}
$$

This cost is not optimal, in view of the $O(n)$ operations that are sufficient to solve the problem on the RAM (by algorithm RAM PREFIX SUMS of Section 2.1, modified for $\circ$).

The observant reader will have noticed that this algorithm is essentially the one developed in Example 1.6 and can be implemented on the combinational circuit of Fig. 1.4, whose size is $O(n \log n)$. This size, like the cost of the PRAM algorithm, is not optimal. It is possible, however, to obtain an optimal PRAM algorithm. The idea is to use fewer processors and exploit once again the associativity of the operation $\circ$.

4.2.2   A Cost-Optimal Algorithm

Let $k = \log n$ and $m = n/k$, where k and m are rounded appropriately. We use a PRAM with m processors P_0, P_1, ..., P_{m-1} and think of the input sequence $\{x_0, x_1, \ldots, x_{n-1}\}$ as being split into m subsequences, each of size k, namely,

$$
\begin{aligned}
Y_0 &= x_0, x_1, \ldots, x_{k-1}, \\
Y_1 &= x_k, x_{k+1}, \ldots, x_{2k-1} \\
&\vdots \\
Y_{m-1} &= x_{n-k}, x_{n-k+1}, \ldots, x_{n-1}.
\end{aligned}
$$

Processor P_i first reads the sequence Y_i for $0 \leq i \leq m - 1$, stores it in memory, and then applies to it algorithm RAM PREFIX SUMS (modified for $\circ$), to obtain

$$ s_{ik}, s_{ik+1}, \ldots, s_{(i+1)k-1}, $$

where

$$ s_{ik+j} = x_{ik} \circ x_{ik+1} \circ \cdots \circ x_{ik+j}, $$

for $j = 0, 1, \ldots, k-1$. This step is executed simultaneously by all processors. Since each processor executes k iterations, the step requires $O(k)$ time.

The parallel algorithm for prefix computation (described in Section 4.2.1) is now applied by processors P_0, P_1, ..., P_{m-1} to the sequence

$$ \{s_{k-1}, s_{2k-1}, \ldots, s_{n-1}\}. $$

When this step is completed, s_{ik-1} will be replaced by

$$ s_{k-1} \circ s_{2k-1} \circ \cdots \circ s_{ik-1}, $$

for $i = 1, 2, \ldots, m$. The time required is $O(\log m)$.

Finally, P_i, for $1 \leq i \leq m - 1$, performs the step

$$ s_{ik+j} \leftarrow s_{ik-1} \circ s_{ik+j} $$

for $j = 0, 1, \ldots, k-2$. This step is executed sequentially by all processors operating in parallel (except P_0) and takes $O(k)$ time. The algorithm is given next as algorithm PRAM PREFIX COMPUTATION. It takes X and $\circ$ as input and returns S as output.

Algorithm PRAM PREFIX COMPUTATION ($X, \circ, S$)

Step 1: for $i = 0$ **to** $m - 1$ **do in parallel**

    (1.1) $s_{ik} \leftarrow x_{ik}$

    (1.2) **for** $j = 1$ **to** $k - 1$ **do**

$$s_{ik+j} \leftarrow s_{ik+j-1} \circ x_{ik+j}$$

    end for

    end for

Step 2: for $j = 0$ **to** $(\log m) - 1$ **do**

    for $i = 2^j + 1$ **to** m **do in parallel**

$$s_{ik-1} \leftarrow s_{(i-2^j)k-1} \circ s_{ik-1}$$

    end for

    end for

Step 3: for $i = 1$ **to** $m - 1$ **do in parallel**

    for $j = 0$ **to** $k - 2$ **do**

$$s_{ik+j} \leftarrow s_{ik-1} \circ s_{ik+j}$$

    end for

    end for. ∎

Analysis. Steps 1 and 3 require $O(k)$ time, while Step 2 runs in $O(\log m)$ time. Since $k = \log n$ and $m = n/\log n$, we have

$$
\begin{aligned}
t(n) &= O(\log n) + O(\log(n/\log n)) \\
&= O(\log n).
\end{aligned}
$$

In other words, the reduction in the number of processors from n to $n/\log n$ does not affect the running time. This is due to the associativity of the operation $\circ$, which allows the computation to be divided among the processors in the manner described. As a result, (sequential) Steps 1 and 3 take no more time than (parallel) Step 2. Since $p(n) = n/\log n$, the algorithm's cost is

$$
\begin{aligned}
c(n) &= p(n) \times t(n) \\
&= n/\log n \times O(\log n) \\
&= O(n),
\end{aligned}
$$

which is optimal in view of the $\Omega(n)$ lower bound derived earlier.

Example 4.4 Let $\circ$ be $+$, $n = 16$, and $X = \{0, 1, \ldots, 15\}$. Here, $m = 16/4$, and we use four processors: P_0, P_1, P_2, and P_3. In Step 1, P_0 operates on $\{0, 1, 2, 3\}$ and obtains the sums $\{0, 1, 3, 6\}$. Simultaneously, P_1 operates on $\{4, 5, 6, 7\}$ and obtains $\{4, 9, 15, 22\}$. Similarly, P_2 and P_3 compute $\{8, 17, 27, 38\}$ and $\{12, 25, 39, 54\}$, respectively. In Step 2, parallel prefix computation on $\{6, 22, 38, 54\}$ yields $\{6, 28, 66, 120\}$. In Step 3, P_1 adds 6 to each element in $\{4, 9, 15\}$, P_2 adds 28 to each element in $\{8, 17, 27\}$, and P_3 adds 66 to each element in $\{12, 25, 39\}$. This gives the prefix sums $\{0, 1, 3, 6, 10, 15, 21, 28, 36, 45, 55, 66, 78, 91, 105, 120\}$. The behavior of the algorithm for this example is illustrated in Fig. 4.2. □

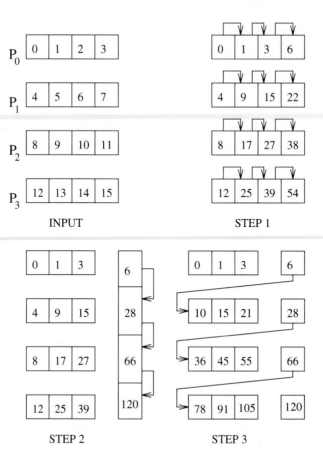

Figure 4.2: Optimal prefix computation on the PRAM.

Some practical implications of algorithm PRAM PREFIX COMPUTATION are worth noting here:

1. The algorithm illustrates how a PRAM with m processors can be made to run an algorithm designed for a PRAM with n processors, where $m < n$. This form of "self-simulation" is useful from a practical point of view. It shows how a parallel computer that is available to solve a problem is able to execute an algorithm for this problem, even if it does not possess the number of processors required theoretically.

2. In the process of designing the algorithm, we were able to establish, to within a constant factor, the minimum number of processors that can be used to solve the problem without increasing the running time achievable using n

processors. In addition to its theoretical significance, this result is important in practice, where the number of processors on a parallel computer is fixed.

3. A certain amount of "overhead" may be present when implementing the algorithm in practice, particularly in the input and output stages. Therefore, if cost optimality is not the main concern, and n processors are indeed available, then the algorithm of Section 4.2.1 may be preferable.

This concludes our discussion of how prefix computation can be performed on the PRAM. Although at first sight the problem may seem a simple one with a fairly straightforward solution, computing prefix sums happens to be one of the most useful tools in parallel computation. We now turn to the presentation of some applications of this computation.

4.3 MAXIMUM SUM SUBSEQUENCE

Given a sequence of numbers $X = \{x_0, x_1, \ldots, x_{n-1}\}$, it is required to find two indices u and v, $u \leq v$, such that the subsequence $\{x_u, x_{u+1}, \ldots, x_v\}$ has the largest possible sum,

$$x_u + x_{u+1} + \cdots + x_v,$$

among all such subsequences of X (i.e., subsequences consisting of consecutive elements of X, with no gaps).

The solution is, of course, plain when all of the numbers are positive: The subsequence with the largest sum is the entire input sequence itself. The presence of negative numbers, however, makes the problem a little more difficult.

Note that an obvious lower bound on the number of operations required is $\Omega(n)$, since any algorithm must examine each of the x_i at least once. In fact, there exists a RAM algorithm that matches this bound up to a constant factor. The algorithm sweeps the sequence exactly once from x_0 to x_{n-1}. It keeps track of the maximum sum subsequence found so far. The maximum is initialized to x_0. Having solved the problem for $x_0, x_1, \ldots, x_{i-1}$, the solution is extended to include x_i by noting that the maximum sum in $x_0, x_1, \ldots, x_i$ is the larger of the following two quantities:

1. The sum of a maximum sum subsequence in $\{x_0, x_1, \ldots, x_{i-1}\}$—that is, the maximum sum seen so far (call it *Maxseen*).

2. The sum of a subsequence ending with x_i (call it *Maxhere*).

This is illustrated in Fig. 4.3. The two indices u and v allow us to keep track of *Maxseen*; similarly, q and i mark the beginning and end, respectively, of the sequence whose sum is *Maxhere*.

The algorithm is given here as algorithm RAM MAXIMUM SUM SUBSEQUENCE. When the algorithm terminates, *Maxseen* contains the sum of a maximum sum subsequence $\{x_u, x_{u+1}, \ldots, x_v\}$.

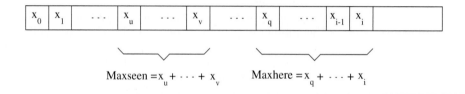

Figure 4.3: Computation of maximum sum subsequence on the RAM.

Algorithm RAM MAXIMUM SUM SUBSEQUENCE

Step 1: (1.1) *Maxseen* $\leftarrow x_0$
       (1.2) $u \leftarrow 0$
       (1.3) $v \leftarrow 0$

Step 2: (2.1) *Maxhere* $\leftarrow x_0$
       (2.2) $q \leftarrow 0$

Step 3: for $i = 1$ **to** $n - 1$ **do**
      (3.1) **if** *Maxhere* ≥ 0
          then *Maxhere* $\leftarrow$ *Maxhere* $+ x_i$
          else   (i) *Maxhere* $\leftarrow x_i$
                 (ii) $q \leftarrow i$
          end if
      (3.2) **if** *Maxseen* $<$ *Maxhere*
          then   (i) *Maxseen* $\leftarrow$ *Maxhere*
                 (ii) $u \leftarrow q$
                 (iii) $v \leftarrow i$
          end if
   end for. ∎

Since the algorithm performs exactly one pass over the input and executes a constant number of constant-time operations for each x_i, its running time is $O(n)$. Any attempt to translate this algorithm into a parallel one would seem hopeless, since each iteration examines just one new element in order to update the maximum sum subsequence encountered so far. By using prefix sums, however, we can surmount this difficulty. An algorithm that uses prefix sums for determining u and v proceeds as follows:

1. The prefix sums $s_0, s_1, \ldots, s_{n-1}$ of $\{x_0, x_1, \ldots, x_{n-1}\}$ are first computed:

$$s_i = \sum_{j=0}^{i} x_j,$$

for $0 \leq i \leq n - 1$.

	i	0	1	2	3	4	5	6	7
INPUT	x_i	-4	2	6	-1	-7	4	2	1
STEP 1	s_i	-4	-2	4	3	-4	0	2	1
STEP 2	m_i	4	4	4	3	2	2	2	1
	a_i	2	2	2	3	6	6	6	7
STEP 3	b_i	4	8	6	-1	-1	6	2	1
STEP 4	$L = 8$, $\quad u = 1$, $\quad v = a_u = 2$								

Figure 4.4: Sequential computation of a maximum sum subsequence.

2. For each i, the maximum s_j to the right, beginning with s_i, is obtained:

$$m_i = \max_{i \leq j \leq n-1} s_j,$$

for $0 \leq i \leq n - 1$. Let a_i be the index at which the maximum m_i is found.

3. For each i, the sum of a maximum sum subsequence is computed:

$$b_i = m_i - s_i + x_i,$$

for $0 \leq i \leq n - 1$.

4. The sum of the overall maximum sum subsequence is then obtained:

$$L = \max_{0 \leq i \leq n-1} b_i.$$

Let u be the index at which the maximum is found. The maximum sum subsequence extends from u to $v = a_u$.

Example 4.5 Let $X = \{-4, 2, 6, -1, -7, 4, 2, 1\}$. The four steps of the computation are illustrated in Fig. 4.4. The maximum sum subsequence is $\{x_1, x_2\}$—that is, $\{2, 6\}$, with a sum of 8. $\square$

Implementation on the PRAM. This algorithm lends itself to direct implementation on the PRAM with $p(n) = n/\log n$ processors $P_0, P_1, \ldots, P_{(n/\log n)-1}$. Step 1 is a prefix computation that can be executed in $O(\log n)$ time using algorithm PRAM PREFIX COMPUTATION of Section 4.2, with operation $\circ$ being $+$. Step 2 is essentially a prefix computation in which the operation $\circ$ is *max*, but with the following two characteristics:

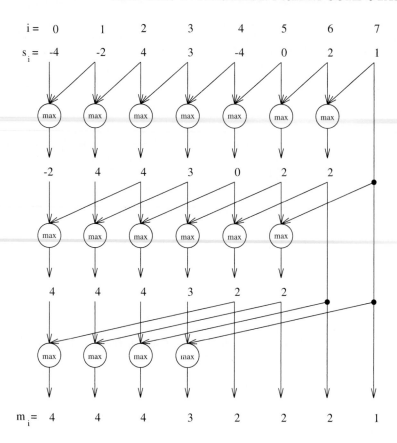

Figure 4.5: Computing the suffix maxima.

1. The direction of the sweep is from $n-1$ to 0, since, for each i, we need to find the maximum s_i from i to $n-1$.

2. In addition to $M = \{m_0, m_1, \ldots, m_{n-1}\}$, the sequence $A = \{a_0, a_1, \ldots, a_{n-1}\}$ is returned.

We refer to the values $M = \{m_0, m_1, \ldots, m_{n-1}\}$ obtained in Step 2 as the *suffix maxima*. This computation is illustrated graphically in Fig. 4.5 for the sequence $\{s_0, s_1, \ldots, s_7\}$ of Example 4.5. Since computing the suffix maxima is a prefix computation, it can be done using algorithm PRAM PREFIX COMPUTATION (with slight modifications). Therefore, Step 2 also requires $n/\log n$ processors and $O(\log n)$ time. In Step 3, each b_i requires one subtraction and one addition and hence takes constant time. Each of the $n/\log n$ processors can thus compute $\log n$ of the b_i's in $O(\log n)$ time. Finally, in Step 4, each processor finds the maximum of

$\log n$ of the b_i's in $O(\log n)$ time. The maximum of these $\log n$ values, namely, L, is then obtained in constant time. Since each step takes $O(\log n)$ time, the algorithm's running time is $t(n) = O(\log n)$, and its cost is

$$
\begin{aligned}
c(n) &= p(n) \times t(n) \\
&= O(n),
\end{aligned}
$$

which is optimal. A formal description of the algorithm is given next. It takes $X = \{x_0, x_1, \ldots, x_{n-1}\}$ as input and returns u and v. We use $k = \log n$.

Algorithm PRAM MAXIMUM SUM SUBSEQUENCE (X, u, v)

> **Step 1:** PRAM PREFIX COMPUTATION $(X, +, S)$
> **Step 2:** Modified PRAM PREFIX COMPUTATION (S, max, M, A)
> **Step 3: for** $i = 0$ **to** $(n/k) - 1$ **do in parallel**
> > **for** $j = 0$ **to** $k - 1$ **do**
> > > $b_{ik+j} \leftarrow m_{ik+j} - s_{ik+j} + x_{ik+j}$
> > **end for**
> **end for**
> **Step 4: for** $i = 0$ **to** $(n/k) - 1$ **do in parallel**
> > (4.1) $d_i \leftarrow b_{ik}$
> > (4.2) $w_i \leftarrow ik$
> > (4.3) **for** $j = 1$ **to** $k - 1$ **do**
> > > **if** $b_{ik+j} > d_i$
> > > > **then** (i) $d_i \leftarrow b_{ik+j}$
> > > > > (ii) $w_i \leftarrow ik + j$
> > > **end if**
> > **end for**
> > (4.4) $L \xleftarrow{\text{MAX}} d_i$
> > (4.5) **if** $L = d_i$
> > > **then** $u \xleftarrow{\text{MIN}} w_i$
> > **end if**
> > (4.6) $v \leftarrow a_u$
> **end for.** ∎

It should be noted that:

1. In Step 2, a modified version of algorithm **PRAM PREFIX COMPUTATION** is used that takes S and max as input, sweeps from $n - 1$ to 0, and returns M and A.

2. In Steps (4.1)–(4.3), processor P_i finds the maximum of the values b_{ik}, b_{ik+1}, $\ldots$, $b_{(i+1)k-1}$. This maximum is stored in d_i and its index in w_i. (This is done simultaneously for all i, $0 \le i \le (n/k) - 1$.)

3. In Step (4.4), a **CW** instruction is used to find the largest d_i and store it in L. (If several d_i hold the maximum value, one is chosen arbitrarily and written in L.)

4. In Step (4.5), the index in X where the maximum sum subsequence begins is stored in u: All processors compare their d_i with L, and the processor P_i for which $d_i = L$ writes w_i in u. (A **CW** is used so that if several processors attempt to write in u, the one writing the smallest value succeeds.)

4.4   SOLVING LINEAR RECURRENCES

Consider the equation

$$z_i = u_{i,1}z_{i-1} + u_{i,2}z_{i-2} + \cdots + u_{i,n}z_{i-n} + v_i,$$

where $i > n$. This equation is known as an *nth-order linear recurrence*, and all of its terms are typically real numbers. It is to be solved for z_i, assuming that z_1, z_2, ..., z_n are known and $u_{i,1}$, $u_{i,2}$, ..., $u_{i,n}$ and v_i are given for all $i > n$. For convenience, we may rewrite the equation in vector form as

$$\boldsymbol{z}_i = \boldsymbol{z}_{i-1}\boldsymbol{U}_i,$$

where

$$\boldsymbol{z}_i = (z_i, z_{i-1}, \ldots, z_{i-n+1}, 1),$$

$$\boldsymbol{z}_{i-1} = (z_{i-1}, z_{i-2}, \ldots, z_{i-n}, 1),$$

and

$$\boldsymbol{U}_i = \begin{pmatrix} u_{i,1} & 1 & 0 & \cdots & 0 & 0 \\ u_{i,2} & 0 & 1 & \cdots & 0 & 0 \\ & & \vdots & & & \\ u_{i,n-1} & 0 & 0 & \cdots & 1 & 0 \\ u_{i,n} & 0 & 0 & \cdots & 0 & 0 \\ v_i & 0 & 0 & \cdots & 0 & 1 \end{pmatrix}.$$

We now let $\boldsymbol{V}_i$ be a product of n matrices $\boldsymbol{U}_i$ as follows:

$$\boldsymbol{V}_i = \boldsymbol{U}_{(i-1)n+1} \times \boldsymbol{U}_{(i-1)n+2} \times \cdots \times \boldsymbol{U}_{in},$$

for $i \geq 2$. We let $\boldsymbol{x}_i$ be the vector

$$\boldsymbol{x}_i = (z_{in}, z_{in-1}, \ldots, z_{(i-1)n+1}, 1),$$

for $i \geq 1$. In other words,

$$\boldsymbol{x}_i = \boldsymbol{x}_1 \boldsymbol{V}_2 \times \boldsymbol{V}_3 \times \cdots \times \boldsymbol{V}_i.$$

Since $\boldsymbol{x}_1 = (z_n, z_{n-1}, \ldots, z_1, 1)$ and $\boldsymbol{V}_i$, $i \geq 2$, are given, $\boldsymbol{x}_i$ can be readily computed for every value of $i > 1$. Each $\boldsymbol{x}_i$ gives the value of n of the unknowns, namely, $z_{in}, z_{in-1}, \ldots, z_{(i-1)n+1}$.

The key step in this approach is the evaluation of

$$\boldsymbol{V}_2 \times \boldsymbol{V}_3 \times \cdots \times \boldsymbol{V}_i,$$

which is essentially a prefix computation, with the operation $\circ$ being matrix multiplication. Suppose that, given $z_1, z_2, \ldots, z_n$, we wish to compute $z_{n+1}, z_{n+2}, \ldots, z_{mn}$ for some $m > 1$. The following PRAM algorithm uses $m - 1$ processors labeled $P_2, P_3, \ldots, P_m$ to obtain these values by evaluating $\boldsymbol{x}_2, \boldsymbol{x}_3, \ldots, \boldsymbol{x}_m$:

Algorithm PRAM LINEAR RECURRENCE

Step 1: for $i = 2$ **to** m **do in parallel**
 Compute $\boldsymbol{V}_i$
 end for
Step 2: Use algorithm PRAM PREFIX COMPUTATION to obtain
 $$\boldsymbol{V}_i = \boldsymbol{V}_2 \times \boldsymbol{V}_3 \times \cdots \times \boldsymbol{V}_i,$$
 for $3 \leq i \leq m$.
Step 3: for $i = 2$ **to** m **do in parallel**
 $$\boldsymbol{x}_i = \boldsymbol{x}_1 \boldsymbol{V}_i$$
 end for. ∎

Analysis. In Step 1, each processor P_i computes $\boldsymbol{V}_i$ by multiplying the n matrices $\boldsymbol{U}_{(i-1)n+1}, \boldsymbol{U}_{(i-1)n+2}, \ldots, \boldsymbol{U}_{in}$. Each of the latter has $n + 1$ rows and $n + 1$ columns. The best available sequential algorithm for multiplying two such matrices runs in $O(n^\epsilon)$ time, where $2 < \epsilon < 2.38$. Thus, Step 1 requires $O(n^{1+\epsilon})$ time. Step 2 runs in $O(n^\epsilon \log m)$ time, since $O(\log m)$ iterations suffice to compute the $m - 2$ prefixes $\boldsymbol{V}_3, \boldsymbol{V}_4, \ldots, \boldsymbol{V}_m$, and each matrix multiplication takes $O(n^\epsilon)$ time. Finally, in Step 3, P_i multiplies the $(n + 1)$-vector $\boldsymbol{x}_1$ by the matrix $\boldsymbol{V}_i$ in $O(n^2)$ time. The algorithm's running time is therefore dominated by the running time of Step 1, assuming that $n > \log m$.

Example 4.6 We illustrate the algorithm for $n = 2$ and $m = 4$. Thus, we assume that z_1 and z_2 are given, and we need to compute

$$z_i = u_{i,1} z_{i-1} + u_{i,2} z_{i-2} + v_i,$$

for $i = 3, 4, \ldots, 8$. We write

$$\boldsymbol{z}_i = (z_i, z_{i-1}, 1)$$

and

$$\boldsymbol{U}_i = \begin{pmatrix} u_{i,1} & 1 & 0 \\ u_{i,2} & 0 & 0 \\ v_i & 0 & 1 \end{pmatrix}.$$

This way, $\boldsymbol{z}_i = \boldsymbol{z}_{i-1} \boldsymbol{U}_i$ translates to

$$\begin{aligned}
z_3 &= z_2 U_3, \\
z_4 &= z_3 U_4 \\
&= z_2 U_3 \times U_4, \\
z_5 &= z_4 U_5 \\
&= z_2 U_3 \times U_4 \times U_5, \\
z_6 &= z_5 U_6 \\
&= z_2 U_3 \times U_4 \times U_5 \times U_6, \\
z_7 &= z_6 U_7 \\
&= z_2 U_3 \times U_4 \times U_5 \times U_6 \times U_7, \\
z_8 &= z_7 U_8 \\
&= z_2 U_3 \times U_4 \times U_5 \times U_6 \times U_7 \times U_8.
\end{aligned}$$

Now,

$$\begin{aligned}
x_1 &= (z_2, z_1, 1) &&= z_2, \\
x_2 &= (z_4, z_3, 1) &&= z_4, \\
x_3 &= (z_6, z_5, 1) &&= z_6, \\
x_4 &= (z_8, z_7, 1) &&= z_8,
\end{aligned}$$

and

$$\begin{aligned}
V_2 &= U_3 \times U_4, \\
V_3 &= U_5 \times U_6, \\
V_4 &= U_7 \times U_8.
\end{aligned}$$

Thus, $x_2 = x_1 V_2$, $x_3 = x_1 V_2 \times V_3$, and $x_4 = x_1 V_2 \times V_3 \times V_4$. $\square$

4.5   POLYNOMIAL INTERPOLATION

Suppose we are given $n + 1$ pairs of numbers (x_i, y_i), $i = 0, 1, \ldots, n$, and an arbitrary real-valued function f, such that

1. f is defined on the x_i over an interval $[a, b]$,

2. $y_i = f(x_i)$,

3. $a \leq x_0 < x_1 < x_2 < \cdots < x_n \leq b$.

The problem of *polynomial interpolation* is that of creating a polynomial $h(x)$ of degree n using the pairs (x_i, y_i) such that $h(x_i) = y_i$ for $i = 0, 1, \ldots, n$. In *Newton's interpolation method*, the polynomial sought is written as

$$h(x) = y_0 + Y_{01}(x - x_0) + Y_{02}(x - x_0)(x - x_1) + Y_{03}(x - x_0)(x - x_1)(x - x_2)$$

$$+ \cdots + Y_{0n}(x - x_0)(x - x_1)\ldots(x - x_{n-1}),$$

where the coefficients Y_{0i}, for $i = 1, 2, \ldots, n$, are called the *divided differences* of f. These are computed as follows:

$$Y_{i,i} = y_i,$$

$$Y_{i,i+j} = \frac{Y_{i,i+j-1} - Y_{i+1,i+j}}{x_i - x_{i+j}},$$

for $i, j = 0, 1, \ldots, n$. For example,

$$Y_{i,i+1} = \frac{y_i - y_{i+1}}{x_i - x_{i+1}},$$

$$Y_{i+1,i+2} = \frac{y_{i+1} - y_{i+2}}{x_{i+1} - x_{i+2}},$$

and

$$Y_{i,i+2} = \frac{Y_{i,i+1} - Y_{i+1,i+2}}{x_i - x_{i+2}}$$

$$= \frac{((y_i - y_{i+1})/(x_i - x_{i+1})) - ((y_{i+1} - y_{i+2})/(x_{i+1} - x_{i+2}))}{x_i - x_{i+2}}$$

$$= \frac{y_i}{(x_i - x_{i+1})(x_i - x_{i+2})} + \frac{y_{i+1}}{(x_{i+1} - x_i)(x_{i+1} - x_{i+2})}$$

$$+ \frac{y_{i+2}}{(x_{i+1} - x_{i+2})(x_i - x_{i+2})}.$$

In general, for $i = 1, 2, \ldots, n$,

$$Y_{0i} = \frac{y_0}{X_{01}X_{02}\ldots X_{0i}} + \frac{y_1}{X_{10}X_{12}\ldots X_{1i}} + \cdots + \frac{y_i}{X_{i0}X_{i1}\ldots X_{i,i-1}},$$

where

$$X_{ij} = (x_i - x_j) \quad \text{for} \quad i \neq j.$$

For each j, where $0 \leq j \leq i$, the denominator of the fraction whose numerator is y_j in Y_{0i}, over $i = 1, 2, \ldots, n$, can be expressed as a prefix computation. For example, when $j = 0$, the denominators are

$$X_{01}$$
$$X_{01}X_{02}$$
$$X_{01}X_{02}X_{03}$$
$$\vdots$$
$$X_{01}X_{02}\ldots X_{0n}.$$

The denominators can be computed using algorithm PRAM PREFIX COMPU-TATION with the operation $\circ$ taken as scalar multiplication. Since one such prefix computation is required for each value of j, there are $n + 1$ prefix computations in all.

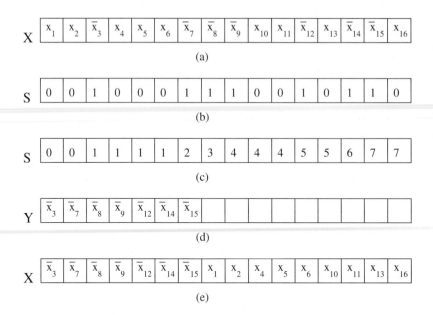

Figure 4.6: Packing labeled and unlabeled data in an array: (a) Input; (b) Secondary array; (c) Prefix sums; (d) Output in Y; (e) Output in X.

4.6   ARRAY PACKING

One of the most common and important applications of prefix computation is in packing an array. Suppose that an array X of n elements is given, some of whose entries are labeled. The labeled entries are scattered arbitrarily throughout the array, as illustrated in Fig. 4.6(a) for the array $X = \{x_1, x_2, \ldots, x_{16}\}$, where a label is denoted by a bar over x_i. Such an array may arise in an application in which a set of data is given and it is required to identify those data satisfying a certain condition. A datum satisfying the condition is labeled.

Once the data have been labeled, it is required to bring the labeled elements into contiguous positions in the same or another array. This may be necessary for a proper output of the results, or because the labeled elements are to undergo further processing and they are expected to appear in adjacent positions in the next stage of the computation.

Sequentially, the problem is solved by "burning the candle at both ends:" Two pointers q and r are used, where $q = 1$ and $r = n$ initially. The pointers are moved in opposite directions, q to the right and r to the left; q advances if x_q is a labeled element, whereas r advances if x_r is an unlabeled element. If at any time x_q is unlabeled and x_r is labeled, these two elements switch positions. When $q \geq r$, the labeled elements appear in adjacent positions in the first part of the array. This takes $O(n)$ time, which is optimal.

In parallel, we use a secondary array of n elements $S = \{s_1, s_2, \ldots, s_n\}$ to compute the destination of each labeled element of X. Initially,

$$
\begin{aligned}
s_i &= 1, & \text{provided that } x_i \text{ is labeled} \\
&= 0 & \text{otherwise,}
\end{aligned}
$$

as illustrated in Fig. 4.6(b). The array S can be created using $n/\log n$ processors in $O(\log n)$ time, each processor filling $\log n$ positions of S. A prefix sums computation is then performed on the elements of S, as shown in Fig. 4.6(c). Finally, each labeled element x_i of X is copied into position s_i of an array Y. This is illustrated in Fig. 4.6(d). Note that the labeled elements of X occupy the first s_n positions of Y. Both the prefix computation and the copying of the labeled elements of X into Y can be done using $n/\log n$ processors in $O(\log n)$ time.

In some cases, it may be necessary to pack the labeled elements of X within X itself: Once their destinations are known, the labeled elements can be copied directly into the first s_n positions of X. However, this would overwrite some unlabeled elements of X. Should this be undesirable, it can be avoided as follows:

1. The destinations of the s_n labeled elements are first computed.

2. The same procedure is then applied to the $n - s_n$ unlabeled elements.

3. Simultaneously, the labeled and unlabeled elements are copied into the first s_n and last $n - s_n$ positions of X, respectively.

This is shown in Fig. 4.6(e). We illustrate the use of array packing through the following two examples:

Example 4.7 Let $Q = \{q_1, q_2, \ldots, q_n\}$ be a finite sequence representing n points in the plane. The *convex hull* of Q, denoted $CH(Q)$, is the smallest convex polygon that contains all the points of Q. In other words, for each $q_i \in Q$:

1. Either q_i is a *corner* of $CH(Q)$,

2. Or q_i lies *inside* $CH(Q)$.

A set of points and its convex hull are shown in Fig. 4.7.

Given Q, it is required to compute $CH(Q)$—that is, to identify those elements of Q which are corners of $CH(Q)$. Suppose that an algorithm, using some property of the corners of the convex hull, has labeled those points $q_i \in Q$ which are corners of $CH(Q)$. These labeled points are now packed into contiguous positions of an array. They are then sorted by polar angle, with a point inside $CH(Q)$ serving as the origin of the coordinates. The corners of $CH(Q)$ are then produced as output, listed in contiguous positions of an array in the order in which they appear on the polygon. $\square$

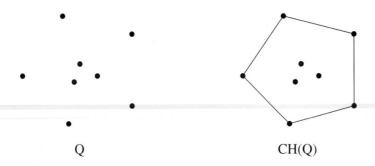

Q   CH(Q)

Figure 4.7: A set of points and its convex hull.

Example 4.8 A sequence of n distinct numbers $X = \{x_1, x_2, \ldots, x_n\}$ in arbitrary order is given, together with an integer k, where $1 \leq k \leq n$. The problem of *selection* calls for determining the kth smallest element of X. For instance, if $X = \{3, 7, 1, 5, 6, 8, 4, 9\}$ and $k = 4$, then the fourth smallest element is 5.

One algorithm for solving this problem chooses an element m of X and labels each element of X that is smaller than m. The outcome of this step determines what to do next. Let the number of labeled elements be L. There are three possibilities:

1. $L > k$: In this case, the kth smallest element of X must be one of the labeled elements. All unlabeled elements are discarded, and the algorithm is applied recursively on the labeled elements.

2. $L = k - 1$: In this case, m is the kth smallest element of X, and the algorithm terminates.

3. $L < k - 1$: In this case, the kth smallest element of X must be one of the unlabeled elements. All labeled elements, as well as m, are discarded, and the algorithm is applied recursively on the unlabeled elements with $k \leftarrow k - L - 1$.

In the two cases where the algorithm is applied recursively, the elements retained must be packed into contiguous positions of an array and passed to the next level of recursion. □

4.7 INTERVAL BROADCASTING

Suppose that an array X of n elements is given. Certain positions of X are referred to as *leaders*. Each leader holds a datum, while all other positions of X are empty. The positions of the leaders are entirely arbitrary. This is illustrated in Fig. 4.8(a) for an array of 16 elements and four leaders, holding the data v, w, x, and y. It is required to copy the datum in each leader into all positions of the array following the leader, up to, but not including, the next leader (if it exists), as shown in

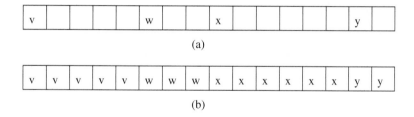

Figure 4.8: Interval broadcasting: (a) Input; (b) Output.

Fig. 4.8(b). This is known as *interval broadcasting*. Sequentially, the problem is solved optimally in $O(n)$ time using one pass over X.

In parallel, once again prefix computation will prove valuable to an efficient execution of this task. We begin by setting up the following conditions:

1. Each leader in X is assumed to hold a pair (i, d_i), where i is the leader's index in the array X and d_i is its datum.

2. Each nonleader in X is assumed to hold a pair $(-1, \#)$, where $\#$ is a dummy datum (or placeholder).

3. The operation $\circ$ of prefix computation is defined such that

$$(i, a) \circ (j, b)$$

results in

$$j \leftarrow i \quad \text{and} \quad b \leftarrow a, \quad \text{provided that} \quad j < i.$$

In other words, (j, b) becomes (i, a) if $j < i$; otherwise, (j, b) remains unchanged.

Interval broadcasting is now performed by applying prefix computation with operation $\circ$ to the array X, as illustrated in Fig. 4.9 for the array of Fig. 4.8. This computation can be performed in $O(\log n)$ time using $n/\log n$ processors.

Example 4.9 Suppose that $X = \{d_1, d_2, \ldots, d_n\}$ is an array of numbers arranged arbitrarily. It is required to sort X in nondecreasing order. A well-known sequential sorting algorithm is Quicksort, which operates as follows: First, an element of X (for instance, d_1) is used to split X into three subarrays X_1, X_2, and X_3 such that:

1. X_1 contains the elements of X smaller than d_1.

2. X_2 contains the elements of X equal to d_1.

3. X_3 contains the elements of X larger than d_1.

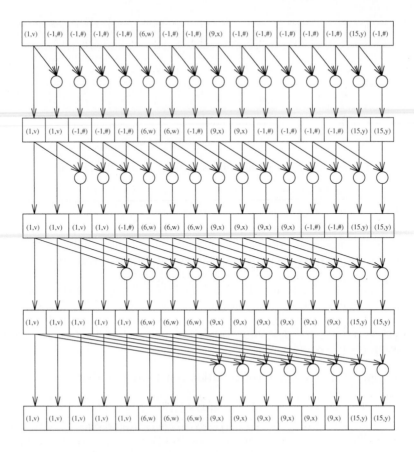

Figure 4.9: Using prefix computation for interval broadcasting.

The two arrays X_1 and X_3 are now treated separately, and each is split into three subarrays as was X. This continues recursively until X is sorted. In parallel, we use interval broadcasting and array packing for a fast execution of each level of the recursion:

1. Interval broadcasting is applied over the entire array X to identify, for each subarray, the elements of the subarray smaller than, equal to, and larger than its first element. Here, the first element of each subarray is the *leader*, and its value is broadcast to all the elements following it in the subarray (i.e., up to, but not including, the first element of the next subarray). Now all the elements in a subarray can be compared simultaneously to the leader, and the outcome of the comparison is used to label each element with a '<', '=', or '>'.

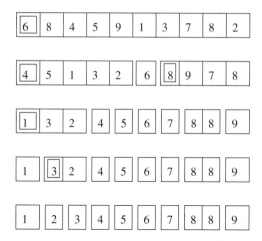

Figure 4.10: Parallel Quicksort using interval broadcasting.

2. Array packing is applied to each subarray using the labels '<', '=', and '>'. The effect is to produce three subarrays of elements smaller than, equal to, and larger than the first element, respectively.

This is illustrated in Fig. 4.10 for an array of 10 elements. □

Interval Prefix Computation. Interval broadcasting can be generalized in the following way: An array X of n elements, $d_1, d_2, \ldots, d_n$ is given. Some positions of X are leaders. It is required to perform prefix computation, for a given operation $\circ$, on the elements d_i of each interval between leaders (i.e., beginning with a leader and continuing up to, but not including, the next leader). As before, we assume that:

1. Each leader holds a pair (i, d_i), where i is its index in X and d_i is the datum it stores.

2. Each nonleader holds a pair $(-1, d_j)$, where d_j is the datum it stores.

3. Prefix computation is executed on the pairs defined in Steps 1 and 2 such that when it is applied to the pairs (i, d_r) and (j, d_s), where $r < s$, the result is

$$j \leftarrow i \quad \text{and} \quad d_s \leftarrow d_r \circ d_s, \quad \text{provided that} \quad j < i.$$

In other words, (j, d_s) becomes $(i, d_r \circ d_s)$ if $j < i$; otherwise, (j, d_s) remains unchanged.

Here $\circ$ could be any binary associative operation defined on $d_1, d_2, \ldots, d_n$, such as addition, multiplication, comparison, and so on. It is easy to see that interval prefix computation can be performed in $O(\log n)$ time using $n/\log n$ processors.

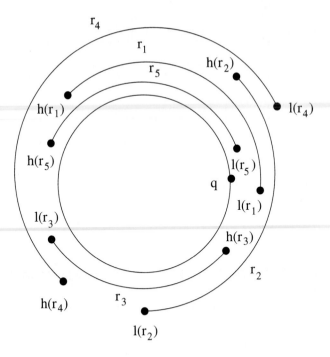

Figure 4.11: A sequence of arcs on a circle.

4.8   COMPUTING CLIQUES OF CIRCULAR ARCS

In this application, we are given a sequence $R = \{r_1, r_2, \ldots, r_n\}$, $n \geq 2$, of arcs on a circle such that:

1. No arc is contained fully in another arc.

2. No two arcs share an endpoint.

3. The arcs are sorted; that is, the endpoints are available in sorted order around the circle.

An example of such a sequence is shown in Fig. 4.11. In what follows, each arc r_i is identified by its *head* $h(r_i)$ and *tail* $l(r_i)$. The labeling is done in such a way that arc r_i is traveled clockwise if one moves from $h(r_i)$ to $l(r_i)$. The foregoing conditions imply that $h(r_1)$, $h(r_2)$, $\ldots$, $h(r_n)$, as well as $l(r_1)$, $l(r_2)$, $\ldots$, $l(r_n)$, are given in sorted cyclic order.

Maximum 1-Overlap Clique.   Given a point q on the circle, the *1-overlap clique* of q is the set of all circular arcs in R that contain q. In Fig. 4.11, the

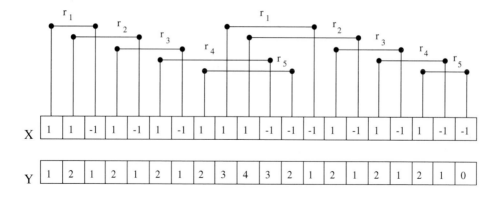

X	1	1	-1	1	-1	1	-1	1	1	1	-1	-1	-1	1	-1	1	-1	1	-1	-1

Y	1	2	1	2	1	2	1	2	3	4	3	2	1	2	1	2	1	2	1	0

Figure 4.12: Using prefix sums to compute cliques of circular arcs.

1-overlap clique of the given point q consists of r_1 and r_2. Clearly, all arcs of a 1-overlap clique mutually intersect. A 1-overlap clique is *maximum* if there does not exist any 1-overlap clique of larger cardinality. Sequentially, a maximum 1-overlap clique may be obtained by examining each of $h(r_1)$, $h(r_2)$, ..., $h(r_n)$ in turn and keeping track of which is contained in most arcs.

In parallel, this traversal is done efficiently through the use of prefix computation. In what follows we describe a PRAM algorithm with $n/\log n$ processors. For each arc r_i of R, the arc's head $h(r_i)$ is labeled with a $+1$, while the arc's tail $l(r_i)$ is labeled with a -1. Two copies of these labels (each listed in clockwise order on the circle) are now stored in an array X, the second copy immediately following the first. The label of an arc's tail is placed in the array after the label of that arc's head. Specifically, the labels are stored in X as follows: First, the label of $h(r_1)$ is placed in $X(1)$. Then, proceeding clockwise, we add the label of each head or tail as it is encountered. The label of $l(r_i)$ is skipped if the label of $h(r_i)$ has not been entered in X yet. The process terminates when each label occurs twice in the array. This is shown in Fig. 4.12 for the set of five arcs of Fig. 4.11. If each of the $n/\log n$ processors creates a section of array X consisting of $2\log n$ elements, this step is completed in $O(\log n)$ time.

By storing two copies of the list of arcs in the array X, a circular scan of the circle to detect all 1-overlap cliques is simulated by one traversal of X from beginning to end.

We now perform a prefix sums computation on X and store the result in an array Y, as shown in Fig. 4.12. A maximum of these sums corresponds to a point where a maximum 1-overlap clique occurs. If there are several such sums, one is chosen arbitrarily. In the figure, the maximum sum is 4; it corresponds to a maximum 1-overlap clique occurring at $h(r_2)$ and containing the arcs r_1, r_2, r_4, and r_5. The prefix sums computation can be performed in $O(\log n)$ time by $n/\log n$ processors using algorithm PRAM PREFIX COMPUTATION. Finding the largest prefix sum and the point where it occurs (for instance, $h(r_j)$ the head of arc r_j) can also be done in $O(\log n)$ time using $n/\log n$ processors: First, with all processors operating in parallel, each processor (sequentially) finds the largest of $\log n$ sums and the point where it occurs; the largest of these and the point where it occurs (i.e., $h(r_j)$) are then determined in constant time using a **MAX CW** instruction.

Once the maximum sum has been determined, all processors read $h(r_j)$ in $O(1)$ time. All processors now "know" where the maximum 1-overlap clique occurs, but do not "know" its members. In order to determine the arcs belonging to the maximum 1-overlap clique, we identify those arcs containing $h(r_j)$. Since testing whether an arc contains a point can be done in constant time, this step is performed in $O(\log n)$ time with $n/\log n$ processors: Each processor takes charge of $\log n$ distinct arcs and checks each arc to see whether it contains $h(r_j)$. As a result, if an arc contains $h(r_j)$, that arc is labeled with a 1; otherwise it is labeled with a 0.

If required, the members of the maximum 1-overlap clique, denoted $A(R) = \{a_1, a_2, \ldots, a_k\}$, are now stored in contiguous positions of an array. Using the array-packing algorithm of Section 4.6 and the array of 1's and 0's just obtained, we pack the members of $A(R)$ into k contiguous positions of an array A in $O(\log n)$ time, using $n/\log n$ processors.

4.9 GENERAL PREFIX COMPUTATION

In this section, a generalization of prefix computation is presented. Two applications of this computation are then described.

A Database Problem. In order to motivate our generalization, we begin by considering the following problem, known as *range searching*: Let $Q = \{q_1, q_2, \ldots, q_n\}$ be a finite sequence of ordered pairs of real numbers. Each entry $q_i = (x_i, y_i)$ of Q can be viewed as the Cartesian coordinates of a point in the plane. A rectangle G is now given whose sides are parallel to the axes of the coordinates; thus, G is defined by the two intervals $[a, b]$ and $[c, d]$ on the x and y axes, respectively. This is illustrated in Fig. 4.13, where all points are located in the first quadrant for simplicity. For some function f and a binary operator $*$, it is required to compute the quantity

$$f(i) * f(j) * \cdots * f(k),$$

where $q_i, q_j, \ldots, q_k$ are those elements of Q which fall inside G. In the figure, the answer would be $f(4) * f(5) * f(7) * f(8)$.

Range searching is a database search problem, where Q is a database and G is the query. More generally, the elements of Q are ordered tuples of the form $(x, y, \ldots, z)$, and it is required to find those elements whose components $x, y, \ldots, z$, fall within given ranges specified in the query $G = \{[a, b], [c, d], \ldots, [e, f]\}$; that is, $a \leq x \leq b, c \leq y \leq d, \ldots, e \leq z \leq f$.

We are now ready to introduce general prefix computation (GPC), a generalization of prefix computation.

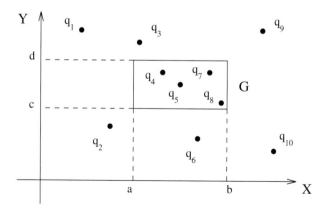

Figure 4.13: Range searching.

GPC. Let $\{f(1), f(2), \ldots, f(n)\}$ and $\{y(1), y(2), \ldots, y(n)\}$ be two sequences of elements with a binary associative operator $*$ defined on the f elements and a linear order $\prec$ defined on the y elements. It is required to compute the sequence

$$\{D(1), D(2), \ldots, D(n)\}$$

whose elements $D(m)$, $m = 1, 2, \ldots, n$ are defined as

$$D(m) = f(j_1) * f(j_2) * \cdots * f(j_k),$$

where

$$j_1 < j_2 < \cdots < j_k$$

and $\{j_1, j_2, \ldots, j_k\}$ is the sequence of indices such that

$$j_i < m \quad \text{and} \quad y(j_i) \prec y(m)$$

for $i = 1, 2, \ldots, k$.

If, for some m, $1 \le m \le n$, no index j satisfies

$$j < m \quad \text{and} \quad y(j) \prec y(m)$$

(i.e., the sequence $\{j_1, j_2, \ldots, j_k\}$ is empty), then $D(m)$ is assigned the value of the neutral (or *identity*) element for $*$. For example, when $*$ is $+$, the neutral element is 0. Since no index is smaller than 1, $D(1)$ is always equal to the neutral element.

With this definition, GPC can be related to the range-searching problem. Let:

1. The sequence Q contain n elements, namely, the pairs $(m, y(m))$ for $m = 1, 2, \ldots, n$.

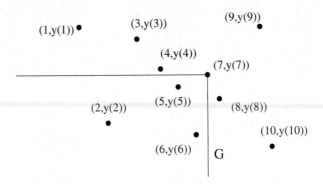

Figure 4.14: GPC related to range searching.

2. The linear order $\prec$ be the usual "less than" relation $<$ defined on numbers.

3. The query G consist of the two intervals $(-\infty, m]$ and $(-\infty, y(m)]$, for every m from 1 to n.

This is illustrated in Fig. 4.14 for the set in Fig. 4.13; taking $m = 7$, we get

$$D(7) = f(2) * f(5) * f(6).$$

4.9.1   Lower Bound

A lower bound is now derived on the number of operations required to perform GPC. In what follows, we take $\prec$ and $*$ to be the usual $<$ and $+$, respectively. The lower bound is obtained by showing that any algorithm for GPC must be able to take a sequence $Z = \{z(1), z(2), \ldots, z(n)\}$ of numbers in arbitrary order and sort it into nondecreasing order. Note that if $z(i) = z(j)$, then $z(i)$ is considered smaller than $z(j)$ if and only if $i < j$. To express the problem of sorting Z as a GPC problem, we let $f(j) = 1$ for $1 \le j \le n$. By first setting $y(j) = z(j)$ for $j = 1$, $2, \ldots, n$ and computing $D(m)$ for $m = 1, 2, \ldots, n$, we obtain the number of elements j such that $z(j) < z(m)$ and $j < m$. Now we set $y(j) = z(n - j + 1)$ for $j = 1, 2, \ldots, n$ and compute $D(n - m + 1)$ for $m = 1, 2, \ldots, n$—that is, the number of elements j such that $z(j) < z(m)$ and $j > m$. By computing $D(m) + D(n - m + 1)$ for $m = 1, 2, \ldots, n$, we obtain the total number of elements in Z which are smaller than $z(m)$—that is, the position of $z(m)$ in Z had the sequence been sorted. Using this information, we can sort Z in $O(n)$ operations (by placing each element in its sorted position). In view of the $\Omega(n \log n)$ lower bound on the number of operations required to sort a sequence of n numbers, the same lower bound on GPC follows.

4.9.2 Performing GPC on the PRAM

We now describe an algorithm for GPC on the PRAM. Some notation will prove useful. Let:

1. $D(m, S)$ be the function $D(m)$ restricted on a sequence of indices S; that is, $D(m, S) = f(j_1) * f(j_2) * \cdots * f(j_k)$, where j_i satisfies all the conditions given earlier, and in addition, $j_i \in S$ for $i = 1, 2, \ldots, k$.

2. $Y(S)$ be the sequence of elements $y(j)$, $j \in S$, listed in sorted order.

3. $B(m, S)$ be the position of element $y(m)$ in $Y(S)$.

4. $J(m, S) = \{j_1, j_2, \ldots, j_r\}$ be the subsequence of S satisfying $y(j_i) \prec y(m)$; for convenience, m itself is included in $J(m, S)$.

5. $E(m, S) = f(j_1) * f(j_2) * \cdots * f(j_r)$.

Suppose that we interpret $(i, y(i))$ as a pair of Cartesian coordinates (as we did earlier) and refer to it as point i. Then point i is *to the left of* point j if $i < j$. Similarly, point i is *below* point j if $y(i) < y(j)$, or if $y(i) = y(j)$ and $i < j$. Using this interpretation, we compute $D(m, S)$ over points in S that are to the left and below point m. Also, $E(m, S)$ is computed over points in S that are below point m (including point m itself).

The algorithm for performing GPC proceeds as follows: Initially, $S = \{1, 2, \ldots, n\}$. Now S is divided into two subsequences, L (for *left*) and R (for *right*), of equal size such that all the points of L are to the left of all the points of R. The algorithm is then applied recursively to L and R (the recursion terminating when a sequence contains one element). This yields $Y(L)$, $Y(R)$, $D(l, L)$, $D(r, R)$, $E(l, L)$, $E(r, R)$, $B(l, L)$, and $B(r, R)$ for all points l in L and all points r in R. Now $Y(L)$ and $Y(R)$ are merged to form $Y(S)$, and the rank $B(m, S)$ in $Y(S)$ for each point m in S is obtained. The latter is used to compute, for each point r in R, the index g_r of the point in L with the largest y-coordinate such that $y(g_r) < y(r)$. Thus,

$$B(g_r, L) = B(r, S) - B(r, R).$$

Similarly, for each point l in L, we compute the index g_l of the point in R with the largest y-coordinate such that $y(g_l) < y(l)$. Hence,

$$B(g_l, R) = B(l, S) - B(l, L).$$

The final result can now be obtained directly from the following relations, for each point l in L and each point r in R:

$$\begin{aligned}
D(l, S) &= D(l, L), \\
D(r, S) &= E(g_r, L) * D(r, R), \\
E(l, S) &= E(l, L) * E(g_l, R), \\
E(r, S) &= E(g_r, L) * E(r, R).
\end{aligned}$$

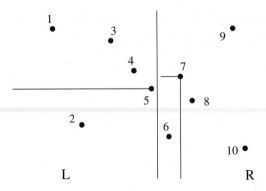

Figure 4.15: Performing GPC recursively.

Example 4.10 Suppose that we want to compute $D(7, S)$ for the sequence $S = \{1,$ $2, \ldots, 10\}$ in Fig. 4.15. Once the algorithm has been applied to L and R, the values of the functions E and D will have been obtained for all points r in R and all points l in L. In particular, we would have $E(5, L) = f(2) * f(5)$ and $D(7, R) = f(6)$. After merging, we get $g_7 = 5$. Therefore,

$$
\begin{aligned}
D(7, S) &= E(5, L) * D(7, R) \\
&= f(2) * f(5) * f(6). \;\square
\end{aligned}
$$

Analysis.   Since the input points are given in the form $\{(1, y(1)),$ $(2, y(2)), \ldots, (n, y(n))\}$, they are already sorted by x-coordinate. Therefore, splitting the sequence S at each level of the recursion into L and R can be done in constant time using n processors. For example, at the first level of recursion, L consists of points $\{(1, y(1)), (2, y(2)), \ldots, (n/2, y(n/2))\}$, and R consists of points $\{((n/2) + 1, y((n/2) + 1)), ((n/2) + 2, y((n/2) + 2)), \ldots, (n, y(n))\}$. This splitting process continues until each sequence L and each sequence R consists of one point. The time required is $O(\log n)$, since there are $\log n$ levels in the recursion. It is helpful to think of the splitting process as a complete binary tree whose root is the input sequence of n points and whose leaves represent a one-point sequence each. If the leaves are numbered from left to right, then leaf i contains $(i, y(i))$.

Once the first phase of the recursion (i.e., splitting the points) has bottomed out, we go back up the tree, merging the points *on the basis of their y-coordinates*, as required by the algorithm. At each level of the tree, a node receives from its children two sequences of points, both sorted by y-coordinate. The two sequences are merged, the functions B, D, and E computed, and the result sent to the node's parent. Eventually, the root receives two sorted sequences of size $n/2$ each, which it merges, and computes the final functions. Thus, the sequence of points emerges at the root *sorted by y-coordinate*. Clearly, the functions B, D, and E require constant time to be computed at each level, using n processors. If merging at each level can also be done in constant time using $O(n)$ processors, then this second phase of the recursion requires $O(\log n)$ time as well. It would follow that the PRAM algorithm for performing GPC runs in $O(\log n)$ time using $O(n)$ processors.

The remainder of this section is used to show how merging can be done in constant time at each level. Specifically, we describe a PRAM algorithm that takes as input the n values $\{y(1), y(2), \ldots, y(n)\}$, stored in arbitrary order in the leaves of a (conceptual) complete binary tree T, one value per leaf. The algorithm moves these values up the tree, at each node merging the sequences received from the left and right children and sending the resulting sorted sequence to its parent. When the algorithm terminates, the initial sequence of n values emerges from the root of the tree sorted in nondecreasing order. In order to achieve a total running time of $O(\log n)$, the merging process is pipelined. Thus, the algorithm works at several levels of the tree at once, overlapping the merging at different nodes over time. Thereafter, we refer to this algorithm as algorithm PRAM SORT.

Algorithm PRAM SORT. Let L_v be the sequence of values stored in the leaves of the subtree of T whose root is an internal (i.e., nonleaf) node v. At the jth time step, v contains a *sorted* sequence $Q_v(j)$ whose elements are selected from L_v. Furthermore, the sequence $Q_v(j)$ is an *increasing* subsequence of L_v. Eventually, when $Q_v(j) = L_v$, node v is said to be *complete*. Also, all leaves are said to be complete by definition. During the algorithm, a node v whose parent is not complete at the jth step sends a sorted subsequence $R_v(j)$ of $Q_v(j)$ to its parent.

How is $Q_v(j)$ created? Let w and z be the children of v. Node v merges $R_w(j)$ and $R_z(j)$ to obtain $Q_v(j)$, where $R_w(j)$ and $R_z(j)$ are themselves formed as follows:

1. If w is not complete during the $(j-1)$st step, then $R_w(j)$ consists of every fourth element of $Q_w(j-1)$.

2. If w becomes complete during the jth step, then:

    (i) $R_w(j+1)$ consists of every fourth element of $Q_w(j)$.

    (ii) $R_w(j+2)$ consists of every second element of $Q_w(j)$.

    (iii) $R_w(j+3) = Q_w(j)$.

Consequently, if w and z become complete during the jth step, then v becomes complete during step $j+3$. It follows that the root of T becomes complete during step $3\log n$. At this point, the root contains the input sequence of n values in sorted order, and the algorithm terminates.

The only detail left is to show how the sequences $R_w(j)$ and $R_z(j)$ are merged in constant time. Given two sequences of values, the *predecessor* of an element in one sequence is the largest element in the other sequence that is smaller than it (if such an element exists). Suppose that each element of $R_w(j)$ $(R_z(j))$ knows the position of its predecessor in $R_z(j)$ $(R_w(j))$. In that case, $R_w(j)$ and $R_z(j)$ can be merged in constant time using $|R_w(j)| + |R_z(j)|$ processors, each processor directly placing one element in its final position in $Q_v(j)$. To make this possible, certain necessary information about predecessors is maintained. To wit, after step $j - 1$:

1. The elements of $R_w(j - 1)$ "know" their predecessors in $R_z(j - 1)$, and vice versa, these two sequences having just been merged to form $Q_v(j - 1)$.

2. Each element of $R_w(j - 1)$ finds its predecessor in $Q_w(j - 1)$ in constant time. Consequently, all elements in $R_w(j - 1)$ can determine their predecessor in $R_w(j)$, also in constant time. Note that no more than four elements of $R_w(j - 1)$ have the same predecessor in $R_w(j)$. Now each element in $R_w(j)$ can determine its predecessor in $R_w(j - 1)$ in constant time.

3. Each element of $R_z(j - 1)$ finds its predecessor in $Q_z(j - 1)$ in constant time. Consequently, all elements in $R_z(j - 1)$ can determine their predecessors in $R_z(j)$, also in constant time. Note that no more than four elements of $R_z(j-1)$ have the same predecessor in $R_z(j)$. Now each element in $R_z(j)$ can determine its predecessor in $R_z(j - 1)$ in constant time.

4. With the preceding "knowledge," the elements of $R_w(j)$ can determine their predecessors in $R_z(j)$, and vice versa, in constant time.

Thus, obtaining the information about predecessors required in the current step, merging, and obtaining the information about predecessors for the following step all require constant time. As mentioned before, there are $3 \log n$ steps in all, and therefore, the algorithm runs in $O(\log n)$ time. Since the sequences involved at each step contain a total of $O(n)$ elements, the number of processors needed is $O(n)$.

4.10   APPLICATIONS OF GPC

We now show how GPC can be used to perform other computations. We assume in what follows that $\prec$ is the usual "less than" relation, $<$.

4.10.1   Computational Geometry

Computational geometry is that branch of computer science concerned with designing efficient algorithms for solving geometric problems—that is, problems involving points, lines, polygons, circles, and so on. Two problems from computational geometry were already used in this chapter to demonstrate the use of prefix computation, namely, the convex hull problem and the clique problem on circular arcs, discussed in Sections 4.6 and 4.8, respectively. Computational geometry also provides our first examples for illustrating the applicability of GPC to the solution of other problems.

Let $S = \{q_1, q_2, \ldots, q_n\}$ be a sequence representing n points in the plane, given by their Cartesian coordinates. The horizontal and vertical coordinates of q_i are denoted $q_i[1]$ and $q_i[2]$, respectively. A point q_i is said to *dominate* a point q_j if

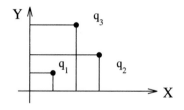

Figure 4.16: Point domination.

and only if $q_i[1] > q_j[1]$ and $q_i[2] > q_j[2]$. For example, in Fig. 4.16, both q_2 and q_3 dominate q_1, but q_2 does not dominate q_3 and q_3 does not dominate q_2.

We use GPC to solve three problems on S. In solving these problems, we begin by sorting the points on their first (i.e., horizontal) coordinate, in ascending and descending order, and denote the resulting lists by $a_1, a_2, \ldots, a_n$ and $d_1, d_2, \ldots, d_n$, respectively. GPC is then applied to each problem by appropriately choosing f, y, and $*$ and then computing D.

> **Problem 1.** For each point q in S, compute the number of points in S that are dominated by q.
>
> **Solution.** Take $*$ to be $+$, and for $m = 1, 2, \ldots, n$, let $f(m) = 1$ and $y(m) = a_m[2]$.
>
> For $m = 1, 2, \ldots, n$, the number of points dominated by a_m is $D(m)$. □

Problem 1 is sometimes referred to as *empirical cumulative distribution function (ECDF) searching*.

> **Problem 2.** Given two disjoint subsequences A and B of S, for each point q in B, count the number of points in A that q dominates.
>
> **Solution.** Take $*$ to be $+$, and for $m = 1, 2, \ldots, n$, let
>
> $$\begin{aligned} f(m) &= \ 1 \ \text{ for } \ a_m \in A \\ &= \ 0 \ \text{ for } \ a_m \in B, \\ y(m) &= \ a_m[2]. \end{aligned}$$
>
> For each point a_m in B, the number of points of A dominated by a_m is $D(m)$. □

Problem 2 is sometimes referred to as *two-set dominance counting*. In Fig. 4.17, $A = \{q_1, q_2, q_3\}$ and $B = \{q_4, q_5, q_6\}$. Here, each of q_4 and q_5 dominates one point of A, namely, q_1 and q_2, respectively, while q_6 dominates no point of A.

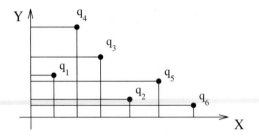

Figure 4.17: Two-set dominance counting.

Problem 3. Determine those points of S which are not dominated by any other point.

Solution. Take $*$ to be *max*, and for $m = 1, 2, \ldots, n$, let $f(m) = d_m[2]$ and $y(m) = m$.

For $m = 1, 2, \ldots, n$, point d_m is not dominated by any other point if and only if $d_m[2] > D(m)$. $\square$

Problem 3 is sometimes referred to as the problem of *computing maximal points* (or *maximal elements*, or *maximal vectors*). In Fig. 4.17, q_3, q_4, q_5, and q_6 are maximal points.

Analysis. Sorting S on the PRAM and then computing the GPC (which itself involves sorting) can be done in $O(\log n)$ time with $O(n)$ processors, as explained earlier, using algorithm PRAM SORT.

4.10.2   Counting Inversions in a Permutation

Suppose that a permutation r of the numbers $\{1, 2, \ldots, n\}$ is given, where $r(i)$ represents the ith number in the permutation, such that $1 \le r(i) \le n$ for $1 \le i \le n$. For example, a permutation of 1 2 3 4 5 6 7 8 is 6 8 1 3 7 4 2 5; that is, $r(1) = 6$, $r(2) = 8, \ldots, r(8) = 5$. This representation of a permutation differs from the one given in Section 3.3, but is more appropriate for our present purpose. An *inversion* in a permutation is a pair $(r(i), r(j))$ such that

$$i < j \quad \text{and} \quad r(i) > r(j).$$

For example, in the permutation 68137425, there are 16 inversions, namely,

$$(6, 1), (6, 3), (6, 4), (6, 2), (6, 5), (8, 1), (8, 3), (8, 7),$$

$$(8, 4), (8, 2), (8, 5), (3, 2), (7, 4), (7, 2), (7, 5), (4, 2).$$

The problem to be solved is that of counting the number of inversions in a given permutation.

We can solve this problem using GPC as follows: Take $*$ as $+$, and for $m = 1$, $2, \ldots, n$, let $f(m) = 1$ and $y(m) = -r(m)$. By computing $D(m)$ for $m = 1, 2, \ldots,$ n, we obtain the number of elements i such that

$$i < m \quad \text{and} \quad r(i) > r(m).$$

The total number of inversions is therefore

$$D(1) + D(2) + \cdots + D(n).$$

Example 4.11 When the permutation is 68137425, we have $D(1) = 0, D(2) = 0, D(3) = 2, D(4) = 2, D(5) = 1, D(6) = 3, D(7) = 5, D(8) = 3$. The total number of inversions is 16. $\Box$

Analysis. On a PRAM with n processors, GPC requires $O(\log n)$ time. Therefore, the problem of counting inversions is solved using the same number of processors and running time.

4.10.3 Reconstructing Trees from Their Traversals

Given a binary tree, a *traversal* of the tree is a listing of the nodes of the tree in some order corresponding to a "walk" along the edges of the tree that visits each node exactly once. Several orders of traversal may be defined. Two such orders of interest in this section are *inorder* and *preorder*.

Inorder traversal (also known as *symmetric* or *lexicographic* order) is defined recursively as follows:

1. Traverse the left subtree in inorder.

2. Visit the root.

3. Traverse the right subtree in inorder.

Example 4.12 For the binary tree of Fig. 4.18, inorder traversal causes the nodes to be visited in the following order: $A, B, C, D, E, F, G, H, I, J, K$. $\Box$

Preorder traversal (also known as *depth-first* order) is defined recursively as follows:

1. Visit the root.

2. Traverse the left subtree in preorder.

3. Traverse the right subtree in preorder.

Example 4.13 For the binary tree of Fig. 4.18, preorder traversal causes the nodes to be visited in the following order: $G, B, A, E, C, D, F, J, H, I, K$. $\Box$

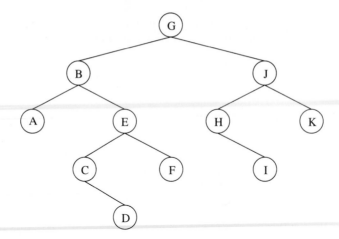

Figure 4.18: Binary tree.

Suppose now that instead of being given the binary tree (as in Fig. 4.18, for example), we are given its inorder and preorder traversals and are asked to *reconstruct* the tree from these traversals. In other words, the problem is to determine each node's parent. We now show how this reconstruction is accomplished using GPC.

We will find it useful to construct, from the inorder and preorder traversals, a third sequence called the *inorder-preorder* sequence, denoted *IP*. For a binary tree of n nodes, the *IP* sequence is a permutation of the numbers $1, 2, \ldots, n$, obtained as follows:

1. Assign to each node of the tree an integer from 1 to n corresponding to its position in the inorder traversal.

2. List the integers assigned to the nodes in a sequence corresponding to a preorder traversal. This is the *IP* sequence.

Example 4.14 For the tree of Fig. 4.18, we have:

$$
\begin{array}{llllllllllll}
\text{INORDER}: & A & B & C & D & E & F & G & H & I & J & K \\
& 1 & 2 & 3 & 4 & 5 & 6 & 7 & 8 & 9 & 10 & 11
\end{array}
$$

$$
\begin{array}{llllllllllll}
\text{PREORDER}: & G & B & A & E & C & D & F & J & H & I & K \\
\quad IP: & 7 & 2 & 1 & 5 & 3 & 4 & 6 & 10 & 8 & 9 & 11. \;\square
\end{array}
$$

In order to reconstruct a binary tree from its *IP* sequence, we make the following observation: Consider $IP(m)$, the mth element of the *IP* sequence, where $2 \le m \le n$. Let:

1. l_m = index of the largest element (if any) in IP such that $l_m < m$ and $IP(l_m) < IP(m)$.

2. r_m = index of the smallest element (if any) in IP such that $r_m < m$ and $IP(r_m) > IP(m)$.

Then, if $l_m > r_m$, $IP(m)$ is a right child of $IP(l_m)$; otherwise, $IP(m)$ is a left child of $IP(r_m)$.

Example 4.15 Continuing with Fig. 4.18, we have:

m	1	2	3	4	5	6	7	8	9	10	11
$IP(m)$	7	2	1	5	3	4	6	10	8	9	11
$IP(l_m)$	–	–	–	2	2	3	5	7	7	8	10
$IP(r_m)$	–	7	2	7	5	5	7	–	10	10	–
Parent of $IP(m)$	–	7	2	2	5	3	5	7	10	8	10. □

The above computation can be carried out through GPC as follows:

1. Take $*$ to be *max*, and let $f(m) = y(m) = IP(m)$ for $m = 1, 2, \ldots, n$. Now compute $D(m)$ for $m = 2, 3, \ldots, n$; this gives $IP(l_m)$.

2. Take $*$ to be *min*, and let $f(m) = IP(m)$ and $y(m) = -IP(m)$ for $m = 1, 2, \ldots, n$. Now compute $D(m)$ for $m = 2, 3, \ldots, n$; this gives $IP(r_m)$.

3. Let $f(m) = m$ and $y(m) = IP(m)$ for $m = 1, 2, \ldots, n$, and define $*$ as follows:

$$
\begin{aligned}
i * j &= i, && \text{provided that } IP(i) > IP(j) \\
&= j && \text{otherwise.}
\end{aligned}
$$

Now compute $D(m)$ for $m = 2, 3, \ldots, n$; this gives l_m.

4. Let $f(m) = m$ and $y(m) = -IP(m)$ for $m = 1, 2, \ldots, n$, and define $*$ as follows:

$$
\begin{aligned}
i * j &= i, && \text{provided that } IP(i) < IP(j) \\
&= j && \text{otherwise.}
\end{aligned}
$$

Now compute $D(m)$ for $m = 2, 3, \ldots, n$; this gives r_m.

Thus, a binary tree can be reconstructed from its inorder and preorder traversals in $O(\log n)$ time on the PRAM, using n processors.

4.11   PROBLEMS

4.1 Design an algorithm that simulates the circuit of Section 3.4.2 on the PRAM, and analyze its running time, number of processors, cost, and work.

4.2 Consider the following PRAM algorithm for prefix computation over the input sequence $\{x_0, x_1, \ldots, x_{n-1}\}$:

  (a) For all odd values of i, do: $x_i \leftarrow x_{i-1} \circ x_i$.

  (b) Permute the elements $x_0 x_1 \ldots x_{n-1}$ using the perfect-unshuffle mapping; this produces $x_0 x_2 \ldots x_{n-2} x_1 x_3 \ldots x_{n-1}$.

  (c) Apply this algorithm recursively to $x_1 x_3 \ldots x_{n-1}$.

  (d) Permute the elements $x_0 x_2 \ldots x_{n-2} x_1 x_3 \ldots x_{n-1}$ using the perfect-shuffle mapping; this produces $x_0 x_1 \ldots x_{n-1}$.

  (e) For all even values of i, $i > 0$, do: $x_i \leftarrow x_{i-1} \circ x_i$.

  The perfect-shuffle and perfect-unshuffle mappings were defined in Section 2.3.6. Show that this algorithm is equivalent to the circuit of Section 3.4.2.

4.3 It is possible to obtain an algorithm that uses the design method of *divide and conquer* to perform prefix computation for some operation $\circ$ (such as *addition*, *multiplication*, *max*, *min*, and so on) on a sequence S of size n in $O(\log \log n)$ time using $O(n/\log \log n)$ processors. Compared with algorithm PRAM PREFIX COMPUTATION of Section 4.2, this algorithm would also have optimal cost, but would be significantly faster while using more processors. To obtain such an algorithm, proceed as follows:

  (a) Divide the sequence S into $n^{1/2}$ subsequences of size $n^{1/2}$ elements each. Perform prefix computation on each subsequence recursively, using $n^{1/2}$ processors. Let the result of this computation over the ith sequence be $\{s(i, 1), s(i, 2), \ldots, s(i, n^{1/2})\}$.

  (b) Perform a prefix computation on the sequence $\{s(1, n^{1/2}), s(2, n^{1/2}), \ldots, s(n^{1/2} - 1, n^{1/2})\}$, using n processors. Let the result of this computation be $\{s'(1, n^{1/2}), s'(2, n^{1/2}), \ldots, s'(n^{1/2} - 1, n^{1/2})\}$.

  (c) Combine $s'(i, n^{1/2})$ with all the elements of $\{s(i + 1, 1), s(i + 1, 2), \ldots, s(i + 1, n^{1/2})\}$ for $i = 1, 2, \ldots, n^{1/2} - 1$, using $n^{1/2}$ processors per subsequence.

  (d) Show that the preceding algorithm uses n processors to run in $O(\log \log n)$ time by solving the recurrence equation $t(n) = t(n^{1/2}) + O(1)$.

  (e) Show how the number of processors can be reduced to $O(n/\log \log n)$ while maintaining the running time at $O(\log \log n)$, to achieve an optimal cost of $O(n)$.

4.4 Discuss the implications of the result obtained in Problem 4.3 on other computations, such as array packing, for example.

4.5 Show how the prefix computation over $x_0, x_1, \ldots, x_{n-1}$ can be performed on each of the following interconnection network parallel computers:

(a) A complete binary tree with n leaf processors.

(b) A linear array with n processors augmented with perfect-unshuffle connections.

(c) A mesh with $n^{1/2} \times n^{1/2}$ processors.

Analyze your algorithms.

4.6 Provide a formal description of algorithm PRAM PREFIX COMPUTATION, as modified in Section 4.3 to compute the suffix maxima of a sequence.

4.7 The problem of computing the suffix maxima of a sequence of n numbers can be solved by first reversing the sequence, then computing its prefix maxima, and, finally, reversing the results. Provide a formal description of a PRAM algorithm based on this approach, and analyze its running time and cost.

4.8 An array X of size n in the shared memory of a PRAM contains labeled and unlabeled elements. It is required to pack the labeled elements at the beginning of X and the unlabeled elements at the end of X. As described in Section 4.6, this can be done by first performing two prefix sum computations (to obtain the destinations of the elements). All elements are then moved to their new positions. If n processors are available, then this last step can be done in constant time: All elements are moved simultaneously, and thus, no element is overwritten before moving. Show how the same operation can be done in $O(\log n)$ time with $n/\log n$ processors.

4.9 For the algorithm of Example 4.9, derive the running time, number of processors required, and cost.

4.10 Suggest another parallel implementation of Quicksort that does not use interval broadcasting.

4.11 A given sequence of n jobs $J = \{j_0, j_1, \ldots, j_{n-1}\}$ is to be processed on a single machine. The machine can execute one job at a time, and when it is assigned a job, it must complete it before the next job can be processed. With each job j_i is associated:

(a) A *processing time* s_i and

(b) A *deadline* d_i by which j_i must be completed.

A *schedule* is a permutation of the jobs in J that determines the order of their execution. A schedule is said to be *feasible* if each job finishes by its deadline. Given a sequence of jobs with their processing times and deadlines, show how prefix computation can be used to determine whether a feasible schedule exists.

4.12 Consider the following variant of Problem 4.11: With each job j_i is associated a profit $q_i \geq 0$. Profit q_i is earned if and only if job j_i is completed by its deadline. It is required to find a subset of the jobs satisfying the following two conditions:

(a) All jobs in the subset can be processed and completed by their deadlines, and

(b) The sum of the profits earned is as large as possible.

Assuming that $s_i = 1$ for all i, describe a parallel algorithm for finding an optimal solution.

4.13 Suppose we are given a knapsack that can carry a maximum weight of W and a sequence of n objects $A = \{a_0, a_1, \ldots, a_{n-1}\}$ whose respective *weights* are $\{w_0, w_1, \ldots, w_{n-1}\}$. Associated with each object is a *profit*, the sequence of profits being denoted by $\{q_0, q_1, \ldots, q_{n-1}\}$. If we place in the knapsack a fraction z_i of the object whose weight is w_i, where $0 \leq z_i \leq 1$, then a profit of $z_i q_i$ is gained. Our purpose is to fill the knapsack with objects (or fractions thereof) such that:

(a) The total weight of the selected objects,

$$\sum_{i=0}^{n-1} z_i w_i,$$

does not exceed W, and

(b) The total profit gained,

$$\sum_{i=0}^{n-1} z_i q_i,$$

is as large as possible.

Use prefix computation to obtain an optimal solution to this problem—that is, a sequence $Z = \{z_0, z_1, \ldots, z_{n-1}\}$ satisfying the given conditions.

4.14 A number s_0 and four sequences of numbers $\{a_1, a_2, \ldots, a_n\}$, $\{b_1, b_2, \ldots, b_n\}$, $\{d_1, d_2, \ldots, d_n\}$, and $\{e_1, e_2, \ldots, e_n\}$ are given. Show how the sequence $\{s_1, s_2, \ldots, s_n\}$ can be computed in parallel for each of the following definitions of s_i, $i = 1, 2, \ldots, n$ (with $s_i = 0$ for $i < 0$):

(a) $s_i = a_i s_{i-1} + b_i$

(b) $s_i = a_i s_{i-1} + b_i s_{i-2}$

(c) $s_i = (a_i s_{i-1} + b_i)/(e_i s_{i-1} + d_i)$

(d) $s_i = (s_{i-1}^2 + a_i^2)^{1/2}$.

4.15 Describe the test used in Section 4.8 to determine whether a point on the circumference of a circle is contained in a given circular arc.

4.16 Consider a set of n numbers, each consisting of b bits (i.e., b 0's and 1's). It is desired to sort the numbers in nondecreasing order. An algorithm known as *radix sort* consists of b iterations. In the first iteration, the numbers are sorted on the basis of the value of their least significant (i.e., rightmost) bit: Numbers with a '0' in that position are placed ahead of numbers with a '1'. In iteration i, $2 \le i \le b$, the numbers (in the order obtained from the previous iteration) are sorted on the basis of the value of their ith least significant bit. Show how this algorithm can be implemented on the PRAM using prefix computation, and analyze the running time of and number of processors used by the algorithm.

4.17 What modifications are needed to the radix sort algorithm of Problem 4.16 in order for the numbers to be sorted on their ith most significant (i.e., ith leftmost) bit in iteration i? Show how the new algorithm can be implemented on the PRAM, and analyze the running time of and number of processors used by the algorithm.

4.18 In a Fibonacci sequence, the first two numbers are equal to 1, and each subsequent number is the sum of the previous two. Use prefix computation to generate the first n Fibonacci numbers.

4.19 Show how prefix computation can be used to solve the following set of n equations:

$$
\begin{aligned}
b_1 &= a_{11}x_1 + a_{12}x_2, \\
b_2 &= a_{21}x_1 + a_{22}x_2 + a_{23}x_3, \\
b_3 &= a_{32}x_2 + a_{33}x_3 + a_{34}x_4, \\
&\vdots \\
b_{n-1} &= a_{n-1,n-2}x_{n-2} + a_{n-1,n-1}x_{n-1} + a_{n-1,n}x_n, \\
b_n &= a_{n,n-1}x_{n-1} + a_{n,n}x_n.
\end{aligned}
$$

This set of equations is known as a *tridiagonal linear system*.

4.20 A sequence of pairs (l_i, r_i), $i = 1, 2, \ldots, n$, is given, representing intervals on a horizontal line, with l_i and r_i the left and right endpoints, respectively, of interval J_i. The left endpoint l_i is *contained* in interval J_k if $l_k \le l_i \le r_k$. It is required to determine, for each l_i, $i = 1, 2, \ldots, n$, the number of intervals in which it is contained. Show how prefix computation can be used to solve this problem.

4.21 Given a polynomial $g(x)$ of degree n, it is required to evaluate g at points $h\varepsilon$, where ε is an arbitrary real and h is an integer taking consecutive values $h = a, a+1, \ldots, b$, for two given integers a and b, $a < b$. Suggest an algorithm for solving this problem using prefix computation.

4.22 A two-dimensional array I of numbers is given. It is required to find a rectangular subarray of I with the largest sum among all such subarrays of I. Use prefix computation to solve this problem on a PRAM. Analyze the running time of your algorithm as a function of the number of rows and columns of I.

4.23 An alphabet $A = \{a_1, a_2, \ldots, a_m\}$ is given over which a linear order $\prec$ is defined such that $a_1 \prec a_2 \prec \cdots \prec a_m$. Consider two different words $u = u_1 u_2 \ldots u_n$ and $v = v_1 v_2 \ldots v_n$ over this alphabet; that is, $u_i \in A$ and $v_i \in A$, for $1 \leq i \leq n$. Word u is said to *precede* word v in *lexicographic order* if there exists a j such that $u_i = v_i$ for $i < j$, and $u_j \prec v_j$. Use prefix computation to determine which of two given words (if any) precedes the other. Assume that p processors are available on your chosen model of computation, where $p < n$. What is the running time of your algorithm?

4.24 Two numbers a and b of n bits each are given, whose binary representations are

$$a_{n-1}a_{n-2}\ldots a_0 \quad \text{and} \quad b_{n-1}b_{n-2}\ldots b_0$$

such that

$$a = \sum_{i=0}^{n-1} a_i 2^i \quad \text{and} \quad b = \sum_{i=0}^{n-1} b_i 2^i.$$

It is desired to compute the sum s of a and b, whose binary representation is $s_n s_{n-1} \ldots s_0$. Adding the numbers bit by bit from right to left takes $O(n)$ time. One property of this approach is that for $i > 0$, s_i cannot be computed until e_i, the carry generated by adding a_{i-1} and b_{i-1}, is available. (Note that s_0 can be computed directly, since $e_0 = 0$ by definition.) In a different approach, known as the *carry–look-ahead adder*, all carries $e_1, e_2, \ldots, e_n$ are computed first, and then the sum bits are computed simultaneously from

$$s_i = a_i \oplus b_i \oplus e_i,$$

where $\oplus$ denotes the **exclusive-or** operation (i.e., $s_i = 0$ if exactly two of a_i, b_i, and e_i are equal to 1; otherwise $s_i = 1$). Since computing the s_i can be done in constant time with n independent processors, the time required to add a and b depends on the first step—that is, producing $e_1, e_2, \ldots, e_n$. The latter is done as follows: The value of e_i depends on a_{i-1}, b_{i-1}, and e_{i-1}; specifically,

$$\begin{aligned} e_i &= 0, & \text{provided that } a_{i-1} = b_{i-1} = 0 \\ &= 1, & \text{provided that } a_{i-1} = b_{i-1} = 1 \\ &= e_{i-1} & \text{otherwise.} \end{aligned}$$

Show how prefix computation can be used to generate $e_1, e_2, \ldots, e_n$ in $O(\log n)$ time.

4.25 In Section 4.9.1, a lower bound of $\Omega(n \log n)$ was derived on the number of operations required to perform GPC when $\prec$ and $*$ are $<$ and $+$, respectively. Can similar lower bounds be derived using other linear orders and other binary operations?

4.26 Give a formal description of a PRAM algorithm for performing GPC.

4.27 For each of the following problems, defined in Section 4.10, derive a lower bound on the number of operations required to solve that problem:

  (a) Empirical cumulative distribution function searching

  (b) Two-set dominance counting

  (c) Computing maximal points

  (d) Counting inversions in a permutation

  (e) Reconstructing trees from their traversals.

4.28 Describe and analyze an algorithm for performing GPC on each of the following models of parallel computation:

  (a) Mesh

  (b) Hypercube

  (c) Star.

4.29 Extend the problem of computing maximal points to a set of points in a three-dimensional space. Then show how the problem can be solved using GPC.

4.30 A finite set S of points in the plane is given. A *triangulation* of S is obtained by connecting pairs of points using straight-line segments, until no segment can be added without intersecting an existing segment. An example of a triangulated point set is shown in Fig. 4.19. Derive an algorithm that uses GPC to obtain a triangulation of a given set S.

4.31 A sequence of parentheses (for example, in a mathematical expression) is *balanced* if every left (right) parenthesis has a matching right (left) parenthesis. For example, the sequence ((()(((()))))) is balanced. Let a balanced sequence of parentheses be represented by $\{h_1, h_2, \ldots, h_n\}$, where h_i represents the ith parenthesis. It is required to determine the matching parenthesis of each parenthesis. We can use GPC to solve this problem as follows:

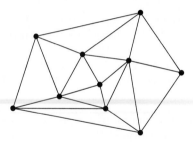

Figure 4.19: A triangulated set of planar points.

Step 1: Create the sequence $\{b_1, b_2, \ldots, b_n\}$, where $b_i = 1$ if h_i is a left parenthesis; otherwise, $b_i = -1$.

Step 2: Create the sequence $\{a_1, a_2, \ldots, a_n\}$, where $a_i = b_1 + b_2 + \cdots + b_i$ if h_i is a left parenthesis; otherwise, $a_i = b_1 + b_2 + \cdots + b_{i-1}$. (Note that, if h_i is a right parenthesis, its matching left parenthesis will be $h_{i'}$, where i' is the largest index smaller than i for which $a_i = a_{i'}$.)

Step 3: Take operation $*$ of GPC to be *max*, and let

$$y(i) = f(i) = a_i - \frac{1}{i+1}$$

for $i = 1, 2, \ldots, n$. (Note that all the $y(i)$ are distinct, and so are all the $f(i)$.)

Step 4: Perform a GPC; this gives

$$D(i) = a_{i'} - \frac{1}{i'+1}$$

for $i = 1, 2, \ldots, n$. (Note that $a_{i'} = \lceil D(i) \rceil$.)

Step 5: For each right parenthesis h_i, the index i' of its matching left parenthesis $h_{i'}$ is obtained from

$$i' = \frac{1}{a_{i'} - D(i)} - 1. \quad \blacksquare$$

(a) Show that the preceding algorithm correctly computes matching parentheses in $O(\log n)$ time using $O(n)$ processors.

(b) Design a different parallel algorithm to solve the parenthesis-matching problem, and analyze the performance of the algorithm.

4.32 Suggest other problems that can be solved using GPC.

4.33 Propose alternative generalizations of basic prefix computation that might lead to the efficient solution of some computational problems.

4.34 Study the effect of using discriminating analysis instead of uniform analysis on the running times of the algorithms presented in this chapter.

4.12   BIBLIOGRAPHICAL REMARKS

Although equations of the form $x_i = f(x_{i-1}, x_i)$ appear in a multitude of contexts, no special attention is paid explicitly to prefix computation in sequential algorithms. One of the earliest references to an operation resembling packing is in the programming language APL, developed by Iverson [309]. Therein, operator COMPRESS is applied to two arrays of the same length—an array A of arbitrary numbers, for example, and an array B of 0's and 1's; the effect is to select those elements of A corresponding to 1's in B and return them in contiguous positions of an output array. (A more general form of COMPRESS, called REPLICATE, is now included in the language; when operating on the two arrays 2031 and *abcd*, for instance, REPLICATE produces *aacccd*; see the APL2 language manual [67].) Another early use of prefix computation is in the design of addition circuits, as described in Ofman [446]. (See also Brent [122, 124], Han et al. [285], Krapchenko [330], and Winograd [642].) Other specialized uses were proposed by Stone [590] to evaluate polynomials, by Chen and Kuck [146], Kogge [326], Kogge and Stone [327], and Stone [591] for recurrence problems (see also Hyafil and Kung [308] and Karp et al. [322]), and by Stone [592] for the solution of tridiagonal systems of equations.

In 1980, three results appeared simultaneously in connection with algorithms to perform prefix computation. An efficient circuit was proposed by Ladner and Fischer [352] (see Section 3.4.2), and its shared-memory counterpart, using the perfect-shuffle and-unshuffle operations, was described by Schwartz [556]. An efficient implementation in VLSI circuits was developed by Brent and Kung [125]. Improved circuits were later obtained in Lakshmivarahan et al. [358], and an asynchronous algorithm for prefix computation was derived in Lubachevsky and Greenberg [393]. An algorithm by Saxena et al. [549] computes the prefix sums of n integers of at most b bits each in $O((\log n/\log\log n)+\log b)$ time on the PRAM, at a cost of $O(n)$, using the **COMMON CW** instruction of the PRAM. Similar algorithms are given in Cole and Vishkin [173], Hagerup [279], Ragde [520], Rajasekaran and Reif [524], and the references therein.

A set $\mathcal{X}$ together with an operation $\circ$, satisfying the conditions in Section 4.1 is called a *semigroup*. (See, for example, Birkhoff and Bartee [108].) Prefix computation is known by many different names. In mathematical circles, prefix sums are referred to as *initial sums*. In Schwartz [556] they are called *all partial sums*, and in Hockney and Jesshope [298] *cascade sums*. It is suggested in Blelloch [111] that an operation called *scan*, which is essentially a prefix computation, be incorporated into parallel computers as an elementary operation (much like addition, comparison, memory access, and so on.). Algorithm PRAM PREFIX COMPUTATION is from Akl [18, 21]. The maximum sum subsequence problem is a special one-dimensional version of a problem that arises in processing pictures. In the more general two-dimensional version, an $n \times n$ array of numbers is given, and it is required to find a rectangular subarray with the maximum sum among all such subarrays. According to Bentley [98], this serves as a maximum likelihood estimator for some patterns occurring in digital pictures. The PRAM algorithm in Section 4.3 was first proposed by Akl and Guenther [38, 39]; see also Perumalla and Deo [490].

The application of prefix computation to the solution of linear recurrences is mentioned in Fich [228]. An approach to polynomial interpolation was developed by Newton (see Hildebrand [293]); its implementation using prefix sums is by Eğecioğlu et al. [214]. (See also Eğecioğlu et al. [212, 213] and Eğecioğlu and Koç [215].) The use of prefix sums to pack an array and the applicability of the latter operation to recursive parallel algorithms were first demonstrated in Akl [15]. Parallel algorithms for computing convex hulls and for selection are described in Akl [21] and Akl and Lyons [42].

Interval prefix computation appears in the literature under different forms and names. It is called *partitioning* in Mago [400], *summing by groups* in Schwartz [556], *generalization* in Nassimi and Sahni [438], *data distribution* in Ullman [615], *interval broadcasting* in Akl et al. [50], and *segmented scanning* in Blelloch [112]. The use of prefix computation in connection with circular arcs is due to Akl et al. [26].

Other applications of prefix computation are described in Akl [21], Bilardi and Preparata [105], Lakshmivarahan and Dhall [356], Liang et al. [383], Reif [533], Volger [629], and Wagner and Han [630]. Algorithms for performing prefix computation on various models of computation appear in Akl and Meijer [43], Dekel and Sahni [198], Goldberg [261], Meijer and Akl [415, 416], and Stone [593]. A PRAM algorithm is described in Cole and Vishkin [173] that computes the prefix sums of n numbers of $\log n$ bits each in $O(\log n / \log \log n)$ time using $O(n \log \log n / \log n)$ processors.

General prefix computation was first proposed in Springsteel and Stojmenović [583], where it is argued that GPC is a generic computation that captures the most common difficult component of many problems. It is shown therein to be an elegant and powerful tool in tackling various problems in computational geometry, graph theory, and combinatorics. Algorithm PRAM SORT (used in the implementation of GPC on the PRAM) was first proposed by Cole [166]. Lower bounds and sequential algorithms for fundamental problems in computational geometry are provided in Preparata and Shamos [500]; see also Mulmuley [435] and O'Rourke [454]. Parallel algorithms for computational geometric problems are described in Akl and Lyons [42]. Another generalization of prefix computation, known as *broadcasting with selective reduction* (BSR), is described in Akl and Guenther [38] and Fava Lindon and Akl [226]. It is shown in Chapter 11 how BSR extends the power of the PRAM.

Chapter 5

Divide and Conquer

An effective approach to designing fast algorithms in sequential computation is the method known as *divide and conquer*. In it, a problem to be solved is broken into a number of subproblems (typically, two) of the same form as the original problem; this is the *divide* step. The subproblems are then solved independently, usually recursively; this is the *conquer* step. Finally, the solutions to the subproblems are combined to provide the answer to the original problem. Thus, strictly speaking, the method should be more accurately called *divide, conquer, and combine*.

Example 5.1 The sorting algorithms Mergesort and Quicksort are both based on the divide-and-conquer approach. In Mergesort, the input sequence to be sorted is divided into two subsequences; the latter are sorted recursively and then merged. Here, the *divide* step is easy: The two subsequences are simply the first half and the second half of the input sequence. The *combine* step is slightly harder: It requires a special procedure for *merging* two sorted subsequences. In Quicksort, the input sequence is broken into three *independent* subsequences consisting of all elements smaller than, equal to, and larger than a *pivot* element, respectively. The first and third of the subsequences are sorted recursively, and then the three subsequences are concatenated. Here, by contrast with Mergesort, the *combine* step (i.e., concatenation) is trivial compared to the *divide* step (i.e., splitting the sequence with respect to a pivot). □

Example 5.2 One approach to computing the convex hull of a finite set Q of points in the plane (see Example 4.7) is to divide the set into two disjoint subsets S_1 and S_2, compute $CH(S_1)$ and $CH(S_2)$ recursively, and then combine the latter to obtain $CH(Q)$. A typical situation illustrating this approach is shown in Fig. 5.1. □

Divide and conquer can also be used successfully in parallel computation. The purpose of this chapter is to provide a number of examples demonstrating the effectiveness of this algorithmic design method in deriving efficient parallel algorithms.

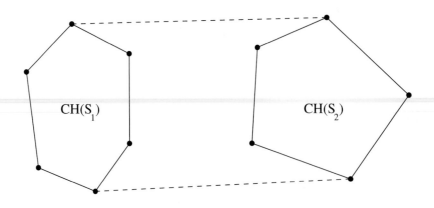

Figure 5.1: Computing the convex hull by divide and conquer.

It may be argued, of course, that *all* parallel algorithms are essentially based on some form of divide and conquer, since, by definition, this is what parallelism is all about: A computational problem is broken into subproblems that are solved simultaneously using several processors. In some sense, this is true. However, such a wide interpretation is too general to allow a true appreciation of the real power of the method. Indeed, there is more to divide and conquer than a straightforward subdivision of tasks among processors: The efficiency of the method derives from the appropriate selection of the subproblems, leading to a fast algorithm.

In fact, parallel divide and conquer was already used in previous chapters of this book. For example, the fast Fourier transform circuit and the permutation circuit (among others) in Chapter 3 and the PRAM algorithm for GPC in Chapter 4 illustrate the subtle application of divide and conquer with optimal results.

In this chapter, divide and conquer is used to solve a number of fundamental problems in computer science. We continue to use the PRAM as the model of computation. In Section 5.1, it is shown how a sorted list can be searched in parallel for a given item. The problem of merging two sorted sequences is then addressed in Section 5.2. In Section 5.3, an algorithm is developed for selecting, in parallel, the kth smallest element of a given input sequence. We conclude in Section 5.4 with a parallel divide-and-conquer algorithm for computing the convex hull of a set of points in the plane. Uniform analysis is used throughout to derive the running time of algorithms, unless otherwise stated.

5.1   SEARCHING

A fundamental operation in parallel processing, and one of the most commonly used, is *searching* a list for a given item. Typically, we are given a *file* of n records, with the ith record, $1 \le i \le n$, consisting of:

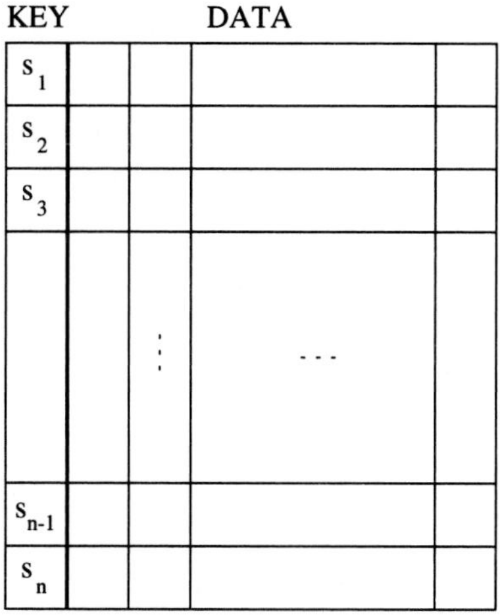

Figure 5.2: A file of records to be searched on the KEY field.

1. A KEY field containing an integer s_i.

2. Several other DATA fields containing information.

This is illustrated in Fig. 5.2.

In what follows, we assume that the sequence $S = \{s_1, s_2, \ldots, s_n\}$ is sorted in nondecreasing order; that is, $s_1 \leq s_2 \leq \cdots \leq s_n$. The search problem is formulated as follows: Given an integer x, where $s_1 \leq x \leq s_n$, it is required to determine whether $x = s_k$ for some s_k in S. In other words, a record is sought whose KEY field equals x. There are three possibilities:

1. A single record is found satisfying the condition; in this case, k is returned, and the information stored in the DATA fields of the kth record are then retrieved.

2. No k is found for which $x = s_k$; in this case, a 0 is returned, indicating failure of the search.

3. Several records satisfy the condition; in this case, an appropriate way of selecting a record is used. For example, the first index k found for which $x = s_k$ is returned, and the information associated with that record is retrieved.

Sequentially, this problem is solved by the well-known procedure, *binary search*. In it, the KEY of the record occupying the middle position of the file is compared to x. If they are equal, the procedure terminates; otherwise, depending on the outcome of the comparison, the top or bottom half of the file is discarded from further consideration, and the procedure is applied recursively to the other half. An iterative version of this procedure is algorithm RAM BINARY SEARCH; it uses two variables i and h to point to the first and last records, respectively, in that portion of the file still under consideration:

Algorithm RAM BINARY SEARCH (S, x, k)

> **Step 1:** (1.1) $i \leftarrow 1$
> (1.2) $h \leftarrow n$
> (1.3) $k \leftarrow 0$
> **Step 2: while** $i \leq h$ **do**
> (2.1) $m \leftarrow \lfloor (i + h)/2 \rfloor$
> (2.2) **if** $x = s_m$
> **then** (i) $k \leftarrow m$
> (ii) $i \leftarrow h + 1$
> **else if** $x < s_m$
> **then** $h \leftarrow m - 1$
> **else** $i \leftarrow m + 1$
> **end if**
> **end if**
> **end while.** ■

Since the number of records under consideration is reduced by one half at each step, algorithm RAM BINARY SEARCH requires $O(\log n)$ time in the worst case.

Binary search is a good example of how divide and conquer can be used to design efficient sequential algorithms. We now show how the same approach can be used in parallel. First an algorithm is described that is based on a simplistic interpretation of divide and conquer. Then a more effective adaptation of the technique that takes better advantage of parallelism is presented.

5.1.1   Searching on the PRAM

Assume that the file of n records is stored in the shared memory of a PRAM with N processors $P_1, P_2, \ldots, P_N$, where $1 < N \leq n$. Assume further that one processor— for example, P_1—has read x and stored it in shared memory and has initialized k to 0, also in shared memory. If $N = n$, then the search problem is solved in constant time:

1. All processors read x.

2. Processor P_i compares x to s_i, $1 \leq i \leq n$.

3. Those processors P_j (if any) for which $x = s_j$ use a **MIN CW** to write the smallest such j in k.

Note that a **MIN CW** instruction is used to select the value of k, from the possibly many indices j found for which $x = s_j$. Since all such j are found simultaneously, choosing the smallest is one way of breaking the tie. Other concurrent write instructions may be used, such as **PRIORITY CW**, **ARBITRARY CW**, and so on.

Suppose now that $N < n$. The sequence $S = \{s_1, s_2, \ldots, s_n\}$ is subdivided into N subsequences of length n/N each, and processor P_i is assigned the subsequence $\{s_{(i-1)(n/N)+1}, s_{(i-1)(n/N)+2}, \ldots, s_{i(n/N)}\}$. The algorithm is now as follows:

1. All processors read x.

2. Those processors P_i (if any) for which $s_{(i-1)(n/N)+1} \leq x \leq s_{i(n/N)}$ perform algorithm RAM BINARY SEARCH on their assigned subsequences.

3. Those processors P_l (if any) for which $x = s_{(l-1)(n/N)+j}$ use a **MIN CW** to write $(l-1)(n/N) + j$ in k.

Steps 1 and 3 take constant time. In Step 2, algorithm RAM BINARY SEARCH is executed on n/N elements (possibly simultaneously by several consecutive processors operating on contiguous subsequences) and requires $O(\log(n/N))$ time. This is faster than the sequential algorithm, but not considerably, since $\log(n/N) = \log n - \log N$.

5.1.2 Parallel Binary Search

One of the limitations of the algorithm described in the previous section, for the case where $N < n$, is that most processors are essentially idle during the binary search. A second limitation is that binary search is executed *sequentially* by those processors which are active. A faster parallel algorithm for searching a sorted sequence when $N < n$ is now obtained by developing a *parallel* version of binary search that uses *all* processors. Recall that during each iteration of Step 2 in algorithm RAM BINARY SEARCH, the middle element s_m of the sequence searched is tested for equality with x: If $x < s_m$, then s_m and all the elements larger than it are discarded; otherwise, s_m and all the elements smaller than it are discarded. The next iteration is therefore applied to a sequence whose length is approximately one-half of that in the previous iteration. The algorithm terminates when the middle element of the sequence still under consideration is found equal to x or when all the elements have been discarded.

In the parallel version, there are N processors, and we can extend binary search to become an $(N+1)$-way search. The algorithm will consist of several stages. At each stage, the sequence still under consideration is divided into $(N+1)$ subsequences of equal length. The N processors simultaneously test the elements at the boundary between adjacent subsequences for equality with x. This is illustrated in Fig. 5.3, where the sequence S is assumed to be sorted from left to right in nondecreasing order.

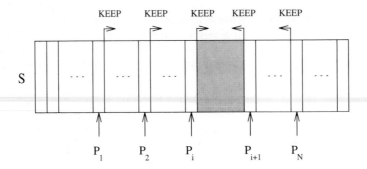

Figure 5.3: Parallel binary search.

Every processor compares an element s of S with x:

1. If $x < s$, then if an element equal to x is in the sequence at all, it must precede s; consequently, s and all the elements that follow it (i.e., that lie to the right of x in Fig. 5.3) are removed from consideration.

2. If $x > s$, then if an element equal to x is in the sequence at all, it must follow s; consequently, s and all the elements that precede it (i.e., that lie to the left of x in Fig. 5.3) are removed from consideration.

3. If $x = s$, then the index of s is returned.

Thus, unless $x = s$, each processor splits the sequence into two parts, namely, those elements to be discarded (as they definitely do not contain an element equal to x) and those which might contain an element equal to x and are hence kept. This narrows down the search to the intersection of all the parts to be kept—that is, the subsequence between two elements tested in the current stage. This subsequence, shown shaded in Fig. 5.3, is searched in the next stage by the same process. The process continues until either an element of S equal to x is found or all the elements of S are discarded.

How Many Stages Are Required?   Intuitively, since every stage is applied to a sequence whose length is $1/(N+1)$ times the length of the sequence searched during the previous stage, less 1, the number of stages needed in the worst case to search a sorted sequence S of length n for an element x is $O(\log_N n)$.

More formally, let g be the smallest integer such that $n \leq (N+1)^g - 1$; that is,

$$g = \lceil \log(n+1) / \log(N+1) \rceil.$$

We show by induction that g stages suffice for the parallel search algorithm. Clearly, this is true for $g = 0$. Now, assume that it is true for $(N+1)^{g-1} - 1$. In order to search a sequence of length $(N+1)^g - 1$, processor P_i, $i = 1, 2, \ldots, N$, compares

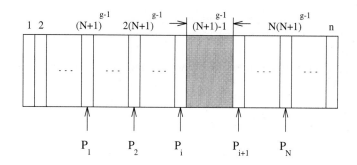

Figure 5.4: Deriving the number of stages in parallel binary search.

x to s_j, where $j = i(N+1)^{g-1}$, as shown in Fig. 5.4. Following this comparison, only a subsequence of length $(N+1)^{g-1} - 1$ needs to be searched. This completes the proof.

In fact, this number of stages (i.e., $\lceil \log(n+1)/\log(N+1) \rceil$) is the minimum required in the worst case by any comparison-based PRAM search algorithm. To see why, note that any algorithm using N processors can compare an input element x to at most N elements of S simultaneously. After these comparisons and the subsequent deletion of elements from S definitely not equal to x, the number of elements left must be at least

$$\lceil (n-N)/(N+1) \rceil \geq (n-N)/(N+1)$$
$$= ((n+1)/(N+1)) - 1.$$

After g repetitions of the same process, we are left with a sequence of length $((n+1)/(N+1)^g) - 1$. It follows that the number of iterations required by any such parallel algorithm is no smaller than the minimum g such that

$$((n+1)/(N+1)^g) - 1 \leq 0,$$

which is

$$\lceil \log(n+1)/\log(N+1) \rceil.$$

Implementation. The only detail of the parallel binary search algorithm that may need some elaboration is how the subsequence to be searched during the next stage is determined. Each processor P_i uses a variable e_i which takes the value *left* or *right* according to whether the part of the sequence that P_i decides to keep is to the left or right of the element it compared to x during the current stage. Initially, the value of each e_i is undefined. Two constants $e_0 = $ *right* and $e_{N+1} = $ *left* are also used. Following the comparison between x and an element $s_{j(i)}$ of S, where $1 \leq i \leq N$ and $1 \leq j(i) \leq n$, P_i assigns a value to e_i (unless $x = s_{j(i)}$, in which case the value of e_i is irrelevant). If $e_{i-1} \neq e_i$ for some i, $1 \leq i \leq N+1$, then the subsequence to be searched next runs from s_q to s_r, where $q = (i-1)(N+1)^{g-1}+1$ and $r = i(N+1)^{g-1} - 1$. Precisely one processor updates q and r in the shared memory, and all remaining processors can simultaneously read the updated values.

The algorithm is given in what follows as algorithm PRAM SEARCH. It takes S and x as input: If $x = s_k$ for some k, then k is returned; otherwise a 0 is returned. If several $j(i)$ are found such that $x = s_{j(i)}$, then the smallest is returned as k.

Algorithm PRAM SEARCH (S, x, k)

> **Step 1:** (1.1) $q \leftarrow 1$
> (1.2) $r \leftarrow n$
> (1.3) $k \leftarrow 0$
> (1.4) $g \leftarrow \lceil \log(n+1)/\log(N+1) \rceil$
> **Step 2: while** $(q \leq r$ **and** $k = 0)$ **do**
> (2.1) $j(0) \leftarrow q - 1$
> (2.2) **for** $i = 1$ **to** N **do in parallel**
> (i) $j(i) \leftarrow (q-1) + i(N+1)^{g-1}$
> (ii) **if** $j(i) \leq r$
> **then if** $x = s_{j(i)}$
> **then** $k \overset{\text{MIN}}{\longleftarrow} j(i)$
> **else if** $x < s_{j(i)}$
> **then** $e_i \leftarrow left$
> **else** $e_i \leftarrow right$
> **end if**
> **end if**
> **else** (a) $j(i) \leftarrow r + 1$
> (b) $e_i \leftarrow left$
> **end if**
> (iii) **if** $e_{i-1} \neq e_i$
> **then** (a) $q \leftarrow j(i-1) + 1$
> (b) $r \leftarrow j(i) - 1$
> **end if**
> (iv) **if** $(i = N$ **and** $e_i \neq e_{i+1})$
> **then** $q \leftarrow j(i) + 1$
> **end if**
> **end for**
> (2.3) $g \leftarrow g - 1$
> **end while.** ∎

Note that, in the case of a successful search, the index k returned by the algorithm is the smallest index *found* such that $x = s_k$. This is not necessarily the smallest *overall* index of an element of S equal to x.

Analysis. Step 1 initializes the indices q and r of the sequence to be searched, as well as the result k and the number of stages g. It can be performed by one processor—for example, P_1—in constant time. The same is true of Steps (2.1) and (2.3). Step (2.2) also takes constant time. Since there are at most g iterations of Step 2, algorithm PRAM SEARCH runs in time

$$
\begin{aligned}
t(n) &= O(\log(n+1)/\log(N+1)) \\
&= O(\log_N n),
\end{aligned}
$$

using $p(n) = N$ processors. The algorithm is therefore time optimal in view of the lower bound of $\Omega(\lceil \log(n+1)/\log(N+1)\rceil)$ on the minimum number of stages required in the worst case by any comparison-based PRAM search algorithm (derived earlier in this section). It should be emphasized here that N is normally a function of n (for example, $N = n^{1/2}$) and not a constant.

Example 5.3 Let $n = 15$, and let $S = \{16, 20, 24, 25, 26, 32, 33, 37, 47, 47, 69, 70, 75, 89, 92\}$ be the sequence to be searched for $x = 47$ using algorithm PRAM SEARCH with $N = 3$ processors P_1, P_2, and P_3. Initially, $q = 1$, $r = 15$, $k = 0$, and $g = 2$. During the first iteration of Step 2, P_1 computes $j(1) = 4$ and compares s_4 to x. Since $47 > 25$, $e_1 = right$. Simultaneously, P_2 and P_3 compare s_8 and s_{12}, respectively, to x. Since $47 > 37$ and $47 < 70$, $e_2 = right$ and $e_3 = left$. Now $e_2 \neq e_3$; therefore, $q = 9$ and $r = 11$. The new sequence to be searched runs from s_9 to s_{11}, as shown in Fig. 5.5(a), and $g = 1$. In the second iteration, illustrated in Fig. 5.5(b), P_1 computes $j(1) = 9$, P_2 computes $j(2) = 10$, and P_3 computes $j(3) = 11$. Since s_9 and s_{10} are both equal to 47, k is set to 9. $\square$

It should be noted that when the assumption regarding x (namely, $s_1 \leq x \leq s_n$) is not satisfied (i.e., if $x < s_1$ or $x > s_n$), the algorithms of this section still return the correct result (i.e., $k = 0$). However, it is clear that in those cases no search is required whatsoever.

5.2 MERGING

Suppose that two sequences of numbers $X = \{x_1, x_2, \ldots, x_n\}$ and $Y = \{y_1, y_2, \ldots, y_m\}$ are given, each sorted in nondecreasing order, with $n \geq m \geq 1$. The problem of *merging* X and Y calls for creating, from these two sequences, a third sequence of numbers $Z = \{z_1, z_2, \ldots, z_{n+m}\}$, also sorted in nondecreasing order, such that each element of X and each element of Y appears exactly once in Z. The elements of X and the elements of Y are to retain in Z their original order. Also, if $x_i = y_j$ for some i and j, then x_i is to precede y_j in Z.

Sequentially, this problem can be solved by a simple algorithm that uses three indices i, j, and k, pointing to an element in X, Y, and Z, respectively: The two elements x_i and y_j are compared, and the smaller of the two becomes z_k. The algorithm is given next as algorithm RAM MERGE. For convenience, the algorithm assumes the presence of two elements $x_{n+1} = \infty$ and $y_{m+1} = \infty$.

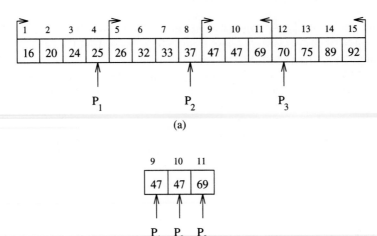

Figure 5.5: Searching a sequence of 15 elements for $x = 47$ using three processors: (a) First Iteration; (b) Second Iteration.

Algorithm RAM MERGE (X, Y, Z)

> **Step 1:** (1.1) $i \leftarrow 1$
> (1.2) $j \leftarrow 1$
> **Step 2: for $k = 1$ to $n + m$ do**
> if $x_i \leq y_j$
> **then** (i) $z_k \leftarrow x_i$
> (ii) $i \leftarrow i + 1$
> **else** (i) $z_k \leftarrow y_j$
> (ii) $j \leftarrow j + 1$
> **end if**
> **end for.** ∎

Since $m = O(n)$, the algorithm runs in $O(n)$ time. This is optimal in view of the $\Omega(n)$ lower bound required to read the input.

In parallel, the problem of merging X and Y can be solved using the odd-even merging circuit of Section 3.1.1, which consists of $O(\log n)$ stages of $O(n)$ processors each. It is straightforward to simulate this circuit on the PRAM using $O(n)$ processors and $O(\log n)$ time. Each stage of the circuit represents one step on the PRAM, and all transfers of data from one stage to the next (through direct links) are performed via the shared memory. This results in a PRAM algorithm whose cost is $O(n \log n)$, which is clearly not optimal in view of the $O(n)$ running time of algorithm RAM MERGE.

The remainder of this section is devoted to the development of a PRAM merging algorithm that improves on the performance of the algorithm described in the previous paragraph. Specifically, the PRAM algorithm uses $O(n/\log \log n)$ processors, runs in $O(\log \log n)$ time, and therefore has a cost of $O(n)$, which is optimal. Our exposition of the parallel merging algorithm begins with a description of a sequence of computations leading to a solution to the main problem. Note that, in order to satisfy the requirement that when $x_i = y_j$ for some i and j, x_i is to precede y_j in Z, we assume in what follows that if $x_i = y_j$, then x_i is considered to be *smaller than* y_j.

5.2.1 Searching for a Predecessor

Assume that we have a sequence $A = \{a_1, a_2, \ldots, a_n\}$ of n numbers, sorted in nondecreasing order. Given a number b, it is required to find the index of the largest element of A that is smaller than b. If no such element exists in A, then the index to be returned is 0. It is easy to see that algorithm PRAM SEARCH of Section 5.1.2 can be slightly modified to solve this problem using N processors in $O(\log(n+1)/\log(N+1))$ time. In the context of the merging problem, a further modification will allow the algorithm to distinguish between the following two cases:

1. If $A = X$ and $b = y_j$ for some $y_j \in Y$, then the algorithm returns the index of the largest element of X that is *smaller than or equal to* y_j (since, if $x_i = y_j$, then x_i is by definition considered smaller than y_j).

2. If $A = Y$ and $b = x_i$ for some $x_i \in X$, then the algorithm returns the index of the largest element of Y that is *strictly smaller than* x_i.

In what follows, we refer to this modified algorithm as algorithm PRAM MODIFIED SEARCH.

5.2.2 Ranking an Arbitrary Sequence

The *rank* of an element b in a given sequence A is the number of elements of A that are smaller than b.

Suppose now that $A = \{a_1, a_2, \ldots, a_n\}$ is a sequence of n numbers sorted in nondecreasing order. Further, let $B = \{b_1, b_2, \ldots, b_k\}$ be an arbitrary sequence of k numbers such that $k = O(n^\varepsilon)$ for a constant ε, $0 < \varepsilon < 1$. It is desired to compute the rank of each element of B in A. In order to determine the rank of *one* element b_i of B in A, we can use algorithm PRAM MODIFIED SEARCH with $N = \lfloor n/k \rfloor = \Omega(n^{1-\varepsilon})$ processors: The rank of b_i in A is equal to the index of the largest element of A smaller than b_i. This takes $O(\log(n+1)/\log(N+1)) = O(1)$ time. It follows that computing the ranks of *all* elements of B in A in constant time requires $kN = O(n)$ processors operating simultaneously, where each group of N processors executes algorithm PRAM MODIFIED SEARCH for one of the k elements of B.

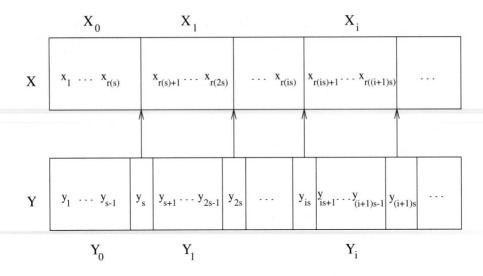

Figure 5.6: Ranking a sorted sequence.

5.2.3   Ranking a Sorted Sequence

Let $X = \{x_1, x_2, \ldots, x_n\}$ and $Y = \{y_1, y_2, \ldots, y_m\}$ be sequences of numbers, each sorted in nondecreasing order, with $n \geq m \geq 1$. It is desired to compute the ranks of all elements of Y in X (under the assumption that if $x_i = y_j$, then x_i is considered smaller than y_j). To accomplish this, we begin by selecting $s = m^{1/2}$ elements of Y, namely, $\{y_s, y_{2s}, \ldots, y_m\}$. These elements split Y into s subsequences Y_0, $Y_1, \ldots, Y_{s-1}$ of $s - 1$ elements each. The ranks of $\{y_s, y_{2s}, \ldots, y_m\}$ in X are now computed. Let $r(is)$ be the rank of y_{is} in X; that is, $x_{r(is)}$ is the largest element of X that is smaller than y_{is} (if such an element exists; otherwise $r(is) = 0$). It follows that the ranks in X of the elements of the subsequence $Y_i = \{y_{is+1}, y_{is+2}, \ldots, y_{(i+1)s-1}\}$ can be determined by examining only the elements $X_i = \{x_{r(is)+1}, x_{r(is)+2}, \ldots, x_{r((i+1)s)}\}$. This is illustrated in Fig. 5.6.

Therefore, the problem of computing the ranks of the elements of Y in X can now be solved by recursively computing the ranks in X_i of the elements of Y_i, in parallel, for $i = 0, 1, \ldots, s - 1$. Note that, while Y_i is guaranteed to have $s - 1$ elements, X_i is of arbitrary length (at most n). Let $r(0) = 0$. If $r(is) = r((i+1)s)$, then the ranks of all the elements of Y_i in X_i are 0, and the recursion terminates. The recursion also terminates when the number of elements for which ranks are to be computed drops below four; in this case, the ranks are found by applying algorithm PRAM MODIFIED SEARCH.

When the recursion terminates, we have the rank in X_i of each element y_{is+j} of Y_i; let this rank be denoted $r_i(j)$. The rank of y_{is+j} in X, denoted $r(is + j)$, is now obtained from

$$r(is + j) = r(is) + r_i(j).$$

The algorithm is given next as algorithm PRAM RANK. The ranks of the elements of Y in X are returned in $R = \{r(1), r(2), \ldots, r(m)\}$, where $r(i)$ is the rank of y_i in X. Similarly, the ranks of the elements of Y_i in X_i are stored in $R_i = \{r_i(1), r_i(2), \ldots, r_i(s-1)\}$.

Algorithm PRAM RANK (X, Y, R)

> **if** $m < 4$
> **then** Algorithm PRAM MODIFIED SEARCH
>> computes the ranks of Y in X
>> using $N = |X|$ processors
> **else** (1) $s \leftarrow |Y|^{1/2}$
>> (2) **for** $i = 1$ **to** s **do in parallel**
>>> (2.1) Algorithm PRAM MODIFIED SEARCH
>>> computes the rank $r(is)$ of y_{is} in X
>>> using $N = |X|^{1/2}$ processors
>>> (2.2) $r(0) \leftarrow 0$
>> **end for**
>> (3) **for** $i = 0$ **to** $s - 1$ **do in parallel**
>>> (3.1) $X_i \leftarrow \{x_{r(is)+1}, x_{r(is+2)+2}, \ldots, x_{r((i+1)s)}\}$
>>> (3.2) $Y_i \leftarrow \{y_{is+1}, y_{is+2}, \ldots, y_{(i+1)s-1}\}$
>>> (3.3) **if** $r(is) = r((i+1)s)$
>>>> **then** $R_i = \{0, 0, \ldots, 0\}$
>>>> **else** PRAM RANK (X_i, Y_i, R_i)
>>> **end if**
>>> (3.4) **for** $j = 1$ **to** $s - 1$ **do in parallel**
>>>> $r(is + j) \leftarrow r(is) + r_i(j)$
>>> **end for**
>> **end for**
> **end if.** ∎

Analysis. To analyze the algorithm, note that before the recursion begins, the ranks of the $s = m^{1/2} = O(n^{1/2})$ elements $\{y_s, y_{2s}, \ldots, y_m\}$ in X can be computed using $O(n)$ processors in constant time. As explained in Section 5.2.2, the rank of each element is computed using $N = \lfloor n/s \rfloor = \Omega(n^{1/2})$ processors by algorithm PRAM MODIFIED SEARCH in $O(\log(n+1)/\log(N+1)) = O(1)$ time. The same applies when algorithm PRAM MODIFIED SEARCH is invoked to terminate the recursion. Thus, the running time of the recursive algorithm is given by

$$
\begin{aligned}
t(n) &= t(n^{1/2}) + O(1) \\
&= O(\log \log n).
\end{aligned}
$$

Since no more than $O(n)$ processors are needed at each level of the recursion, we have

$$p(n) = O(n).$$

This leads to a cost of

$$
\begin{aligned}
c(n) &= p(n) \times t(n) \\
&= n \times O(\log \log n) \\
&= O(n \log \log n).
\end{aligned}
$$

Example 5.4 Let $X = \{5, 7, 12, 15, 15, 16, 18, 20\}$ and $Y = \{3, 9, 15, 19\}$; that is, $n = 8$ and $m = 4$. Initially, $s = 4^{1/2} = 2$ and $r(0) = 0$. The ranks of $y_2 = 9$ and $y_4 = 19$ in X are found, namely, $r(2) = 2$ and $r(4) = 7$. The sequences $X_0 = \{5, 7\}$, $X_1 = \{12, 15, 15, 16, 18\}$, $Y_0 = \{3\}$, and $Y_1 = \{15\}$ are created. The algorithm is now called to find the ranks of Y_0 in X_0 and Y_1 in X_1. Since each of the sequences Y_0 and Y_1 consists of one element, the ranks are computed using PRAM MODIFIED SEARCH: The rank of 3 in X_0 is $r_0(1) = 0$, and the rank of 15 in X_1 is $r_1(1) = 3$. Finally, the ranks of 3 and 15 in X are obtained from $r(1) = r(0) + r_0(1) = 0$ and $r(3) = r(2) + r_1(1) = 5$, respectively. $\square$

5.2.4 A Fast Merging Algorithm

We are now ready to solve the problem of merging in parallel the two sequences $X = \{x_1, x_2, \ldots, x_n\}$ and $Y = \{y_1, y_2, \ldots, y_m\}$ (each sorted in nondecreasing order), to produce a third sequence $Z = \{z_1, z_2, \ldots, z_{n+m}\}$ (also sorted in nondecreasing order). The idea is to use algorithm PRAM RANK, developed in the previous section, twice; first to compute the ranks $R = \{r(1), r(2), \ldots, r(m)\}$ in X of the elements of Y and then to compute the ranks $R' = \{r'(1), r'(2), \ldots, r'(n)\}$ in Y of the elements of X. The final position of each element of X and each element of Y in Z is now the sum of two ranks, namely, the element's rank in its own sequence and its rank in the other sequence. The algorithm is given next as algorithm PRAM MERGE. It is important to keep in mind that to compute the ranks, "smaller than" means "smaller than or equal to" when the rank of y_j in X is computed and "strictly smaller than" when the rank of x_i in Y is computed.

Algorithm PRAM MERGE (X, Y, Z)

    Step 1: (1.1) PRAM RANK (X, Y, R)
            (1.2) **for** $i = 1$ **to** m **do in parallel**

$$z_{i+r(i)} \leftarrow y_i$$

             end for
    Step 2: (2.1) PRAM RANK (Y, X, R')
            (2.2) **for** $i = 1$ **to** n **do in parallel**

$$z_{i+r'(i)} \leftarrow x_i$$

             end for. ■

Example 5.5 Suppose that $X = \{5, 7, 12, 15, 15, 16, 18, 20\}$ and $Y = \{3, 9, 15, 19\}$ are to be merged. After Step (1.1), we have the ranks of Y in X; that is, $r(1) = 0, r(2) = 2, r(3) = 5$, and $r(4) = 7$. Therefore, after Step (1.2), $z_1 = 3, z_4 = 9, z_8 = 15$, and $z_{11} = 19$. Similarly, after Step (2.1), we have the ranks of X in Y; that is,

$$r'(1) = 1, \quad r'(2) = 1, \quad r'(3) = 2, \quad r'(4) = 2,$$
$$r'(5) = 2, \quad r'(6) = 3, \quad r'(7) = 3, \quad r'(8) = 4.$$

Therefore, after Step (2.2), $z_2 = 5, z_3 = 7, z_5 = 12, z_6 = 15, z_7 = 15, z_9 = 16$, $z_{10} = 18$, and $z_{12} = 20$. $\square$

Analysis. Using $O(n)$ processors, Steps (1.1) and (2.1) run in $O(\log \log n)$ time, while Steps (1.2) and (2.2) take constant time. Thus, for algorithm PRAM MERGE,

$$
\begin{aligned}
p(n) &= O(n), \\
t(n) &= O(\log \log n), \\
c(n) &= O(n \log \log n).
\end{aligned}
$$

This algorithm is therefore faster and uses fewer processors than a simulation of odd-even merging on the PRAM. Its cost, however, is not optimal (despite the fact that the $\log \log n$ factor is very small for all but extremely large values of n). In the next section, we show how the number of processors can be reduced without increasing the running time, to achieve an an optimal cost of $O(n)$.

5.2.5   An Optimal Merging Algorithm

In order to attain cost optimality, we need to use a more subtle form of divide and conquer. The idea is to apply algorithm PRAM MERGE with fewer processors to solve a smaller version of the original problem. The solution obtained allows the larger problem to be broken into small independent problems that can be solved simultaneously, each by algorithm RAM MERGE and a small number of processors. The details follow.

Solving a Smaller Problem.   The sequence X is subdivided into $u = n/\log \log n$ subsequences $X_1, X_2, \ldots, X_u$ of $\log \log n$ elements each. Similarly, the sequence Y is subdivided into $v = m/\log \log m$ subsequences $Y_1, Y_2, \ldots, Y_v$ of $\log \log m$ elements each. Let a_i be the first element of X_i and b_i be the first element of Y_i, as shown in Fig. 5.7. We form the two sequences $X' = \{a_1, a_2, \ldots, a_u\}$ and $Y' = \{b_1, b_2, \ldots, b_v\}$.

The sequences X' and Y' (each of which is sorted in nondecreasing order) can now be merged using algorithm PRAM MERGE. The number of processors used is $O(n/\log \log n)$, the time required is $O(\log \log(n/\log \log n))$—that is, $O(\log \log n)$. The cost is $O(n)$.

Breaking Down the Larger Problem.   As a result of merging X' and Y', we have the rank in Y' of every element in X' and the rank in X' of every element in Y'. These ranks are now used to compute:

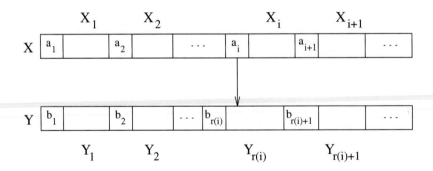

Figure 5.7: Solving a small merging problem.

1. The rank in Y of every element in X'.

2. The rank in X of every element in Y'.

We proceed as follows: Let the rank of a_i in Y' be $r(i)$. In other words,

$$b_{r(i)} < a_i \le b_{r(i)+1},$$

as shown in Fig. 5.7. Thus, the rank of a_i in Y is obtained by determining its rank in $Y_{r(i)}$. This is done by traversing $Y_{r(i)}$ sequentially to find its largest element smaller than a_i. Since $Y_{r(i)}$ has $\log \log m$ elements, the time taken is $O(\log \log m)$. With u processors, the ranks in Y of all elements of X' can be obtained simultaneously in $O(\log \log m)$ time. Similarly, with v processors, the ranks in X of all elements of Y' can be obtained simultaneously in $O(\log \log n)$ time. This step, therefore, uses $O(n/\log \log n)$ processors and runs in $O(\log \log n)$ time, for a cost of $O(n)$.

Solving Many Small Problems.   Now that the ranks of $\{a_1, a_2, \ldots, a_u\}$ in Y and the ranks of $\{b_1, b_2, \ldots, b_v\}$ in X are all known, the problem of merging X and Y reduces to solving several independent merging problems. Each such problem involves a subsequence of X and a subsequence of Y, disjoint from all other subsequences. To see this, let the rank of a_i in Y be $k(i)$. Clearly, every element x_j of X_i must be such that

$$y_{k(i)} \le x_j \le y_{k(i+1)},$$

as shown in Fig. 5.8(a). Similarly, let the rank of b_i in X be $q(i)$. Every element y_j of Y_i must satisfy

$$x_{q(i)} \le y_j \le x_{q(i+1)},$$

as shown in Fig. 5.8(b).

This defines a collection of disjoint merge problems, each involving $O(\log \log n)$ elements. Each such problem can be solved by one processor using algorithm RAM

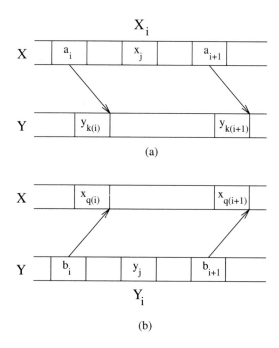

Figure 5.8: Solving independent merging problems: (a) Merging each X_i with Y; (b) Merging Y_i with X (to be used whenever one of the merging problems shown in (a) involves more than $O(\log \log n)$ elements of Y).

MERGE in $O(\log \log n)$ time. Since there are $O(n/\log \log n)$ such disjoint merge problems, $O(n/\log \log n)$ processors are required, and the cost is $O(n)$.

Analysis. Each of the three steps of the preceding PRAM algorithm uses $O(n/\log \log n)$ processors and runs in $O(\log \log n)$ time. These are therefore the processor and time requirements of the entire algorithm, leading to a cost of $O(n)$, which is optimal. We refer to this algorithm in what follows as algorithm PRAM OPTIMAL MERGE.

5.3   SELECTION

An example of a computation in which the technique of divide and conquer plays a key role in the design of an efficient algorithm is provided by the problem of selection. Given a sequence $S = \{s_1, s_2, \ldots, s_n\}$ of numbers listed in arbitrary order and an integer k, where $1 \leq k \leq n$, the problem of *selection* calls for determining the kth smallest element of S. In other words, we are looking for an element s_i of S such that exactly $k - 1$ elements of S are smaller than s_i. As usual, ties between elements are broken using their indices: If two elements of S are equal, then the one with the smaller index is considered to be smaller (i.e., if $s_j = s_k$, then s_j is considered smaller than s_k if and only if $j < k$).

Example 5.6 If $S = \{5, -20, 3, 6, 0, -1, 12\}$ and $k = 4$, then the fourth smallest element of S is 3. $\square$

An interesting special case of the selection problem occurs when $k = \lceil n/2 \rceil$. Here, the kth smallest element of S is called the *median*, a quantity often arising in statistical analyses.

The definition of the kth smallest element suggests that, if S is given sorted in nondecreasing order, then the element sought occupies the kth position. This gives an algorithm for solving the selection problem: Sort S, and then pick the kth element of the sorted sequence. On the RAM, this solution requires $O(n \log n)$ time if an optimal sorting algorithm (such as Heapsort or Mergesort) is used. The approach, however, solves the problem for every value of k from 1 to n, implying that perhaps a more efficient algorithm may exist that finds the kth smallest element only for the given k. In fact, a better sequential algorithm is known whose running time is $O(n)$, and this is optimal: Since every element of S must be examined, $\Omega(n)$ is a lower bound on the total number of steps required to solve the selection problem. In what follows, we refer to this algorithm as algorithm RAM SELECT.

In parallel, we can take advantage of the fact that sorting can be performed very quickly: On a PRAM with $O(n)$ processors, S can be sorted in $O(\log n)$ time by algorithm PRAM SORT. This means that the selection problem can be solved in $O(\log n)$ time using $O(n)$ processors. The cost of this solution, however, is $O(n \log n)$, which is not optimal in view of the $O(n)$ running time of algorithm RAM SELECT.

In what follows, we show how divide and conquer can be used in conjunction with parallel sorting to obtain a fast PRAM algorithm for selection whose cost is optimal. An algorithm is first described that runs in $O(\log n \log \log n)$ time and uses $O(n / \log n)$ processors. Although the running time of this parallel algorithm is higher than that of the solution, mentioned in the previous paragraph, which directly sorts the sequence S, its cost of $O(n \log \log n)$ is lower. Furthermore, the *work* of this algorithm—that is, the total number of steps it executes—is $O(n)$, which is indeed optimal. Finally, we show how the algorithm leads to another one whose cost is optimal.

5.3.1 Reducing the Number of Candidates

In solving the selection problem by divide and conquer, we invoke an idea similar to the one used in Section 5.1. Since one particular element of S is being looked for, namely, the kth smallest, it may be possible to devise a test that allows the number of potential candidates to be reduced from n to a smaller number.

Suppose that we can find an element m of S such that:

1. At least $n/4$ elements of S are guaranteed to be smaller than m.

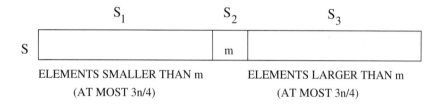

Figure 5.9: Splitting S into three subsequences.

2. At least $n/4$ elements of S are guaranteed to be larger than m.

Then we can use m to split S into three subsequences:

1. A sequence S_1 of elements of S that are smaller than m. (This includes elements equal to m, but whose indices in S are smaller than m's index.)

2. A sequence S_2 consisting of m itself.

3. A sequence S_3 of elements of S that are larger than m. (This includes elements equal to m but whose indices in S are larger than m's index.)

Since at least $n/4$ elements of S are guaranteed to be larger than m, we have

$$|S_1| \leq \frac{3n}{4}.$$

Similarly, since at least $n/4$ elements of S are guaranteed to be smaller than m, we have

$$|S_3| \leq \frac{3n}{4}.$$

The situation at this point is illustrated in Fig. 5.9.

We can now reduce the number of candidates for the title of kth smallest element of S as follows:

1. If $k = |S_1| + 1$, then m is the kth smallest element of S.

2. If $k \leq |S_1|$, then the kth smallest element of S must be in S_1.

3. If $k > |S_1| + 1$, then the kth smallest element of S must be in S_3.

In the first case, the algorithm returns m and terminates. In the second and third cases, the number of candidates is reduced to at most three-fourths of the size of S.

The same reduction process can now be applied to either S_1 or S_3. At the end of $O(\log \log n)$ such iterations, we would be left with $O(n/\log n)$ candidates, since

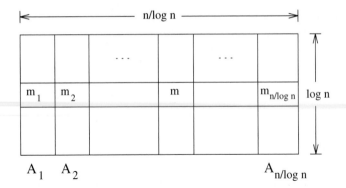

Figure 5.10: Divide and conquer using the median of medians.

$$\left(\frac{3}{4}\right)^{O(\log\log n)} n \;=\; \frac{n}{\left(\frac{4}{3}\right)^{O(\log_{4/3}\log n)}}$$

$$=\; O(\frac{n}{\log n}).$$

Having reduced the number of candidates to $O(n/\log n)$, we can now use the parallel sorting solution alluded to before. By sorting the remaining candidates in nondecreasing order using algorithm PRAM SORT, the kth smallest element of S is identified. Since there are $O(n/\log n)$ elements to be sorted, this final step requires $O(\log(n/\log n))$—that is, $O(\log n)$—time and $O(n/\log n)$ processors.

5.3.2   The Median of Medians

The discussion in the previous section was based on the assumption that an element m of S satisfying the given conditions is available. We now show how to find m. Suppose that S is divided into $n/\log n$ subsequences $A_1, A_2, \ldots, A_{n/\log n}$, each of size $\log n$. The result is illustrated in Fig. 5.10 as a rectangle of $n/\log n$ columns of $\log n$ rows each.

Now the median m_i of A_i is found, for $i = 1, 2, \ldots, n/\log n$. The median of the sequence of medians $\{m_1, m_2, \ldots, m_{n/\log n}\}$ is the desired element m. In Fig. 5.10, each m_i is shown in the middle of A_i, and m is shown in the middle of its row; this, of course, is for the purpose of illustration only, as each m_i, as well as m, can occur anywhere in their respective sequences.

Since m_i is the median of A_i, for $i = 1, 2, \ldots, n/\log n$, $(\log n)/2$ elements of A_i are smaller than it. Also, because m is the median of $\{m_1, m_2, \ldots, m_{n/\log n}\}$,

$(n/\log n)/2$ of these medians are smaller than it. Therefore, at least

$$\frac{\log n}{2} \times \frac{n}{2\log n} = \frac{n}{4}$$

elements of S are guaranteed to be smaller than m. By a similar reasoning, we establish that at least $n/4$ elements of S are guaranteed to be larger than m.

5.3.3 A Parallel Selection Algorithm

We are now ready to bring together the various pieces of the selection algorithm. The full algorithm is given next as algorithm PRAM SELECT. It takes the sequence S and an integer k as input and returns the kth element of S in a variable a.

> **Algorithm PRAM SELECT (S, k, a)**
>
> **Step 1:** *found* ← **false**
> **Step 2: while** $(|S| > n/\log n$ **and not** *found*) **do**
>   (2.1) Divide S into subsequences A_i, $i = 1, 2, \ldots, |S|/\log|S|$,
>   each consisting of $\log|S|$ elements of S
>   (2.2) **for** $i = 1$ **to** $|S|/\log|S|$ **do in parallel**
>   Find the median m_i of A_i
>   **end for**
>   (2.3) Find the median m of $\{m_1, m_2, \ldots, m_{|S|/\log|S|}\}$
>   (2.4) Create the subsequences S_1 and S_3
>   consisting of those elements of $|S|$
>   smaller than and larger than m, respectively
>   (2.5) **if** $k = |S_1| + 1$
>   **then** (i) $a \leftarrow m$
>   (ii) *found* ← **true**
>   **else** **if** $k < |S_1|$
>   **then** $S \leftarrow S_1$
>   **else** (i) $S \leftarrow S_3$
>   (ii) $k \leftarrow k - |S_1| - 1$
>   **end if**
>   **end if**
>   **end while**
> **Step 3: if not** *found*
>   **then** (3.1) Sort the sequence S
>   (3.2) $a \leftarrow k$th element of S
>   **end if.** ∎

Example 5.7 Suppose that $S = \{15, 4, 6, 18, 20, 3, 2, 6, 8, 10, 6, 8, 13, 17, 9, 7\}$—that is, $n = 16$ and $k = 14$. Since $\log n = 4$, we create the subsequences

$$
\begin{aligned}
A_1 &= \{15, 4, 6, 18\}, \\
A_2 &= \{20, 3, 2, 6\}, \\
A_3 &= \{8, 10, 6, 8\}, \\
A_4 &= \{13, 17, 9, 7\},
\end{aligned}
$$

whose medians are $m_1 = 15$, $m_2 = 6$, $m_3 = 8$, and $m_4 = 13$, respectively. The median m of these medians is 13. Therefore,

$$S_1 = \{4, 6, 3, 2, 6, 8, 10, 6, 8, 9, 7\}$$

and

$$S_3 = \{15, 18, 20, 17\}.$$

Now, $k > |S_1| + 1$, and we let

$$S = \{15, 18, 20, 17\} \quad \text{and} \quad k = 14 - 12 = 2.$$

Since $|S| = n/\log n$, S is sorted in Step 3, and its 2nd smallest element, namely, 17, is the 14th smallest element of the original input sequence. $\square$

Implementation. In order to complete the specification of algorithm PRAM SELECT, we must provide several details of its implementation. Dividing S into subsequences is easy: A_i is the ith sequence of $\log |S|$ consecutive elements of S. The median of A_i can be found by assigning one processor to it and using algorithm RAM SELECT. The median m of medians is obtained by sorting the sequence $\{m_1, m_2, \ldots, m_{|S|/\log |S|}\}$ and picking the element in position $(|S|/2\log |S|)$ of the resulting sequence.

The sequences S_1 and S_3 are created by comparing each element of S with m and labeling that element with a '$<$' if it is smaller than m and with a '$>$' if it is larger than m. All the elements labeled '$<$' are now packed into $|S_1|$ contiguous positions within S, using the array-packing algorithm of Section 4.6. The same is done for S_3. Finally, assigning S_1 (or S_3) to S in preparing for the next iteration is done simply by updating one of two indices, namely, either the one pointing to the beginning of S or the one pointing to the end of S.

Analysis. Steps 1, (2.1), and (2.5) take constant time. Step (2.2) uses $|S|/\log |S|$ processors (each executing algorithm RAM SELECT on a sequence of length $\log |S|$) and runs in $O(\log |S|)$ time. In Step (2.3), a sequence of $|S|/\log |S|$ elements is sorted (by algorithm PRAM SORT) using $O(|S|/\log |S|)$ processors in $O(\log(|S|/\log |S|)) = O(\log |S|)$ time. Creating each of S_1 and S_3 by means of array packing is a prefix computation requiring $O(|S|/\log |S|)$ processors to complete in $O(\log |S|)$ time. Therefore, each iteration of Step 2 uses $O(|S|/\log |S|)$ processors and runs in $O(\log |S|)$ time.

Since $|S| \leq n$, it follows that the processor and time requirements of one iteration of Step 2 are $O(n/\log n)$ and $O(\log n)$, respectively. Because Step 2 is iterated

$O(\log \log n)$ times, its total running time is $O(\log n \log \log n)$. Similarly, the number of elementary steps (operations) executed during one iteration of Step 2 is

$$O(\frac{|S|}{\log |S|}) \times O(\log |S|) = O(|S|).$$

Therefore, the total number of operations executed over all iterations of Step 2 is

$$O(n + \left(\frac{3}{4}\right) n + \left(\frac{3}{4}\right)^2 n + \cdots + \left(\frac{3}{4}\right)^{O(\log \log n)} n) = O(n).$$

As mentioned at the end of Section 5.3.1, Step 3 requires $O(\log n)$ time and $O(n/\log n)$ processors and executes a total of $O(n)$ elementary steps. To sum up, algorithm PRAM SELECT has a running time of

$$t(n) = O(\log n \log \log n)$$

and uses

$$p(n) = O(n/\log n)$$

processors, while performing a total of $O(n)$ elementary steps. Its cost is

$$\begin{aligned} c(n) &= p(n) \times t(n) \\ &= O(n \log \log n), \end{aligned}$$

which is not optimal in view of the $O(n)$ operations sufficient for selection.

5.3.4 An Optimal Selection Algorithm

Algorithm PRAM SELECT executes an optimal number of elementary steps, namely, $O(n)$. Its cost, on the other hand, is not optimal. This suggests that a number of processors are idle during significant periods of the computation. In order to obtain an optimal cost, we seek to reduce the number of processors. This can be achieved by appealing to the slowdown folklore theorem, since selection is one of the standard problems to which it applies. As it turns out, the running time in this particular case, instead of *increasing* when fewer processors are used, remains unchanged.

From the "proof" of the slowdown folklore theorem, we know that if q processors are used to execute W operations, then these operations can be distributed among the processors (in those cases where the theorem applies). In the case of algorithm PRAM SELECT, $W = O(n)$, and each component of the algorithm (finding the medians, sorting, packing, and so on) lends itself to this redistribution. It follows that with q processors, the running time is $O(\log n \log \log n + n/q)$, and the cost is $O(q \log n \log \log n + n)$. Choosing

$$q = \frac{n}{\log n \log \log n},$$

we find that the algorithm's running time is $O(\log n \log \log n)$, the same as before, while the cost is now $O(n)$, which is optimal.

5.4   COMPUTING THE CONVEX HULL

Our final algorithm in this chapter computes the convex hull of a set of points in the plane. Recall the definition given in Example 4.7. Let $Q = \{q_1, q_2, \ldots, q_n\}$ be a finite sequence representing n points in the plane. The convex hull of Q, denoted $CH(Q)$, is the convex polygon with the smallest area containing all the points of Q. Thus, each $q_i \in Q$ either lies inside $CH(Q)$ or is a corner of $CH(Q)$. Given Q, the problem we wish to solve is to compute $CH(Q)$. Since $CH(Q)$ is a polygon, an algorithm for this problem must produce the corners of $CH(Q)$ in the order in which they appear on the boundary of the polygon (in clockwise order, for example). In arriving at this algorithm, we make the following assumptions to simplify the presentation:

1. Each point q_i of Q is given by a pair of Cartesian coordinates (x_i, y_i).

2. No two points of Q have the same x- or y-coordinate.

3. No three points of Q lie on the same straight line.

4. The set Q consists of four or more points (since, when $n \leq 3$, $CH(Q) = Q$).

A divide-and-conquer approach to computing the convex hull is given in Example 5.2. It begins by dividing the set into two disjoint subsets—a left subset S_1 and a right subset S_2. Then it computes $CH(S_1)$ and $CH(S_2)$ recursively. Finally, it merges the latter to obtain $CH(Q)$. The merge is performed by computing two "tangents" common to $CH(S_1)$ and $CH(S_2)$: An *upper* tangent and a *lower* tangent. Each tangent touches exactly one corner of each polygon. All corners of $CH(S_1)$ and $CH(S_2)$ fall below (above) the infinite straight line supporting the upper (lower) tangent. Together, these tangents combine the two polygons $CH(S_1)$ and $CH(S_2)$ into one polygon $CH(Q)$, as shown in Fig. 5.1. The merge operation is expressed as follows:

$$CH(Q) \leftarrow CH(S_1) \ \cup \ CH(S_2).$$

This approach works well sequentially and can also be used in a parallel setting. We opt, however, for a different parallel implementation of the basic idea. As was done before in this chapter, particularly in Section 5.2, the approach used here is to divide the problem into several, instead of two, subproblems. The subproblems are solved individually, and their solutions are combined into one global solution to the original problem. This technique is sometimes called *multiway divide and conquer*. The parallel algorithm consists of four steps and is given next as algorithm PRAM CONVEX HULL:

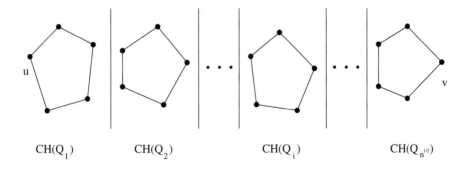

Figure 5.11: Convex polygons to be merged in the computation of $CH(Q)$.

Algorithm PRAM CONVEX HULL $(n, Q, CH(Q))$

> **Step 1:** Sort the points of Q by their x-coordinates.
> **Step 2:** Partition Q into $n^{1/2}$ subsets $Q_1, Q_2, \ldots, Q_{n^{1/2}}$,
> separated by vertical lines,
> such that Q_i is to the left of Q_j if $i < j$.
> **Step 3: for $i = 1$ to $n^{1/2}$ do in parallel**
> > **if** $|Q_i| \leq 3$
> > **then** $CH(Q_i) \leftarrow Q_i$
> > **else** PRAM CONVEX HULL $(n^{1/2}, Q_i, CH(Q_i))$
> > **end if**
> > **end for**
> **Step 4:** $CH(Q) \leftarrow CH(Q_1) \cup CH(Q_2) \cup \cdots \cup CH(Q_{n^{1/2}})$. ∎

Step 1 is performed using algorithm PRAM SORT. Step 2 is immediate: Since the points are sorted by their x-coordinates, it suffices to take the ith set of $n^{1/2}$ points in the sorted list and call it Q_i, $i = 1, 2, \ldots, n^{1/2}$. Step 3 applies the algorithm recursively to all the Q_i simultaneously. Finally, Step 4 merges the convex hulls obtained in Step 3 to compute $CH(Q)$. We now show how this step is implemented.

5.4.1 Merging a Set of Disjoint Polygons

The situation at the end of Step 3 is illustrated in Fig. 5.11. Let u and v be the points of Q with the smallest and largest x-coordinates, respectively, as shown in the figure. The convex hull $CH(Q)$ consists of two parts:

1. The *upper hull*—that is, the sequence of corners of $CH(Q)$ in clockwise order, beginning with u and ending with v.

2. The *lower hull*—that is, the sequence of corners of $CH(Q)$ in clockwise order, beginning with v and ending with u.

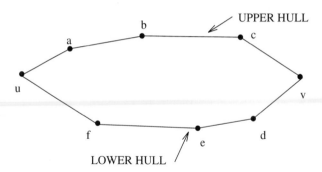

Figure 5.12: The upper and lower hulls of $CH(Q)$.

This is depicted in Fig. 5.12, in which the upper hull consists of the corners u, a, b, c, and v, while v, d, e, f, and u are the corners of the lower hull. Step 4 computes the upper hull and lower hull separately and then concatenates them. Since computing the lower hull is symmetric to computing the upper hull, we only explain how the latter is performed.

Identifying the Upper Hull. Suppose that n processors are available. We assign $n^{1/2}-1$ processors to $CH(Q_i)$, for $i = 1, 2, \ldots, n^{1/2}$. Each processor assigned to $CH(Q_i)$ finds the upper tangent common to $CH(Q_i)$ and one of the remaining $n^{1/2} - 1$ convex polygons $CH(Q_j)$, $j \neq i$. Among all tangents to polygons to the left of $CH(Q_i)$, let L_i be the one with the smallest slope and tangent to $CH(Q_i)$ at corner l_i. Similarly, among all tangents to polygons to the right of $CH(Q_i)$, let R_i be the one with the largest slope and tangent to $CH(Q_i)$ at point r_i. As shown in Fig. 5.13(a), if the angle α formed by L_i and R_i is smaller than 180 degrees, then none of the corners of $CH(Q_i)$ is on the upper hull. Otherwise, as shown in Fig. 5.13(b), all corners from l_i to r_i are on the upper hull.

These computations are done simultaneously for all $CH(Q_i)$, each yielding a (possibly empty) list of points of Q on the upper hull. The lists are then compressed into one list using the array-packing algorithm of Section 4.6. This way, all upper-hull points (from u to v) occupy contiguous locations of an array. A similar computation yields all the lower-hull points (from v to u) in contiguous positions of an array. By putting the two arrays side by side (and omitting v and u from the second array), we obtain $CH(Q)$.

One detail still requires some attention, namely, the way in which the tangents are found. This computation is a major component of the merge step, and it is important that we perform it efficiently, as explained next.

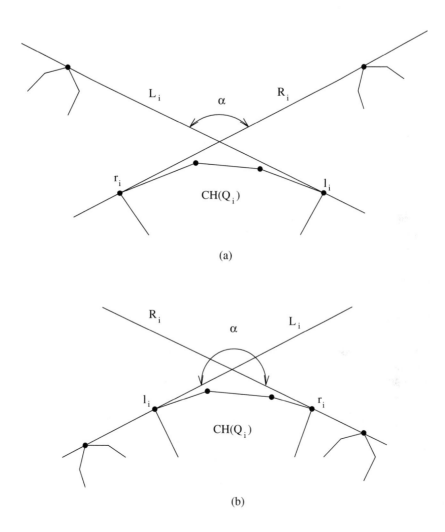

Figure 5.13: Identifying points on the upper hull of $CH(Q)$: (a) α smaller than 180 degrees; (b) α larger than 180 degrees.

5.4.2   Computing Tangents

Given two convex polygons $CH(Q_i)$ and $CH(Q_j)$, each with $O(n^{1/2})$ corners, it is required to find their upper common tangent (k, m)—that is, a straight-line segment with endpoints k and m, tangent to $CH(Q_i)$ at k and to $CH(Q_j)$ at m. Here, k and m are on the upper hulls of $CH(Q_i)$ and $CH(Q_j)$, respectively. We now show how the upper common tangent (k, m) can be obtained by one processor in $O(\log n^{1/2})$—that is, $O(\log n)$—time. The approach is based on the same idea as binary search. Consider the sorted sequence of corners forming the upper hull of $CH(Q_i)$, and let s be the corner in the middle of the sequence. Similarly, let w be the corner in the middle of the sorted sequence of corners forming the upper hull of $CH(Q_j)$. For illustration purposes, suppose that $CH(Q_j)$ is to the right of $CH(Q_i)$. There are two possibilities:

1. Either (s, w) is the upper common tangent of $CH(Q_i)$ and $CH(Q_j)$; that is, $k = s$ and $m = w$, as shown in Fig. 5.14(a), in which case we are done;

2. Or one half of the (remaining) corners of $CH(Q_i)$ and/or $CH(Q_j)$ can be removed from further consideration as upper tangent points. This is illustrated in Figs. 5.14(b)–(h) and Fig. 5.15, in which those parts of a polygon removed from consideration are highlighted. The process is now repeated by finding the corners s and w in the middle of the remaining sequence of corners in $CH(Q_i)$ and $CH(Q_j)$, respectively.

The sections of $CH(Q_i)$ and/or $CH(Q_j)$ to be removed from further consideration are fairly straightforward to determine in Figs. 5.14(b)–(h). The cases illustrated in Figs. 5.15(a) and (b) require a word of explanation. Consider Fig. 5.15(a). The line through s and w crosses $CH(Q_j)$ at some point o (this point being used for argument purposes only; it is not a corner, and its position is not computed). Let S and W be tangents at s and w, respectively, and let L be the vertical line separating $CH(Q_i)$ and $CH(Q_j)$. The lines S and W intersect at a point z that lies above the line through s and w and to the left of (or on) L. Consequently, m must lie to the right of o. Therefore, k cannot lie to the left of s. It follows that all corners which precede s on the upper hull of $CH(Q_i)$ can be deleted from further consideration. The case in Fig. 5.15(b) is symmetric.

5.4.3   Analysis

As mentioned earlier, Step 1 of algorithm PRAM CONVEX HULL is performed using algorithm PRAM SORT. This requires $O(n)$ processors and $O(\log n)$ time. If $\{q_1', q_2', \ldots, q_n'\}$ represents the sorted sequence, then points q_j', $j = (i - 1)n^{1/2} + 1$, $(i - 1)n^{1/2} + 2, \ldots, in^{1/2}$, belong to Q_i, for $i = 1, 2, \ldots, n^{1/2}$. Therefore, with n processors, Step 2 requires constant time: Processor P_j reads q_j', then uses j and $n^{1/2}$ to compute i, and finally assigns q_j' to Q_i, $j = 1, 2, \ldots, n$. If $t(n)$ is the running time of algorithm PRAM CONVEX HULL, then Step 3 requires $t(n^{1/2})$

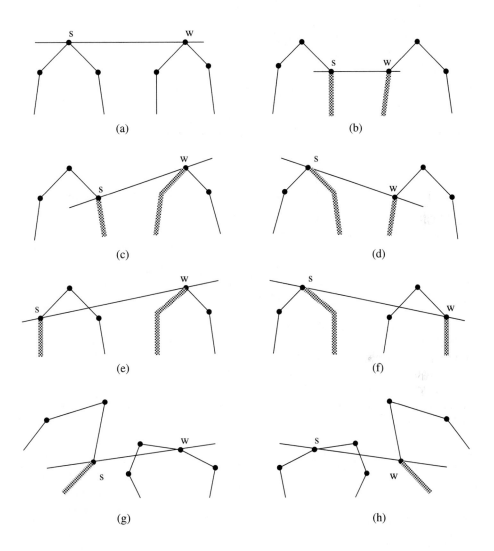

Figure 5.14: Computing the upper tangent: (a)–(h) Eight simple cases.

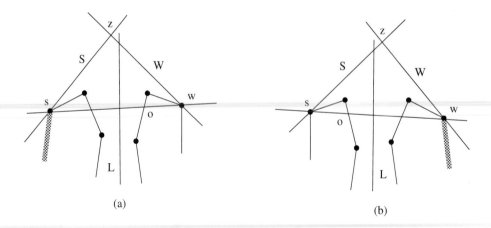

Figure 5.15: Computing the upper tangent: (a)–(b) Two more involved cases.

time, with $n^{1/2}$ processors computing $CH(Q_i)$. In Step 4, each of $(n^{1/2} - 1)n^{1/2}$ processors computes one tangent in $O(\log n)$ time. For each $CH(Q_i)$, the tangents L_i and R_i are found in constant time using a **MIN CW** instruction, executed on the tangent slopes. It also takes constant time to determine whether the corners from l_i to r_i belong to the upper hull. Finally, array packing is done in $O(\log n)$ time using n processors.

Putting all the pieces together, the overall running time of the algorithm is given by

$$t(n) = t(n^{1/2}) + \beta \log n,$$

for some constant β. Thus, $t(n) = O(\log n)$. Since $p(n) = n$, the algorithm's cost is $c(n) = O(n \log n)$.

A Lower Bound. That the preceding cost is optimal can be established by deriving an $\Omega(n \log n)$ lower bound on the number of operations required to compute the convex hull of n planar points. To obtain this lower bound, we show that any convex hull algorithm must be capable of sorting a sequence of positive real numbers $X = \{x_1, x_2, \ldots, x_n\}$ in nondecreasing order.

Consider the sequence $Q = \{(x_1, x_1^2), (x_2, x_2^2), \ldots, (x_n, x_n^2)\}$, and view each pair as the Cartesian coordinates of a point in the plane. Thus, all points of Q fall on the curve $y = x^2$. Now apply to Q *any* algorithm that computes the convex hull. Since all the points of Q are corners of $CH(Q)$, the algorithm returns them *sorted* in nondecreasing order on the x_i. Therefore, the $\Omega(n \log n)$ lower bound on the number of operations required to sort a sequence of n numbers applies also to computing the convex hull of n points in the plane.

5.5 PROBLEMS

5.1 Trace the behavior of algorithm PRAM SEARCH for the sequence S of Example 5.3 in the following two cases:

(a) $N = 2$ and $x = 22$.

(b) $N = 4$ and $x = 89$.

5.2 For algorithm PRAM SEARCH, analyze the following:

(a) The speedup it provides with respect to the sequential algorithm, RAM BINARY SEARCH.

(b) Its cost.

5.3 Let S be a sorted sequence of n integers, and let x be a given integer. A cost-optimal parallel search algorithm which determines whether x occurs in S would use $p(n)$ processors and run in time $t(n)$ such that $p(n) \times t(n) = O(\log n)$. Is such an algorithm possible?

5.4 Algorithm PRAM SEARCH solves the *discrete* search problem—that is, the problem of searching for a value in a given sequence. Similar algorithms can be derived for the *continuous* case—that is, searching for a point at which a continuous function takes a given value. Describe a parallel algorithm for locating (within a given tolerance) the point at which a certain function:

(a) Takes its largest value inside a specified interval.

(b) Is equal to zero.

5.5 A binary sequence of length n consists of a (possibly empty) string of 0's followed by a (possibly empty) string of 1's.

(a) Given a PRAM with N processors, $1 < N \leq n$, describe an algorithm for determining the number of 1's in the sequence.

(b) Repeat (a) for the case where the sequence consists of a string of 0's, followed by a string of 1's, followed by a string of 0's.

5.6 Compare algorithm PRAM SEARCH to the algorithm for searching on a binary tree of processors described in Example 1.5. Specifically, contrast the assumptions, running time, number of processors, cost, and ability to handle a sequence of queries of one algorithm to the other.

5.7 Let us consider again the following ranking problem presented in Section 5.2.3: Two sequences of numbers $X = \{x_1, x_2, \ldots, x_n\}$ and $Y = \{y_1, y_2, \ldots, y_m\}$ are given, each sorted in nondecreasing order, with $n \geq m \geq 1$. For each element y_j of Y, it is required to find two elements of X such that

$$x_i \leq y_j < x_{i+1}.$$

For completeness, we assume the existence of two additional elements $x_0 = -\infty$ and $x_{n+1} = +\infty$.

Sequentially, the problem can be solved in $O(n)$ time by merging X and Y. Alternatively, when m is asymptotically smaller than $n/\log n$, a faster solution is obtained by performing m binary searches in X, one for each element of Y, leading to an $O(m \log n)$ running time. An even faster solution is obtained when $\log(n/m)$ is asymptotically smaller than $\log n$. The idea is to first partition X into m consecutive subsequences of size n/m each, by selecting $m - 1$ elements of X, namely, $x_{n/m}$, $x_{2(n/m)}$, $\ldots$, $x_{n-(n/m)}$. These elements are now merged with Y; as a result, we know, for each element y_j, the subsequence of X into which it falls. Finally, a binary search for every element of Y is performed in the corresponding subsequence of X (such search being, of course, unnecessary for elements of Y that are smaller than x_1 or larger than x_n). This algorithm requires $O(m \log(n/m))$ time.

We are particularly interested here in the case where m is significantly smaller than n. Such a situation arises when X is a very large database of n elements and Y is a sequence of m queries of the database, submitted at the same time, where $m < n$. In a parallel computing environment, we would expect the number of processors to be closer to m than to n. How is the problem solved in parallel? Each of the foregoing sequential solutions can be adapted in a parallel environment as follows:

(a) The two sequences X and Y could be merged using algorithm PRAM OPTIMAL MERGE. This requires $O(\log \log n)$ time and $O(n/\log \log n)$ processors. The cost is $O(n)$.

(b) When m is asymptotically smaller than $n/\log n$, an algorithm that uses fewer processors (namely, m) is obtained by conducting m simultaneous binary searches over X. This solution is slower than the previous one, requiring $O(\log n)$ time, but has a smaller cost of $O(m \log n)$.

(c) Consider now the following algorithm, based on the third sequential solution: The sequence S is partitioned into m subsequences X_1, X_2, $\ldots$, X_m using $x_{n/m}$, $x_{2(n/m)}$, $\ldots$, $x_{n-(n/m)}$. These $m - 1$ elements are merged with Y using algorithm PRAM OPTIMAL MERGE. This requires $O(m/\log \log m)$ processors and $O(\log \log m)$ time. A binary search for each element y_j is now conducted in the appropriate X_i. This requires m processors and $O(\log(n/m))$ time. For $n > m \log m$, the overall running time is $O(\log(n/m))$. This solution is faster than the previous one and has a smaller cost of $O(m \log(n/m))$ when $\log(n/m)$ is asymptotically smaller than $\log n$.

Assuming that m is significantly smaller than n and that only m processors are available, discuss possible ways to improve the preceding parallel solutions.

5.8 Analyze the work of algorithm PRAM MERGE.

5.9 Design and analyze a parallel algorithm for merging two sequences of numbers of total length n, each sorted in nondecreasing order, on a pyramid with n base processors.

5.10 Let X and Y be two sorted sequences of numbers of length n and m, respectively.

    (a) Develop a RAM algorithm for finding the kth smallest element among all elements of X and Y.

    (b) Use the algorithm in **(a)** to obtain a PRAM algorithm for merging X and Y into a third sorted sequence Z of length $n + m$.

5.11 Show how algorithm PRAM OPTIMAL MERGE can be used to obtain a parallel algorithm for sorting into nondecreasing order a sequence of numbers given in arbitrary order.

5.12 Design a PRAM algorithm for merging two sorted sequences of total length n in $O((n/N) + \log n)$ time using N processors, where $1 < N \leq n$, such that the sequences are merged *in place*—that is, without using an additional array of size n.

5.13 Can you find an algorithm for selecting the kth smallest element of a sequence of n numbers $S = \{s_1, s_2, \ldots, s_n\}$ that uses $O(n/\log^\varepsilon n)$ processors and runs in $O(\log^\varepsilon n)$ time, for some $0 \leq \varepsilon \leq 1$?

5.14 Design parallel algorithms for solving the selection problem on each of the following models of computation:

    (a) Tree

    (b) Mesh

    (c) Hypercube.

5.15 Given a sequence of numbers $S = \{s_1, s_2, \ldots, s_n\}$ and an integer k, $1 \leq k \leq n$, it is desired to find the k smallest elements of S. Design and analyze a parallel algorithm for solving this problem on your chosen model of computation.

5.16 Show how algorithm PRAM SELECT can be used to derive a parallel algorithm for sorting on the PRAM a sequence of numbers given in arbitrary order.

5.17 Use algorithm PRAM SELECT to design a parallel divide-and-conquer algorithm for computing the convex hull of a set of n points in the plane.

5.18 A *triangulation* of a simple n-vertex polygon Q is the augmentation of Q with diagonal edges connecting vertices of Q such that, in the resulting decomposition, every face is a triangle. Design and analyze a parallel algorithm for solving this problem based on the divide-and-conquer approach.

5.19 Given a simple polygon Q with n vertices and two points s and d in Q, the *interior shortest path* problem asks for computing the shortest path from s to d that lies completely inside Q. Design a parallel divide-and-conquer algorithm for solving this problem.

5.20 Design a parallel divide-and-conquer algorithm for determining whether any two of n given straight-line segments in the plane intersect.

5.21 Given a set of geometric objects, a point r is said to be *visible* from a point s if the line segment with endpoints r and s is not intersected by any object. For example, two points r and s in a simple polygon Q are visible from one another if the line segment with endpoints r and s does not intersect any edge of Q. (See Problem 2.11.) Assume that a set of n (opaque) nonintersecting line segments in the plane are given. Design a parallel divide-and-conquer algorithm for determining all parts of the plane that are visible from a point r in the plane.

5.22 For a set S of n points in the plane, it is required to determine which two points are closest to one another.

   (a) Design and analyze a PRAM algorithm for solving this problem based on the divide-and-conquer approach.

   (b) Extend your solution to find, for each point of S, its closest neighbor, also in S.

5.23 Suppose that two b-bit integers x and y, where b is a power of 2, are to be multiplied together. A divide-and-conquer algorithm can be used for this purpose. Each of x and y is first divided into two equal parts of $b/2$ bits and expressed as follows:

$$x = u2^{b/2} + v,$$
$$y = w2^{b/2} + z.$$

The product xy is now computed from

$$(uw)2^b + (uz + vw)2^{b/2} + vz,$$

where the products $uw, uz, vw,$ and vz are obtained by the same algorithm recursively. Let $q(b)$ be the number of bit operations required to compute xy by this algorithm. Since the algorithm involves four multiplications of two $(b/2)$-bit integers, three additions of integers with at most $2b$ bits, and two shifts (multiplication by 2^b and $2^{b/2}$), we have

$$q(1) = 1,$$
$$q(b) = 4q(b/2) + ab,$$

for some constant a. It follows that $q(b) = O(b^2)$.

(a) Suggest a parallel implementation of the foregoing algorithm.

(b) If the quantity $uz + vw$ is obtained from

$$(u + v)(w + z) - uw - vz,$$

then only three multiplications of $(b/2)$-bit integers are required. Consequently,

$$q(1) = 1,$$
$$q(b) = 3q(b/2) + a'b,$$

for some constant a'. (There are now four additions and two subtractions, instead of three additions, of integers with at most $2b$ bits.) Therefore, $q(b) = O(b^{\log 3}) = O(b^{1.59})$. Repeat **(a)** for this version of the algorithm.

5.24 Given two sequences $\{a_1, a_2, \ldots, a_n\}$, where $a_1 = 0$, and $\{b_1, b_2, \ldots, b_n\}$, a closed-form solution to the first-order linear recurrence

$$x_1 = b_1,$$
$$x_i = a_i x_{i-1} + b_i, \quad i = 2, 3, \ldots, n,$$

is given by

$$x_i = \sum_{j=0}^{i} \left(\prod_{k=j+1}^{i} a_k \right) b_j$$

for $i = 2, 3, \ldots, n$. Design a parallel divide-and-conquer approach for computing $x_2, x_3, \ldots, x_n$.

5.25 In Problem 1.23, the trapezoidal rule was described for computing an approximation to the definite integral

$$D = \int_a^b f(x)dx.$$

There, the interval $[a, b]$ was divided into N subintervals of equal size, and D was approximated by a summation of the values of $f(x)$ at the interval points. An alternative approach is provided by *adaptive quadrature*, whereby the interval $[a, b]$ is divided into unequal subintervals such that the required accuracy is achieved with the fewest evaluations of f. Assume that D is to be computed to within an accuracy of ε. We proceed as follows:

(a) The trapezoidal rule is used with $N = 1$ and $N = 2$ to compute D_1 and D_2, respectively, where

$$\begin{array}{rcl} D_1 & = & \frac{b-a}{2}(f(a) + f(b)), \\ D_2 & = & \frac{b-a}{4}(f(a) + 2f(\frac{a+b}{2}) + f(b)). \end{array}$$

(b) If the absolute value of $(D_2 - D_1)$ is smaller than or equal to ε, then $D = D_2$. Otherwise, the same method is applied to each of the subintervals $[a, (a + b)/2]$ and $[(a + b)/2, b]$ with an accuracy of $\varepsilon/2$.

Develop a parallel implementation of adaptive quadrature.

5.26 Given a bipartite graph G, it is required to color the edges of G with a minimum number of colors such that each edge is assigned a color and no two edges adjacent to the same vertex receive the same color. Design a parallel divide-and-conquer algorithm to solve this problem.

5.27 Study the effect of using discriminating analysis instead of uniform analysis on the running times of the algorithms presented in this chapter.

5.6   BIBLIOGRAPHICAL REMARKS

Sequential algorithms based on the divide-and-conquer approach are well documented; see, for example, Aho et al. [7], Brassard and Bratley [120], Cormen et al. [185], Horowitz and Sahni [303], and Smith [574]. Descriptions of, and references to, parallel divide-and-conquer algorithms can be found in Akl [18, 21], Akl and Lyons [42], Gibbons and Rytter [258], JáJá [310], Quinn [515], and Reif [533].

Parallel algorithms for searching a sorted sequence are proposed in Baer et al. [82], Kruskal [336], and Snir [576]. Algorithm PRAM SEARCH was first proposed by Snir [576], who also established its optimality. Other parallel search algorithms for a variety of models and inputs appear in Akl and Dehne [30], Akl and Meijer [44], Atallah and Kosaraju [74], Carey and Thompson [129], Chan and Choi [135], Chang [139], Chung et al. [160], Meijer and Akl [417], Ottman et al. [462], Potter [494], Ramamoorthy et al. [525], Schmeck and Schröder [551], Stanfill and Kahle [584], Stone [595], and Wen [639].

Algorithms for merging two sorted sequences on the PRAM are described in Akl and Santoro [51], Barlow et al. [84], Borodin and Hopcroft [118], Guan and Langston [271], Hagerup and Rüb [280], Kruskal [336], and Shiloach and Vishkin [564]. The ideas used in algorithm PRAM MERGE are presented in Kruskal [336] and Valiant [618]. Parallel merging algorithms for other models were also proposed. These include the odd-even and bitonic merging circuits of Chapter 3, due to Batcher [89], and their implementations on the linear array and mesh interconnection networks by Kumar and Hirschberg [342], Nassimi and Sahni [437], and Thompson and Kung [612]. Algorithms for merging on a tree, a star, and a pyramid are given in Akl [18], Menn and Somani [420], and Stout [596], respectively. An $\Omega(\log \log n)$ lower bound on the time required to merge two sorted sequences on the *comparison tree* model, where only comparisons are counted, is derived in Borodin and Hopcroft [118] and Häggkvist and Hell [281]. Parallel merging algorithms for this model are described by Gavril [256] and Valiant [618].

Descriptions of algorithm RAM SELECT can be found in Aho et al. [7], Akl [21], and Cormen et al. [185]. The first parallel algorithm for selection was proposed in Akl [15]. Other PRAM algorithms are described in Cole and Vishkin [170] and Vishkin [627]. Algorithm PRAM SELECT is based on ideas presented in Akl [15] and Vishkin [627]. A lower bound of $\Omega(\log \log n)$ on the running time required for selection on the comparison tree model is derived in Valiant [618], and algorithms for this model are given in Ajtai et al. [8], Cole and Yap [174], and Reischuck [536]. A number of selection algorithms for various other parallel models were proposed. These include algorithms for the tree (see, for example, Aggarwal [3], Cooper and Akl [183], Greenberg and Manber [268], Stout [596], and Tanimoto [604]) and the star (see Qiu and Akl [508]), as well as for variants of the mesh (see Stout [597]) and the hypercube (see Chandran and Rosenfeld [137] and Plaxton [492]). A lower bound of $\Omega((n/p) \log \log p + \log p)$ on the time required for selection using p processors on a class of networks that includes the tree, the mesh, the hypercube, the butterfly, and the shuffle exchange is derived by Plaxton [493]. A special-purpose architecture for selecting the kth smallest out of n elements is described in Wah and Chen [631].

The convex hull problem has attracted a good deal of attention in both sequential and parallel computation. The problem's origins and applications, as well as sequential algorithms for its solution, are described in Preparata and Shamos [500]. PRAM algorithms for the convex hull are described, for example, in Aggarwal et al. [5], Akl [17], and Atallah and Goodrich [72]. Algorithm PRAM CONVEX HULL was first proposed in Aggarwal et al. [5] and Atallah and Goodrich [72]. Examples of parallel convex hull algorithms for other models are provided in Akl [14] (combinational circuits), Akl [21] (mesh of trees), Chazelle [141] (linear array), Chow [155] (cube-connected cycles), Miller and Stout [427] (mesh), and Stojmenović [585] (hypercube). Parallel algorithms for computing the convex hull and closely related geometric objects on the PRAM and various other models of computation are reviewed in Akl and Lyons [42], Atallah [69], Atallah and Chen [70], Atallah and Goodrich [73], and Ó'Dúnlaing [445].

Parallel divide-and-conquer algorithms were proposed for a host of other problems, including problems in computational geometry (see, for example, Aggarwal et al. [5], Akl [16, 17], Akl and Lyons [42], Akl et al. [50], Atallah et al. [71], Cole and Goodrich [167], Cole et al. [168], ElGindy and Goodrich [216], Goodrich [264],

JáJá [310], and Reif [533]), numerical analysis (see, for example, Akl [21], Freeman and Phillips [251], and Lakshmivarahan and Dhall [355]), optimization (see, for example, Chalmers and Akl [132, 133]), and graph theory (see, for example, Akl [19], Gibbons and Rytter [258], and Reif [533]). Various other aspects of parallel divide and conquer are studied in Cvetanović [192], Horowitz and Zorat [304], Kumar and Rao [344], Lo et al. [392], Madala and Sinclair [398], Rao and Kumar [527], Stout [599], and Zorat [651].

Chapter 6

Pointer-Based Data Structures

In the previous two chapters, we focused on problems whose input data were stored in *arrays* in shared memory. Thus, data were known to occupy contiguous locations in memory, and a datum could be accessed using its index in an array. In this chapter, we turn our attention to problems whose data are stored in pointer-based data structures such as linked lists, trees, and general graphs.

We begin in Section 6.1 by describing the *pointer-jumping* technique, a basic tool behind the algorithms of this chapter. Two fundamental related problems are then addressed in Section 6.2, namely, *prefix computation* on linked lists and *linked list ranking*. Fast algorithms for these two problems allow a host of other computations to be performed efficiently. In fact, the importance of these algorithms extends beyond computations defined strictly on linked lists. Many computational problems occurring in the context of other data structures can be solved by transforming those structures into linked lists and then applying the prefix computation or list-ranking algorithms. This is possible, in particular, when a powerful approach known as the *Euler tour* method is used. The approach is presented in Section 6.3, together with several algorithms for solving problems defined on trees. Finally, we show in Section 6.4 how the *connected components* of a graph can be computed. Applications of the connected components algorithm are explored in Section 6.5.

Our chosen model of parallel computation in this chapter continues to be the PRAM. Note that we use the term *node* when speaking of the basic component of a data structure and the term *vertex* when referring to the elements of a graph, although strictly speaking, the two terms are synonymous. Running times of algorithms are derived using uniform analysis, unless otherwise stated.

6.1   POINTER JUMPING

The main idea behind the algorithms in this chapter is a simple technique known as *pointer jumping*. Consider the data structure in Fig. 6.1 consisting of a tree of nodes, where each node has a pointer to its parent. Suppose that the node labeled *LEAF* wishes to communicate a value to the *ROOT* node. One way to do this is to follow the pointers from *LEAF* up the tree, through nodes A, B, C, D, E, F and G, to *ROOT*. This requires eight steps. The same thing can be accomplished in just three steps, provided that all nodes are instructed to modify their pointers at each step as follows: If node x points to node y and node y points to node z, then node x makes its pointer point to node z. In Fig. 6.1, the updated pointers are shown in dotted lines (only for the path from node *LEAF* to node *ROOT*) and labeled by the number of the step in which they were created. In the cases where it applies, pointer jumping allows a computation that takes $O(n)$ time sequentially to be performed in parallel in $O(\log n)$ time.

6.2   COMPUTATIONS ON A LINKED LIST

Suppose that we are given a singly linked list L as shown in Fig. 6.2(a). The list is composed of *nodes* linked by *pointers*. As shown in Fig. 6.2(b), each node i consists of:

1. An information field *info*(i), containing some information.

2. A value field *val*(i) holding a number x_j.

3. A pointer field *succ*(i) pointing to the successor of node i in L.

Since the last node in the list, the *tail*, has no successor, its pointer is equal to *nil*. In what follows, we omit the *info* field from the discussion and figures, referring to it only when required; similarly, the *succ* field is represented by an arrow, provided that it is not *nil*.

There are three important aspects to stress here:

1. The nodes forming the linked list are stored in memory in *arbitrary locations*. In particular, no assumption is made about the nodes (including their pointer fields) being stored in an array. In fact, we assume that the number of nodes in L is unknown in advance.

2. Since L is a linked list, the notion of a node's *index* is essentially meaningless. However, we use indices in our exposition in order to be able to distinguish among nodes and their respective fields. Thus, we speak of node i and field *val*(i), although the index i cannot tell us the node's position in the list. For example, in Fig. 6.2(a), node 7 is the fourth node in the list.

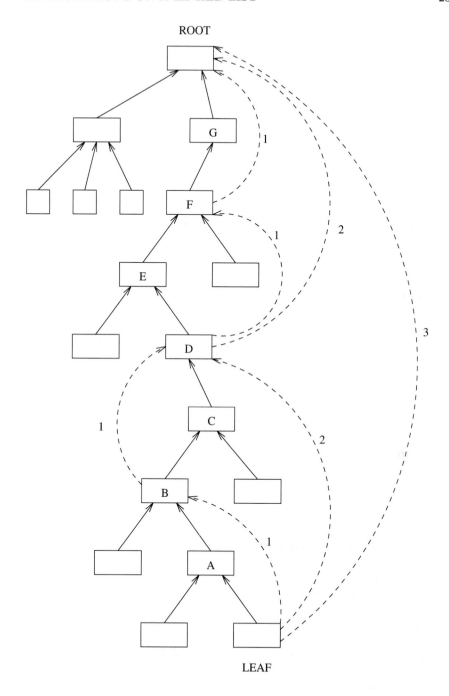

Figure 6.1: Pointer jumping on a tree.

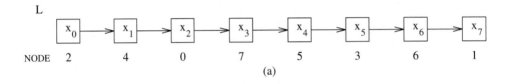

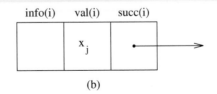

Figure 6.2: (a) A linked list and (b) the format of each of its nodes.

Figure 6.3: Linked list after prefix computation on *val* field.

3. Each node i holds in its value field $val(i)$ a datum x_j. Here also, the index j of x_j is for illustration purposes only: It allows us to distinguish among the data held by the different nodes. Thus, x_j is just a number, and there is no way of telling that it is the $(j+1)$st element in an ordered list of numbers x_0, x_1, x_2, and so on. Why then are the x's indexed in Fig. 6.2(a) in the order in which they appear in L? Again, this is just an artifact that simplifies the presentation, as will become apparent shortly.

6.2.1 Prefix Computation

Given a linked list L as shown in Fig. 6.2(a), it is required to perform the prefix computation

$$x_0, \quad x_0 \circ x_1, \quad x_0 \circ x_1 \circ x_2, \quad \ldots,$$

for some operation $\circ$, as shown in Fig. 6.3, where the symbol X_{ij} is used to denote $x_i \circ x_{i+1} \circ \cdots \circ x_j$.

In a sequential setting, all we are given is a pointer to the *head* of the list—that is, the address of the first node (node 2 in Fig. 6.2(a)). The prefix computation is then performed by a single traversal of L, and the time required is *linear* in the number of nodes in the list.

How is the problem to be solved in parallel? Assume that the linked list is stored in the shared memory of a PRAM. If all that we are given is a pointer to the

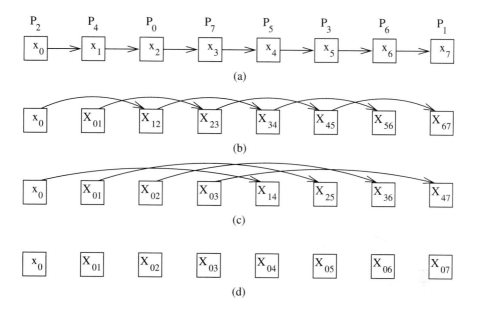

Figure 6.4: Prefix computation by pointer jumping: (a) Initially; (b) After one iteration; (c) After two iterations; (d) After three iterations.

head, then there is not much hope to improve on the running time of the sequential solution. In a typical parallel setting, however, it is quite likely that each node in L is "known" to a distinct processor; indeed, L itself may have been constructed in parallel, each processor contributing a node. In what follows, therefore, we assume that processor P_i is assigned node i and is in charge of that node throughout the computation: P_i "knows" the address of node i and can gain access to its contents in $O(1)$ time. By our earlier assumption, however, node i can appear anywhere in the list, and so P_i does not "know" its position relative to the other processors. Furthermore, no processor "knows" the number of nodes in L. A processor assignment for the list of Fig. 6.2(a) is shown in Fig. 6.4(a).

A parallel algorithm for prefix computation on L uses pointer jumping. In each iteration, a processor:

1. Uses ∘ to combine the value in the *val* field of its node with the value held in the *val* field of its successor's node.

2. Makes the *succ* field of its node equal to the *succ* field of its successor's node.

This is illustrated in Fig. 6.4 for the list of Fig. 6.2(a). It is easy to see that, except for the pointer jumping, the algorithm is essentially the same as the one described at the beginning of Section 4.2. Indeed, the similarity between Fig. 6.4 and Fig. 4.1

is remarkable. (Of course, in Fig. 4.1, the arrows do not represent pointers, but rather illustrate which values are combined.) One important difference between the present algorithm and that in Fig. 4.1 is that in the latter we knew exactly how many iterations would be executed, namely, $\log n$, since the size n of the input sequence was known. How does the present algorithm terminate, given that the processors do not "know" initially how many of them there are? From Fig. 6.4(d), it is clear that no more computations are required once all pointer fields are equal to *nil*. A simple way for testing this is to use a location in memory holding a Boolean variable *finished*. At the end of each iteration, all processors whose node's *succ* field is not *nil* use a **COMMON CW** to write the value **false** in *finished*. At the beginning of each iteration, all processors read *finished* and, if it is **false**, determine that another iteration is required. This way, all processors will "know" simultaneously when the algorithm has terminated.

The algorithm is given next as algorithm PRAM LINKED LIST PREFIX. In it, it is assumed that the PRAM has N processors, where $N \geq |L|$. In case $N > |L|$, those processors not in charge of a node of L are assumed to be associated with a node whose pointer field is *nil*. Note that in order to protect the *succ* fields, the algorithm applies pointer jumping to a subfield *next* of the *info* field, where $next(i)$ is initialized to $succ(i)$ for all nodes i.

Algorithm PRAM LINKED LIST PREFIX

Step 1: for all i **do in parallel**
$\qquad next(i) \leftarrow succ(i)$
$\quad$ **end for**
Step 2: *finished* $\leftarrow$ **false**
Step 3: while not *finished* **do**
$\qquad$ (3.1) *finished* $\leftarrow$ **true**
$\qquad$ (3.2) **for all** i **do in parallel**
$\qquad\qquad$ (i) **if** $next(i) \neq nil$
$\qquad\qquad\qquad$ **then** (a) $val(next(i)) \leftarrow val(i) \circ val(next(i))$
$\qquad\qquad\qquad\qquad\quad$ (b) $next(i) \leftarrow next(next(i))$
$\qquad\qquad$ **end if**
$\qquad\qquad$ (ii) **if** $next(i) \neq nil$
$\qquad\qquad\qquad$ **then** *finished* $\overset{\text{COMMON}}{\longleftarrow}$ **false**
$\qquad\qquad$ **end if**
$\qquad$ **end for**
$\quad$ **end while.** ∎

Analysis. Steps 1 and 2 and each iteration of Step 3 require constant time. Since the number of final answers doubles after each iteration of Step 3, the number of iterations is the logarithm of the number of nodes in L. Assuming that this number is n, algorithm PRAM LINKED LIST PREFIX runs in $t(n) = O(\log n)$ time and uses $p(n) = n$ processors.

6.2.2   List Ranking

Another useful computation is that of determining, in a given linked list L, the location of each node in the list—in particular, its distance from the end of the list. For example, in Fig. 6.2(a), node 2 is at distance 7 from the end of the list (since this many pointers need to be traversed to reach the node with a *nil* pointer). Specifically, for each node i for which $succ(i) \neq nil$, we wish to compute

$$rank(i) = rank(succ(i)) + 1.$$

Of course, if $succ(i) = nil$, then $rank(i) = 0$.

Sequentially, this problem is solved as follows:

1. Beginning from the *head*, traverse the list, reversing each pointer, until the end of the list is reached.

2. Now traverse the list in the opposite direction, assigning a rank to each node visited.

If L has n nodes, then this RAM algorithm takes $O(n)$ time. Equivalently, we could traverse L from *head* to *tail* to find out how many nodes it has and then once again from *head* to *tail* to assign a rank to each node.

On a PRAM with one processor per node, the ranks can be computed quite simply by using the prefix "sums" algorithm presented in the previous section:

1. For all i, if $succ(i) \neq nil$, then $val(i) \leftarrow 1$; else $val(i) \leftarrow 0$.

2. For all i, let the *succ* field of $succ(i)$ point to node i. This reverses the list, and the old *head* now has a pointer equal to *nil*. Copies of the pointers are used, as in the previous section, in order to avoid modifying the *succ* fields.

3. Algorithm PRAM LINKED LIST PREFIX is now applied to the new linked list, with operation ∘ taken as +: The *val* field of each node now contains the node's rank in L.

This is illustrated in Fig. 6.5. The first two steps take constant time, and the third step is a prefix computation. The algorithm therefore requires $O(\log n)$ time for a linked list of n nodes. Since n processors are used, this yields a cost of $O(n \log n)$, which is not optimal in view of the $O(n)$ RAM algorithm described earlier.

It is interesting to note that the same performance (i.e., $O(\log n)$ time using n processors) can be obtained by a different parallel algorithm that does not perform any pointer reversal. This algorithm, whose structure is similar to that of algorithm PRAM LINKED LIST PREFIX is given next as algorithm PRAM LIST RANKING. For clarity, we use *rank* in the algorithm to refer to the *val* field of each node.

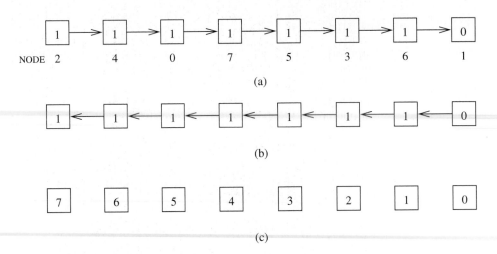

Figure 6.5: List ranking using prefix computation: (a) Initially; (b) After list reversal; (c) After prefix computation.

Algorithm PRAM LIST RANKING

Step 1: for all i **do in parallel**

    (1.1) **if** $succ(i) \neq nil$

        then $rank(i) \leftarrow 1$

        else $rank(i) \leftarrow 0$

        end if

    (1.2) $next(i) \leftarrow succ(i)$

    end for

Step 2: $finished \leftarrow$ **false**

Step 3: while not $finished$ **do**

    (3.1) $finished \leftarrow$ **true**

    (3.2) **for all** i **do in parallel**

        (i) **if** $next(i) \neq nil$

            then (a) $rank(i) \leftarrow rank(i) + rank(next(i))$

                  (b) $next(i) \leftarrow next(next(i))$

            end if

        (ii) **if** $succ(i) \neq nil$

            then $finished \xleftarrow{\text{COMMON}}$ **false**

            end if

        end for

    end while. ∎

The algorithm is illustrated in Fig. 6.6.

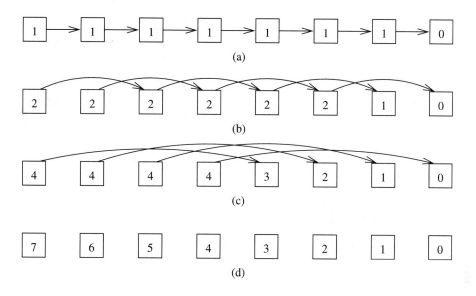

Figure 6.6: Algorithm PRAM LIST RANKING in action: (a) At the end of Step 1; (b) After one iteration of Step 3; (c) After two iterations of Step 3; (d) After three iterations of Step 3.

A variant of the problem occurs when it is required to compute the distance of each node in L from the *beginning* of the list—that is, the sequence number of the node in the list; this is called the *list-sequencing problem*. In this case, a simple traversal of the list (without pointer reversal) suffices sequentially. In parallel, the problem is solved using prefix sums (also without pointer reversal) or by reversing the pointers and using algorithm PRAM LIST RANKING. Note that if L has n nodes, then the sequence number of node i is $n - rank(i) - 1$.

In the preceding discussion, we used an algorithm for prefix computation to solve the list-ranking and list-sequencing problems. It should be easy to see that the converse is also true. Suppose that we assign $val(i)$ to $rank(i)$ and replace $+$ with $\circ$ in algorithm PRAM LIST RANKING. The latter applied to L (with pointers reversed) is equivalent to prefix computation. If the pointers are not reversed, then the result would be a *suffix* computation; that is, the resulting values would be

$$x_0 \circ x_1 \circ \cdots \circ x_{n-1}, \quad x_1 \circ x_2 \circ \cdots \circ x_{n-1}, \quad \ldots, \quad x_{n-1},$$

assuming that L has n nodes.

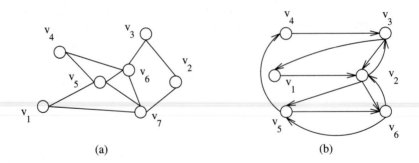

Figure 6.7: (a) An undirected and (b) a directed graph.

6.3 EULER TOURS AND THEIR APPLICATIONS

In Chapter 4, we showed how prefix computation on an array can be used to obtain efficient parallel algorithms to solve problems in a variety of different applications. The same is true of prefix computation on a linked list. This section shows how prefix computation, coupled with another effective computation known as the *Euler tour* method, can be used to address a variety of problems defined on trees. Our treatment begins with some definitions from graph theory, followed by an algorithm for computing an Euler tour in a tree. Several applications are then described.

6.3.1 Euler Tours

A graph $G = (V, E)$ is a set of vertices V connected by a set of edges E. If the edges have no orientation, then the graph is *undirected*; thus, the edge connecting two vertices v_1 and v_2 can be traversed in either way, from v_1 to v_2 or from v_2 to v_1. By contrast, a graph is *directed* if each edge has an orientation; thus, an edge connecting v_1 to v_2 can only be traversed from v_1 to v_2. A *path* in a graph is an ordered list of edges of the form $(v_i, v_j), (v_j, v_k), (v_k, v_l)$, and so on. If, for every pair of vertices v_p and v_q in an undirected graph, there is a path leading from v_p to v_q, then the graph is said to be *connected*. An undirected connected graph with seven vertices is shown in Fig. 6.7(a). A directed graph is connected if the undirected graph obtained from it by ignoring the edge orientations is connected. A directed connected graph with six vertices is shown in Fig. 6.7(b).

A *cycle* in a graph is a path that begins and ends at the same vertex. A cycle is said to be an *Euler tour* if every edge of the graph appears in the cycle exactly once. An Euler tour of the graph in Fig. 6.7(a) is $(v_3, v_2), (v_2, v_7), (v_7, v_1), (v_1, v_5),$ $(v_5, v_7), (v_7, v_6), (v_6, v_5), (v_5, v_4), (v_4, v_6), (v_6, v_3)$. An Euler tour of the graph in Fig. 6.7(b) is $(v_4, v_3), (v_3, v_1), (v_1, v_2), (v_2, v_3), (v_3, v_2), (v_2, v_5), (v_5, v_6), (v_6, v_2),$ $(v_2, v_6), (v_6, v_5), (v_5, v_4)$. The *degree* of a vertex in an undirected graph is the number of edges adjacent to the vertex. An undirected graph has an Euler tour

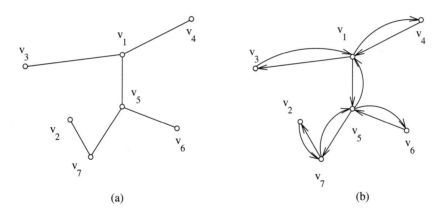

Figure 6.8: (a) A tree and (b) its directed version.

if every one of its vertices is connected to an even number of other vertices—that is, if each vertex has an even *degree*. Indeed, for every edge (v_i, v_j) of the tour, there must be some other edge (v_j, v_k) used by the tour to "exit" vertex v_j. The *in-degree* of a vertex v in a directed graph is the number of vertices connected to the given vertex—that is, the number of edges "entering" v. The *out-degree* of v is the number of vertices to which v is connected—that is, the number of edges "leaving" v. It is straightforward to see that a directed graph has an Euler tour if the in-degree of each vertex is equal to the out-degree of the vertex.

An undirected graph is a *tree* if it is connected and contains no cycles, as shown in Fig. 6.8(a). Clearly, a tree with n vertices has exactly $n - 1$ edges. Suppose that we replace each edge (v_i, v_j) in a tree with two *oriented* edges (v_i, v_j) and (v_j, v_i), as shown in Fig. 6.8(b). Then the resulting directed graph is guaranteed to have an Euler tour, since it satisfies the property that, for each vertex, the in-degree is equal to the out-degree. In what follows, we denote a directed tree such as the one in Fig. 6.8(b) by DT. An Euler tour defined on DT is denoted ET. Note that a DT with n vertices has $2n - 2$ edges, and hence ET is a sequence of $2n - 2$ edges.

6.3.2 Building an Euler Tour

Given a directed tree DT with n vertices, we now describe a parallel algorithm for computing an Euler tour ET of DT. The input to the algorithm is a data structure where DT is stored. The data structure consists of n linked lists, one for each vertex; the nodes of the linked list are the edges "leaving" that vertex. This data structure is illustrated in Fig. 6.9 for the DT of Fig. 6.8(b). A node ij in the linked list for vertex v_i consists of two fields, namely, a field *edge* containing edge (v_i, v_j) and a field *next* containing a pointer to the next node. As shown in Fig. 6.9, a pointer $head(v_i)$ gives access to the first node in the linked list for vertex v_i.

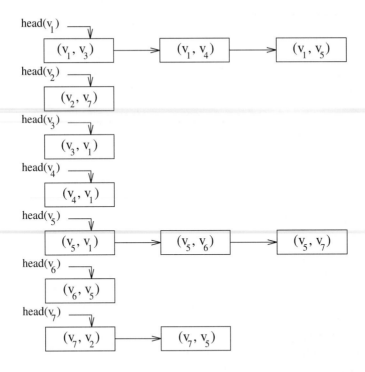

Figure 6.9: Data structure for a directed tree.

The purpose of an algorithm for computing ET is to arrange *all* the edges of DT in a *single* linked list such that each edge (v_i, v_j) is followed by an edge (v_j, v_k). Also, if the first edge in ET "leaves" some vertex v_l, then the last edge in ET "enters" v_l. Such a linked list for the DT of Fig. 6.8(b) is shown in Fig. 6.10 (in which the pointer from (v_5, v_1) to (v_1, v_3) is omitted). Note that each node in the linked list ET consists of two fields, namely, a field *edge* containing an edge and a field *succ* containing a pointer to the successor of the node.

On a PRAM, we assume the availability of $n - 1$ processors, with each processor P_{ij}, $i < j$, in charge of two edges of DT, namely, (v_i, v_j) and (v_j, v_i). The job of processor P_{ij} is to determine the position in ET of the two nodes holding (v_i, v_j) and (v_j, v_i), denoted by ij and ji, respectively. It does so by determining the *successor* of each of these two nodes in the linked list as follows: If, in the linked list for v_j, edge (v_j, v_i) is followed by some edge (v_j, v_k), then the successor of (v_i, v_j) in ET is (v_j, v_k). Otherwise—that is, if (v_j, v_i) is the *last* edge in the linked list for v_j—then the successor of (v_i, v_j) in ET is the *first* edge in the linked list of v_j. The successor of (v_j, v_i) in ET is determined similarly. Thus, we have the following rule:

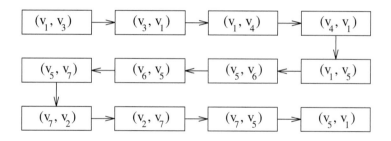

Figure 6.10: The Euler tour as a linked list.

Successor of (v_i, v_j)

    if $next(ji) = jk$
    then $succ(ij) \leftarrow jk$
    else $succ(ij) \leftarrow head(v_j)$
    end if

Successor of (v_j, v_i)

    if $next(ij) = im$
    then $succ(ji) \leftarrow im$
    else $succ(ji) \leftarrow head(v_i)$
    end if. ∎

Applying this rule to the linked lists of Fig. 6.9 gives the Euler tour of Fig. 6.10. (Note again that the pointer from (v_5, v_1) to (v_1, v_3) is omitted.) That this algorithm indeed builds an Euler tour (and not several small cycles) can be seen intuitively as follows: Suppose that the successor of (v_i, v_j) has been selected as (v_j, v_k). This means that in the linked list for v_j, (v_j, v_k) follows (v_j, v_i). Now the only way for (v_j, v_i) to be selected as the successor of (v_k, v_j) is that (v_j, v_i) and (v_j, v_k) are the first and last edges, respectively, in the linked list for v_j.

    Analysis.   The successor of each edge is found in constant time. Therefore, the algorithm builds an Euler tour ET of a directed tree DT with n vertices in constant time using $n - 1$ processors.

    Depth-First Traversal.   So far we have dealt with *unrooted* trees. In many situations, it is useful to designate a special vertex of a tree as its *root*. For example, we could choose vertex v_1 in Fig. 6.8(a) as the root of the tree. Vertices connected to the root are the root's *children*, and vertices connected to these are their children, and so on. A *depth-first* traversal of a rooted tree corresponds to visiting the vertices of the tree in the following order:

1. Visit the root.

2. Visit each of the subtrees of the root (recursively) in depth-first order.

This traversal is also known as a *preorder* traversal. A depth-first traversal of the tree in Fig. 6.8(a) is $v_1 v_3 v_4 v_5 v_6 v_7 v_2$.

An Euler tour of a rooted directed tree DT can be made to correspond to a depth-first traversal of DT by choosing an edge "leaving" the root as the first edge of ET. This is true because in an ET one returns to the root of a subtree only after all vertices in the subtree have been visited. The Euler tour in Fig. 6.10 is a depth-first traversal of the tree in Fig. 6.8(b), with v_1 as the root and (v_1, v_3) the first edge traversed.

Trees as Linked Lists. To conclude this discussion, suppose that v_r is the root of a directed tree DT and (v_r, v_j) is the first edge in an Euler tour ET of DT. Further, let (v_k, v_r) be the last edge in ET—that is, the edge whose successor is (v_r, v_j). In Fig. 6.10, the last edge in ET is (v_5, v_1). Now, the processor associated with node kr can set $succ(kr) = nil$. Finally, suppose that each node ij of ET is in the format given in Fig. 6.2(b), in which the *info* field stores the edge (v_i, v_j) and the *val* field is to be defined when required. With these changes, the linked list representing the ET, as shown in Fig. 6.10, is exactly in the form of linked list L of Fig. 6.2(a). Therefore, all the computations described for L in Section 6.2 can be applied to ET—in particular, prefix computation and list ranking.

We assume in what follows that a prefix sums computation has been applied to the linked list ET, with all the *val* fields initialized to 1. This gives the position in ET of each edge (v_i, v_j), denoted $pos(v_i, v_j)$ and stored in the *val* field of node ij. Thus, if (v_r, v_j) and (v_k, v_r) are the first and last edges in ET, respectively, then $pos(v_r, v_j) = 1$ and $pos(v_k, v_r) = 2n - 2$. In Fig. 6.10, $pos(v_1, v_3) = 1$ and $pos(v_5, v_1) = 12$. Clearly, computing the positions of the edges in ET requires $O(\log n)$ time and $O(n)$ processors.

6.3.3 Basic Tree Computations

In this section, we describe some simple computations on trees with n vertices that can be carried out efficiently in parallel using the Euler tour. The following terminology simplifies the presentation: For an edge (v_i, v_j) of the directed tree DT, if $pos(v_i, v_j) < pos(v_j, v_i)$, then (v_i, v_j) is called an *advance* edge; otherwise, (v_i, v_j) is called a *retreat* edge. In Fig. 6.10, $pos(v_5, v_7) = 8$ and $pos(v_7, v_5) = 11$; thus, (v_5, v_7) is an advance edge and (v_7, v_5) is a retreat edge.

Finding Parents. Suppose that we wish to determine the parent of each vertex v_j (other than the root) in a rooted directed tree. This can be easily accomplished by setting

$$parent(v_j) \leftarrow v_i$$

for each advance edge (v_i, v_j). Indeed, since $pos(v_i, v_j) < pos(v_j, v_i)$ in ET, this means that in a depth-first traversal of the tree, edge (v_i, v_j) is traversed first (from v_i to v_j), implying that v_i is v_j's parent. In Fig. 6.10, $parent(v_7) = v_5$. If v_r is the root, we can set $parent(v_r) \leftarrow nil$.

Enumerating Descendants. For every vertex v_j (other than the root) in a rooted directed tree, the number of descendants of v_j, including v_j itself, can be determined from

$$des(v_j) \leftarrow \frac{pos\ (v_j, parent(v_j)) - 1 - pos\ (parent(v_j), v_j)}{2} + 1.$$

This can be easily seen, since the number of descendants of v_j is the number of advance edges in the subtree rooted at v_j, plus one. These advance edges appear in the section of ET between the advance edge $(parent(v_j), v_j)$ and the retreat edge $(v_j, parent(v_j))$, each advance edge coupled with a retreat edge. For example, in the ET of Fig. 6.10, $pos(v_1, v_5) = 5$ and $pos(v_5, v_1) = 12$; the number of descendants of v_5 is $des(5) = ((11 - 5)/2) + 1 = 4$, as can be verified from Fig. 6.8(b). Note that if v_r is the root, then $des(v_r) \leftarrow n$.

Numbering the Vertices. Suppose that we wish to assign numbers to the vertices of a rooted tree corresponding to the order in which they are visited in a preorder traversal. As mentioned earlier, an Euler tour represents a preorder traversal of DT. Thus, the preorder number of a vertex v_j is the number of advance edges traversed before reaching v_j for the first time, plus one. This number can be computed as follows: First, we assign values to the *val* fields of ET. If (v_i, v_j) is an advance edge, then $val(ij) = 1$; otherwise, $val(ij) = 0$. We now perform a prefix sums computation over the *val* fields. Finally, if (v_i, v_j) is an advance edge, then

$$preorder(v_j) \leftarrow val(ij) + 1.$$

This is illustrated in Fig. 6.11(a) for the ET of Fig. 6.10. Note that if v_r is the root, then $preorder(v_r) \leftarrow 1$.

In a *postorder* traversal of a rooted tree (also known as a *bottom-up* traversal), the vertices are visited in the following order:

1. Visit each of the subtrees of the root (recursively) in postorder.

2. Visit the root.

In other words, a vertex is visited only after all of its descendants have been visited. A postorder traversal of the tree in Fig. 6.8(a), in which v_1 is the root, is $v_3v_4v_6v_2v_7v_5v_1$. We can use ET to assign numbers to the vertices of a rooted tree corresponding to the order in which they are visited in a postorder traversal. In ET, the edge $(v_i, parent(v_i))$ is traversed after all the descendants of v_i have been traversed. Thus, the postorder number of a vertex v_i is the number of retreat edges traversed before reaching v_i for the last time, plus one. This number can be computed as follows: First, assign values to *val* fields of ET. If (v_i, v_j) is a retreat edge, then $val(ij) = 1$; otherwise, $val(ij) = 0$. We now perform a prefix sums computation over the *val* fields. Finally, if (v_i, v_j) is a retreat edge, then

$$postorder(v_i) \leftarrow val(ij).$$

EDGE (v_i, v_j)	(v_1, v_3)	(v_3, v_1)	(v_1, v_4)	(v_4, v_1)	(v_1, v_5)	(v_5, v_6)	(v_6, v_5)	(v_5, v_7)	(v_7, v_2)	(v_2, v_7)	(v_7, v_5)	(v_5, v_1)
val	1	0	1	0	1	1	0	1	1	0	0	0
PREFIX SUMS	1	1	2	2	3	4	4	5	6	6	6	6
PREORDER (v_j)	2		3		4	5		6	7			

(a)

EDGE (v_i, v_j)	(v_1, v_3)	(v_3, v_1)	(v_1, v_4)	(v_4, v_1)	(v_1, v_5)	(v_5, v_6)	(v_6, v_5)	(v_5, v_7)	(v_7, v_2)	(v_2, v_7)	(v_7, v_5)	(v_5, v_1)
val	0	1	0	1	0	0	1	0	0	1	1	1
PREFIX SUMS	0	1	1	2	2	2	3	3	3	4	5	6
POSTORDER (v_i)		1		2			3			4	5	6

(b)

Figure 6.11: Numbering the vertices of a tree in (a) preorder and (b) postorder.

This is illustrated in Fig. 6.11(b) for the *ET* of Fig. 6.10. Note that if v_r is the root, then $postorder(v_r) \leftarrow n$.

Evaluating Binary Relations. Two binary relations between vertices are "is a descendant of" and "is an ancestor of." For two vertices v_i and v_j, vertex v_i is an ancestor of vertex v_j (and hence, vertex v_j is a descendant of vertex v_i) if and only if the following inequalities hold simultaneously:

$$
\begin{aligned}
preorder(v_i) &\leq preorder(v_j) \\
preorder(v_j) &< preorder(v_i) + des(v_i).
\end{aligned}
$$

For example, in Fig. 6.8(b), vertex v_1 is an ancestor of vertex v_2, since $preorder(v_1) = 1$, $preorder(v_2) = 7$, and $des(v_1) = 7$, and hence,

$$
\begin{aligned}
preorder(v_1) &\leq preorder(v_2) \\
preorder(v_2) &< preorder(v_1) + des(v_1).
\end{aligned}
$$

On the other hand, vertex v_3 is not an ancestor of vertex v_5, since $preorder(v_3) = 2$, $preorder(v_5) = 4$, and $des(v_3) = 1$, and hence,

$$
preorder(v_5) > preorder(v_3) + des(v_3).
$$

If the preorder number and the number of descendants of each vertex are available, then the two binary relations can be readily evaluated.

EDGE (v_i, v_j)	(v_1, v_3)	(v_3, v_1)	(v_1, v_4)	(v_4, v_1)	(v_1, v_5)	(v_5, v_6)	(v_6, v_5)	(v_5, v_7)	(v_7, v_2)	(v_2, v_7)	(v_7, v_5)	(v_5, v_1)
val	-1	1	-1	1	-1	-1	1	-1	-1	1	1	1
SUFFIX SUMS	0	1	0	1	0	1	2	1	2	3	2	1
LEVEL (v_j)	1		1		1	2		2	3			

Figure 6.12: Computing levels of vertices in a tree.

Determining Levels of Vertices.   The *level* of a vertex in an undirected rooted tree is the number of unoriented edges on a shortest path from the root to the vertex. In an ET of a DT, the level of a vertex v_j equals the number of retreat edges minus the number of advance edges following the first occurrence of v_j in ET. We compute this level as follows: First, we assign values to the *val* fields of ET. If (v_j, v_i) is a retreat edge, then $val(ji) = 1$; otherwise, $val(ji) = -1$. A suffix sums computation is now performed over the *val* fields. Finally, if (v_i, v_j) is an advance edge, then

$$level(v_j) \leftarrow val(ij) + 1.$$

This is illustrated in Fig. 6.12 for the ET of Fig. 6.10. Note that if v_r is the root, then $level(v_r) \leftarrow 0$.

Analysis.   Let T be the rooted tree with n vertices for all of the problems of this section. Assuming that $pos(v_i, v_j)$ has already been computed for all edges of ET, $parent(v_j)$ and $des(v_j)$ can be computed in $O(1)$ time with $O(n)$ processors for all vertices of T. On the other hand, computing each of $preorder(v_j)$, $postorder(v_j)$, and $level(v_j)$, for all vertices v_j of T, involves a prefix type of computation and hence runs in $O(\log n)$ time using $O(n)$ processors. Given $preorder(v_i)$, $preorder(v_j)$, and $des(v_i)$, the question whether v_i is an ancestor of v_j can be answered in constant time using one processor.

6.3.4   Computing Minima

Suppose that each vertex in a rooted tree T with n vertices stores a certain (arbitrary) number. It is required to find, for each vertex v_i of T, the minimum (equivalently, the maximum) of all numbers stored in the subtree rooted at v_i. This problem can be easily solved by making each node other than the root point to its parent and then using pointer jumping. We present an alternative solution based on the Euler tour because of its general applicability to other problems and the fact that it allows us to describe the solution to another interesting problem, namely, the computation of interval minima.

Consider the sequence $S = \{s_1, s_2, \ldots, s_n\}$, where s_k is the number stored in

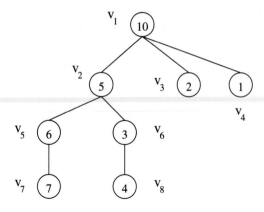

Figure 6.13: Tree for which minima are to be found.

some node v_i of the tree whose preorder number is k; that is,

$$k = preorder(v_i).$$

Thus, the subsequence of S containing the numbers stored in the subtree rooted at v_i is

$$\{s_k, s_{k+1}, \dots, s_{k+des(v_i)-1}\}.$$

Example 6.1 Consider the tree of Fig. 6.13, whose root is v_1. The number stored by each vertex is shown inside the vertex. A preorder traversal of the tree visits the vertices in the order $v_1 v_2 v_5 v_7 v_6 v_8 v_3 v_4$. Thus,

$$\{s_1, s_2, s_3, s_4, s_5, s_6, s_7, s_8\} = \{10, 5, 6, 7, 3, 4, 2, 1\}.$$

The numbers stored in the subtree rooted at v_2 appear in s_2, s_3, s_4, s_5, and s_6, since $preorder(v_2) = 2$ and $des(v_2) = 5$. □

A parallel algorithm for finding the minimum number stored in the tree rooted at v_i, for all v_i in T, proceeds as follows: The tree T is made into a directed tree DT for which an Euler tour ET is computed. From ET, the preorder number and the number of descendants of each vertex are obtained. We now know that the minimum number stored in the tree rooted at v_i is the minimum number in the sequence $\{s_k, s_{k+1}, \dots, s_l\}$, where $k = preorder(v_i)$ and $l = k + des(v_i) - 1$.

Since each vertex v_i generates a pair (k, l) as just defined, there are n such pairs and hence n subsequences of S. There are, therefore, n minima to be found, one per subsequence, or *interval*, of S. We now show how these minima are computed. We refer to this as the *interval minima* problem. For ease of presentation, we assume that n is a power of 2.

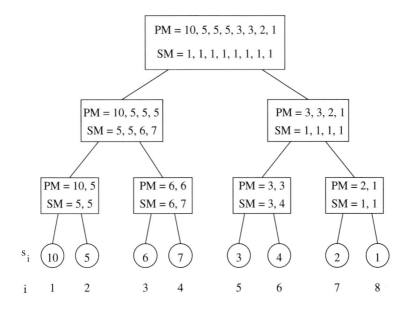

Figure 6.14: Tree for computing interval minima.

Recall that the prefix minima of a sequence $\{a_1, a_2, \ldots, a_n\}$ are given by a sequence $\{b_1, b_2, \ldots, b_n\}$, where $b_i = \min(a_1, a_2, \ldots, a_i)$, while the suffix minima are given by the sequence $\{d_1, d_2, \ldots, d_n\}$, where $d_i = \min(a_i, a_{i+1}, \ldots, a_n)$. We build a complete binary tree T' whose leaves are $s_1, s_2, \ldots, s_n$; that is, leaf i holds s_i (the leaves being numbered from left to right). Each internal (i.e., nonleaf) vertex x contains two subsequences, namely, the prefix minima and the suffix minima of the values held by leaves in the subtree rooted at x. This is shown in Fig. 6.14 for the tree in Fig. 6.13. Inside each internal vertex, the two sequences PM and SM give the prefix minima and suffix minima, respectively.

The array PM in each vertex of T' is constructed by first concatenating the two PM arrays of its children. In the resulting array PM, let u be the last element in the first half of the array. Each element v in the second half is now replaced with $\min(u, v)$. Similarly, the array SM in each vertex is constructed by concatenating the two SM arrays of its children. In the resulting array SM, let u be the first element in the second half. Each element v in the first half is now replaced with $\min(u, v)$.

Given two indices k and l in the sequence S, the information in the complete binary tree T' allows the minimum of the sequence $\{s_k, s_{k+1}, \ldots, s_l\}$, to be found as follows: Let w be the lowest common ancestor in T' of the two leaves k and l, holding s_k and s_l, respectively; in other words, w is that ancestor of both k and l which is the farthest away from the root of T'. Suppose that x and y are the left and right children, respectively, of w. Then the minimum of the sequence $\{s_k,$ $s_{k+1}, \ldots, s_l\}$, is the smaller of two numbers:

1. The suffix minimum corresponding to k in the *SM* array of x.

2. The prefix minimum corresponding to l in the *PM* array of y.

Example 6.2 For the tree T' of Fig. 6.14, let $k = 2$ and $l = 6$; that is, we wish to find the minimum of the sequence $\{s_2, s_3, s_4, s_5, s_6\} = \{5, 6, 7, 3, 4\}$. The lowest common ancestor of leaves 2 and 6 is the root of T'. In the *SM* array of the root's left child, the suffix minimum corresponding to leaf 2 is 5. In the *PM* array of the root's right child, the prefix minimum corresponding to leaf 6 is 3. Therefore, the minimum sought is $\min(5, 3) = 3$. Note that this is the minimum number stored in the subtree rooted at v_2 in Fig. 6.13. $\square$

The only detail left is how vertex w, the lowest common ancestor of the two leaves k and l, is found. Since each internal vertex of T' "knows" the range of leaves in its subtree, we can begin at the root and descend the tree until the furthest vertex from the root is reached, whose subtree contains the leaves i, $i + 1$, $\ldots$, j, where $i \leq k$ and $l \leq j$.

Analysis.   On a PRAM with n processors, the preorder numbers of all the vertices of T can be found in $O(\log n)$ time, as shown in Section 6.3.3. The tree T' has n leaves and hence $\log n$ levels. In each level, all arrays *PM* and *SM* are computed in constant time with n processors: An array *PM* (or *SM*) of size m at a certain vertex requires $m/2$ processors to copy an array *PM* of $m/2$ elements from the left child of the vertex and $m/2$ processors to copy an array *PM* of $m/2$ elements from the right child; this is followed by one comparison and an update involving the last $m/2$ elements of *PM*. For each interval $[k, l]$, one processor can find the lowest common ancestor w of leaves k and l in $O(\log n)$ time, beginning from the root. This is followed by one comparison between elements from the left and right children of w, which can be done in constant time. The overall time and processor requirements are therefore

$$\begin{aligned} t(n) &= O(\log n), \\ p(n) &= n, \end{aligned}$$

for a cost of $O(n \log n)$.

6.3.5   Breadth-First Traversal

In many applications, it is required to traverse the vertices of a rooted tree T in the order of their distance from the root. Vertices at the same level are visited from left to right. For example, the vertices of the tree in Fig. 6.15, whose root is v_2, would be traversed in the following order: $v_2 v_1 v_5 v_7 v_4 v_6 v_3 v_8 v_9$. This is called *breadth-first* traversal. We next describe an algorithm that produces the vertices of a tree in breadth-first order.

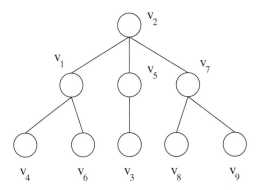

Figure 6.15: A tree to be traversed in breadth-first order.

The first step is to compute an Euler tour of the DT obtained from T. Such a tour ET for the tree of Fig. 6.15 is given in Fig. 6.16. We now assign a level to each edge in ET: If (v_i, v_j) is an advance edge, then its level is equal to $level(v_j)$; otherwise, the level of (v_i, v_j) is $level(v_i)$. This is illustrated in Fig. 6.16. The third step is to identify the leftmost and rightmost edges at each level in ET and delete them therefrom. Note that the first and last edges of ET are the leftmost and rightmost edges, respectively, in level 1. In order to find the leftmost and rightmost edges at each level, we perform a prefix maxima computation and a suffix maxima computation on the edge levels. This gives the sequences $\{a_1, a_2, \ldots, a_{2n-2}\}$ and $\{b_1, b_2, \ldots, b_{2n-2}\}$, respectively. Then, the ith edge in ET, $1 < i < 2n - 2$, is a leftmost edge if $a_i - a_{i-1} > 0$ and a rightmost edge if $b_{i-1} - b_i > 0$. These edges, marked '∗' in Fig. 6.16, are removed from consideration.

We now assign a left parenthesis to each remaining retreat edge and a right parenthesis to each remaining advance edge. This is illustrated in the figure. By matching each left parenthesis with a right parenthesis, we associate with each retreat edge an advance edge called its *mate*. For the deleted edges, mates are defined as follows: If (v_i, v_j) is a rightmost edge at level k, then its mate is the leftmost edge at level $k + 1$, if such an edge exists. The *mate* function is illustrated in Fig. 6.17.

A linked list L of the vertices is now created as follows: A node of L is created for each vertex v_i, and the *info* field of the node stores v_i. Suppose that the advance edge (v_i, v_j) is the mate of the retreat edge (v_k, v_l); in L, $succ(v_k) = v_j$. If (v_i, v_j) is the first edge in ET, then $succ(v_i) = v_j$. This is illustrated in Fig. 6.18 for the tree in Fig. 6.15. Note that since (v_2, v_1) is the first edge in ET, we have $succ(v_2) = v_1$.

The final step is to assign breadth-first numbers to the vertices. This is accomplished by performing a prefix sums computation on the *val* fields of L, where all *val* fields are set to 1 initially. The resulting values in the *val* fields are the breadth-first numbers of the vertices. For example, in Fig. 6.18, the breadth-first number of v_7 is 4, and that of v_3 is 7.

EULER TOUR	LEVEL	LEFTMOST EDGES	RIGHTMOST EDGES	PARENTHESIS SEQUENCE
(v_2, v_1)	1	*		
(v_1, v_4)	2	*		
(v_4, v_1)	2			(
(v_1, v_6)	2			)
(v_6, v_1)	2			(
(v_1, v_2)	1			(
(v_2, v_5)	1			)
(v_5, v_3)	2			)
(v_3, v_5)	2			(
(v_5, v_2)	1			(
(v_2, v_7)	1			)
(v_7, v_8)	2			)
(v_8, v_7)	2			(
(v_7, v_9)	2			)
(v_9, v_7)	2		*	
(v_7, v_2)	1		*	

Figure 6.16: Breadth-first traversal using the Euler tour.

EDGE	(v_4, v_1)	(v_6, v_1)	(v_1, v_2)	(v_3, v_5)	(v_5, v_2)	(v_8, v_7)	(v_9, v_7)	(v_7, v_2)
MATE	(v_1, v_6)	(v_5, v_3)	(v_2, v_5)	(v_7, v_8)	(v_2, v_7)	(v_7, v_9)	NIL	(v_1, v_4)

Figure 6.17: The mates of edges in the Euler tour.

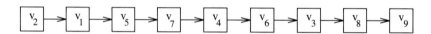

Figure 6.18: Linked list corresponding to breadth-first traversal.

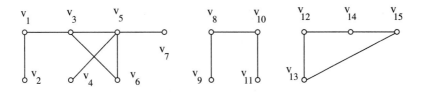

Figure 6.19: A graph with three connected components.

Analysis. For a tree with n vertices, all steps of the preceding algorithm can be executed using n processors in $O(\log n)$ time. In particular, note that parenthesis matching is performed using GPC. (See Problem 4.31.)

6.4   COMPUTING CONNECTED COMPONENTS

Let $G = (V, E)$ be an undirected graph. A *subgraph* $G' = (V', E')$ of G is a graph such that $V' \subseteq V$ and $E' \subseteq E$. As defined in the previous section, G' is connected if there is a path between every pair of its vertices. A *connected component* of a graph G is a connected subgraph C of G of maximum size. In other words, C is not a subgraph of a connected subgraph of G with more vertices. A graph G with three connected components is shown in Fig. 6.19.

The problem we examine in this section is that of identifying the connected components of G, where the latter is given as a list of edges. Due to its many applications, this problem occupies a central place in algorithmic graph theory in general and in parallel computation in particular.

Sequentially, the problem is solved by a searching and labeling approach. The search (which could use a depth-first or breadth-first traversal) begins at an arbitrary vertex v of G. All vertices that can be reached from v are given the label v to identify them as a connected component. When no more vertices can be reached from v, a new search begins from an unlabeled vertex w, and all vertices that can be reached from w are then given the label w. This continues until all connected components have been found. Assuming that $|V| = n$ and $|E| = m$, the approach requires $O(n + m)$ time.

In parallel, a more efficient approach is obtained using the pointer-jumping technique. This approach is based on building rooted directed trees from the vertices of G such that each vertex points to its parent in the tree. At any time during execution of the algorithm, all the vertices in a rooted tree belong to a connected subgraph of G.

Initially, the algorithm begins with the set of vertices V, each vertex representing a separate tree: The vertex is a root with no children and points to itself. These

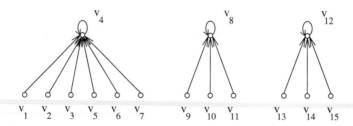

Figure 6.20: Three bushes, each representing a connected component.

n trees are then merged to form larger trees, and the process is repeated several times until the trees can no longer be merged; at this point, the vertices in each tree represent one connected component of G. The pointer-jumping technique is used after each merge to reduce the depth of the trees, so that when the algorithm terminates, each tree has depth 1, and all of its vertices point to the root. Each of these trees is called a *bush*. The connected components of the graph in Fig. 6.19, each represented as a bush, are shown in Fig. 6.20. It is worth noting here that the pointer from each root to itself does not count as a cycle and hence does not violate the condition that a tree has no cycles.

6.4.1   Merging Directed Rooted Trees

We now explain the ideas behind, and the method used in, merging two or more trees into one. Let $parent(v_i)$ denote the parent of vertex v_i in a directed tree constructed by the algorithm. Consider two such trees T_x and T_y, as shown in Fig. 6.21(a), where v_i is the root of T_x and v_j is some vertex in T_y. We say that T_x has been *merged with* T_y to yield a tree T_z if v_j is made the parent of v_i—that is, if $parent(v_i) \leftarrow v_j$, as shown in Fig. 6.21(b).

A number of conditions, however, need to be satisfied before the merging process is fully specified:

1. The vertices of the new tree T_z must form a connected subgraph of G.

2. The merge should introduce no cycles: Whenever two or more trees are merged, the result must be a *tree*.

3. It should be possible to execute the merge quickly—preferably in constant time.

4. The merge should be such that the total number of iterations required is small.

In order to satisfy the first condition, we insist that when two trees T_x and T_y are to be merged, there should be an edge (v_k, v_l) in E connecting a vertex v_k in

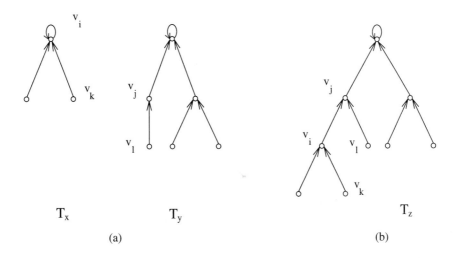

$$T_x \qquad\qquad T_y \qquad\qquad\qquad\qquad T_z$$

(a) (b)

Figure 6.21: Merging directed rooted trees: (a) Two trees to be merged; (b) Tree resulting from merging them.

T_x to a vertex v_l in T_y. The second condition is satisfied by first defining a total order $\prec$ on the vertices: We say that $v_j \prec v_i$, for any two distinct vertices of V, if and only if $j < i$. Then we insist that whenever two trees T_x and T_y are merged as in Fig. 6.21, such that the parent of v_i becomes v_j, it must be the case that T_x is a bush and that $v_j \prec v_i$. If one or the other of these two requirements is not met, then a cycle may be introduced when T_x is merged with T_y and, simultaneously, T_y is merged with T_x. These two situations are illustrated, for an arbitrary set of trees, in Fig. 6.22(a) (where T_y is not a bush) and Fig. 6.22(b) (where $v_5 \not\prec v_3$), respectively.

Let (v_k, v_l) be an edge in E such that $v_k \in T_x$ and $v_l \in T_y$. Clearly, T_x and T_y must be merged. This can be done in constant time if we insist that v_k be a root or the child of a root. All the vertices of a bush satisfy this condition; therefore, by requiring that T_x be a bush, the third condition is satisfied.

While guaranteeing that no cycles will be formed, the requirement that T_x be a bush and $v_j \prec v_i$ is too restrictive, and in the worst case certain graphs will force the algorithm to execute $\Omega(n)$ iterations (i.e., one vertex is merged in each iteration). In order to avoid this situation and reduce the number of iterations required by the algorithm, we introduce a second merge step: Here, for an edge (v_k, v_l) in E such that $v_k \in T_x$ and $v_l \in T_y$, where T_x is a bush different from T_y, T_x is merged with T_y; that is, $parent(v_i) \leftarrow v_j$, but it is not necessarily the case that $v_j \prec v_i$. This means that we now have two distinct merging steps, executed in the following order, in each iteration:

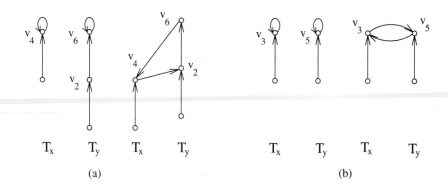

Figure 6.22: Incorrect merging of trees: (a) T_y is not a bush; (b) $v_5 \not\prec v_3$.

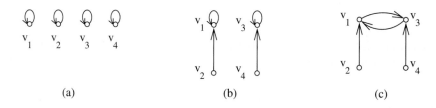

Figure 6.23: Second merge step creating a cycle: (a) Initially; (b) After first merge step; (c) After second merge step.

1. **If** $(v_k, v_l) \in E$ **and** v_k is in a bush **and** $parent(v_l) \prec parent(v_k)$
   then $parent(parent(v_k)) \leftarrow parent(v_l)$.

2. **If** $(v_k, v_l) \in E$ **and** v_k is in a bush **and** $parent(v_l) \neq parent(v_k)$
   then $parent(parent(v_k)) \leftarrow parent(v_l)$.

The first merge step allows a bush to be merged with another bush or with a nonbush without creating any cycles. The second merge step allows a bush to be merged with a nonbush; no cycles are created here either, since a nonbush is never merged with a bush. However, because we begin with n isolated vertices, each representing a tree, the second merge step may merge two bushes *in the first iteration*, thus creating a cycle, as shown in Fig. 6.23, for some arbitrary graph of four vertices.

Creating such a cycle can be easily circumvented by associating each vertex v_i initially with a fictitious vertex v_i' such that $parent(v_i') \leftarrow v_i$. We are now guaranteed to begin the algorithm with n bushes. If any two of these are eligible for merging, this would be done during the first merging step, which guarantees that no cycles

Figure 6.24: A tree that is not a bush.

are created. Since, in addition, the first merging step itself never generates any new bushes, it follows that at no time during execution of the algorithm are two bushes ever merged in the second merging step.

Finally, note that for bush T_x, there may be several edges $(v_k, v_l) \in E$ satisfying the condition in the first or second merge step. If so, *one* of these is chosen arbitrarily to merge T_x with another tree.

6.4.2 A Parallel Algorithm

As explained in the previous section, when a tree T_x is to be merged with a tree T_y, we require that T_x be a bush. Therefore, when an edge $(v_k, v_l) \in E$ has been identified whose endpoints are in distinct trees T_x and T_y, respectively, it is important to be able to check quickly whether v_k belongs to a bush. Recall that in a bush every vertex points directly to the root, and the root points to itself; in other words, the parent of each vertex (including the root) is also its "grandparent." As shown in Fig. 6.24, all vertices in the tree T_x, except the root and its children, can tell that T_x is not a bush using the test

$$parent(v_i) = parent(parent(v_i))?$$

The root and its children can also be informed that T_x is not a bush immediately following this test: Every vertex v_i for which $parent(v_i) \neq parent(parent(v_i))$ informs its parent and grandparent that they are not in a bush. The following algorithm takes as input the *parent* information for all vertices and creates an array *bush*, where $bush(v_i) = $ **true** if vertex v_i is in a bush; otherwise, $bush(v_i) = $ **false**.

Algorithm PRAM BUSH (*parent*)

   for $i = 1$ **to** n **do in parallel**
     (1) $bush(v_i) \leftarrow$ **true**
     (2) **if** $parent(v_i) \neq parent(parent(v_i))$
       then (2.1) $bush(v_i) \leftarrow$ **false**
           (2.2) $bush(parent(v_i)) \overset{\text{COMMON}}{\longleftarrow}$ **false**
           (2.3) $bush(parent(parent(v_i))) \overset{\text{COMMON}}{\longleftarrow}$ **false**
     end if
     (3) $bush(v_i) \leftarrow bush(parent(v_i))$
   end for. ∎

In algorithm PRAM BUSH, if v_r is the root of a nonbush, then:

1. Step (2.2) sets *bush* to **false** for the children of v_r (provided that they have children of their own).

2. Step (2.3) sets $bush(v_r)$ to **false**.

3. Step 3 sets *bush* to **false** for those children of v_r without children of their own.

4. A **COMMON CW** is used, since several children may be setting *bush* for a parent or grandparent simultaneously. (**ARBITRARY CW** may also be used.)

The algorithm requires n processors and runs in constant time.

We are now ready to present the main parallel algorithm for computing the connected components of an undirected graph $G = (V, E)$ with n vertices and m edges. The graph is assumed to be given as a list of edges in arbitrary order. Since the edges have no orientation, each edge appears in the list twice: An edge between v_i and v_j appears as (v_i, v_j) and (v_j, v_i). The algorithm produces as output the connected components of G, each expressed as a bush.

Algorithm PRAM CONNECTED COMPONENTS

   Step 1: for $i = 1$ **to** n **do in parallel**
         (1.1) $parent(v_i) \leftarrow v_i$
         (1.2) $parent(v_i') \leftarrow v_i$
       end for
   Step 2: *finished* $\leftarrow$ **false**
   Step 3: while not *finished* **do**
         (3.1) Algorithm PRAM BUSH (*parent*)
         (3.2) **for all** $(v_k, v_l) \in E$ **do in parallel**
             if $bush(v_k)$ **and** $parent(v_l) \prec parent(v_k)$
             then $parent(parent(v_k)) \overset{\text{ARBITRARY}}{\longleftarrow} parent(v_l)$
             end if
         end for

(3.3) Algorithm PRAM BUSH (*parent*)

(3.4) **for all** $(v_k, v_l) \in E$ **do in parallel**

    if $bush(v_k)$ **and** $parent(v_k) \neq parent(v_l)$

    then $parent(parent(v_k)) \xleftarrow{\text{ARBITRARY}} parent(v_l)$

    end if

   end for

(3.5) *finished* ← **true**

(3.6) **for** $i = 1$ **to** n **do in parallel**

    if $parent(parent(v_i)) \neq parent(v_i)$

    then (i) $parent(v_i) \leftarrow parent(parent(v_i))$

        (ii) *finished* $\xleftarrow{\text{COMMON}}$ **false**

    end if

   end for

end while. ■

Remarks. The loop in Step 3 is repeated as long as there are trees that are not bushes. Clearly, no new bushes are created in the merging Steps (3.2) and (3.4). Every time a new bush is produced by the pointer-jumping step, Step (3.6), a new iteration is required. It may be worth pointing out that pointer jumping never introduces new cycles. Also, note that **ARBITRARY CW** is used in Steps (3.2) and (3.4): Of the several trees to which the bush containing v_k can be merged, one is selected arbitrarily. Similarly, a **COMMON CW** is used in Step (3.6) to update the value of *finished*. (**ARBITRARY CW** could also be used.) Finally, note that Step (3.6) is executed as well for the fictitious vertices v_i'; the corresponding statements are omitted for simplicity, as they are inconsequential after the first iteration of Step 3.

Correctness. In order to show that the algorithm works correctly—that is, that when it terminates and returns a set of bushes, each bush is a complete connected component—we need the following simple observation: A bush T_i that exists at the end of Step (3.4) is a complete connected component. Clearly, T_i must have been created during the previous iteration by the pointer-jumping step, Step (3.6), since neither Step (3.2) nor Step (3.4) creates new bushes. If T_i were not a complete connected component, there would be an edge (v_k, v_l) in E connecting one of its vertices v_k to a vertex v_l in another tree T_j. But then T_i would have been merged with T_j in either of the two merging steps and would no longer be a bush.

Example 6.3 Consider the graph of Fig. 6.19, consisting of 15 vertices, 14 edges, and three connected components. Step 1 of algorithm PRAM CONNECTED COMPONENTS creates the bushes in Fig. 6.25(a). In the first iteration of Step 3, four rooted trees are created by Step (3.2), as shown in Fig. 6.25(b). Note here that the bush rooted at v_6 could have been merged with either the bush rooted at v_3 or the bush rooted at v_5, since both (v_6, v_5) and (v_6, v_3) are edges of E; the choice shown in Fig. 6.25(b) was made by the **ARBITRARY CW**. The same is true of the bush

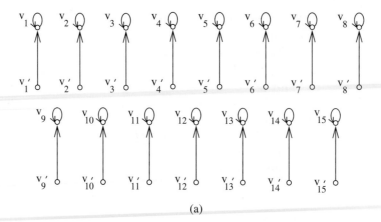

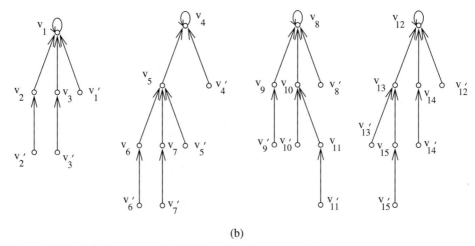

(b)

Figure 6.25: (a) Step 1 and (b) Step (3.2) of algorithm PRAM CONNECTED COMPONENTS.

rooted at v_5, which could have been merged with the bush rooted at v_3 instead of that rooted at v_4. Since none of the trees resulting from Step (3.2) is a bush, Step (3.4) does nothing. In Step (3.6), pointer jumping yields the trees in Fig. 6.26.

In the second iteration, there are two edges in E, namely, (v_3, v_5) and (v_3, v_6), that could be used to merge the bush rooted at v_1 with the tree rooted at v_4; however, since $v_4 \not\prec v_1$, the merge is postponed until Step (3.4), as shown in Fig. 6.27. The ensuing pointer jumping yields the three bushes illustrated in Fig. 6.28. In the third iteration, no further merging takes place, and consequently, no pointer jumping is required. Since all trees are now bushes, the algorithm terminates in the next iteration and returns the bushes shown in Fig. 6.20 (in which the fictitious vertices, no longer needed, are not shown). $\square$

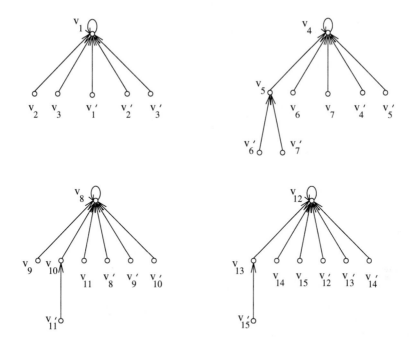

Figure 6.26: Step (3.6) of algorithm PRAM CONNECTED COMPONENTS.

Analysis. Each of Steps 1, (3.1), (3.3), and (3.6) requires n processors, while Steps (3.2) and (3.4) require m processors each. The algorithm therefore uses $\max(n, m)$ processors. Each of Steps 1, 2, and (3.1) through (3.6) takes constant time. It follows that the algorithm's running time is a function of the number of iterations of Step 3. We derive this result as follows:

1. The *height* of a rooted tree is the number of edges separating the root from the farthest leaf. Let h be the height of a nonbush T_i before the pointer-jumping step, Step (3.6). After pointer jumping, the height of T_i is $h/2$ for h even and $(h+1)/2$ for h odd. The worst case occurs when $h = 3$, where the new height is 2—that is, $2h/3$. Thus, at worst, the height of T_i after pointer jumping is $2h/3$.

2. Now, let C be a connected component of G, and let $h_C(i)$ denote the sum of the heights of all the trees containing the vertices of C at the end of the ith iteration of Step 3, for $i \geq 0$. Clearly, $h_C(i) < n$ for all C and i, since G has n vertices in all. In particular, $h_C(0) < n$. For $i \geq 1$, if all the vertices of C were not in a single bush at the beginning of the ith iteration, then we would have

$$h_C(i) \leq \frac{2}{3} h_C(i-1).$$

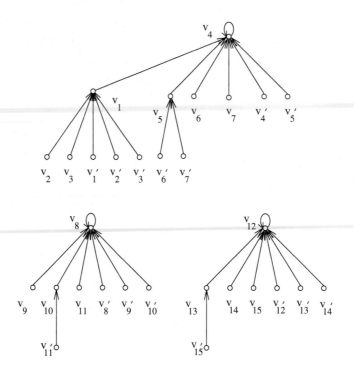

Figure 6.27: Step (3.4) of algorithm PRAM CONNECTED COMPONENTS.

To see this, note that during any iteration, when two trees T_x and T_y are merged, the height of the resulting tree is at most the sum of the heights of T_x and T_y. After pointer jumping, the height of each tree, and hence the sum of the heights, is at most two-thirds of its previous value.

3. The preceding recurrence on $h_C(i)$ allows us to write

$$\left(\frac{3}{2}\right)^i h_C(i) \le h_C(0).$$

Suppose that the vertices of C are all in one bush after the jth iteration; that is, $h_C(j) = 1$. Then

$$\left(\frac{3}{2}\right)^j < n,$$

and $j < \log_{\frac{3}{2}} n$. This means that after $\log_{\frac{3}{2}} n$ iterations, the vertices of each connected component form a bush, and the algorithm terminates in the next iteration (when it discovers that no more pointer jumping is needed). The algorithm's running time is therefore $t(n) = O(\log n)$.

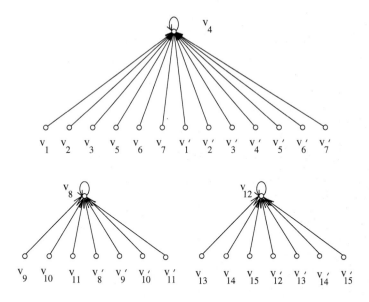

Figure 6.28: Step (3.6) of algorithm PRAM CONNECTED COMPONENTS.

6.5   PROBLEMS

6.1 Suppose that we are given m directed and rooted binary trees with a total of n vertices. Each vertex has a pointer to its parent. The trees are identified by their roots, but no vertex (unless it is a root) knows the identity of the tree to which it belongs. Design an algorithm that allows each vertex to know the identity of its tree, and analyze the processor and time requirements of your algorithm.

6.2 In Section 6.2, prior to executing algorithm PRAM LINKED LIST PREFIX, those processors involved in performing the prefix computation over L can determine their number (and hence the number of nodes in L) by writing a 1 in a location $size$ of memory, using a **SUM CW**. Discuss how this information can be used to provide an alternative termination condition for the algorithm.

6.3 The cost of algorithm PRAM LINKED LIST PREFIX is

$$c(n) = p(n) \times t(n) = n \times O(\log n) = O(n \log n).$$

This cost is not optimal in view of the $O(n)$ time sufficient for solving the same problem on the RAM. Modify the assumptions about the input to obtain a cost-optimal parallel algorithm.

NODE	0	1	2	3	4	5	6	7
INFO								
VAL	x_2	x_7	x_0	x_5	x_1	x_4	x_6	x_3
SUCC	7	NIL	4	6	0	3	1	5

Figure 6.29: A linked list stored in an array.

6.4 Suppose that a partially ordered list of n elements is given, represented by an integer array K of $n + 1$ elements and an index array $NEXT$ of n elements, where

$$K(i) \quad = \quad \text{value of the element at the } i\text{th location,}$$
$$NEXT(i) \quad = \quad \text{location of the element that follows } K(i) \text{ in the list,}$$

for $i = 1, 2, \ldots, n$. If no element follows $K(i)$ in the list, then $NEXT(i) = n+1$ and $K(n + 1) = 0$. For $i = 1, 2, \ldots, n$, it is required to replace $K(i)$ with the sum of $K(i)$ and all the integers that follow it in the list. Design a parallel algorithm for solving this problem, and analyze its running time, number of processors, and cost.

6.5 Suppose that a linked list is stored in an array of contiguous locations. For example, the linked list L of Fig. 6.2(a) may be organized as shown in Fig. 6.29. This representation may be exploited to obtain a cost-optimal parallel algorithm for prefix computation on a linked list. Show how the fast and cost-optimal parallel algorithm for prefix computation obtained in Problem 4.3 can be used for this purpose.

6.6 In Problem 6.5, the linked list is given as an array, where each array location contains a pointer to another (not necessarily adjacent) location. If, however, the linked list L is given in the form of Fig. 6.2(a)—that is, as a collection of nodes in arbitrary locations in memory—it may be reorganized as an array (as in Fig. 6.29) during a preprocessing step: Processor P_i, in charge of node i, writes the contents of the node in location i of the array. For a list with n nodes, this requires n processors and hence eliminates the possibility of a cost-optimal algorithm for prefix computation. There are two ways of avoiding the difficulty:

(a) Modify the definition of *cost* so that only the processors involved in the actual computation (and not those performing the preprocessing step) are counted.

(b) Seek a *work-optimal* algorithm instead of a cost-optimal one. (The preprocessing step requires n operations; if the actual computation requires

$O(n)$ operations, then the algorithm is work optimal, regardless of how many processors are used.)

6.7 A method is given in Section 6.3.3 for determining the level of a vertex in a rooted tree. Suggest alternative ways to perform this computation. (*Hint*: Try using functions such as *pos*, *des*, *preorder*, and so on.)

6.8 Suppose that each vertex in a rooted directed tree DT knows its parent. Design a PRAM algorithm (different from the one given in Section 6.3.3) for enumerating the descendants of each vertex in DT. (*Hint*: Use pointer jumping.)

6.9 Repeat Problem 6.8 for the case where the level of each vertex in the tree is to be determined.

6.10 Let a directed and rooted complete binary tree with n leaves be given. Each vertex stores a number and points to its parent, with the root's pointer equal to *nil*. It is required to perform a prefix computation on the tree such that each vertex stores the minimum of all numbers in its subtree. Design a parallel algorithm for solving this problem that uses $O(n/\log\log n)$ processors and runs in $O(\log\log n)$ time. Generalize your algorithm so that it runs in $O(\log n)$ time on arbitrary trees. Compare your solution to that described in Section 6.3.4.

6.11 Given a linked list L of n nodes, it is required to solve the list-ranking problem in $O(\log n)$ time using $O(n/\log n)$ processors. Design an algorithm that uses the following approach:

(a) Reduce the list L to a list L' of $O(n/\log n)$ nodes.

(b) Solve the list-ranking problem on L' using algorithm PRAM LIST RANKING.

(c) Restore the nodes removed in Step 1 and compute their ranks.

What assumptions need you make regarding the input?

6.12 We are given m linked lists with a total of n nodes. Each node stores a number. Initially, the nodes "know" neither their ranks in their respective lists nor the list to which they belong. It is required to find the smallest number in each list in $O(\log n)$ time.

6.13 Section 6.2 allows us to identify two interesting computations, namely, one that is *inherently sequential* and one that is *inherently parallel*. Consider a linked list L, as in Fig. 6.2(a), and assume, for simplicity, that it is required to compute the sum of the values stored in the *val* fields.

(a) *Inherently sequential computation:* If only a pointer to the *head* of the list is available, then the computation requires $\Omega(n)$ steps, where n is the number of nodes in L, since the list must be traversed one node at a time from *head* to *tail*. This lower bound holds, regardless of how many processors are available.

(b) *Inherently parallel computation:* If several processors are available, each of which is capable of gaining access to a different node of L, then the computation can be completed in $O(\log n)$ time (using one of the algorithms of Section 6.2). On the other hand, if there are fewer processors than nodes in L, then in the worst case this computation will require $\Omega(n)$ steps.

Discuss the foregoing two situations and suggest alternative settings.

6.14 Prove, by induction on the number of nodes, that the algorithm of Section 6.3.2 builds an Euler tour and not several small cycles.

6.15 Show how the breadth-first traversal algorithm of Section 6.3.5 can be completed in $O(n/N + \log n)$ time using N processors, where $N \le n$.

6.16 Let T be a rooted tree and v_1 and v_2 two of its vertices. The *lowest common ancestor* of v_1 and v_2 is a vertex u that is an ancestor of both v_1 and v_2 and is farthest from the root. (This definition is the same as the one given in Section 6.3.4 for binary trees.) It is desired to preprocess T such that, given any two vertices, their lowest common ancestor can be determined quickly. Specifically, show how a tree T with n leaves can be preprocessed in parallel in $O(\log n)$ time such that for *any* two vertices v_1 and v_2, the lowest common ancestor can be obtained by *one* processor in constant time.

6.17 As defined in Section 4.10.3, the *inorder* traversal of a binary tree visits the vertices in the following order: The left subtree is traversed recursively in inorder, then the root is visited, and finally, the right subtree is traversed recursively in inorder. Given a binary tree T with n nodes, show how the Euler tour technique can be used to number the vertices of T in the order of the inorder traversal of T. Analyze the running time and processor requirements of your algorithm.

6.18 Suppose that the vertices of a binary tree T have been assigned inorder numbers, as in Problem 6.17. Show that the lowest common ancestor of any pair of vertices of T (as defined in Section 6.3.4) can be obtained in constant time by one processor.

6.19 The algorithm of Section 6.3.4 solves the interval minima problem in $O(\log n)$ time using $O(n)$ processors.

(a) Show that this algorithm is not cost optimal by describing an $O(n)$-time sequential algorithm to solve the interval minima problem.

(b) Obtain a cost-optimal parallel algorithm for the interval minima problem—that is, an algorithm which runs in $O(\log n)$ time using $O(n/\log n)$ processors—based on the following approach:

(i) Divide the sequence S into $n/\log n$ subsequences, each of size $\log n$.

(ii) Solve the interval minima problem for each subsequence sequentially, using the optimal algorithm developed in (a).

(iii) Compute the prefix and suffix minima of each subsequence of S; let a_i be the smallest element of the ith subsequence.

(iv) Apply the algorithm of Section 6.3.4 to the sequence $\{a_1, a_2, \ldots, a_{n/\log n}\}$.

6.20 It is possible to obtain a cost-optimal PRAM algorithm for the interval minima problem that runs in $O(\log \log n)$ time and uses $O(n/\log \log n)$ processors. Proceed as follows:

(a) Show how the prefix and suffix minima of a sequence of size n can be obtained in $O(\log \log n)$ time using $O(n/\log \log n)$ processors by a recursive divide-and-conquer approach that splits the sequence into subsequences of size $n^{1/2}$.

(b) Construct the binary tree of Section 6.3.4 at a cost of $O(n \log n)$ operations.

(c) Reduce the cost of your algorithm to $O(n)$ by combining your solution with that of Problem 6.19.

6.21 Let T be a directed rooted tree such that each vertex v_i points to its parent and holds a certain value $val(v_i)$. In Section 6.3.4, it was required to compute, for each vertex v of T, the minimum of all values stored in T_v, the subtree rooted at v. Now let $\circ$ be a commutative and associative binary operation (such as addition, multiplication, and so on) defined on the set of values stored in T. A generalized version of the problem in Section 6.3.4 calls for computing a function $F(v)$ for every nonleaf vertex v of T, where $F(v)$ is the result of applying $\circ$ to all the values stored in T_v. For example, if $\circ$ is $+$, then

$$F(v) = \sum_{v_i \in T_v} val(v_i).$$

Design a parallel algorithm for solving this problem.

6.22 Algorithm PRAM CONNECTED COMPONENTS of Section 6.4 has a cost of $O(\max(n, m) \times \log n)$. This is not optimal in view of the $O(n + m)$-time sequential algorithm for solving the same problem. Can you obtain a cost-optimal parallel algorithm for solving the problem?

6.23 Suggest possible ways of reducing the running time of algorithm PRAM CONNECTED COMPONENTS, including using more processors.

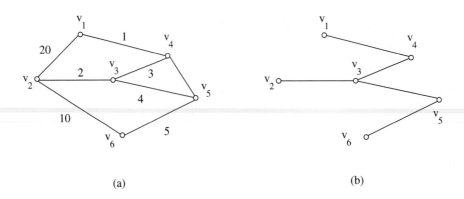

(a)   (b)

Figure 6.30: (a) A weighted graph and (b) its minimum-weight spanning tree.

6.24 Suppose that for graph $G = (V, E)$, where $|V| = n$ and $|E| = m$, $m = O(n^2)$. The graph is given as an $n \times n$ matrix $\boldsymbol{A}$, called the *adjacency* matrix, where each entry a_{ij} of $\boldsymbol{A}$ is defined as follows: If (v_i, v_j) is an edge of G, then $a_{ij} = 1$; otherwise, $a_{ij} = 0$. Design an algorithm for finding the connected components of G in $O(\log^2 n)$ time using $O(n^2/\log^2 n)$ processors.

6.25 Given an undirected and connected graph $G = (V, E)$, a *spanning tree* of G is a subgraph $G' = (V', E')$ of G such that G' is a tree and $V' = V$. If each edge of G is associated with a real number called its *weight*, then a *minimum-weight* spanning tree (MST) of G has the smallest edge-weight sum among all spanning trees of G. A weighted graph and its MST are shown in Figs. 6.30(a) and 6.30(b), respectively.

Consider the following algorithm for computing the MST of a weighted graph G of n vertices and m edges:

> **Step 1:** Sort the edges in nondecreasing order of their weights.
>   Denote the ith edge of the sorted list by e_i.
> **Step 2:** Include e_1 and e_2 in the MST.
> **Step 3: for** $i = 3, 4, \ldots, m$ **do in parallel**
>   **if** the endpoints of e_i belong to the same
>   connected component of the graph generated
>   by $e_1, e_2, \ldots, e_{i-1}$
>   **then** $e_i \notin$ MST
>   **else** $e_i \in$ MST
>   **end if**
>   **end for.** ∎

It is required to:

(a) Describe an implementation of this algorithm on the PRAM.

(b) Analyze the running time and processor requirements of the PRAM algorithm.

6.26 A *biconnected component* of an undirected graph $G = (V, E)$ is a connected component $G' = (V', E')$ such that the deletion of any vertex of V' does not disconnect G'. Design a parallel algorithm for decomposing a given undirected graph into the smallest possible number of biconnected components.

6.27 Let G be an undirected graph. A *bridge* in G is an edge whose removal divides one connected component into two. Design a parallel algorithm for finding the bridges of G.

6.28 An *articulation point* of a connected undirected graph G is a vertex whose removal splits G into two or more connected components. Design a parallel algorithm for finding all articulation points of a given graph.

6.29 An undirected graph is *bipartite* if and only if it has no cycle of odd length. Design and analyze a parallel algorithm for determining whether a given graph is bipartite.

6.30 A *weak component* of a directed graph G is a subgraph G' of G such that every two vertices are joined by a path in which the direction of each edge is ignored. Design a parallel algorithm for decomposing a given graph into the smallest number of weak components.

6.31 An arithmetic expression such as

$$(3 \times 2) + ((7 + 4) \times (6 \times 5))$$

can be stored in a binary tree as shown in Fig. 6.31, in which each leaf stores a constant and each internal node stores a binary operator. Design an efficient parallel algorithm for evaluating an expression stored in such a binary tree, and analyze the running time and processor requirements of your algorithm.

6.32 Let T be a binary rooted directed tree with root v_r such that each vertex v has a pointer *parent(v)* to its parent and a pointer *sibling(v)* to its sibling. (These pointers are equal to *nil* for the root.) The process of obtaining, from T, another tree T' with fewer vertices by combining vertices with their parents is known as *tree contraction*. Ultimately, a tree may shrink to a single vertex if so desired.

(a) Design an algorithm for tree contraction based on the Euler tour method.

(b) Design a different algorithm for tree contraction that uses the following operation: Let v be a leaf such that *parent(v)* $\neq v_r$. Delete v and *parent(v)*, and let *parent(sibling(v))* $\leftarrow$ *parent(parent(v))*.

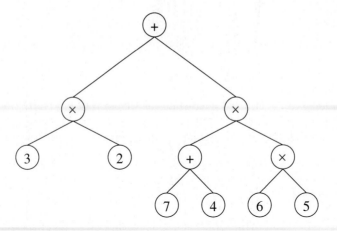

Figure 6.31: Binary tree representing an arithmetic expression.

6.33 Use your algorithms in Problem 6.32 to solve Problem 6.31.

6.34 Let T be a rooted directed tree that is not necessarily binary. Denote by a the maximum number of children a vertex in T can have. Design an algorithm for performing tree contraction over T in each of the following two cases:

    (a) a is a constant.

    (b) a is unbounded.

6.35 Study the effect of using discriminating analysis instead of uniform analysis on the running times of the algorithms presented in this chapter.

6.6   BIBLIOGRAPHICAL REMARKS

Pointer jumping was first proposed in Wyllie [645], where it was used to derive the first, and probably only, parallel algorithm for prefix computation and list ranking that adheres as closely as possible to the requirements of the linked list data structure. That algorithm runs in $O(\log n)$ time and uses $O(n)$ processors. Because prefix computation and list ranking can be easily solved sequentially in $O(n)$ time, the cost of the parallel algorithm is not optimal. However, one must keep in mind that this is the best possible performance under the assumption that the list's nodes are stored in arbitrary memory locations, with a pointer linking each node to its successor. By modifying this assumption, it is possible to reduce the number of processors to $O(n/\log n)$ while maintaining the running time at $O(\log n)$. The idea is to store the linked lists in contiguous locations of an array in the shared memory of a PRAM (each node not necessarily adjacent to its successor) and assign a subarray of $O(\log n)$ elements to each processor. This approach is exploited successfully in Anderson and Miller [66] and Cole and Vishkin [169, 172, 173]. Other algorithms were also derived that attempt to reduce further the number of processors at the expense of increasing the running time. (See, for example, Cole and Vishkin [170, 171], Kruskal et al. [338], Snir [577], and Wagner and Han [630].) Algorithms that achieve cost optimality with a high probability are described in Anderson and Miller [65], Das and Halverson [194], and Vishkin [624, 626]. Parallel algorithms that solve the prefix computation and list-ranking problems on other models of computation were also derived; these include algorithms for variants of the PRAM (see, for example, Han [286, 287], Hillis and Steele [295], Kruskal et al. [337], and Martel and Subramonian [408]), the hypercube (see, for example, Ryu and Já Já [542] and Sanz and Cypher [547]), and various extensions of the mesh (see, for example, Deo et al. [200] and Olariu et al. [449]).

There are numerous applications of prefix computation and list ranking to other problems defined on pointer-based structures; see, for example, Abrahamson et al. [1] (tree contraction), Chen and Das [142], and Chen et al. [143] (tree traversals), Eppstein and Galil [219] (ear decomposition), Kruskal et al. [339] (computing spanning trees), and Lin and Olariu [387] (lowest common ancestor). An extensive survey of parallel algorithms for list ranking and their applications is given in Halverson and Das [282]; see also Lakshmivarahan and Dhall [356]. The Euler tour method traces its origin to the Ph.D. thesis by Wyllie [645], although it appears to have been used effectively for the first time by Tarjan and Vishkin [607] and Vishkin [625]. A survey of its applications is given in Karp and Ramachandran [323].

Early parallel algorithms for computing connected components of an undirected graph appear in Hirschberg [296] and Hirschberg et al. [297]. Improvements were described by Awerbuch and Shiloach [77, 78], Savage and Já Já [548], and Shiloach and Vishkin [565]. An extensive coverage of parallel algorithms for graph-theoretic problems is provided in Gibbons and Rytter [258]; see also Eppstein and Galil [219], Já Já [310], and Reif [533].

Chapter 7

Linear Arrays

The previous three chapters used the PRAM model for developing parallel algorithms to solve a variety of computational problems. It is now time to turn our attention to the interconnection models, to which this and the next two chapters are devoted. In this chapter, we focus on the linear array model introduced in Section 2.3.1 and illustrated in Fig. 2.8. There are theoretical and practical reasons for our interest in this model:

1. From the theoretical point of view, an algorithmic result is more valuable if it is derived on a parallel model of computation that makes the fewest assumptions possible about processor connectivity. Indeed, the weaker the model, the stronger will be an optimality result, since a more powerful model can simulate an algorithm designed for a weaker model with no increase in running time. Evidently, the linear array is the simplest of all models that allow some form of communication among processors. For example, all of the links in the linear array are contained in networks such as the mesh and the hypercube, making it weaker than these two models. (In turn, the latter are weaker than the PRAM, which can simulate any link between two processors by a transfer of data through shared memory.)

2. In addition, the linear array is practical: It can be readily implemented in virtually any technology owing to its minimal connectivity requirements.

This chapter is organized as follows: We begin in Section 7.1 by describing two algorithms for sorting a sequence of numbers on a linear array. Section 7.2 is devoted to matrix computations; in particular, we show how to perform matrix-by-vector multiplication and how to solve a triangular system of equations on a linear array. We then turn in Section 7.3 to the problem of convolution and develop four different linear array algorithms for solving it. For definiteness, all data in Sections 7.2 and 7.3 are assumed to be real numbers. Finally, in Section 7.4 we present parallel algorithms for generating combinatorial objects, particularly combinations and

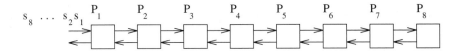

Figure 7.1: Linear array for sorting $S = \{s_1, s_2, \ldots, s_n\}$.

permutations. These algorithms satisfy a number of strict conditions, in addition to running on the weakest of all models of parallel computation. As a result, the algorithms are optimal in every known and reasonable sense. Additional algorithms for the linear array are described in Chapters 8 and 9.

We assume in this chapter that the two-way link connecting two adjacent processors in the linear array has enough *bandwidth* (i.e., capacity) to allow a constant number of data transfers to take place between the two processors simultaneously when so desired. For example, P_i can send two values a and b to P_{i+1} and at the same time receive two values d and e from P_{i+1}. For clarity, we draw as many one-way links between P_i and P_{i+1} as there are data transfers.

7.1 SORTING

The first problem for which we develop solutions on the linear array is that of sorting a sequence of numbers $S = \{s_1, s_2, \ldots, s_n\}$ in nondecreasing order. We assume throughout this section that the elements of S are *not* all available at once. Instead, as is the case in many applications, the elements arrive one at a time. For example, there may be a device that takes certain measurements and feeds them into the linear array for sorting. We will see how the linear array can sort this input *on the fly*. Note that since n time units are required for the entire input to arrive, $\Omega(n)$ is a lower bound on the running time of any algorithm designed to solve this problem (regardless of the model of computation). In Section 7.1.1, a simple algorithm is described that uses n processors to sort the input in optimal time. We then show in Section 7.1.2 how the same performance can be obtained using only $1 + \log n$ processors.

7.1.1 Sorting by Comparison-Exchange

Suppose that a linear array of n processors is available and that it receives the elements of S one at a time, as shown in Fig. 7.1 for $n = 8$. The inputs arrive at P_1. Initially, P_1 reads s_1. During the jth input step, $j > 1$, the contents of P_1, $P_2, \ldots, P_{j-1}$ are shifted to the right, making room in P_1 for the next input element s_j. This is followed by a *comparison-exchange*: For all odd i, $i < j$, the elements in P_i and P_{i+1} are compared, with the smaller going to P_i and the larger to P_{i+1}. The shift and comparison-exchange together require one time unit. After $n - 1$ repetitions of these two steps, input is complete and output can start. During the *j*th output step, $j \geq 1$, the contents of the array are shifted to the left, producing as output from P_1 the current smallest element in the array. This is followed by a comparison-exchange: For all odd i, $i < n - j$, the elements in P_i and P_{i+1} are compared, with the smaller going to P_i and the larger to P_{i+1}. After n repetitions of these two steps, output is complete.

The algorithm is given next as algorithm LINEAR ARRAY COMPARISON-EXCHANGE SORT. In it, "compare-exchange (P_i, P_{i+1})" denotes the operation of comparing the numbers held by P_i and P_{i+1} and placing the smaller in P_i and the larger in P_{i+1}.

Algorithm LINEAR ARRAY COMPARISON-EXCHANGE SORT

Step 1: P_1 reads s_1.
Step 2: for $j = 2$ **to** n **do**
    (2.1) **for** $i = 1$ **to** $j - 1$ **do in parallel**
        P_i sends its datum to P_{i+1}
    end for
    (2.2) P_1 reads s_j
    (2.3) **for all** odd $i < j$ **do in parallel**
        compare-exchange (P_i, P_{i+1})
    end for
    end for
Step 3: for $j = 1$ **to** n **do**
    (3.1) P_1 produces its datum as output
    (3.2) **for** $i = 2$ **to** $n - j + 1$ **do in parallel**
        P_i sends its datum to P_{i-1}
    end for
    (3.3) **for all** odd $i < n - j$ **do in parallel**
        compare-exchange (P_i, P_{i+1})
    end for
    end for. ∎

Example 7.1 A few steps of the algorithm are illustrated in Fig. 7.2 for the input sequence $S = \{5, 1, 3, 8, 6, 4, 7, 2\}$. Let u denote the number of time units elapsed. The first input, namely, 5, is in P_1 when $u = 1$, as shown in Fig. 7.2(a), while the first output, namely, 1, leaves P_1 when $u = 9$, as shown in Fig. 7.2(d). □

Analysis. The algorithm has a running time of $t(n) = O(n)$, which is optimal for the case where inputs arrive one at a time. Since $P(n) = n$, however, the algorithm's cost of $O(n^2)$ is not optimal in view of the $O(n \log n)$ operations sufficient to sort sequentially.

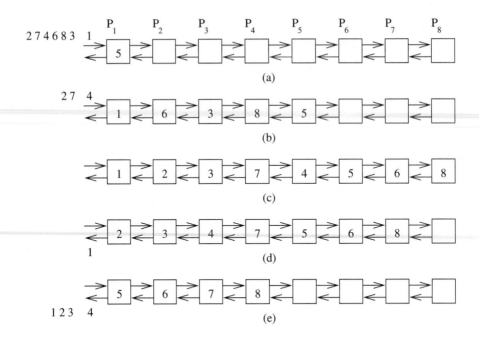

Figure 7.2: Sorting by comparison-exchange on a linear array: (a) $u = 1$; (b) $u = 5$; (c) $u = 8$; (d) $u = 9$; (e) $u = 12$.

7.1.2   Sorting by Merging

A powerful sorting algorithm, and one that has been used successfully in various parallel settings (see Sections 3.1.1 and 4.9.2, for example), is sorting by merging. Recall that for an input sequence $S = \{s_1, s_2, \ldots, s_n\}$, where n is a power of 2 for simplicity of exposition, the algorithm first performs a comparison-exchange on each of the pairs (s_1, s_2), (s_3, s_4), $\ldots$, (s_{n-1}, s_n), thus creating $n/2$ sorted subsequences. In the second step, consecutive pairs of subsequences (of two elements) are merged to form sorted subsequences of length 4. The ith step creates sorted subsequences of length 2^i. After $\log n$ steps, the input sequence is sorted. We now show how this algorithm can be adapted to run on a linear array of $1 + \log n$ processors in $O(n)$ time, thus achieving cost optimality.

The main idea of the linear array algorithm is essentially the same as the one used in algorithm PRAM SORT: Several merging steps are overlapped and executed in a pipelined fashion. The difference here is that the pipeline is not conceptual (as in PRAM SORT), but real: The processors of the array and the links connecting them form the physical pipeline. During execution of the algorithm, the processors and links serve as temporary storage for part of the sequence to be sorted. Let $n = 2^r$ for some positive integer r, and assume that $1 + r$ processors P_1, P_2, $\ldots$,

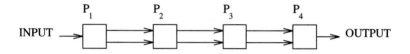

Figure 7.3: A pipeline for sorting.

P_{r+1} are available on the linear array, as shown in Fig. 7.3 for $r = 3$. In one time unit, each processor is capable of receiving one number as input, performing a comparison between two numbers, and producing one number as output.

We distinguish between the top and bottom lines connecting P_i to P_{i+1}, $1 \leq i \leq r$. The input sequence is fed into P_1: During step j, $1 \leq j \leq n$, P_1 receives s_j and sends it to P_2 on the top line if j is odd and on the bottom line if j is even. For $2 \leq i \leq r + 1$:

1. Two subsequences of length 2^{i-2} are sent from P_{i-1} to P_i, each on a different line.

2. These subsequences are merged by P_i into one subsequence of length 2^{i-1}.

The merged subsequences produced by $P_2, P_3, \ldots, P_r$ alternate between the top and bottom lines. Processor P_{r+1} produces the output sequence in sorted order. The key to the efficiency of the algorithm is that P_i, $2 \leq i \leq r + 1$, *does not wait* until P_{i-1} has delivered two complete subsequences of length 2^{i-2}: It starts merging when P_{i-1} has produced a subsequence of length 2^{i-2} on one line and the *first element* of the next subsequence on the other line.

Formally, processor P_1 performs the following steps:

Step 1: Read s_1 from the input sequence.
Step 2: $j \leftarrow 1$
Step 3: for $i = 2$ **to** n **do**
      (3.1) **if** j is odd
             then place s_{i-1} on the top output line
             else place s_{i-1} on the bottom output line
             end if
      (3.2) Read s_i from the input sequence.
      (3.3) $j \leftarrow j + 1$
      end for
Step 4: Place s_n on the bottom output line. ∎

Meanwhile, each processor P_i, $2 \leq i \leq r$, performs the following steps:

Step 1: $j \leftarrow 1$
Step 2: $k \leftarrow 1$

Step 3: while $k < n$ **do**

if the top input line contains 2^{i-2} elements

and the bottom input line contains one element

then (3.1) **for** $m = 1$ **to** 2^{i-1} **do**

(i) For the two subsequences to be merged,
compare the current first element (if any)
of the subsequence on the top input line
to the current first element (if any)
of the subsequence on the bottom input line

(ii) Denote by x the larger of the two
elements in (i), and remove it
from its subsequence
(in case one of the two subsequences
has become empty, the first element
of the other subsequence is taken as x)

(iii) **if** j is odd

then place x on the top output line

else place x on the bottom output line

end if

end for

(3.2) $j \leftarrow j + 1$

(3.3) $k \leftarrow k + 2^{i-1}$

end if

end while. ■

Similarly, processor P_{r+1} performs the following step:

if the top input line contains 2^{r-1} elements

and the bottom input line contains one element

then for $m = 1$ **to** 2^r **do**

(1) Compare the current first element
in the top input line (if any)
to the current first element
in the bottom input line (if any)

(2) Denote the larger of the two elements in (i) by x
(in case one of the two input lines is currently empty,
then the first element on the other input line is x)

(3) Remove x, and produce it as the next
element of the output sequence

end for

end if. ■

Example 7.2 A few steps of the algorithm are illustrated in Fig. 7.4 for $S = \{5, 1, 3, 8, 6, 4, 7, 2\}$. The number of time units elapsed is denoted by u. When

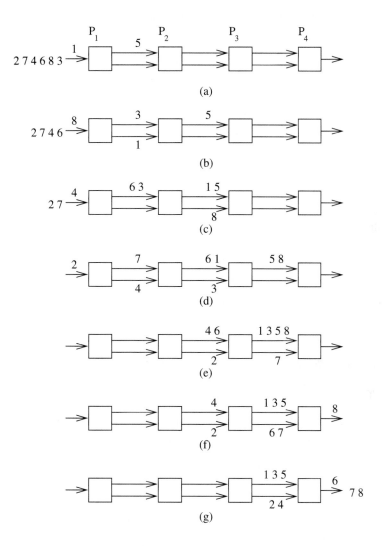

Figure 7.4: Sorting by merging in a pipeline on a linear array: (a) $u = 1$; (b) $u = 3$; (c) $u = 5$; (d) $u = 7$; (e) $u = 10$; (f) $u = 11$; (g) $u = 13$.

$u = 3$, P_2 begins merging, as shown in Fig. 7.4(b). In Fig. 7.4(c), the subsequence $\{1, 5\}$ and the first element, namely, 8, of another subsequence are available, so P_3 can begin merging in the next step. When $u = 10$, P_4 is ready to merge. As shown in Fig. 7.4(f), P_4 produces its first output when $u = 11$. □

Analysis. Processor P_1 produces its first output when $u = 1$. Since processor P_i requires a subsequence of size 2^{i-2} on one line and another of size 1 on the other to begin merging, it starts operating $2^{i-2} + 1$ time units after P_{i-1}. That is, when

$$
\begin{aligned}
u &= 1 + (2^0 + 1) + (2^1 + 1) + \cdots + (2^{i-2} + 1) \\
&= 2^{i-1} + i - 1,
\end{aligned}
$$

P_i produces its first output. Then, $n - 1$ time units later, P_i produces its last output. The last processor to terminate is P_{r+1}, when

$$
\begin{aligned}
u &= (n - 1) + 2^r + r \\
&= 2n + \log n - 1.
\end{aligned}
$$

Therefore, $t(n) = O(n)$. Since $p(n) = 1 + \log n$, the algorithm's cost is $O(n \log n)$, and this is optimal in view of the $\Omega(n \log n)$ lower bound on the number of operations required for sorting.

7.2 · MATRIX COMPUTATIONS

This section is concerned with computational problems defined on matrices and how they can be solved using a linear array. In particular, we are interested in two computations, namely, multiplying a matrix by a vector and solving a triangular system of equations.

7.2.1   Matrix-by-Vector Multiplication

Given an $m \times n$ matrix A and an $n \times 1$ vector u, it is required to compute the $m \times 1$ vector v obtained by multiplying A by u, as shown in the following equation for $m = 4$ and $n = 5$:

$$
\begin{pmatrix}
a_{11} & a_{12} & a_{13} & a_{14} & a_{15} \\
a_{21} & a_{22} & a_{23} & a_{24} & a_{25} \\
a_{31} & a_{32} & a_{33} & a_{34} & a_{35} \\
a_{41} & a_{42} & a_{43} & a_{44} & a_{45}
\end{pmatrix}
\begin{pmatrix}
u_1 \\ u_2 \\ u_3 \\ u_4 \\ u_5
\end{pmatrix}
=
\begin{pmatrix}
v_1 \\ v_2 \\ v_3 \\ v_4
\end{pmatrix}.
$$

Each element v_i of v, $1 \le i \le m$, is obtained from

$$
v_i = \sum_{j=1}^{n} a_{ij} u_j.
$$

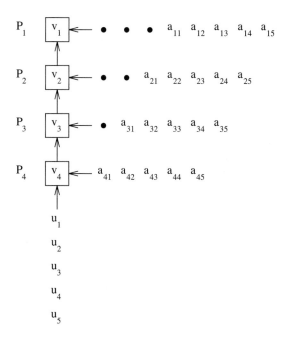

Figure 7.5: Multiplying a matrix by a vector.

On a linear array with m processors P_1, P_2, ..., P_m, the problem is solved as follows: Processor P_i is used to compute v_i. Initially, v_i is 0. Matrix A and vector u are fed into the array as shown in Fig. 7.5 for $m = 4$ and $n = 5$. The rows of A are fed into the array, one row per processor, with P_i receiving the ith row. Also, the ith row lags one time unit behind the $(i+1)$st row, for $1 \le i \le m-1$. Simultaneously, the elements u_1, u_2, ..., u_n are fed into P_m in that order and move up the array until u_n reaches P_1. Upon receipt of two inputs a_{ij} and u_j, processor P_i:

1. Computes $v_i \leftarrow v_i + a_{ij}u_j$.

2. Sends u_j to P_{i-1} (unless $i = 1$).

Note that a_{ij} and u_j meet at the right time, since both arrive at P_i after $(j-1) + (m-i)$ time units.

Analysis. The number of time units required by a_{1n} to reach P_1 is $n+m-2$. One time unit later, computation of v_1 is complete. Since P_1 is the last processor to terminate, this many steps are required to compute the product. Assuming that $m \le n$, the algorithm runs in time $t(n) = O(n)$, for a cost of $O(n^2)$. This is optimal in view of the $\Omega(n^2)$ steps required to read the input sequentially.

7.2.2   Solution of Triangular Systems

A *lower triangular* matrix is a square matrix, all of whose entries above the main diagonal are 0. Given an $n \times n$ lower triangular matrix $\boldsymbol{A}$ with elements a_{ij} such that $a_{ii} \neq 0$ for $i = 1, 2, \ldots, n$ and an $n \times 1$ vector $\boldsymbol{b}$, it is required to solve the equation

$$\boldsymbol{A}\boldsymbol{x} = \boldsymbol{b}$$

for the $n \times 1$ vector $\boldsymbol{x}$. For example, when $n = 4$, the system of equations to be solved is

$$\begin{pmatrix} a_{11} & 0 & 0 & 0 \\ a_{21} & a_{22} & 0 & 0 \\ a_{31} & a_{32} & a_{33} & 0 \\ a_{41} & a_{42} & a_{43} & a_{44} \end{pmatrix} \begin{pmatrix} x_1 \\ x_2 \\ x_3 \\ x_4 \end{pmatrix} = \begin{pmatrix} b_1 \\ b_2 \\ b_3 \\ b_4 \end{pmatrix}.$$

Sequentially, this problem is solved in $O(n^2)$ time by a technique known as *forward substitution*. Initially, the first equation, namely, $a_{11}x_1 = b_1$, is solved for x_1, yielding $x_1 = b_1/a_{11}$. Using this value, the second equation, namely, $a_{21}x_1 + a_{22}x_2 = b_2$, is solved for x_2, yielding $x_2 = (b_2 - a_{21}x_1)/a_{22}$. In general, the value of x_i is obtained from

$$x_i = (b_i - \sum_{j=1}^{i-1} a_{ij}x_j)/a_{ii},$$

where $x_1, x_2, \ldots, x_{i-1}$ have already been computed. This equation for x_i can be rewritten as the following recurrence, where $j < i$:

$$\begin{aligned} y_i^{(1)} &= 0, \\ y_i^{(j+1)} &= y_i^{(j)} + a_{ij}x_j, \\ x_i &= (b_i - y_i^{(i)})/a_{ii}. \end{aligned}$$

This formulation allows us to solve the system of equations on a linear array of n processors. The general setup is shown in Fig. 7.6 for $n = 4$. The input to the array is specified as follows:

1. The elements of the matrix $\boldsymbol{A}$ are fed into the linear array, one diagonal per processor. The elements of the ith diagonal, namely, a_{i1}, $a_{(i+1),2}$, $\ldots$, $a_{n,(n-i+1)}$, are fed into P_i in that order. Each a_{ij} is separated from the following $a_{i+1,j+1}$ by two time units. Also, for $i \geq 2$, the ith diagonal lags behind the $(i-1)$st by one time unit. The elements of $\boldsymbol{A}$ do not travel within the array of processors: P_i is the final destination of a_{ij}.

2. The sequence of y's, namely, $\{y_1, y_2, \ldots, y_n\}$, is fed into P_n in that order. Each y_i is equal to 0 when it enters P_n. It then moves up the array (using the upward links) until it reaches P_1. Two time units separate each pair of consecutive y's.

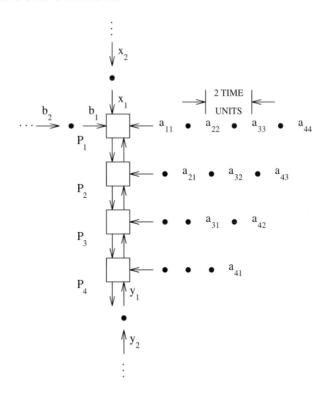

Figure 7.6: Setup for solving a triangular system of equations.

3. The elements of the vector $\boldsymbol{x}$, namely, x_1, x_2, ..., x_n, enter the array at P_1 in that order. Each x_i moves downwards (using the downward links) until it reaches P_n, whereupon it exits the array as output. Two time units separate each pair of consecutive x's.

4. The elements of the vector $\boldsymbol{b}$, namely, b_1, b_2, ..., b_n, are fed into P_1 in that order. Two time units separate each pair of consecutive b's. No element of $\boldsymbol{b}$ goes any further than P_1.

These inputs are then subjected to two kinds of computations:

1. In processor P_k, $2 \leq k \leq n$, a_{ij}, x_j, and y_i arrive simultaneously, and the computation

$$y_i \leftarrow y_i + a_{ij}x_j$$

is performed. Note here that $k = i - j + 1$.

2. When y_i reaches P_1, it is equal to

$$a_{i1}x_1 + a_{i2}x_2 + \cdots + a_{i,i-1}x_{i-1}.$$

Simultaneously, x_i, a_{ii}, and b_i arrive at P_1, and the computation

$$x_i \leftarrow (b_i - y_i)/a_{ii}$$

is performed, giving the desired value of x_i.

It should now be clear why each two consecutive inputs are separated by two time units: By slowing down the input, we guarantee that appropriate data from streams flowing towards one another meet at the right processor at the right time. Also, it is important to note that no computation takes place until y_1 has reached P_1, where x_1 is computed. Therefore, input is timed so that the first values to enter the array (besides the y's), namely, a_{11}, b_1, and x_1, are fed into P_1 at the same time as y_1. This occurs during time unit $n - 1$.

Example 7.3 The first few steps of the algorithm are illustrated in Fig. 7.7 for $n = 4$. Let u denote the number of time units elapsed. When $u = 0$, input begins by feeding y_1 into P_4. When $u = 3$, y_1 enters P_1 simultaneously with a_{11}, b_1, and x_1, as shown in Fig. 7.7(a), and x_1 is computed from: $x_1 \leftarrow (b_1 - y_1)/a_{11}$. Subsequent computations are as follows:

$$
\begin{aligned}
u &= 4: & y_2 &\leftarrow a_{21}x_1 \\
u &= 5: & x_2 &\leftarrow (b_2 - y_2)/a_{22}, \quad y_3 \leftarrow a_{31}x_1 \\
u &= 6: & y_3 &\leftarrow a_{31}x_1 + a_{32}x_2, \quad y_4 \leftarrow a_{41}x_1 \\
u &= 7: & \text{output } &x_1, \quad x_3 \leftarrow (b_3 - y_3)/a_{33}, \quad y_4 \leftarrow a_{41}x_1 + a_{42}x_2 \\
u &= 8: & y_4 &\leftarrow a_{41}x_1 + a_{42}x_2 + a_{43}x_3 \\
u &= 9: & \text{output } &x_2, \quad x_4 \leftarrow (b_4 - y_4)/a_{44}. \quad \Box
\end{aligned}
$$

Analysis. It takes $n - 1$ time units for y_1 to reach P_1; n time units later, x_1 emerges from P_n. The subsequent $n - 1$ elements of x are produced at intervals of 2 time units. The time required by the entire computation is therefore $t(n) = 4n - 3$. Note, however, that only half of the n processors are busy at any given time.

The algorithm can be improved in a number of ways:

1. We can avoid having to feed the b values into P_1 by simply initializing y_i to b_i (instead of 0). Now the computation inside P_k is changed to

$$y_i \leftarrow y_i - a_{ij}x_j$$

   and that inside P_1 to

$$x_i \leftarrow y_i/a_{ii}.$$

2. There is no need for x_i to travel all the way to P_n to be produced as output; it can be sent out from P_1 to the outside world, while a copy of it travels down the array. This way, x_1 is produced in time unit n, and x_n is produced $2n - 2$ time units later, yielding a running time of $3n - 2$. This time can be further reduced by making the trivial observation that y_1 is equal to 0 when reaching P_1; therefore, there is no need to wait for $n - 1$ time units before beginning the computation. This brings the running time down to $t(n) = 2n - 1$.

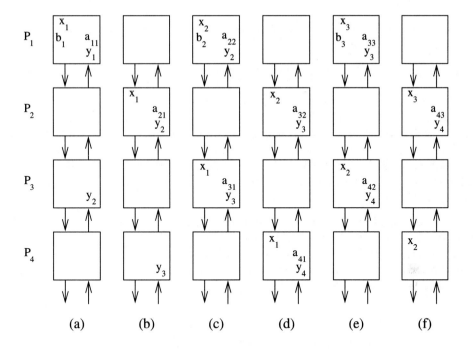

Figure 7.7: Solving a triangular system of equations on a linear array: (a) $u = 3$; (b) $u = 4$; (c) $u = 5$; (d) $u = 6$; (e) $u = 7$; (f) $u = 8$.

3. The utilization of processors can be significantly improved by employing an array of $n/2$ processors, each simulating two processors in the algorithm. Alternatively, the n processors can be used to solve *two* triangular systems of equations simultaneously.

7.3 CONVOLUTION

Suppose that we are given a sequence of values $W = \{w_1, w_2, \ldots, w_k\}$ called *weights*. For an *input* sequence $X = \{x_1, x_2, \ldots, x_n\}$, it is required to compute the *output* sequence $Y = \{y_1, y_2, \ldots, y_{n+1-k}\}$, where

$$y_i = \sum_{j=1}^{k} w_j x_{i+j-1}.$$

In other words,

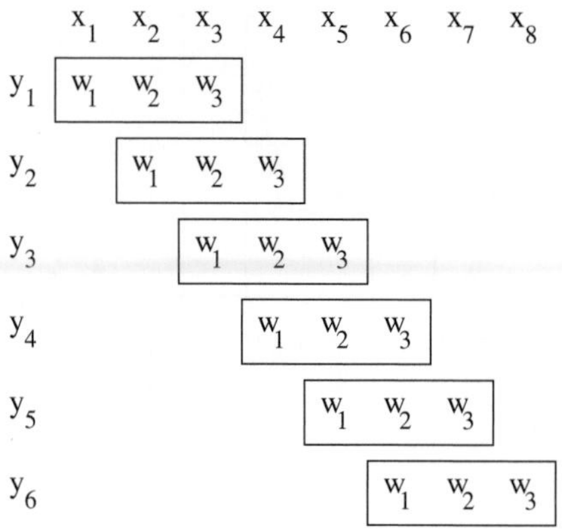

$$x_1 \quad x_2 \quad x_3 \quad x_4 \quad x_5 \quad x_6 \quad x_7 \quad x_8$$

Figure 7.8: Computing the convolution of two sequences.

$$
\begin{aligned}
y_1 &= w_1 x_1 + w_2 x_2 + \cdots + w_k x_k, \\
y_2 &= w_1 x_2 + w_2 x_3 + \cdots + w_k x_{k+1}, \\
&\quad\vdots \\
y_i &= w_1 x_i + w_2 x_{i+1} + \cdots + w_k x_{i+k-1}, \\
&\quad\vdots \\
y_{n+1-k} &= w_1 x_{n+1-k} + w_2 x_{n+2-k} + \cdots + w_k x_n.
\end{aligned}
$$

Example 7.4 Let $n = 8$ and $k = 3$. The three weights $\{w_1, w_2, w_3\}$ slide across the sequence $\{x_1, x_2, \ldots, x_8\}$, or vice versa, to compute the sequence $\{y_1, y_2, \ldots, y_6\}$, as shown in Fig. 7.8. $\square$

The preceding computation is referred to as *convolution*. Sequentially, the sequence Y can be computed in $(n + 1 - k) \times k = O(nk)$ time. In this section, we develop simple algorithms for performing convolution on a linear array of k processors. All of the algorithms run in $O(n)$ time. However, each is based on different design criteria and, as a consequence, has its own advantages.

7.3.1   Inputs and Weights Travel in Opposite Directions

Our first algorithm uses the setup illustrated in Fig. 7.9 for $k = 3$, with the processors indexed from right to left. Here the weights arrive one at a time to the rightmost processor P_1; they travel in a trainlike fashion across the array from right to left. Note that the sequence of weights is fed repeatedly into the array—that is, $w_1, w_2, \ldots, w_k, w_1, w_2, \ldots, w_k, w_1, w_2, \ldots, w_k$, and so on. At the same time, the inputs arrive from the left, through the leftmost processor P_k, and travel across the

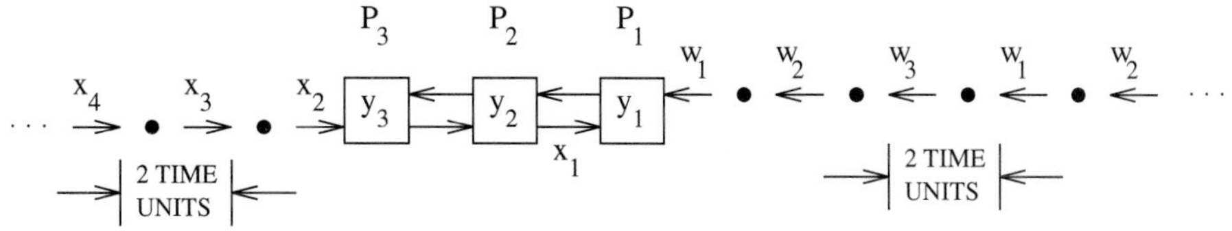

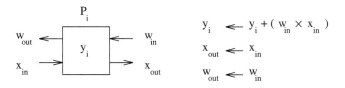

Figure 7.9: Inputs and weights travel in opposite directions.

$$y_i \leftarrow y_i + (w_{in} \times x_{in})$$
$$x_{out} \leftarrow x_{in}$$
$$w_{out} \leftarrow w_{in}$$

Figure 7.10: Behavior of processor P_i in first convolution algorithm.

array from left to right. In order to ensure that each input x is able to meet the appropriate weight w at the right time and place, consecutive x's and consecutive w's are separated by two time units, as illustrated in the figure. Also, w_1 is fed into the array for the first time when x_1 reaches P_1—that is, $k-1$ time units after the beginning of the computation. Each processor P_i has a register y_i holding the partial value of an output y. Initially, this register contains the value 0. When an input x and a weight w meet in a processor, they are multiplied, and the product is added to y. This takes one time unit. The behavior of processor P_i is illustrated in Fig. 7.10, in which the subscripts 'in' and 'out' are used to indicate values coming in and going out, respectively. It is important to note that P_i performs a computation of the form $y_i \leftarrow y_i + (w \times x)$ only when it receives both a w and an x.

How are the outputs produced? Processor P_i knows that y_i is ready for output once it has performed a computation using w_k. In order to allow the processor to recognize w_k, the latter travels with a special tag bit. As soon as the computation of y_i is complete, y_i is sent through the array to exit from P_1. (An alternative would be to produce y_i directly on an output device attached to P_i.)

From the observation in the previous paragraph, it is now clear that y_i in Fig. 7.9 represents y_{i+sk}, where $s = 0, 1, \ldots, \lfloor \frac{n+1-k-i}{k} \rfloor$. Once y_{i+jk} has been produced as output, the register holding it is reinitialized to 0. Computation of $y_{i+(j+1)k}$ now begins in P_i, provided that $i + (j+1)k \leq n + 1 - k$.

Analysis. Let $q = (n+1-k) \bmod k$. Suppose that P_i is the last processor to produce an output. If $q > 0$, then $i = q$; otherwise $i = k$. It takes $(2n-2) + k - i$ time units for x_n to reach P_i, where it meets w_k. Since outputs are sent through the array to exit from P_1, the last output requires an additional i time units to be

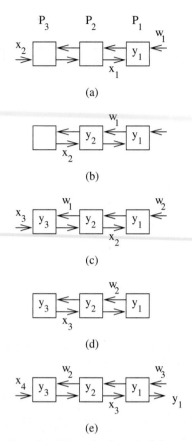

Figure 7.11: First convolution algorithm for $k = 3$: (a) $u = 2$, $y_1 = w_1 x_1$; (b) $u = 3$, $y_2 = w_1 x_2$; (c) $u = 4$, $y_1 = w_1 x_1 + w_2 x_2$, $y_3 = w_1 x_3$; (d) $u = 5$, $y_2 = w_1 x_2 + w_2 x_3$; (e) $u = 6$, $y_1 = w_1 x_1 + w_2 x_2 + w_3 x_3$, $y_3 = w_1 x_3 + w_2 x_4$.

produced. The total time is therefore $2n + k - 2$. Note, however, that at any given time, only $\lceil k/2 \rceil$ processors (at most) are performing computations.

Example 7.5 Three steps of the computation are illustrated in Fig. 7.11 for $k = 3$. Let u denote the number of time units elapsed. When $u = 0$, x_1 enters P_3. It leaves P_3 and enters P_2 when $u = 1$. The first computation occurs when x_1 enters P_1, as shown in Fig. 7.11(a). Note that in Fig. 7.11(e), y_1 is produced as output. $\square$

7.3.2   Inputs and Weights Travel in the Same Direction

In an attempt to keep all processors busy all the time, our second algorithm uses the setup illustrated in Fig. 7.12 for $k = 3$, with the processors indexed from left to right. Here the weights and the inputs arrive at the leftmost processor P_1 and

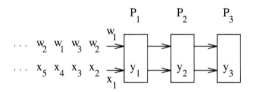

Figure 7.12: Inputs and weights travel in the same direction.

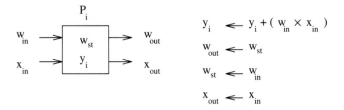

Figure 7.13: Behavior of processor P_i in second convolution algorithm.

travel in the same direction through the array, but at different speeds. The x's move twice as fast as the w's: Each w stays inside every processor it goes through for an extra time unit, thus taking twice as long to go across the array as an x does. It follows that processor P_i requires two registers, namely, one for y_i and one for the passing w's. When a w and an x meet in P_i, they are multiplied and added to y_i (in one time unit). The behavior of P_i is illustrated in Fig. 7.13, where the subscript 'st' denotes a value that stays inside the processor. As in the previous algorithm, a processor P_i:

1. Performs a computation only when it receives *two* values, namely, a w and an x.

2. Produces the contents of register y_i as output and reinitializes y_i to 0 when it has used w_k in a computation.

3. Sends its output through the array to exit from the rightmost processor P_k.

Also as before:

1. Weights are fed repeatedly to the array: $w_1, w_2, \ldots, w_k, w_1, w_2, \ldots, w_k$, and so on.

2. Register y_i serves to hold y_{i+sk} for $s = 0, 1, \ldots, \lfloor \frac{n+1-k-i}{k} \rfloor$.

   Analysis.   Let P_i be the last processor to produce an output. The number of time units taken by x_n to reach P_i is $(n-1) + (i-1)$. The output requires another

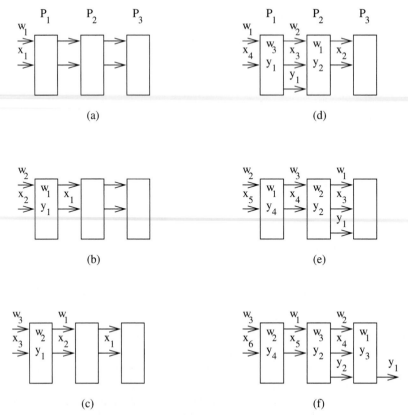

Figure 7.14: Second convolution algorithm for $k = 3$: (a) $u = 0$; (b) $u = 1$, $y_1 = w_1 x_1$; (c) $u = 2$, $y_1 = w_1 x_1 + w_2 x_2$; (d) $u = 3$, $y_1 = w_1 x_1 + w_2 x_2 + w_3 x_3$, $y_2 = w_1 x_2$; (e) $u = 4$, $y_4 = w_1 x_4$, $y_2 = w_1 x_2 + w_2 x_3$; (f) $u = 5$, $y_4 = w_1 x_4 + w_2 x_5$, $y_2 = w_1 x_2 + w_2 x_3 + w_3 x_4$, $y_3 = w_1 x_3$.

$k - i + 1$ time units to be produced to the outside world. The total time is therefore $n + k - 1$.

Example 7.6 The first few steps of computation are illustrated in Fig. 7.14 for $k = 3$. The number of time units elapsed is denoted by u. In Fig. 7.14(d) the computation of y_1 is complete, and therefore, y_1 is sent across the array to emerge eventually as output from P_3. Similarly, in Fig. 7.14(f), y_2 is ready for output. □

7.3.3   Inputs and Outputs Travel in Opposite Directions

The third algorithm, by contrast with the previous two, keeps the weights stationary while moving inputs and outputs. The setup is shown in Fig. 7.15 for $k = 3$, with the processors indexed from right to left. Here P_i stores w_i in a local register.

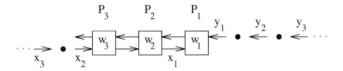

Figure 7.15: Inputs and outputs travel in opposite directions.

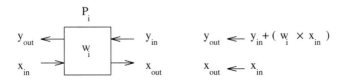

Figure 7.16: Behavior of processor P_i in third convolution algorithm.

The outputs, all initialized to 0, are fed into the array through P_1, the rightmost processor, and travel to the left. The inputs are fed into P_k and travel to the right. When an x and a y meet in a processor, x is multiplied with the resident w and added to y. The behavior of P_i is illustrated in Fig. 7.16. A processor performs a computation only when it receives an x and a y. It produces an output only when it has performed a computation. Note that consecutive x's and consecutive y's are separated by two time units, in order to guarantee that each y will meet the appropriate x's involved in its computation at the right time and place. An output y_i is produced from P_k every two time units.

One interesting property of this algorithm is that for each i, y_i emerges from P_k one time unit after the last input required to compute it, namely, x_{i+k-1}, enters that processor. Therefore, we say that that algorithm has a *constant response time*.

Analysis. Since $2n-2$ time units elapse before x_n reaches P_k, the time required by the algorithm is $2n-1$. Note, however, that only $\lceil k/2 \rceil$ processors (at most) are busy at any time.

Example 7.7 A few steps of the algorithm are illustrated in Fig. 7.17 for $k = 3$. The number of time units elapsed is denoted by u. Note that y_1 is produced as output when $u = 3$, as shown in Fig. 7.17(c). □

7.3.4 Inputs and Outputs Travel in the Same Direction

Our final algorithm, as did the algorithm of Section 7.3.2, reduces the running time by keeping all processors busy. It is based on the setup shown in Fig. 7.18 for $k = 3$, with the processors indexed from right to left. The idea is to feed both the inputs and the outputs into the array at P_k, the leftmost processor, and let them

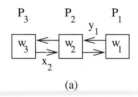

(a)

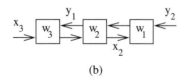

(b)

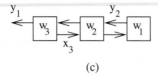

(c)

Figure 7.17: Third convolution algorithm for $k = 3$: (a) $u = 1$, $y_1 = w_1 x_1$; (b) $u = 2$, $y_1 = w_1 x_1 + w_2 x_2$; (c) $u = 3$, $y_1 = w_1 x_1 + w_2 x_2 + w_3 x_3$, $y_2 = w_1 x_2$.

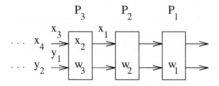

Figure 7.18: Inputs and outputs travel in the same direction.

propagate through the array, moving in the same left-to-right direction, with the y's moving twice as fast as the x's. Each processor P_i has two registers; one stores w_i, while the second stores a passing x for one additional time unit. When an x and a y reach P_i, w_i and x are multiplied, and the result is added to y. Initially, all y's are equal to 0. The behavior of P_i is illustrated in Fig. 7.19. As usual, a processor P_i performs a computation only if it receives an x and y and produces an output only if it has performed a computation. All processors work all the time. However, there are two phases, each lasting $k - 1$ time units, in which the processors are idle (i.e., do not perform any computations):

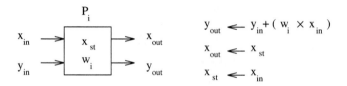

Figure 7.19: Behavior of processor P_i in fourth convolution algorithm.

1. An initial phase, during which the input simply propagates down the array until x_k reaches w_k.

2. A final phase, during which the output propagates out of the array.

Note also that response time is no longer constant: y_i is produced as output k time units after the last input required to compute it, namely, x_{i+k-1}, starts entering the leftmost processor of the array.

Analysis. It takes $n-1$ time units for x_n to reach P_k and an additional k time units to reach P_1. Therefore, the running time of this algorithm is $n+k-1$. Another way to see this is to note that y_1 waits $k-1$ time units before entering P_k and leaves P_1 after another k time units. The subsequent $n-k$ outputs take another $n-k$ time units in all.

Example 7.8 A few steps of the algorithm are illustrated in Fig. 7.20 for $k=3$. The number of time units elapsed is denoted by u. As shown in Fig. 7.20(a), y_1 enters P_3 after $k-1=2$ time units. It leaves P_1 after an additional $k=3$ time units, as shown in Fig. 7.20(d). In each of the subsequent $n-k$ time units, a new output is produced by P_1. □

7.4 GENERATING COMBINATORIAL OBJECTS (⋆)

A fundamental class of algorithms in computer science is concerned with the generation of combinatorial objects. A combinatorial object consists of n elements selected from a sequence $S = \{s_1, s_2, \ldots, s_m\}$ of m elements, arranged in a particular way. A total order relation $\prec$ is defined on the elements of S such that $s_1 \prec s_2 \prec \cdots \prec s_m$. There are usually many *instances* of a combinatorial object. For example, two *combinations* of n out of m elements are distinct if they differ in the elements they contain, while two *permutations* of m given elements are distinct if they differ in the order of their elements. Given a certain combinatorial object, it is required to design an efficient algorithm which will *generate* (i.e., produce as output in a list) all distinct instances of that object.

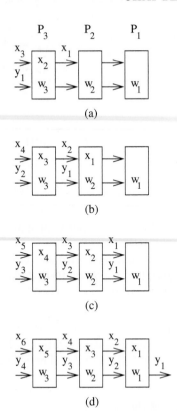

Figure 7.20: Fourth convolution algorithm for $k = 3$: (a) $u = 2$; (b) $u = 3$, $y_1 = w_3 x_3$; (c) $u = 4$, $y_1 = w_3 x_3 + w_2 x_2$, $y_2 = w_3 x_4$; (d) $u = 5$, $y_1 = w_3 x_3 + w_2 x_2 + w_1 x_1$, $y_2 = w_3 x_4 + w_2 x_3$, $y_3 = w_3 x_5$.

Example 7.9 Suppose that we want to generate all distinct permutations of n elements chosen from S. When $m = 3$ and $n = 2$, the output should be (s_1, s_2), (s_1, s_3), (s_2, s_1), (s_2, s_3), (s_3, s_1), and (s_3, s_2). In general, there are $m!/(m - n)!$ such permutations, and we seek an algorithm to produce each of them exactly once. □

In this section, we show how combinatorial objects can be generated on a linear array. We begin in Section 7.4.1 by presenting an algorithm for generating binary strings. This algorithm illustrates many of the ideas to be used later in the section. It also provides some motivation for the general design criteria described in Section 7.4.2. These criteria, to be satisfied by algorithms for generating combinatorial objects, lead to algorithms that are optimal in more than one sense. Sections 7.4.3 and 7.4.4 are devoted to the presentation of algorithms for generating combinations and permutations, respectively.

We assume henceforth that each of the processors of the linear array has the ability to produce its output to the outside world, either on a display device or by feeding it directly into another parallel computer for further processing, depending on the application.

7.4.1 A Binary Counter

A *binary counter* is a device that behaves like a car odometer or a digital clock. For some $n \geq 1$, such a counter produces binary strings of n bits—that is, strings of 0's and 1's—representing the numbers from 0 to $2^n - 1$. Initially, the counter is to display a string of n 0's. At each subsequent step, it is to generate the next binary string $b_1 b_2 \ldots b_n$, in increasing numerical order. For example, if $n = 6$, then the counter should produce 000000, 000001, 000010, 000011, ..., 111111.

Suppose that a binary counter is to be implemented as a linear array of n processors P_1, P_2, ..., P_n, where P_i is in charge of producing bit b_i. We require the counter to satisfy the following two design criteria:

1. Constant Space. Each processor P_i is to have a constant amount of storage space. Specifically, there is a fixed number of registers, or *words*, per processor. Each register consists of $O(\log n)$ bits, since P_i needs $\log n$ bits to represents its index i.

2. Constant Time. The time elapsed between any two consecutive binary strings displayed by the counter is constant. This requirement assumes that basic operations such as addition or the comparison of two words of size $O(\log n)$ bits each take $O(1)$ time.

Simple Solutions. Consider the output of a processor P_i when bits $b_1 b_2 \ldots b_i$ are fixed (i.e., do not change). We refer to this as a *block* of processor P_i.

Example 7.10 A block of processor P_4 when $n = 6$ is shown in Fig. 7.21. Note that the bit produced by each processor is shown inside the processor. The block shown in the figure occurs while strings 000100 to 000111 are being generated. □

In general:

1. A block of processor P_i consists of bit b_i repeated 2^{n-i} times.

2. Blocks producing a 0 2^{n-i} times and those producing a 1 2^{n-i} times follow each other in a cyclic manner.

One can use the foregoing observation to design the following algorithm for the binary counter:

Algorithm 1: Instruct P_i to produce a 0 2^{n-i} times, then a 1 2^{n-i} times, then a 0 2^{n-i} times, and so on. ■

The problem with this solution, however, is that for small values of i, 2^{n-i} is a large number, and the constant-space design criterion is violated. For example, when

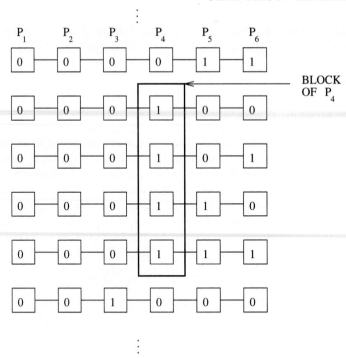

Figure 7.21: A block of processor P_4.

$i = 1$, P_1 needs $n - 1$ bits to store the integer 2^{n-1}, which is required to keep track of how many successive times a certain bit (0 or 1) has been produced.

We can avoid this difficulty by modifying the algorithm so that P_i does *not* need to keep track of how many times it has generated the same bit in succession. Again, refer to Fig. 7.21. In the last step shown, the output of P_4 changes from 1 to 0 and that of P_3 from 0 to 1. This is true in general: When a block of 1's in processor P_i ends, it is time for processor P_{i-1} to begin a new block. Therefore, the new algorithm is as follows:

Algorithm 2:   When b_i changes from 1 to 0, P_i sends a message to P_{i-1} to update b_{i-1} (from 1 to 0 or from 0 to 1). Also, instruct P_n to alternate between 0 and 1. ∎

Example 7.11 In the last step shown in Fig. 7.21, P_6 informs P_5 that it has switched from 1 to 0, and so P_5 also switches from 1 to 0 and informs P_4, which does the same and informs P_3. The latter switches from 0 to 1, and the new string 001000 has now been generated. □

The problem with this solution, as demonstrated by the example, is that the delay between one string and the next is not constant: The message has to travel from P_6 to P_3 before the new string is available. In the worst case this delay is $O(n)$, thus violating the constant-time design criterion.

Split and Plan. The two straightforward solutions just described illustrate the difficulty in trying to develop a parallel algorithm that simultaneously satisfies the two design criteria of constant space and constant time. We now show how this can be accomplished by, in fact, combining the two basic ideas outlined. The algorithm uses a technique called *split and plan*. *Split* refers to splitting the processors into two groups, each using a different algorithm to solve the problem. *Plan* refers to planning ahead of time to produce a binary string that represents a major change with respect to the string preceding it.

Let $s = n - \lceil \log n \rceil$. Processor P_s plays a special role in the algorithm. The processors are split into two groups: $P_1, P_2, \ldots, P_{s-1}$ and $P_s, P_{s+1}, \ldots, P_n$.

Algorithm for $P_s, P_{s+1}, \ldots, P_n$. When $i \geq s$, we have $2^{n-i} < 2n$. In other words, the number of binary strings for which b_i is unchanged when $i \geq s$ is less than $2n$. Consequently, every P_i, $s \leq i \leq n$, can store the number 2^{n-i} locally and use Algorithm 1 to produce its blocks. This requires less than $\lceil \log 2n \rceil$ bits of storage space per processor—that is, a constant number of words of $O(\log n)$ bits. It follows that the two design criteria of constant space and constant time are satisfied. ∎

Algorithm for $P_1, P_2, \ldots, P_{s-1}$. For these processors, Algorithm 2 is used: $P_i, 1 \leq i \leq s-1$, continually produces the same bit until it is informed to change its output. Preparation for a major update in the output of $P_1, P_2, \ldots, P_{s-1}$ begins a number of steps before it is supposed to take place. The process is started by P_s every time it produces the first 1 in a block (of 2^{n-s} 1's). A message is sent from P_s to P_{s-1} and continues to move to the left, advancing to a new processor for each new binary string generated. A processor P_i receiving this message forwards it (updated) to the left if $b_i = 1$ and does not forward it if $b_i = 0$ (thus ending the message's journey).

What does the message contain? When it reaches processor P_i, the message is an integer v_i equal to the number of steps that P_i needs to wait before switching its current output bit b_i. Initially, $v_{s-1} = 2^{n-s}$. Upon receipt of the message, P_i computes $v_{i-1} \leftarrow v_i - 1$ and sends it to P_{i-1} (provided that $b_i = 1$). Since $2^{n-s} > s - 1$, there is enough time for the message to visit all processors P_i, $i < s$, if necessary before the end of the current block of processor P_s. ∎

Example 7.12 Let $n = 8$. Then $s = 8 - \log 8 = 5$. Consider Fig. 7.22, in which a subset of the strings generated by the linear array is depicted. The column beneath P_i represents the output of P_i at each step. As soon as processor P_5 generates the first 1 of its current block, it sends a message to P_4 informing it that a major change is to occur in $2^{8-5} = 8$ steps. The message travels to the left, reaching P_3 and then P_2, where it stops. Six steps later, processors P_2, P_3, and P_4 are ready to change their respective bits simultaneously. □

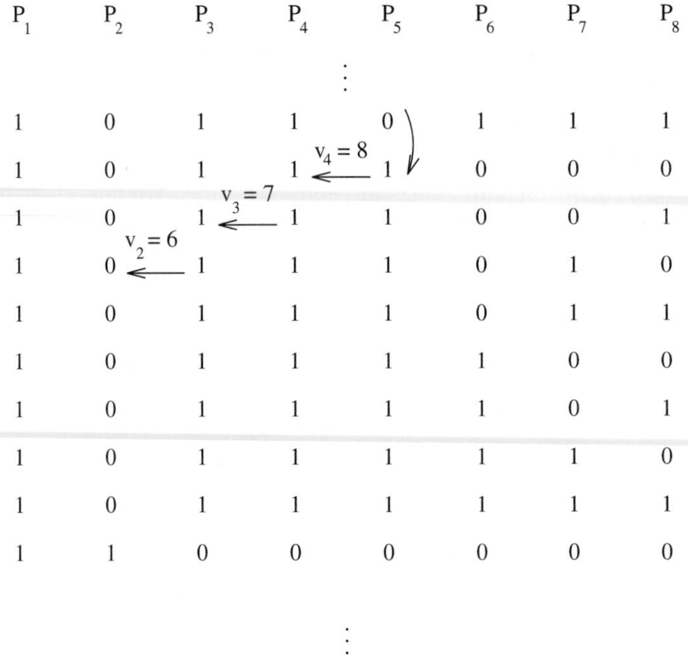

P_1	P_2	P_3	P_4	P_5	P_6	P_7	P_8
			$\vdots$				
1	0	1	1	0	1	1	1
1	0	1	1	1	0	0	0
1	0	1	1	1	0	0	1
1	0	1	1	1	0	1	0
1	0	1	1	1	0	1	1
1	0	1	1	1	1	0	0
1	0	1	1	1	1	0	1
1	0	1	1	1	1	1	0
1	0	1	1	1	1	1	1
1	1	0	0	0	0	0	0
			$\vdots$				

In the upper rows, $v_4 = 8$ (arrow into P_4 from P_5), $v_3 = 7$ (arrow into P_3 from P_4), $v_2 = 6$ (arrow into P_2 from P_3).

Figure 7.22: Planning for a major change in P_2, P_3, and P_4.

Termination.   The only detail left is to specify how all processors stop simultaneously after the last binary string is produced. Processor P_1 has only two blocks, each of size 2^{n-1}, namely, a block of 0's followed by a block of 1's. When this processor produces a 1 for the first time, it sends a termination message, END, to processor P_2. Each processor P_i, $i \geq 2$, forwards this message to the right when it also produces a 1 for the first time after receiving it. This way, all processors receive the message and terminate, all at the same time, the moment every one is supposed to produce a 0 for the first time (after a block of 1's). Since $2^{n-1} > n-1$, the termination message has enough time to reach all of the processors.

Example 7.13 The termination condition is illustrated in Fig. 7.23 for $n = 4$. $\square$

By combining the algorithm for P_1, P_2, $\ldots$, P_{s-1} with the algorithm for P_s, $P_{s+1}, \ldots, P_n$ and the termination condition, we obtain a binary counter for a linear array of processors, to which we refer as algorithm LINEAR ARRAY BINARY COUNTER.

Analysis.   There are 2^n distinct binary strings of length n. On a linear array of n processors, the algorithm generates each of these strings exactly once, in constant

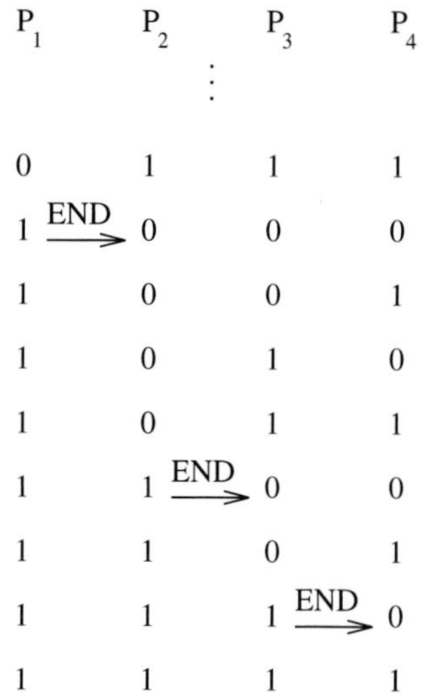

$$P_1 \qquad P_2 \qquad P_3 \qquad P_4$$

$$\vdots$$

0	1	1	1
1 $\xrightarrow{\text{END}}$ 0	0	0	
1	0	0	1
1	0	1	0
1	0	1	1
1	1 $\xrightarrow{\text{END}}$ 0	0	
1	1	0	1
1	1	1 $\xrightarrow{\text{END}}$ 0	
1	1	1	1

Figure 7.23: Termination condition for binary counter.

time. The cost of this algorithm is $O(n2^n)$, which is optimal in view of the $\Omega(n2^n)$ operations required to produce the output.

7.4.2 Optimality Conditions

Algorithm **LINEAR ARRAY BINARY COUNTER** runs on a linear array of n processors, with a memory of constant size per processor, and generates consecutive strings with a constant delay. We now explain the importance of these properties for parallel algorithms that generate *all* instances of a combinatorial object defined on a sequence $S = \{s_1, s_2, \ldots, s_m\}$ on whose elements a total order relation is defined. An algorithm that runs on a linear array of processors and satisfies these conditions is optimal in the most general sense.

1. Constant Space. Each processor has a constant number of words, each of $O(\log m)$ bits. □

Each word is thus capable of storing a binary encoding of one of the elements of S, or of an integer no larger than m. Theoretically, given a collection of algorithms for a certain problem, all with the same running time but different memory requirements, the one needing the least memory is usually the best. In practice, when the algorithm is implemented using a collection of tiny processors on a chip, small memory usage is preferable, if not necessary. The constant-space property implies that no processor can by itself store an array of size m, or a large combinatorial number such as $m!$.

2. Constant Time. The time required by the algorithm between the production of any two consecutive instances of an object is constant. □

Constant time to produce each instance of an object is, of course, the best any algorithm can aim to achieve, from the theoretical point of view. As usual, we are assuming here that a processor requires constant time to perform an elementary operation, such as addition or comparison, on two numbers of $O(\log m)$ bits each. A constant time delay between outputs is also important in practice, particularly in applications where the output of one computation serves as input to another.

3. Cost Optimality. The algorithm is cost optimal. □

Suppose that each instance of a combinatorial object J consists of n elements and that there are $I(n, m)$ distinct instances in all. Then a lower bound on the number of elementary operations required to generate all instances of S is $\Omega(nI(n, m))$. A parallel algorithm for generating (i.e., producing as output a list of) all instances of J will be cost optimal if the product of its running time and the number of processors it uses is $O(nI(n, m))$.

In what follows, we describe algorithms that generate combinations and permutations on a linear array, while satisfying the preceding three optimality conditions.

7.4.3   Combinations

An *n-combination* of $S = \{s_1, s_2, \ldots, s_m\}$ is obtained by selecting n distinct elements of S. The elements of the *n*-combination are listed in increasing order, using an order relation $\prec$ defined on S. Thus, for $m = 12$ and $n = 5$, $s_4 s_7 s_9 s_{10} s_{11}$ is a 5-combination. There are $C(n, m) = m!/(m - n)!n!$ distinct *n*-combinations of m elements, requiring $\Omega(nC(n, m))$ operations to be generated.

In this section, we describe an algorithm for generating *n*-combinations of $S = \{1, 2, \ldots, m\}$, with the order relation defined on the elements of S being $<$ (i.e., the usual "less than" relation). The algorithm uses a linear array of n processors $P_1, P_2, \ldots, P_n$, indexed from left to right. Each processor is in charge of producing one element of each combination. The special case of $n = m$ is easily handled: Since there is only one combination to be generated, processor P_i produces the integer i and terminates. In what follows, we examine the case where $1 \leq n \leq m - 1$. We also use *combination* to mean *n-combination* of S.

Let $A = a(1)a(2)\ldots a(n)$ and $B = b(1)b(2)\ldots b(n)$ be two combinations. We say that A *precedes* B *lexicographically* if and only if for some $k \geq 1$, $a(i) = b(i)$ when $i < k$, and $a(k) < b(k)$. The first combination in lexicographic order is $12\ldots n$, and the last one is $(m - n + 1)(m - n + 2)\ldots m$.

Example 7.14 Let $m = 5$ and $n = 3$. Then there are 10 distinct 3-combinations, in the following lexicographic order: 1 2 3, 1 2 4, 1 2 5, 1 3 4, 1 3 5, 1 4 5, 2 3 4, 2 3 5, 2 4 5, 3 4 5. □

Suppose that we want to generate all combinations of S in lexicographic order. We begin by developing some intuition. By a *run* of processor P_i, $1 \leq i \leq n$, we mean that processor's output when the output of P_1, P_2, $\ldots$, P_{i-1} is fixed. Processor P_1 produces one run of numbers $a(1)$ such that each number $a(1)$ is repeated $C(n-1, m-a(1))$ times in succession, for $a(1) = 1, 2, \ldots, m-n+1$. Processors P_2, P_3, $\ldots$, P_n will each produce several runs. One run of processor P_i, $2 \le i \le n$, consists of numbers $a(i)$ such that $a(i)$ is repeated $C(n-i, m-a(i))$ times in succession, for $a(i) = a(i-1) + 1$, $a(i-1) + 2$, $\ldots$, $m-n+i$. Note that the largest number produced by P_i is $m-n+i$, $1 \le i \le n$. This is easily verified by referring to Example 7.14.

We now need to refine the preceding observation so as to guarantee that each processor P_i will "know" when to begin and end a run, will have $a(i-1)$ available, and will produce its output, all while using a constant amount of space and a constant amount of time between outputs.

We denote the jth combination in a lexicographic ordering of combinations by $a_j(1)a_j(2)\ldots a_j(n)$, where

$$1 \le a_j(i) \le m, \quad 1 \le i \le n, \quad \text{and} \quad 1 \le j \le C(n,m).$$

For $1 \le i \le n$ and $1 \le j < C(n,m)$, the following properties hold:

Property 1. $a_{j+1}(i) = 1 + a_{j+1}(i-1)$ if $a_j(i) = m-n+i$. □

To see this, note that since $a_j(1)a_j(2)\ldots a_j(n)$ is an ascending series of values from $\{1, 2, \ldots, m\}$, we have

$$a_j(i) = m-n+i, \quad a_j(i+1) = m-n+i+1, \quad \ldots, \quad a_j(n) = m,$$

and therefore, $a_j(i)$ to $a_j(n)$ must be updated in the next combination, having attained their largest possible values. In order to guarantee that $a_{j+1}(1)$ $a_{j+1}(2)$ $\ldots$ $a_{j+1}(n)$ is also in ascending order and that it follows in lexicographic order, $a_{j+1}(i)$ takes the smallest possible value it can, namely, $a_{j+1}(i-1) + 1$.

Property 2. $a_{j+1}(i) = 1 + a_j(i)$, if $a_j(i) < m-n+i$ and $a_{j-k}(i+1) = m-n+i$, for all k, $k = 1, 2, \ldots, n-i$. □

To see this, let $a_j(i) = v$, where $v < m-n+i$, and $a_j(1)a_j(2)\ldots a_j(i-1) = X$ for some series of values X. Suppose that the jth combination is the last combination with prefix Xv. Now consider the following combinations, listed in lexicographic order, for some q series of values Y_1, Y_2, $\ldots$, Y_q:

$j - q$:	X	v	$m-n+i$		Y_1
$j - q + 1$:	X	v	$m-n+i$		Y_2
			$\vdots$		
$j - 1$:	X	v	$m-n+i$		Y_q
j :	X	v	$m-n+i+1$	$m-n+i+2$	$\ldots$
$j + 1$:	X	$v+1$	$v+2$		$\ldots$

Clearly, $a_j(i+1) = m-n+i+1$, $a_j(i+2) = m-n+i+2$, $\ldots$, $a_j(n) = m$. To guarantee that the next combination is in lexicographic order, $a_{j+1}(i) = v+1$.

Also, as shown, there are q previous combinations with $m - n + i$ in position $i + 1$. What is q? Since each of the q series Y_1, Y_2, $\ldots$, Y_q consists of $n - (i + 1)$ integers chosen from the $n - i$ integers $m - n + i + 1$, $m - n + i + 2$, $\ldots$, m, the number of such series is $q = C(n - i - 1, n - i) = n - i$.

Property 3. $a_{j+1}(i) = a_j(i)$, if $a_j(i) < m - n + i$ and $a_{j-k}(i + 1) \neq m - n + i$, for some k, $k = 1, 2, \ldots, n - i$. $\square$

To see this, we continue with the same argument as for property 2. Any combination with prefix Xv, except the last, is *not* preceded by $n - i$ combinations with $m - n + i$ in position $i + 1$, and therefore, v in position i remains unchanged.

Example 7.15 Consider the third and fourth 3-combinations in Example 7.14, namely, $a_3(1)a_3(2)a_3(3) = 1\ 2\ 5$ and $a_4(1)a_4(2)a_4(3) = 1\ 3\ 4$.

1. For $i = 1, m - n + i = 5 - 3 + 1 = 3$. Since $a_3(1) = 1 < 3$ and $a_1(2) = a_2(2) = 2 < 5 - 3 + 2$, we have $a_4(1) = a_3(1) = 1$.

2. For $i = 2, m - n + i = 5 - 3 + 2 = 4$. Since $a_3(2) = 2 < 4$ and $a_2(3) = 4$, we have $a_4(2) = 1 + a_3(2) = 3$.

3. For $i = 3, m - n + i = 5 - 3 + 3 = 5$. Since $a_3(3) = 5$, we have $a_4(3) = 1 + a_4(2) = 4$. $\square$

The algorithm consists of $C(n, m)$ iterations; during the jth iteration, it generates the jth combination $a_j(1)a_j(2)\ldots a_j(n)$, with processor P_i producing $a_j(i)$. Each processor P_i maintains a variable $D(i)$. Initially, $D(i) = a_{n-i+1}(i)$; that is, P_i is one step ahead of P_{i+1}. The latter property is maintained throughout the algorithm, as shown in Fig. 7.24 for $m = 5$ and $n = 3$, where a sequence of lines connecting integers indicates the values that are in the variables $D(i)$ at each step. As a result, when $D(n) = a_j(n)$, for $j = C(n, m)$, processors P_1, P_2, $\ldots$, P_{n-1} will have calculated further values. These, as well as two special values, $a_j(0)$ and $a_j(n + 1)$, are defined as follows:

1. For $j \geq 1$, $a_j(0) = m - n$, and $a_j(n + 1) = m$.

2. For $j \geq C(n, m)$ and $1 \leq i \leq n$, $a_j(i) = m - n + i$.

Thus, for $1 \leq j \leq C(n, m)$ and $0 \leq i \leq n + 1$, we can write $D(i) = a_{j+n-i}(i)$.

The key to the algorithm is the efficient calculation of each $D(i)$ at each step when j is increased by 1. For this purpose, a number of values must be maintained by P_i:

1. During the jth iteration, P_i must produce $a_j(i)$ as output; however, at that moment, $D(i) = a_{j+n-i}(i)$. Thus, P_i needs to store $a_j(i)$, $a_{j+1}(i)$, $\ldots$, $a_{j+n-i}(i)$.

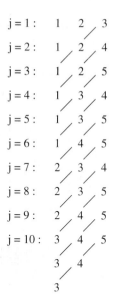

Figure 7.24: Processor P_i is one step ahead of P_{i+1} in the generation of combinations.

2. During the jth iteration, P_{i+1} updates $D(i + 1)$; the new value is $a_k(i + 1)$, where $k = (j + 1) + n - (i + 1) = j + n - i$. Since this calculation may require reference to $a_{j+n-i}(i)$, the latter needs to be stored by P_i.

3. During the jth iteration P_{i-1} updates $D(i - 1)$; the new value is $a_k(i - 1)$, where $k = (j + 1) + n - (i - 1)$. Since this calculation may require references to $a_{j+1}(i)$, $a_{j+2}(i)$, ..., $a_{j+n-i}(i)$, these values need to be stored by P_i.

The preceding analysis leads us to conclude that P_i needs to maintain $a_j(i)$, $a_{j+1}(i)$, ..., $a_{j+n-i}(i)$. We observe, however, that within any $n - i + 1$ successive combinations, where the elements in positions 1, 2, ..., $i - 1$ are kept fixed, the element in position i has at most three different values: $D(i)$ and two other values, denoted by $d_1(i)$ and $d_2(i)$. This can be easily seen by noting that, at position i, any element v, where $v \leq m - n + i$, occurs $C(n - i, m - v)$ times in successive combinations:

1. If $v = m - n + i$, then it appears once.

2. If $v = m - n + i - 1$, then it appears $n - i + 1$ times.

3. If $v < m - n + i - 1$, then it appears more than $n - i + 1$ times.

Therefore, P_i needs to store only five local variables, namely, the three values of v and the number of repetitions $r(i)$ and $r_1(i)$ when v appears more than once. All processors terminate when $D(i) = m - n + i$ has been repeated n times; this occurs simultaneously for all i, $1 \le i \le n$. The algorithm is given next as algorithm LINEAR ARRAY COMBINATIONS. Note that $d_1(i)$, $d_2(i)$, and $r_1(i)$ can be initialized arbitrarily, since each is needed only *after* it has been assigned a value.

Algorithm LINEAR ARRAY COMBINATIONS

Step 1: (1.1) $D(0) \leftarrow m - n$

(1.2) $D(n+1) \leftarrow m$

(1.3) $r(n+1) \leftarrow 0$

Step 2: for $i = 1$ **to** n **do in parallel**

(2.1) $D(i) \leftarrow i$

(2.2) $r(i) \leftarrow n - i + 1$

(2.3) **while not** $(D(i) = m - n + i$ **and** $r(i) > n)$ **do**

    (i) **if** $r(i) > n - i$

        then output $D(i)$

        else if $r(i) + r_1(i) > n - i$

            then output $d_1(i)$

            else output $d_2(i)$

            end if

        end if

    (ii) $x \leftarrow D(i-1)$

    (iii) $y \leftarrow D(i+1)$

    (iv) $z \leftarrow r(i+1)$

    (v) **if** $D(i) = m - n + i$

        then (a) $d_2(i) \leftarrow d_1(i)$

            (b) $d_1(i) \leftarrow D(i)$

            (c) $r_1(i) \leftarrow r(i)$

            (d) $D(i) \leftarrow x + 1$

            (e) $r(i) \leftarrow 1$

        else if $y = m - n + i$ **and** $z = n - i$

            then (a) $d_2(i) \leftarrow d_1(i)$

                (b) $d_1(i) \leftarrow D(i)$

                (c) $r_1(i) \leftarrow r(i)$

                (d) $D(i) \leftarrow D(i) + 1$

                (e) $r(i) \leftarrow 1$

            else if $r(i) \le n$

                then $r(i) \leftarrow r(i) + 1$

                end if

            end if

        end if

    end while

end for. ∎

Analysis.   The algorithm uses n processors, each with a constant amount of storage space, and generates all $C(n, m)$ combinations, in constant time per combination. It therefore has a cost of $O(nC(n, m))$, which is optimal, in view of the $\Omega(nC(n, m))$ lower bound on the number of operations required to generate all n-combinations of m elements.

7.4.4 Permutations

A *permutation* of $S = \{s_1, s_2, \ldots, s_n\}$ is an arrangement of the elements of S in a certain order. Thus, for $n = 5$, $s_4 s_2 s_5 s_1 s_3$ and $s_2 s_3 s_5 s_4 s_1$ are two different permutations. There are $n!$ distinct permutations of n elements, requiring $\Omega(nn!)$ operations to be generated. In this section, we describe an algorithm for generating all permutations of n *arbitrary* elements on which a total order is defined such that $s_1 \prec s_2 \prec \cdots \prec s_n$. The algorithm runs on a linear array of n processors P_1, $P_2, \ldots, P_n$, indexed from left to right. Each processor is responsible for producing one element of every permutation generated. Once a permutation has been generated, each processor updates the element it just produced, and the next permutation is generated.

The algorithm generates permutations such that each permutation differs from the previous one in the least possible way. This is accomplished by creating each new permutation through a transposition of two neighboring elements in the previous one. The resulting permutations are said to be generated in *minimal-change order*. This approach is particularly suitable for the linear array, since each processor P_i has direct access only to its two adjacent processors P_{i-1} and P_{i+1}.

Let $E(i)$ be the output of processor P_i. After each adjacent transposition, P_i generates an updated $E(i)$, $1 \leq i \leq n$, resulting in an entire new permutation being produced as output. Initially, $E(i) \leftarrow s_i$, $1 \leq i \leq n$. The following steps are then repeated until the algorithm terminates:

1. Move element s_n to the left, from P_n to P_1, by repeatedly exchanging it with its left neighbor.

2. Generate the next permutation of $\{s_1, s_2, \ldots, s_{n-1}\}$ in $P_2, P_3, \ldots, P_n$.

3. Move element s_n to the right, from P_1 to P_n, by repeatedly exchanging it with its right neighbor.

4. Generate the next permutation of $\{s_1, s_2, \ldots, s_{n-1}\}$ in $P_1, P_2, \ldots, P_{n-1}$. ■

The algorithm is based on the idea of generating the permutations of $\{s_1, s_2, \ldots, s_n\}$ from the permutations of $\{s_1, s_2, \ldots, s_{n-1}\}$ by taking each such permutation and inserting s_n in all n possible positions of it. For example, taking the permutation $s_1 s_2 \ldots s_{n-1}$ of $\{s_1, s_2, \ldots, s_{n-1}\}$, we get n permutations of $\{s_1, s_2, \ldots, s_n\}$ as follows:

$$
\begin{array}{cccccc}
s_1 & s_2 & \cdots & s_{n-2} & s_{n-1} & \boldsymbol{s_n} \\
s_1 & s_2 & \cdots & s_{n-2} & \boldsymbol{s_n} & s_{n-1} \\
s_1 & s_2 & \cdots & \boldsymbol{s_n} & s_{n-2} & s_{n-1} \\
 & & \vdots & & & \\
\boldsymbol{s_n} & s_1 & \cdots & s_{n-3} & s_{n-2} & s_{n-1}
\end{array}
$$

In Step 1 of the algorithm, we are given a permutation of $\{s_1, s_2, \ldots, s_{n-1}\}$ in $P_1, P_2, \ldots, P_{n-1}$ and the element s_n in P_n. The element s_n is moved to the left $n-1$ times, thus generating $n-1$ distinct permutations of $\{s_1, s_2, \ldots, s_n\}$. Therefore, Step 1 can be viewed as consisting of $n-1$ pulses, each producing a distinct permutation.

With s_n in P_1, Step 2 generates the next permutation of $\{s_1, s_2, \ldots, s_{n-1}\}$ in $P_2, P_3, \ldots, P_n$. Step 3 moves s_n to the right $n-1$ times, and $n-1$ additional permutations of $\{s_1, s_2, \ldots, s_n\}$ are obtained. Like Step 1, Step 3 can be viewed as consisting of $n-1$ pulses, each producing a new permutation. Finally, Step 4 generates the next permutation of $\{s_1, s_2, \ldots, s_{n-1}\}$ in $P_1, P_2, \ldots, P_{n-1}$ while s_n is in P_n, and the loop is restarted at Step 1.

Steps 1 and 3 are trivial to implement on a linear array of processors: During each pulse, the processor holding s_n exchanges it with its left neighbor in Step 1 and its right neighbor in Step 3. It remains to show how Steps 2 and 4 are implemented.

To generate the $(n-1)! - 1$ permutations of $\{s_1, s_2, \ldots, s_{n-1}\}$ that follow $s_1 s_2 \ldots s_{n-1}$, also by adjacent transpositions, we assign a *direction* to every element. This is denoted by an arrow above the element, for illustration. Initially, all arrows point to the left. Thus, if the permutations of $\{s_1, s_2, s_3, s_4\}$ are to be generated, we would have

$$
\overset{\leftarrow}{s_1}\ \overset{\leftarrow}{s_2}\ \overset{\leftarrow}{s_3}\ \overset{\leftarrow}{s_4}\ .
$$

Now, an element is said to be *mobile* if its direction points to a "smaller" adjacent neighbor—that is, a neighbor which precedes it according to the order relation $\prec$. (Recall that $s_1 \prec s_2 \prec \cdots \prec s_n$.) In the foregoing example, s_2, s_3, and s_4 are mobile, while in

$$
\overset{\rightarrow}{s_3}\ \overset{\leftarrow}{s_1}\ \overset{\leftarrow}{s_2}\ \overset{\rightarrow}{s_4},
$$

only s_2 and s_3 are mobile. The algorithm is as follows:

> **while** there are mobile elements **do**
>   (1) Find the largest mobile element; call it s_m.
>   (2) Switch s_m with the adjacent neighbor to which its direction points.
>   (3) Reverse the direction of all elements larger than s_m.
> **end while.** ∎

To implement this idea on the linear array of processors, we set the direction of $E(1), E(2), \ldots, E(n-1)$ to the left initially. The direction of s_n is immaterial to the proper execution of the algorithm and can be defined arbitrarily. How do all processors in Steps 2 and 4 know the largest mobile element? This is done by propagating that information during the $n-1$ pulses that precede each of these steps. A variable can be used that travels along with s_n and holds at any given time the largest mobile element in $\{s_1, s_2, \ldots, s_{n-1}\}$ it has encountered so far. When s_n reaches its destination at the end of Step 1 (Step 3), the largest mobile element is "known" to P_1 (P_n). It would appear that $n-1$ additional pulses are needed to make this information "known" to the other processors, thus violating the constant-time condition. In order to avoid this, a second variable is used that travels in the direction opposite to s_n; this variable also holds at any given time the largest mobile element it has encountered so far. Thus, each processor P_i stores two variables:

leftmax(i) = index of the largest mobile element from the sequence $\{s_1, s_2, \ldots,$
   $s_{n-1}\}$ in $P_1, P_2, \ldots, P_i$.

rightmax(i) = index of the largest mobile element from the sequence $\{s_1, s_2, \ldots,$
   $s_{n-1}\}$ in $P_i, P_{i+1}, \ldots, P_n$.

These two variables are initialized at the beginning of Steps 1 and 3 as follows: Let $E(i) = s_k$; then:

$$leftmax(i) = rightmax(i) \ = \ k, \qquad \text{provided that} \ \ E(i) \prec s_n \ \ \text{and} \ E(i) \ \text{is mobile}$$
$$= \ 0 \qquad \text{otherwise.}$$

The variables are then updated during the $n-1$ pulses of Steps 1 and 3.

Example 7.16 Let $n = 5$. The values of $E(i)$, *leftmax*(i), and *rightmax*(i) during the first iteration of Step 1 are shown in Figs. 7.25 and 7.26. $\square$

The complete algorithm is given next as algorithm LINEAR ARRAY PERMUTATIONS. It begins with an initialization phase A in which the first permutation is produced as output. This is followed by a second phase B in which Steps 1–4 are iterated to generate the remaining permutations. Note that:

1. Whenever the index k is used, it is assumed that $E(i) = s_k$.

2. The direction of $E(i)$ is stored in a variable *arrow*(i), taking one of the two values **left** and **right**.

3. Two additional variables $E(0)$ and $E(n+1)$ are used for convenience such that $E(0) = E(n+1) = \Delta$, where $s_n \prec \Delta$.

4. The algorithm terminates when no mobile element is found, a condition that is detected simultaneously by all processors, since in this case *leftmax*$(i) =$ *rightmax*(i) for all $1 \leq i \leq n$. Each processor for which this equality holds checks whether the same is true for one of its two neighbors, and if so, the processor terminates execution.

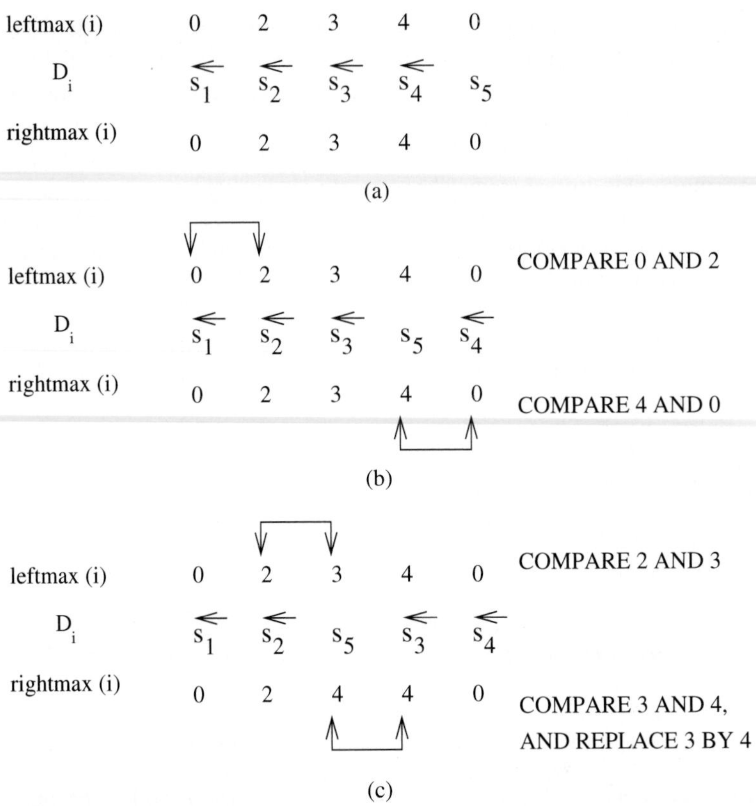

leftmax (i)   0   2   3   4   0

D_i $\overset{\leftarrow}{s_1}$ $\overset{\leftarrow}{s_2}$ $\overset{\leftarrow}{s_3}$ $\overset{\leftarrow}{s_4}$ s_5

rightmax (i)   0   2   3   4   0

(a)

leftmax (i)   0   2   3   4   0   COMPARE 0 AND 2

D_i $\overset{\leftarrow}{s_1}$ $\overset{\leftarrow}{s_2}$ $\overset{\leftarrow}{s_3}$ s_5 $\overset{\leftarrow}{s_4}$

rightmax (i)   0   2   3   4   0   COMPARE 4 AND 0

(b)

leftmax (i)   0   2   3   4   0   COMPARE 2 AND 3

D_i $\overset{\leftarrow}{s_1}$ $\overset{\leftarrow}{s_2}$ s_5 $\overset{\leftarrow}{s_3}$ $\overset{\leftarrow}{s_4}$

rightmax (i)   0   2   4   4   0   COMPARE 3 AND 4,
                                                        AND REPLACE 3 BY 4

(c)

Figure 7.25: Finding the largest mobile element on a linear array (first two pulses): (a) Initially; (b) After one pulse; (c) After two pulses.

Algorithm LINEAR ARRAY PERMUTATIONS

A. Initialization

Step 1: for $i = 1$ to n **do in parallel**
        (1.1) $E(i) \leftarrow s_i$
        (1.2) $arrow(i) \leftarrow$ **left**
        (1.3) **output** $E(i)$
        end for
Step 2: $E(0) \leftarrow \Delta, \quad E(n+1) \leftarrow \Delta$

B. Repeat

Step 1: (1.1) **for** $i = 1$ to n **do in parallel**
        if $(arrow(i) =$ **left and** $E(i-1) \prec E(i) \prec s_n)$
          or $(arrow(i) =$ **right and** $E(i+1) \prec E(i) \prec s_n)$
        then $leftmax(i) \leftarrow k$, $rightmax(i) \leftarrow k$
        else $leftmax(i) \leftarrow 0$, $rightmax(i) \leftarrow 0$
        end if
        end for

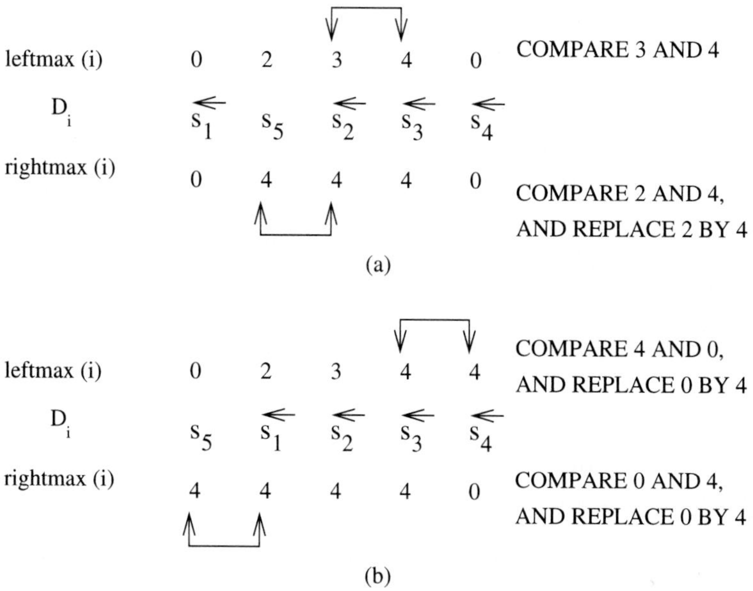

leftmax (i)   0   2   3   4   0   COMPARE 3 AND 4

D_i $\overleftarrow{s}_1$ $\overleftarrow{s}_5$ $\overleftarrow{s}_2$ $\overleftarrow{s}_3$ $\overleftarrow{s}_4$

rightmax (i)   0   4   4   4   0   COMPARE 2 AND 4,
                                               AND REPLACE 2 BY 4

(a)

COMPARE 4 AND 0,
leftmax (i)   0   2   3   4   4   AND REPLACE 0 BY 4

D_i s_5 $\overleftarrow{s}_1$ $\overleftarrow{s}_2$ $\overleftarrow{s}_3$ $\overleftarrow{s}_4$

rightmax (i)   4   4   4   4   0   COMPARE 0 AND 4,
                                               AND REPLACE 0 BY 4

(b)

Figure 7.26: Finding the largest mobile element on a linear array (second two pulses): (a) After three pulses; (b) After four pulses.

(1.2) **for** $i = 1$ **to** $n - 1$ **do**
    (i) $E(n - i) \leftrightarrow E(n - i + 1)$, $arrow(n{-}i) \leftrightarrow arrow(n{-}i{+}1)$
    (ii) **for** $j = 1$ **to** n **do in parallel**
        output $E(j)$
        end for
    (iii) $leftmax(i{+}1) \leftarrow \max(leftmax(i),\ leftmax(i{+}1))$
    (iv) $rightmax(n{-}i) \leftarrow \max(rightmax(n{-}i),\ rightmax(n{-}i{+}1))$
    end for
Step 2: (2.1) **for** $i = 2$ **to** n **do in parallel**
    if $\max(leftmax(i),\ rightmax(i)) < k$
    then reverse the direction of $arrow(i)$
    else if $\max(leftmax(i),\ rightmax(i)) = k$
        then if $arrow(i) = $ **left**
            then $E(i - 1) \leftrightarrow E(i)$, $arrow(i - 1) \leftrightarrow arrow(i)$
            else $E(i) \leftrightarrow E(i + 1)$, $arrow(i) \leftrightarrow arrow(i{+}1)$
            end if
        end if
    end if
    end for
(2.2) **for** $i = 1$ **to** n **do in parallel**
    output $E(i)$
    end for

Step 3: (3.1) Same as Step (1.1) of phase B

         (3.2) **for** $i = 1$ **to** $n - 1$ **do**

               (i) $E(i) \leftrightarrow E(i + 1)$, $arrow(i) \leftrightarrow arrow(i{+}1)$

               (ii) **for** $j = 1$ **to** n **do in parallel**

                     output $E(j)$

                  end for

               (iii) $leftmax(i{+}1) \leftarrow \max(leftmax(i), leftmax(i{+}1))$

               (iv) $rightmax(n{-}i) \leftarrow \max(rightmax(n{-}i), rightmax(n{-}i{+}1))$

             end for

Step 4: (4.1) **for** $i = 1$ **to** $n - 1$ **do in parallel**

             Same as body of loop in Step (2.1)

             end for

         (4.2) **for** $i = 1$ **to** n **do in parallel**

               output $E(i)$

             end for

until there are no mobile elements. ∎

Analysis. The algorithm generates the $n!$ permutations in constant time per permutation, using a linear array of n processors, each with a constant amount of storage space. The algorithm is cost optimal, in view of the $\Omega(nn!)$ operations required to generate the $n!$ permutations.

7.5   PROBLEMS

7.1 Prove the correctness of the sorting algorithm in Section 7.1.1.

7.2 One interesting feature of the algorithm in Section 7.1.1 is that, once input is complete and output starts, the array can begin processing a new input sequence of n elements. This is useful when several sequences are queued for sorting. Discuss the changes required in order for the algorithm to be able to handle m consecutive input sequences, and analyze the performance of the modified algorithm.

7.3 Another variant of the algorithm of Section 7.1.1 allows both P_1 and P_n to handle input and output. While P_1 is producing output, P_n can receive input, and conversely. Sorted sequences are produced alternately in nondecreasing order (through P_1) and in nonincreasing order (through P_n). Analyze the performance of this algorithm in the case where m sequences are queued for sorting.

7.4 Consider the following algorithm for sorting a sequence of numbers $S = \{s_1, s_2, \ldots, s_n\}$ on a linear array of n processors $P_1, P_2, \ldots, P_n$. Initially, P_i holds s_i, $1 \leq i \leq n$. As in Section 7.1.1, let "compare-exchange (P_i, P_{i+1})" denote the operation of comparing the numbers held by P_i and P_{i+1} and

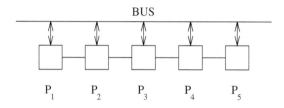

Figure 7.27: Linear array augmented with a bus.

then placing the smaller number in P_i and the larger in P_{i+1}. The algorithm, known as *odd-even transposition sort*, consists of two steps that are performed repeatedly:

> **Step 1: for** $i = 1, 3, \ldots, 2\lfloor n/2 \rfloor - 1$ **do in parallel**
>   compare-exchange (P_i, P_{i+1})
>   **end for**
> **Step 2: for** $i = 2, 4, \ldots, 2\lfloor (n-1)/2 \rfloor$ **do in parallel**
>   compare-exchange (P_i, P_{i+1})
>   **end for.** ∎

Show that after $\lceil n/2 \rceil$ repetitions of the preceding two steps, in that order, P_i holds the ith smallest number. (*Hint*: Refer to Section 8.1.2.)

7.5 The algorithm in Problem 7.4 uses n processors and runs in $O(n)$ time, for a cost of $O(n^2)$, which is not optimal. Suppose instead that $\log n$ processors are used, each capable of storing $n/\log n$ elements of the input sequence. The 'compare-exchange (P_i, P_{i+1})' operation is now replaced with a 'merge-split (P_i, P_{i+1})' operation. Assuming that each of P_i and P_{i+1} holds a sorted subsequence, this operation merges the two subsequences into one and then splits the latter into two halves, the first going to P_i and the second to P_{i+1}. Provide a complete description of the new algorithm, and analyze its running time and cost.

7.6 One limitation of the linear array is its large diameter: It takes $n - 1$ steps for a datum to travel from P_1 to P_n on an n-processor array. In an attempt to circumvent this weakness, a variant of the model is used in which a further communication path, known as a *bus*, is available in addition to the usual links connecting the processors. The setup is shown in Fig. 7.27 for $n = 5$. At any given time during the execution of an algorithm, exactly one processor is allowed to *broadcast* a datum to the other processors using the bus. All processors receive the datum simultaneously. The time required by the broadcast operation is assumed to be constant; thus to go from P_1 to P_n, a datum now takes one time unit. The bus can also be used to provide input to the array from the outside world. An input sequence $S = \{s_1, s_2, \ldots, s_n\}$ is to be sorted on this model so that when the algorithm terminates, P_i holds the ith smallest element. Show how this can be done using the following approach to sorting: An element occupies position i of the sorted sequence if exactly $i - 1$ elements are found to be smaller than it. Analyze the resulting algorithm's running time.

7.7 As defined in Section 2.3.1, a *ring* is a linear array of processors P_1, P_2, $\ldots$, P_m in which P_1 and P_m are directly connected. Show how a ring can be used to compute an $m \times 1$ vector $\boldsymbol{v}$ resulting from multiplying an $m \times n$ matrix $\boldsymbol{A}$ and an $n \times 1$ vector $\boldsymbol{u}$. Compare the running time of your solution to that of the algorithm in Section 7.2.1.

7.8 Design an algorithm for multiplying two $n \times n$ matrices on a linear array of processors, and analyze the running time, number of processors, and cost of the algorithm.

7.9 An *upper triangular* matrix is a square matrix, all of whose elements below the main diagonal are 0. Design a parallel algorithm for solving the system of equations $\boldsymbol{Ax} = \boldsymbol{b}$, where $\boldsymbol{A}$ is a given $n \times n$ upper triangular matrix, $\boldsymbol{b}$ is a given $n \times 1$ vector, and $\boldsymbol{x}$ is an $n \times 1$ vector of unknowns.

7.10 Two methods were mentioned at the end of Section 7.2.2 to improve the utilization of processors:

(a) Using $n/2$ processors instead of n.

(b) Solving two systems simultaneously, using n processors.

Provide the details of these two methods.

7.11 Describe a dual to the algorithm of Section 7.3.2 in which the w's move twice as fast as the x's, and analyze the performance of the new algorithm.

7.12 Describe a dual to the algorithm of Section 7.3.4 in which the x's move twice as fast as the y's, and analyze the performance of the new algorithm.

7.13 Describe an algorithm for performing convolution on a linear array such that inputs, weights, and outputs all move during each time unit. Analyze your algorithm.

7.14 Consider an array of processors P_1, P_2, $\ldots$, P_k, where P_k is the leftmost processor. A convolution can be performed on this array as follows: Let P_i store w_i. The inputs x_1, x_2, $\ldots$, x_n are fed into P_k and travel to the right. When x_1 reaches P_1, each P_i holds x_i and w_i; it computes $w_i x_i$ and sends the result into an adder attached to the linear array, where $y_1 = w_1 x_1 + w_2 x_2 + \cdots + w_k x_k$ is computed. The sequence of x's is now shifted to the right, discarding

x_1 and bringing in x_{k+1}. Again, all processors compute a product, and the adder produces y_2. This continues until y_{n+1-k} has been obtained. Discuss this algorithm and analyze its performance, paying particular attention to the design of the adder.

7.15 Consider the linear array augmented with a bus, as described in Problem 7.6. It is desired to solve the convolution problem on this model. Let the array consist of k processors P_1, P_2, ..., P_k (the leftmost processor being P_1), with P_i holding w_i. The outputs y_1, y_2, ..., y_{n+1-k} are fed into P_1 (with y_1 entering first) and travel down the array from left to right. The bus is used to provide the sequence $\{x_1, x_2, \ldots, x_n\}$ as input to the array. Give the details of this algorithm and analyze its performance.

7.16 A variant of the approach in Problem 7.15 uses a ring (instead of an array) augmented with a bus. Here, P_i holds y_i (which, as in Section 7.3.1, stands for y_{i+sk}, where $s = 0, 1, \ldots, \lfloor \frac{n+1-k-i}{k} \rfloor$), while the bus brings x_1, x_2, ..., x_n into the array, in that order. The weights w_1, w_2, ..., w_k, are shifted cyclically around the ring so that, at each step, each weight enters a processor. Specify what computations are performed by the processors, and analyze the resulting algorithm.

7.17 Describe an algorithm for performing convolution on a mesh-of-trees interconnection network in $O(\log k)$ time using $n \times k$ processors.

7.18 The following definition of convolution (slightly different from the one in Section 7.3) is sometimes used: Given two sequences $\{a_1, a_2, \ldots, a_n\}$ and $\{b_1, b_2, \ldots, b_n\}$, a sequence $\{y_1, y_2, \ldots, y_{2n-1}\}$ is computed from

$$y_i = \sum_{j=1}^{n} a_{i-j+1} b_j, \qquad 1 \le i \le 2n - 1.$$

For example, when $n = 3$,

$$
\begin{aligned}
y_1 &= a_1 b_1, \\
y_2 &= a_1 b_2 + a_2 b_1, \\
y_3 &= a_1 b_3 + a_2 b_2 + a_3 b_1, \\
y_4 &= a_2 b_3 + a_3 b_2, \\
y_5 &= a_3 b_3.
\end{aligned}
$$

Express this computation as a matrix-by-vector product, and show how it can be performed on a linear array.

7.19 Show how algorithm LINEAR ARRAY BINARY COUNTER of Section 7.4.1 can be used to generate all *subsets* of a set S of m elements.

7.20 Design an algorithm for the linear array that generates subsets of a set in the *minimal-change* order (as defined in Section 7.4.4). In other words, each subset should differ from the previous one in the least possible way.

7.21 An *n-subset* of a set of m elements is a subset with exactly n members. Combinations of n out of m elements are n-subsets. Show how an algorithm for generating binary strings can be used to generate n-subsets.

7.22 Given a sequence $S = \{s_1, s_2, \ldots, s_m\}$ of arbitrary elements, an *n-variation* of S is a string $v_1 v_2 \ldots v_n$ such that $v_i \in S$ for all $1 \leq i \leq n$. Note that repeated elements are allowed. For example, $DCABA$ and $ACCDD$ are both 5-variations of $\{A, B, C, D\}$. The number of variations of n elements out of m is m^n. Special instances of m-variations are binary and decimal counters, where $S = \{0, 1\}$, and $S = \{0, 1, \ldots, 9\}$, respectively.

   (a) Design an algorithm for generating all n-variations of $S = \{0, 1, \ldots, m - 1\}$.

   (b) Extend your algorithm in **(a)** to the case where the elements of S are arbitrary symbols, all stored in the local memory of one processor.

7.23 Algorithm LINEAR ARRAY COMBINATIONS of Section 7.4.3 works for the case where $S = \{1, 2, \ldots, m\}$. Design a linear array algorithm for generating all n-combinations of a set of m arbitrary elements. One of the processors is allowed to store all the elements of S.

7.24 A *composition* of a positive integer m into n parts (or *n-composition*) is any sequence $\{x_1, x_2, \ldots, x_n\}$ of positive integers such that $x_1 + x_2 + \cdots + x_n = m$. Show how an algorithm for generating n-combinations of m elements can be used to generate all n-compositions of m.

7.25 Show how an algorithm for generating all subsets of a set can be used to generate compositions of an integer into *any* number of parts.

7.26 Design a parallel algorithm for generating compositions of an integer m, given that the largest part in each composition is k, for some integer $k \leq m$.

7.27 A combination of n out of m elements *with repetitions* is an unordered set of n elements taken from a set of m elements such that elements are allowed to repeat. In other words, $x_1 x_2 \ldots x_n$ is a combination with repetitions from $S = \{1, 2, \ldots, m\}$ if and only if $1 \leq x_1 \leq x_2 \leq \cdots \leq x_n \leq m$. Design an algorithm for generating combinations with repetitions on a linear array of processors.

7.28 Use the *split-and-plan* technique to design an algorithm for generating all permutations of n arbitrary elements on a linear array of n processors, in *lexicographic order*.

7.29 Let S be a set of m arbitrary elements. An *n-permutation* of S is obtained by selecting n distinct elements of S and arranging them in some order. (See Example 7.9.) Two n-permutations are distinct if they differ with respect to the elements they contain or with respect to the order of the elements. Design a parallel algorithm for generating all n-permutations of S.

7.30 Design a linear array algorithm for generating *random* permutations of n elements.

7.31 A permutation of the sequence $S = \{s_1, s_2, \ldots, s_n\}$ is a *derangement* if s_i does not appear in (its identity) position i, for all i, $1 \le i \le n$. Thus, for $n = 5$, $s_2 s_3 s_5 s_1 s_4$ and $s_5 s_4 s_2 s_3 s_1$ are derangements. There are $D_n = (n-1)(D_{n-1} + D_{n-2})$ derangements of n elements, with $D_0 = 1$ and $D_1 = 0$, requiring $\Omega(nD_n)$ operations to be generated. Describe an algorithm that uses the split-and-plan technique to generate all derangements of n arbitrary elements on a linear array of n processors.

7.32 A *partition* of an integer n is given by a sequence $\{x_1, x_2, \ldots, x_m\}$ of positive integers, where $x_1 \ge x_2 \ge \cdots \ge x_m$ and $x_1 + x_2 + \cdots + x_m = n$. Design a parallel algorithm for generating all partitions of an integer:

(a) Into m parts.

(b) Into any number of parts.

7.33 Let S be a set of n elements. An *equivalence relation* (or *partition*) of S consists of subsets $S_1, S_2, \ldots, S_k$ whose union is equal to S, such that the intersection of any two subsets is empty. Design a parallel algorithm for generating all equivalence relations of a set.

7.34 An *m-ary* tree is a data structure with n nodes that either is empty (i.e., $n = 0$) or consists of a root and m disjoint children, each of which is the root of an m-ary subtree. Design a parallel algorithm for generating all m-ary trees with n nodes.

7.35 A sequence of n left parentheses and n right parentheses is *balanced* if the number of right parentheses encountered when scanning from left to right never exceeds the number of left parentheses. (See Problem 4.31.)

(a) Show how an algorithm for generating binary trees on n nodes can be used to generate all balanced sequences of (n left and n right) parentheses.

(b) Design a parallel algorithm different from the one in **(a)** for generating balanced sequences of parentheses.

7.36 Suppose that each instance of a combinatorial object consists of n elements. When n processors are available on a linear array, each processor can be made responsible for producing one element. This approach was used in this chapter.

Now, let the number of processors be N, where $N < n$ or $N > n$. In this case, an *adaptive* algorithm is needed that adjusts its behavior according to the number of available processors. Discuss various approaches to obtaining adaptive algorithms for generating combinatorial objects in parallel.

7.37 In this chapter, when deriving a lower bound on the number of operations required to generate all instances of a combinatorial object, we took into account the number of operations needed to actually produce as output each instance in full. For example, all permutations of n elements require $\Omega(nn!)$ operations to be generated. An alternative definition simply takes into account the number of operations required to "create" each instance, without actually producing it in full as output. According to this second definition, the lower bound on generating all permutations of n elements is $\Omega(n!)$, since it may be possible to "create" each permutation from the previous one using a constant number of operations. Discuss approaches to designing parallel algorithms (for generating combinatorial objects) that are cost optimal under the new definition.

7.38 Given two n-bit numbers, show how they can be multiplied on a $2n$-processor linear array, and analyze the running time of your algorithm.

7.39 Extend the algorithm of Problem 7.38 so that the linear array multiplies *two* pairs of n-bit numbers in about the same time as it multiplies one pair.

7.40 Design an algorithm for dividing an integer x by an integer y on a linear array of processors. Make any appropriate assumptions about the input and the form of the output.

7.41 Pattern matching in strings is the problem of determining whether a string S_1 of n symbols occurs within a string S_2 of m symbols. For example, $S_1 = ABA$ occurs within $S_2 = AACCAABAC$. Design an algorithm for solving this problem on a linear array of processors.

7.42 Let W be a string of symbols from a given finite alphabet. The *reverse* of W, denoted W^R, consists of the symbols of W listed backwards. Given a string W, design an algorithm for determining, on a linear array of processors, whether $W = W^R$.

7.43 Given two sequences X and Y of symbols, a third sequence Z is a *common subsequence* of X and Y if Z is a subsequence of both X and Y. For example, if $X = \{a, c, b, c, d, a\}$ and $Y = \{b, a, c, c, b, a\}$, then $Z = \{c, c, a\}$ is a common subsequence of X and Y. Design a linear array algorithm that finds the longest common subsequence of two given sequences X and Y.

7.44 Given a sequence $X = \{x_1, x_2, \ldots, x_n\}$ of distinct integers, an *increasing subsequence* of X is a subsequence $\{x_i, x_j, \ldots, x_k\}$, where $i < j < \cdots < k$

and $x_i < x_j < \cdots < x_k$. Design a linear array algorithm that finds the longest increasing subsequence of a given sequence X.

7.45 Let $X = x_1 x_2 \ldots x_n$ and $Y = y_1 y_2 \ldots y_m$ be two strings of symbols from a finite alphabet. It is required to change X symbol by symbol, until it turns into Y. This is done by insertion, deletion, or replacement of symbols. It is required to minimize the number of single-symbol changes. Design a linear array algorithm to solve this problem.

7.46 Design an algorithm for computing the discrete Fourier transform on a linear array, and analyze the running time of the algorithm.

7.47 Given two sequences of weights $\{w_0, w_1, \ldots, w_h\}$ and $\{v_1, v_2, \ldots, v_k\}$, a sequence of initial values $\{y_{-k}, y_{-k+1}, \ldots, y_{-1}\}$, and an input sequence $\{x_{-h}, x_{-h+1}, \ldots, x_0, x_1, \ldots, x_n\}$, a process known as *filtering* calls for computing the output sequence $\{y_0, y_1, \ldots, y_n\}$ whose elements are defined by

$$y_i = \sum_{j=0}^{h} w_j x_{i-j} + \sum_{j=1}^{k} v_j y_{i-j}.$$

Design a linear array algorithm for filtering.

7.48 Let $U = \{u_0, u_1, \ldots, u_{n-1}\}$ and $V = \{v_0, v_1, \ldots, v_{n-1}\}$ be two given sequences of values. The *correlation* between U and V is defined as

$$R = \frac{nA - BC}{((nD - B^2)(nE - C^2))^{1/2}},$$

where

$$A = \sum_{j=0}^{n-1} u_j v_j, \quad B = \sum_{j=0}^{n-1} u_j, \quad C = \sum_{j=0}^{n-1} v_j, \quad D = \sum_{j=0}^{n-1} u_j^2, \quad \text{and } E = \sum_{j=0}^{n-1} v_j^2.$$

Design an algorithm for computing R on a linear array.

7.49 Describe a linear array algorithm for computing the convex hull of a set of n points in the plane (as defined in Example 4.7)

7.6 BIBLIOGRAPHICAL REMARKS

Interest in linear arrays as a viable model of parallel computation was fostered by the pioneering work of Kung [346, 347, 348, 349]. Linear array algorithms for sorting are described in Akl [18, 21], Akl and Schmeck [52], Baudet and Stevenson [92], Chen et al. [147], Goodman and Hedetniemi [263], Knuth [325], Kumar and Hirschberg [342], Kung [348], Lee et al. [362], Miranker et al. [430], Orton et al. [455], Thompson and Kung [612], Todd [613], and Yasuura et al. [647]. Algorithm LINEAR ARRAY COMPARISON-EXCHANGE SORT was first proposed in Lee et al. [362] and Miranker et al. [430]. The algorithm of Section 7.1.2 is derived in Todd [613]. Algorithms for multiplying a matrix by a vector, solving tridiagonal systems of equations, performing convolution, filtering, computing Fourier transforms, and performing related computations on a linear array are described in Kung and Leiserson [351].

The design of algorithms to generate combinatorial objects has long fascinated mathematicians and computer scientists. Some of the earliest papers on the interplay between mathematics and computer science are devoted to the subject; see, for example, Lehmer [364] and Thompkins [609]. Because of their many applications in science and engineering, combinatorial algorithms continue to receive much attention, and interest has naturally been paid to the development of parallel algorithms for generating combinatorial objects; see, for example, Akl [20], Akl et al. [41], Chan and Akl [134], Cosnard and Ferreira [186], and Gupta and Bhattacharjee [275]. Several linear array algorithms have been proposed, including algorithms for counters (see Akl et al. [32]), combinations (see Akl et al. [37], Chen and Chern [144], Elhage and Stojmenović [217], Lin and Tsay [385], and Stojmenović [587]), permutations (see Akl et al. [46], Akl and Stojmenović [53], Chen and Chern [144], and Lin [384]), derangements (see Akl et al. [27]), binary trees (see Akl and Stojmenović [54]), t-ary trees (see Akl and Stojmenović [59]), integer partitions and compositions (see Akl and Stojmenović [55]), subsets and set partitions (see Djokić et al. [206]), and equivalence relations (see Stojmenović [586]). Algorithms for generating combinatorial objects at random are given in Rajan et al. [522] and Stojmenović [588]. The algorithms of Sections 7.4.1, 7.4.3, and 7.4.4 were first proposed in Akl et al. [32], Akl et al. [37], and Akl and Stojmenović [53], respectively. A survey of linear array algorithms for generating combinatorial objects is provided in Akl and Stojmenović [58].

Other algorithms for linear arrays are described in Asano and Umeo [68], Atallah and Tsay [75], Chaudhuri [140], Chazelle [141], Chen et al. [145], Holey and Ibarra [299], Kung and Lam [350], Leighton [367], Moldovan [432], Quinn [515], Quinton and Robert [517], Robert [537], and Ullman [615].

Chapter 8

Meshes and Related Models

In Chapter 7 we saw how a linear array of processors, despite its limited connectivity, could solve many different problems efficiently, sometimes with an optimal running time, sometimes at an optimal cost. A limitation of the linear array, however, is its large diameter: In an array with n processors, $n - 1$ steps are needed to transfer a datum from the leftmost to the rightmost processor. Another topology is therefore sought to solve those computational problems in which such transfers of data are frequent and necessary.

A model that offers a significantly smaller diameter, while retaining most of the advantages of the linear array, is the two-dimensional array, or *mesh*, of processors defined in Section 2.3.2 and illustrated in Fig. 2.9. Like the linear array, the model is simple from a theoretical point of view, as well as being appealing in practice. In it, the maximum degree of a processor is four. The topology is *regular*, as all rows (and columns) are connected to their successors in exactly the same way. The topology is also *modular*, in the sense that any of its regions can be implemented with the same basic component. These properties allow the mesh to be easily extended by the simple addition of a row or a column. Given N processors, the mesh can be organized as a square array with $n = N^{1/2}$ rows and $n = N^{1/2}$ columns. This yields a mesh whose diameter is $2N^{1/2} - 2$ (i.e., the number of links on the shortest path from the processor in the top left corner to the processor in the bottom right corner). Another configuration of the mesh arranges the processors into m rows and n columns, where $m \neq n$ and $N = m \times n$.

Despite all of its advantages, the mesh is inadequate for those computational problems in which its diameter is still considered too large. For those problems, other topologies are used. Some of these, like the *pyramid* of Section 2.3.5, are based on the idea of combining the *tree* and mesh models, thus obtaining the best of both worlds: A complete binary tree with $N^{1/2}$ leaves has a diameter of $\log N$, while an $N^{1/2} \times N^{1/2}$ mesh allows $2N^{1/2}$ processors (in adjacent rows, for example) to exchange their data in one step. Alternatively, the *mesh-of-trees* model of Section 2.3.4 is appropriate. Other models, not based on the mesh or tree, and used primarily for their small diameter, are studied in Chapter 9. They include the *hypercube* and *star* interconnection networks. A third approach, in which the mesh is augmented with *buses* to reduce its diameter, is presented in Chapter 10.

Algorithms for five fundamental computations are derived in this chapter. In Section 8.1, we describe an algorithm for sorting a sequence of numbers on a mesh of processors. We then show in Section 8.2 how a dynamic programming computation can be performed on a subnetwork of the mesh, the *triangular array*. Sorting is revisited in Section 8.3.1 and solved this time on a mesh of trees. Two other algorithms for the mesh of trees are the subjects of Sections 8.3.2 and 8.3.3. The first solves a system of n linear equations in n unknowns, while the second computes the convex hull of a set of n points in the plane.

8.1   SORTING ON THE MESH

Our algorithm for a mesh of processors solves the following problem: Let $S = \{x_0, x_1, \ldots, x_{N-1}\}$ be a sequence of numbers stored in a mesh of $N = m \times n$ processors arranged in m rows and n columns. The processors, $P_0, P_1, \ldots, P_{N-1}$, are indexed in *row-major order*; that is, P_i is placed in row j and column k of the mesh, where $i = jn + k$ for $0 \leq i \leq N - 1$, $0 \leq j \leq m - 1$, and $0 \leq k \leq n - 1$. Initially, P_i holds x_i for $i = 0, 1, \ldots, N - 1$. It is required to *sort* the sequence S into a sequence $S' = \{y_0, y_1, \ldots, y_{N-1}\}$, where $y_0 \leq y_1 \leq \cdots \leq y_{N-1}$, such that when the algorithm terminates, P_i holds y_i.

Example 8.1 Let $S = \{4, 3, 7, 1, 2, 5, 6, 8, 4, 9, 3, 8\}$, and let $m = 4$ and $n = 3$. The initial configuration of a 4×3 mesh holding S is shown in Fig. 8.1(a). When sorting is complete, the mesh holds $S' = \{1, 2, 3, 3, 4, 4, 5, 6, 7, 8, 8, 9\}$ in row-major order, as shown in Fig. 8.1(b). $\square$

Our presentation of the algorithm is greatly simplified if we begin by establishing two simple results, first encountered in Problems 3.2 and 7.4.

8.1.1   The 0–1 Principle

Consider a sorting algorithm $\mathcal{A}$ based on a predetermined sequence of comparisons and exchanges among the elements of the input sequence. The algorithm compares x_i (held by P_i) to x_j (held by P_j) and places the smaller in P_i and the larger in P_j. Here the pair (i, j) is predetermined and does not depend in any way on the values in the sequence being sorted. Examples of algorithms that operate in this way are the odd-even-merge sorting circuit of Section 3.1.1 and the algorithm for sorting by comparison-exchange on the linear array, described in Section 7.1.1.

Suppose that we want to establish the correctness of $\mathcal{A}$; that is, we wish to show that $\mathcal{A}$ sorts, in nondecreasing order, any sequence of numbers on which it operates. Let Z be a sequence of N 0's and 1's in arbitrary order. The *0–1 principle* says that if $\mathcal{A}$ can correctly sort each one of the 2^N possible sequences Z so that for every

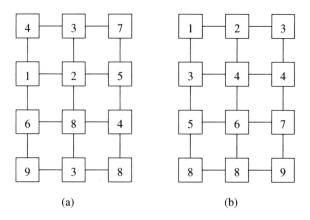

Figure 8.1: Sorting a sequence on a mesh in row-major order: (a) Initial configuration; (b) Sorted sequence.

sequence, all 0's are followed by all 1's, then it can correctly sort *any* sequence of *arbitrary* numbers.

To see this, let $S = \{x_0, x_1, \ldots, x_{N-1}\}$ be a sequence of arbitrary numbers whose sorted form is $S' = \{y_0, y_1, \ldots, y_{N-1}\}$, where $y_0 \leq y_1 \leq \cdots \leq y_{N-1}$. Also, suppose that $\mathcal{A}$ (the sorting algorithm whose correctness is to be established) is guaranteed to be able to sort all sequences of N 0's and 1's correctly. Now, proceeding by contradiction, assume that, when applied to S, algorithm $\mathcal{A}$ incorrectly produces $S'' = \{y_0', y_1', \ldots, y_{N-1}'\}$. Let j be the smallest index such that $y_j' \neq y_j$. This implies that

$$
\begin{aligned}
y_i' &= y_i \leq y_j && \text{for } 0 \leq i < j, \\
y_j' &> y_j, \\
\text{and } \quad y_k' &= y_j && \text{for some } k > j.
\end{aligned}
$$

We now create a sequence $Z = \{z_0, z_1, \ldots, z_{N-1}\}$ of 0's and 1's from S as follows:

$$
\begin{aligned}
z_i &= 0 && \text{if } x_i \leq y_j \\
&= 1 && \text{if } x_i > y_j,
\end{aligned}
$$

for $i = 0, 1, \ldots, N - 1$. Note that for any pair of indices i and l,

$$
\begin{aligned}
x_i &\leq x_l \leq y_j && \text{implies } z_i = z_l = 0, \\
x_i &\leq y_j < x_l && \text{implies } z_i = 0, z_l = 1, \\
y_j &< x_i \leq x_l && \text{implies } z_i = z_l = 1.
\end{aligned}
$$

In other words, if $x_i \leq x_l$, then $z_i \leq z_l$, for every pair of indices i and l. Thus, when $\mathcal{A}$ is given Z to sort, the result of every comparison-exchange is the same as for S, and the output Z' will be of the following form:

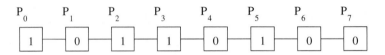

Figure 8.2: Sorting a sequence of 0's and 1's on a linear array.

$$Z' : \quad 0 \quad 0 \quad \ldots \quad 1 \quad \ldots \quad 0 \quad \ldots$$
$$\updownarrow \quad \updownarrow \quad\quad \updownarrow \quad\quad \updownarrow$$
$$S'' : \quad y'_0 \quad y'_1 \quad \ldots \quad y'_j \quad \ldots \quad y'_k \quad \ldots$$

In Z', (at least) one 0 follows a 1. This means that $\mathcal{A}$, contrary to its definition, has failed to sort a sequence of 0's and 1's correctly. Therefore, the assumption regarding $\mathcal{A}$'s failure to sort S correctly must be wrong, and the validity of the 0–1 principle is established.

8.1.2 Transposition Sort

Suppose that a linear array of N processors $P_0, P_1, \ldots, P_{N-1}$ holds a sequence of numbers $S = \{x_0, x_1, \ldots, x_{N-1}\}$ such that P_i stores x_i, for $0 \le i \le N - 1$. It is required to sort S into $S' = \{y_0, y_1, \ldots, y_{N-1}\}$, where $y_0 \le y_1 \le \cdots \le y_{N-1}$, such that P_i holds y_i. This can be done by the following algorithm, where "compare-exchange (P_i, P_{i+1})" means that P_i and P_{i+1} compare their values, placing the smaller in P_i and the larger in P_{i+1}:

Algorithm LINEAR ARRAY TRANSPOSITION SORT
>**for** $j = 0$ **to** $N - 1$ **do**
>>**for** $i = 0$ **to** $N - 2$ **do in parallel**
>>>**if** $i \bmod 2 = j \bmod 2$
>>>**then** compare-exchange (P_i, P_{i+1})
>>>**end if**
>>**end for**
>**end for.** ∎

That this algorithm correctly sorts S is established by showing that it can sort any sequence Z of N 0's and 1's (and then using the 0–1 principle). Suppose that Z is stored one element per processor and that it consists of q 0's and $N - q$ 1's. This is illustrated in Fig. 8.2 for $N = 8$ and $q = 4$. We show that when the algorithm terminates, the $N - q$ 1's are in processors $P_q, P_{q+1}, \ldots, P_{N-1}$. Note first that the algorithm moves 1's only to the right (and 0's only to the left). Suppose that the lth rightmost 1, $l = 1, 2, \ldots, N - q$, is initially in P_i. Depending on whether i is even or odd, the lth rightmost 1 begins traveling to the right during either the lth or the $(l+1)$st iteration of the algorithm (i.e., when $j = l - 1$ or $j = l$ in the outer loop), at the latest. It then continues to travel to the right, at each iteration, until it reaches P_{N-j}.

The worst case occurs when the $N-q$ 1's are initially in processors $P_0, P_1, \ldots,$ P_{N-q-1} and $N-q$ is even. The rightmost 1 (in P_{N-q-1}) moves to the right when $j = 1$ (i.e., during the second iteration), thus allowing the second rightmost 1 to move when $j = 2$. This continues until the element in P_0 (i.e., the $(N-q)$th rightmost 1) begins moving when $j = N-q$ (i.e., during the $(N-q+1)$st iteration) and travels to the right until it reaches P_q, $q-1$ iterations later. Therefore, $(N-q+1)+(q-1) = N$ iterations suffice to sort S correctly.

8.1.3 Sorting by Row and Column Operations

We are now ready to present an algorithm for sorting a sequence of numbers on the mesh. The results of Sections 8.1.1 and 8.1.2 are used as follows:

1. The 0–1 principle allows us to restrict our attention to sequences of 0's and 1's. If the algorithm sorts all such sequences correctly, then it can do the same for any sequence of arbitrary numbers.

2. Algorithm LINEAR ARRAY TRANSPOSITION SORT allows us to describe the mesh algorithm in terms of row and column operations. Thus, any reference in what follows to "sorting a row" or "sorting a column" by a SORT operation simply means a call to the linear array algorithm.

In the discussion that follows, we therefore assume that an $m \times n$ mesh containing a sequence of 0's and 1's is given as shown in Fig. 8.3(a) for $m = 5$ and $n = 4$. When the sorting algorithm terminates, the contents of the mesh should be as shown in Fig. 8.3(b). The presentation is also made easier by assuming that $m = 2^s$ and $n = 2^{2r}$, where $s \geq r$. We begin with some definitions:

Cyclic Shift. A row of the mesh is cyclically shifted k positions to the right, $k \geq 1$, by moving the element in column i of the row, for $i = 0, 1, \ldots, n-1$, through the row's processors, until it reaches column j of the same row, where $j = (i + k)$ mod n. Note that if $j < i$, the element in column i actually moves *to the left* to reach its destination in column j.

Horizontal Slice. This is a submesh of $n^{1/2}$ rows and n columns containing all rows i such that $i = kn^{1/2}, kn^{1/2} + 1, \ldots, (k+1)n^{1/2} - 1$ for a nonnegative integer k, as shown in Fig. 8.4(a). Note that the mesh is represented by a rectangle for simplicity.

Vertical Slice. This is a submesh of m rows and $n^{1/2}$ columns containing all columns j such that $j = ln^{1/2}, ln^{1/2} + 1, \ldots, (l+1)n^{1/2} - 1$ for a nonnegative integer l, as shown in Fig. 8.4(b).

Block. This is a submesh of $n^{1/2}$ rows and $n^{1/2}$ columns consisting of all processors $P(i, j)$ such that $i = kn^{1/2}, kn^{1/2} + 1, \ldots, (k+1)n^{1/2} - 1$ and $j = ln^{1/2}, ln^{1/2}+1, \ldots, (l+1)n^{1/2}-1$, for nonnegative integers k and l, as shown in Fig. 8.4(c).

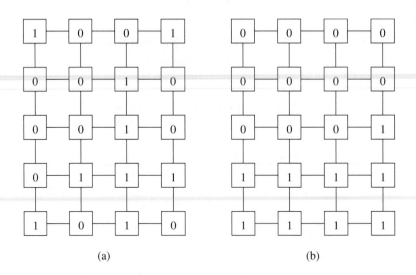

(a)   (b)

Figure 8.3: Sorting a sequence of 0's and 1's on a mesh: (a) Input sequence stored in the mesh, one element per processor; (b) Sorted sequence.

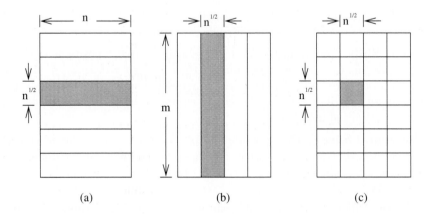

(a)   (b)   (c)

Figure 8.4: Dividing a mesh into submeshes: (a) Horizontal slice; (b) Vertical Slice; (c) Block.

Uniform Region. This is a row, horizontal slice, vertical slice, or block consisting only of 0's or only of 1's.

Nonuniform Region. This is a row, horizontal slice, vertical slice, or block consisting of both 0's and 1's.

It should be clear that when the sorting algorithm terminates, the mesh consists of (zero or more) uniform rows filled with 0's (at the top), followed by at most one nonuniform row consisting of 0's followed by 1's, and, finally, (zero or more) uniform rows filled with 1's (at the bottom), as shown in Fig. 8.3(b).

The sorting algorithm uses three operations based on SORT, called BALANCE, UNBLOCK, and SHEAR. Operations BALANCE and UNBLOCK also use the cyclic shift. These three operations are presented next.

Operation BALANCE. This operation is applied to a submesh of size $v \times w$. Its purpose is to even out the distribution of 0's and 1's among the w columns. As a result, the number of nonuniform rows is reduced to at most $\min(v, w)$. The operation consists of three steps:

1. Each column in the submesh is sorted in nondecreasing order from top to bottom using SORT.

2. Each row i in the submesh is cyclically shifted $i \bmod w$ positions to the right.

3. Each column in the submesh is sorted in nondecreasing order from top to bottom using SORT. ∎

Suppose that the number of nonuniform rows in the $v \times w$ submesh is initially v. If $v \leq w$, operation BALANCE promises no reduction in the maximum number of nonuniform rows (since $\min(v, w) = v$). By contrast, if $v > w$, and operation BALANCE works as claimed, then the maximum number of nonuniform rows left in the submesh after the operation is applied is $\min(v, w) = w$. In other words, BALANCE *reduces* the number of nonuniform rows from v to at most w. Let us therefore focus on this case.

To see that the desired effect is indeed achieved when $v > w$, note that in Step 2 the elements of each column are distributed, in round-robin fashion, among all the columns. Consider any three distinct columns i, j, and k. Since the columns were sorted in Step 1, the number of 0's received from column k by columns i and the number of 0's received from column k by columns j differ by at most 1. It follows that the total difference in the number of 0's held by columns i and j after Step 2 is at most w (for any i and j). Thus, once the columns are sorted in Step 3:

(a) At most w nonuniform rows are created.

(b) These rows are all consecutive and separate the uniform rows filled with 0's from the uniform rows filled with 1's.

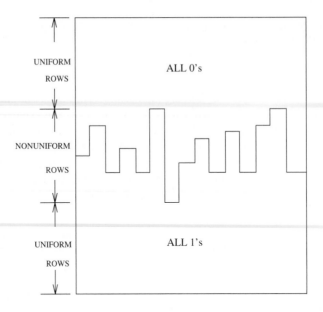

Figure 8.5: Effect of operations BALANCE, UNBLOCK, and SHEAR.

The effect of operation BALANCE is shown in Fig. 8.5.

Operation UNBLOCK.   This operation distributes the elements of each block in the mesh among all the columns of the mesh. As a result, a uniform row is created for every uniform block. Similarly, a nonuniform row is (possibly) created for every nonuniform block. This is done using the following two steps:

1. Each row i of the mesh is cyclically shifted $in^{1/2}$ mod n positions to the right.

2. All columns of the mesh are sorted in nondecreasing order from top to bottom using SORT. ■

Suppose that operation UNBLOCK is applied to a mesh with b nonuniform blocks. Step 1 transfers each of the n elements of a block to a different column of the mesh. Thus, the difference in the number of 0's between any two columns is now at most b. After the columns are sorted in Step 2, at most b nonuniform rows remain in the mesh. Furthermore, these rows are all consecutive and separate the uniform rows filled with 0's from the uniform rows filled with 1's, as shown in Fig. 8.5.

Operation SHEAR.   This operation is applied to the entire mesh. Each pair of adjacent rows is transformed into one uniform row and (possibly) one nonuniform

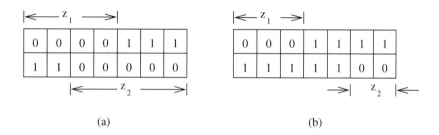

Figure 8.6: Effect of Step 1 of operation SHEAR on adjacent rows: (a) $z_1 + z_2 \geq n$; (b) $z_1 + z_2 < n$.

row, by sorting the initial two rows in opposite directions. The operation consists of two steps:

1. All even-numbered rows of the mesh are sorted in nondecreasing order to the right, and all odd-numbered rows of the mesh are sorted in nondecreasing order to the left, using SORT.

2. Each column of the mesh is sorted in nondecreasing order from top to bottom using SORT. ∎

Suppose that operation SHEAR is applied to a mesh with b consecutive nonuniform rows. Step 1 places the 0's in opposite ends of adjacent nonuniform rows, as shown in Fig. 8.6, where z_1 and z_2 denote the number of 0's in the top and bottom rows, respectively.

When $z_1 + z_2 \geq n$, there is at least one 0 in each column of the pair of rows. When $z_1 + z_2 < n$, there is at least one 1 in each column. This means that, within the pair of rows, any column has at most one more 0 than any other column. Because there are $\lceil b/2 \rceil$ pairs of adjacent nonuniform rows, the total difference in the number of 0's held by any two columns of the mesh after Step 1 is at most $\lceil b/2 \rceil$. Sorting the columns in Step 2 causes at most $\lceil b/2 \rceil$ nonuniform rows to be left. These rows are consecutive and separate a sequence of uniform rows filled with 0's from a sequence of uniform rows filled with 1's, as shown in Fig. 8.5.

The complete algorithm for sorting a sequence of 0's and 1's on a mesh of processors is given next as algorithm MESH SORT. Note that when operation BALANCE is applied to a horizontal slice (i.e., a submesh of $n^{1/2}$ rows and n columns), the latter is treated as a mesh of n rows and $n^{1/2}$ columns lying on its side, with its topmost row to the left (i.e., the leftmost *column* of this mesh is the bottommost *row* of the horizontal slice).

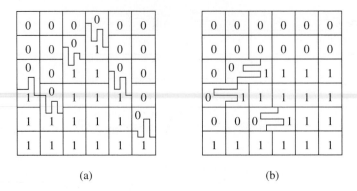

(a)   (b)

Figure 8.7: Proving the correctness of MESH SORT: (a) After Step 1; (b) After Step 3.

Algorithm MESH SORT

> **Step 1: for all** vertical slices **do in parallel**
> > BALANCE
> > **end for**
> **Step 2:** UNBLOCK
> **Step 3: for all** horizontal slices **do in parallel**
> > BALANCE
> > **end for**
> **Step 4:** UNBLOCK
> **Step 5: for** $i = 1$ to 3 **do**
> > SHEAR
> > **end for**
> **Step 6: for all** rows **do in parallel**
> > SORT
> > **end for.** ∎

Correctness. We establish the correctness of the algorithm by examining the effect of each step on the contents of the mesh:

1. Operation BALANCE in Step 1, applied to a vertical slice, leaves at most $n^{1/2}$ nonuniform rows in the slice. Furthermore, these rows are consecutive, implying that there are at most *two* nonuniform blocks in the slice, as illustrated in Fig. 8.7(a). Since the mesh consists of $n^{1/2}$ vertical slices, there are at most $2n^{1/2}$ nonuniform blocks left after Step 1.

2. Operation UNBLOCK in Step 2, applied to a mesh with at most $2n^{1/2}$ nonuniform blocks, leaves at most $2n^{1/2}$ nonuniform rows, and these rows are consec-

utive. This means that at the end of Step 2, there are at most *three* nonuniform horizontal slices in the mesh.

3. Operation BALANCE in Step 3, applied to a nonuniform horizontal slice (treated as an $n \times n^{1/2}$ mesh) leaves at most two nonuniform blocks in the slice (as did Step 1). Because there are three such nonuniform slices, the number of nonuniform blocks at the end of Step 3 is at most six, as shown in Fig. 8.7(b).

4. Operation UNBLOCK in Step 4, applied to a mesh with at most six nonuniform blocks, leaves at most six nonuniform rows in the mesh.

5. Operation SHEAR is applied three times in Step 5 to a mesh with at most six nonuniform rows. The first iteration reduces the number to $6/2 = 3$, the second to $\lceil 3/2 \rceil = 2$, and the third to 1. Thus, there remains at most one nonuniform row after Step 5, and this row separates a sequence of uniform rows filled with 0's (at the top of the mesh) from a sequence of uniform rows filled with 1's (at the bottom of the mesh).

6. There is (possibly) one nonuniform row left in the mesh at the end of Step 5; once it is sorted in Step 6 by operation SORT, the contents of the mesh are completely sorted.

Analysis. Each step of the algorithm involves sorting the rows or columns of the mesh or cyclically shifting the rows by at most $n - 1$ positions each. Specifically, there are nine column-sorting steps, four row-sorting steps, and four row-shifting steps. Using algorithm LINEAR ARRAY TRANSPOSITION SORT, each sorting step requires $O(n)$ or $O(m)$ time, depending on whether it is applied to the rows or columns of the mesh. Similarly, each shift operation takes $O(n)$ time. The algorithm's running time is therefore $O(n + m)$. To see that this time is the best possible on the mesh, suppose that $P(0,0)$ initially holds the largest number in the sequence to be sorted. When the sequence is finally sorted, this number must occupy $P(m - 1, n - 1)$. The shortest path from $P(0,0)$ to $P(m - 1, n - 1)$ consists of $(m - 1) + (n - 1)$ links to be traversed, thus establishing an $\Omega(m + n)$ lower bound on the number of elementary operations required to sort a sequence of mn elements on an $m \times n$ mesh.

To derive the algorithm's cost, assume for simplicity that $m = n = N^{1/2}$. Therefore, $p(N) = N$ and $t(N) = O(N^{1/2})$, for a cost of $c(N) = O(N^{3/2})$, which is not optimal in view of the $O(N \log N)$ elementary operations sufficient for sorting sequentially.

8.2   DYNAMIC PROGRAMMING

Dynamic programming is a powerful algorithmic method used in the solution of optimization problems in which a discrete function is to be minimized or maximized. The approach is to compute optimal solutions to subproblems of the main problem and then combine them to obtain a global optimal solution. This method has been applied successfully to a wide variety of problems, including scheduling problems, computing shortest paths in directed and weighted graphs, constructing binary search trees, and finding the longest common subsequence of two sequences. (See Problem 1.21.)

In this section we are interested in one class of dynamic programming computations, a general characterization of which is provided next.

8.2.1   A Minimization Problem

Let $f(i,j)$ be a real-valued function of two integer variables i and j, $1 \leq i \leq j \leq n$. Initially, $f(i,j) = w(i,j)$ for $1 \leq i < j \leq n$, and $f(i,i) = 0$ for $1 \leq i \leq n$. Here, the values $w(i,j)$ are chosen as appropriate for the specific application at hand. The final value of $f(i,j)$ is to be obtained according to the rule

$$f(i,j) = \min_{i \leq k \leq j} \left(f(i,k) + f(k,j) \right) \quad \text{for} \ \ 1 \leq i < j \leq n.$$

This equation assumes that when $f(i,j)$ is to be computed for two given integers i and j, all values required for its computation, namely, $f(i,k)$ and $f(k,j)$ for $i \leq k \leq j$, have been previously obtained by the same rule and stored, and are hence available. Note also that for $k = i$ or $k = j$, the quantity $(f(i,k) + f(k,j))$ equals the given initial value $w(i,j)$. Once $f(i,j)$ is computed, it, too, is stored and later used to compute subsequent values of f, for other values of i and j.

The computation just described is typical of those arising in many dynamic programming algorithms. The following example illustrates one instance of such a computation;

Example 8.2 Suppose that G is a connected and weighted graph with n vertices $v_1, v_2, \ldots, v_n$. Further, let $w(i,j) \geq 0$ be the weight (also referred to as the *length*) of edge (v_i, v_j), which connects vertices v_i and v_j. If v_i and v_j are not directly connected by an edge, then $w(i,j) = \infty$. The weight (or length) of a path from v_i to v_j is the sum of the weights of the edges forming it. Under these conditions, $f(i,j)$ represents the length of a shortest path (i.e., a path with minimum weight) from v_i to v_j, which is allowed to go through intermediate vertices v_k, provided that $i < k < j$. Note that if the path does indeed go through other vertices $v_h, v_l, \ldots, v_m$, then

$$w(i,h) + w(h,l) + \cdots + w(m,j) < w(i,j). \ \ \square$$

8.2.2 An Algorithm for the Triangular Array

We now show how the equation

$$f(i,j) = \min_{i \leq k \leq j} \left(f(i,k) + f(k,j) \right)$$

can be computed on a mesh interconnection network, for $1 \leq i < j \leq n$. Specifically, we use a triangular array.

The Triangular Array. This is essentially a subnetwork of a mesh that is composed of those processors above the main diagonal, as shown in Fig. 8.8 for $n = 6$. In this network, the standard mesh links are modified slightly for the purposes of the computation to be performed. Thus, each processor $P(i,j)$ is connected to processors $P(i-1,j)$ and $P(i,j+1)$ by two links, namely, a simple (or *fast*) link and a buffer (or *slow*) link. The buffer link contains a register that slows down the communication by one time unit. Thus, if $P(i,j)$ sends a datum to $P(i-1,j)$ and/or to $P(i,j+1)$ on the fast link, the datum arrives at its destination during *the same* time unit. If, on the other hand, the datum is sent on the slow link, it arrives during *the following* time unit.

Processor $P(i,j)$ will be in charge of computing $f(i,j)$ and will finish doing so at time unit $2(j-i)$. Once $f(i,j)$ has been computed, it is sent to $P(i-1,j)$ and $P(i,j+1)$ on the fast links. After leaving $P(i,j)$, a datum travels (simultaneously up and to the right) for $j-i$ time units on the fast links and then continues its motion on the slow links. Typically, a processor receives up to four inputs and produces up to four outputs, as shown in Fig. 8.9. Each processor holds a variable F in an internal register. Initially, $F = w(i,j)$ for processor $P(i,j)$.

Timing Analysis. Suppose that the algorithm begins during time unit 1 and that subsequent time units are numbered 2, 3, and so on. Let u denote the number of the current time unit at any point during the execution of the algorithm. When $u = 2(j-i)$, the final value of $f(i,j)$ has been computed by $P(i,j)$, and it is sent up and to the right on the fast links. Now, $f(i,j)$ stays on the fast links for $j-i$ time units. Therefore, it reaches $P(i,j+j-i)$ traveling right and $P(i-j+i,j)$ traveling up when $u = 2(j-i) + (j-i) = 3(j-i)$, at which point it must switch to the slow links. Thus, a datum switches from a fast to a slow link as it goes through a processor $P(r,s)$ if $u = 3(s-r)/2$.

The Algorithm. Using the notation in Fig. 8.9, we see that each processor $P(i,j)$ performs the following computations whenever it receives input:

    Step 1: $F \leftarrow \min(F, f_1 + f_3, f_2 + f_4)$
    Step 2: if $u = 3(j-i)/2$
            then (i) $f_2' \leftarrow f_1$
                  (ii) $f_4' \leftarrow f_3$
            else (i) $f_2' \leftarrow f_2$
                  (ii) $f_4' \leftarrow f_4$
            end if

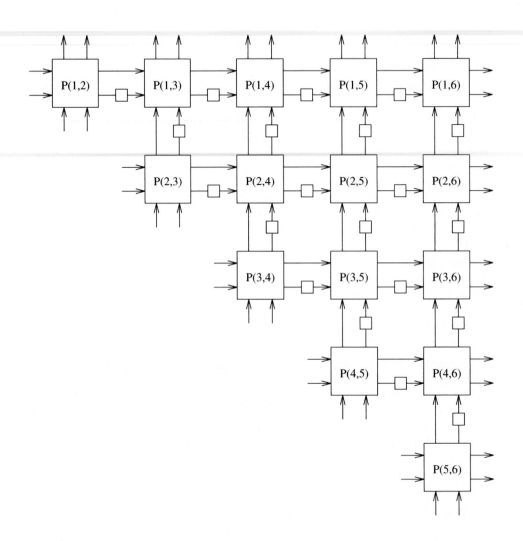

Figure 8.8: A triangular network for dynamic programming.

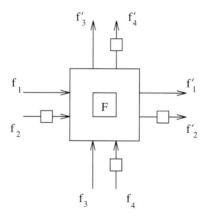

Figure 8.9: A processor of the triangular array.

Step 3: if $u = 2(j - i)$
      then (i) $f_1' \leftarrow F$
            (ii) $f_3' \leftarrow F$
      else (i) $f_1' \leftarrow f_1$
            (ii) $f_3' \leftarrow f_3$
      end if. ∎

It is important to note that:

1. A processor $P(i,j)$ uses f_l, $1 \le l \le 4$, in the computation of F, provided that f_l was received during the current time unit. Similarly, $P(i,j)$ produces f_l as output, provided that it was received in the previous time unit.

2. Processors $P(i, i+1)$ do not receive any input and begin operating when $u = 1$. They perform no computations and, when $u = 2$, produce F as $f(i, i+1)$.

Example 8.3 Let $n = 6$. We illustrate how $f(1,6)$ is computed on the network of Fig. 8.8, where

$$
\begin{aligned}
f(1,6) = \min (\, & w(1,6), \quad f(1,2) + f(2,6), \\
& f(1,3) + f(3,6), \\
& f(1,4) + f(4,6), \\
& f(1,5) + f(5,6)).
\end{aligned}
$$

The computation is illustrated in Fig. 8.10, in which only the top row of the triangular array is shown and u denotes the number of time units elapsed. The first values to emerge from their respective processors are $f(1,2)$ and $f(5,6)$, when $u = 2$. Subsequent computations are as follows:

$u = 3$: $f(1,2)$ and $f(5,6)$ are placed by $P(1,3)$ and $P(4,6)$ on the slow links.

$u = 4$: $f(1,3)$ and $f(4,6)$ are placed by $P(1,3)$ and $P(4,6)$ on the fast links.

$u = 5$: $f(1,3)$ and $f(4,6)$ reach $P(1,5)$ and $P(2,6)$, respectively.

$u = 6$: $f(1,4)$ and $f(3,6)$ are placed by $P(1,4)$ and $P(3,6)$ on the fast links;
$\quad\quad\;\; f(1,3)$ and $f(4,6)$ are placed by $P(1,5)$ and $P(2,6)$ on the slow links.

$u = 7$: $f(1,4)$ and $f(1,3)$ reach $P(1,6)$ from the left;
$\quad\quad\;\; f(4,6)$ and $f(3,6)$ reach $P(1,6)$ from the bottom.

$u = 8$: $P(1,6)$ computes $F \leftarrow \min\,(w(1,6), f(1,3) + f(3,6), f(1,4) + f(4,6))$;
$\quad\quad\;\; f(1,5)$ and $f(1,2)$ reach $P(1,6)$ from the left;
$\quad\quad\;\; f(5,6)$ and $f(2,6)$ reach $P(1,6)$ from the bottom.

$u = 9$: $P(1,6)$ computes $F \leftarrow \min\,(F, f(1,5) + f(5,6), f(1,2) + f(2,6))$.

When $u = 10$, $F = f(1,6)$ is produced as output by $P(1,6)$. $\square$

Analysis. A problem of size n uses a triangular array of $n(n-1)/2$ processors. Since the last output to be produced is $f(1,n)$, and this requires $2(n-1)$ time units, the algorithm has a running time of $t(n) = 2(n-1)$.

8.3   COMPUTING WITH A MESH OF TREES

The mesh-of-trees model of parallel computation was defined in Section 2.3.4 and illustrated in Fig. 2.11. In this model, N processors are arranged in $N^{1/2}$ rows numbered 0, 1, ..., $N^{1/2} - 1$ and $N^{1/2}$ columns numbered 0, 1, ..., $N^{1/2} - 1$. The processor in row i and column j is denoted $P(i,j)$. Each row is connected as a binary tree whose root is the leftmost processor in the row. The children of $P(i,j)$ in the tree over row i are $P(i, 2j+1)$ (provided that $2j+1 \le N^{1/2} - 1$) and $P(i, 2j+2)$ (provided that $2j+2 \le N^{1/2} - 1$). Similarly, each column is connected as a binary tree whose root is the topmost processor in the column. The children of $P(i,j)$ in the tree over column j are $P(2i+1, j)$ (provided that $2i+1 \le N^{1/2} - 1$) and $P(2i+2, j)$ (provided that $2i+2 \le N^{1/2} - 1$).

The diameter of the mesh of trees is the smallest distance between $P(0,0)$ and $P(N^{1/2} - 1, N^{1/2} - 1)$, which is $O(\log N)$: There are $O(\log N)$ links separating $P(0,0)$ from $P(0, N^{1/2} - 1)$ and $O(\log N)$ links separating the latter from $P(N^{1/2} - 1, N^{1/2} - 1)$. All links in the mesh of trees are of course *bidirectional*, or *two-way*, links, thus allowing any processor to send a datum to any other processor.

8.3.1   Sorting

Suppose that it is required to sort a sequence of numbers $S = \{x_0, x_1, \ldots, x_{n-1}\}$ in nondecreasing order. A sorting algorithm known as *enumeration sort* computes, for each element x_i, the number of elements of S smaller than x_i. This number, denoted by $s(i)$, is the position of x_i in a sorted S.

We show how to implement the algorithm on an $n \times n$ mesh of trees. The processors in the first column, $P(0,0), P(1,0), \ldots, P(n-1, 0)$, receive the input,

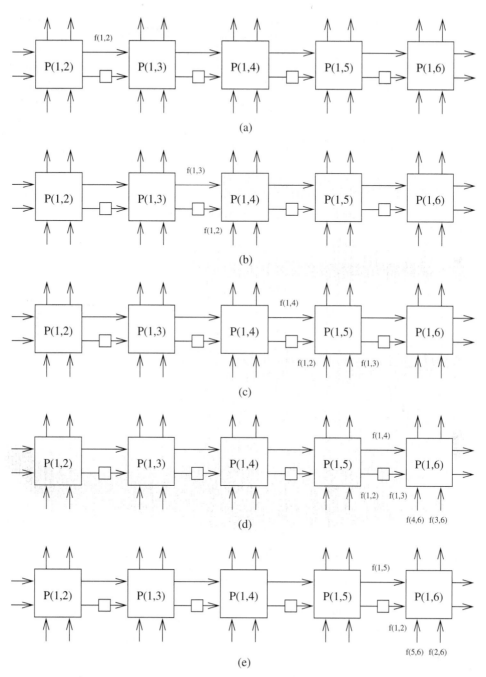

Figure 8.10: Computing $f(1,6)$ by dynamic programming on the triangular array: (a) $u = 2$; (b) $u = 4$; (c) $u = 6$; (d) $u = 7$; (e) $u = 8$.

one number per processor, as shown in Fig. 8.11(a) for $n = 5$. When the algorithm terminates, the processors in the first column will contain S, sorted from top to bottom; that is, the smallest number will be in $P(0,0)$ and the largest in $P(n-1,0)$.

The algorithm consists of three steps and is given next as algorithm MESH-OF-TREES SORT.

Algorithm MESH-OF-TREES SORT

Step 1: The ith row of the mesh will be in charge of computing the position of x_i in a sorted S, for $0 \leq i \leq n-1$. To do this, x_i is distributed to all the processors in the row using the binary tree over the ith row. Each processor receiving x_i keeps a copy of it and sends x_i to its two children. Following this, the tree over the ith column is used to distribute x_i to all processors in the column. The situation at this point is illustrated in Fig. 8.11(b).

Step 2: Processor $P(i, j)$, $0 \leq i \leq n - 1$, $0 \leq j \leq n - 1$, now contains x_i and x_j. The processor sets a variable $r(i, j)$ as follows:

> **if** $x_i > x_j$ **or** $(x_i = x_j$ **and** $i > j)$
> **then** $r(i, j) \leftarrow 1$
> **else** $r(i, j) \leftarrow 0$
> **end if**.

The tree over row i is now used to sum the $r(i, j)$: Each processor adds the two values received from its children to its own and sends the result to its parent. Eventually, for $i = 0, 1, \ldots, n - 1$, $P(i, 0)$ will hold

$$s(i) = \sum_{j=0}^{n-1} r(i, j),$$

that is, the number of elements smaller than x_i.

Step 3: It is now required to route each x_i to its final destination, processor $P(s(i), 0)$. This is done as follows, for $i = 0, 1, \ldots, n - 1$:

(3.1) The value $s(i)$ is sent to processor $P(i, i)$ using the tree over row i.

(3.2) Processor $P(i, i)$ uses the tree over column i to send x_i to $P(s(i), i)$.

(3.3) The tree over row $s(i)$ is now used to send x_i to $P(s(i), 0)$. ■

Analysis. A binary tree with $O(n)$ leaves has $O(\log n)$ levels. Therefore, the algorithm requires $O(\log n)$ time, since each of Steps 1, 2, and 3 essentially consists of routing data up and down the trees. (Step 2 also includes one constant-time comparison and assignment to compute $r(i, j)$ and a constant-time addition at each processor during the computation of $s(i)$.) Since $p(n) = n^2$, the algorithm has a cost of $O(n^2 \log n)$, which is not optimal in view of the $O(n \log n)$ elementary operations sufficient for sorting sequentially.

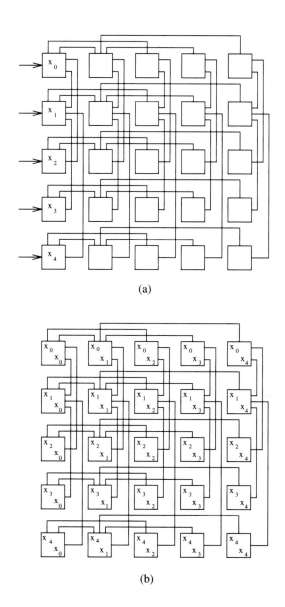

(a)

(b)

Figure 8.11: Input and distribution of data to be sorted on a mesh of trees: (a) The processors in the first column receive the numbers to be sorted; (b) The trees over the rows and the columns are used to distribute the data.

Example 8.4 The algorithm is illustrated in Fig. 8.12 for $S = \{8, 3, 2, 8, 6\}$. The tree links over rows and columns are omitted for simplicity. The $r(i, j)$ computed are shown inside the processors in Fig. 8.12(c). In Fig. 8.12(d), the path taken during Step 3 to route $x_4 = 6$ to $P(s(4), 0)$ is depicted. □

Reducing the Cost. The algorithm's cost can be reduced to $O(n^2)$ by using a mesh of trees with $n \times (n/\log n)$ processors arranged in n rows numbered 0 to $n - 1$ and $n/\log n$ columns numbered 0 to $(n/\log n) - 1$. The processors in row i are in charge of computing $s(i)$ for x_i. However, each processor now must store $O(\log n)$ distinct elements of S besides x_i. The algorithm proceeds as follows:

1. As before, $P(i, 0)$, $0 \le i \le n - 1$, reads x_i and propagates it along its row.

2. $P(0, j)$, $0 \le j \le (n/\log n) - 1$, now reads $x_{j \log n}$, $x_{j \log n + 1}$, $\ldots$, $x_{(j+1) \log n - 1}$, one by one, and sends each, as soon as it is read, down column j to the processors in the column.

3. Each processor $P(i, j)$ now holds x_i and $\log n$ other values. Sequentially, it counts how many of these are smaller than x_i; let this number be $r(i, j)$.

4. As before, the $r(i, j)$ are summed over row i, to obtain $s(i)$ in $P(i, 0)$.

5. $P(i, 0)$ forwards $s(i)$ to $P(i, \lfloor i/\log n \rfloor)$, using the tree over row i. This is depicted in Fig. 8.13 for $n = 16$. Now x_i is sent to $P(s(i), \lfloor i/\log n \rfloor)$, using the tree over column $\lfloor i/\log n \rfloor$. Note here that $\log n$ of the elements share the tree over column $\lfloor i/\log n \rfloor$, and hence, pipelining is used when sending them from their current rows to their respective destination rows. Finally, the tree over row $s(i)$ is used to send x_i to $P(s(i), 0)$.

Each of these steps requires $O(\log n)$ time. Since $O(n^2/\log n)$ processors are used, the algorithm's cost is $O(n^2)$.

8.3.2   Solving a System of Equations

Consider the following system of linear equations:

$$
\begin{array}{ccccccccc}
a_{11}x_1 & + & a_{12}x_2 & + & \cdots & + & a_{1n}x_n & = & b_1, \\
a_{21}x_1 & + & a_{22}x_2 & + & \cdots & + & a_{2n}x_n & = & b_2, \\
& & & & \vdots & & & & \\
a_{n1}x_1 & + & a_{n2}x_2 & + & \cdots & + & a_{nn}x_n & = & b_n.
\end{array}
$$

This system is usually written in matrix form as:

$$
\begin{pmatrix}
a_{11} & a_{12} & \cdots & a_{1n} \\
a_{21} & a_{22} & \cdots & a_{2n} \\
& & \vdots & \\
a_{n1} & a_{n2} & \cdots & a_{nn}
\end{pmatrix}
\begin{pmatrix}
x_1 \\
x_2 \\
\vdots \\
x_n
\end{pmatrix}
=
\begin{pmatrix}
b_1 \\
b_2 \\
\vdots \\
b_n
\end{pmatrix},
$$

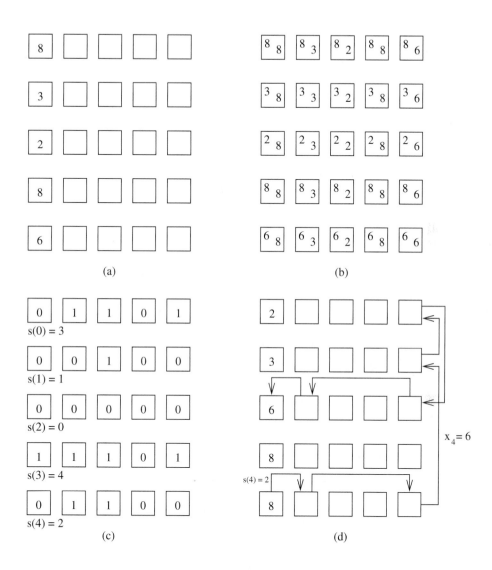

Figure 8.12: Sorting the sequence $S = \{8, 3, 2, 8, 6\}$ on a mesh of trees: (a) Initially; (b) After Step 1; (c) After Step 2; (d) After Step 3.

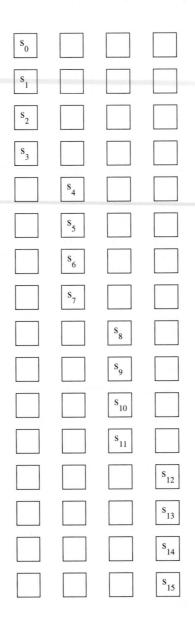

Figure 8.13: Sorting n elements with $n^2/\log n$ processors.

or $\boldsymbol{A}\boldsymbol{x} = \boldsymbol{b}$. Typically, the elements of $\boldsymbol{A}$, $\boldsymbol{x}$, and $\boldsymbol{b}$ are real numbers. Now suppose that the matrix $\boldsymbol{A}$ and the vector $\boldsymbol{b}$ are given, and it is required to solve the foregoing system for the n unknowns forming the vector $\boldsymbol{x}$. In what follows, we assume that the matrix $\boldsymbol{A}$ has an *inverse*; that is, there exists a matrix $\boldsymbol{A}^{-1}$ such that $\boldsymbol{A}^{-1}\boldsymbol{A} = \boldsymbol{A}\boldsymbol{A}^{-1} = \boldsymbol{I}$, where $\boldsymbol{I}$ is the *identity* matrix (an $n \times n$ matrix, all of whose entries are 0, except the entries on the main diagonal, which are all equal to 1). This assumption guarantees that the system of equations possesses a solution (and that this solution is unique).

In theory, the problem can be solved by computing $\boldsymbol{A}^{-1}$ and then obtaining the elements of $\boldsymbol{x}$ from

$$\boldsymbol{x} = \boldsymbol{A}^{-1}\boldsymbol{b}.$$

But how is $\boldsymbol{A}^{-1}$ itself computed? We show in Section 9.9 that the inverse of a matrix can be obtained through matrix multiplication. As mentioned in Example 1.25, the fastest known sequential algorithm for multiplying two $n \times n$ matrices has a running time of $O(n^\epsilon)$, where $2 < \epsilon < 2.38$. Once $\boldsymbol{A}^{-1}$ is available, the matrix-by-vector product $\boldsymbol{A}^{-1}\boldsymbol{b}$ can be performed using $O(n^2)$ basic operations. Therefore, the system $\boldsymbol{A}\boldsymbol{x} = \boldsymbol{b}$ requires $O(n^\epsilon)$ time to be solved on a RAM. This approach is seldom used, however, due to the numerical errors usually involved in computing $\boldsymbol{A}^{-1}$: Round-off errors, resulting from using floating-point numbers instead of ideal real numbers, tend to accumulate, leading to numerical instability. Instead, other techniques are used. We now describe the most famous of these, known as *Gaussian elimination*.

Gaussian Elimination. This is an algorithm for solving $\boldsymbol{A}\boldsymbol{x} = \boldsymbol{b}$ by applying a sequence of n transformations to $\boldsymbol{A}$ and $\boldsymbol{b}$ such that the system is transformed into the equation

$$\boldsymbol{A}^{(n)}\boldsymbol{x}^{(n)} = \boldsymbol{b}^{(n)},$$

where $\boldsymbol{A}^{(n)} = \boldsymbol{I}$. In this case, $x_i^{(n)} = b_i^{(n)}$, and the system is solved.

Initially, $\boldsymbol{A}^{(0)} = \boldsymbol{A}$ and $\boldsymbol{b}^{(0)} = \boldsymbol{b}$. The ith transformation obtains $\boldsymbol{A}^{(i)}$, $\boldsymbol{x}^{(i)}$, and $\boldsymbol{b}^{(i)}$ from $\boldsymbol{A}^{(i-1)}$, $\boldsymbol{x}^{(i-1)}$, and $\boldsymbol{b}^{(i-1)}$, respectively, by reducing a diagonal element of $\boldsymbol{A}^{(i-1)}$ to 1 and all other $n - 1$ elements in the same column to 0. This is accomplished by the following four steps:

Step 1: The largest element in the submatrix of $\boldsymbol{A}^{(i-1)}$ formed by rows i, $i + 1, \ldots, n$ and columns $i, i + 1, \ldots, n$ is found. Let this element, called the *pivot*, be $a_{kl}^{(i-1)}$.

Step 2: If $k \neq i$, then the ith and kth rows of $\boldsymbol{A}^{(i-1)}$ are interchanged, and so are $b_i^{(i-1)}$ and $b_k^{(i-1)}$; thus,

$$a_{ij}^{(i-1)} \quad \leftrightarrow \quad a_{kj}^{(i-1)} \qquad \text{for } 1 \leq j \leq n,$$

$$\text{and} \quad b_i^{(i-1)} \quad \leftrightarrow \quad b_k^{(i-1)}.$$

If $l \neq i$, then the ith and lth columns of $\boldsymbol{A}^{(i-1)}$ are interchanged, and so are $x_i^{(i-1)}$ and $x_l^{(i-1)}$; thus,

$$a_{ji}^{(i-1)} \quad \leftrightarrow \quad a_{jl}^{(i-1)} \qquad \text{for } 1 \leq j \leq n,$$

$$\text{and} \quad x_i^{(i-1)} \quad \leftrightarrow \quad x_l^{(i-1)}.$$

Step 3: All the elements in the (new) ith row of $\boldsymbol{A}^{(i-1)}$ and (the new) $b_i^{(i-1)}$ are divided by $a_{ii}^{(i-1)}$; thus,

$$a_{ii}^{(i)} \quad \leftarrow \quad 1,$$

$$a_{ij}^{(i)} \quad \leftarrow \quad \frac{a_{ij}^{(i-1)}}{a_{ii}^{(i-1)}} \qquad \text{for } j \neq i,$$

$$b_i^{(i)} \quad \leftarrow \quad \frac{b_i^{(i-1)}}{a_{ii}^{(i-1)}}.$$

Step 4: All remaining elements $a_{rj}^{(i-1)}$ and $b_r^{(i-1)}$, $r \neq i$, are updated to

$$a_{rj}^{(i)} \quad \leftarrow \quad a_{rj}^{(i-1)} \quad - \quad \frac{a_{ri}^{(i-1)} a_{ij}^{(i-1)}}{a_{ii}^{(i-1)}},$$

$$b_r^{(i)} \quad \leftarrow \quad b_r^{(i-1)} \quad - \quad \frac{a_{ri}^{(i-1)} b_i^{(i-1)}}{a_{ii}^{(i-1)}}.$$

In particular,

$$a_{ri}^{(i)} \quad = \quad a_{ri}^{(i-1)} - \frac{a_{ri}^{(i-1)} a_{ii}^{(i-1)}}{a_{ii}^{(i-1)}}$$

$$= \quad 0. \quad \blacksquare$$

The division by $a_{ii}^{(i-1)}$ in Steps 3 and 4 is the reason why we sought, in Step 1, the largest value in the submatrix. This avoids the possibility of division by 0 (causing an abrupt termination of the algorithm!) or by a very small value (causing large round-off errors). Note also that the interchange of rows in Step 2 requires no change in the order of the unknowns; however if columns i and l are swapped, then $x_i^{(i-1)}$ and $x_l^{(i-1)}$ must also change places in $\boldsymbol{x}^{(i-1)}$ to yield $\boldsymbol{x}^{(i)}$.

Correctness of the method follows from the fact that each of the preceding steps is such that the resulting system $\boldsymbol{A}^{(i)} \boldsymbol{x}^{(i)} = \boldsymbol{b}^{(i)}$ is equivalent to $\boldsymbol{A}^{(i-1)} \boldsymbol{x}^{(i-1)} = \boldsymbol{b}^{(i-1)}$, since both sides are affected equally by a division, multiplication, subtraction, or swap. Finally, note that for each pivot, $O(n^2)$ elements need to be updated. Since there are n pivots, the algorithm requires $O(n^3)$ time sequentially.

Example 8.5 Consider the system

$$\begin{pmatrix} 3 & 6 & 2 \\ 1 & 2 & 1 \\ 2 & 1 & 2 \end{pmatrix} \begin{pmatrix} x_1 \\ x_2 \\ x_3 \end{pmatrix} = \begin{pmatrix} 29 \\ 10 \\ 14 \end{pmatrix}.$$

The largest element in the matrix is 6. Therefore, the first and second columns are swapped, and consequently, x_1 and x_2 are also swapped, yielding

$$\begin{pmatrix} 6 & 3 & 2 \\ 2 & 1 & 1 \\ 1 & 2 & 2 \end{pmatrix} \begin{pmatrix} x_2 \\ x_1 \\ x_3 \end{pmatrix} = \begin{pmatrix} 29 \\ 10 \\ 14 \end{pmatrix}.$$

Once all the elements have been updated, we have

$$\begin{pmatrix} 1 & 1/2 & 1/3 \\ 0 & 0 & 1/3 \\ 0 & 3/2 & 5/3 \end{pmatrix} \begin{pmatrix} x_2 \\ x_1 \\ x_3 \end{pmatrix} = \begin{pmatrix} 29/6 \\ 1/3 \\ 55/6 \end{pmatrix}.$$

The largest element among 0, $1/3$, $3/2$, and $5/3$ is the last of these. Therefore, we swap rows 2 and 3 and columns 2 and 3 to obtain

$$\begin{pmatrix} 1 & 1/3 & 1/2 \\ 0 & 5/3 & 3/2 \\ 0 & 1/3 & 0 \end{pmatrix} \begin{pmatrix} x_2 \\ x_3 \\ x_1 \end{pmatrix} = \begin{pmatrix} 29/6 \\ 55/6 \\ 1/3 \end{pmatrix}.$$

Updating the elements, we get

$$\begin{pmatrix} 1 & 0 & 1/5 \\ 0 & 1 & 9/10 \\ 0 & 0 & -3/10 \end{pmatrix} \begin{pmatrix} x_2 \\ x_3 \\ x_1 \end{pmatrix} = \begin{pmatrix} 3 \\ 11/2 \\ -3/2 \end{pmatrix}.$$

We now have no choice but to use $-3/10$ as the pivot. Updating the elements one last time, we obtain

$$\begin{pmatrix} 1 & 0 & 0 \\ 0 & 1 & 0 \\ 0 & 0 & 1 \end{pmatrix} \begin{pmatrix} x_2 \\ x_3 \\ x_1 \end{pmatrix} = \begin{pmatrix} 2 \\ 1 \\ 5 \end{pmatrix}.$$

Therefore, $x_1 = 5, x_2 = 2$, and $x_3 = 1$. $\square$

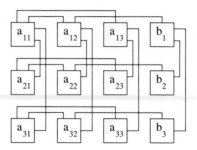

Figure 8.14: Gaussian elimination on a mesh of trees.

Implementation on a Mesh of Trees. The Gaussian elimination algorithm is immediate to implement on an $n \times (n+1)$ mesh of trees, as shown in Fig. 8.14 for $n = 3$. For convenience of notation, the rows and columns of the mesh are numbered 1 to n and 1 to $n+1$, respectively. The matrix $\boldsymbol{A}$ is stored in rows 1 to n and columns 1 to n. The vector $\boldsymbol{b}$ is stored in column $n+1$. The processors in the latter column also keep track of the unknowns x_1, x_2, ..., x_n and swap x_i and x_j whenever the values in columns i and j are exchanged. The algorithm is given in what follows as algorithm MESH-OF-TREES GAUSSIAN ELIMINATION.

Algorithm MESH-OF-TREES GAUSSIAN ELIMINATION

Step 1: During the ith iteration, the largest element in row j, $j = i, i+1, \ldots$, n, is found using the binary tree on row j. Each processor sends to its parent the largest of three elements, namely, its own element and the two elements received from its children. It also forwards to its parent the row and column numbers of this largest value. Eventually, the largest value in each row is "known" to the processors in column 1. They use their column tree to find the overall largest value $a_{kl}^{(i-1)}$ and its row and column numbers, k and l, respectively.

Step 2: If $k \neq i$ and/or $l \neq i$, then the processors in rows i and k and/or columns i and l are informed that their values are to be exchanged. Two rows are exchanged using column trees, with each pair of elements using a distinct tree. Similarly, two columns are exchanged using row trees.

Step 3: The tree over row i is used to distribute $a_{ii}^{(i-1)}$ to all processors, and the values $a_{ij}^{(i)}$ and $b_i^{(i)}$ are computed.

Step 4: For each row $r \neq i$, the tree over the row is used to distribute $a_{ri}^{(i-1)}$ to all processors in the row. Simultaneously, the tree over each column j, $1 \leq j \leq n$, is used to distribute $a_{ij}^{(i-1)}/a_{ii}^{(i-1)}$, while the tree over column $n+1$ is used to distribute $b_i^{(i-1)}/a_{ii}^{(i-1)}$, to all processors in the column. The processors then compute the new values of $a_{rj}^{(i)}$ and $b_r^{(i)}$, $r \neq i$, $1 \leq j \leq n$. ■

Analysis. Each of the steps is easily seen to require $O(\log n)$ time since a binary tree with $O(n)$ leaves has $O(\log n)$ levels. Because there are n pivots, the algorithm has a running time of

$$t(n) = O(n \log n).$$

The number of processors is $p(n) = O(n^2)$, leading to a cost of

$$c(n) = O(n^3 \log n).$$

This cost exceeds the $O(n^3)$ time required sequentially.

Reducing the Cost. The cost can be reduced by a factor of $O(\log n)$ as follows: Let $m = \log^{1/2} n$, and consider a mesh of trees with $(n/m) \times ((n/m) + 1)$ processors arranged in n/m rows by $((n/m) + 1)$ columns. Each processor in the first n/m columns stores an $m \times m$ submatrix of $\boldsymbol{A}$. Each processor in the last column also holds m elements of the vector $\boldsymbol{b}$. During the ith iteration, each of the four steps is executed partly sequentially and partly in parallel. For example, when finding the pivot, each processor first determines sequentially the largest of the $\log n$ elements it holds that also belongs to the submatrix currently under consideration. Then the mesh of trees is used to find the global maximum. Similarly, when performing updates, the global values are broadcast using the mesh of trees, then each processor computes sequentially the new values of the elements it holds. Since each processor holds $O(\log n)$ elements, and the binary trees over rows and columns have $O(\log(n/m))$—that is, $O(\log n)$—levels each, the algorithm still requires $O(\log n)$ time per iteration. The total time for all pivots is still $O(n \log n)$, but since only $O(n/\log n)$ processors are used, the cost is now $O(n^3)$.

8.3.3 Computing the Convex Hull

Our third algorithm for the mesh of trees computes the convex hull of a set of planar points. Recall from Example 4.7 and Section 5.4 that we are given a set Q of $n \geq 4$ points in the plane, each identified by its Cartesian coordinates. For simplicity of presentation, we assume, as before, that no two points have the same x- or y-coordinate and that no three points fall on the same straight line. It is required to compute $CH(Q)$, the convex hull of Q.

Corners of $CH(Q)$ satisfy the following condition: A point $q_i \in Q$ is a corner of $CH(Q)$ if and only if no other three points q_k, q_j, and q_l of Q can be found such that q_i falls inside the triangle formed by q_k, q_j, and q_l. This condition is the basis of our algorithm.

Consider Fig. 8.15(a), showing a set Q of planar points. The following properties of Q are immediate:

1. The point *XMAX* with maximum x-coordinate is a corner of $CH(Q)$. The same is true of *XMIN*, *YMAX*, and *YMIN*, the points with minimum x-coordinate, maximum y-coordinate, and minimum y-coordinate, respectively,

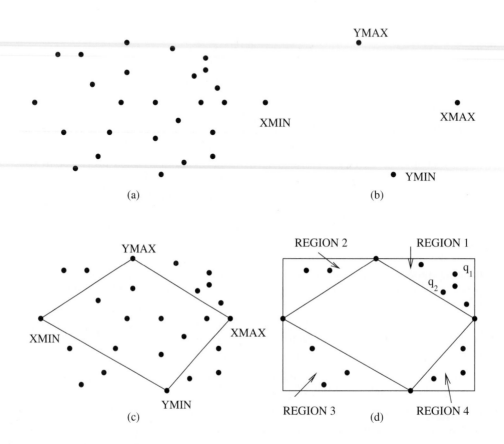

Figure 8.15: Identifying four regions involved in the computation of the convex hull: (a) A set Q of planar points for which the convex hull is to be computed; (b) The four extreme points of Q, namely, *XMAX* (the point with maximum x-coordinate), *XMIN* (the point with minimum x-coordinate), *YMAX* (the point with maximum y-coordinate), and *YMIN* (the point with minimum y-coordinate); (c) All points falling inside the quadrilateral formed by the extreme points are discarded from further consideration, as they cannot be corners of the convex hull; (d) The corners of $CH(Q)$ falling inside each of the four regions can now be computed.

as shown in Fig. 8.15(b). This follows from the fact that none of these points (called the *extreme points*) falls inside a triangle formed by three other points, and therefore, none of them can be interior to $CH(Q)$. Of course, two extreme points may coincide; for example, $XMAX$ and $YMAX$ may be the same point. We continue, however, to refer to them as distinct points for generality.

2. Any point falling inside the polygon $\mathcal{L}$ formed by $XMIN, YMAX, XMAX,$ and $YMIN$ cannot be a corner of $CH(Q)$. This is shown in Fig. 8.15(c).

3. Having discarded all points falling inside the polygon $\mathcal{L}$, we can now focus on the four regions shown in Fig. 8.15(d). The corners of $CH(Q)$ falling inside each region can be found independently of those falling inside the other regions.

4. For each point q in REGION 1, we find two points q' and q'' such that, among all points in REGION 1 (including $YMAX$ and $XMAX$):

   (a) q' forms the smallest angle α_1 with q and the positive x-axis.

   (b) q'' forms the largest angle α_2 with q and the positive x-axis.

   Now, q is a corner of $CH(Q)$ if and only if $\alpha_2 - \alpha_1 < 180$ degrees. Consider, for example, points q_1 and q_2 in Fig. 8.15(d). The angles α_1 and α_2 associated with q_1 are shown in Fig. 8.16(a). Here, $\alpha_2 - \alpha_1 < 180$ degrees, and no triangle can be found that includes q_1. By contrast, $\alpha_2 - \alpha_1 > 180$ degrees in Fig. 8.16(b), and the polygon formed by $YMAX, XMAX, q_2',$ and q_2'' includes q_2. The same rule applies to the points in REGION 4; it also applies to the points in REGIONS 2 and 3, except that we measure the angles with respect to the negative x-axis.

Implementation on a Mesh of Trees.   We use an $n \times n$ mesh of trees. As in Section 8.3.2, we number the rows 1 to n, and similarly for the columns, for notational convenience. The sequence

$$Q = \{(x_1, y_1), (x_2, y_2), \ldots, (x_n, y_n)\},$$

where x_i and y_i are the x- and y-coordinates, respectively, of the ith point, represents the points for which the convex hull is to be computed. Initially, processor $P(1, i)$, $i = 1, 2, \ldots, n$, reads (x_i, y_i) and distributes the pair of coordinates to all processors in column i, using the tree over that column. The algorithm is given next as algorithm MESH-OF-TREES CONVEX HULL:

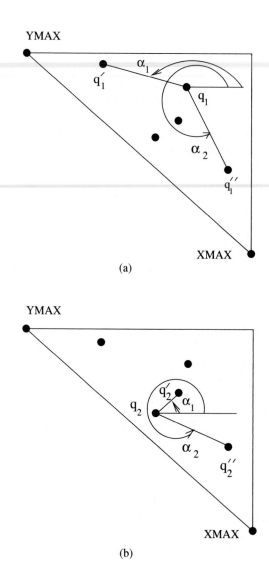

Figure 8.16: (a) Point q_1 is a corner of the convex hull, whereas (b) point q_2 is not.

Algorithm MESH-OF-TREES CONVEX HULL

Step 1:

(1.1) The processors in rows 1, 2, 3, and 4 compute *XMAX, YMAX, XMIN,* and *YMIN* and store their coordinates in $P(1,1)$, $P(2,1)$, $P(3,1)$, and $P(4,1)$, respectively.

(1.2) By means of the tree over column 1, these four values are "made known" to $P(1,1)$. The latter then forwards these values to all processors in row 1, using the tree over that row.

Step 2:

(2.1) The four processors in row 1 corresponding to the extreme points produce a 1 as output, indicating that these points are vertices of $CH(Q)$.

(2.2) All processors in row 1 corresponding to points *inside* the quadrilateral formed by the extreme points produce a 0, indicating that these points are not vertices of $CH(Q)$ and should therefore be removed from further consideration.

(2.3) Each of the remaining processors $P(1,j)$ in row 1 identifies the region (1, 2, 3, or 4) in which point (x_j, y_j) falls and communicates this information to all processors $P(i,j)$ in column j.

(2.4) *YMAX* is assigned to REGIONS 1 and 2, *XMAX* to REGIONS 1 and 4, *YMIN* to REGION 3 and 4, and *XMIN* to REGION 2 and 3.

Step 3:

If processor $P(1,i)$, corresponding to point $q_i = (x_i, y_i)$ of Q, produced neither a 1 nor a 0 in Step 2, then the following steps are executed by the processors in row i:

(3.1) The points q_j and q_k (in the same region as q_i) are found such that the straight-line segments (q_i, q_j) and (q_i, q_k) form the smallest angle α_1 and the largest angle α_2, respectively, with respect to:

(i) The positive x-axis if q_i is in REGION 1 or 4,

(ii) The negative x-axis if q_i is in REGION 2 or 3.

(3.2) If $\alpha_2 - \alpha_1 < 180$ degrees, then q_i is a corner of $CH(Q)$, and $P(1,i)$ produces a 1 as output; otherwise, $P(1,i)$ produces a 0.

Step 4:

(4.1) It is now necessary to pack the points which have been identified as being corners of the convex hull in contiguous positions of row 1 such that, if $CH(Q)$ has h corners, they appear in processors $P(1, 1)$, $P(1, 2)$, ..., $P(1, h)$. In order to do so, we perform a prefix sums computation on the 1's and 0's produced in Steps 2 and 3. This is done as follows:

    (i) $P(1, i)$ propagates its 0 or 1 to all the processors in its column.

    (ii) In row i, processors $P(i, 1)$, $P(i, 2)$, ..., $P(i, i)$ compute the sum of the 0's and 1's they contain; call this sum $w(i)$.

    (iii) $P(i, 1)$ sends $w(i)$ to $P(1, i)$.

    (iv) If $P(1, i)$ holds a corner (x_i, y_i) of the convex hull, then it sends it to $P(w(i), 1)$.

(4.2) $P(1, 1)$ now chooses an arbitrary point in the plane that is guaranteed to fall inside $CH(Q)$. For example, the centroid of the polygon $\mathcal{L}$ formed by the extreme points can be used. This point is designated as an origin for polar coordinates and sent to processors $P(2, 1)$, $P(3, 1)$, ..., $P(h, 1)$. Each of $P(1, 1)$, $P(2, 1)$, ..., $P(h, 1)$ now computes the polar angle formed by the point it holds.

(4.3) The angles computed in Step (4.2) are sorted in nondecreasing order using algorithm MESH-OF-TREES SORT. This gives the corners of the convex hull, listed in counterclockwise order, exactly in the sequence in which they appear along the boundary of $CH(Q)$. ∎

Analysis.   Each of the four steps requires $O(\log n)$ time. Thus, $t(n) = O(\log n)$. Since $p(n) = n^2$, the algorithm has a cost of $O(n^2 \log n)$. This cost can be reduced to $O(n^2)$ by using a mesh of n rows and $n/\log n$ columns, as described in Section 8.3.1. Note also that the algorithm can be easily modified to produce the corners of $CH(Q)$ in clockwise order (as in Section 5.4).

8.4   PROBLEMS

8.1 Apply algorithm MESH SORT to a mesh of processors with eight rows and four columns, initially holding the sequence $\{32, 31, \ldots, 1\}$, one number per processor, in row-major order. Show the contents of the processors after each step of the algorithm.

8.2 How can algorithm MESH SORT be modified to produce the sorted sequence in snakelike row-major order (as defined in Section 2.3.2)?

8.3 Describe an implementation on a mesh of processors of the *odd-even-merge sorting* algorithm on which the combinational circuit of Section 3.1.1 is based. For an input sequence of n elements, the mesh should have n processors, arranged in $n^{1/2}$ rows and $n^{1/2}$ columns, and the sort should be complete in $O(n^{1/2})$ time. The sequence, once sorted, should be in snakelike row-major order (as defined in Section 2.3.2).

8.4 Show how the *bitonic sorting* algorithm of Problem 3.8 can be implemented on a mesh of processors. For an input sequence of n elements, the mesh should have n processors, arranged in $n^{1/2}$ rows and $n^{1/2}$ columns, and the sort should be complete in $O(n^{1/2})$ time. The sequence, once sorted, should be in shuffled row-major order (as defined in Section 2.3.2).

8.5 Prove the following properties of the triangular array algorithm in Section 8.2:

(a) If a processor receives inputs f_1 and f_2 during time unit u, then during time unit $u + 1$ its outputs f_1' and f_2' are such that $f_1' = f_1$ and $f_2' = f_2$ (i.e., the input arriving on the fast input link is *not* switched to the slow output link).

(b) If a processor's output f_2' is such that $f_2' = f_1$ during time unit $u+1$, then the processor received no input f_2 during time unit u. (This property, together with (a), establishes that a processor never has to place two values on its slow output link simultaneously).

(c) If $F = f(i, j)$ is produced as output during time unit $u+1$, then processor $P(i, j)$ received no input during time unit u (i.e., a processor never has to place two values on its fast output link simultaneously).

8.6 Explain why, in the triangular array algorithm of Section 8.2, processor $P(i, j)$ finishes computing $f(i, j)$ when $u = 2(j - i)$.

8.7 In the triangular array of Section 8.2, each processor needs to keep track of u, the number of time units elapsed, in order to "decide" whether it is time to produce the contents of F as output or to switch a value received on a fast link onto a slow link. Show that by using $2(n - 1)$ control signals, one per row and one per column, which travel at appropriate speeds from left to right and from bottom to top, respectively, each processor receiving these signals can determine what needs to be done (without having to store u).

8.8 A sequence $S = \{s_1, s_2, \ldots, s_n\}$ whose elements are listed in arbitrary order is stored in an $n^{1/2} \times n^{1/2}$ mesh of processors, one element per processor. Given an element x, it is required to determine whether $x = s_i$ for some $1 \leq i \leq n$ and, if so, return the index i as the answer to the query. If x is not equal to any element in S, then a 0 is returned. Design an algorithm for solving this problem, and analyze its running time and cost.

8.9 Problem 8.8 can be generalized to the case where several queries are to be answered. Here m elements $x_1, x_2, \ldots, x_m$ are queued, and it is required to determine, for each x_j, $1 \leq j \leq m$, whether $x_j = s_i$ for some $1 \leq i \leq n$. A naive algorithm handles each query by repeatedly applying the solution to Problem 8.8. Show that a better performance can be obtained through pipelining. Analyze the running time of the new algorithm, under the assumption that each processor has a constant amount of local storage.

8.10 Given an $n \times n$ matrix

$$A = \begin{pmatrix} a_{11} & a_{12} & \cdots & a_{1n} \\ a_{21} & a_{22} & \cdots & a_{2n} \\ & & \vdots & \\ a_{n1} & a_{n2} & \cdots & a_{nn} \end{pmatrix},$$

it is required to compute the *transpose* of A; that is,

$$A^T = \begin{pmatrix} a_{11} & a_{21} & \cdots & a_{n1} \\ a_{12} & a_{22} & \cdots & a_{n2} \\ & & \vdots & \\ a_{1n} & a_{2n} & \cdots & a_{nn} \end{pmatrix}.$$

In other words, every row in matrix A is a column in matrix A^T. The transpose of an $n \times n$ matrix can be computed on an $n \times n$ mesh by assigning a_{ij} to $P(i, j)$ and then routing a_{ij} to $P(j, i)$, for all $1 \leq i, j \leq n$. Show how this is done in each of the following two cases:

(a) The element a_{ij} carries along the indices of its destination processor, namely, j and i, as it travels from $P(i, j)$ to $P(j, i)$.

(b) The element a_{ij} carries no information whatsoever concerning i and j as it travels from $P(i, j)$ to $P(j, i)$.

8.11 Let $n = 2^q$, and assume that an $n \times n$ matrix A is to be transposed using a perfect-shuffle interconnection network parallel computer with n^2 processors $P_0, P_1, \ldots, P_{2^{2q}-1}$. Initially, element a_{ij} of A is stored in P_k, where $k = 2^q(i-1) + (j-1)$. A *shuffle operation* moves the element held by P_l into P_m, for every processor P_l connected to a processor P_m by a perfect-shuffle link. Show that after q shuffle operations, processor P_k contains element a_{ji}. Compare the running time and cost of this algorithm to the running time and cost of the algorithm in Problem 8.10.

8.12 Given an $m \times n$ matrix A and an $n \times k$ matrix B, it is required to compute an $m \times k$ matrix C equal to the product of A and B. The elements of $C = A \times B$ are given by

$$c_{ij} = \sum_{s=1}^{n} a_{is} \times b_{sj},$$

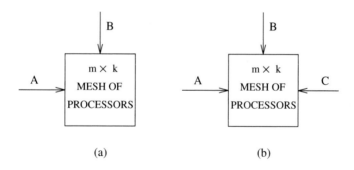

Figure 8.17: Matrix multiplication on a mesh of processors with sequential input: (a) The elements of the product matrix, all initialized to 0, reside in the mesh at the beginning of the computation; (a) The elements of the product matrix, all initialized to 0, are fed into the mesh sequentially.

for $1 \leq i \leq m$ and $1 \leq j \leq k$. Design an algorithm for performing this computation on a mesh of processors with m rows and k columns. Initially, processor $P(i,j)$ holds $c_{ij} = 0$. Matrices A and B are fed into the mesh as shown in Fig. 8.17(a). Tell how to organize the input and subsequent computations so that, when the algorithm terminates, $P(i,j)$ contains the final value of c_{ij}.

8.13 Assume that several pairs of matrices (A_1, B_1), (A_2, B_2), ..., (A_q, B_q) are queued, waiting to be multiplied on the mesh in Problem 8.12. Show how the algorithm can be modified to allow this computation to be carried out in a *pipeline* fashion.

8.14 In Problem 8.13, once processor $P(i,j)$ has finished computing c_{ij} for one pair of matrices, it should produce it as output immediately before it becomes involved in computing the product of a new pair of matrices. This is because the product matrix may be needed for another computation once it is available and/or because $P(i,j)$ has storage room for only one c_{ij} at a time. If $P(i,j)$ is directly connected to an output device, then it can send c_{ij} to the outside world once it is computed. Alternatively, suppose that only boundary processors in the mesh are connected to output devices. Discuss how the c_{ij} are produced as output in this case.

8.15 Repeat Problem 8.12 for the case where matrices A, B, and C are fed to the mesh as shown in Fig. 8.17(b), with all the elements of C initialized to 0.

8.16 Consider an $n \times n$ mesh of processors where the processors in each row and the processors in each column are connected to form a *ring*. (The additional links are called *wraparound connections*, and the mesh is now referred to as a *torus.*) Initially, $P(i,j)$ stores elements a_{ij} and b_{ij} of two matrices $\boldsymbol{A}$ and $\boldsymbol{B}$, respectively. Design an algorithm for computing $\boldsymbol{C} = \boldsymbol{A} \times \boldsymbol{B}$ on this model, so that at the end of the computation $P(i,j)$ also holds c_{ij}.

8.17 Repeat Problem 8.16 for the mesh under the same initial conditions, but without the wraparound connections.

8.18 An $n \times n$ matrix of 0's and 1's (representing the pixels of a black-and-white image) is stored in an $n \times n$ mesh of processors, one pixel per processor. We assume that every 1-pixel has a label: All pixels with the same label form an *object*.

(a) Design an algorithm that finds the nearest object to each pixel.

(b) Extend your solution in **(a)** to find the nearest object to each object.

Your algorithms should work for any natural definition of *distance*.

8.19 Let $n = 2^{2s}$, and consider a mesh of n processors P_0, P_1, ..., P_{n-1} arranged in 2^s rows and 2^s columns, in row-major order. The mesh contains a sequence $\{a_0, a_1, \ldots, a_{n-1}\}$ and computes its discrete Fourier transform $\{b_0, b_1, \ldots, b_{n-1}\}$. Initially, P_i holds a_i; when the computation terminates, P_i holds b_i, for $i = 0, 1, \ldots, n-1$. The algorithm used is an implementation of the FFT on the mesh and is given next as algorithm MESH FFT. In it, rev(k) denotes the integer obtained by reversing the binary representation of an integer k, and ω_n is a primitive nth root of unity.

> **Algorithm MESH FFT**
> **Step 1: for** $k = 0$ **to** $n-1$ **do in parallel**
> $\quad\quad d_k \leftarrow a_k$
> **end for**
> **Step 2: for** $h = (\log n) - 1$ **downto** 0 **do**
> $\quad\quad$ **for** $k = 0$ **to** $n-1$ **do in parallel**
> $\quad\quad\quad$ (2.1) $g \leftarrow 2^h$
> $\quad\quad\quad$ (2.2) $q \leftarrow n/g$
> $\quad\quad\quad$ (2.3) $z \leftarrow (\omega_n^g)^{\text{rev}(k) \bmod q}$
> $\quad\quad\quad$ (2.4) **if** $(k \bmod g) = (k \bmod 2g)$
> $\quad\quad\quad\quad$ **then** (i) $r \leftarrow d_k$
> $\quad\quad\quad\quad\quad\quad$ (ii) $d_k \leftarrow r + z d_{k+g}$
> $\quad\quad\quad\quad\quad\quad$ (iii) $d_{k+g} \leftarrow r - z d_{k+g}$
> $\quad\quad\quad$ **end if**
> $\quad\quad$ **end for**
> $\quad$ **end for**
> **Step 3: for** $k = 0$ **to** $n-1$ **do in parallel**
> $\quad\quad b_k \leftarrow d_{\text{rev}(k)}$
> **end for.** ∎

Analyze the running time of this algorithm, taking into account both the computational and routing steps involved.

8.20 Let A be a given $m \times n$ matrix, where $m > n$, and b be a given $m \times 1$ vector. Now consider the system of linear equations described by $Ax = b$, where x is an $n \times 1$ vector of unknowns. Since there are more equations than unknowns, the system is said to be *overdetermined*: In general, there is no (unique) solution. Because there is no way of satisfying all of the equations at the same time, a compromise solution is to compute a vector x that approximately satisfies them. One approach is to find an x that minimizes the quantity

$$\sum_{i=1}^{m} \left(b_i - \sum_{j=1}^{n} a_{ij} x_j \right)^2.$$

This is known as a *least squares solution*. Design a parallel algorithm for performing the computation.

8.21 The convolution problem of Section 7.3 can be extended to two dimensions as follows: Let X be an $n \times n$ input matrix and W be a $k \times k$ weight matrix, where $k < n$. The weight matrix slides across the input matrix: For each position of W within X, the weights w are multiplied by the corresponding inputs x, and the sum of these products is computed. Specifically, if the input value at the top left corner of the submatrix of X covered by W is x_{rs}, then we compute

$$\sum_{i=1}^{k} \sum_{j=1}^{k} w_{ij} x_{r+i-1,s+j-1},$$

for $r = 1, 2, \ldots, n - k + 1$ and $s = 1, 2, \ldots, n - k + 1$. Show how this computation can be performed on a parallel computer consisting of $n - k + 1$ meshes of k rows and k columns each.

8.22 Show how the prefix sums of a sequence $\{x_0, x_1, \ldots, x_{n-1}\}$ can be computed on an $m^{1/2} \times m^{1/2}$ mesh of processors, where $m < n$.

8.23 Let R and S denote the interior and boundary, respectively, of a region in two-dimensional space, and let $f(x, y)$ and $g(x, y)$ be continuous functions defined on S and R, respectively. It is required to compute a function $u(x, y)$ that is equal to $f(x, y)$ on S and that satisfies the following partial differential equation on R, known as *Poisson's equation*:

$$u_{xx} + u_{yy} = g(x, y), \quad \text{where} \quad u_{xx} = \frac{\partial^2 u(x, y)}{\partial x^2}, \quad \text{and} \quad u_{yy} = \frac{\partial^2 u(x, y)}{\partial y^2}.$$

This is a special case of the *boundary value problem* called the *model problem*. It is solved numerically by first deriving a discrete version of it. Here R and S

are the interior and boundary, respectively, of the unit square $0 \le x \le 1, 0 \le y \le 1$. A uniform grid of $n + 1$ horizontal and $n + 1$ vertical lines, where n is an arbitrary positive integer, is superimposed over the unit square, with a spacing of $d = 1/n$ between lines. The $(n + 1)^2$ intersections of these lines are called *grid points*. For a grid point (x, y) in R, u_{xx} and u_{yy} are approximated by *difference quotients* as follows:

$$u_{xx} = (u(x + d, y) + u(x - d, y) - 2u(x, y))/d^2,$$

$$u_{yy} = (u(x, y + d) + u(x, y - d) - 2u(x, y))/d^2.$$

This leads to the following form of Poisson's equation, known as a *difference equation*:

$$u(x, y) = (u(x + d, y) + u(x - d, y) + u(x, y + d) + u(x, y - d) - d^2 g(x, y))/4.$$

An iterative process called *successive overrelaxation* is used to obtain an approximate value for $u(x, y)$ at each of the $(n - 1)^2$ interior grid points. Beginning with an arbitrary value $u_0(x, y)$, the iteration

$$u_k(x, y) = u_{k-1}(x, y) + w(u'_k(x, y) - u_{k-1}(x, y))$$

is used for successive integer values of k, $k \ge 1$, where

$$w = 2/(1 + \sin(\pi d))$$

and

$$u'_k(x, y) = (u_{k-1}(x + d, y) + u_k(x - d, y) + u_{k-1}(x, y + d)$$

$$+ u_k(x, y - d) - d^2 g(x, y))/4.$$

Let e_k denote the absolute value of the difference between $u_k(x, y)$ and the *exact* value of u at (x, y). The iterative process continues until $e_k \le e_0/10^v$, where v is a positive integer representing the desired accuracy. Neither e_0 nor e_k is known, of course. However, it can be shown that the process converges and the preceding inequality is true after $k = qn$ iterations, where $q = v/3$. Since there are $(n - 1)^2$ interior points, the entire process takes $O(n^3)$ time. Show how this algorithm can be implemented on an $N \times N$ mesh of processors, where $N = n - 1$.

8.24 Show that the discrete model problem of Problem 8.23 can be solved by reducing it to a system of $(n - 1)^2$ linear equations in $(n - 1)^2$ unknowns.

8.25 *Jacobi's method* is another iterative approach to solving the model problem of Problem 8.23. Given "old" values u_{k-1} at grid points, the following equation is used to generate "new" values:

$$u_k(x, y) = (u_{k-1}(x + d, y) + u_{k-1}(x - d, y) + u_{k-1}(x, y + d)$$

$$+u_{k-1}(x, y - d) - d^2 g(x, y))/4.$$

Although slow in its convergence, requiring $O(n^2)$ iterations, this method is easier to implement in parallel than is successive overrelaxation. Show how the methods works on a mesh of processors.

8.26 A *q-dimensional lattice* is an interconnection network parallel computer that generalizes the linear array and the mesh to dimensions higher than two. In this lattice, the processors are placed at points $(i_1, i_2, \ldots, i_q)$ of q-dimensional space, where i_k is an integer for $1 \leq k \leq q$. Exactly one processor is placed at each point. Processor P_i at $(i_1, i_2, \ldots, i_q)$ is connected by a direct two-way link to processor P_j at $(j_1, j_2, \ldots, j_q)$ if and only if the distance between P_i and P_j, denoted $d(P_i, P_j)$ and defined as

$$d(P_i, P_j) = \sum_{k=1}^{q} \text{abs}(i_k - j_k),$$

is equal to 1, where $\text{abs}(i_k - j_k)$ represents the absolute value of $(i_k - j_k)$. A q-dimensional lattice with 24 processors is shown in Fig. 8.18 for $q = 3$. It consists of two stacked 4×3 meshes, with the processor in row i and column j of one mesh connected to the corresponding processor in the other mesh. Show that two $n \times n$ matrices can be multiplied in $O(n^{3/4})$ time on a three-dimensional lattice consisting of $n^{3/4}$ stacked $n^{3/4} \times n^{3/4}$ meshes.

8.27 Show how a sequence of numbers $S = \{s_0, s_1, \ldots, s_{n-1}\}$ can be sorted in nondecreasing order on a PRAM with n^2 processors in $O(1)$ time.

8.28 The *Gauss-Jordan method* is an algorithm for solving the system of linear equations $\boldsymbol{Ax} = \boldsymbol{b}$, where $\boldsymbol{A}$ is a given $n \times n$ matrix, $\boldsymbol{b}$ is a given $n \times 1$ vector, and $\boldsymbol{x}$ is the unknown $n \times 1$ vector. The idea is to eliminate all the unknowns but x_i from the ith equation. This is done as follows: Let b_i be denoted by $a_{i,n+1}$. For $1 \leq j \leq n, 1 \leq i \leq n, j \leq k \leq n + 1$, and $i \neq j$, we compute

$$a_{ik} \leftarrow a_{ik} - (a_{ij}/a_{jj})a_{jk}.$$

Then, for $1 \leq i \leq n$, $x_i \leftarrow a_{i,n+1}/a_{ii}$. Show how this algorithm can be implemented on a mesh of trees.

8.29 The elements a_{jj} used in the Gauss-Jordan method of Problem 8.28 are called *pivots*. If a pivot equals 0 at any point, then the method fails. Similarly, if the value of a pivot is too close to 0, then the errors of computation grow, and the method becomes numerically unstable. Show how the method can be changed to avoid these problems, and modify your mesh-of-trees implementation in Problem 8.28 to include the changes.

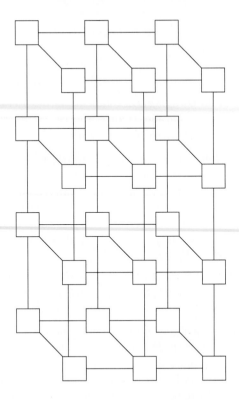

Figure 8.18: A three-dimensional lattice.

8.30 The system of linear equations $\boldsymbol{Ax} = \boldsymbol{b}$ can also be solved by decomposing the matrix $\boldsymbol{A}$ into two matrices $\boldsymbol{L}$ and $\boldsymbol{U}$ such that $\boldsymbol{LU} = \boldsymbol{A}$, where $\boldsymbol{U}$ is *upper triangular* ($u_{kj} = 0$ if $k > j$) and $\boldsymbol{L}$ is *lower triangular* ($l_{ik} = 0$ if $i < k$) with diagonal elements equal to 1 ($l_{ik} = 1$ if $i = k$). Now the systems $\boldsymbol{Ly} = \boldsymbol{b}$ and $\boldsymbol{Ux} = \boldsymbol{y}$ are solved using forward and back substitution, respectively. Assume that $\boldsymbol{A}$ is *positive definite*, that is:

(a) $\boldsymbol{A}$ is *symmetric* ($a_{ij} = a_{ji}, 1 \leq i, j \leq n$);

(b) For all $n \times 1$ nonzero vectors $\boldsymbol{v}$, $\boldsymbol{v}^T \boldsymbol{Av} > 0$, where $\boldsymbol{v}^T$ is the *transpose* of $\boldsymbol{v}$ (i.e., the vector obtained by writing the elements of $\boldsymbol{v}$ as a $1 \times n$ vector).

In this special case, the elements of $\boldsymbol{L}$ and $\boldsymbol{U}$ are obtained from

$$
\begin{aligned}
l_{ik} &= a_{ik}^k / u_{kk} & i > k, \\
u_{kj} &= a_{kj} & k \leq j,
\end{aligned}
$$

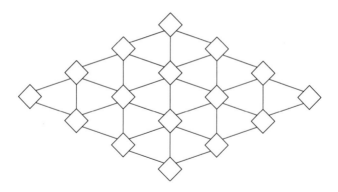

Figure 8.19: Hexagonal array with 16 processors.

where $a_{ij}^1 = a_{ij}$ and $a_{ij}^{k+1} = a_{ij}^k - (l_{ik} \times u_{kj})$. Show how the matrices $\boldsymbol{L}$ and $\boldsymbol{U}$ can be computed on an interconnection network parallel computer in which the processors form a *hexagonal array*, as shown in Fig. 8.19. This two-dimensional network can be viewed as variant of the mesh in which a typical processor is connected to its six closest neighbors.

8.31 The convex hull algorithm of Section 8.3.3 needs to determine whether a given point falls inside a given quadrilateral.

   (a) Develop a sequential constant-time algorithm to perform such a test.

   (b) Develop a parallel algorithm for the general case where it is required to determine whether a point falls inside a polygon with n sides.

8.32 Design a parallel algorithm for computing the convex hull of a set Q of points in the plane using only the property that a point is a corner of $CH(Q)$ if and only if it does not fall inside a triangle formed by any three points of Q other than itself.

8.33 Design a parallel algorithm for computing the convex hull of a set Q of points in the plane using the following property: The straight-line segment connecting two points q_i and q_j of Q is a side of $CH(Q)$ if and only if all remaining $n-2$ points of Q fall on the same side of the infinite straight line through q_i and q_j.

8.34 Modify the algorithm in Problem 8.33 to take advantage of the following additional property: If (q_i, q_j) is a side of $CH(Q)$, then q_j (among all the points of Q) forms the smallest angle with q_i (with respect to the positive x-axis in REGIONS 1 and 4 and the negative x-axis in REGIONS 2 and 3 of Fig. 8.15).

8.35 Describe an algorithm for multiplying two matrices on the hexagonal array of Problem 8.30.

8.36 Design an algorithm for multiplying two matrices on a mesh-of-trees interconnection network.

8.37 Extend the mesh-of-trees interconnection network to three dimensions.

8.38 Show how the network of Problem 8.37 can be used to multiply two $n \times n$ matrices in $O(\log n)$ time using n^3 processors.

8.39 Using the results of Problems 8.37 and 8.38, show that m pairs of $n \times n$ matrices can be multiplied in $O(m + 2 \log n)$ time.

8.40 A graph is said to be *planar* if it can be drawn in the plane so that no two of its edges intersect (except at a vertex). If the edges are drawn as straight-line segments, the resulting drawing of the graph is called a *planar subdivision*. For example, the triangulation of Fig. 4.19 (used in Problem 4.30) is a planar subdivision. In general, a planar subdivision consists of a collection of adjacent *polygons* in the plane (i.e., not necessarily *triangles*, as in Fig. 4.19). These polygons can be convex or concave, but they must be *simple*, meaning that no two sides of a polygon may intersect, except at a corner. Note also that two adjacent polygons must share a side. Thus, a polygon with n sides can be adjacent to at most n other polygons. Given a planar subdivision S and a point q, it is required to determine whether a polygon of S contains q and, if so, to identify that polygon. Design an algorithm for solving this problem on a mesh of trees.

8.41 Suppose that a pyramid with $O(n^2)$ processors can solve a problem of size n in time $t(n)$. Show that a mesh of trees with $O(n^2)$ processors can solve the same problem in $O(t(n) \log n)$ time.

8.42 Show that there exist problems of size n which can be solved by a mesh of trees with $O(n^2)$ processors in time $t(n)$, but which require $O(t(n) \times n^{1/2} / \log^{3/2} n)$ on a pyramid with $O(n^2)$ processors.

8.43 Consider the two-dimensional representation of a pyramid with three levels shown in Fig. 8.20. Dotted lines represent links connecting processors at the same level, and solid lines represent connections between a processor and its children. Compare this layout to that of a mesh of trees shown in Fig. 2.11, and identify the advantages and disadvantages of each.

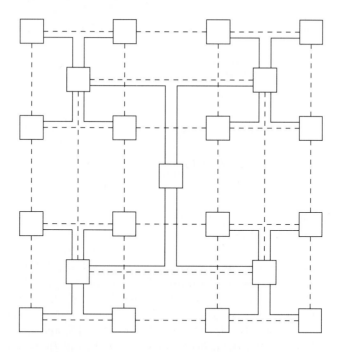

Figure 8.20: Two-dimensional representation of a pyramid with three levels.

8.5   BIBLIOGRAPHICAL REMARKS

Two-dimensional arrays of processors were among the earliest models of parallel computation proposed in theory and in practice; see, for example, Barnes et al. [85], Batcher [90], Bouknight et al. [119], Flanders et al. [232], Hord [302], and Siegel [571]. The many attractive properties of the mesh as a prime candidate for implementation using VLSI circuits were soon recognized. Kung [346, 347, 348, 349], in particular, emphasized its suitability for developing parallel algorithms which he called *systolic*—that is, algorithms in which data and control signals travel in rhythmic fashion across a two-dimensional topology. The mesh model continues to appeal, and several computers have been built based on it; see, for example, Moldovan [432], Quinn [515], and Trew and Wilson [614].

A proof of the 0–1 principle is provided in Knuth [325]. Algorithms for sorting by odd-even transposition on the linear array appear in Akl [18], Knuth [325], and Kung [348]. Sorting algorithms for the mesh are described in Kumar and Hirschberg [342], Lang et al. [359], Nassimi and Sahni [437], and Thompson and Kung [612]. These algorithms are essentially implementations on the mesh of the odd-even-merge and bitonic sorting algorithms and are recursive in nature. By contrast, the algorithms in Leighton [366], Marberg and Gafni [404], Sado and

Igarashi [544], Scherson et al. [550], and Schnorr and Shamir [553] are based on row and column operations and are expressed solely in terms of these operations. In particular, algorithm MESH SORT, originally proposed by Marberg and Gafni [404] under the name *ROTATESORT*, was the first such algorithm to sort in a constant number of row and column operations. Other sorting algorithms for the mesh and closely related models are described in Chern and Murata [151], Flanders and Reddaway [233], Krizanc and Narayanan [333], Kunde [345], Leighton [366], and Schröder [554]. Many algorithms for solving a variety of computational problems on the mesh are documented in Akl [21], Akl and Lyons [42], Akl et al. [45], Bertsekas and Tsitsiklis [99], Chaudhuri [140], Kumar et al. [343], Leighton [367], Mead and Conway [412], Moldovan [432], Preston and Uhr [504], Quinn [514], Quinton and Robert [517, 518], Robert [537], Snyder et al. [580], and Ullman [615]. The dynamic programming approach of Section 8.2.1 is used in Knuth [325] to construct optimal binary search trees. An algorithm for computing a dynamic programming solution on a triangular array was first proposed in Guibas et al. [272].

The mesh-of-trees model was proposed independently by several authors as an extension to the mesh; see, for example, Capello and Steiglitz [128], Hsiao and Snyder [305], Leighton [365], Muller and Preparata [434], Nath et al. [441], and Preparata and Vuillemin [501]. Surveys of parallel sorting algorithms are provided in Akl [18], Bitton et al. [109], Lakshmivarahan et al. [357], and Rajasekaran [523]. Parallel algorithms for numerical problems are described in Bertsekas and Tsitsiklis [99], Freeman and Phillips [251], Golub and Ortega [262], Lakshmivarahan and Dhall [355], and Modi [431]. The monograph by Robert [537] is devoted to a study of parallel implementations of the Gaussian elimination method. An introduction to computational geometry is provided in Preparata and Shamos [500]. Several parallel algorithms for computing the convex hull and other geometric problems are presented in Akl and Lyons [42] and Reif [533].

The pyramid model and a number of its variations are described in Dyer [210], Jamieson et al. [311], Snyder et al. [580], Suaya and Birtwistle [600], Tanimoto [604, 605], and Tanimoto and Pavlidis [606].

Chapter 9

Hypercubes and Stars

In Chapter 8, we studied the mesh interconnection network parallel computer. The model was seen to be an attractive one, both theoretically and practically, thanks to its simplicity and regularity. Despite all of its advantages, however, the model is inherently slow for many applications. Indeed, an $N^{1/2} \times N^{1/2}$ mesh has a diameter of $2N^{1/2}-2$. Three general approaches were proposed to allow faster communication among the processors. One of these approaches was presented in Chapter 8; it consists in modifying the mesh by either replacing or augmenting its existing edges with links forming "tree connections" among the processors. The mesh of trees and the pyramid are among the networks resulting from such replacement and augmentation, respectively. Another approach, also based on modifying the mesh, is described in Chapter 10; it extends the mesh through the addition of various forms of *buses*.

In this chapter, an alternative approach is examined that does not take the mesh as its starting point. Instead, different interconnection networks are used whose diameters are smaller than that of the mesh. Among these are the *perfect-shuffle*, the *hypercube*, the *cube-connected cycles*, the *de Bruijn*, and the *star* networks. Here, we focus on the hypercube and star interconnection networks. Specifically, the first part of the chapter shows how a fundamental operation, namely, matrix multiplication, can be used to solve a variety of computational problems on the hypercube. It is important to note that the emphasis here, as elsewhere in the book, is not only on the *model*, but also on the *method*. Thus, in this context, there is nothing special about matrix multiplication on the hypercube. Rather, our objective is to show how matrix multiplication is an important algorithm design technique in parallel computation. The hypercube is used as a vehicle of illustration, since it happens to be one of the two models studied in this chapter. The second part of the chapter shows how several operations are executed on the star. In particular, we describe solutions to a number of data-routing problems and demonstrate how the fast Fourier transform can be performed.

We begin in Section 9.1 by presenting an algorithm for matrix multiplication on the hypercube. A second matrix operation, which will prove useful in our subsequent development, namely matrix transposition on the hypercube, is illustrated in Section 9.2. Sections 9.3–9.10 describe parallel algorithms that use matrix multiplication (and occasionally matrix transposition) as a basic technique. Sections 9.11–9.14 are devoted to the star interconnection network and its algorithms.

9.1 MATRIX MULTIPLICATION

In this section, we provide a formal specification of the hypercube model of parallel computation. This is followed by a definition of the problem of matrix multiplication. Finally, an algorithm for multiplying two matrices on a hypercube is described.

9.1.1 The Hypercube Interconnection Network

The hypercube model was introduced in Section 2.3.7 and illustrated in Figs. 2.16 and 2.17. A formal specification and a different pictorial representation are given in what follows. Note that we ignore the case (considered for completeness in Section 2.3.7) of a zero-dimensional hypercube, since a hypercube with one processor is not a parallel computer.

Let $N = 2^g$ processors P_0, P_1, ..., P_{N-1} be available, for $g \geq 1$. Further, let i and $i^{(b)}$ be two integers, $0 \leq i, i^{(b)} \leq N - 1$, whose binary representations differ only in position b, $0 \leq b < g$. Specifically, if $i_{g-1}i_{g-2} \ldots i_{b+1}i_bi_{b-1} \ldots i_1i_0$ is the binary representation of i, then $i_{g-1}i_{g-2} \ldots i_{b+1}i_b'i_{b-1} \ldots i_1i_0$ is the binary representation of $i^{(b)}$, where i_b' is the binary complement of bit i_b. A *g-dimensional hypercube interconnection network* is formed by connecting each processor P_i, $0 \leq i \leq N - 1$, to $P_{i^{(b)}}$ by a two-way link, for all $0 \leq b < g$. This is illustrated in Fig. 9.1 for $g = 4$. (The representation shown is often used to illustrate the model, perhaps because it is slightly more convenient than those depicted in Figs. 2.16 and 2.17.)

9.1.2 Computing the Product of Two Matrices

Let A and B be two $n \times n$ matrices whose elements are numerals (for example, reals), and let $n = 2^q$. It is required to compute a third $n \times n$ matrix C equal to the product of A and B. The elements of C are defined as follows:

$$c_{jk} = \sum_{i=0}^{n-1} a_{ji} \times b_{ik} \qquad 0 \leq j, k \leq n - 1.$$

As indicated in Example 1.25, a lower bound on the number of operations required to perform this computation is $\Omega(n^2)$. This is the highest known lower bound. On the other hand, the lowest available upper bound is $O(n^\epsilon)$, $2 < \epsilon < 2.38$, also mentioned in Example 1.25. Since C has n^2 entries, each of which, by definition, equals the sum of n products, a straightforward RAM algorithm requires $O(n^3)$ time.

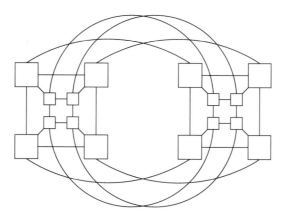

Figure 9.1: A hypercube with 2^4 processors.

9.1.3 A Parallel Algorithm

The parallel algorithm for matrix multiplication that we now describe is essentially an implementation on the hypercube of the straightforward RAM algorithm mentioned at the end of the previous section. In order to multiply the two $n \times n$ matrices $\boldsymbol{A}$ and $\boldsymbol{B}$, where $n = 2^q$, we use a hypercube with $N = n^3 = 2^{3q}$ processors. It is helpful to visualize the processors as being arranged in an $n \times n \times n$ array, with processor P_r occupying position (i, j, k), where $r = in^2 + jn + k$ and $0 \le i, j, k \le n - 1$. Thus, if the binary representation of r is

$$r_{3q-1} r_{3q-2} \dots r_{2q} r_{2q-1} \dots r_q r_{q-1} \dots r_0,$$

then the binary representations of i, j, and k are

$$r_{3q-1} r_{3q-2} \dots r_{2q}, \qquad r_{2q-1} r_{2q-2} \dots r_q, \qquad \text{and} \quad r_{q-1} r_{q-2} \dots r_0,$$

respectively. Note that in the $n \times n \times n$ array, all processors agreeing on one or two of the coordinates (i, j, k) form a hypercube. Specifically, all processors with the same index value in one of the three coordinates form a hypercube with n^2 processors; similarly, all processors with the same index values in two fixed coordinates form a hypercube with n processors.

Let each processor P_r have three registers A_r, B_r, and C_r, also denoted $A(i, j, k)$, $B(i, j, k)$, and $C(i, j, k)$, respectively. Initially, processor P_s in position $(0, j, k)$, $0 \le j \le n - 1$, $0 \le k \le n - 1$, contains a_{jk} and b_{jk} in registers A_s and B_s, respectively. The registers of all other processors are initialized to 0. At the end of the computation, register C_s of P_s should contain element c_{jk} of $\boldsymbol{C}$. The algorithm is designed to perform the n^3 multiplications involved in computing the n^2 entries of $\boldsymbol{C}$ simultaneously. It proceeds in three steps:

Step 1: The elements of matrices A and B are distributed over the n^3 processors so that the processor in position (i, j, k) contains a_{ji} and b_{ik}. This is done as follows:

(1.1) Copies of data initially in $A(0, j, k)$ and $B(0, j, k)$, are sent to the processors in positions (i, j, k), where $1 \leq i \leq n-1$. As a result, $A(i, j, k) = a_{jk}$ and $B(i, j, k) = b_{jk}$, for $0 \leq i \leq n - 1$.

(1.2) Copies of the data in $A(i, j, i)$ are sent to the processors in positions (i, j, k), where $0 \leq k \leq n-1$. As a result, $A(i, j, k) = a_{ji}$ for $0 \leq k \leq n-1$.

(1.3) Copies of the data in $B(i, i, k)$ are sent to the processors in positions (i, j, k), where $0 \leq j \leq n-1$. As a result, $B(i, j, k) = b_{ik}$ for $0 \leq j \leq n-1$.

Step 2: Each processor in position (i, j, k) computes the product

$$C(i, j, k) \leftarrow A(i, j, k) \times B(i, j, k).$$

Thus, $C(i, j, k) = a_{ji} \times b_{ik}$ for $0 \leq i, j, k \leq n - 1$.

Step 3: The sum

$$C(0, j, k) \leftarrow \sum_{i=0}^{n-1} C(i, j, k)$$

is computed for $0 \leq j, k \leq n - 1$.

The algorithm is given next as algorithm HYPERCUBE MATRIX MULTIPLI-CATION. In it, we denote by $N(r_m = d)$ the set of integers r, $0 \leq r \leq N-1$, whose binary representation is $r_{3q-1} \ldots r_{m+1} d r_{m-1} \ldots r_0$.

Algorithm HYPERCUBE MATRIX MULTIPLICATION (A, B, C)

    Step 1: (1.1) **for** $m = 3q - 1$ **downto** $2q$ **do**
            for all $r \in N(r_m = 0)$ **do in parallel**
               (i) $A_{r(m)} \leftarrow A_r$
               (ii) $B_{r(m)} \leftarrow B_r$
            end for
        end for
        (1.2) **for** $m = q - 1$ **downto** 0 **do**
            for all $r \in N(r_m = r_{2q+m})$ **do in parallel**
               $A_{r(m)} \leftarrow A_r$
            end for
        end for
        (1.3) **for** $m = 2q - 1$ **downto** q **do**
            for all $r \in N(r_m = r_{q+m})$ **do in parallel**
               $B_{r(m)} \leftarrow B_r$
            end for
        end for

Step 2: for $r = 0$ **to** $N - 1$ **do in parallel**
$\quad\quad C_r \leftarrow A_r \times B_r$
$\quad$**end for**
Step 3: for $m = 2q$ **to** $3q - 1$ **do**
$\quad\quad$**for all** $r \in N(r_m = 0)$ **do in parallel**
$\quad\quad\quad C_r \leftarrow C_r + C_{r(m)}$
$\quad\quad$**end for**
$\quad$**end for.** ∎

A three-dimensional geometric interpretation of the algorithm may be helpful. The $n \times n \times n$ array representation of the hypercube consists of n layers, each of n^2 processors. Let these layers be numbered 0 to $n-1$. Initially, each processor in layer 0 (i.e., the base layer) holds a distinct element of matrix $\boldsymbol{A}$ in its A register and a distinct element of matrix $\boldsymbol{B}$ in its B register. The A and B registers of processors in layers 1 to $n-1$ are "empty"— that is, contain irrelevant data. Similarly, the C registers of *all* processors are "empty."

During the first iteration of Step (1.1)—that is, when $m = 3q-1$—each processor in layer 0 sends a copy of its data to the corresponding processor in layer $n/2$. (The processors in layers 1 to $(n/2) - 1$ also execute this operation; however, since no relevant data are held initially in their A and B registers, they perform no useful transfers.) During the second iteration of Step (1.1), copies of the inputs are sent from layer 0 to layer $n/4$ and simultaneously from layer $n/2$ to layer $3n/4$. Continuing in this fashion, the distance separating the senders and receivers is halved at each iteration. Thus, $q = \log n$ iterations suffice to copy the data initially in layer 0 to the processors in layers 1 to $n-1$. It is important to note that during this step, those processors P_r for which $r_m = 0$ are the only ones to send copies of their data. Furthermore, the latter overwrite the contents of the A and B registers of processors $P_{r(m)}$, for $m = 3q - 1, 3q - 2, \ldots, 2q$. Therefore, input data are never overwritten by (irrelevant) data initially in the A and B registers of processors in layers 1 to $n-1$.

The same approach is used in Steps (1.2) and (1.3). In Step (1.2), each processor in column i of layer i, $0 \le i \le n - 1$, sends the contents of its A register to all processors in its row. Similarly, in Step (1.3), each processor in row i of layer i, $0 \le i \le n - 1$, sends the contents of its B register to all processors in its column. Step 2 involves only a local computation. Finally, Step 3 can be interpreted in the same way as Step (1.3): Pairs of corresponding processors in different layers, separated by a distance that doubles at each iteration, add the contents of their C registers.

Analysis. Each of Steps (1.1), (1.2), (1.3), and 3 consists of q constant-time iterations. Step 2 requires constant time. Therefore, the algorithm has a running time of $O(q)$—that is, $t(n) = O(\log n)$. Since $p(n) = n^3$, the algorithm's cost is $c(n) = O(n^3 \log n)$. This cost is not optimal in view of the $O(n^3)$ basic operations sufficient for multiplying two $n \times n$ matrices on the RAM by the straightforward algorithm based on the definition of the matrix product.

Example 9.1 Let $n = 2$, and consider the two matrices

$$A = \begin{pmatrix} 1 & 2 \\ 3 & 4 \end{pmatrix} \quad \text{and} \quad B = \begin{pmatrix} -1 & -2 \\ -3 & -4 \end{pmatrix},$$

whose product $C = A \times B$ it is desired to compute. Applying algorithm HYPERCUBE MATRIX MULTIPLICATION, we use $N = 2^3 = 8$ processors P_0, P_1, ..., P_7, as shown in Fig. 9.2, in which, for each processor P_r, the index r is given in binary representation. In Figs. 9.2(a)–(d), the contents of A_r are shown above those of B_r, for each processor P_r holding input data. In Fig. 9.2(e) the contents of C_r are indicated for all P_r, while in Fig. 9.2(f) only the contents of those registers C_r holding the product matrix are displayed.

Initially, the inputs are stored as shown in Fig. 9.2(a). The data transfers taking place in Steps (1.1), (1.2), and (1.3) are illustrated in Figs. 9.2(b), (c), and (d), respectively. At this point, the processor in position (i, j, k) holds a_{ji} and b_{ik}; it computes their product and stores it in $C(i, j, k)$, as shown in Fig. 9.2(e). Finally, all processors with the same indices j and k add their $C(i, j, k)$ and place the result in $C(0, j, k)$. The product matrix

$$C = \begin{pmatrix} -7 & -10 \\ -15 & -22 \end{pmatrix}$$

now resides in processors P_0, P_1, P_2, and P_3, as shown in Fig. 9.2(f). $\square$

9.2   MATRIX TRANSPOSITION

Let A be an $n \times n$ matrix whose transpose A^T (as defined in Problem 8.10) we wish to compute. Each element a_{ji}^T of A^T is such that

$$a_{ji}^T = a_{ij},$$

where a_{ij} is an element of A. Let $n = 2^q$. The transpose can be computed on a hypercube with $N = n^2 = 2^{2q}$ processors P_0, P_1, ..., P_{N-1}. It is helpful to visualize the processors as being arranged in an $n \times n$ array in row-major order. Thus, processor P_r occupies position (i, j) of this array, where $r = in + j$ and $0 \le i, j \le n - 1$. Initially, element a_{ij} of A is held by processor P_r in a register A_r, where $r = in + j$. When the algorithm terminates, element a_{ij} of A is to be held by processor P_s in a register A_s, where $s = jn + i$.

Let the binary representations of r and s be $r_{2q-1}r_{2q-2} \ldots r_q r_{q-1} \ldots r_1 r_0$ and $s_{2q-1}s_{2q-2} \ldots s_q s_{q-1} \ldots s_1 s_0$, respectively. Here, $r_{2q-1}\, r_{2q-2} \ldots r_q$ and $r_{q-1}\, r_{q-2} \ldots r_0$ are the binary representations of i and j, respectively. Similarly, $s_{2q-1}s_{2q-2} \ldots s_q$ and $s_{q-1}s_{q-2} \ldots s_0$ are the binary representations of j and i, respectively. Thus,

$$r_{2q-1}r_{2q-2} \ldots r_q = s_{q-1}s_{q-2} \ldots s_0,$$

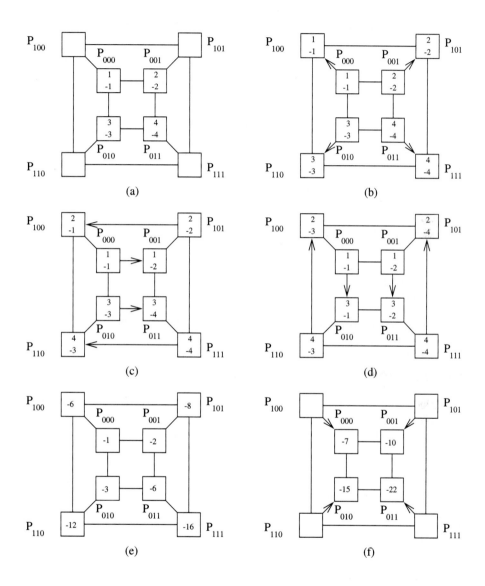

Figure 9.2: Multiplying two matrices on a hypercube: (a) Initially; (b) After Step (1.1); (c) After Step (1.2); (d) After Step (1.3); (e) After Step 2; (f) After Step 3.

and

$$r_{q-1}r_{q-2}\dots r_0 = s_{2q-1}s_{2q-2}\dots s_q.$$

Therefore, element a_{ij} can be routed from P_r to P_s in at most $2q$ steps. The algorithm is given next as algorithm HYPERCUBE MATRIX TRANSPOSE. In it, register A_u of P_u is assumed to hold initially element a_{kl} of A, where $u = kn + l$. When the algorithm terminates, A_u holds a_{kl}^T. An additional register B_u is also used by P_u for routing data sent to it by other processors. The index of P_u is $u = u_{2q-1}u_{2q-2}\dots u_0$.

Algorithm HYPERCUBE MATRIX TRANSPOSE (A)

for $m = 2q - 1$ downto q do
  for $u = 0$ to $N - 1$ do in parallel
    (1) if $u_m \neq u_{m-q}$
      then $B_{u^{(m)}} \leftarrow A_u$
      end if
    (2) if $u_m = u_{m-q}$
      then $A_{u^{(m-q)}} \leftarrow B_u$
      end if
  end for
end for. ■

A recursive interpretation of the algorithm provides the best intuition for understanding it. Suppose that the $n \times n$ matrix is subdivided into four $(n/2) \times (n/2)$ submatrices. In the first level of the recursion, the elements of the bottom left submatrix are swapped with the corresponding elements of the top right submatrix. The elements of the other two submatrices are untouched. This corresponds to the first iteration of the algorithm (i.e., when $m = 2q - 1$). The same step is now applied to each of the four $(n/2) \times (n/2)$ matrices (each viewed as four $(n/4) \times (n/4)$ submatrices). This continues until 2×2 matrices are transposed, whereupon the algorithm terminates.

Analysis. The algorithm consists of q constant-time iterations. Therefore, $t(n) = O(\log n)$. Since $p(n) = n^2$, the algorithm's cost is $c(n) = O(n^2 \log n)$. This cost is not optimal in view of the $n(n-1)/2$ basic operations sufficient to transpose an $n \times n$ matrix on the RAM by swapping a_{ij} with a_{ji} for all $i < j$.

Example 9.2 Let $n = 4$ (i.e., $q = 2$), and suppose that the 4×4 matrix to be transposed is

$$A = \begin{pmatrix} 1 & b & c & d \\ e & 2 & f & g \\ h & v & 3 & w \\ x & y & z & 4 \end{pmatrix}.$$

As required by algorithm HYPERCUBE MATRIX TRANSPOSE, a hypercube with 16 processors $P_0, P_1, \dots, P_{15}$, is used, with each processor holding one element of $\boldsymbol{A}$. The processor indices, in binary representation, are arranged in a 4×4 array, in row-major order, as follows:

$$
\begin{array}{cccc}
0000 & 0001 & 0010 & 0011 \\
0100 & 0101 & 0110 & 0111 \\
1000 & 1001 & 1010 & 1011 \\
1100 & 1101 & 1110 & 1111.
\end{array}
$$

Thus, P_{0000} holds 1, P_{0001} holds b, P_{0010} holds c, and so on. In the first iteration of the algorithm, $m = 2q-1 = 3$. During Step (1), each processor P_u for which $u_3 \neq u_1$ sends the element it holds in A_u to $P_{u^{(3)}}$, which stores it in $B_{u^{(3)}}$. Specifically, P_{0010}, P_{0011}, P_{0110}, and P_{0111} send their elements to P_{1010}, P_{1011}, P_{1110}, and P_{1111}, respectively, while P_{1000}, P_{1001}, P_{1100}, and P_{1101} send their elements to P_{0000}, P_{0001}, P_{0100}, and P_{0101}, respectively. In other words, referring to the 4×4 array of indices, each of the four processors in the top right corner sends its element to the corresponding processor in the bottom right corner, while each of the four processors in the bottom left corner sends its element to the corresponding processor in the top left corner. The processors receiving the elements (i.e., those in the top left and bottom right corners) serve as temporary locations for these data and will now forward them to their intended destinations. Thus, during Step (2), each processor P_u for which $u_3 = u_1$ (i.e., a processor that received a datum in Step (1)) sends the datum it holds in B_u to $P_{u^{(1)}}$, which stores it in $A_{u^{(1)}}$. Specifically, P_{0000}, P_{0001}, P_{0100}, and P_{0101} send data to P_{0010}, P_{0011}, P_{0110}, and P_{0111}, respectively, while P_{1010}, P_{1011}, P_{1110}, and P_{1111} send data to P_{1000}, P_{1001}, P_{1100}, and P_{1101}, respectively. At the end of the first iteration, the contents of the A_u registers, for $0 \leq u \leq 15$, are as follows:

$$
\begin{array}{cccc}
1 & b & h & v \\
e & 2 & x & y \\
c & d & 3 & w \\
f & g & z & 4.
\end{array}
$$

In the second (and final) iteration, $m = q = 2$. During Step (1), each processor P_u for which $u_2 \neq u_0$ sends the element it holds in A_u to $P_{u^{(2)}}$, which stores it in $B_{u^{(2)}}$. Thus, elements are transferred simultaneously from P_{0100} to P_{0000}, from P_{0001} to P_{0101}, from P_{0110} to P_{0010}, from P_{0011} to P_{0111}, from P_{1100} to P_{1000}, from P_{1001} to P_{1101}, from P_{1110} to P_{1010}, and from P_{1011} to P_{1111}. Then, in Step (2), each processor P_u for which $u_2 = u_0$ sends the datum it holds in B_u to $P_{u^{(0)}}$, which stores it in $A_{u^{(0)}}$. Thus, data are transferred simultaneously from P_{0000} to P_{0001}, from P_{0101} to P_{0100}, from P_{0010} to P_{0011}, from P_{0111} to P_{0110}, from P_{1000} to P_{1001}, from P_{1101} to P_{1100}, from P_{1010} to P_{1011}, and from P_{1111} to P_{1110}. In other words, the effect of the second iteration is to swap the element in the top right corner processor with that in the bottom left corner processor, within each of the four 2×2 subarrays. Therefore, after the second iteration, the contents of the A_u registers, for $0 \leq u \leq 15$, are as follows:

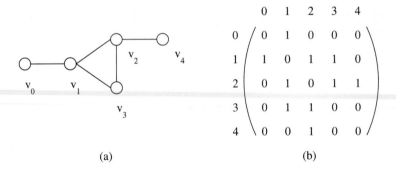

(a)   (b)

Figure 9.3: (a) An undirected graph and (b) its adjacency matrix.

$$
\begin{array}{cccc}
1 & e & h & x \\
b & 2 & v & y \\
c & f & 3 & z \\
d & g & w & 4.
\end{array}
$$

The algorithm now terminates, with the processors in the hypercube holding A^T, as required. □

9.3 CONNECTED COMPONENTS

In this section we revisit the problem of computing the connected components of a graph, first studied in Section 6.4. Let $G = (V, E)$ be a graph whose vertex set is given by the sequence $V = \{v_0, v_1, \ldots, v_{n-1}\}$. This graph is represented by an $n \times n$ *adjacency matrix* A, whose entries a_{ij}, $0 \le i, j \le n-1$, are defined as follows:

$$
\begin{aligned}
a_{ij} &= 1, && \text{provided that } v_i \text{ is connected to } v_j \\
&= 0 && \text{otherwise.}
\end{aligned}
$$

Example 9.3 An undirected graph with five vertices and its adjacency matrix are shown in Figs. 9.3(a) and (b), respectively. Note that since the graph in Fig. 9.3(a) is undirected, the matrix in Fig. 9.3(b) is symmetric. A directed graph with five vertices and its adjacency matrix are shown in Figs. 9.4(a) and (b), respectively. □

As defined in Section 6.4, a *connected component* of an undirected graph G is a connected subgraph of G of maximum size. Given such a graph G, we develop an algorithm for computing its connected components on a hypercube interconnection network parallel computer. A key step in the algorithm is the computation of the so-called *connectivity matrix* of G. We use this as our starting point.

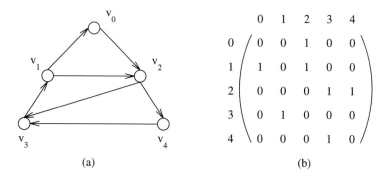

Figure 9.4: (a) A directed graph and (b) its adjacency matrix.

9.3.1 Computing the Connectivity Matrix

The connectivity matrix of a (directed or undirected) graph G with n vertices is an $n \times n$ matrix C whose elements are defined as follows:

$$
\begin{aligned}
c_{jk} \quad &= \quad 1, \quad \text{provided that there is a path of length 0 or more from } v_j \text{ to } v_k \\
&\qquad\qquad \text{in which no vertex appears more than once} \\
&= \quad 0 \quad \text{otherwise,}
\end{aligned}
$$

for $0 \le j, k \le n - 1$. Here the length of a path is the number of edges on the path. Thus, a path of length 0 begins and ends at a vertex without using any edges, while a path of length 1 consists of one edge. The matrix C is also known as the *reflexive and transitive closure* of the graph G. Given the adjacency matrix A of G, it is required to compute C. The approach we take uses *Boolean matrix multiplication*, which differs from regular matrix multiplication (usually defined on reals) in that:

1. The matrices to be multiplied, as well as the product matrix, are all binary; that is, each of their entries is either 0 or 1.

2. The Boolean (i.e., logical) **and** operation replaces regular multiplication; that is, 0 **and** 0 = 0, 0 **and** 1 = 0, 1 **and** 0 = 0, and 1 **and** 1 = 1.

3. The Boolean (i.e., logical) **or** operation replaces regular addition; that is, 0 **or** 0 = 0, 0 **or** 1 = 1, 1 **or** 0 = 1, and 1 **or** 1 = 1.

Thus, if X, Y, and Z are $n \times n$ Boolean matrices, where Z is the Boolean product of X and Y, then

$$
z_{ij} = (x_{i1} \text{ and } y_{1j}) \text{ or } (x_{i2} \text{ and } y_{2j}) \text{ or } \ldots \text{ or } (x_{in} \text{ and } y_{nj}),
$$

for $i, j = 0, 1, \ldots, n - 1$.

The first step in the computation of the connectivity matrix C is to obtain an $n \times n$ matrix B from A as follows:

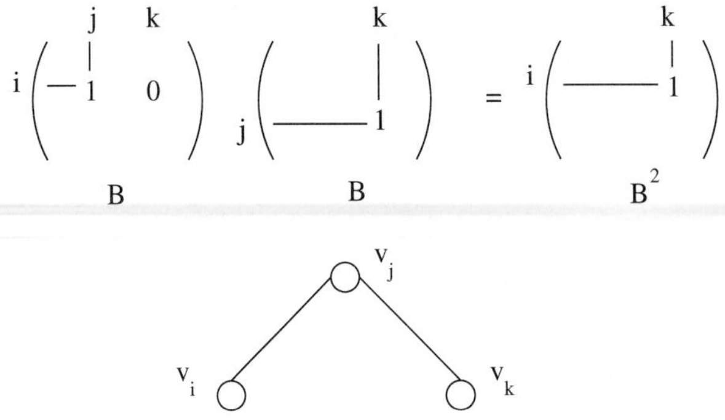

$$i\begin{pmatrix} \overset{j}{\underset{|}{-1}} & \overset{k}{} \\ & 0 \end{pmatrix} \quad j\begin{pmatrix} \overset{k}{\underset{|}{}} \\ \underline{\qquad}\; 1 \end{pmatrix} \;=\; i\begin{pmatrix} \overset{k}{\underset{|}{}} \\ \underline{\qquad}\; 1 \end{pmatrix}$$

$$B \qquad\qquad B \qquad\qquad B^2$$

Figure 9.5: A path from v_i to v_k goes through v_j.

$$\begin{aligned} b_{jk} &= a_{jk}, & \text{provided that } j \neq k \\ &= 1 & \text{otherwise,} \end{aligned}$$

for $j, k = 0, 1, \ldots, n-1$. In other words, matrix $\boldsymbol{B}$ is equal to matrix $\boldsymbol{A}$ augmented with 1's along the diagonal; that is, $b_{jj} = 1$ for all j. Therefore, $\boldsymbol{B}$ represents all paths in G of length less than 2, or

$$\begin{aligned} b_{jk} &= 1, & \text{provided that there is a path of length 0 or 1 from } v_j \text{ to } v_k \\ & & \text{in which no vertex appears more than once} \\ &= 0 & \text{otherwise.} \end{aligned}$$

Now let $\boldsymbol{B}^2$ be the Boolean product of $\boldsymbol{B}$ with itself. The matrix $\boldsymbol{B}^2$ represents paths of length 2 or less, as illustrated in Fig. 9.5, in which only the entries b_{ij}, b_{ik}, and b_{jk} are shown. Since $b_{ij} = 1$ and $b_{jk} = 1$, it follows that $b_{ik}^2 = 1$, representing a path of length 2 from v_i to v_k (through v_j). Similarly, $\boldsymbol{B}^3$ represents paths of length 3 or less, $\boldsymbol{B}^4$ represents paths of length 4 or less, and $\boldsymbol{B}^n$ represents paths of length n or less.

We now observe that if there is a path from v_i to v_j, it cannot have length more than $n-1$, since G has only n vertices. Consequently, $\boldsymbol{C} = \boldsymbol{B}^{n-1}$. The matrix $\boldsymbol{B}^{n-1}$ is computed by successive squaring—that is, by computing $\boldsymbol{B}^2$, $\boldsymbol{B}^4$, and so on. This means that the connectivity matrix $\boldsymbol{C}$ is obtained after $\lceil \log(n-1) \rceil$ Boolean matrix multiplications. Note that when $n-1$ is not a power of 2, $\boldsymbol{C}$ is obtained from $\boldsymbol{B}^m$, where m is the smallest power of 2 larger than $n-1$; that is, $m = 2^{\lceil \log(n-1) \rceil}$. This is correct, since $\boldsymbol{B}^m = \boldsymbol{B}^{\,n-1}$ for $m > n-1$.

Implementation.   In order to implement the preceding algorithm, we can use algorithm HYPERCUBE MATRIX MULTIPLICATION, adapted to perform Boolean matrix multiplication. The new algorithm is given next as algorithm HYPERCUBE CONNECTIVITY. It takes the adjacency matrix $\boldsymbol{A}$ of G as input and returns the connectivity matrix $\boldsymbol{C}$ as output. The hypercube used has $N = n^3$

processors P_0, P_1, ..., P_{N-1}. The latter are thought of as being arranged in an $n \times n \times n$ array, as in Section 9.1.3. In this array, P_r occupies position (i, j, k), where $r = in^2 + jn + k$ and $0 \leq i, j, k \leq n - 1$. Processor P_r has three registers: $A(i, j, k)$, $B(i, j, k)$, and $C(i, j, k)$. Initially, the processors in positions $(0, j, k)$, $0 \leq j, k \leq n - 1$, contain the adjacency matrix; that is, $A(0, j, k) = a_{jk}$. At the end of the computation, these processors contain the connectivity matrix; that is, $C(0, j, k) = c_{jk}, 0 \leq j, k \leq n - 1$.

Algorithm HYPERCUBE CONNECTIVITY (A, C)

Step 1: for $j = 0$ **to** $n - 1$ **do in parallel**
$\qquad A(0, j, j) \leftarrow 1$
end for
Step 2: for $j = 0$ **to** $n - 1$ **do in parallel**
$\qquad$ **for** $k = 0$ **to** $n - 1$ **do in parallel**
$\qquad\qquad B(0, j, k) \leftarrow A(0, j, k)$
$\qquad$ **end for**
end for
Step 3: for $i = 1$ **to** $\lceil \log(n - 1) \rceil$ **do**
$\qquad$ (3.1) HYPERCUBE MATRIX MULTIPLICATION (A, B, C)
$\qquad$ (3.2) **for** $j = 0$ **to** $n - 1$ **do in parallel**
$\qquad\qquad$ **for** $k = 0$ **to** $n - 1$ **do in parallel**
$\qquad\qquad\qquad$ (i) $A(0, j, k) \leftarrow C(0, j, k)$
$\qquad\qquad\qquad$ (ii) $B(0, j, k) \leftarrow C(0, j, k)$
$\qquad\qquad$ **end for**
$\qquad$ **end for**
end for. ∎

Analysis. Steps 1, 2, and (3.2) take constant time. In step (3.1), algorithm HYPERCUBE MATRIX MULTIPLICATION requires $O(\log n)$ time. This step is iterated $\lceil \log(n - 1) \rceil$ times. It follows that the running time of algorithm HYPERCUBE CONNECTIVITY is $t(n) = O(\log^2 n)$. Since $p(n) = n^3$, the algorithm's cost is $c(n) = O(n^3 \log^2 n)$.

9.3.2 An Algorithm for Connected Components

Having computed the connectivity matrix C of G, we can use it to construct an $n \times n$ matrix D whose entries are defined as follows:

$$\begin{aligned} d_{jk} &= v_k, &\quad \text{provided that } c_{jk} = 1 \\ &= 0 &\quad \text{otherwise,} \end{aligned}$$

for $0 \leq j, k \leq n - 1$. In other words, row j of D contains the names of vertices to which v_j is connected by a path. The connected components of G are then found by assigning each vertex to a component as follows: v_j is assigned to a component l if l is the smallest index for which $d_{jl} \neq 0$.

Implementation.   This approach is implemented on the hypercube using algorithm HYPERCUBE CONNECTIVITY. The algorithm is given next as algorithm HYPERCUBE CONNECTED COMPONENTS. It runs on a hypercube with $N = n^3$ processors, each with three registers A, B, and C. The processors are arranged in an $n \times n \times n$ array, as is required for algorithm HYPERCUBE CONNECTIVITY. Initially, $A(0, j, k) = a_{jk}$ for $0 \le j, k \le n - 1$; that is, the processors in positions $(0, j, k)$ contain the adjacency matrix of G. When the algorithm terminates, $C(0, j, 0)$ contains the component number for vertex v_j, where $j = 0, 1, \ldots, n - 1$.

Algorithm HYPERCUBE CONNECTED COMPONENTS (A, C)

Step 1: HYPERCUBE CONNECTIVITY (A, C)
Step 2: for $j = 0$ **to** $n - 1$ **do in parallel**
        for $k = 0$ **to** $n - 1$ **do in parallel**
         if $C(0, j, k) = 1$
         then $C(0, j, k) \leftarrow v_k$
         end if
        end for
        end for
Step 3: for $j = 0$ **to** $n - 1$ **do in parallel**
        (3.1) The n processors in row j find the smallest l for which
          $C(0, j, l) \ne 0$
        (3.2) $C(0, j, 0) \leftarrow l$
        end for. ∎

Note that the algorithm creates the matrix $\boldsymbol{D}$ in Step 2 and stores it in the C registers of the processors. In Step 3, the number of the component to which v_j belongs overwrites the contents of register $C(0, j, 0)$. The algorithms's output is therefore $C(0, 0, 0)$, $C(0, 1, 0)$, $\ldots$, $C(0, n - 1, 0)$, giving the component numbers of $v_0, v_1, \ldots, v_{n-1}$, respectively.

Analysis. Step 1 requires $O(\log^2 n)$ time. Steps 2 and (3.2) take constant time. In step (3.1), the n processors in row j form a $\log n$-dimensional hypercube. Therefore, this step is executed in the same way as Step 3 of algorithm HYPERCUBE MATRIX MULTIPLICATION by replacing operation '+' with operation 'min'. The overall running time of algorithm HYPERCUBE CONNECTED COMPONENTS is $t(n) = O(\log^2 n)$. Since $p(n) = n^3$, the algorithm's cost is $c(n) = O(n^3 \log^2 n)$.

Example 9.4 Consider the graph in Fig. 9.6(a), whose adjacency and connectivity matrices are given in Figs. 9.6(b) and (c), respectively. Matrix $\boldsymbol{D}$ is shown in Fig. 9.6(d). The assignment of components is therefore:

$$\begin{array}{ll} \text{Component 0:} & v_0, v_2, v_4, v_5 \\ \text{Component 1:} & v_1, v_3, v_6. \end{array} \quad \square$$

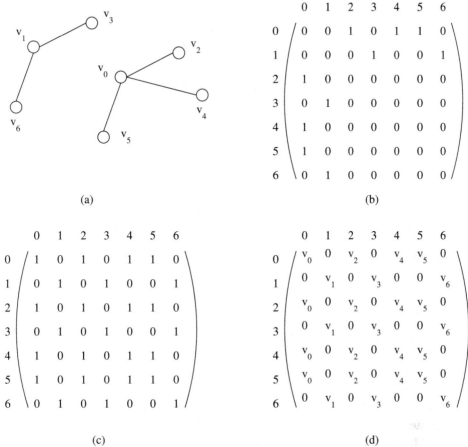

Figure 9.6: Computing connected components on a hypercube: (a) Graph with two connected components; (b) Adjacency matrix; (c) Connectivity matrix; (d) Matrix of connected components.

9.4 STRONG COMPONENTS

Let $G = (V, E)$ be a directed graph with n vertices. A *strong component* of G is a subgraph $G' = (V', E')$ of G such that:

1. There is a path from every vertex in V' to every other vertex in V' along edges in E'.

2. G' is *maximal*; that is, G' is not a subgraph of a strong component with more vertices.

Example 9.5 The directed graph of Fig. 9.7 has two strong components, namely, $\{v_0, v_1, v_2, v_3\}$ and $\{v_4, v_5, v_6\}$. □

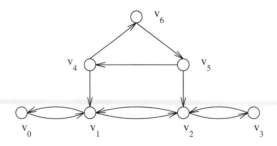

Figure 9.7: A directed graph with two strong components.

We can compute strong components in much the same way as connected components. Let A be the adjacency matrix of G. The algorithm is given next as algorithm HYPERCUBE STRONG COMPONENTS:

Algorithm HYPERCUBE STRONG COMPONENTS (A, C)

   Step 1: HYPERCUBE CONNECTIVITY (A, C)
   Step 2: $D \leftarrow C$
   Step 3: HYPERCUBE MATRIX TRANSPOSE (D)
   Step 4: Compute the matrix F where:
                  $f_{ij} = 1$, provided that $c_{ij} = 1$ and $d_{ij} = 1$
                        $= 0$ otherwise
   Step 5: for $i = 0$ to $n - 1$ do in parallel
                  (5.1) Find the smallest j for which $f_{ij} = 1$
                  (5.2) $c_{i0} \leftarrow j$
                  end for. ∎

Note that in Step 2 matrix C is copied into D, and after Step 3, $D = C^T$. These two steps are necessary, as they allow the processor holding c_{ij} to obtain c_{ji} as well (since $d_{ij} = c_{ji}$). Therefore, in Step 4, $f_{ij} = 1$ if and only if there is a path from v_i to v_j and a path from v_j to v_i, meaning that v_i and v_j belong to the same strong component. Finally, the j found in Step 5 and returned in $C(0, i, 0)$ is the number of the strong component to which v_i belongs.

Analysis.   Step 1 requires $O(\log^2 n)$ time and n^3 processors. Steps 2 and 4 use n^2 processors and run in constant time, while Steps 3 and 5 are performed in $O(\log n)$ time by n^2 processors. Thus, $t(n) = O(\log^2 n)$, $p(n) = n^3$, and $c(n) = O(n^3 \log^2 n)$.

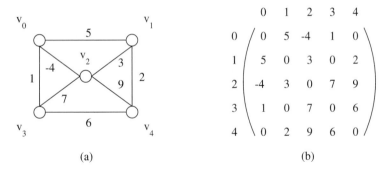

Figure 9.8: (a) A weighted graph and (b) its weight matrix.

9.5 ALL-PAIRS SHORTEST PATHS

When each edge of a graph is associated with a real number, called its *weight*, the graph is said to be *weighted*. A weighted graph may be directed or undirected. An undirected weighted graph with five vertices is shown in Fig. 9.8(a). The meaning of an edge's weight varies from one application to another; it may represent distance, cost, time, probability, and so on. A *weight matrix* W is used to represent a weighted graph, as shown in Fig. 9.8(b). Here, entry w_{ij} of W represents the weight of edge (v_i, v_j). If v_i and v_j are not connected by an edge, then w_{ij} may be equal to zero, infinity, or any appropriate value, depending on the application.

Suppose that we are given a directed and weighted graph $G = (V, E)$, with n vertices, as shown in Fig. 9.9(a). The graph is defined by its weight matrix W, as shown in Fig. 9.9(b). We assume that W has positive, zero, or negative entries, as long as there is no cycle in G such that the sum of the weights of the edges on the cycle is negative. For convenience, we refer in this section to the weight of edge (v_i, v_j) as its *length* (as was done in Example 8.2).

The problem that we address here is known as the *all-pairs shortest paths problem* and is stated as follows: For every pair of vertices v_i and v_j in V, it is required to find the length of the shortest path from v_i to v_j along edges in E. Specifically, a matrix D is to be constructed such that d_{ij} is the length of the shortest path from v_i to v_j in G, for all i and j. Here, the length of a path (or cycle) is the sum of the lengths of the edges forming it. In Fig. 9.9, the shortest path from v_0 to v_4 is along edges (v_0, v_1), (v_1, v_2), (v_2, v_4) and has length 6. It may be obvious now why we insisted that G have no cycle of negative length: If such a cycle were to exist within a path from v_i to v_j, then one could traverse this cycle indefinitely, producing paths of ever shorter lengths from v_i to v_j.

Let d_{ij}^k denote the length of the shortest path from v_i to v_j that goes through at most $k - 1$ intermediate vertices. Thus, $d_{ij}^1 = w_{ij}$—that is, the length of the edge from v_i to v_j. In particular, if there is no edge from v_i to v_j, where $i \neq j$, then

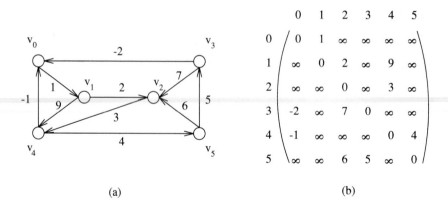

Figure 9.9: (a) A directed and weighted graph and its (b) weight matrix.

$d_{ij}^1 = w_{ij} = \infty$. Also, $d_{ii}^1 = w_{ii} = 0$. Given that G has no cycles of negative length, there is no advantage in visiting any vertex more than once in a shortest path from v_i to v_j. It follows that $d_{ij} = d_{ij}^{n-1}$, since there are only n vertices in G.

In order to compute d_{ij}^k for $k > 1$, we can use the recurrence

$$d_{ij}^k = \min_l (d_{il}^{k/2} + d_{lj}^{k/2}).$$

The validity of this relation is established as follows: Suppose that d_{ij}^k is the length of the *shortest* path from v_i to v_j and that two vertices v_r and v_s are on this shortest path (with v_r preceding v_s). It must be the case that the edges from v_r to v_s (along the shortest path from v_i to v_j) form a shortest path from v_r to v_s. (If a shorter path from v_r to v_s existed, it could be used to obtain a shorter path from v_i to v_j, which is absurd.) Therefore, to obtain d_{ij}^k, we can compute all combinations of *optimal subpaths* (whose concatenation is a path from v_i to v_j) and then choose the shortest one. The fastest way to do this is to combine pairs of subpaths with at most $k/2$ vertices each. This guarantees that a recursive computation of d_{ij}^k can be completed in $O(\log k)$ steps.

Let $\boldsymbol{D}^k$ be the matrix whose entries are d_{ij}, for $0 \le i, j \le n-1$. In accordance with the discussion in the previous two paragraphs, the matrix $\boldsymbol{D}$ can be computed from $\boldsymbol{D}^1$ by evaluating $\boldsymbol{D}^2, \boldsymbol{D}^4, \ldots, \boldsymbol{D}^m$, where m is the smallest power of 2 larger than or equal to $n-1$ (i.e., $m = 2^{\lceil \log(n-1) \rceil}$), and then taking $\boldsymbol{D} = \boldsymbol{D}^m$. In order to obtain $\boldsymbol{D}^k$ from $\boldsymbol{D}^{k/2}$, we use a special form of matrix multiplication in which the operations '+' and 'min' replace the standard operations of matrix multiplication— that is, '×' and '+', respectively. Hence, if a matrix multiplication algorithm is available, it can be modified to generate $\boldsymbol{D}^m$ from $\boldsymbol{D}^1$. Exactly $\lceil \log(n-1) \rceil$ such matrix products are required.

Implementation.   Algorithm HYPERCUBE MATRIX MULTIPLICATION, appropriately modified, can be used to compute the shortest path matrix D. The modified algorithm is given next as algorithm HYPERCUBE SHORTEST PATHS. It runs on a hypercube with n^3 processors, each with three registers A, B, and C. As before, the processors are regarded as being arranged in an $n \times n \times n$ array. Initially, $A(0, j, k) = w_{jk}$ for $0 \le j, k \le n - 1$; that is, the processors in positions $(0, j, k)$ contain $D^1 = W$. When the algorithm terminates, $C(0, j, k)$ contains the length of the shortest path from v_j to v_k for $0 \le j, k \le n - 1$.

Algorithm HYPERCUBE SHORTEST PATHS (A, C)

   Step 1: for $j = 0$ **to** $n - 1$ **do in parallel**
         for $k = 0$ **to** $n - 1$ **do in parallel**
            $B(0, j, k) \leftarrow A(0, j, k)$
         end for
      end for
   Step 2: for $i = 1$ **to** $\lceil \log(n - 1) \rceil$ **do**
            (2.1) HYPERCUBE MATRIX MULTIPLICATION (A, B, C)
            (2.2) **for** $j = 0$ **to** $n - 1$ **do in parallel**
                  for $k = 0$ **to** $n - 1$ **do in parallel**
                     (i) $A(0, j, k) \leftarrow C(0, j, k)$
                     (ii) $B(0, j, k) \leftarrow C(0, j, k)$
                  end for
               end for
         end for. ∎

Analysis.   Steps 1 and (2.2) require constant time. There are $\lceil \log(n - 1) \rceil$ iterations of Step (2.1), each requiring $O(\log n)$ time. The overall running time of algorithm HYPERCUBE SHORTEST PATHS is therefore $t(n) = O(\log^2 n)$. Since $p(n) = n^3$, the algorithm's cost is $c(n) = O(n^3 \log^2 n)$.

Example 9.6 Consider the graph in Fig. 9.9(a), whose weight matrix W is shown in Fig. 9.9(b). By setting $D^1 = W$, we compute the matrices D^2, D^4, and $D^8 = D$, as follows:

$$
D^2 = \begin{pmatrix}
0 & 1 & 3 & \infty & 10 & \infty \\
8 & 0 & 2 & \infty & 5 & 13 \\
\infty & \infty & 0 & \infty & 3 & 7 \\
-2 & -1 & 7 & 0 & 10 & \infty \\
-1 & 0 & 10 & 9 & 0 & 4 \\
3 & \infty & 6 & 5 & 9 & 0
\end{pmatrix}, \quad
D^4 = \begin{pmatrix}
0 & 1 & 3 & 19 & 6 & 10 \\
4 & 0 & 2 & 14 & 5 & 9 \\
2 & 3 & 0 & 12 & 3 & 7 \\
-2 & -1 & 1 & 0 & 4 & 12 \\
-1 & 0 & 2 & 9 & 0 & 4 \\
3 & 4 & 6 & 5 & 9 & 0
\end{pmatrix},
$$

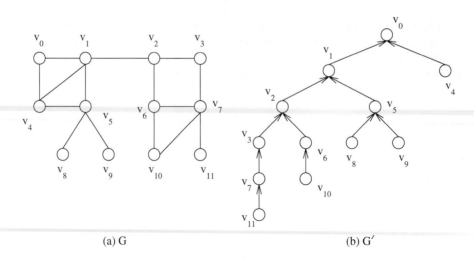

(a) G   (b) G′

Figure 9.10: (a) A graph G and (b) its spanning tree G'.

$$\boldsymbol{D}^8 = \begin{pmatrix} 0 & 1 & 3 & 15 & 6 & 10 \\ 4 & 0 & 2 & 14 & 5 & 9 \\ 2 & 3 & 0 & 12 & 3 & 7 \\ -2 & -1 & 1 & 0 & 4 & 8 \\ -1 & 0 & 2 & 9 & 0 & 4 \\ 3 & 4 & 6 & 5 & 9 & 0 \end{pmatrix} . \ \Box$$

9.6   SPANNING TREES

A *spanning tree* of an undirected and connected graph G is a connected subgraph $G' = (V, E')$ that contains no cycles. In this section, we use algorithm HYPER-CUBE SHORTEST PATHS to compute a spanning tree of G. Specifically, we obtain a *breadth-first spanning tree*; that is:

1. The spanning tree is *rooted*.

2. The length of the path in G'—that is, the number of edges—from any vertex v_i to the root is the smallest possible in G.

Example 9.7 A graph G with 12 vertices is shown in Fig. 9.10(a). A breadth-first spanning tree G' of G rooted at v_0 is shown in Fig. 9.10(b). $\Box$

Let $\boldsymbol{A}'$ be the adjacency matrix of G'. In order to compute $\boldsymbol{A}'$, we use the adjacency matrix $\boldsymbol{A}$ of G as a weight matrix. Thus,

$$\begin{aligned} w_{ij} &= 1, & \text{provided that } (v_i, v_j) \in E \\ &= \infty & \text{otherwise.} \end{aligned}$$

We now find the length of the shortest path from v_0 to every other vertex v_i. This length is the level at which v_i appears in the tree. Once v_i "knows" its level, it chooses its own parent by selecting a vertex one level up the tree (i.e., one edge closer to v_0). The algorithm is given next as algorithm HYPERCUBE SPANNING TREE:

Algorithm HYPERCUBE SPANNING TREE (A)

Step 1: Compute the shortest paths in G using algorithm HYPERCUBE SHORT-EST PATHS. The value d_{ij} obtained by this algorithm is the number of edges on the shortest path from vertex v_i to vertex v_j. Thus, d_{0j} is the level of v_j, denoted $level(j)$.

Step 2: A matrix A' representing a directed spanning tree G' of G, where each vertex points to its parent, is now obtained as follows: View the hypercube with n^3 processors used in Step 1 as an $n \times n \times n$ array with processors in positions (k, i, j). Now consider the n^2 processors in positions $(0, i, j)$ holding the d_{ij} and the w_{ij}.

    (2.1) For $j = 0, 1, \ldots, n-1$, $level(j)$ is sent to all processors in column j.

    (2.2) In row i, $1 \leq i \leq n-1$, the processor in position $(0, i, 0)$ holds d_{i0}, which is equal to d_{0i} (since the graph is undirected) and hence to $level(i)$. Row i is now searched for a processor holding a value $level(l) = level(i)-1$ such that $w_{il} = 1$, $1 \leq i \leq n-1$. The entries a'_{ij} in row i of A' are set as follows:

$$\begin{aligned} a'_{il} &\leftarrow 1, \\ a'_{ij} &\leftarrow 0, \qquad j \neq l. \end{aligned}$$

    (2.3) Row 0 of A' is filled with 0's, since v_0 has no parent:

$$a'_{0j} \leftarrow 0, \qquad 0 \leq j \leq n-1. \blacksquare$$

When the algorithm terminates, the n^2 processors in positions $(0, i, j)$, $0 \leq i, j \leq n-1$, hold the matrix A', one element per processor. Each row of this matrix has exactly one 1 and $n-1$ 0's, except for row 0, which is filled with 0's.

Analysis. The algorithm runs in $t(n) = O(\log^2 n)$ time and uses $p(n) = n^3$ processors. Its cost is $c(n) = O(n^3 \log^2 n)$.

9.7 BRIDGES

Let G be an undirected graph with adjacency matrix A. A *bridge* of G is an edge whose removal splits a connected component into two. For the graph G of Fig. 9.10(a), the bridges are (v_1, v_2), (v_5, v_8), (v_5, v_9), and (v_7, v_{11}). An algorithm for finding the bridges of G is given next as algorithm HYPERCUBE BRIDGES:

Algorithm HYPERCUBE BRIDGES (A)

Step 1:   Find a spanning tree G' of G.

Step 2:   Find the connectivity matrix C' of G'. We note that for every vertex v_i, the set of vertices with a path to v_i is exactly the set of descendants of v_i in G'.

Step 3:   Construct a graph G'' consisting of:

(3.1) The edges of G'.

(3.2) Two oriented edges (v_i, v_j) and (v_j, v_i), for every edge $(v_i, v_j) \in G$, such that neither $(v_i, v_j) \in G'$ nor $(v_j, v_i) \in G'$.

Step 4:   Find the connectivity matrix C'' of G''.

Step 5:   The bridges of G are those edges (v_k, v_l) such that:

(5.1) In G', vertex v_l is the parent of vertex v_k.

(5.2) The set of vertices with a path to v_k is the same in G' and G'', that is, $c'_{ik} = c''_{ik}$ for $0 \leq i \leq n - 1$. ∎

Example 9.8 The graph G'' for the graphs G and G' of Fig. 9.10 is shown in Fig. 9.11. Note that edge (v_2, v_1) is a bridge of G, since in both G' and G'' the set of vertices with a path to v_2 is the same. (These vertices are descendants of v_2, namely, v_3, v_6, v_7, v_{10}, and v_{11}.) On the other hand, (v_4, v_0) is not a bridge of G, since in G'' there is a path from v_9 to v_4, even though v_9 is not a descendant of v_4 in G'. □

Correctness. The fact that the edges identified by algorithm HYPERCUBE BRIDGES are indeed the bridges of the graph G is established as follows:

1. Let $(v_i, v_j) \in G$, but $(v_i, v_j) \notin G'$. By condition (5.1) of the algorithm, (v_i, v_j) cannot be a bridge. Correctness of this condition is seen by observing that the sequence of edges leading from v_i to v_0 (the root of G') and from v_j to v_0 forms a path linking v_i to v_j in G. This path does not contain edge (v_i, v_j), since $(v_i, v_j) \notin G'$. Thus, if (v_i, v_j) is removed from G, v_i and v_j remain connected, and therefore, (v_i, v_j) is not a bridge. For example, consider the edge (v_1, v_4) in Fig. 9.10. This edge belongs to G, but not to G'. It is not a bridge, since we know that v_1, v_0, v_4 is a path in G.

2. Let (v_k, v_l) be an edge in G' such that v_l is the parent of v_k.

   (a) If (v_k, v_l) is a bridge, then its removal disconnects the descendants of v_k from the remaining vertices of G. In other words, no edge of G connects a descendant of v_k to a nondescendant of v_k. For example,

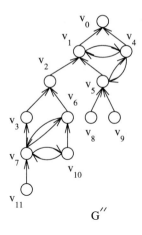

Figure 9.11: The graph G'' used to identify bridges.

(v_2, v_1) is a bridge in the graph G of Fig. 9.10. Its removal disconnects v_2's descendants $\{v_3, v_6, v_7, v_{10}, v_{11}\}$ from the remaining vertices
$\{v_0, v_1, v_4, v_5, v_8, v_9\}$. Consequently, in G'' there is still no path to v_k
from a nondescendant of v_k, and $c'_{ik} = c''_{ik}$ for $0 \leq i \leq n-1$, as required
by condition (5.2) of the algorithm.

(b) If (v_k, v_l) is not a bridge, then there must exist an edge (v_i, v_j) of G
connecting a vertex v_i in the subtree rooted at v_k to a vertex v_j not in
that subtree. Consequently, there is a path from v_j to v_k in G'', but
not in G'. For example, (v_5, v_1) is not a bridge of G, since $c'_{45} = 0$ and
$c''_{45} = 1$.

Implementation. Let A'' denote the adjacency matrix of graph G''. Steps
1, 2, and 4 are immediate to implement on the hypercube using the algorithms in
Sections 9.6 and 9.3.1. Step 3 is implemented as follows:

1. The adjacency matrix A' of G' is transposed. The resulting matrix $(A')^T$
   represents a spanning tree $(G')^T$ that is essentially the same as G', but with
   the edges oriented from each parent to its child. For simplicity of notation,
   the elements of $(A')^T$ are denoted by g_{ij}.

2. Compute the elements a''_{ij} of A'' from the pair of conditions

$$
\begin{aligned}
a''_{ij} &\leftarrow 1, && \text{provided that } a_{ij} = 1 \text{ and } g_{ij} = 0, \\
a''_{ij} &\leftarrow 0 && \text{otherwise,}
\end{aligned}
$$

   for $0 \leq i, j \leq n-1$, where $a_{ij} \in A$, the symmetric adjacency matrix of G.

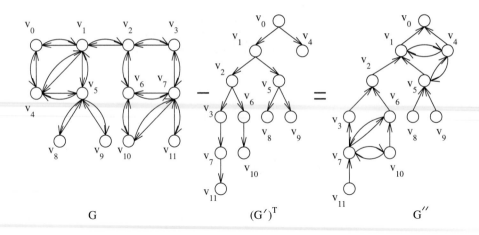

Figure 9.12: Computing the graph G''.

To see why the preceding assignment correctly computes A'', note first that since G is an undirected graph, every edge $(v_i, v_j) \in G$ appears twice in A; that is, $a_{ij} = a_{ji} = 1$. Thus, we can view A as the adjacency matrix of a directed graph. Now the adjacency matrix of G'' is obtained from A by removing the edges of $(G')^T$—that is, the edges oriented from parents to children. This is illustrated in Fig. 9.12 for the graphs G and G' of Fig. 9.10. Finally, in Step 5, column j of C' is compared to column j of C'' for $j = 0, 1, \ldots, n-1$: If $c'_{ij} = c''_{ij}$ for $0 \le i \le n-1$, then some edge (v_j, v_l) of G', where v_j is a child of v_l, is a bridge; otherwise, no such bridge exists. If it is determined that v_j is the endpoint of a bridge, then row j of A' is searched for its only nonzero entry. Suppose that this entry is $a'_{jl} = 1$; in that case, the parent of v_j is v_l, and the bridge has been identified.

Analysis.   Steps 1, 2, and 4 require $O(\log^2 n)$ time and n^3 processors, while Steps 3 and 5 require $O(\log n)$ time and n^2 processors. Therefore, $t(n) = O(\log^2 n)$. Since $p(n) = n^3$, $c(n) = O(n^3 \log^2 n)$.

9.8   MINIMUM SPANNING TREE

Let $G = (V, E)$ be an undirected, connected, and weighted graph with n vertices. A *minimum-weight spanning tree* (MST) of G is a spanning tree of G with the smallest edge-weight sum. (See Problem 6.25.) In this section, we show how algorithm HYPERCUBE SHORTEST PATHS can be used to compute an MST for a given graph G.

Let w_{ij} be the weight of edge $(v_i, v_j) \in E$. In what follows, we assume that all w_{ij} are distinct. (If, for two edges (v_i, v_j) and $(v_{i'}, v_{j'})$, $w_{ij} = w_{i'j'}$, then w_{ij} is considered smaller than $w_{i'j'}$ if $in + j < i'n + j'$; otherwise, $w_{i'j'}$ is considered

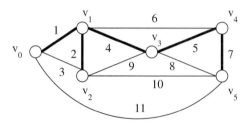

Figure 9.13: A graph and its MST.

smaller than w_{ij}.) Our algorithm uses the following property of MST edges: Edge $(v_i, v_j) \in$ MST if and only if, on every path from v_i to v_j consisting of two or more edges, there is an edge $(v_{i'}, v_{j'})$ such that $w_{i'j'} > w_{ij}$. This property is established by contradiction as follows:

1. Let (v_i, v_j) be an edge of MST. Now assume that there exists a path $H(i, j)$ from v_i to v_j in G, all of whose edges have weights smaller than w_{ij}. If (v_i, v_j) is removed from MST, two disjoint subtrees are obtained, MST^i (containing v_i) and MST^j (containing v_j). Since MST^i and MST^j together contain all the vertices in V, and since $H(i, j)$ goes from v_i to v_j, $H(i, j)$ must have an edge $(v_{i'}, v_{j'})$ with $v_{i'}$ in MST^i and $v_{j'}$ in MST^j. A new spanning tree of G can thus be obtained consisting of MST^i, MST^j, and $(v_{i'}, v_{j'})$, whose weight is smaller than that of MST. But this is absurd, and we conclude that no such path $H(i, j)$ exists.

2. To prove the converse, let every path consisting of two or more edges from v_i to v_j have an edge whose weight is larger than w_{ij}. Now assume that $(v_i, v_j) \notin$ MST. Let $H(i, j)$ be the path from from v_i to v_j, all of whose edges are in MST, and let $(v_{i'}, v_{j'})$ be an edge of $H(i, j)$ whose weight is larger than w_{ij}. By replacing $(v_{i'}, v_{j'})$ with (v_i, v_j) in MST, a new spanning tree with smaller weight is obtained, again leading to a contradiction.

Example 9.9 A graph G is illustrated in Fig. 9.13, with its MST shown by thick lines. Note that edge $(v_1, v_3) \in$ MST, since every path of length 2 or more from v_1 to v_3 contains an edge whose weight is larger than w_{13}. On the other hand, $(v_0, v_5) \notin$ MST, since every edge on the path from v_0 to v_5 in MST has weight less than w_{05}. □

Given G, an algorithm for computing MST is now obtained as follows: Algorithm **HYPERCUBE SHORTEST PATHS** is modified so that the length of a path is now equal to the longest edge it contains (as opposed to the sum of the lengths of the edges). With this new definition, all shortest paths are computed by replacing the statement

$$d_{ij}^k \leftarrow \min_l (d_{il}^{k/2} + d_{lj}^{k/2})$$

in algorithm HYPERCUBE SHORTEST PATHS with

$$d_{ij}^k \leftarrow \min_l(\max(d_{il}^{k/2}, d_{lj}^{k/2})).$$

This means that, for every path from v_i to v_j, we find the longest edge in the path, and then we determine the shortest of these edges, whose length is d_{ij}^{n-1}.

It is now possible to determine those edges of E which belong in the minimum-weight spanning tree. This is done using the condition

$$(v_i, v_j) \in \text{MST} \quad \text{if and only if} \quad w_{ij} = d_{ij}^{n-1}.$$

Note that the requirement in Section 9.5 that G have no cycle of negative total weight is not needed here, since the operation '+' has been replaced with 'max.' This is fortunate, for otherwise the applicability of algorithm HYPERCUBE SHORTEST PATHS to the computation of MST would have been seriously restricted: While forbidding negative cycles made sense when computing shortest paths, it is certainly meaningless for minimum-weight spanning trees.

Analysis. The MST of a graph G with n vertices can be computed in $O(\log^2 n)$ time on a hypercube with n^3 processors.

9.9   MATRIX INVERSION

Let A be an $n \times n$ matrix whose inverse A^{-1} we seek to compute, such that $AA^{-1} = A^{-1}A = I$. Here I is an $n \times n$ identity matrix (whose main diagonal elements are 1, and all the rest are 0). Sequentially, the inverse may be computed in the following way: We begin by writing

$$A = \begin{pmatrix} A_{11} & A_{12} \\ A_{21} & A_{22} \end{pmatrix}$$

$$= \begin{pmatrix} I & Z \\ A_{21}A_{11}^{-1} & I \end{pmatrix} \begin{pmatrix} A_{11} & Z \\ Z & B \end{pmatrix} \begin{pmatrix} I & A_{11}^{-1}A_{12} \\ Z & I \end{pmatrix},$$

where the A_{ij} are are $(n/2) \times (n/2)$ submatrices of A and $B = A_{22} - A_{21}A_{11}^{-1}A_{12}$. The $(n/2) \times (n/2)$ matrix Z is the *zero matrix*. (All of its elements are 0.) The inverse of A is then given by the matrix product

$$A^{-1} = \begin{pmatrix} I & -A_{11}^{-1}A_{12} \\ Z & I \end{pmatrix} \begin{pmatrix} A_{11}^{-1} & Z \\ Z & B^{-1} \end{pmatrix} \begin{pmatrix} I & Z \\ -A_{21}A_{11}^{-1} & I \end{pmatrix},$$

where A_{11}^{-1} and B^{-1} are computed by applying the same process recursively. This requires two inversions, six multiplications, and two additions of $(n/2) \times (n/2)$ matrices. Denoting the sequential-processing time required to perform these operations by the functions $i(n/2), m(n/2)$, and $a(n/2)$, respectively, we get

$$i(n) = 2i(n/2) + 6m(n/2) + 2a(n/2).$$

Since $a(n/2) = n^2/4$ and $m(n/2) = O((n/2)^\epsilon))$, where $2 < \epsilon < 2.38$, it follows that $i(n) = O(n^\epsilon)$. Thus, on the RAM, the time required to compute the inverse of an $n \times n$ matrix matches, up to a constant factor, the time required to multiply two $n \times n$ matrices.

In a parallel setting, $\boldsymbol{B}^{-1}$ and $\boldsymbol{A}_{11}^{-1}$ cannot be obtained simultaneously, since $\boldsymbol{A}_{11}^{-1}$ must first be available in order for the computation of $\boldsymbol{B}^{-1}$ to be possible. Consequently, the running time of any parallel algorithm based on this approach would be $t(n) \geq 2t(n/2)$; that is, $t(n) = \Omega(n)$. We therefore seek a better parallel algorithm. As a first step, we develop a parallel algorithm for inverting a matrix $\boldsymbol{A}$ in the special case where $\boldsymbol{A}$ is lower triangular.

9.9.1 Inverting a Lower Triangular Matrix

Let $\boldsymbol{A}$ be an $n \times n$ lower triangular matrix—that is, a matrix all of whose entries above the main diagonal are 0. It is desired to compute the inverse $\boldsymbol{A}^{-1}$ of $\boldsymbol{A}$. We begin by writing

$$\boldsymbol{A} = \begin{pmatrix} \boldsymbol{B} & \boldsymbol{Z} \\ \boldsymbol{C} & \boldsymbol{D} \end{pmatrix}$$

where $\boldsymbol{B}$, $\boldsymbol{C}$, and $\boldsymbol{D}$ are $(n/2) \times (n/2)$ submatrices of $\boldsymbol{A}$ and $\boldsymbol{Z}$ is an $(n/2) \times (n/2)$ zero matrix. It follows that

$$\boldsymbol{A}^{-1} = \begin{pmatrix} \boldsymbol{B}^{-1} & \boldsymbol{Z} \\ -\boldsymbol{D}^{-1}\boldsymbol{C}\boldsymbol{B}^{-1} & \boldsymbol{D}^{-1} \end{pmatrix}.$$

If $\boldsymbol{B}^{-1}$ and $\boldsymbol{D}^{-1}$ are computed recursively and simultaneously, a parallel algorithm for $\boldsymbol{A}^{-1}$ would have a running time of

$$t(n) = t(n/2) + 2r(n/2),$$

where $r(n/2)$ is the time it takes to multiply two $(n/2) \times (n/2)$ matrices. Using algorithm HYPERCUBE MATRIX MULTIPLICATION, we have $r(n) = O(\log n)$. Therefore, $t(n) = O(\log^2 n)$.

Example 9.10 Consider the 4×4 lower triangular matrix

$$\boldsymbol{A} = \begin{pmatrix} 2 & 0 & 0 & 0 \\ -2 & 1 & 0 & 0 \\ 3 & 0 & -4 & 0 \\ -2 & 4 & 6 & 3 \end{pmatrix}.$$

In order to compute $\boldsymbol{A}^{-1}$, we must compute the inverses $\boldsymbol{B}^{-1}$ and $\boldsymbol{D}^{-1}$ of the matrices

$$\boldsymbol{B} = \begin{pmatrix} 2 & 0 \\ -2 & 1 \end{pmatrix} \quad \text{and} \quad \boldsymbol{D} = \begin{pmatrix} -4 & 0 \\ 6 & 3 \end{pmatrix},$$

respectively. Applying the recursive algorithm to B, we first compute the inverses of the two 1×1 submatrices 2 and 1 to get $1/2$ and 1, respectively. The lower left element of B^{-1} is then computed from $-(1 \times (-2) \times (1/2)) = 1$, yielding

$$B^{-1} = \begin{pmatrix} 1/2 & 0 \\ 1 & 1 \end{pmatrix}.$$

Similarly, applying the recursive algorithm to D, we first compute the inverses of the 1×1 submatrices -4 and 3 to obtain $-1/4$ and $1/3$, respectively. The lower left element of D^{-1} is then computed from $-((1/3) \times 6 \times (-1/4)) = 1/2$, yielding

$$D^{-1} = \begin{pmatrix} -1/4 & 0 \\ 1/2 & 1/3 \end{pmatrix}.$$

The final step computes the lower left 2×2 submatrix of A^{-1} from

$$-D^{-1}CB^{-1} = -\begin{pmatrix} -1/4 & 0 \\ 1/2 & 1/3 \end{pmatrix} \begin{pmatrix} 3 & 0 \\ -2 & 4 \end{pmatrix} \begin{pmatrix} 1/2 & 0 \\ 1 & 1 \end{pmatrix},$$

which gives

$$A^{-1} = \begin{pmatrix} 1/2 & 0 & 0 & 0 \\ 1 & 1 & 0 & 0 \\ 3/8 & 0 & -1/4 & 0 \\ -7/4 & -4/3 & 1/2 & 1/3 \end{pmatrix}. \quad \Box$$

9.9.2   The Characteristic Polynomial of a Matrix

We now provide two definitions that are useful in the treatment to follow:

Determinant.   Let A be an $n \times n$ matrix. When $n > 1$, we denote by A_{ij} the $(n-1) \times (n-1)$ matrix obtained from A by deleting row i and column j. The *determinant* of A, denoted $det(A)$, is defined as follows:

$$\begin{aligned} det(A) \;=\;& a_{11}, & n = 1 \\ =\;& a_{11}\,det(A_{11}) \quad -a_{12}\,det(A_{12}) + \dots \\ & \qquad\qquad\quad +(-1)^{i+j}a_{ij}\,det(A_{ij}) \quad + \dots \\ & \qquad\qquad\qquad\qquad\quad +(-1)^{n+1}a_{1n}\,det(A_{1n}), \quad n > 1. \end{aligned}$$

If $det(A) \neq 0$, then A is said to be *nonsingular*; in this case, the inverse A^{-1} is guaranteed to exist (and, conversely, if A^{-1} exists, then $det(A) \neq 0$).

Characteristic Polynomial.   The *characteristic polynomial* $\phi(x)$ of an $n \times n$ matrix A is defined to be

$$\begin{aligned} \phi(x) \;=\;& det(xI - A) \\ =\;& x^n + h_1 x^{n-1} + h_2 x^{n-2} + \dots + h_n. \end{aligned}$$

Note, in particular, that for $x = 0$, $det(-A) = h_n$. Therefore, $det(A) = (-1)^n h_n$.

9.9.3   The Characteristic Equation of a Matrix

The *Cayley-Hamilton Theorem* of linear algebra states that every $n \times n$ matrix $\boldsymbol{A}$ satisfies its own characteristic polynomial. Thus, taking $x = \boldsymbol{A}$ yields the *characteristic equation*

$$\boldsymbol{A}^n + h_1\boldsymbol{A}^{n-1} + h_2\boldsymbol{A}^{n-2} + \cdots + h_{n-1}\boldsymbol{A} + h_n\boldsymbol{I} \; = \; 0.$$

Multiplying by $\boldsymbol{A}^{-1}$ yields

$$\boldsymbol{A}^{n-1} + h_1\boldsymbol{A}^{n-2} + h_2\boldsymbol{A}^{n-3} + \cdots + h_{n-1}\boldsymbol{I} + h_n\boldsymbol{A}^{-1} \; = \; 0.$$

Therefore,

$$\boldsymbol{A}^{-1} \; = \; -\frac{1}{h_n}(\boldsymbol{A}^{n-1} + h_1\boldsymbol{A}^{n-2} + \cdots + h_{n-2}\boldsymbol{A} + h_{n-1}\boldsymbol{I}).$$

Now, the coefficients $h_1, h_2, \ldots, h_n$ satisfy

$$\begin{pmatrix} 1 & 0 & 0 & \ldots & 0 \\ s_1 & 2 & 0 & \ldots & 0 \\ s_2 & s_1 & 3 & \ldots & 0 \\ & & \vdots & & \\ s_{n-1} & \ldots & s_2 & s_1 & n \end{pmatrix} \begin{pmatrix} h_1 \\ h_2 \\ h_3 \\ \vdots \\ h_n \end{pmatrix} = - \begin{pmatrix} s_1 \\ s_2 \\ s_3 \\ \vdots \\ s_n \end{pmatrix},$$

or $\boldsymbol{Sh} = -\,\boldsymbol{s}$, where s_i denotes the *trace* of $\boldsymbol{A}^i$—that is, the sum of the diagonal elements of $\boldsymbol{A}^i$, for $1 \leq i \leq n$. The system of equations $\boldsymbol{Sh} = -\,\boldsymbol{s}$ can be solved for $\boldsymbol{h}$ by computing the inverse of $\boldsymbol{S}$ and writing: $\boldsymbol{h} = -\,\boldsymbol{S}^{-1}\boldsymbol{s}$. Since $\boldsymbol{S}$ is lower triangular, it can be inverted using the algorithm of Section 9.9.1.

9.9.4   Inverting an Arbitrary Matrix

The algorithm for inverting an arbitrary $n \times n$ matrix $\boldsymbol{A}$ is now straightforward and is given next as algorithm HYPERCUBE MATRIX INVERSION:

Algorithm HYPERCUBE MATRIX INVERSION ($\boldsymbol{A}$)

Step 1: Compute the powers $\boldsymbol{A}^2$, $\boldsymbol{A}^3$, $\ldots$, $\boldsymbol{A}^n$ of the matrix $\boldsymbol{A}$ (taking $\boldsymbol{A}^1 = \boldsymbol{A}$).

Step 2: Compute s_i by summing the diagonal elements of $\boldsymbol{A}^i$ for $i = 1, 2, \ldots, n$.

Step 3: Compute $h_1, h_2, \ldots, h_n$ from the equation $\boldsymbol{h} = -\,\boldsymbol{S}^{-1}\boldsymbol{s}$.

Step 4: Compute $\boldsymbol{A}^{-1} = (-1/h_n)(\boldsymbol{A}^{n-1} + h_1\boldsymbol{A}^{n-2} + \cdots + h_{n-2}\boldsymbol{A} + h_{n-1}\boldsymbol{I})$. ∎

Implementation.   Each of the powers $\boldsymbol{A}^i$ in Step 1 can be computed in $O(\log n) \times O(\log i)$ time with n^3 processors by repeated squaring and multiplication of matrices, using algorithm HYPERCUBE MATRIX MULTIPLICATION. Let $\boldsymbol{X} = \boldsymbol{A}$ and $\boldsymbol{Y} = \boldsymbol{I}$. The computation proceeds as follows:

> **while** $i \neq 0$ **do**
>   (1) **if** i is odd
>   **then** $Y \leftarrow X \times Y$
>   **end if**
>   (2) $i \leftarrow \lfloor i/2 \rfloor$
>   (3) $X \leftarrow X^2$
> **end while.** ∎

When the iteration terminates, $Y = A^i$.

Step 2 is performed as follows: The elements of the matrix A^i reside in the base layer of a hypercube with n^3 processors, viewed as an $n \times n \times n$ array. In particular, the diagonal elements are held by the processors in positions $(0, j, j)$ of the array, for $j = 0, 1, \ldots, n - 1$. These processors do not form a hypercube. However, because each row of the base layer is a hypercube of n processors, the diagonal elements can be routed to the processors in positions $(0, 0, 0)$, $(0, 1, 0)$, $\ldots$, $(0, n - 1, 0)$, respectively, in $O(\log n)$ time. The latter processors, in turn, form a hypercube and can compute the sum of the diagonal elements in $O(\log n)$ time.

Step 3 involves inverting a lower triangular matrix, followed by a matrix-by-vector product. The latter computation is easy to execute on the hypercube as a special case of matrix-by-matrix multiplication. Finally, in Step 4, the simple operation of multiplying a matrix by a real number is immediate, while computing the sum of a collection of matrices consists in applying the method used in Step 3 of algorithm HYPERCUBE MATRIX MULTIPLICATION.

Analysis.   Step 1 requires $O(n^4)$ processors and $O(\log^2 n)$ time if all matrices A^i, $2 \leq i \leq n$, are to be computed simultaneously. In Step 2, each of the s_i can be computed in $O(\log n)$ time using n processors. Inverting S in Step 3 requires $O(\log^2 n)$ time and n^3 processors. In the same step, computing h_1, h_2, $\ldots$, h_n requires $O(\log n)$ time and n^2 processors. Finally, Step 4 can be performed in $O(\log n)$ time using $O(n^3)$ processors. The overall running time is therefore $t(n) = O(\log^2 n)$, while the number of processors used is $p(n) = O(n^4)$, resulting in a cost of $c(n) = O(n^4 \log^2 n)$. While fast, this algorithm is not cost optimal, in view of the $O(n^\epsilon)$ operations sufficient to invert a matrix on the RAM, where $2 < \epsilon < 2.38$.

Computing the Determinant.   Since $det(A) = (-1)^n h_n$, computing the coefficients of the characteristic polynomial as in Section 9.9.3, and in particular h_n, leads to an immediate evaluation of $det(A)$.

9.10   EIGENVALUES AND EIGENVECTORS

A system of n simultaneous linear differential equations of first order with constant coefficients is written as

$$\frac{dx}{dt} = Ax,$$

where A is an $n \times n$ matrix and x is an $n \times 1$ vector. For some vector $u \neq 0$, $x = ue^{\lambda t}$ is a solution to $dx/dt = Ax$ if and only if $\lambda u = Au$. Here, λ is called an *eigenvalue* and u an *eigenvector*. The *algebraic eigenvalue problem* is to determine such λ and u. There are always n eigenvalues, to each of which there corresponds at least one eigenvector.

9.10.1 Jacobi's Algorithm

For an $n \times n$ matrix B and an $n \times 1$ vector y, if we apply the transformation $x = By$ to the system of differential equations, we get

$$\frac{dy}{dt} = (B^{-1}AB)y.$$

The eigenvalues of $B^{-1}AB$ are the same as those of A. We therefore choose B such that the eigenvalues of $B^{-1}AB$ are easily obtainable. For example, if $B^{-1}AB$ is a *diagonal* matrix (i.e., a matrix all of whose elements are 0, except those on the diagonal), then the diagonal elements are the eigenvalues. One method of transforming a symmetric matrix A to diagonal form is *Jacobi's algorithm*. The method is an iterative one, where the kth iteration is defined by

$$A_k = R_k A_{k-1} R_k^T$$

for $k \geq 1$, and $A_0 = A$. The $n \times n$ matrices R_k are known as *plane rotations*. Let a_{ij}^k denote the elements of A_k. The purpose of R_k is to reduce the two elements a_{pq}^{k-1} and a_{qp}^{k-1} to 0 (for some $p < q$, depending on k). In reality, each iteration decreases the sum of the squares of the nondiagonal elements, so that A_k converges to a diagonal matrix. The process stops when the sum of the squares is sufficiently small, or, more specifically, when

$$d_k = \left(\sum_{i=1}^{n} \sum_{j \neq i} (a_{ij}^k)^2 \right)^{1/2} < \delta$$

for some small tolerance δ. At that point, the columns of the matrix $R_1^T R_2^T \cdots R_k^T$ are the eigenvectors.

The plane rotations are chosen as follows: If a_{pq}^{k-1} is a nonzero off-diagonal element of A_{k-1}, we wish to define R_k so that $a_{pq}^k = a_{qp}^k = 0$. Denote the elements of R_k by r_{ij}^k. We take

$$r_{pp}^k = r_{qq}^k = \cos\theta_k, \qquad r_{pq}^k = -r_{qp}^k = \sin\theta_k,$$

$$r_{ii}^k = 1, \quad \text{provided that } i \neq p \text{ or } q, \quad \text{and} \quad r_{ij}^k = 0 \text{ otherwise},$$

where $\cos\theta_k$ and $\sin\theta_k$ are obtained in the following way: Let

$$\alpha_k = (a_{qq}^{k-1} - a_{pp}^{k-1})/2a_{pq}^{k-1} \quad \text{and} \quad \beta_k = 1/(\text{sign}(\alpha_k))(\text{abs}(\alpha_k) + (1 + \alpha_k^2)^{1/2}),$$

where $\text{sign}(\alpha_k)$ is $+1$ or -1, depending on whether α_k is positive or negative, respectively, and $\text{abs}(\alpha_k)$ denotes the absolute value of α_k. Then

$$\cos\theta_k = 1/(1 + \beta_k^2)^{1/2} \quad \text{and} \quad \sin\theta_k = \beta_k \cos\theta_k.$$

The only question remaining is, which nonzero element a_{pq}^{k-1} is selected for reduction to 0 during the kth iteration? Many approaches are possible, one of which is to choose the element of greatest magnitude, since this would lead to the greatest reduction in d_k.

As described, this algorithm converges in $O(n^2)$ iterations. Since each iteration consists of two matrix multiplications, the entire process takes $O(n^{2+\epsilon})$ time on the RAM, where $2 < \epsilon < 2.38$.

9.10.2   Computing Eigenvalues in Parallel

Jacobi's algorithm lends itself naturally to a parallel implementation. Let $n = 2^s$ for some positive integer s. We use a hypercube with $n^3 = 2^{3s}$ processors. As in Section 9.1.3, we view the processors as being arranged in an $n \times n \times n$ array. Initially, the matrix A (i.e., A_o) is stored in the n^2 processors occupying positions $(0, j, m)$, $0 \le j, m \le n-1$, one element per processor. At the beginning of iteration k, these same processors contain A^{k-1}. They find the largest off-diagonal element of A^{k-1} and create R_k and R_k^T. All n^3 processors are then used to obtain $C_k = R_k A_{k-1}$ and $A_k = C_k R_k^T$. At the end of the iteration, if $d_k < \delta$, the process terminates. The algorithm is given next as algorithm HYPERCUBE EIGENVALUES. In it, the subscript k is omitted from A_k, R_k, R_k^T, and d_k, since new values replace old ones. Also, a_{pq} denotes the off-diagonal element of A with the largest absolute value.

> **Algorithm HYPERCUBE EIGENVALUES (A, δ)**
>
>   **while** $d > \delta$ **do**
>   (1) Find a_{pq}
>   (2) Create R
>   (3) $A \leftarrow RA$
>   (4) Create R^T
>   (5) $A \leftarrow AR^T$
>   **end while.** ∎

Analysis. The n^2 processors holding A form a $2s$-dimensional hypercube. They can compute d_k in $O(\log n)$ time. Similarly, Step (1) takes $O(\log n)$ time. Steps (2) and (4) require constant time, since each of the n^2 processors in positions $(0, j, m)$, $0 \le j, m \le n-1$, creates one element of R_k and one element of R_k^T. (Alternatively, only R_k is computed in Step (2); its transpose is then obtained by algorithm HYPERCUBE MATRIX TRANSPOSE in Step (4).) Algorithm HYPERCUBE MATRIX MULTIPLICATION is used in Steps (3) and (5) to compute $R_k A R_k^T$. The time per iteration is thus $O(\log n)$. Since convergence is attained after $O(n^2)$ iterations, the overall running time is $O(n^2 \log n)$. Since $p(n) = n^3$, the algorithm's cost is $c(n) = O(n^5 \log n)$.

Example 9.11 Let $n = 2$ (i.e., $s = 1$), $\delta = 10^{-5}$, and

$$A = \begin{pmatrix} 1 & 1 \\ 1 & 1 \end{pmatrix}.$$

Algorithm HYPERCUBE EIGENVALUES uses eight processors forming a three-dimensional hypercube. Fig. 9.14(a) shows the elements of A_o inside the processors to which they are assigned. In the first iteration, the off-diagonal element $a_{12} = 1$ is chosen for reduction to 0 (i.e., $p = 1$ and $q = 2$). Thus,

$$R_1 = \begin{pmatrix} \cos\theta_1 & \sin\theta_1 \\ -\sin\theta_1 & \cos\theta_1 \end{pmatrix} = \begin{pmatrix} 1/\sqrt{2} & 1/\sqrt{2} \\ -1/\sqrt{2} & 1/\sqrt{2} \end{pmatrix},$$

as shown in Fig. 9.14(b). Now

$$R_1 A_o = \begin{pmatrix} 1/\sqrt{2} & 1/\sqrt{2} \\ -1/\sqrt{2} & 1/\sqrt{2} \end{pmatrix} \begin{pmatrix} 1 & 1 \\ 1 & 1 \end{pmatrix} = \begin{pmatrix} \sqrt{2} & \sqrt{2} \\ 0 & 0 \end{pmatrix}$$

is computed, using all eight processors to execute the eight multiplications involved simultaneously, as shown in Fig. 9.14(c). The elements of $R_1 A_o$ replace those of A_o, and R_1^T replaces R_1, as shown in Fig. 9.14(d). Finally, $A R_1^T$ is computed, and the value of A_1 at the end of the first iteration is shown in Fig. 9.14(e). Since the two off-diagonal elements are both 0, the procedure terminates. The eigenvalues are 2 and 0, and the eigenvectors are

$$(1/\sqrt{2} \ \ 1/\sqrt{2})^T \quad \text{and} \quad (-1/\sqrt{2} \ \ 1/\sqrt{2})^T. \ \ \Box$$

9.11 AN INTRODUCTION TO THE STAR

Let V_m be the set of all $m!$ permutations of the symbols $\{1, 2, \ldots, m\}$. For any permutation $v \in V_m$, if we denote the ith symbol of v by $v(i)$, then v can be written as $v(1)v(2)\ldots v(m)$. A *star interconnection network* on m symbols, denoted by $\mathcal{S}_m$, is represented by an undirected graph with $m!$ vertices, where each vertex P_v is a processor. Here, permutation v is referred to as the *label* of P_v. Processor P_v is connected to $m - 1$ processors P_u, where u is obtained by interchanging the first and ith symbols of v; that is, $u = v(i)v(2)\ldots v(i-1)v(1)v(i+1)\ldots v(m)$ for $i = 2, 3, \ldots, m$. Thus, each processor is connected to $m - 1$ processors through *connections* $2, 3, \ldots, m$. Starting at P_v, one *visits* connection i by traversing the link connecting P_v to P_u, where v and u are as just defined. The network $\mathcal{S}_m$ is also called an *m-star*. Networks $\mathcal{S}_1$, $\mathcal{S}_2$, $\mathcal{S}_3$, and $\mathcal{S}_4$ are shown in Fig. 9.15. ($\mathcal{S}_4$ was also shown in Fig. 2.20 and is repeated here for completeness.)

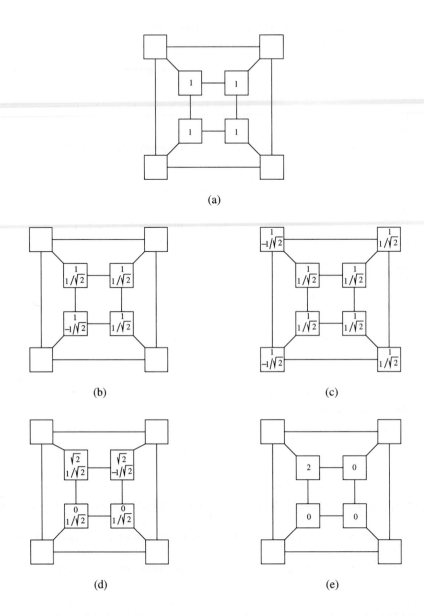

Figure 9.14: Computing eigenvalues on a hypercube: (a) Elements of the input matrix stored in the hypercube, one element per processor; (b) After Steps (1) and (2) of algorithm HYPERCUBE EIGENVALUES ; (c) Executing Step (3) of the algorithm; (d) After Step (4) of the algorithm; (e) Input matrix at the end of the first iteration of the algorithm.

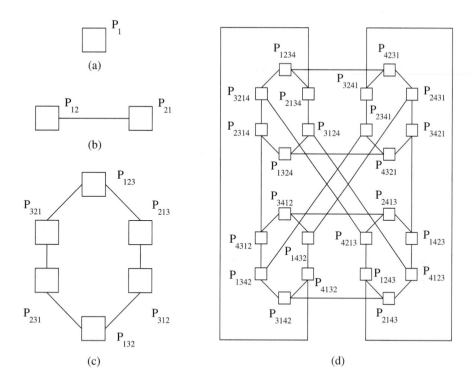

Figure 9.15: The star interconnection network: (a) $\mathcal{S}_1$; (b) $\mathcal{S}_2$; (c) $\mathcal{S}_3$; (d) $\mathcal{S}_4$.

The star compares favorably with the hypercube in several aspects. To see this, we examine two properties of a star $\mathcal{S}_m$ with $m!$ processors and a hypercube with $O(m!)$ processors, denoted here by $\mathcal{H}_m$ for convenience. (Since $m!$ is not necessarily a power of 2, as is required for the number of processors of a hypercube, we take the number of processors of $\mathcal{H}_m$ to be the smallest power of 2 larger than $m!$.)

Degree. The degree of $\mathcal{H}_m$ is $O(\log m!) = O(m \log m)$. By contrast, the degree of $\mathcal{S}_m$ is $m - 1 = O(\log m! / \log m)$.

Diameter. The diameter of $\mathcal{H}_m$ is $O(\log m!) = O(m \log m)$. By contrast, the diameter of $\mathcal{S}_m$ is $O(m) = O(\log m! / \log m)$.

In other words, $\mathcal{S}_m$ has a degree and a diameter that are asymptotically smaller than those of $\mathcal{H}_m$, for approximately the same number of vertices. We now introduce some simple terminology and notation that will prove useful in designing algorithms for the star.

9.11.1 Decomposing $\mathcal{S}_m$ into Substars

Let $\mathcal{S}_k(e_{k+1}e_{k+2}\ldots e_m)$ be a subgraph of $\mathcal{S}_m$ induced by all the processors P_v whose labels v have the same $m - k$ last symbols $e_{k+1}e_{k+2}\ldots e_m$, $1 \le k \le m$, where $e_{k+1}e_{k+2}\ldots e_m$ is a permutation of $m - k$ distinct symbols in $\{1, 2, \ldots, m\}$. Thus, $\mathcal{S}_k(e_{k+1}e_{k+2}\ldots e_m)$ is a k−star. There are $m!/k!$ such substars. In particular, $\mathcal{S}_m$ can be decomposed into m substars $\mathcal{S}_{m-1}$, namely, $\mathcal{S}_{m-1}(i)$, $1 \le i \le m$. For example, $\mathcal{S}_4$ in Fig. 9.15(d) contains four 3-stars, namely, $\mathcal{S}_3(1)$, $\mathcal{S}_3(2)$, $\mathcal{S}_3(3)$, and $\mathcal{S}_3(4)$, by fixing the last symbol at 1, 2, 3, and 4, respectively.

9.11.2 A Processor Ordering

We now describe an ordering of the processors of $\mathcal{S}_m$ and give a function that maps this ordering to the positive integers. Let P_u and P_v be two processors of $\mathcal{S}_m$, where $u = e_1e_2\ldots e_m$ and $v = d_1d_2\ldots d_m$. The ordering $\prec$ on the processors is defined as follows: $P_u \prec P_v$ if there exists an i, $1 \le i \le m$, such that $e_j = d_j$ for $j > i$ and $e_i > d_i$. In order to provide some intuition, we relate $\prec$ to the more common lexicographic ordering. Assume that the processor labels (i.e., the permutations of $\{1, 2, \ldots, m\}$) have been listed according to $\prec$. If this list were to be traversed in reverse order while reading the symbols of each permutation from right to left, lexicographic order would be obtained.

Example 9.12 For $m = 4$, the 24 permutations of $\{1, 2, 3, 4\}$, ordered according to $\prec$, are as follows (in row-major order):

1234	2134	1324	3124	2314	3214
(0)	(1)	(2)	(3)	(4)	(5)

1243	2143	1423	4123	2413	4213
(6)	(7)	(8)	(9)	(10)	(11)

1342	3142	1432	4132	3412	4312
(12)	(13)	(14)	(15)	(16)	(17)

2341	3241	2431	4231	3421	4321
(18)	(19)	(20)	(21)	(22)	(23). $\square$

Processor Rank. The *rank* of a processor is the number of processors that precede it. We now describe a function that maps the permutations, ordered according to $\prec$, into the integers $0, 1, \ldots, m! - 1$. The latter will represent the processor ranks.

Let $e_1e_2\ldots e_m$ be a permutation. For each e_i, we define

$$q_i = \mathrm{abs}\!\left(e_i - i - \sum_{j=i+1}^{m} [e_i > e_j]\right) \times (i - 1)!$$

for $2 \leq i \leq m$, where $[e_i > e_j]$ equals 1 when $e_i > e_j$ and equals 0 otherwise. Then the rank of P_u, where $u = e_1 e_2 \ldots e_m$ is

$$rank(e_1 e_2 \ldots e_m) = \sum_{i=2}^{m} q_i.$$

The rank of each processor in $\mathcal{S}_4$ is shown below its label in Example 9.12.

A Notation for Processor Labels. Let i_1 and i_2 be two distinct symbols from $\{1, 2, \ldots, m\}$. Further, let σ_{m-2} be any permutation of the $m - 2$ symbols $\{1, 2, \ldots, m\} - \{i_1, i_2\}$. We use the notation $i_1 \sigma_{m-2} i_2$ to represent a permutation of $\{1, 2, \ldots, m\}$. For example, if $m = 9$, $i_1 = 6$, $i_2 = 2$, and $\sigma_7 = 5497183$, then $i_1 \sigma_7 i_2 = 654971832$. Similarly, σ_{m-1} stands for a permutation of $m - 1$ symbols. Thus, $i_1 \sigma_{m-1}$ and $\sigma_{m-1} i_2$ are permutations of m symbols.

9.12 DATA COMMUNICATION ON A STAR

In this section, we describe a number of algorithms for communicating data among the processors of $\mathcal{S}_m$. As usual, we assume that each processor contains a datum of constant size, that this datum requires one time unit to traverse a link between two processors, and that a processor can send *one* datum to *one* of its neighbors in any given time unit.

9.12.1 Routing in Arbitrary Order

Consider the following problem: Given $\mathcal{S}_{m-1}(i)$ and $\mathcal{S}_{m-1}(j)$, with $i \neq j$, it is required to send the data in the processors in $\mathcal{S}_{m-1}(i)$ to the processors in $\mathcal{S}_{m-1}(j)$. Specifically, the datum in each processor in $\mathcal{S}_{m-1}(i)$ is to be routed to one processor in $\mathcal{S}_{m-1}(j)$ such that no two processors in $\mathcal{S}_{m-1}(i)$ send their contents to the same processor in $\mathcal{S}_{m-1}(j)$. This can be accomplished in three steps as follows:

1. In the first step, those $(m - 2)!$ processors P_v in $\mathcal{S}_{m-1}(i)$, where $v = j\sigma_{m-2}i$, send their data to $(m - 2)!$ processors P_u in $\mathcal{S}_{m-1}(j)$, where $u = i\sigma_{m-2}j$, through connection m. These data have now reached their final destinations. At the same time, the remaining $(m-1)! - (m-2)!$ processors P_w in $\mathcal{S}_{m-1}(i)$, where $w = k\sigma_{m-2}i$ and $k \neq i, j$, send their data (also through connection m) to the processors P_x in $\mathcal{S}_{m-1}(k)$, where $x = i\sigma_{m-2}k$.

2. In the second step, processors P_x in $\mathcal{S}_{m-1}(k)$, where $x = i\sigma_{m-2}k$, send the data they have received to the processors P_y, where $y = j\sigma_{m-2}k$.

3. In the third step, processors P_y, where $y = j\sigma_{m-2}k$, send the data they have received through connection m to the processors P_z in $\mathcal{S}_{m-1}(j)$, where $z = k\sigma_{m-2}j$.

The algorithm is given next as algorithm STAR COPY:

Algorithm STAR COPY (i, j)

Step 1: for all $s = \sigma_{m-1}i$ **do in parallel**

P_s sends datum to neighbor along connection m

end for

Step 2: for all $x = i\sigma_{m-2}k$, $k \neq j$, **do in parallel**

P_x sends datum to neighbor P_v with $v(1) = j$

end for

Step 3: for all $y = j\sigma_{m-2}k$, $k \neq i$, **do in parallel**

P_y sends datum to neighbor along connection m

end for. ∎

The correctness of this algorithm follows from the fact that the datum in processor P_s of $\mathcal{S}_{m-1}(i)$, where $s = \alpha_1 j \alpha_2 i$, is mapped to processor P_r of $\mathcal{S}_{m-1}(j)$, where $r = \alpha_1 i \alpha_2 j$. Here α_1 and α_2 are permutations of symbols in $\{1, 2, \ldots, m\} - \{i, j\}$ such that the symbols in α_1 are different from those in α_2, and α_1 and α_2 together contain $m - 2$ symbols.

Example 9.13 Suppose that $m = 4$ and that the six processors in $\mathcal{S}_3(1)$ wish to send their data to the six processors in $\mathcal{S}_3(3)$. The data transfers that occur during the three steps are as follows:

Step 1 : $P_{3241} \rightarrow P_{1243}$ $P_{3421} \rightarrow P_{1423}$

$P_{4231} \rightarrow P_{1234}$ $P_{4321} \rightarrow P_{1324}$

$P_{2341} \rightarrow P_{1342}$ $P_{2431} \rightarrow P_{1432}$

Step 2 : $P_{1234} \rightarrow P_{3214}$ $P_{1324} \rightarrow P_{3124}$

$P_{1342} \rightarrow P_{3142}$ $P_{1432} \rightarrow P_{3412}$

Step 3 : $P_{3214} \rightarrow P_{4213}$ $P_{3124} \rightarrow P_{4123}$

$P_{3142} \rightarrow P_{2143}$ $P_{3412} \rightarrow P_{2413}.$ □

Analysis. Since each of the three steps of the algorithm involves a constant time computation, $t(m) = O(1)$.

9.12.2   Generalized Routing in Arbitrary Order

Let $I = \{i_1, i_2, \ldots, i_l\}$ and $J = \{j_1, j_2, \ldots, j_l\}$ be two sequences from $\{1, 2, \ldots, m\}$ such that no two elements of I are equal, no two elements of J are equal, and no element of I is equal to an element of J. It is desired to send the data in $\mathcal{S}_{m-1}(i_1), \mathcal{S}_{m-1}(i_2), \ldots, \mathcal{S}_{m-1}(i_l)$ to $\mathcal{S}_{m-1}(j_1), \mathcal{S}_{m-1}(j_2), \ldots, \mathcal{S}_{m-1}(j_l)$ such that the contents of $\mathcal{S}_{m-1}(i_k)$ are sent to $\mathcal{S}_{m-1}(j_k)$, $1 \leq k \leq l$. This routing can also be achieved in constant time by algorithm STAR GROUP COPY, given next.

Algorithm STAR GROUP COPY (I, J)

    for $k = 1$ **to** l **do in parallel**
        STAR COPY (i_k, j_k)
    end for. ∎

Note that in algorithm STAR COPY, certain processors in an intermediate substar are used to route the data from the origin substar to the destination substar. In the present routing, however, l substars are origins and l are destinations. Since the l routings (each using STAR COPY) are performed in parallel, a processor may play more than one role—as origin, intermediate, or destination processor. Therefore, in algorithm STAR GROUP COPY, a processor is allowed to send and receive data simultaneously if necessary.

9.12.3 Ordered Routing

Suppose that we wish to move all the data held by the processors in $\mathcal{S}_{m-1}(i)$ to the processors in $\mathcal{S}_{m-1}(i+1)$ while preserving their relative order within the substar. In other words, the datum held by a processor in $\mathcal{S}_{m-1}(i)$ is to be copied to a processor *with the same rank* in $\mathcal{S}_{m-1}(i+1)$. Let α_1 and α_2 be defined as in Section 9.12.1. We note that if P_u, where $u = \alpha_1(i+1)\alpha_2 i$, is a processor of $\mathcal{S}_{m-1}(i)$, then the processor with the same rank in $\mathcal{S}_{m-1}(i+1)$ is P_v, where $v = \alpha_1 i \alpha_2 (i+1)$. This means that we can use algorithm STAR COPY with $j = i + 1$ to perform this ordered routing.

9.12.4 Broadcasting

The problem of broadcasting is defined as follows: A given processor P_v, where $v = j\sigma_{m-2}i$, wishes to broadcast a datum D to all processors in $\mathcal{S}_m$. The problem is solved by algorithm STAR BROADCASTING, given next:

Algorithm STAR BROADCASTING (D)

Step 1: The technique of *recursive doubling* (see Example 2.5) is used to distribute D to $m - 2$ processors P_u, where $u = k\sigma_{m-2}i$ and $1 \le k \le m$, with $k \ne i, j$.

Step 2: The $m - 1$ processors P_x, where $x = 1\sigma_{m-2}i, 2\sigma_{m-2}i, \ldots, (i-1)\sigma_{m-2}i,$ $(i+1)\sigma_{m-2}i, \ldots, m\sigma_{m-2}i$, in $\mathcal{S}_{m-1}(i)$ send D to the $m - 1$ processors P_y, where $y = i\sigma_{m-2}1, i\sigma_{m-2}2, \ldots, i\sigma_{m-2}(i-1), i\sigma_{m-2}(i+1), \ldots, i\sigma_{m-2}m$, respectively.

Step 3: Each processor P_y, where $y = i\sigma_{m-2}l$ and $1 \le l \le m$, with $l \ne i$, recursively broadcasts D to all the processors of $\mathcal{S}_{m-1}(l)$, while P_v, $v = j\sigma_{m-2}i$, recursively broadcasts D in $\mathcal{S}_{m-1}(i)$. ∎

The algorithm is illustrated in Fig. 9.16, in which the processors holding D at each step are shown shaded.

Analysis. Let $t(m)$ be the running time of the algorithm. Then Steps 1 and 2 require $O(\log m)$ and $O(1)$ time, respectively. Therefore,

$$\begin{aligned} t(m) &= t(m-1) + O(\log m) \\ &= O(m \log m). \end{aligned}$$

9.13   PREFIX COMPUTATION

Let a sequence of elements $\{x_0, x_1, \ldots, x_{m!-1}\}$ be given, stored in the processors of $\mathcal{S}_m$, one element per processor. Thus x_i is initially stored in $P_{(i)}$, where the index i is the *rank* of the processor, based on the processor ordering defined in Section 9.11.2. Also given is a binary associative operation $\circ$. A prefix computation, as defined in Section 4.1, is to compute all the quantities $s_j = x_0 \circ x_1 \circ \cdots \circ x_j$, $j = 0, 1, \ldots,$ $m! - 1$, such that at the end of the computation $P_{(j)}$ holds s_j. An algorithm for this problem is given shortly. We refer to the s_j as the prefix *sums* for convenience.

Suppose that we have computed prefix sums for two groups of substars as follows:

> *Group 1* : $\mathcal{S}_{m-1}(i)$, $\mathcal{S}_{m-1}(i+1)$, $\ldots$, $\mathcal{S}_{m-1}(i+k)$
> *Group 2* : $\mathcal{S}_{m-1}(i+k+1)$, $\mathcal{S}_{m-1}(i+k+2)$, $\ldots$, $\mathcal{S}_{m-1}(i+2k+1)$.

Suppose also that each processor holds two variables, s and r, for storing the partial prefix sum so far and the total sum of values in the group to which it belongs, respectively. Let the total sum in *Group 1* be r_1 and the total sum in *Group 2* be r_2. We first use algorithm STAR GROUP COPY to send r_1 to every processor in *Group 2* and r_2 to every processor in *Group 1*. Then, the prefix sums in processors in *Group 1* remain the same, while the prefix sum s in a processor in *Group 2* becomes $s \circ r_1$. The total sum for all processors in both groups becomes $r_1 \circ r_2$. All of these steps require $O(1)$ time. *Group 1* and *Group 2* now form a single group. The steps just described are then used to merge the new group with another group formed in the same way. This continues until all the prefix sums have been computed.

Initially, there are m groups, each containing only one substar $\mathcal{S}_{m-1}$, and the algorithm is applied recursively to that substar. When the recursion terminates, each processor in the group holds the two variables s and r required at the beginning of the merging phase. The groups are now merged in pairs, as described in the previous paragraph. This leads to a running time of $t(m) = t(m-1) + O(\log m) = O(m \log m)$.

9.14   COMPUTING THE FFT $(\star)$

In this section, we revisit the problem of computing the fast Fourier transform (FFT) of a sequence (first studied in Section 3.2) and show how it can be performed efficiently on the star interconnection network. The algorithm is based on decomposing

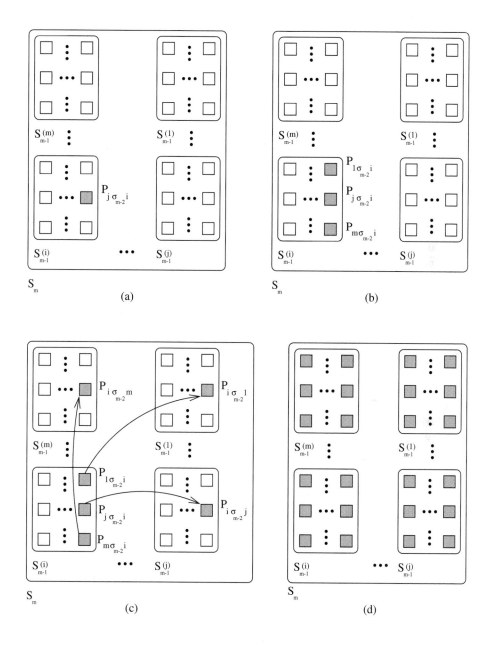

Figure 9.16: Broadcasting on the star: (a) Initially; (b) After Step 1; (c) After Step 2; (d) After Step 3.

the star into disjoint paths, computing the FFT on these paths, treated as linear arrays of processors, and then combining the answers. A number of preliminary results are presented first, culminating in the algorithm for the FFT.

9.14.1 Decomposing the Star into Cycles

We begin by describing a decomposition scheme that partitions $\mathcal{S}_m$ into $(m-2)!$ disjoint cycles, each of length $(m-1)m$. Each cycle can be defined by its initial permutation of the form $\sigma = 1\sigma_{m-2}m$. Let d_i represent the position of symbol i in σ, where $d_1 = 1$. In the discussion which follows we use the permutations v—that is, the labels of processors P_v—when talking about the processors of $\mathcal{S}_m$.

Starting at σ and visiting connections $d_2, d_3, \ldots, d_{m-1}$, in that order, we obtain a path $1\sigma_{m-2}m, 2\sigma_{m-2}m, \ldots, (m-1)\sigma_{m-2}m$, of length $m-1$, in which all permutations end with the symbol m. If we now visit connection d_m, we obtain the permutation $m\sigma_{m-2}(m-1)$, in which symbol i is in position d_l, where $l = (i \bmod m) + 1$. Now, starting from $m\sigma_{m-2}(m-1)$, we visit once again connections $d_2, d_3, \ldots, d_{m-1}$, and we obtain the path $m\sigma_{m-2}(m-1), 1\sigma_{m-2}(m-1), \ldots, (m-2)\sigma_{m-2}(m-1)$, of $m-1$ permutations, all of which end with the symbol $m-1$. In general, the jth time we visit connections $d_2, d_3, \ldots, d_{m-1}, 1 \le j \le m$, we obtain the path $(m-j+2)\sigma_{m-2}(m-j+1), (m-j+3)\sigma_{m-2}(m-j+1), \ldots, m\sigma_{m-2}(m-j+1), 1\sigma_{m-2}(m-j+1), \ldots, (m-j)\sigma_{m-2}(m-j+1)$, of length $m-1$, in which all permutations end with the symbol $m-j+1$. If we call the jth group of $m-1$ permutations *path j*, we can make the following observations:

1. The first permutation of path j is obtained from the last permutation of path $j-1$ through connection d_m.

2. In the first permutation of path j (obtained the $(j-1)$st time we visit connection d_m), symbol i is in position d_k, where $k = ((i+j-1) \bmod m) + 1$. The mth time we visit connection d_m, we get a permutation in which symbol i is in position d_i, since $1 \le i \le m$ and $((i+m-1) \bmod m) + 1 = i$. In other words, we get σ, signifying that a cycle is obtained.

3. We have m paths of $m-1$ permutations each. The permutations in each path are distinct, and each permutation in path i is different from each permutation in path j, $i \ne j$, because permutations in different paths end with different symbols. As a consequence, a cycle contains $(m-1)m$ distinct permutations.

4. Because each cycle is generated by an initial permutation of the form $1\sigma_{m-2}m$, there are $(m-2)!$ cycles in total, one for each permutation of the symbols $2, 3, \ldots, m-1$.

5. All the cycles of $\mathcal{S}_m$ are disjoint.

Example 9.14 When $m = 4$, there are $(4-2)! = 2$ cycles in $\mathcal{S}_4$, as follows:

Cycle 1 : Path 1 : 1234 $\overset{d_2=2}{\Longrightarrow}$ 2134 $\overset{d_3=3}{\Longrightarrow}$ 3124 $\overset{d_4=4}{\Longrightarrow}$
Path 2 : 4123 $\overset{d_2=2}{\Longrightarrow}$ 1423 $\overset{d_3=3}{\Longrightarrow}$ 2413 $\overset{d_4=4}{\Longrightarrow}$
Path 3 : 3412 $\overset{d_2=2}{\Longrightarrow}$ 4312 $\overset{d_3=3}{\Longrightarrow}$ 1342 $\overset{d_4=4}{\Longrightarrow}$
Path 4 : 2341 $\overset{d_2=2}{\Longrightarrow}$ 3241 $\overset{d_3=3}{\Longrightarrow}$ 4231 $\overset{d_4=4}{\Longrightarrow}$ 1234

Cycle 2 : Path 1 : 1324 $\overset{d_2=3}{\Longrightarrow}$ 2314 $\overset{d_3=2}{\Longrightarrow}$ 3214 $\overset{d_4=4}{\Longrightarrow}$
Path 2 : 4213 $\overset{d_2=3}{\Longrightarrow}$ 1243 $\overset{d_3=2}{\Longrightarrow}$ 2143 $\overset{d_4=4}{\Longrightarrow}$
Path 3 : 3142 $\overset{d_2=3}{\Longrightarrow}$ 4132 $\overset{d_3=2}{\Longrightarrow}$ 1432 $\overset{d_4=4}{\Longrightarrow}$
Path 4 : 2431 $\overset{d_2=3}{\Longrightarrow}$ 3421 $\overset{d_3=2}{\Longrightarrow}$ 4321 $\overset{d_4=4}{\Longrightarrow}$ 1324. □

The decomposition of $\mathcal{S}_m$ into disjoint cycles can be combined with its decomposition into substars. As observed in Section 9.11.1, $\mathcal{S}_m$ can be decomposed into $m!/k!$ substars $\mathcal{S}_k$, $k < m$. Using the decomposition scheme described in the current section, $\mathcal{S}_k$ can be partitioned into $(k-2)!$ cycles, each of length $(k-1)k$. As a consequence, $\mathcal{S}_m$ can be decomposed into $m!/(k-1)k$ disjoint cycles of length $(k-1)k$ each.

9.14.2 The Fast Fourier Transform

Given a sequence of numbers $\{a_0, a_1, \ldots, a_{n-1}\}$, its discrete Fourier transform (DFT) is the sequence $\{b_0, b_1, \ldots, b_{n-1}\}$, where

$$b_j = \sum_{k=0}^{n-1} a_k \times \omega_n^{jk}, \quad \text{for} \quad j = 0, 1, \ldots, n-1,$$

and ω_n is a primitive nth root of unity (as defined in Section 3.2.1). Suppose that n, the number of input elements, is composite; that is, $n = r_1 \times r_2$, where r_1 and r_2 are positive integers larger than 1. If we arrange the n input elements into an $r_1 \times r_2$ two-dimensional grid, using row-major order, the DFT can be written as

$$b(j_1, j_0) = \sum_{k_0=0}^{r_2-1} \sum_{k_1=0}^{r_1-1} a(k_1, k_0) \times \omega_n^{(j_1 r_1 + j_0)(k_1 r_2 + k_0)},$$

where $a(k_1, k_0)$ refers to the input element in row k_1 and column k_0 of the grid, $b(j_1, j_0)$ refers to the output element in row j_1 and column j_0 of the grid, and the original indices j and k are related to the new ones by the following equations:

$$
\begin{array}{rlrl}
j &= j_1 r_1 + j_0, & j_0, k_1 &= 0, 1, \ldots, r_1 - 1, \\
k &= k_1 r_2 + k_0, & j_1, k_0 &= 0, 1, \ldots, r_2 - 1.
\end{array}
$$

Since

$$\omega_n^{j_1 k_1 r_1 r_2} = (e^{2\pi i/n})^{j_1 k_1 n} = 1,$$

we have

$$b(j_1, j_0) = \sum_{k_0=0}^{r_2-1} \omega_n^{j_1 k_0 r_1} \left(\omega_n^{j_0 k_0} \sum_{k_1=0}^{r_1-1} a(k_1, k_0) \omega_n^{j_0 k_1 r_2} \right).$$

According to this decomposition, the DFT can be computed in three steps:

1. The DFT of each column of the grid is computed:

$$b'(j_0, k_0) = \sum_{k_1=0}^{r_1-1} a(k_1, k_0) \omega_{r_1}^{j_0 k_1}.$$

2. Local multiplications are performed:

$$b''(j_0, k_0) = \omega_n^{j_0 k_0} b'(j_0, k_0).$$

3. The DFT of each row of the grid is computed:

$$b(j_1, j_0) = \sum_{k_0=0}^{r_2-1} b''(j_0, k_0) \omega_{r_2}^{j_1 k_0}.$$

Note that at the end of these three steps, the matrix $\boldsymbol{B}$ whose entries are $b(j_1, j_0)$ is transposed. This approach to computing the DFT is referred to as the *fast Fourier transform (FFT) algorithm*. It requires nr_1 operations to obtain the $b''(j_0, k_0)$ and nr_2 operations to obtain the $b(j_1, j_0)$, for a total of $n(r_1 + r_2)$ operations. If n can be decomposed into h factors (i.e., if $n = r_1 \times r_2 \times \cdots \times r_h$), then successive applications of the foregoing algorithm give an h-step algorithm. Let us view the n input elements as being arranged into an $r_1 \times r_2 \times \cdots \times r_h$, h-dimensional grid. During the ith step of the computation, elements that are adjacent over dimension $h - i + 1$ of the grid participate in Fourier transform computations. This algorithm requires a total of $n(r_1 + r_2 + \cdots + r_h)$ operations. When n is a power of 2, $r_i = 2$ for every i, and we get the *radix-2* FFT algorithm requiring $n \log n$ operations (as shown in Section 3.2.2). Another situation of particular interest in the current chapter occurs when $n = 1 \times 2 \times \cdots \times m$, in which case the number of operations required is $O(nm^2)$.

9.14.3 A Star Algorithm for the FFT

Suppose we are given a sequence of n numbers $\{a_0, a_1, \ldots, a_{m!-1}\}$, stored in the $m!$ processors of $\mathcal{S}_m$, one element per processor. An algorithm is now presented that computes the FFT on the star interconnection network. In what follows, the phrase "rearrangement of elements over connection i" means that all of the processors of $\mathcal{S}_m$ adjacent through the connection i exchange their data.

Mapping the FFT to the Star.   Since $n = m!$, we can write

$$n = 1 \times 2 \times 3 \times 4 \times \cdots \times (m-1) \times m.$$

If we denote the ith factor by r_i and exclude the initial 1, then n can be written as

$$n = r_2 \times r_3 \times r_4 \times \cdots \times r_{m-1} \times r_m.$$

Let the input elements be arranged into an $r_2 \times r_3 \times \cdots \times r_m$ $(m-1)$-dimensional grid, and denote by DFT(k) the DFT of a sequence of length k. Then DFT($m!$) is obtained in $m-1$ steps by computing

$$
\begin{array}{ll}
r_2 \times r_3 \times \cdots \times r_{m-1} & \text{DFT}(r_m)'s \\
r_2 \times r_3 \times \cdots \times r_{m-2} \times r_m & \text{DFT}(r_{m-1})'s \\
\quad\vdots & \\
r_2 \times r_3 \times \cdots \times r_{m-i} \times r_{m-i+2} \times \cdots \times r_m & \text{DFT}(r_{m-i+1})'s \\
\quad\vdots & \\
r_2 \times r_4 \times \cdots \times r_m & \text{DFT}(r_3)'s \\
r_3 \times r_4 \times \cdots \times r_m & \text{DFT}(r_2)'s.
\end{array}
$$

In other words, during the ith step, $r_2 \times r_3 \times \cdots \times r_{m-i} \times r_{m-i+2} \times \cdots \times r_m$ DFTs (of sequences of length r_{m-i+1} each) are computed among elements that are adjacent over dimension $m-i$ of the grid. Now recall that the star possesses

$$
\begin{array}{ll}
r_2 \times r_3 \times \cdots \times r_{m-2} & \text{cycles of length } r_{m-1} \times r_m \\
r_2 \times r_3 \times \cdots \times r_{m-3} \times r_m & \text{cycles of length } r_{m-2} \times r_{m-1} \\
\quad\vdots & \\
r_2 \times r_3 \times \cdots \times r_{m-i-1} \times r_{m-i+2} \times \cdots \times r_m & \text{cycles of length } r_{m-i} \times r_{m-i+1} \\
\quad\vdots & \\
r_4 \times r_5 \times \cdots \times r_m & \text{cycles of length } r_2 \times r_3 \\
r_3 \times r_4 \times \cdots \times r_m & \text{cycles of length } r_2.
\end{array}
$$

We note that $\mathcal{S}_m$ possesses $r_2 \times r_3 \times \cdots \times r_{m-i-1} \times r_{m-i+2} \times \cdots \times r_m$ cycles, each of length $r_{m-i} \times r_{m-i+1}$, or $r_2 \times r_3 \times \cdots \times r_{m-i-1} \times r_{m-i} \times r_{m-i+2} \times \cdots \times r_m$ paths of length r_{m-i+1} each. Thus, the number and length of the paths match exactly the number and length of the DFTs required in the ith step of the computation.

However, in order to always have the appropriate elements in adjacent positions in the cycles of the star, a special initial arrangement of the elements is needed, and every Fourier transform step is separated from the next by a rearrangement of the elements. Thus, the ith step is followed by a rearrangement of the elements over connection $(m-i+1)$ of the star. If we imagine that the elements are arranged into an $r_2 \times r_3 \times \cdots \times r_m$ $(m-1)$-dimensional grid and are indexed by following successively dimensions 1, 2, $\ldots$, $m-1$, this rearrangement is needed at the end of the ith step in order to bring into adjacent processors of the star groups of r_{m-i}

elements that are adjacent over dimension $m - i - 1$ of the grid and that should participate in the same DFT computation in the $(i + 1)$st step. For example, in the two-dimensional case, the rearrangement corresponds to a change from columns to rows. In the next two sections, we show how, using the ordering described in Section 9.11.2, together with successive rearrangements, elements that participate in the same $\mathrm{DFT}(r_m - i + 1)$ during the ith step are brought together into processors of the star, forming a linear array.

9.14.4   Embedding a Grid into a Star

Let the $m!$ input elements be thought of as being organized into a $2 \times 3 \times \cdots \times m$ $(m - 1)$-dimensional grid following successively dimensions 1, 2, ..., $m - 1$. Further, assume that these elements are initially loaded into the processors of the star according to the $\prec$ ordering and then rearranged successively over connections 2, 3, ..., m. We now show that after rearrangement over connection i of the star, the i elements that are adjacent over dimension $i - 1$ of the grid reside in processors of the star that form a linear array.

We first establish a property of the $m!$ permutations (i.e., processor labels), arranged in an $(m - 1)$-dimensional grid. The permutations are first ordered according to $\prec$ and then are placed into the (conceptual) $2 \times 3 \times \cdots \times m$ grid following successively dimensions 1, 2, ..., $m - 1$. Thus, each permutation v is associated with one input element on the grid (the element held by processor P_v on the star). Because the ordering $\prec$ is used initially, the permutations associated with the i elements that are adjacent over dimension $i - 1$ of the grid can be obtained from each other as follows: Let $e_1 e_2 \ldots e_i \ldots e_m$ be the permutation associated with the last of the i elements. Then the permutation associated with the $(i - 1)$st element is obtained from the permutation associated with the ith element by exchanging the symbols in positions i and d_2, where d_l, $2 \leq l \leq i$, is the position of the lth smallest symbol among $e_1, e_2, \ldots, e_i$. In general, the permutation associated with the $(i - k)$th element, $1 \leq k \leq i - 1$, is obtained from the permutation associated with the $(i - k + 1)$st element by exchanging the symbols in positions i and d_{k+1}. In other words, the permutation associated with the $(i - k + 1)$st element has the kth smallest symbol among $e_1, e_2, \ldots, e_i$ in position i. This is a property of the $\prec$ ordering.

Example 9.15 Consider the labels of the processors of $\mathcal{S}_4$ (ordered according to $\prec$ as shown in Example 9.12). Let these labels be arranged into a $2 \times 3 \times 4$ three-dimensional grid, following successively dimensions 1, 2, and 3, as follows:

$$
\begin{array}{lll}
(1234 \quad 2134) & (1324 \quad 3124) & (2314 \quad 3214) \\
(1243 \quad 2143) & (1423 \quad 4123) & (2413 \quad 4213) \\
(1342 \quad 3142) & (1432 \quad 4132) & (3412 \quad 4312) \\
(2341 \quad 3241) & (2431 \quad 4231) & (3421 \quad 4321).
\end{array}
$$

Now take the three permutations 1342, 1432, and 3412, adjacent over dimension 2. The second of these (i.e., 1432) can be obtained from the third (i.e., 3412) by exchanging the symbol in position 3 (i.e., 1) with the second smallest symbol among 3, 4, and 1 (i.e., 3). □

Now suppose that the elements held by the star processors are rearranged over connections 2, 3, ..., i. As a result, the permutation $e_1 e_2 \ldots e_i \ldots e_m$ (associated with some element) is transformed into $e_i e_1 \ldots e_{i-1} e_{i+1} \ldots e_m$. Therefore, among the i elements that are adjacent over dimension $i - 1$ of the grid, the permutation associated with the $(i-k)$th element, $1 \le k \le i-1$, is obtained from the permutation associated with the $(i - k + 1)$st element by exchanging the symbols in positions 1 and d_{k+1}. However, we know from Section 9.14.1 that the permutations obtained by visiting successively connections $d_2, d_3, \ldots, d_i$ of the star are adjacent and form the cycles which are embedded in a substar $\mathcal{S}_i$ of $\mathcal{S}_m$. In other words, after the ith rearrangement of the elements in the star, elements that are adjacent over dimension $i - 1$ of the grid reside in processors forming a linear array.

Example 9.16 Let us consider again the three processors whose labels are 1342, 1432, and 3412. These processors hold elements that are adjacent over dimension 2 of the grid. After rearrangement over connections 2 and 3, these elements are now held by the processors whose labels are 4132, 3142, and 1342, respectively. The second of these permutations is obtained from the third by exchanging the first and second symbols (i.e., by visiting connection d_2), and the first is obtained from the second by exchanging the first and third symbols (i.e., by visiting connection d_3). The three processors whose labels are 4132, 3142, and 1342 form a linear array in $\mathcal{S}_3(2)$, as can be verified in Fig. 9.15(d). □

9.14.5 Initial Ordering and Rearrangements

Initially, we want elements that are adjacent over dimension $m - 1$ of the grid to reside in processors forming a linear array. This can be done if we first rearrange the elements, ordered according to the $\prec$ order, over connections 2, 3, ..., m of the star. If an element is initially stored in the processor labeled with the permutation $e_1 e_2 \ldots e_m$, then after the $m-1$ rearrangements, it is stored in the processor labeled with the permutation $e_m e_1 \ldots e_i \ldots e_{m-1}$. In other words, the processor whose label is $e_m e_1 \ldots e_i \ldots e_{m-1}$ holds the input element a_k, where $k = rank(e_1 e_2 \ldots e_i \ldots e_m)$. Therefore, the label of each processor is cyclically shifted to the left once, before applying the mapping function to it.

Subsequently, the elements are rearranged over connections m, $m - 1$, ..., 2 during the execution of the algorithm. Therefore, when the algorithm terminates, each processor P_u, where $u = e_1 e_2 \ldots e_i \ldots e_m$, contains the element b_j, where $j = rank(e_1 e_2 \ldots e_i \ldots e_m)$.

Example 9.17 For $m = 4$, the initial ordering of the (labels of the) processors of S_4 is as follows (in row-major order), along with the index of the input element that each processor contains:

$$
\begin{array}{cccccc}
4123 & 4213 & 4132 & 4312 & 4231 & 4321 \\
(0) & (1) & (2) & (3) & (4) & (5) \\[6pt]
3124 & 3214 & 3142 & 3412 & 3241 & 3421 \\
(6) & (7) & (8) & (9) & (10) & (11) \\[6pt]
2134 & 2314 & 2143 & 2413 & 2341 & 2431 \\
(12) & (13) & (14) & (15) & (16) & (17) \\[6pt]
1234 & 1324 & 1243 & 1423 & 1342 & 1432 \\
(18) & (19) & (20) & (21) & (22) & (23).
\end{array}
$$

This is illustrated in Fig. 9.17(a), in which the index beside each processor is that of the input element it contains.

The first step computes DFT(4)'s over the elements connected by thick lines. At the end of this step, the elements are rearranged over connection 4 (along the links shown in dashed lines in Fig. 9.17(b)). The second step computes DFT(3)'s over the elements connected by thick lines in Fig. 9.17(b) and then rearranges the elements over connection 3 (along the links shown in dashed lines in Fig. 9.17(c)).

The third step computes DFT(2)'s over the elements connected by thick lines in Fig. 9.17(c). The final distribution of the elements is shown in Fig. 9.17(d) (after rearrangement, at the end of the third step, over connection 2, shown in dashed lines).

The labels of the processors of S_4, along with the index of the element that each processor contains at the end of the computation, are given in Example 9.12. $\square$

9.14.6   The Algorithm

We are now ready to provide a formal statement of the algorithm for computing the FFT on the star. The algorithm consists of $m - 1$ steps. Each step views S_m as a set of disjoint cycles of different lengths, as follows:

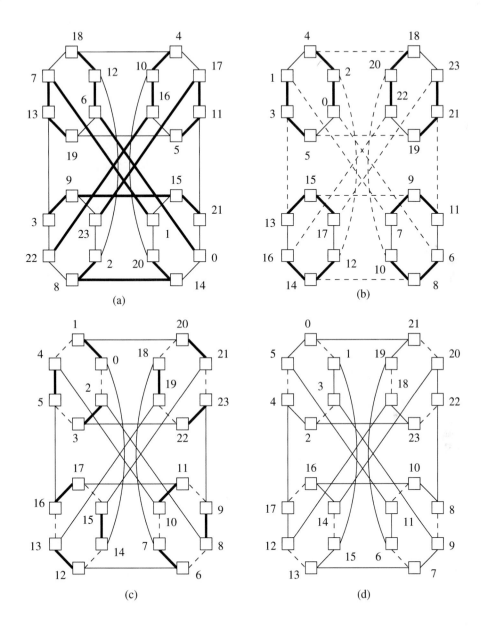

Figure 9.17: Computing the FFT on the star: (a) Initial ordering of the input elements and computation of DFT(4)'s; (b) Rearrangement and computation of DFT(3)'s; (c) Rearrangement an computation of DFT(2)'s; (d) Final distribution of elements.

Step	Number of Cycles	Length of Cycle
1	$(m-2)!$	$(m-1) \times m$
2	$(m-3)! \times m$	$(m-2) \times (m-1)$
3	$(m-4)! \times (m-1) \times m$	$(m-3) \times (m-2)$
$\vdots$	$\vdots$	$\vdots$
i	$(m-i-1)! \times (m-i+2) \times \cdots \times m$	$(m-i) \times (m-i+1)$
$\vdots$	$\vdots$	$\vdots$
$m-2$	$4 \times 5 \times \cdots \times (m-1) \times m$	2×3
$m-1$	$3 \times 4 \times \cdots \times (m-1) \times m$	1×2

In Step i, DFT$(m-i+1)$'s are computed among $m-i+1$ adjacent processors, on the disjoint cycles of the star, starting in each cycle from the processor whose label is the cycle's initial permutation. Note that in Step i, $m-i$ sets of $m-i+1$ adjacent processors form a cycle of length $(m-i) \times (m-i+1)$. The algorithm is given next as algorithm STAR FFT. In it, we assume that the input elements have been loaded into the processors according to the initial arrangement.

Algorithm STAR FFT (m)

    for $i = 1$ to $m-1$ **do**
        (1) Perform DFT$(m-i+1)$'s
        (2) Multiply each element locally with the appropriate coefficient
        (3) Rearrange the elements over connection $(m-i+1)$
    end for. ∎

9.14.7 The Fourier Transform on a Linear Array

The only detail left is how the DFTs are computed on linear arrays of processors, as required by algorithm STAR FFT. An algorithm for this purpose is now described. One can view the DFT as the evaluation of the polynomial

$$a_0 + a_1 x + a_2 x^2 + \cdots + a_{n-1} x^{n-1}$$

at $x = 1, \omega_n, \omega_n^2, \ldots, \omega_n^{n-1}$. It is helpful here to use *Horner's rule* to write the polynomial as

$$a_0 + x(a_1 + \cdots + x(a_{n-3} + x(a_{n-2} + x a_{n-1})) \ldots).$$

The computation can now be performed on a linear array of n (multiply-and-add) processors, as shown in Fig. 9.18(a). Initially, each processor holds one element of the input sequence. The behavior of a typical processor is shown in Fig. 9.18(b). Note that the leftmost processor receives no input from the left; it produces the two sequences $\{a_{n-1}, a_{n-1}, \ldots, a_{n-1}\}$ and $\{1, \omega_n, \ldots, \omega_n^{n-1}\}$. The rightmost processor produces one sequence of outputs, namely, $\{b_0, b_1, \ldots, b_{n-1}\}$—that is, the DFT

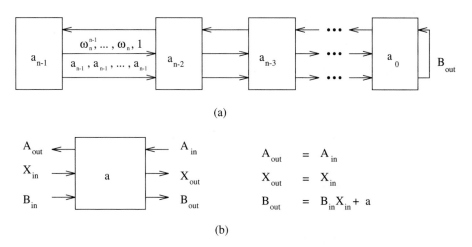

(a)

(b)

Figure 9.18: Computing the DFT on a linear array of processors: (a) Movement of data; (b) Behavior of a typical processor.

of the input sequence. The elements of this output sequence are computed in a pipelined fashion, in a total of $O(n)$ steps. Note that the outputs which emerge from the rightmost processor are fed back into the array and stored one element per processor, in preparation for the next iteration of algorithm STAR FFT (in which they are used as the input sequence).

Analysis. The linear array algorithm used to compute the DFT requires $O(k)$ basic operations for an input sequence of length k. Therefore, algorithm STAR FFT executes $r_m + r_{m-1} + \cdots + r_3 + r_2$ such operations. Given that $r_i \leq m$, for $2 \leq i \leq m$, the algorithm has a running time of $t(n) = O(m^2)$ for an input sequence of length $n = m!$. Since $p(n) = n$, the algorithm's cost is $c(n) = O(nm^2)$. As shown in Section 9.14.2, the running time of the sequential algorithm is $n(2+3+\cdots+m) = O(nm^2)$ when $n = 2 \times 3 \times \cdots \times m$. Therefore, algorithm STAR FFT has an optimal cost with respect to the sequential algorithm on which it is based.

9.15 PROBLEMS

9.1 Assume that $N = 2^g$ data are stored in the processors of a hypercube, one element per processor. Thus, datum x_i is stored in P_i, $0 \leq i \leq 2^g - 1$. An algorithmic technique of wide applicability when solving problems on the hypercube is known as the DESCEND paradigm. It consists of g iterations: During the jth iteration, $0 \leq j \leq g-1$, a basic operation is performed on pairs of data whose indices differ by 2^j. Let OPERATION (P_i, P_l) be a sequence of instructions applied to data in processors P_i and P_l. Also, let $i_{g-1}i_{g-2}\ldots i_1i_0$

be the binary representation of index i. The general DESCEND paradigm is as follows:

DESCEND

      for $j = g - 1$ **downto** 0 **do**
        for $i = 0$ **to** $2^g - 1$ **do in parallel**
          if $i_j = 0$
          then OPERATION (P_i, P_{i+2^j})
          end if
        end for
      end for. ■

If OPERATION (P_i, P_{i+2^j}) requires constant time, then DESCEND runs in $O(\log N)$ time. A dual to the DESCEND paradigm is the ASCEND paradigm, in which j in the outer loop varies from 0 to $g - 1$.

(a) Show how the DESCEND paradigm can be used to obtain an algorithm that computes the sum of all the x_i and places it in P_0.

(b) Use either of the two paradigms (ASCEND or DESCEND) to broadcast the datum held by one processor (for example, processor P_k) to all other processors.

(c) Suggest other problems that can be solved using these paradigms.

9.2 Let A and B be sorted sequences of numbers stored in a hypercube with $N = 2^g$ processors, one element per processor, such that A resides in P_0, P_1, ..., $P_{2^{g-1}-1}$ and B resides in $P_{2^{g-1}}$, $P_{2^{g-1}+1}$, ..., P_{2^g-1}. Consider the following algorithm, in which operation "compare-exchange (P_k, P_l)" is as defined in Problem 7.4:

Algorithm HYPERCUBE MYSTERY (A, B)

    Step 1: for $j = 0$ **to** $g - 2$ **do**
        for $i = 0$ **to** $2^{g-1} - 1$ **do in parallel**
          P_i sends its datum to $P_{i(j)}$
        end for
      end for
    Step 2: for $j = g - 1$ **downto** 0 **do**
        for $i = 0$ **to** $2^g - 1$ **do in parallel**
          if $i_j = 0$
          then compare-exchange $(P_i, P_{i(j)})$
          end if
        end for
      end for. ■

What does this algorithm do?

9.3 Compare Step 3 of algorithm HYPERCUBE MATRIX MULTIPLICATION to algorithm HYPERCUBE PREFIX SUMS of Example 2.5, stating their similarities and differences.

9.4 Show how algorithm HYPERCUBE MATRIX MULTIPLICATION can be modified to have a cost of $O(n^3)$.

9.5 Compare the running time and cost of algorithm HYPERCUBE MATRIX TRANSPOSE to the running time and cost of the algorithm in Problem 8.11.

9.6 Compare the performance of algorithm HYPERCUBE CONNECTED COMPONENTS to that of algorithm PRAM CONNECTED COMPONENTS.

9.7 Step 3 of algorithm HYPERCUBE MATRIX INVERSION requires a hypercube algorithm that uses n^2 processors to multiply an $n \times n$ matrix by an $n \times 1$ vector in $O(\log n)$ time. Provide the details of such an algorithm.

9.8 Show how Step 4 of algorithm HYPERCUBE MATRIX INVERSION is implemented.

9.9 Design an algorithm for sorting a sequence of numbers on the hypercube.

9.10 Design an algorithm for computing the FFT of a sequence of numbers on the hypercube.

9.11 Let a set of n numbers be distributed arbitrarily among the N processors of a hypercube such that each processor holds n/N numbers. Show that the kth smallest number can be found in $O((n/N)\log^{1/2} N + \log^2 N \log(n/N))$ time.

9.12 Design an algorithm for multiplying two $n \times n$ matrices on a cube-connected cycles interconnection network.

9.13 Design an algorithm for sorting a sequence of numbers, stored one per processor, on a de Bruijn interconnection network.

9.14 Show how two $n \times n$ matrices can be multiplied in $O(1)$ time on the PRAM.

9.15 Consider the following *greedy* algorithm for computing the MST of a weighted, undirected graph with n vertices. Beginning with an arbitrarily chosen vertex (v_0, for example), each iteration adds one vertex and an associated edge to the tree. If v_i is a vertex not yet in the tree, let $s(v_i)$ denote a vertex already in the tree that is closest to v_i. The algorithm therefore consists of two steps:

Step 1: Include v_0 in the MST, and let $s(v_i) = v_0$ for $i = 1, 2, \ldots, n-1$.

Step 2: Repeat the following steps, as long as there are vertices not yet in the MST:

(2.1) Include in the tree the closest vertex not yet in the tree; that is, for all $v_i \notin$ MST, find the edge $(v_i, s(v_i))$ for which $w_{v_i,s(v_i)}$ is smallest, and add it to the tree.

(2.2) For all $v_i \notin$ MST, update $s(v_i)$; that is, assuming that v_j was the most recently added vertex to the tree, $s(v_i)$ is updated by determining the smaller of $w_{v_i,s(v_i)}$ and w_{v_i,v_j}. ∎

Derive a parallel implementation of this algorithm, and analyze its running time and cost.

9.16 Derive a parallel algorithm based on the following approach to computing the MST of a weighted, undirected graph G with n vertices and m edges:

Step 1: The edges of G are sorted in order of increasing weight.

Step 2: The $n-1$ edges with smallest weight *that do not include a cycle* are selected as the edges of the MST. ∎

9.17 Consider the following algorithm for computing the MST of a weighted, undirected graph G with n vertices:

Step 1: for $i = 0$ **to** $n-1$ **do**
    (1.1) Determine, for vertex v_i, its closest neighbor v_j
    (1.2) Add the edge (v_i, v_j) to MST
    end for
Step 2: (2.1) $k \leftarrow$ number of distinct edges added to MST in Step 1
    (2.2) Each collection of edges added to MST in Step 1
        and forming a connected component
        is called a subtree of MST
Step 3: while $k < n-1$ **do**
    (3.1) Let $T_1, T_2, \ldots, T_m$ be the distinct subtrees formed so far
    (3.2) **for** $i = 1$ **to** m **do**
        (i) Among all edges adjacent to vertices in T_i,
            find the edge of smallest weight
            (connecting T_i to another subtree—for example, T_j)
        (ii) Add the edge found in (a) to MST
        (iii) Merge T_i and T_j into one subtree
        end for
    (3.3) $k \leftarrow k +$ number of distinct edges added to MST in (3.2)
    end while. ∎

Applying this algorithm to the graph of Fig. 9.19, we get the following edges after Step 1: $(v_0, v_1), (v_2, v_0), (v_3, v_4)$, and (v_5, v_3). (Ties are broken by selecting the vertex with smallest index as v_j.) These form two subtrees $T_1 = \{(v_0, v_1), (v_2, v_0)\}$ and $T_2 = \{(v_3, v_4), (v_5, v_3)\}$. Since $k = 4$, we execute Step 3

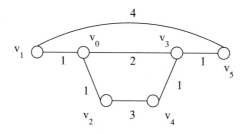

Figure 9.19: An undirected, weighted graph.

and find that the edge of smallest weight connecting T_1 and T_2 is (v_0, v_3). Design a parallel algorithm based on this approach, and analyze its performance.

9.18 Let A be an $n \times n$ nonsingular matrix, and assume that a nonsingular lower triangular matrix L and a nonsingular upper triangular matrix U exist such that $A = LU$. This is called an *LU-decomposition* of A. (See Problem 8.30.) Design a parallel algorithm for computing L and U, and analyze its running time and cost. (*Hint*: Partition A, L, and U into $(n/2) \times (n/2)$ submatrices such that

$$\left(\begin{array}{cc} A_{11} & A_{12} \\ A_{21} & A_{22} \end{array} \right) = \left(\begin{array}{cc} L_{11} & Z \\ L_{12} & L_{22} \end{array} \right) \left(\begin{array}{cc} U_{11} & U_{12} \\ Z & U_{22} \end{array} \right),$$

where Z is an $(n/2) \times (n/2)$ zero matrix.)

9.19 Let A be an $n \times n$ nonsingular matrix. It is desired to compute two matrices Q and R such that $A = QR$, where Q is an *orthogonal* matrix (i.e., $Q^T Q = QQ^T = I$) and R is a nonsingular upper triangular matrix. Develop a parallel algorithm for computing Q and R, and analyze its running time and cost. (*Hint*: Begin by computing an LU-decomposition, as defined in Problem 9.18, of $A^T A$.)

9.20 A set of rows of an $m \times n$ matrix A whose indices are given by the sequence $\{r(1), r(2), \ldots, r(l)\}$ are said to be *linearly dependent* if coefficients d_1, d_2, $\ldots$, d_l (not all equal to 0) can be found such that

$$d_1 a_{r(1)j} + d_2 a_{r(2)j} + \cdots + d_l a_{r(l)j} = 0, \quad \text{for } 1 \le j \le n;$$

otherwise, the rows are said to be *linearly independent*. The *rank* of a nonzero $m \times n$ matrix, denoted $rank(A)$, is the size of the largest set of linearly independent rows. Two alternative definitions of the rank are as follows:

(a) $rank(A)$ = number of nonzero eigenvalues of AA^T.

(b) $rank(A)$ = largest k for which $h_k \neq 0$ in the characteristic polynomial of AA^T.

Design a parallel algorithm for computing $rank(A)$ according to each of these two definitions.

9.21 Given l processors P_i, $0 \leq i \leq l - 1$, on a parallel computer, and N data distributed arbitrarily among the l processors, define $load(P_i)$ to be the number of elements stored in P_i. In the problem *of load balancing*, it is required to balance the load among the processors such that

$$\max_{0 \leq i,j \leq l-1} (load(P_i) - load(P_j)) \leq 1.$$

Let M and μ be the maximum and minimum loads, respectively. Clearly, $0 \leq \mu \leq M \leq N$. The quantity $M - \mu$ is called the *maximum load difference*. When the load is balanced, the maximum load difference is at most 1. Describe an algorithm for load balancing on a hypercube with l processors whose running time is $O(M \log^{1/2} l + \log^2 l)$.

9.22 Prove that the diameter of the star interconnection network $\mathcal{S}_m$ is $\lfloor 3(m-1)/2 \rfloor$.

9.23 Suppose that (the labels of) all the processors in $\mathcal{S}_m$ are arranged into an $m \times (m-1)!$ array in row-major order (in terms of the processor ordering $\prec$ of Section 9.11.2), as illustrated in Example 9.12 for $m = 4$. Show that:

(a) Row i of this array is $\mathcal{S}_{m-1}(i)$.

(b) All processors in the same column have the same *rank* in their respective $\mathcal{S}_{m-1}$'s.

9.24 Suppose that the first and mth symbols of each processor label are exchanged in the $m \times (m-1)!$ array of Problem 9.23, representing $\mathcal{S}_m$. Show that in the resulting $m \times (m-1)!$ array, the processors in each column are connected to form a linear array.

9.25 Consider the $m \times (m-1)!$ array of Problem 9.23, and suppose that it is required to perform a linear array operation on each of its columns (such as, for example, sorting the data held by the processors in the column, using algorithm LINEAR ARRAY TRANSPOSITION SORT). This can be accomplished as follows:

Step 1: Copy the datum in each P_u, where $u = i\sigma_{m-2}j$, to P_v, where $v = j\sigma_{m-2}i$.

Step 2: In the resulting $m \times (m-1)!$ array, perform a linear array operation on the processors of each column. (They form a linear array by the result in Problem 9.24.)

Step 3: Copy the datum in each P_v, where $v = j\sigma_{m-2}i$, back into P_u, where $u = i\sigma_{m-2}j$. ∎

Describe an algorithm that takes advantage of the transformations in Steps 1 and 3 to sort a sequence of numbers on $\mathcal{S}_m$, viewed as an $m \times (m-1)!$ array.

9.26 Let $P_{(0)}, P_{(1)}, \ldots, P_{(m!-1)}$ be the processors of $\mathcal{S}_m$, indexed according to the ordering of processors $\prec$ defined in Section 9.11.2. Each processor $P_{(i)}$ holds a datum x_i. It is required to reverse the sequence of data such that x_i is stored in $P_{(m!-1-i)}$. Show how this can be done.

9.27 Repeat Problem 9.23 for the pancake interconnection network defined in Problem 2.28.

9.28 Recursive doubling is used by processor P_v, where $v = j\sigma_{m-2}i$, in Step 1 of algorithm STAR BROADCASTING to distribute the datum D to $m-2$ processors P_u, where $u = k\sigma_{m-2}i$ such that $1 \leq k \leq m$ and $k \neq i, j$. For example, if $m = 5$ and $v = 12345$, then recursive doubling consists of the following two iterations (equivalently, two levels of recursion):

(a) In the first iteration, P_{12345} sends D to P_{32145}, where 3 is the middle symbol in 12345.

(b) In the second iteration, P_{12345} and P_{32145} simultaneously send D to P_{21345} and P_{42135}, respectively.

Give a formal description of recursive doubling (as used in Step 1 of algorithm STAR BROADCASTING) for any value of m.

9.29 Show how broadcasting in the star interconnection network can be performed by simulating a permutation circuit.

9.30 Analyze the following algorithm for broadcasting on $\mathcal{S}_m$: Let a processor in $\mathcal{S}_{m-1}(i)$ hold a datum D that it is to broadcast. It begins by broadcasting the datum recursively to all processors in $\mathcal{S}_{m-1}(i)$. Algorithm STAR COPY is now used to copy D from each processor in $\mathcal{S}_m(i)$ to each processor in $\mathcal{S}_{m-1}(i+1)$. Recursive doubling and algorithm STAR GROUP COPY are now used to propagate D to all the remaining processors of $\mathcal{S}_m$.

9.31 The following is yet another broadcasting algorithm for $\mathcal{S}_m$. Again, let a processor in $\mathcal{S}_{m-1}(i)$ hold a datum D that it is to broadcast. It copies the datum to a processor in $\mathcal{S}_{m-1}(j)$, for some $j \neq i$. Recursive doubling is now used to copy D to one processor in each $\mathcal{S}_{m-1}(k)$, $k = 1, 2, \ldots, m$, $k \neq i, j$. The algorithm is now applied recursively to each $\mathcal{S}_{m-1}$ to complete the broadcast. Analyze this algorithm's running time.

9.32 Derive a lower bound on the number of elementary steps required to broadcast a datum held by one processor to all other processors on the star interconnection network $\mathcal{S}_m$.

9.33 Suppose that in $\mathcal{S}_m$ some processors are marked. Define the rank of a marked processor as the number of marked processors that precede it in the ordering $\prec$ of Section 9.11.2. Show how this rank can be computed.

9.34 In $\mathcal{S}_m$ is a subset of k processors $l_1, l_2, \ldots, l_k$ marked as *leaders*, with $l_i \prec l_j$ if $i < j$ and $k \leq m!$. Each leader l_i holds a datum that it is to distribute to all higher numbered processors (in terms of the processor ordering $\prec$), up to, but not including, the next leader l_{i+1} (if the latter exists). Show how this operation (called *interval broadcasting* in Section 4.7) can be performed.

9.35 Let A and B be two sorted sequences of numbers stored in two groups of $\mathcal{S}_{m-1}$'s (in the star interconnection network $\mathcal{S}_m$), one number per processor, as follows:

$$\text{Group 1 (storing } A)\text{:} \quad \mathcal{S}_{m-1}(i), \ \mathcal{S}_{m-1}(i+1), \ \ldots, \ \mathcal{S}_{m-1}(j)$$
$$\text{Group 2 (storing } B)\text{:} \quad \mathcal{S}_{m-1}(k), \ \mathcal{S}_{m-1}(k+1), \ \ldots, \ \mathcal{S}_{m-1}(l).$$

Here, $i \leq j < k \leq l$. We assume that A is sorted in nondecreasing order, that B is sorted in nonincreasing order, and that *Group 1* and *Group 2* do not necessarily contain the same number of $\mathcal{S}_{m-1}$'s. Show how A and B can be merged into a sequence C, sorted in either nondecreasing or nonincreasing order, and stored in a group of $\mathcal{S}_{m-1}$'s (one number per processor) as follows:

$$\mathcal{S}_{m-1}(i), \mathcal{S}_{m-1}(i+1), \ldots, \mathcal{S}_{m-1}(j), \mathcal{S}_{m-1}(k), \mathcal{S}_{m-1}(k+1), \ldots, \mathcal{S}_{m-1}(l).$$

Analyze your algorithm.

9.36 Use the algorithms developed in Problems 9.34 and 9.35 to perform GPC (defined in Section 4.9) on a star interconnection network.

9.37 Let a set of $m!$ points in the plane be stored in $\mathcal{S}_m$, one point per processor. It is required to compute the convex hull of this set. Use the divide-and-conquer approach to derive an algorithm for computing the convex hull on the star interconnection network.

9.38 Suppose that the processors of $\mathcal{S}_m$ have been indexed $P_{(0)}, P_{(1)}, \ldots, P_{(m!-1)}$, according to the ordering $\prec$ of Section 9.11.2. Each processor $P_{(i)}$ holds a datum x_i. Now assume that k of the data are "active," where k is not necessarily known and $0 \leq k \leq m!$. The rank of an "active" element x_i is defined as the number of "active" elements x_j such that $j < i$. It is required to *compress* (or *concentrate*) the "active" elements so that they move to processors $P_{(0)}$, $P_{(1)}, \ldots, P_{(k-1)}$ such that "active" element x_i moves to $P_{(j)}$, where j is the rank of x_i. Show that concentration can be performed on $\mathcal{S}_m$ in $O(m^2)$ time.

9.39 Let $P_{(0)}$, $P_{(1)}$, ..., $P_{(m!-1)}$ be the processors of $\mathcal{S}_m$, indexed according to the $\prec$ ordering. For some k, $0 \leq k \leq m! - 1$, the first k processors are "active": Processor $P_{(i)}$, $0 \leq i \leq k - 1$, holds a distinct integer x_i such that $0 \leq x_i \leq m! - 1$. It is required to *distribute* the x_i as follows: Integer x_i is to be sent to processor $P_{(x_i)}$. Show how this operation can be performed on $\mathcal{S}_m$.

9.40 Let $P_{(0)}$, $P_{(1)}$, ..., $P_{(m!-1)}$ be the processors of $\mathcal{S}_m$, indexed according to the $\prec$ ordering. Some of the processors are "active." Each "active" processor $P_{(i)}$ holds a distinct integer x_i, where $0 \leq x_i \leq m! - 1$. It is required to *permute* the x_i as follows: Integer x_i is to be sent to processor $P_{(x_i)}$. Show how this operation can be performed on $\mathcal{S}_m$.

9.41 Let $P_{(0)}$, $P_{(1)}$, ..., $P_{(m!-1)}$ be the processors of $\mathcal{S}_m$, indexed according to the $\prec$ ordering, with $P_{(i)}$ holding a datum x_i. It is required to perform a *cyclic shift* of the data. Specifically, given some integer s, $P_{(i)}$ is to send x_i to $P_{(j)}$, where $j = i + s \bmod m!$, simultaneously for all i, $0 \leq i \leq m! - 1$. Show that this operation can be performed on $\mathcal{S}_m$ in $O(m^2)$ time. (Note that if $s > 0$, the cyclic shift is to the right, while $s < 0$ implies a cyclic shift to the left.)

9.42 Consider again Problem 9.21 for the star interconnection network. When solving the load-balancing problem on $\mathcal{S}_m$, in addition to the requirement that the maximum load difference be no more than 1, the following condition must be satisfied as well: If $P_i \prec P_j$, then $load(P_i) \geq load(P_j)$. Design an algorithm for load balancing on $\mathcal{S}_m$ that runs in $O(mM + m^3 \log m)$ time, where M is the maximum load among the processors in the network.

9.43 Let a set of N numbers be distributed arbitrarily among the processors of $\mathcal{S}_m$ such that each processor holds $\lceil N/m! \rceil$ numbers, where $N \geq m!$. It is required to find the kth smallest of the set of numbers. Show how this can be done in $O((N/(m - 1)!) + (\log(N/m!))m^3 \log m)$ time.

9.44 A *bubblesort interconnection network* on m symbols, denoted by $\mathcal{B}_m$, is represented by an undirected graph with $m!$ vertices, where each vertex P_v is a processor. The *label* v of a processor is a distinct permutation of the m symbols $\{1, 2, ..., m\}$. Two processors P_u and P_v are directly connected by a link if u can be obtained from v by exchanging two adjacent symbols of v. Thus, for $m = 4$, P_{2134} and P_{2314} are connected. It should be clear that the bubblesort network is defined in a way very similar to the way the star and pancake networks are defined, the three networks being distinguished from one another by the way their processors are connected.

(a) What are the degree and diameter of $\mathcal{B}_m$?

(b) Design an algorithm for broadcasting a datum from one processor to all other processors of $\mathcal{B}_m$.

9.45 The value of the polynomial

$$b_0 + b_1 x + \cdots + b_{n-2} x^{n-2} + b_{n-1} x^{n-1}$$

at $x = (\omega^{-1})^k$ is given by

$$a_k = \frac{1}{n} \sum_{j=0}^{n-1} b_j (\omega^{-1})^{jk} \quad \text{for } k = 0, 1, \ldots, n-1.$$

The sequence $\{a_0, a_1, \ldots, a_{n-1}\}$ is the *inverse* DFT of $\{b_0, b_1, \ldots, b_{n-1}\}$. Show how an algorithm for computing the FFT can be modified to compute the inverse DFT.

9.46 Suppose that we want to multiply the two polynomials

$$f(x) = \sum_{j=0}^{n-1} a_j x^j \quad \text{and} \quad g(x) = \sum_{k=0}^{n-1} d_k x^k$$

to obtain the product polynomial $h = fg$. Show how efficient algorithms for computing the FFT and inverse DFT can be used to obtain the coefficients of h. (*Hint*: Let N be the smallest integer that is a power of 2 and is greater than $2n - 1$. Begin by padding each of the two sequences $\{a_0, a_1, \ldots, a_{n-1}\}$ and $\{d_0, d_1, \ldots, d_{n-1}\}$ with $N - n$ 0's and computing its FFT.)

9.47 Algorithm STAR FFT requires the input sequence to have size $m!$. Show how the algorithm can be modified to run for input sequences of any length.

9.48 Design algorithms for performing the following three operations on a star interconnection network:

(**a**) Simultaneous broadcasting of a message from *every* processor to all other processors.

(**b**) Sending a *distinct* message from a *single* processor to each one of the remaining processors.

(**c**) Sending a *distinct* message from *every* processor to each one of the remaining processors.

The algorithms are to work under the usual assumption whereby, in one time unit, a processor can send a message of fixed length over one of its links to a neighbor and at the same time receive a message of fixed length from one of its neighbors.

9.49 Modify the algorithms in Problem 9.48 to work under the following assumption: In one time unit, a processor can send (receive) messages of fixed length to (from) all of its neighbors simultaneously.

9.16 BIBLIOGRAPHICAL REMARKS

The hypercube and hypercubelike models were among the earliest interconnection networks proposed for parallel computation. The perfect shuffle was known since the early 1950s (as were the various circuits based on it, such as, for example, the butterfly and omega circuits); see Beneš [96], Clos [161], Pease [483, 484], and Stone [590]. Early references to the hypercube can be found in Pease [485] and Schwartz [556]. The model's popularity is well documented, both in theoretical works (see, for example, Akl [18, 21], Akl and Lyons [42], Das et al. [193], Ferreira [227], Leighton [367], and Ranka and Sahni [526]) and in publications that are more practically oriented (see, for example, Blelloch [112], Fox et al. [240], Hatcher and Quinn [289], Hillis [294], Seitz [558, 559], and Trew and Wilson [614]).

A number of algorithms for matrix multiplication on the hypercube, together with their applications, are presented in Dekel et al. [197]. In particular, the algorithm of Section 9.1.3 was first proposed in Dekel et al. [197]. References to, and descriptions of, other parallel algorithms for matrix multiplication and their applications to graph-theoretic and numerical problems, can be found in Akl [21], Leighton [367], Reif [533], and Ullman [615].

The problem of computing the transpose of a matrix efficiently on various models of parallel computation is studied in Akl [21], Bertsekas and Tsitsiklis [99], and Kumar et al. [343]. Parallel algorithms for matrix inversion are described in Csanky [190] and Pease [483]. Algorithm HYPERCUBE EIGENVALUES first appeared in Akl [21]. Original algorithms for the cube-connected cycles and de Bruijn networks are given in Preparata and Vuillemin [502] and Samatham and Pradhan [545, 546], respectively.

The star interconnection network was proposed by Akers et al. [11] as an alternative to the hypercube. Besides its smaller degree and diameter, other attractive properties of the star, compared with the hypercube, are its rich structure and its symmetry properties, as well as many fault tolerance characteristics, as shown, for example, in Akers et al. [11], Akers and Krishnamurthy [12, 13], Dietzfelbinger et al. [205], and Sur and Srimani [603].

In fact, the star interconnection network belongs to a large class of graphs called *Cayley graphs*. Given a set of generators for a finite group $\mathcal{G}$, the Cayley graph with respect to $\mathcal{G}$ is defined in Akers and Krishnamurthy [13] as follows: The vertices of the graph correspond to the elements of the group $\mathcal{G}$, and there is an edge (a, b) for $a, b \in \mathcal{S}$ if and only if there is a generator γ such that $a\gamma = b$. If the set of generators is closed under inversion, then the resulting graph is undirected. Now let $\mathcal{G}_m$ be a symmetric group on m symbols, and let V_m be the set of all $m!$ permutations of symbols $1, 2, \ldots, m$. A star interconnection network on m symbols,

$\mathcal{S}_m = (V_m, E(\mathcal{S}_m))$, is a Cayley graph with generators $\rho_i = i23\ldots(i-1)1(i+1)\ldots n, 2 \le i \le m$. Similarly, a pancake interconnection network on m symbols, $\mathcal{P}_m = (V_m, E(\mathcal{P}_m))$, is a Cayley graph with generators $\kappa_i = i(i-1)\ldots 321(i+1)(i+2)\ldots n, 2 \le i \le m$. Several properties of the star, as well as algorithms for solving a variety of problems on it, are described in Akl et al. [33, 49, 50], Akl and Qiu [47, 48], Fragopoulou [243], Fragopoulou and Akl [244, 245, 246, 247, 248, 249], Fragopoulou et al. [250], Jwo et al. [319], Menn and Somani [420], Nigam et al. [443], Qiu [507], Qiu and Akl [508, 509], and Qiu et al. [510, 511, 512, 513]. Generalizations of the star interconnection network are proposed in Chiang and Chen [152] and the references therein. The algorithm of Section 9.14.7 for computing the discrete Fourier transform on a linear array was originally presented in Zhang and Yun [648].

Chapter 10

Models Using Buses

As mentioned in Chapter 8, the mesh of processors is one of the most attractive models of computation in theory and in practice. Its large diameter, however, seems to limit its usefulness in most applications. This problem is somewhat mitigated, but by no means solved, through the addition of *wraparound connections* linking the rightmost processor in each row to the leftmost and the topmost processor in each column to the bottommost. Traversing a wraparound link is assumed to take as much time as traversing a standard mesh link. Thus, a datum can go from one corner of the mesh to the opposite corner in two constant time "hops." Unfortunately, on an $N^{1/2} \times N^{1/2}$ mesh, it still takes $d = N^{1/2} - 1$ "hops" to go from the corner processor $P(0,0)$ to the central processor $P(d/2, d/2)$. This means that the addition of wraparound connections reduces the mesh's diameter only by a factor of one-half.

Effective solutions to the diameter problem are described in Chapters 8 and 9. Thus, the mesh-of-trees model is obtained by replacing the standard mesh links with tree connections. Alternatively, the mesh itself may be abandoned altogether and a different topology used, such as the hypercube, for example. There are, however, at least two difficulties with these approaches:

1. Architectures based on such models are not easily extended to accommodate a larger number of processors. For example, in the hypercube, the neighbors of *each* of the existing processors need to be updated when the new processors are included.

2. The models have links whose lengths grow with the number of processors. Their diameters are small (typically logarithmic in the number of processors), provided that the propagation time along a link is assumed to be constant, *regardless of the length of the link.* In the absence of this assumption, the diameters are significantly larger.

By contrast, the mesh does not suffer from these disadvantages. Indeed, a mesh is easily extended (through the addition of a row or a column of processors, affecting only the existing boundary processors), and its links are all of equal length (implying that the propagation time along a link is always the same, regardless of whether one assumes it to be constant or not). In an attempt to retain these and other advantages of the mesh, a third alternative is sought to reduce its diameter. In this approach, the mesh is augmented with a certain number of *buses*. Here, a bus is simply a communication link to which some or all of the processors of the mesh are attached. Through the bus, processors that are not neighbors on the mesh can communicate directly. (The idea was introduced for the linear array in Problem 7.6 and illustrated in Fig. 7.27.)

This chapter is devoted to the study of meshes enhanced with buses. We describe algorithms for three types of buses:

1. *Fixed Buses.* A mesh can be augmented with fixed buses in two ways. In the first model of this kind, all processors of the mesh are connected to a single static bus. At any given time, *one* processor can *broadcast* a datum by placing it on the bus. The datum will be accessible for reading by *all* the remaining processors on the mesh. In the second model, the processors of each row and the processors of each column are connected by a bus. For each row, a *single* processor can use the row bus at any given time to broadcast a datum to the other processors in its row. The column buses are used in exactly the same way.

2. *Reconfigurable Buses.* This model allows buses to be created dynamically on the mesh while a problem is being solved. The number, shape, and length of these buses are not fixed and are defined by the algorithm, as needed, at each step. As with fixed buses, one processor can place a datum on the bus, to be read by all other processors.

3. *Optical Buses.* Traditionally, buses used to connect processors (whether fixed or reconfigurable) are assumed to be *electronic*, and consequently, access to the bus for the purpose of broadcasting is *exclusive*, as described in the previous two paragraphs. An *optical bus*, by contrast, allows several processors to inject data on the bus simultaneously, each datum destined for one or several processors. This capability leads to an entirely new range of techniques for parallel algorithm design.

Writing a (fixed-size) datum on a bus and reading a (fixed-size) datum from the bus are considered basic operations requiring constant time. But how long does it take to traverse a bus, whether electronic or optical? Let $B(L)$ represent a bus of length L, and let $\tau_{B(L)}$ be the time taken by a datum of fixed size to go from one end of the bus to the other. Clearly, $\tau_{B(L)}$ is a function of L. There are many choices for this function. On an electronic bus it could be, for example, quadratic, linear or logarithmic, depending on the technology used to implement the bus. Moreover, it is usually impossible to predict how long it will take a datum to traverse a given section of an electronic bus. For example, the time required by a datum to traverse a given section of the bus may depend on the position of that section relative to the point on the bus where the datum originated. It may also depend on how long the bus has been in use (and hence on its present temperature). On an optical bus, on the other hand, the time required to travel a distance L is typically linear in L. In theoretical analyses of algorithms for meshes enhanced with buses, it is best, therefore, to leave $\tau_{B(L)}$ as a parameter when expressing the running time of an algorithm. Thus, if S steps of an algorithm use the bus, the time consumed by these steps would be $S \times \tau_{B(L)}$. However, for simplicity, we take

$$\tau_{B(L)} = O(1)$$

in this chapter. This choice also ensures consistency, since it is in keeping with our earlier assumptions regarding other models. Specifically, the following times were assumed to be constant:

1. The time to gain access to an arbitrary location of a memory of size M on the RAM model of sequential computation.

2. The time to gain access to an arbitrary location of a memory of size M on the PRAM model of a shared-memory parallel computer.

3. The time to traverse a link of arbitrary length on an interconnection network parallel computer with N processors, such as the mesh of trees, the hypercube, or the star.

4. The time taken by a datum to go from one stage to the next (by traversing a line of arbitrary length) in a combinational circuit.

For definiteness, we take $\tau_{B(L)}$ to be smaller than or equal to the time required by a basic computational operation, such as adding or comparing two numbers.

The chapter is organized as follows: Section 10.1 describes the fixed-bus models. In Section 10.2, we study meshes with reconfigurable buses. Optical buses are introduced in Section 10.3.

10.1 FIXED BUSES

In this section, we describe two ways of enhancing a mesh with fixed (electronic) buses. In the first approach, all of the processors in the mesh are connected to a global bus. In the second approach, row and column buses are used. We demonstrate how each of the two models is used by exhibiting an algorithm for finding the maximum of a sequence of numbers. A lower bound for this problem on each model is also derived.

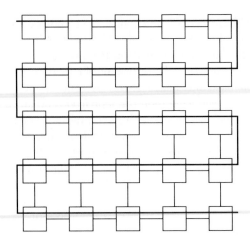

Figure 10.1: Mesh augmented with a global bus.

10.1.1   Global Bus

In the global-bus model, an $n^{1/2} \times n^{1/2}$ mesh of processors $P(i,j)$, $0 \le i,j \le n^{1/2} - 1$, is augmented with a single global bus, as illustrated in Fig. 10.1. All processors of the mesh are attached to the bus. At any given time, at most one processor can write a datum onto the bus. This datum is instantly available for reading simultaneously by *all* the other processors. The global-bus model also enjoys the following property: If two or more processors attempt to place a datum on the bus at the same time, exactly one, selected arbitrarily by the bus, succeeds. Communication with neighbors in the mesh (using standard links) proceeds as usual. Thus, during an elementary step, a processor can either write to or read from the bus or communicate with a neighbor in the mesh.

Computing the Maximum.   Suppose that n input data (for example, real numbers) are stored in an $n^{1/2} \times n^{1/2}$ mesh, one datum per processor. It is required to determine the maximum of these data and place it in processor $P(0,0)$. On a standard mesh—that is, one *without* a bus—the problem clearly requires $\Omega(n^{1/2})$ elementary steps: If the maximum happens to reside initially in $P(n^{1/2}-1, n^{1/2}-1)$, then it takes $2n^{1/2} - 2$ steps simply to move it to $P(0,0)$. In fact, if the maximum is already in $P(0,0)$ initially, then we cannot be sure that it is indeed the maximum until we have compared it, directly or indirectly, to the datum in $P(n^{1/2}-1, n^{1/2}-1)$, and this also requires $\Omega(n^{1/2})$ elementary steps.

An $O(n^{1/2})$-time algorithm for the standard mesh is also easy to derive. The algorithm consists of two phases. In the first phase, each processor in the rightmost column sends its datum to its left neighbor. Subsequently, each processor $P(i,j)$ receiving a datum from its right neighbor compares it to its own datum and forwards the larger to the left, provided that $j > 0$. Eventually, $P(i,0)$, $i = 0, 1, \ldots,$ $n^{1/2} - 1$, determines the largest datum in row i, denoted by x_i. This phase requires $n^{1/2} - 1$ elementary steps. In the second phase, $P(n^{1/2} - 1, 0)$ sends $x_{n^{1/2}-1}$ to $P(n^{1/2} - 2, 0)$. The latter compares the datum received with $x_{n^{1/2}-2}$ and sends the larger to $P(n^{1/2} - 3, 0)$. The process continues until $P(0,0)$ determines the overall largest datum of the original sequence. This phase also requires $n^{1/2} - 1$ elementary steps. In what follows, we refer to this algorithm as algorithm MESH MAXIMUM.

On a mesh enhanced with a global bus, the maximum can be found much faster. The algorithm here also consists of two phases, namely, a local data-gathering phase, in which only standard mesh links are used, and a global data communication phase, in which the bus is used. In the first phase, K iterations of two elementary steps are performed. Here, K is a parameter whose value is derived in the analysis that follows the presentation of the algorithm. The processors receive data from their neighbors, and a processor replaces the datum it currently holds with one it has received if the latter is larger. In the second phase, one processor broadcasts its datum to all other processors during each iteration. A processor replaces the datum it currently holds with the one received through the bus if the latter is no smaller. The algorithm is given next as algorithm GLOBAL-BUS MESH MAXIMUM. The n input data are assumed to be stored in the mesh, one datum per processor. At any point during the execution of the the the algorithm, the set of processors whose data have not been changed is denoted by $\mathcal{G}$. When the algorithm terminates, all processors "know" the maximum.

Algorithm GLOBAL-BUS MESH MAXIMUM

Phase 1: for $i = 1$ **to** K **do**

    (1.1) Each processor sends its datum
        to its (at most four) neighbors in the mesh

    (1.2) Each processor replaces its datum with one
        it has received if the latter is larger

  end for

Phase 2: while $|\mathcal{G}| > 0$ **do**

    (2.1) One processor in $\mathcal{G}$ broadcasts its datum

    (2.2) Each processor replaces its datum with the one
        that has been broadcast if the latter is no smaller

  end while. ∎

Note that in Step (2.2), the broadcasting processor also "replaces" its datum to ensure that it is removed from $\mathcal{G}$.

Analysis. We first observe that if the two steps of Phase 1 were to be executed $n^{1/2}$ times, then the maximum of the input data would be held by each of the n processors of the mesh. Instead, Phase 1 is executed K times, where $K < n^{1/2}$, and requires $4K$ time units. Now, let S_i be the set of processors whose data were not replaced after the ith iteration of Phase 1. Thus, Phase 2 requires at most

$|S_K|$ iterations. This number of iterations is needed if the processor holding the maximum is the last to have access to the bus for writing. The algorithm's worst case running time is therefore

$$t(n) = 4K + |S_K|.$$

We now determine the value of K that minimizes $t(n)$. First, recall that the distance between two processors is the number of links on the shortest path joining them. After i steps, the distance between the elements of S_i cannot be less than $i + 1$. Now, note that the number of processors at a distance $i + 1$ or less from a given processor (including the processor itself) is

$$2(i + 1)^2 + 2(i + 1) + 1.$$

This quantity is larger than $i^2/2$. It follows that $|S_i| \leq n/(i^2/2)$. Hence,

$$t(n) \leq 4K + \frac{2n}{K^2}.$$

The expression $4K + 2n/K^2$ is minimized when $K = n^{1/3}$, leading to a running time of $O(n^{1/3})$. This is clearly an improvement over the $\Omega(n^{1/2})$ time required to find the maximum on the standard mesh. We now show that it is the best that can be done on a mesh enhanced with a global bus, provided that the algorithm used does not allow any values other than input data to be exchanged by the processors.

A Lower Bound. In algorithm GLOBAL-BUS MESH MAXIMUM, the only values exchanged by the processors are the input data themselves. An algorithm of this type, in which the processors are not allowed to communicate any modified or encoded form of the input data, is called a *conservative flow* algorithm. We now derive a lower bound on the running time of any conservative flow algorithm that finds the maximum of n data, stored one datum per processor, on a mesh augmented with a global bus.

We begin by observing that a meaningful lower bound for the present model cannot be based on *distance* considerations. Indeed, the global bus reduces the diameter of the mesh to a constant. Instead, we use the notion of *information content*. Suppose that the n processors of the $n^{1/2} \times n^{1/2}$ mesh are numbered from 0 to $n - 1$, using the snakelike row-major order (defined in Section 2.3.2). Also, let $I_i(k)$ be the largest number of data that processor P_i can receive in k time units. We say that P_i contains the data information of $I_i(k)$ processors at time k. The information accumulated by P_i consists of:

1. Messages received by P_i through *local communications* (i.e., via the standard mesh links), denoted by $I_i'(k)$.

2. Messages received by P_i through *global communications* (i.e., via the global bus), denoted by $I_i''(k)$.

At $k = 0$, $I_i'(0) = I_i''(0) = 0$ and $I_i(0) = 1$. For any $k > 0$, $I_i(k) \leq I_i'(k) + I_i''(k) + 1$. Here the inequality is justified, since $I_i'(k)$ and $I_i''(k)$ may contain some common information.

Let $k = l + g$, where l and g are the times taken by l and g unit-time local and global communications, respectively. Suppose that processors $P_{i(1)}$, $P_{i(2)}$, ..., $P_{i(m)}$, where $0 \leq i(j) \leq n - 1$ and $m \leq g$, broadcast until this time. Although for any j, $P_{i(j)}$ broadcasts all its accumulated information at some time unit u_j, only $I_{i(j)}''(u_j)$ was accumulated by it through the global bus. However, the same amount of information was also received by all other processors from various broadcasts before time unit u_j. Therefore, the nonredundant information transmitted by $P_{i(j)}$ in its broadcast is at most

$$I_{i(j)}(u_j) - I_{i(j)}''(u_j) \leq I_{i(j)}'(u_j) + 1.$$

Since this argument holds for any $P_{i(j)}$, $1 \leq j \leq m$, it follows that

$$I_i''(k) \leq g + \sum_{j=1}^{m} I_{i(j)}'(u_j),$$

after g broadcasts. Consequently,

$$I_i(k) \leq I_i'(k) + 1 + g + \sum_{j=1}^{m} I_{i(j)}'(u_j).$$

What about $I_i'(k)$? Note that processor P_i receives the information held by all those processors which are at a distance k or less from P_i, using the standard mesh links. The information previously received by these processors through various broadcasts and transmitted to P_i via the standard mesh links is redundant, as processor P_i has already read it. Since the number of processors at a distance k or less from P_i (including itself) is at most $2k^2 + 2k + 1$,

$$I_i'(k) \leq 2k^2 + 2k + 1 \leq (2k + 1)^2.$$

Taking $u_j = j + l$, we have

$$I_{i(j)}'(u_j) \leq (2(j + l) + 1)^2 \leq (2(g + l) + 1)^2 = (2k + 1)^2.$$

Hence,

$$I_i(k) \leq (2k + 1)^2 + 1 + g + \sum_{j=1}^{m} (2k + 1)^2.$$

Since $m \leq g \leq k$, we get

$$I_i(k) \leq (2k + 1)^2 + 1 + k + k(2k + 1)^2 = 4k^3 + 8k^2 + 6k + 2,$$

for $0 \leq i \leq n - 1$ and $k \geq 0$.

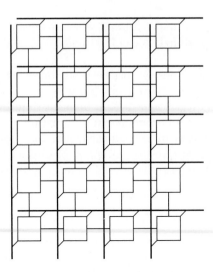

Figure 10.2: Mesh augmented with row and column buses.

Suppose that it takes H time units to compute the maximum in the worst case, and let some processor P_i have the result. Then

$$n \leq I_i(H) \leq 4H^3 + 8H^2 + 6H + 2.$$

It follows that $\Omega(n^{1/3})$ is a lower bound on the time required by any conservative flow algorithm which finds the maximum of n numbers on an $n^{1/2} \times n^{1/2}$ mesh of processors enhanced with a global bus.

10.1.2   Row and Column Buses

One limitation of the global-bus model is that no more than one processor can broadcast a datum at any given time. This problem can be solved partially by augmenting the mesh with several global buses (instead of just one). Such an enhancement, however, does not appreciably improve the performance of the standard mesh in those computations requiring large transfers of data from one end of the mesh to the other. Examples of these problems are merging, sorting, matrix multiplication, convolution, and computing the discrete Fourier transform. Furthermore, for large values of n, the time taken by a message to propagate from one end of the bus to the other becomes significant (regardless of which nonconstant function of n is used to describe the propagation time).

A definite improvement is obtained by enhancing the mesh with row and column buses. Here, an $X \times Y$ mesh of processors with X rows and Y columns is augmented with one bus on each row and one bus on each column, as shown in Fig. 10.2. In this model, a processor can either communicate locally with its four neighbors using standard mesh links or broadcast along its row or column bus. All processors connected to the same bus can read a value being broadcast simultaneously. Therefore, a datum can be broadcast by one processor to *all* other processors in *two* steps: First the processor broadcasts the datum along its row, and then each processor on that row broadcasts the received datum along its own column. As before, only one processor is allowed to broadcast on a given bus at any given time.

The power of this new model is now illustrated by deriving an algorithm for finding the maximum of a sequence of n data. The algorithm runs in $O(n^{1/8})$ time, thus overcoming the $\Omega(n^{1/3})$ lower bound derived for the mesh with a global bus.

Computing the Maximum. Let n data (for example, real numbers) be given, stored one per processor in an $X \times Y$ mesh, augmented with row and column buses, where $X \geq Y$ and $XY = n$. An algorithm for finding the maximum of n input data is given next as algorithm ROW AND COLUMN BUSES MESH MAXIMUM. The algorithm partitions the mesh into blocks of size $m \times m$. The values of X, Y, and m are to be determined in the analysis following the description of the algorithm. The only assumption made here, for ease of presentation, is that X and Y are multiples of m and m^2, respectively. We refer to a row of $m \times m$ blocks as a *band*. The algorithm is illustrated throughout using an example in which $X = 16$, $Y = 12$, and $m = 2$.

Algorithm ROW AND COLUMN BUSES MESH MAXIMUM

Step 1:

(1.1) Use algorithm MESH MAXIMUM to find the maximum datum in each $m \times m$ block. This is illustrated in Fig. 10.3(a), in which links and buses are omitted and the processor holding the maximum of each block is shown as a shaded square. Note that in each band there are Y/m partial maxima.

(1.2) Copy the partial maximum in each block to all the processors in the first column of the block, using standard mesh links. This is shown in Fig. 10.3(b).

Step 2:

(2.1) The Y/m partial maxima in each band are divided into m groups, each containing Y/m^2 elements. Since there are m row buses in each band, each row bus is assigned one group of Y/m^2 elements, as illustrated in Fig. 10.3(c), in which the elements assigned to each row are shown in shaded squares.

(2.2) Each row bus is used to find the maximum of the Y/m^2 data assigned to it. This is done in Y/m^2 iterations. During the ith iteration, the ith of the Y/m^2 data is broadcast on the row bus, and the leftmost processor in the row keeps track of the maximum seen so far.

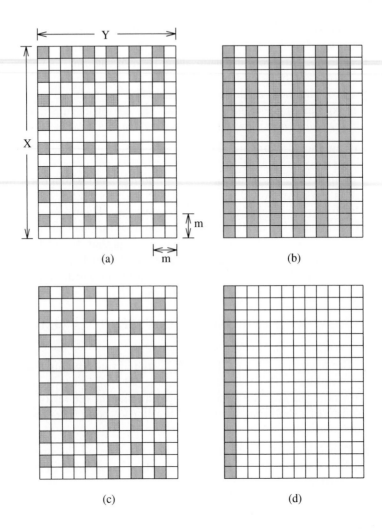

Figure 10.3: Steps 1 and 2 of maximum-finding algorithm: (a) The maximum datum in each $m \times m$ block is found; (b) The maximum in each block is copied to all processors in the first column of the block; (c) Each row bus is assigned Y/m^2 partial maxima; (d) The largest of the partial maxima in each row is found and placed in the leftmost processor of that row.

(2.3) There are now X partial maxima; each band contains m such maxima in its leftmost column, as shown in Fig. 10.3(d).

Step 3: Find the maximum of the elements in the leftmost column in each band (using the second phase of algorithm MESH MAXIMUM). There are now X/m partial maxima left, as shown in Fig. 10.4(a).

Step 4:

(4.1) Row buses are used to broadcast each of the X/m partial maxima to all processors in its row.

(4.2) The X/m partial maxima are divided into Z groups, where $Z \leq Y$, each containing at most $\lceil X/(Ym) \rceil$ elements and each assigned to a distinct column. This is shown in Fig. 10.4(b), where eight groups of one element each are created. (Alternatively, the maximum in band j, $j = 0, 1, \ldots, (X/m) - 1$, is assigned to column $j \bmod Y$, with the number of columns used in this manner being $Z = \min(Y, X/m)$.)

Step 5: For each of the Z columns, use the column bus to find the maximum element among the partial maxima assigned to that column in Step (4.2). This is done in $\lceil X/(Ym) \rceil$ iterations. During the ith iteration, the ith of the (at most) $\lceil X/(Ym) \rceil$ partial maxima is broadcast on the column bus, and the topmost processor in the column keeps track of the maximum seen so far. At the end of this step, there are Z partial maxima left, stored one per processor in the first Z columns of the topmost row, as shown in Fig. 10.4(c).

Step 6:

(6.1) Consider the submesh M of the original mesh determined by the first Z rows and Z columns. The first row of processors of M contains the Z partial maxima left.

(6.2) Subdivide M into four $Z/2 \times Z/2$ submeshes M_1, M_2, M_3, and M_4. Using the column buses, send the elements in the top row of M_2 to the top row of M_4, as shown in Fig. 10.4(d). Submeshes M_1 and M_4 are now viewed as independent meshes, with separate row and column buses. Step (6.2) is applied recursively to find the maximum in each of M_1 and M_4. The recursion terminates when two 1×1 meshes are created. Suppose that the maxima in M_1 and M_4 have been found; call them m_1 and m_4, respectively. Each of m_1 and m_4 is located in the top left processor of its respective submesh. Using the column bus in the first column of M_4, send element m_4 to the first row of M. Then, using the row bus in the top row of M, send element m_4 to the top left processor of M. The latter computes and stores the larger of m_1 and m_4. ■

When the algorithm terminates, $P(0,0)$ produces as output the maximum of the n input data. Note that in Step (6.2), if Z is odd, $Z/2$ is appropriately rounded.

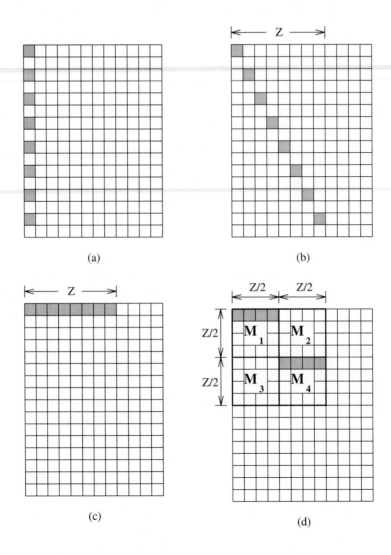

Figure 10.4: Steps 3–6 of maximum-finding algorithm: (a) The largest of the m partial maxima in each band is found; (b) The partial maximum in band j is assigned to column $j \bmod Y$; (c) Each column finds the largest of the elements assigned to it and places it in its topmost processor; (d) The largest of the partial maxima is found recursively.

Analysis. Steps 1 and 3 use only standard mesh links and run in $O(m)$ time. Steps 2 and 4 use the row buses and require $O(Y/m^2)$ and $O(1)$ time, respectively. Step 5 uses the column buses and runs in $O(X/(Ym))$, which is $O(n/(Y^2m))$. Finally, Step 6 requires $O(\log Y)$ time. The overall running time is therefore:

$$t(n) = O(\max(m, \frac{Y}{m^2}, \frac{n}{Y^2m}, \log Y)).$$

This quantity reaches its minimum when $m = n^{1/8}$ and $Y = n^{3/8}$. Thus, with a rectangular $n^{5/8} \times n^{3/8}$ mesh, augmented with row and column buses, the maximum of n data, stored one per processor, can be found in $O(n^{1/8})$ time.

A Lower Bound. We now derive a lower bound on any conservative flow algorithm that finds the maximum of n data on an $x \times y$ mesh of processors augmented with row and column buses, where $x \geq y$ and $xy = n$. Let $I_i(k)$, $I_i'(k)$, and $I_i''(k)$ be defined as in Section 10.1.1, and recall that $I_i(k) \leq I_i'(k) + I_i''(k) + 1$. We have

$$I_i'(k) \leq 2k^2 + 2k + 1.$$

In order to derive an upper bound on $I_i''(k)$, we assume that every datum placed on a row or column bus is received simultaneously by all processors in the mesh. Since there are $x + y$ buses, a processor may receive information about at most $(x + y)(2(h-1)^2 + 2(h-1) + 1)$ values during time unit h. Therefore,

$$I_i''(k) \leq (x + y) \sum_{h=1}^{k} (2(h-1)^2 + 2(h-1) + 1).$$

Hence, after H time units,

$$I_i(H) \leq (2H^2 + 2H + 1) + 1 + (x + y) \sum_{h=1}^{H} (2h^2 - 2h + 1).$$

In other words,

$$I_i(H) = O(H^3(x + y)) = O(H^3x) = O(H^3n/y).$$

If an algorithm finds the maximum in H time units, it must be the case that $I_i(H) \geq n$, for some i. Therefore, $H^3 = \Omega(y)$. If $x = y = n^{1/2}$, then $H = \Omega(n^{1/6})$.

An improved lower bound is now obtained for the case where $x > y$. Suppose that we need to find the maximum of the x data in the first column of the mesh. We assume that a value known to one processor is also known instantly by all remaining processors in the same row. After k time units, a processor has received at most $1 + 2k$ distinct values via the (vertical) mesh links. Since only one processor can use a column bus at time unit k, it can tell the other processors about at most

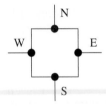

Figure 10.5: The four ports of a mesh processor.

$1 + 2(k-1) = 2k - 1$ new values. As there are y such column buses, at time H_1 a processor possesses information about at most

$$(1 + 2H_1) + 1 + y \sum_{k=1}^{H_1} (2k - 1)$$

values, which is $O(yH_1^2)$. If an algorithm finds the maximum of the x values in the first column in H_1 time units, it must be the case that $H_1^2 = \Omega(x/y)$. Because $H_1 < H$, we have

$$(H^3)^2 \times H^2 = \Omega(y^2 \times (x/y)) = \Omega(n),$$

and consequently, $H = \Omega(n^{1/8})$. This implies that algorithm ROW AND COLUMN BUSES MESH MAXIMUM achieves (asymptotically) the best possible running time for finding the maximum of n data on a mesh with n processors and row and column buses.

We note in concluding this section that any algorithm for finding the maximum of a sequence of values can be easily modified to perform other functions on these values, such as computing their minimum, their sum, their product, their logical AND, and so on. These associative functions are known as *semigroup operations*.

10.2   RECONFIGURABLE BUSES

Consider a typical processor in a mesh-of-processors interconnection network. Such a processor has four links connecting it to its neighbors. Each of these links is attached to the processor itself via an interface, commonly referred to as a *port*. A mesh processor therefore has four ports, called its north (N), south (S), west (W), and east (E) ports, as illustrated in Fig. 10.5. Suppose that a processor is capable of connecting its ports internally in pairs in any one of the 10 configurations depicted in Fig. 10.6. Each of these configurations either creates a connection between two ports for exactly one pair of ports, or creates a connection in two *disjoint* pairs of ports, or connects no ports at all. These internal connections, combined with the standard mesh links, allow for paths of arbitrary lengths and shapes to be created in the mesh. This is illustrated in Fig. 10.7 for a 4×4 mesh in which three paths

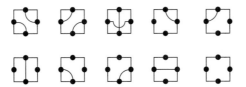

Figure 10.6: Possible internal connections of a processor's ports.

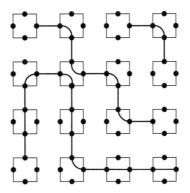

Figure 10.7: A mesh with three configured buses.

have been established. These paths created by the processors have the following properties:

1. The paths are *dynamic* (or *reconfigurable*), in the sense that they can be created by the processors and then modified as many times as necessary during the execution of an algorithm.

2. In order to connect its ports internally, a processor relies on a condition dictated by the algorithm. This condition may depend on the processor's row and column indices in the mesh or on the values of some variables held by the processor in its registers. For example, the algorithm may specify that all processors in odd rows are to connect their W and E ports or that all processors holding a 0 in some register are to connect their W and S ports.

3. It takes a constant number of time units for a processor to connect its ports internally, and hence, at any given step of an algorithm, *all* needed paths can be set up in constant time.

4. Each path created by a set of processors among themselves is viewed as a *bus* to which these processors are connected. It therefore possesses all the properties of (electronic) buses, namely:

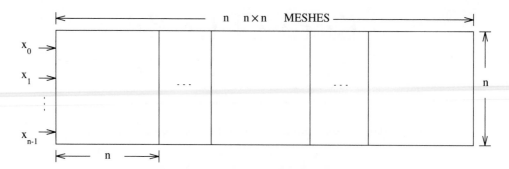

Figure 10.8: A mesh of meshes with reconfigurable buses.

(a) Only *one* processor can place (i.e., write) a datum on the bus at any given time.

(b) A datum placed on the bus can be obtained (i.e., read) by *all* processors connected to the bus simultaneously.

(c) It takes constant time for a datum to travel from one end of the bus to the other.

These specifications yield a new model of computation, called the *mesh with reconfigurable buses*. Since this model can establish a single global bus among its processors or a bus on each row and on each column, it can execute any algorithm for the models of Section 10.1, using the same number of processors and with no increase in the running time. In what follows, we illustrate the power of the mesh with reconfigurable buses by deriving an algorithm for it that sorts n numbers in nondecreasing order.

10.2.1   A First Attempt at Sorting

Suppose that it is desired to sort the sequence of numbers $Q = \{x_0, x_1, \ldots, x_{n-1}\}$ on a mesh with reconfigurable buses. We begin by developing an algorithm for the model that does the job in constant time, while using $O(n^3)$ processors. Consider a mesh with reconfigurable buses consisting of n rows and n^2 columns of processors. We view this mesh as n meshes, numbered 0 to $n-1$, each with n rows and n columns, also numbered 0 to $n-1$, placed side by side, as shown in Fig. 10.8. Each processor in the leftmost column receives as input one of the numbers to be sorted.

The sorting algorithm to be used is based on the idea of *sorting by enumeration*. (See Section 8.3.1.) Each number x_i is compared to each one of the other numbers to determine how many elements of the input sequence are smaller than it. This determines the rank (or position) of x_i in the sorted sequence. The sequence is now permuted in order to place each number in the position corresponding to its rank.

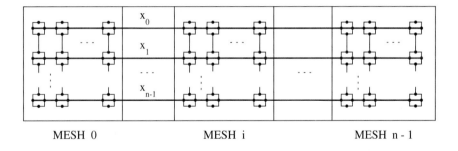

Figure 10.9: Distribution along rows in sorting by enumeration.

As usual, if two numbers are equal, then the one with the smaller index in the input sequence is considered to be the smaller of the two (for the purpose of computing its rank). The algorithm is given next as algorithm RECONFIGURABLE BUSES MESH SORT. It consists of four steps: distribution, comparison, ranking, and permutation.

Algorithm RECONFIGURABLE BUSES MESH SORT (Q)

Step 1:

    (1.1) All processors connect their W and E ports, thus creating a bus on each row of the mesh, as illustrated in Fig. 10.9.

    (1.2) The sequence Q is distributed to all meshes by having processor $P(i,0)$ of mesh 0 broadcast x_i on its row bus.

    (1.3) The processors in column 0 of each $n \times n$ mesh connect their N and S ports, thus creating a bus on that column.

    (1.4) Processor $P(i,0)$ of mesh i, $0 \leq i \leq n-1$, broadcasts x_i on its column bus. As a result, each processor $P(j,0)$, $0 \leq j \leq n-1$, of mesh i, $0 \leq i \leq n-1$, now contains the pair (x_j, x_i), as shown in Fig. 10.10(a).

Step 2: In mesh i, $0 \leq i \leq n-1$, processor $P(j,0)$, $0 \leq j \leq n-1$, compares x_j to x_i: If $x_j < x_i$, it stores a 1 in a special register R; otherwise it stores a 0 in R. At the end of this step, the processors in column 0 of mesh i contain three values, as shown in Fig. 10.10(b).

Step 3: By adding the 1's in column 0 of mesh i, the rank of x_i is obtained for $i = 0, 1, \ldots, n-1$. The following three steps are executed for mesh i, $0 \leq i \leq n-1$ (i.e., for all $n \times n$ meshes simultaneously):

    (3.1) All processors in columns 1 to $n-2$ connect their W and E ports. This creates a bus on each row. Processor $P(j,0)$, $0 \leq j \leq n-1$, broadcasts the value in its R register (i.e., 0 or 1) on the bus in row

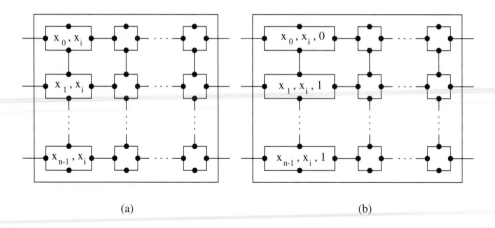

(a)   (b)

Figure 10.10: Distribution along column 0 and comparison in mesh i: (a) Each processor $P(j,0)$ of mesh i contains x_j and x_i; (b) If $x_j < x_i$, $P(j,0)$ stores a 1 in a special register R (otherwise it stores a 0 in R).

j. All processors in row j store the received value (i.e., 0 or 1) in their respective R registers. An example illustrating the contents of the R registers at the end of this step is shown in Fig. 10.11(a).

(3.2) If a processor contains a 0 in its R register, it connects its N and S ports; otherwise (i.e., if R contains a 1) it connects its W and N ports and its S and E ports. The buses created as a result of applying this step on the processors in Fig. 10.11(a) are shown in Fig. 10.11(b).

(3.3) Processor $P(n-1,0)$—that is, the processor in the bottom left corner— places a special symbol (for example, $*$) on the bus to which its S port is connected. If the processor in the jth column of the topmost row, namely, $P(0,j)$, receives that symbol, then the number of 1's in column 0 (i.e., the rank of x_i) is j. In Fig. 10.11(c), the rank of x_i is 3.

Step 4: The element of Q whose rank is k is produced as output on row k, $0 \leq k \leq n-1$. This is done by executing the following steps, for $i = 0, 1, \ldots,$ $n-1$, in parallel:

(4.1) In mesh i, each processor connects its N and S ports. This creates column buses. Processor $P(0,j)$, containing the special symbol, broadcasts j (i.e., the rank of x_i) down its column bus, as shown in Fig. 10.12(a).

(4.2) From Step 1, all processors in row i of mesh i contain x_i. After j is broadcast in (4.1), processor $P(i,j)$ in mesh i contains (x_i,j). Using the column bus created in (4.1), this processor broadcasts (x_i,j) along its column bus, as shown in Fig. 10.12(b).

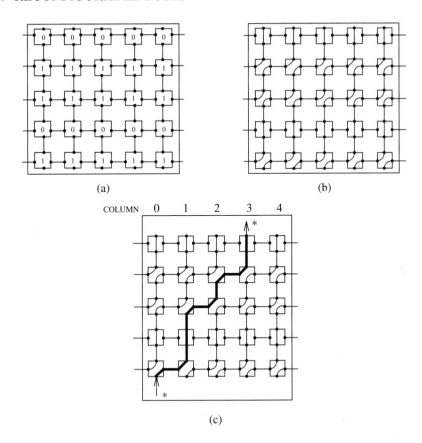

(a)

(b)

(c)

Figure 10.11: Ranking in mesh i: (a) Each processor in the leftmost column broadcasts the value contained in its register R to all processors in its row; (b) A processor containing a 0 connects its N and S ports, whereas a processor containing a 1 connects its W and N ports and its S and E ports; (c) The processor in the bottom left corner sends a special symbol on the bus to which its S port is connected.

(4.3) All processors of the $n \times n^2$ mesh connect their W and E ports. This creates row buses across the mesh. Processor $P(j, j)$ of mesh i broadcasts x_i along its row bus, as shown in Fig. 10.12(c). ■

When the algorithm terminates, the input sequence is stored in the leftmost column of the mesh, sorted in nondecreasing order from top to bottom (i.e., the smallest number is in processor $P(0,0)$ and the largest in processor $P(n-1,0)$ of mesh 0).

Analysis. Each step of the algorithm runs in constant time. Therefore, $t(n) = O(1)$, $p(n) = n^3$, and $c(n) = O(n^3)$.

While extremely fast, requiring constant time to sort, this algorithm is also exorbitant in its use of processors. It is worthwhile to study, however, for a number of reasons:

1. It demonstrates the power and flexibility of the mesh with reconfigurable buses. Indeed, no interconnection network parallel computer studied so far is capable of sorting at this speed, regardless of how many processors it uses.

2. Certain aspects of the algorithm are interesting in their own right. In particular, the technique used in Step 3 to compute the sum of n bits in constant time is quite unique. Similarly, the technique used in Step 4 allows any permutation of $\{x_0, x_1, \ldots, x_{n-1}\}$ to be performed in constant time using only mesh 0.

3. The algorithm will be used in the next section to develop another algorithm for sorting n numbers on a mesh with reconfigurable buses that requires a smaller number of processors.

10.2.2   A More Efficient Sorting Algorithm

In this section, we design an algorithm for sorting on a mesh with reconfigurable buses that uses fewer processors asymptotically than the algorithm of Section 10.2.1. Our starting point will be algorithm MESH SORT of Section 8.1.3. Recall that this algorithm sorts n numbers organized in a rectangular array A of 2^s rows and 2^{2r} columns, with $s \geq r$ (each element of which is stored in one processor of a rectangular mesh). Algorithm MESH SORT consists of six steps, each involving one or more of the following fundamental operations:

1. Sorting a row of A.

2. Sorting a column of A.

3. Cyclically shifting a row of A.

Now, imagine that the n numbers we wish to sort here (i.e., the elements of $Q = \{x_0, x_1, \ldots, x_{n-1}\}$) are organized in an array A with $X = n^{2/3}$ rows and $Y = n^{1/3}$ columns. We assign each row of the array A of numbers to Y^3 processors, organized as a mesh with reconfigurable buses consisting of Y rows and Y^2 columns, using the same arrangement as in Fig. 10.8. In other words, each row of A is associated with Y meshes, numbered 0 to $Y - 1$, of $Y \times Y$ processors each, and the elements of that row are stored one per processor in the first column of processors of mesh 0. Similarly, each column of the array A of numbers is assigned to X^3 processors, organized as a mesh with reconfigurable buses with X rows and X^2 columns, also as in Fig. 10.8. In other words, each column of A is associated with X meshes, numbered 0 to $X - 1$, of $X \times X$ processors each, and the elements of that column are stored one per processor in the first column of mesh 0. The entire setup is

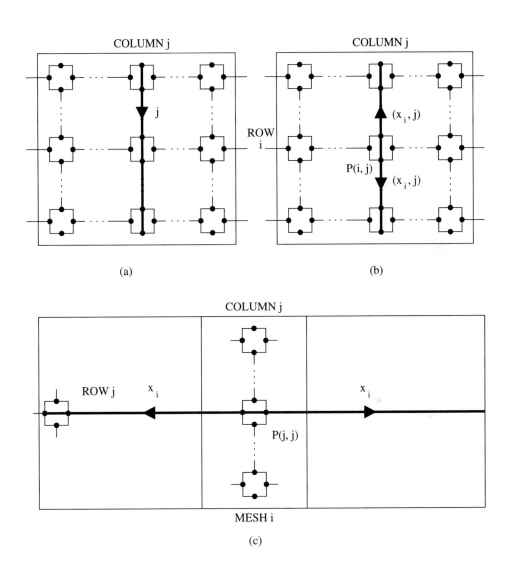

Figure 10.12: Permutation step in sorting by enumeration: (a) In mesh i, all processors having connected their N and S ports, processor $P(0, j)$, containing the special symbol, broadcasts j (i.e., the rank of x_i) down its column; (b) Processor $P(i, j)$ broadcasts (x_i, j) along its column; (c) All processors of the $n \times n^2$ mesh having connected their W and E ports, processor $P(j, j)$ of mesh i broadcasts x_i along its row.

illustrated in Fig. 10.13; note that the array A in the figure is an array of numbers (*not* processors).

Algorithm MESH SORT can now be used directly to sort the elements of the input sequence Q, organized in an $X \times Y$ array A:

1. Whenever algorithm MESH SORT calls for a row of A to be sorted, the Y^3 processors associated with that row implement algorithm RECONFIGURABLE BUSES MESH SORT.

2. Whenever algorithm MESH SORT calls for a column of A to be sorted, the X^3 processors associated with that column implement algorithm RECONFIGURABLE BUSES MESH SORT.

3. Whenever algorithm MESH SORT calls for a row of A to be cyclically shifted, the shift is implemented by the processors of mesh 0 associated with the given row. Since a cyclic shift is just a special permutation, it can be executed using the same approach as in Step 4 of algorithm RECONFIGURABLE BUSES MESH SORT.

Analysis. Each of the six steps of algorithm MESH SORT can be executed in a constant number of time units. This algorithm therefore runs in $t(n) = O(1)$ time. The total number of processors it requires is

$$
\begin{aligned}
p(n) &= XY^3 + YX^3 \\
&= n^{2/3}n + n^{1/3}n^2 \\
&= O(n^{7/3}).
\end{aligned}
$$

Since $7/3 < 3$, this is an improvement over the algorithm of Section 10.2.1 with respect to processor utilization.

10.2.3 A Recursive Algorithm

The number of processors used to sort n numbers in constant time on a mesh with reconfigurable buses can be reduced even further by applying the algorithm just described recursively. In order to convey the idea, we begin by assuming that recursion is applied just once. Specifically, whenever a row or a column of the $X \times Y$ array A is to be sorted:

1. That row or column is viewed as a rectangular $X_1 \times Y_1$ array A_1.

2. Array A_1 is sorted by algorithm MESH SORT, implemented using meshes with reconfigurable buses, as in Section 10.2.2.

Thus, each row is sorted using

$$ Y^{7/3} = (n^{1/3})^{7/3} = n^{7/9} $$

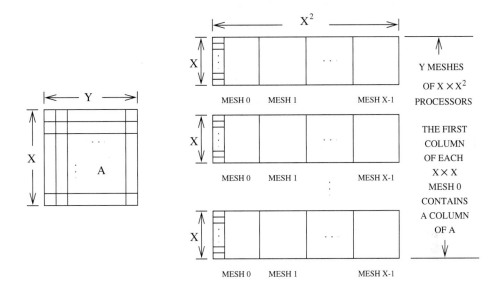

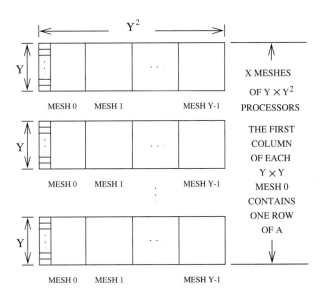

Figure 10.13: Organization of processors for a more efficient sorting algorithm.

processors, while each column is sorted using

$$X^{7/3} = (n^{2/3})^{7/3} = n^{14/9}$$

processors. The total number of processors required is therefore

$$(X \times n^{7/9}) + (Y \times n^{14/9}) = O(n^{17/9}).$$

Note that $17/9 < 7/3$, and so an improvement has been achieved.

Suppose now that the recursion is applied twice. Each row and each column of A_1 is viewed as a rectangular $X_2 \times Y_2$ array A_2, which is sorted using the algorithm of Section 10.2.2. The total number of processors now is

$$(X \times Y^{17/9}) + (Y \times X^{17/9}) = O(n^{43/27}),$$

again an asymptotic improvement.

In general, if the recursion is applied d times, for $d \geq 0$, then the number of processors used is

$$p(n) = O(n^{1+\epsilon}),$$

where $\epsilon = 2(2/3)^{d+1}$. The running time is $t(n) = O(9^{d+1})$, which is $O(9^d)$, where 9 is the number of times the columns of A are sorted by algorithm MESH SORT.

10.3   OPTICAL BUSES

Although our models of computation are abstract devices whose behavior is not tied to any particular technology, their usefulness depends a great deal on their ability to reflect true computing engines. In fact, the very assumptions made in connection with a model are rooted in what is currently feasible and what will be possible in the foreseeable future. These assumptions concern such considerations as, for example:

1. Which aspects of computation are important and need to be included in the model.

2. Which aspects are of secondary nature and can be ignored.

3. How long certain operations take.

4. How long it takes a datum to travel from one point to another.

Accordingly, a good model of computation is one that strikes the right balance between realism and mathematical tractability. Indeed, it often happens that a new technology renders some theoretical assumptions obsolete and leads us to re-define our models. These observations are best illustrated by the main topic of this chapter, namely, *buses as agents of computation*. The study of buses, not only as communication channels among the processors of a parallel computer, but also as active components of the computing device, exemplifies the interplay between theory and practice. Let us take a close look at these buses.

In the previous two sections, it was assumed that the buses used to enhance the mesh were *electronic*. Two characteristics of the abstract buses used in our models justified this assumption:

1. The *bidirectionality* of the buses. This means that once a datum is placed on the bus by a processor P, that datum travels on the bus in both directions away from P (e.g., to the left and to the right) simultaneously, reaching (at once) *all* processors attached to the bus.

2. The lack of a precise function that describes the time taken by a signal to propagate along a given section of a wire. Therefore, it is customary to assume, as we did, that signals travel on a bus at infinite speed.

(We note in passing that, strictly speaking, the buses in Sections 10.1 and 10.2 need not be electronic. Any medium satisfying the preceding two assumptions will do.)

An alternative to electronic buses is provided by *optical buses*. Here, *light signals* are used instead of electrical signals. The bus itself is called an *optical waveguide*. Optical buses offer numerous advantages from a technological point of view (including high bandwidth and low interference). From our point of view, however, the two most relevant properties of optical buses are:

1. Their *unidirectionality*, which means that a datum placed by any processor on an optical bus travels in only one (always the same) direction.

2. The predictability of the propagation delay per unit length along them, meaning that the time it takes a light signal to travel a certain distance along an optical waveguide is directly proportional to that distance.

These two simple, yet important, properties lead to the definition of entirely new computational models and open up rich avenues for algorithmic design. Specifically, let n processors $P_0, P_1, \ldots, P_{n-1}$ be connected to an optical bus. The first property (i.e., unidirectionality) allows several processors to place data on the bus simultaneously, one datum per processor. The data form a *pipeline* and travel down the bus, all in the same direction, as shown in Fig. 10.14, where $d_i, d_j,$ and d_k are the data placed at the same time on the bus by processors $P_i, P_j,$ and P_k, respectively. The second property of optical buses (i.e., the predictability of the propagation delay) allows the difference between the arrival times of two data d_i and d_j at a processor P_l (for example) to be determined by the distance separating P_i and P_j.

The remainder of this section is devoted to a study of optical buses and a demonstration of how their characteristics lead to novel and interesting algorithms. We begin by defining the behavior of optical buses more precisely and then show how they can be used to enhance the mesh of processors. Finally, we develop an algorithm capable of sorting n numbers in $O(\log n)$ time on a mesh of n processors

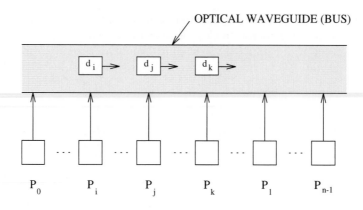

Figure 10.14: A pipeline of data on an optical bus.

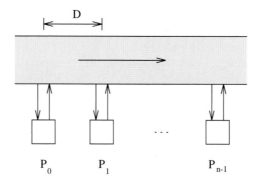

Figure 10.15: A linear array of processors with an optical bus.

enhanced with optical buses. It is important to stress here that while the algorithms of this section are motivated, and made possible, by the properties of optical buses, they could run equally well on any model of computation which uses buses satisfying these same properties. For definiteness, however, the algorithms are expressed and analyzed in terms of optical buses.

10.3.1   Linear Arrays with Optical Buses

Suppose that n processors are connected to an optical waveguide, as shown in Fig. 10.15. The processors are numbered P_0, P_1, ..., P_{n-1} from left to right. Each processor is attached to the bus via a two-way link. We represent this link as two oriented edges, one for receiving (i.e., reading) data from the bus, the second for sending (i.e., writing) data to the bus. Data travel on the bus in one direction only, from left to right, as indicated by the arrow in the figure. The bus is the only medium available to the processors for communicating among themselves. We call this model a *linear array with optical buses*. (The term *linear array* is used simply to refer to the fact that the processors are arranged in a one-dimensional pattern. Note that no processor is directly connected to another processor by a standard linear-array link.) Since the bus is unidirectional, P_i can send a message to P_j, provided that $j > i$.

Let each datum (or message) to be placed on the bus consist of b bits. A bit is represented by a light pulse of width w; that is, w is the duration of the pulse, in time units (seconds, for example). The presence of a light pulse indicates a binary '1', its absence a binary '0'. The *optical distance* between two processors P_i and P_j is the length of the waveguide separating them (which may or may not be equal to the physical distance separating them). Let D be the optical distance separating any two consecutive processors in the system, as shown in Fig. 10.15. Thus, D is a constant. The number of time units required by a light pulse to traverse D is denoted by τ_D. In other words, $\tau_D = D/v$, where v is the speed of light in the waveguide. If P_i sends a message to P_j, where $j > i$, then the message arrives at P_j after $(j - i)\tau_D$ time units.

The parallel computer of Fig. 10.15 allows several—indeed, all—processors to place data on the bus simultaneously. In order to avoid overlapping messages, however, the following conditions must be satisfied:

1. $D > bwv$.

2. Processors wishing to write on the bus do so synchronously; that is, they place their data on the bus at prespecified times separated by regular intervals.

These two conditions ensure that if P_i and P_{i+1} begin transmitting d_i and d_{i+1} at the same time, the first bit of d_i will not reach P_{i+1} until the last bit of d_{i+1} has departed. Therefore, no two messages d_i and d_j ever collide on the bus; that is, d_i and d_j never reach P_l at the same time.

The time taken by an optical signal (a light pulse) to traverse the optical bus from one end (at P_0) to the other (at P_{n-1})—that is, $\tau_{B(L)}$—is known as the *bus cycle*. Since the optical length of the bus is $L = (n-1)D$, it follows that $\tau_{B(L)} = L/v$. Time is divided into bus-cycle intervals. As stated at the beginning of this chapter, we take $\tau_{B(L)} = O(1)$.

Waiting Function. When is a processor P_j to read a message d_i from the bus? This is, of course, controlled by the algorithm. There are two cases to consider:

1. In the first case, P_j "knows" the identity of the sender P_i. Here, all processors wishing to place a datum on the bus do so only at the *beginning* of a bus cycle. We can define a function $wait(i, j)$ which specifies the time that P_j should wait, *relative to the beginning of the bus cycle*, before reading d_i. Thus,

$$wait(i, j) = (j - i)\tau_D.$$

Since τ_D is a constant by definition, we omit it henceforth from the definition of the function, and write $wait(i,j) = j - i$. In fact, there is an alternative way of defining the function $wait$ that does not depend on D or τ_D. Suppose that, during each bus cycle, every one of the processors is required to place a message on the bus. (Processors without any real message to send place a dummy message on the bus.) Now, $wait(i,j) - 1$ gives the number of messages that P_j should skip before reading d_i. Specifically, if $wait(i,j) = k$, then P_j reads the kth message that passes by it. The two definitions are equivalent, and in either case, the transmission of d_i from P_i to P_j is completed within one bus cycle.

Example 10.1 Suppose that $n = 5$ and that P_3 expects to receive d_0 (from P_0), while P_4 expects d_2 (from P_2). At the beginning of the bus cycle, P_0 and P_2 place d_0 and d_2 on the bus as shown in Fig. 10.16(a). Relative to the beginning of the bus cycle, P_4 receives d_2 at time $4 - 2 = 2$, as shown in Fig. 10.16(b), while P_3 receives d_0 at time $3 - 0 = 3$, as shown in Fig. 10.16(c). □

It is important to note that the same message may be destined to, and can be read by, multiple processors during the same bus cycle. However, a processor cannot receive more than one message during the same bus cycle.

2. In the second case, the receiver P_j does not "know" the identity of the sender P_i, but the sender knows the identity of the receiver. Here, the sender P_i writes its message d_i, destined to P_j, on the bus at time $((n-1) - j + i)\tau_D$ relative to the beginning of the bus cycle. All processors read the bus simultaneously at the *end* of the bus cycle—that is, at time $(n-1)\tau_D$ relative to the beginning of the bus cycle. If there is a message destined to a processor, the latter will find it at that time. Therefore, the transmission of d_i from P_i to P_j takes one bus cycle. As before, we omit τ_D when discussing this form of communication.

Example 10.2 Suppose that $n = 5$ and that P_0 wishes to send d_0 to P_3, while P_2 wishes to send d_2 to P_4. Relative to the beginning of the bus cycle, P_0 places d_0 on the bus at time $(5 - 1) - 3 + 0 = 1$, as shown in Fig. 10.17(a), while P_2 places d_2 on the bus at time $(5 - 1) - 4 + 2 = 2$, as shown in Fig. 10.17(b), and the data reach their destinations at time 4, as shown in Fig. 10.17(c). □

In the remainder of this section, we use the *wait* function approach in all algorithms developed for optical buses. We emphasize here that a receiving processor P_j must compute $wait(i,j)$ before the sender P_i actually begins its transmission of d_i along the bus. This is because the bus cycle $\tau_{B(L)}$ is smaller than or equal to the time taken by any basic computational operation, as assumed at the beginning

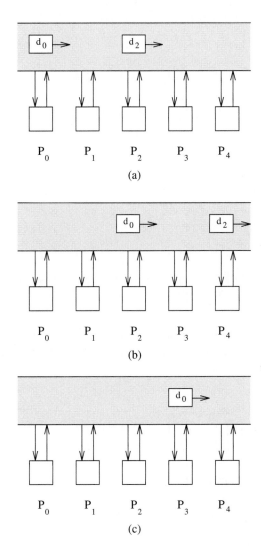

Figure 10.16: Routing data when receiver "knows" sender: (a) At the beginning of the bus cycle, P_0 places d_0 (destined to P_3) on the bus, while P_2 places d_2 (destined to P_4) on the bus; (b) P_4 receives d_2 two time units after the beginning of the bus cycle; (c) P_3 receives d_0 three time units after the beginning of the bus cycle.

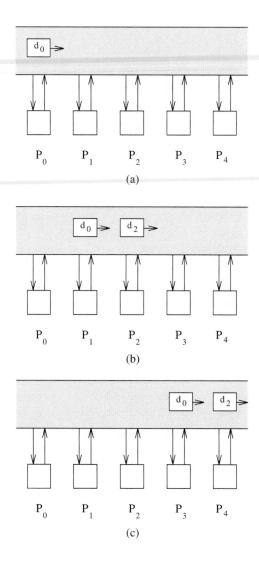

Figure 10.17: Routing data when sender "knows" receiver: (a) P_0 places d_0 (destined to P_3) on the bus one time unit after the beginning of the bus cycle; (b) P_2 places d_2 (destined to P_4) on the bus two time units after the beginning of the bus cycle; (c) Each datum reaches its destination at the end of the bus cycle.

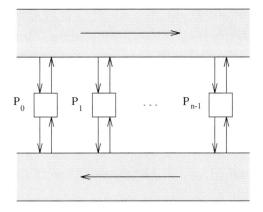

Figure 10.18: Two-way communication using optical buses.

of the chapter. As usual, the actions of the processors and the time at which each action is to take place are fully controlled by the algorithm.

Two-Way Communication. The system in Fig. 10.15 allows for messages to travel only in one direction. In order to allow messages to be sent in both directions, the arrangement shown in Fig. 10.18 is used. Here two optical buses are used. The upper bus allows data to be sent from left to right, while the lower bus allows data to travel from right to left. Each processor can read and write to either of the two buses, as required by the algorithm. The two buses are completely independent from one another and accommodate separate pipelines. The *wait* function is now interpreted as follows:

> **if** $wait(i,j) > 0$
> **then** P_j reads d_i from the upper bus at time $wait(i,j)$
> **else if** $wait(i,j) < 0$
> > **then** P_j reads d_i from the lower bus at time $-wait(i,j)$
> > **else** P_j does not read in this cycle
> > **end if**
> **end if.** ■

As before, the transmission of d_i from P_i to P_j takes constant time.

10.3.2   Data Communication

The linear array with optical buses shown in Fig. 10.18 can be used to execute a variety of data communication schemes. Such schemes include sending a datum from one processor to all other processors and performing an arbitrary permutation of the data held by the processors. All these schemes are uniquely determined by the *wait* function. Thus, in order to transfer a datum from P_i to P_j, for given i and j, the algorithm specifies

$$wait(i,j) = j - i.$$

Therefore, we can define a communication pattern simply by giving the *wait* function, as shown next for the cases of broadcasting, executing an arbitrary permutation, and distributing data in general.

Broadcasting.   Suppose that P_i wishes to broadcast a datum d_i to all other processors. It suffices to set

$$wait(i,j) = j - i, \quad \text{for a specific } i \text{ and all } j \neq i.$$

Example 10.3 A broadcast by P_2 is illustrated in Fig. 10.19 for $n = 5$. At the beginning of a bus cycle, P_2 places d_2 on the upper and lower buses, as shown in Fig. 10.19(a). The datum reaches P_1 and P_3 simultaneously, as shown in Fig. 10.19(b), and then it reaches P_0 and P_4 simultaneously, as shown in Fig. 10.19(c). The broadcast is complete within one bus cycle. $\square$

Permutation.   Suppose that an arbitrary permutation r of the indices $\{0, 1, \ldots, n-1\}$ is to be executed, where $0 \leq i, r(i) \leq n-1$, such that d_i is to be sent to $P_{r(i)}$, for every i and each processor receives exactly one datum. It suffices to set

$$wait(i, r(i)) = r(i) - i, \quad \text{for all } i.$$

Example 10.4 Suppose that $n = 5$ and that P_i holds d_i for $0 \leq i \leq n-1$. It is required to perform a permutation of the data such that P_0, P_1, P_2, P_3, and P_4 hold d_4, d_3, d_1, d_0, and d_2, respectively. The permutation, as it is executed on the linear array with optical buses, is illustrated in Fig. 10.20, where only the relevant data are shown on each waveguide. Initially, each processor places its datum on the upper and lower waveguides, at the beginning of a bus cycle; this is depicted in Fig. 10.20(a). In Fig. 10.20(b), d_1 reaches its destination at P_2, and the latter reads it from the upper bus. In Fig. 10.20(c), d_3 and d_2 reach their destinations, and they are read by P_1 and P_4, respectively. In Fig. 10.20(d), P_3 reads d_0, and finally, P_0 reads d_4, as shown in Fig. 10.20(e). The entire permutation is completed in one bus cycle. $\square$

Data Distribution.   In general, it may be required to send datum d_i, held by P_i, to two or more processors or to no processor at all. In this case, we can define $s(j)$ as the index of the processor from which P_j receives a datum, where $0 \leq j, s(j) \leq n-1$. This allows for the possibility that

$$s(j) = s(k) = i, \quad \text{for } j \neq k.$$

In other words, the function s is not necessarily a permutation. In order to perform

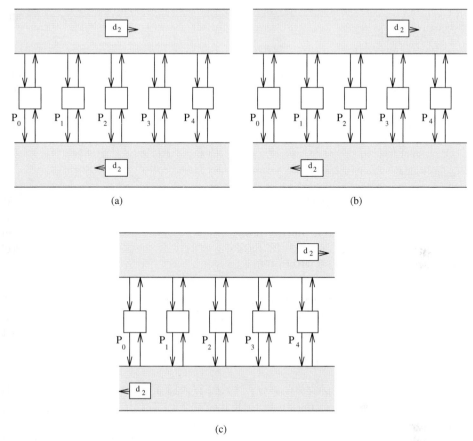

Figure 10.19: Broadcasting using optical buses: (a) At the beginning of the bus cycle, P_2 places d_2 on the upper and lower buses; (b) One time unit later, d_2 reaches P_1 and P_3 simultaneously; (c) Two time units after the beginning of the bus cycle, d_2 reaches P_0 and P_4 simultaneously.

this operation, we define the waiting function as

$$wait(s(j), j) = j - s(j), \qquad \text{for all } j.$$

Example 10.5 Suppose that $n = 5$ and that P_i holds d_i for $0 \le i \le n - 1$. It is required to distribute the data such that P_0, P_1, P_2, P_3, and P_4 hold d_3, d_3, d_0, d_1, and d_0, respectively. As shown in Fig. 10.20, the data distribution is performed in the same way as a permutation, except that this time P_0 and P_1 receive d_3, P_2 and P_4 receive d_0, and P_3 receives d_1. No processor receives d_2 or d_4. The entire data distribution operation is completed in one bus cycle. $\square$

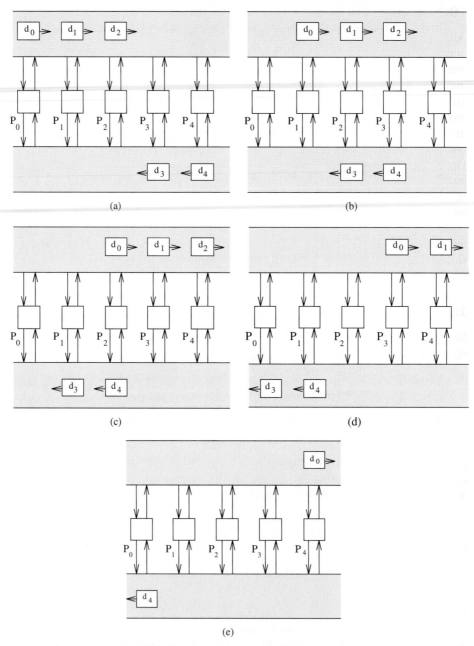

Figure 10.20: Data permutation and distribution using optical buses: (a) All data are placed on the buses, as described in Examples 10.4 and 10.5; (b)–(e) Each datum is read from the appropriate bus, as required.

10.3.3 PRAM Simulation

All three data communication operations of Section 10.3.2, namely, broadcasting, permutation, and data distribution, can be performed within one bus cycle and hence require constant time. It is particularly interesting to observe that the permutation and data distribution operations allow a linear array of n processors with optical buses and $O(1)$ memory locations per processor to simulate in constant time any form of memory access allowed on a PRAM with n processors and $O(n)$ shared memory locations (except for the concurrent-write operation **CW**). This is true because **ER** and **EW** are essentially permutations of the data, while **CR** can be viewed as a data distribution operation. On the other hand, **CW** cannot be simulated in constant time. To see this, recall that $\tau_{B(L)}$ is assumed to be smaller than or equal to the time required by a basic operation, such as adding or comparing two numbers, whereas a **CW** typically involves an arbitrary number of such operations.

It follows that any PRAM algorithm involving **ER**, **CR**, or **EW** can be performed in the same amount of time on a linear array with optical buses as on the PRAM (the processors used in the two models being identical in kind and in number).

10.3.4 Meshes with Optical Buses

In practice, two problems may arise in attempting to implement linear arrays with optical buses for large values of n:

1. Optical signals weaken rapidly as they travel over long distances.

2. The time taken by a message to travel from one end of the bus to the other (i.e., the bus cycle) grows considerably (as observed also for global electronic buses).

One solution to these problems is to use a two-dimensional array of processors augmented with row and column optical buses. The arrangement is shown in Fig. 10.21. The array consists of X rows, numbered 0 to $X - 1$, and Y columns, numbered 0 to $Y - 1$, where $XY = n$. Here, each processor is connected to four optical buses. The two buses on each row are used to send messages horizontally, as described for the linear array with optical buses. Similarly, the two buses on each column are used to send messages vertically. We refer to this model as a *mesh with optical buses*. (Note that, although the term *mesh* is used, no two processors are directly connected by a standard mesh-of-processors link.) A message can be sent from $P(i, j)$ to $P(k, l)$ in two bus cycles: First the message is sent from $P(i, j)$ to $P(i, l)$ and then from $P(i, l)$ to $P(k, l)$.

A Sorting Algorithm. We conclude our description of meshes with row and column optical buses by showing how n numbers can be sorted on the model. For the second time in this chapter, we invoke algorithm MESH SORT. As mentioned in Section 10.2.2, this algorithm sorts n numbers arranged in a rectangular array

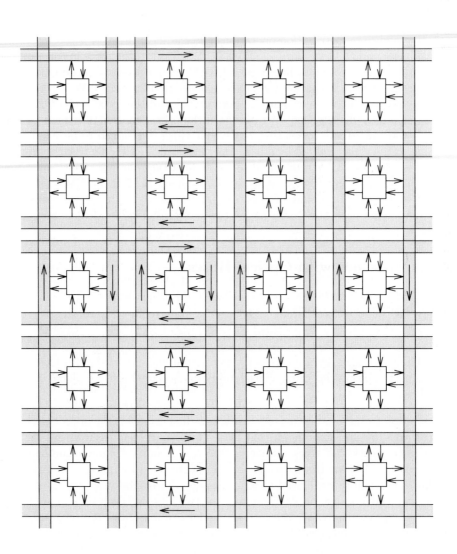

Figure 10.21: A mesh of processors with optical buses.

A, of 2^s rows and 2^{2r} columns, with $s \geq r$. Each step of the algorithm executes one or more of the following operations on A: Sorting a row, sorting a column, and cyclically shifting a row.

Now, suppose that A consists of $X = 2^s$ rows and $Y = 2^{2r}$ columns, where $s \geq r$ and $XY = n$. The elements of A are stored, one per processor, in the mesh of Fig. 10.21. Algorithm MESH SORT is now implemented as follows:

1. Whenever a row is to be sorted, the linear array with optical buses on that row simulates algorithm PRAM SORT.

2. Whenever a column is to be sorted, the linear array with optical buses on that column simulates algorithm PRAM SORT.

3. Whenever a row is to be cyclically shifted, this is done using function $wait(i, j)$, since a cyclic shift is just a permutation.

Analysis. We first note that algorithm PRAM SORT involves no **CW** instructions, and consequently, each memory access required by that algorithm can be simulated in constant time by a linear array with optical buses. Now, algorithm PRAM SORT sorts $n^{1/2}$ numbers in $O(\log n^{1/2}) = O(\log n)$ time, using $O(n^{1/2})$ processors. It follows that each application of algorithm PRAM SORT requires $O(\log n)$ bus cycles. There are 13 such steps in algorithm MESH SORT (nine column sorts and four row sorts). Each cyclic shift requires one bus cycle. There are four cyclic shifts in algorithm MESH SORT. Therefore, a mesh with row and column optical buses can sort a sequence of n numbers in time

$$t(n) = O(\log n),$$

using $p(n) = n$ processors, for a cost of $c(n) = O(n \log n)$, which is optimal.

10.4 PROBLEMS

10.1 Consider a linear array of n processors P_0, P_1, ..., P_{n-1}, augmented with a single global (electronic) bus (as defined in Problem 7.6 and illustrated in Fig. 7.27). Each processor P_i holds a number x_i. It is required to find the *median* of $\{x_0, x_1, \ldots, x_{n-1}\}$—that is, the $\lceil n/2 \rceil$nd smallest number in the sequence.

    (a) Show how the problem can be solved on the given model of computation in $O((n \log n)^{1/2})$ time.

    (b) Derive an $\Omega((n \log n)^{1/2})$ lower bound on the time required by *any* conservative flow algorithm for finding the median of n numbers on this model.

10.2 In Section 10.1.1, it is shown how the mesh of processors is enhanced with a single global bus. This idea can be extended to the q-dimensional lattice (a generalization of the mesh described in Problem 8.26 and illustrated, for three dimensions, in Fig. 8.18). Here, one bus connects all n processors P_1, P_2, ..., P_n of a q-dimensional lattice. Now, suppose that each processor P_i contains a number x_i. It is required to find the maximum of $\{x_1, x_2, \ldots, x_n\}$ such that when the algorithm terminates, P_1 holds the largest number in the sequence.

   (a) Derive an algorithm for the given model of computation that finds the maximum in $O(n^{1/(q+1)})$ time.

   (b) Show that $\Omega(n^{1/(q+1)})$ is a lower bound on the time required by any conservative flow algorithm for finding the maximum of n numbers on this model.

10.3 Given an n^q-processor q-dimensional lattice augmented with a single global bus, it is required to find the maximum of n numbers stored in the lattice.

   (a) Show how this computation can be performed in $O(n^{q/(q+1)})$ time.

   (b) Derive an $\Omega(n^{q/(q+1)})$ lower bound on the time required by any conservative flow algorithm for finding the maximum on this model.

10.4 Suppose that each processor P_i of an n-processor q-dimensional lattice augmented with a single global bus holds a number x_i, $1 \le i \le n$. It is required to sort $\{x_1, x_2, \ldots, x_n\}$ such that when the algorithm terminates, P_i holds the ith smallest number in the sequence. Show that, with or without broadcasting, any conservative flow algorithm requires $\Omega(n^{1/q})$ basic operations to complete the sort on this model. (*Hint*: First show that for any processor, the maximum number of processors at distance r is $2^q((r+q-1)!/(r-1)!q!)+1$. Then construct a permutation of the input that forces any sorting algorithm to execute at least $n^{1/q}$ separate data movement steps.)

10.5 Consider an $n^{1/2} \times n^{1/2}$ mesh augmented with l global buses. Each processor P_i stores a number x_i, $0 \le i \le n-1$. Derive a lower bound on the number of basic operations required by any conservative flow algorithm that sorts the sequence $\{x_0, x_1, \ldots, x_{n-1}\}$.

10.6 Suppose that an n^q-processor q-dimensional lattice is augmented with l global buses.

   (a) Design an algorithm for this model that finds the maximum of n numbers in $O((n^q/l)^{1/(q+1)} + \log n)$ time.

   (b) Derive an $\Omega((n^q/l)^{1/(q+1)} + \log n)$ lower bound on the number of basic operations required by any conservative flow algorithm that finds the maximum of n numbers on this model.

10.7 Two $n \times n$ matrices are stored, one element of each per processor, in an $n \times n$ mesh of processors augmented with l global buses. Show that $\Omega(n^2/(n+l))$ is a lower bound on the number of basic operations required to compute the product of the two matrices.

10.8 Suppose that an $n^{1/2} \times n^{1/2}$ mesh of processors is augmented with one bus per row. Each processor in the mesh holds either a 0 or a 1. It is required to find the location of the leftmost 1 in each row.

   (a) Show that if the problem is solved on each row independently of other rows (using the row buses and horizontal mesh links), the number of operations required is $\Omega(n^{1/4})$.

   (b) Derive an algorithm for solving the problem in $O(n^{1/4})$ time.

   (c) Show that if, in addition, vertical mesh links are used, the problem can be solved in $O(n^{1/6})$ time.

   (d) Derive an $\Omega(n^{1/6})$ lower bound on the number of operations required to solve this problem by any algorithm that uses all links and buses.

10.9 Consider again the model in Problem 10.8. Each processor P_i holds a number x_i. It is required to find the largest number in each row.

   (a) Derive an $\Omega(n^{1/6} \log^{1/3} n)$ lower bound on the number of operations required to solve this problem by any conservative flow algorithm that uses all links and buses.

   (b) Develop an $O(n^{1/6} \log^{1/3} n)$-time algorithm to solve the problem on this model.

10.10 An $n^{1/2} \times n^{1/2}$ mesh of processors augmented with b global buses holds a b-bit number in each processor. It is required to find the maximum of these numbers. We are allowed to use *any* type of algorithm; that is, the conservative flow restriction is removed. How fast can this problem be solved?

10.11 Repeat Problem 10.10 for the case where the n b-bit numbers are to be sorted in nondecreasing order.

10.12 Repeat Problem 10.10 for an n-processor q-dimensional lattice augmented with b global buses.

10.13 Repeat Problem 10.10 for an n^q-processor q-dimensional lattice augmented with b global buses and n input numbers of b bits each.

10.14 Repeat Problem 10.11 for an n^q-processor q-dimensional lattice augmented with b global buses.

10.15 Consider an $N^{1/2} \times N^{1/2}$ mesh augmented with row and column buses, as described in Section 10.1.2. Each processor holds a number. Show that the maximum of these numbers can be found in $O(N^{1/6})$ time.

10.16 Let n numbers be stored by the first column of processors in the model of Problem 10.15, one number per processor, where $n \le N^{1/2}$.

    (a) Show that the maximum of these numbers can be found on this model in $O(\log n)$ time.

    (b) Derive an $\Omega(\log n)$ lower bound on the number of basic operations required to solve the problem by any conservative flow algorithm running on this model.

10.17 Let n numbers be stored in the model of Problem 10.15, one number per processor, in column-major order, where $N^{1/2} \le n \le N$.

    (a) Design an algorithm for finding the maximum of these numbers on this model in $O(\max(\log(N^{2/3}/n^{1/3}), n^{1/3}/N^{1/6}))$ time.

    (b) Derive an $\Omega(\max(\log(N^{2/3}/n^{1/3}), n^{1/3}/N^{1/6}))$ lower bound on the number of operations required to solve the problem by any conservative flow algorithm running on this model.

10.18 Assume that n numbers are stored in the first $n^{3/8}$ columns of an $n^{5/8} \times n^{5/8}$ mesh augmented with row and column buses. Use the lower bound derived in Problem 10.17 to show that the running time of algorithm ROW AND COLUMN BUSES MESH MAXIMUM cannot be improved by using $n^{5/4}$ processors.

10.19 Design an algorithm for finding the median of n numbers in $O(n^{1/6})$ time on an $n^{1/2} \times n^{1/2}$ mesh of processors augmented with row and column buses.

10.20 Show that the median of n numbers can be found in $O(n^{1/8} \log n)$ time on an $n^{3/8} \times n^{5/8}$ mesh of processors augmented with row and column buses.

10.21 Design an algorithm that finds the kth smallest of n numbers for some k, $1 \le k \le n$, in $O(n^{1/8} \log n)$ time on the model of Problem 10.20.

10.22 Show that the kth smallest of n numbers for some k, $1 \le k \le n$, can be found in $O(n^{1/8} \log^{3/4} n)$ time on an $(n^{3/8} \log^{1/4} n) \times (n^{5/8}/\log^{1/4} n)$ mesh of processors augmented with row and column buses.

10.23 Suppose that each processor of an $n^{1/3} \times n^{5/9}$ mesh augmented with row and column buses has a memory of size $n^{1/9}$. Develop an algorithm that finds the kth smallest of n numbers for some k, $1 \le k \le n$, on this model in $O(n^{1/9} \log n)$ time.

10.24 A sequence of n numbers is stored, one number per processor, in the first column of an $n \times n$ mesh augmented with row and column buses. Show that the largest of these numbers can be found in $O(\log n)$ time.

10.25 Repeat Problem 10.24 for the case where the kth smallest number for some k, $1 \le k \le n$, is to be found.

10.26 Repeat Problem 10.24 for the case where the numbers are to be sorted in nondecreasing order.

10.27 A set of n points in the plane is stored in the first column of an $n \times n$ mesh augmented with row and column buses, each point being given by its x- and y-coordinates. Design an algorithm for computing the convex hull of the set on this model in $O(\log n)$ time.

10.28 Show that the convex hull of n points can be computed in $O(n^{1/8} \log^{3/4} n)$ time on an $(n^{3/8} \log^{1/4} n) \times (n^{5/8} / \log^{1/4} n)$ mesh augmented with row and column buses.

10.29 Given n points in the plane, it is required to determine, for each point, the closest of the other $n - 1$ points. Design an $O(\log n)$-time algorithm for solving this problem on an $n \times n$ mesh augmented with row and column buses.

10.30 A sorted sequence S_1 of n numbers is stored in row-major order, one number per processor, in a $n^{1/2} \times n^{1/2}$ mesh augmented with row and column buses. Given a second sequence S_2 of m numbers, it is required to design an algorithm that determines, for each element s of S_2, whether s belongs to S_1.

10.31 A q-dimensional lattice with n processors is augmented with a bus on each dimension. Design an algorithm for this model that finds the maximum of n numbers.

10.32 Repeat Problem 10.31 for the case where the number of processors on the q-dimensional lattice augmented with buses is n^q.

10.33 Suppose that an $n^{1/2} \times n^{1/2}$ mesh is augmented with l buses on each row and l buses on each column. How fast can the maximum of n numbers, stored one per processor, be found on this model?

10.34 How fast can the median of n numbers be found on the model of Problem 10.33?

10.35 How fast can the kth smallest of n numbers for some k, $1 \le k \le n$, be found on the model of Problem 10.33?

10.36 How fast can n numbers be sorted on the model of Problem 10.33?

10.37 Suppose that a q-dimensional lattice with n processors is augmented with l buses on each dimension. Given a set of n points in the plane, how fast can the closest point, among points in the set, to each of the n points, be found on this model?

10.38 A q-dimensional lattice with n^q processors is augmented with l buses on each dimension. Design an algorithm for computing the convex hull of n planar points on this model.

10.39 Suppose that n numbers $x_0, x_1, \ldots, x_{n-1}$, of b bits each, are stored one per processor in an $n^{1/2} \times n^{1/2}$ mesh augmented with row and column buses. The maximum of $\{x_0, x_1, \ldots, x_{n-1}\}$ can be found in $2b$ elementary steps by a nonconservative flow algorithm as follows: In the first b iterations, only row buses are used. During the ith iteration:

    (a) A processor P_j whose x_j has a '1' in bit position i places a '1' on its row bus.

    (b) All processors in a row read the bit on their row bus, and if it is '1', every processor P_k whose x_k has a '0' in bit position i turns itself 'off'.

    (c) A processor P_j whose x_j has a '1' in bit position i places a '0' on its row bus.

At the end of the b iterations, (at least) one processor per row is still on, and it holds the maximum number for that row. Each row maximum is now placed (using the row bus) in the leftmost processor of the row. The column bus on the leftmost column is now used to find the overall maximum in another b iterations, using the same approach as used for the rows. Design a similar algorithm for finding the kth smallest of n numbers for some k, $1 \le k \le n$.

10.40 How fast can the maximum of n numbers, of b bits each, be found by a nonconservative flow algorithm on an $n^{1/2} \times n^{1/2}$ mesh augmented with b buses per row and b buses per column?

10.41 Use the approach in Problem 10.39 to develop an algorithm for sorting n numbers on a mesh augmented with row and column buses.

10.42 Show how any permutation of n values $\{x_0, x_1, \ldots, x_{n-1}\}$ can be executed in constant time on a mesh with reconfigurable buses consisting of n rows and n columns of processors.

10.43 Design and analyze an algorithm for computing the reflexive and transitive closure of an undirected graph (as defined in Section 9.3.1) on a mesh with reconfigurable buses.

10.44 Design and analyze an algorithm for computing the connected components of an undirected graph on a mesh with reconfigurable buses.

10.45 Suppose that a linked list with n nodes is stored in an array, as described in Problem 6.5. Show how the list-ranking problem (defined in Section 6.2.2) can be solved in $O(\log n / \log m)$ time on a mesh with reconfigurable buses using $(m(n+1)+2) \times 3n$ processors, where $2 \leq m \leq n$.

10.46 Given a sequence with n parentheses, design an algorithm for solving the parenthesis-matching problem (defined in Problem 4.31) in $O(1)$ time using $O(n^2)$ processors on a mesh with reconfigurable buses.

10.47 Design an algorithm for adding two n-bit numbers in $O(1)$ time on a mesh with reconfigurable buses, and analyze the processor requirements of the algorithm.

10.48 Given n numbers $x_0, x_1, \ldots, x_{n-1}$, where $0 \leq x_i < 2^b$ for $0 \leq i \leq n-1$, and some positive integer b, show how their sum can be computed on a mesh with reconfigurable buses in $O(b + \log \log n)$ time and $O(n)$ processors.

10.49 Show how two n-bit numbers can be multiplied in $O(\log n)$ time on an $n \times 2n$ mesh with reconfigurable buses.

10.50 Design and analyze an algorithm for solving the lowest common ancestor problem (as defined in Section 6.3.4) on a mesh with reconfigurable buses.

10.51 Design and analyze an algorithm for computing the convex hull of a set of n planar points on a mesh with reconfigurable buses.

10.52 The *Hough transform* is a method of detecting the boundaries of objects in binary images. Consider the special case where straight-line edges are to be detected. We are given an $N \times N$ binary image with n pixels, where $n \leq N^2$. The pixels are given by their coordinates (x_i, y_i), assuming that they all fall in the first quadrant. We assume also that the image has been preprocessed, so that potential edge pixels are given the value '1', while all other pixels are given the value '0'. Each pixel (x_i, y_i) with value '1' is mapped into a point (θ, ρ) in parameter space, where θ is the slope of a line through (x_i, y_i) and ρ is the perpendicular distance from the origin to the line. Thus,

$$\rho = \lfloor x_i \cos \theta + y_i \sin \theta \rfloor.$$

This transformation maps collinear pixels to the same point (θ, ρ). In practice, the parameter space is divided into k discrete values for θ, namely, $\theta_0, \theta_1, \ldots, \theta_{k-1}$, and k discrete values for ρ, namely, $\rho_0, \rho_1, \ldots, \rho_{k-1}$. There are therefore k^2 points in the parameter space. For each of the pixels (x_i, y_i) and each θ_j, $0 \leq j \leq k-1$, $\rho(i, j)$ is computed, and a counter associated with $(\theta_j, \rho(i, j))$ is incremented. Detecting straight-line edges in the image now reduces to detecting points in the parameter space to which a large number of pixels (for example, δ or more, for some threshold δ) are mapped. Design an algorithm for computing the Hough transform on a mesh with reconfigurable buses.

10.53 In a black-and-white digitized image, two pixels are said to be *connected* if they are adjacent horizontally or vertically. It is required to assign a label to each black pixel such that two black pixels q_1 and q_2 have the same label if and only if there is a connected path consisting only of black pixels from q_1 to q_2. Show how this problem can be solved on a mesh with reconfigurable buses.

10.54 Given n bits, design and analyze an algorithm that computes their **xor** (i.e., their **exclusive-or**) on a mesh with reconfigurable buses.

10.55 A sequence $S = \{x_1, x_2, \ldots, x_{n^2}\}$ is given, where $x_i \in \{1, 2, \ldots, n\}$ for $1 \le i \le n^2$. It is required to construct a histogram of the elements of S—that is, to count, for each i, $1 \le i \le n$, how many elements of S are equal to i. Design an algorithm that solves this problem in $O(1)$ time on an $n \times n$ mesh with reconfigurable buses.

10.56 Design and analyze an algorithm for computing the prefix sums of a sequence $S = \{x_0, x_1, \ldots, x_{n-1}\}$ on a mesh with reconfigurable buses.

10.57 The idea of enhancing a mesh with reconfigurable buses can be extended to q-dimensional lattices. Design and analyze an algorithm for sorting n numbers on a three-dimensional lattice augmented with reconfigurable buses.

10.58 A linear array with optical buses and n processors is given. Each processor P_i holds a binary value v_i, $0 \le i \le n - 1$. It is required to compute the binary **or** of the values held by an arbitrary, but specified, subset of processors S. The result is to be stored in the memory of an arbitrary, but known, processor $P_j \in S$. Show how this computation is performed on the model.

10.59 Repeat Problem 10.58 for the case of several disjoint subsets $S_1, S_2, \ldots, S_l$ of processors. The binary **or** of the values held by the processors in each subset S_i is to be computed and placed in a distinct processor $P_j \in S_i$.

10.60 Can all data communication patterns described in Section 10.3.2 be implemented *in a constant number of bus cycles* on the mesh with optical buses? If not, suggest mechanisms that would make this possible. (*Hint*: Suppose that an arbitrary permutation needs to be performed. If the datum in processor $P(i, j)$ is to be sent to processor $P(k, l)$ through an intermediate processor $P(i, l)$, as described in Section 10.3.4, then this takes *two* bus cycles. Now, consider the case where $P(i, l)$ is used as an intermediate processor for an arbitrary number of such data transfers from one set of

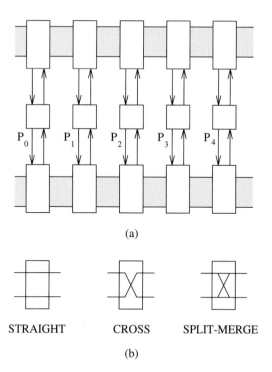

(a)

STRAIGHT   CROSS   SPLIT-MERGE

(b)

Figure 10.22: Linear array with reconfigurable optical buses: (a) Processor P_i is connected to each of the two waveguides by a switch; (b) The three states of a switch.

processors to another, and recall that a basic operation, such as comparison of indices, requires at least as much time as a bus cycle.)

10.61 Show how the *Gaussian elimination* algorithm of Section 8.3.2 can be implemented on a mesh with optical buses.

10.62 Solve Problem 5.4 on a mesh with optical buses.

10.63 It is possible to combine reconfigurable buses with optical buses to obtain a new communication medium that enjoys the powerful properties of the original ones. Consider the following model of computation illustrated in Fig. 10.22(a): The model consists of n processors P_0, P_1, ..., P_{n-1} connected to two optical buses. A processor P_i is connected to each of the two waveguides by a switch. The latter can be in one of three states, as shown in Fig. 10.22(b). In the STRAIGHT state, messages traveling on the bus are allowed to propagate through the switch, and the processor has no access to the bus. When the switch is in the CROSS state, a message traveling on the bus is not allowed to traverse the switch, while the processor can both read from and write to the bus. In the third state, namely, SPLIT-MERGE, messages traveling on the bus are allowed to propagate through the switch, and the processor can read from and write to the bus. This way, different subbuses can be created, as required by the algorithm. Such a model is known as the *linear array with reconfigurable optical buses*. Suppose that each processor of this model holds a binary value v_i, $0 \leq i \leq n - 1$. Let S be an arbitrary, but specified, subset of processors $P_{j(0)}, P_{j(1)}, \ldots, P_{j(k-1)}$ holding the values $v_{j(0)}, v_{j(1)}, \ldots, v_{j(k-1)}$, where $j(0) < j(1) < \cdots < j(k-1)$. It is required to perform a binary prefix **or** operation over the k binary values $v_{j(0)}, v_{j(1)}, \ldots, v_{j(k-1)}$ such that $P_{j(i)}$ stores $v_j(0)$ **or** $v_{j(1)}$ **or** $\cdots$ **or** $v_{j(i)}$ at the end of the computation, for $0 \leq i \leq k - 1$. Show how this computation can be performed on a linear array with reconfigurable optical buses.

10.64 Repeat Problem 10.63 for the case of several disjoint subsets $S_1, S_2, \ldots, S_l$ of processors, where a binary prefix **or** is to be performed on the binary values held by the processors in each subset.

10.65 Show how each of the following two PRAM concurrent write instructions involving an arbitrary number of processors can be simulated on a linear array with reconfigurable optical buses:

(a) **COMMON CW**.

(b) **PRIORITY CW**.

10.66 Given n one-bit values v_i, $0 \leq i \leq n - 1$, the binary prefix sums problem requires the computation of $b_i = v_0 + v_1 + \cdots + v_i$ for all $0 \leq i \leq n - 1$, where '+' denotes addition. Show how this computation can be performed on a linear array with reconfigurable optical buses.

10.67 Each processor P_i of a linear array with reconfigurable optical buses holds a datum x_i, $0 \leq i \leq n - 1$, where k of the x_i are nonzero. It is required to pack the k nonzero values (in their original order) in processors P_0, $P_1, \ldots, P_{k-1}$. Show how this can be done in $O(1)$ time.

10.68 Describe a model of computation in which an $n^{1/2} \times n^{1/2}$ mesh of processors is augmented with reconfigurable optical buses. (*Hint*: Extend the model in Problem 10.63 to two dimensions.)

10.69 Show that the model in Problem 10.68 can simulate, in constant time, all data-routing steps that can take place at the same time on an n-processor constant-degree interconnection network parallel computer.

10.70 A set of k nonzero data x_{ij} are arbitrarily dispersed, one datum per processor, among the n processors of an $n^{1/2} \times n^{1/2}$ mesh with reconfigurable optical buses. All other processors hold zero values. It is required to pack the k nonzero data in the first $\lceil k/n^{1/2} \rceil$ rows of the mesh. Show how this packing can be performed in constant time.

10.71 Consider a PRAM with N processors and M shared-memory locations, where $M = \Omega(N)$. Show how all memory access operations allowed on this model (as defined in Section 2.2.1) can be simulated on the model of Problem 10.68.

10.5   BIBLIOGRAPHICAL REMARKS

The properties of meshes and, more generally, q-dimensional lattices, augmented with global buses, were studied extensively in the literature. Algorithms and lower bounds for solving a variety of problems on these models are known, including such problems as semigroup computations (see, for example, Aggarwal [4], Bokhari [114], auf der Heide and Pham [290] and Stout [597]), finding the median (see, for example, Stout [597]), sorting (see, for example, auf der Heide and Pham [290], and Stout [597]), and matrix multiplication (see, for example, Aggarwal [4]). Algorithm GLOBAL BUS MESH MAXIMUM was first proposed in Bokhari [114] and shown to be time optimal by Aggarwal [4]. In Gurla [276] and Stout [598], algorithms are described for meshes augmented with one bus per row, while auf der Heide and Pham [290] consider meshes augmented with buses to which "concurrent writes" are possible. Machines that incorporate the global bus concept are described in Jordan [317] and Maresca and Li [406].

Algorithms for solving numerous problems were designed for the mesh augmented with row and column buses, including such problems as semigroup computations (see, for example, Bhagavathi et al. [104], Blais and ElGindy [110], Chen et al. [150], and Lin et al. [388]), finding the median (see, for example, Chen et al. [149, 150] and Prasanna Kumar and Raghavendra [498]), selection (see, for example, Bhagavathi et al. [101, 102] and Lin et al. [388]), sorting (see, for example, Krishnan and Murthy [332] and Lin et al. [388]), searching (see, for example, Bhagavathi et al. [104]), computational geometry (see, for example, Bhagavathi et al. [100, 103] and Bokka et al. [115]), and dynamic programming (see, for example, Ulm and Baker [616]). Algorithm ROW AND COLUMN BUSES MESH MAXIMUM was originally described in Chen et al. [150]; its time optimality was established by Bar-Noy and Peleg [86]. In Prasanna Kumar and Raghavendra [498] and Bar-Noy and Peleg [86], q-dimensional lattices augmented with a bus in each dimension are studied. Extensions to and variations of these models are described in Carlson [130], Chung [158, 159], Maeba et al. [399], Raghavendra [521], and Serrano and Parhami [560].

A considerable amount of attention has been paid to meshes enhanced with reconfigurable buses. Algorithms exist for solving computational problems on this model in many different areas, such as graph theory (see, for example, Alnuweiri [62],

Lin [386], and Wang and Chen [635]), image processing (see, for example, Al-nuweiri [61], Jenq and Sahni [314], Kao et al. [320], Lin et al. [389], Merry and Baker [423], and Pan [463]), sorting (see, for example, Chen and Chen [148], Jang and Prasanna [312], Merry and Baker [422], Nakano et al. [436], Nigam and Sahni [442], Olariu and Schwing [447], Olariu et al. [451, 452], and Wang et al. [636]), computer arithmetic (see, for example, Fragopoulou [241] and Thangavel and Muthuswamy [608]), and optimization (see, for example, Merry and Baker [421] and Olariu et al. [450]), as well as problems on sequences and linked lists (see, for example, Ben-Asher and Shuster [95] and Olariu et al. [449, 451]). Algorithm RECON-FIGURABLE BUSES MESH SORT was first presented in Wang et al. [636], while the improved algorithm of Section 10.2.3 was developed by Ben-Asher et al. [94]. The power of the model is investigated in Ben-Asher et al. [94], Fragopoulou [242], Olariu et al. [448], and Wang and Chen [634]. It should be noted that many interconnection networks are referred to in the literature as being *reconfigurable*, yet these models differ from one another, sometimes greatly and sometimes in subtle details. (See, for example, Li and Maresca [378], Li and Stout [380], Maresca [405], Miller et al. [425], Miller and Shuster [426], Rothstein [540], Shi et al. [563], Snyder [578], and Wang et al. [636].) Typical machines that use reconfigurable buses are described in Li and Maresca [379], Li and Stout [380], Maresca et al. [407], and Shu and Nash [570]. The problem of fault tolerance through reconfiguration in three-dimensional meshes is addressed in Chandra and Melhem [136].

As mentioned at the beginning of this chapter, different functions of L, the length of an electronic bus, may be used to describe the time taken by a datum of fixed size to go from one end of the bus to the other. These functions may be of the form L^2, L, or $\log L$, depending on the physical properties of the components used to implement the bus. Similarly, the time taken by a signal to traverse a given section of the bus is not always the same. Other difficulties usually associated with electronic buses are low bandwidth, capacitive loading, and cross talk caused by mutual inductance. All of these issues are discussed in Chiarulli et al. [153], Guo et al. [274], Melhem et al. [418], Qiao and Melhem [505], Ullman [615], and the references therein. Linear arrays and meshes augmented with optical buses are investigated in Chiarulli et al. [153], Guo [273], Guo et al. [274], Hamdi [283], Hamdi and Pan [284], Levitan et al. [374], Melhem et al. [418], Qiao and Melhem [505], and Qiao et al. [506]. Algorithms for sorting a sequence of numbers on a mesh with optical buses are described in Hamdi [283]. A model that combines optical buses with reconfiguration is proposed in Pavel and Akl [477, 479, 481, 480, 478]. A survey of results obtained on meshes enhanced with various forms of buses (electronic and optical) is provided in Pavel and Akl [482].

Chapter 11

Broadcasting with Selective Reduction

The most powerful model of parallel computation studied so far in this book is the PRAM. An algorithm that solves a problem of size n in $t(n)$ time units using $p(n)$ processors on any other model (interconnection network or combinational circuit) can be executed by the PRAM in *at most* $t(n)$ time units and using *at most* $p(n)$ processors. Our purpose in this chapter is to present a model even more powerful than the PRAM. Surprisingly, this model, which we call *broadcasting with selective reduction* (BSR), requires asymptotically no more resources than the PRAM for its implementation.

BSR is essentially an extension of the PRAM. As such, it consists of N processors, M shared-memory locations, and a memory access unit (MAU), as shown in Fig 11.1. All forms of memory access allowed by the PRAM, namely, exclusive read **ER**, exclusive write **EW**, concurrent read **CR**, and all forms of concurrent write **CW**, are allowed by BSR. Thus, during the execution of an algorithm, several processors may read from or write to the same memory location simultaneously, such that each processor gains access to at most one location. However, an additional type of memory access (not present on the PRAM) is permitted in BSR by means of which *all* processors may gain access to *all* memory locations at the same time for the purpose of writing. At each memory location, a subset of the incoming *broadcast* data is selected (according to an appropriate *selection* criterion) and reduced to one value (using an appropriate *reduction* operator). This value is finally stored in the memory location. We use the term *broadcasting with selective reduction* to refer to this form of memory access, which distinguishes BSR from the PRAM.

A memory access unit for the PRAM was designed as a combinational circuit in Section 2.4.2. In this chapter we show that a memory access unit for BSR, which accommodates all forms of memory access allowed on the PRAM, *plus* broadcasting with selective reduction, can be obtained by modifying the PRAM's MAU. The

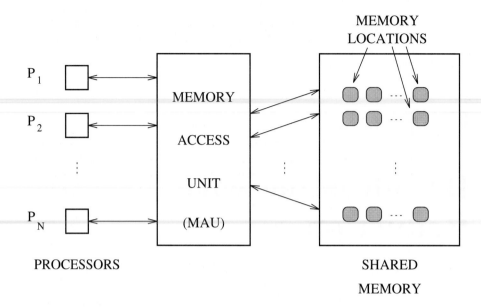

Figure 11.1: The BSR model of parallel computation.

width, depth, and size of the resulting MAU for BSR are the same as the PRAM's, namely, $O(M)$, $O(\log M)$, and $O(M \log M)$, respectively.

How Long Does a Step Take in BSR?   Since the BSR's MAU has asymptotically the same width, depth, and size as the PRAM's MAU, memory access in both models should require $\tau_a(N, M) = O(\log M)$. However, we assume here (as we did for the PRAM in Section 2.2.2) that

$$\tau_a(N, M) = O(1).$$

This means that broadcasting with selective reduction, as well as each of **ER**, **EW**, **CR**, and **CW**, takes constant time.

Similarly, a computational operation (arithmetic or logical) is also assumed to take constant time (as is the case for all computational models in this book); thus,

$$\tau_c(N, M) = O(1).$$

In other words, we use *uniform analysis* for BSR (as we did for the PRAM in Chapters 4, 5, and 6). Therefore, in the subsequent treatment, any elementary step in BSR requires constant time, unless otherwise stated.

The chapter is organized as follows: BSR is described formally in Section 11.1. BSR solutions to a number of computational problems are presented in Section 11.2. In Section 11.3, we construct a memory access unit for BSR. Finally, in Section 11.4, a generalization of the model is obtained in which several selection criteria are used. For convenience of notation, all indexing (for processors, memory locations, and data) begins at 1.

11.1 THE BSR MODEL

The BSR model of parallel computation is a PRAM augmented with an additional form of concurrent access to shared memory. Thus, BSR's repertoire of instructions is the same as that of the PRAM, plus one instruction called **BROADCAST**. This instruction allows all processors to write to all shared-memory locations simultaneously. Each **BROADCAST** consists of three phases:

1. A *broadcasting* phase, in which each processor P_i broadcasts a *datum d_i* and a *tag g_i*, $1 \leq i \leq N$, destined to all M memory locations.

2. A *selection* phase, in which each memory location U_j uses a *limit l_j*, $1 \leq j \leq M$, and a *selection rule σ* to test the condition $g_i \ \sigma \ l_j$. Here, g_i and l_j are variables of the same type (e.g., integers), and σ is a *relational operator* selected from the set
$$<, \ \leq, \ =, \ \geq, \ >, \ \neq \, .$$
If $g_i \ \sigma \ l_j$ is **true**, then d_i is selected for reduction in the next phase; otherwise d_i is rejected by U_j.

3. A *reduction* phase, in which all data d_i selected by U_j during the selection phase are combined into one datum that is finally stored in U_j. This phase uses an appropriate binary associative *reduction operator $\mathcal{R}$* selected from the set

$$\text{SUM, PRODUCT, AND, OR, EXCLUSIVE-OR,}$$

$$\text{MAXIMUM, MINIMUM.}$$

All three phases are performed simultaneously for all processors P_i, $1 \leq i \leq N$, and all memory locations U_j, $1 \leq j \leq M$, as illustrated in Fig. 11.2.

It is important to note here that all the data to be broadcast by the processors during the **BROADCAST** instruction are already available to the processors prior to the execution of this instruction. If a *datum* or a *tag* is not already stored in a processor's local register, the processor can obtain it from the shared memory by executing either an **ER** or a **CR** instruction. Similarly, the *limits*, as well as the selection rule σ and the reduction operator $\mathcal{R}$, are assumed to be known by the memory locations. If not, they can be stored in memory using appropriate **EW** or **CW** instructions.

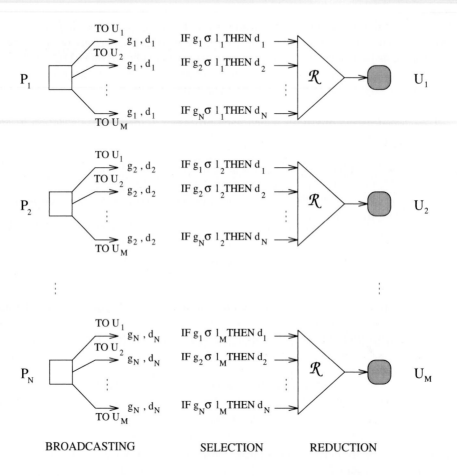

Figure 11.2: The three phases of the **BROADCAST** instruction.

Notation for the BROADCAST Instruction. Let $\mathcal{R}$ represent one of the following reduction operators:

$$\sum, \prod, \wedge, \vee, \oplus, \cap, \cup.$$

These operators denote the binary associative operations

SUM, PRODUCT, AND, OR, EXCLUSIVE-OR, MAXIMUM, MINIMUM,

respectively, applied to the elements of a set. The instruction **BROADCAST** of BSR is written as follows:

$$\mathop{U_j}_{1 \leq j \leq M} \leftarrow \mathop{\mathcal{R}}_{\substack{g_i \, \sigma \, l_j \\ 1 \leq i \leq N}} d_i.$$

This notation is interpreted as saying that, for each memory location U_j associated with the limit l_j, the proposition $g_i \, \sigma \, l_j$ is evaluated over all broadcast *tag* and *datum* pairs (g_i, d_i). In every case where the proposition is **true**, d_i is *accepted* by U_j. The set of all *data* accepted by U_j is reduced to a single value by means of the binary associative operation $\mathcal{R}$ and is stored in that memory location. If no *data* are accepted by a given memory location, the value (of the shared variable) held by that location is not affected by the **BROADCAST** instruction. If only one *datum* is accepted, U_j is assigned the value of that datum.

The preceding notation for the **BROADCAST** instruction is defined for all processors P_i, $1 \leq i \leq N$, and all memory locations U_j, $1 \leq j \leq M$. It is, of course, possible to specify that the instruction is to be executed for an arbitrary set of processors P_i, $i \in S_1$, and an arbitrary set of memory locations U_j, $j \in S_2$, where S_1 and S_2 are two sets of indices.

Comparing BSR to the PRAM. Two points are worth making when comparing BSR to the PRAM:

1. In BSR, the **BROADCAST** instruction requires $\tau_a(N, M)$—that is, $O(1)$—time. By contrast, on a PRAM with the same number of processors and memory locations, this mode of memory access would require $M \times \tau_a(N, M)$—that is, $O(M)$—time, since a **BROADCAST** is equivalent to M **CW** instructions.

2. Because all forms of memory access allowed on the PRAM are also allowed in BSR, the latter is *at least as powerful* as the former. The **BROADCAST** instruction, however, makes BSR *strictly more powerful* than the PRAM. To see this, consider the following computation: Suppose we are given a sequence of numbers $X = \{x_1, x_2, \ldots, x_n\}$, sorted in nondecreasing order, and a second sequence of distinct numbers $L = \{l_1, l_2, \ldots, l_n\}$, sorted in increasing order. It is required to compute, for $1 \leq i \leq n$, the sum s_i of all those elements of X not equal to l_i. On the RAM, the problem can be solved in $O(n)$ time, which is obviously optimal. This is done in three steps:

(a) The sum S of all the elements of X is first computed.

(b) The sequences X and L are merged into a third sequence Y, sorted in nondecreasing order, such that every element of L precedes every element of X that is equal to it.

(c) The sequence Y is scanned, and s_i, $1 \leq i \leq n$, is computed by subtracting from S all the elements of X equal to l_i.

On the PRAM, it is clear that no algorithm can solve this problem in constant time using n processors. Indeed, n processors can compute *one* of the s_i in $O(\tau_a(N, M))$—that is, $O(1)$—time, but not all of s_1, s_2, ..., s_n. On the other hand, n processors perform this computation in BSR using one **BROADCAST** instruction:

(a) Processor P_i, $1 \leq i \leq n$, broadcasts (x_i, x_i) as the *tag* and *datum* pair.

(b) Memory location U_j selects those x_i not equal to l_j, $1 \leq j \leq n$.

(c) Those x_i selected by U_j are added up to obtain s_j, $1 \leq j \leq n$.

This requires $\tau_a(N, M)$—that is, $O(1)$—time (and, in fact, does not depend on X and L being sorted).

11.2   BSR ALGORITHMS

We now illustrate the use of BSR in solving a number of fundamental computational problems. The power and elegance of the model are demonstrated by the efficiency and conciseness of the algorithms it affords.

11.2.1   Prefix Sums

Given a sequence of n numbers $\{x_1, x_2, \ldots, x_n\}$, it is required to compute their prefix sums $s_j = x_1 + x_2 + \cdots + x_j$, for all j, $1 \leq j \leq n$. A BSR algorithm for performing this computation is given next as algorithm BSR PREFIX SUMS. It uses n processors and n memory locations. Processor P_i broadcasts its index i as *tag* and the number x_i as *datum*. Memory location U_j uses its index j as *limit*, the relation $\leq$ for selection, and $\sum$ as a reduction operator. When the algorithm terminates, U_j holds s_j, $1 \leq j \leq n$.

> **Algorithm BSR PREFIX SUMS**
>
> **for** $j = 1$ **to** n **do in parallel**
>   **for** $i = 1$ **to** n **do in parallel**
> $s_j \leftarrow \sum_{i \leq j} x_i$
>   **end for**
> **end for.** ■

Analysis. The algorithm consists of one **BROADCAST** instruction. Thus, $p(n) = n$, $t(n) = O(1)$, and $c(n) = p(n) \times t(n) = O(n)$, which is optimal in view of the $\Omega(n)$ operations required to solve the problem.

Example 11.1 Algorithm BSR PREFIX SUMS is illustrated for the case $n = 3$ in Fig. 11.3. Let us consider P_1. It broadcasts the pair $(1, x_1)$ to the three memory locations U_1, U_2, and U_3, whose respective limits are 1, 2, and 3. Since the *tag* 1 satisfies the three propositions

$$1 \leq 1, \quad 1 \leq 2, \quad 1 \leq 3,$$

the *datum* x_1 is accepted by U_1, U_2, and U_3. Similarly, P_2 broadcasts $(2, x_2)$. Since $2 \nleq 1$, $2 \leq 2$, and $2 \leq 3$, the *datum* x_2 is accepted by U_2 and U_3. Finally, P_3 broadcasts $(3, x_3)$. Since $3 \nleq 1$, $3 \nleq 2$, and $3 \leq 3$, the *datum* x_3 is accepted by U_3 only. The data accepted by U_1, U_2, and U_3 are reduced using summation, and hence, x_1, $x_1 + x_2$, and $x_1 + x_2 + x_3$ are stored in U_1, U_2, and U_3, respectively, as required. $\square$

11.2.2 Sorting

Given a sequence of n numbers $X = \{x_1,\ x_2,\ \ldots,\ x_n\}$, it is required to rearrange the elements of X into a sequence $S = \{s_1,\ s_2,\ \ldots,\ s_n\}$ whose elements are sorted in nondecreasing order. The following solution to this problem is based on the approach known as *sorting by enumeration* (previously used in Sections 8.3.1 and 10.2.1):

A BSR algorithm for sorting $\{x_1,\ x_2,\ \ldots,\ x_n\}$ requires n processors and n memory locations and consists of two steps:

1. In the first step, the rank r_j of each element x_j is computed: Using a **BROADCAST** instruction, we count the number of elements x_i that are smaller than x_j. Each processor P_i broadcasts the pair $(x_i, 1)$, where x_i is the *tag* and 1 is the *datum*. Memory location U_j uses the value x_j as *limit*, the relation $<$ for selection, and $\sum$ as a reduction operator. When this step terminates, U_j holds r_j, for $1 \leq j \leq n$.

2. In the second step, x_j is placed in position $1 + r_j$ of the sorted sequence S. However, since several elements of X may be equal, they need to be placed in distinct positions of the sorted sequence. For example, if x_j, x_k, and x_m are equal, they all have the same rank; that is, $r_j = r_k = r_m$. We place x_j in position $1 + r_j$, x_k in position $2 + r_j$, and x_m in position $3 + r_j$ of S. The element with the next higher rank is placed in position $4 + r_j$ of S. This is done using a **BROADCAST** instruction: Processor P_i broadcasts the pair (r_i, x_i), where r_i is the *tag* and x_i is the *datum*. Memory location U_j uses its index j as the limit, the relation $\leq$ for selection, and $\bigcap$ as a reduction

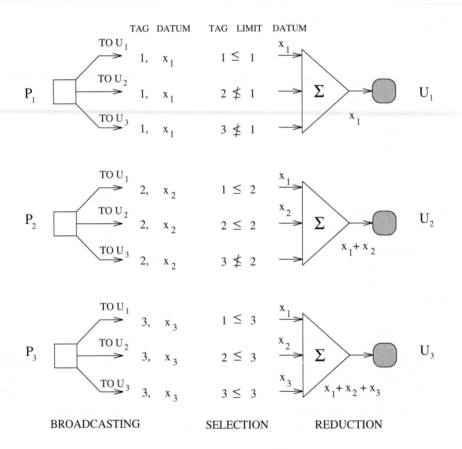

Figure 11.3: Computing prefix sums in BSR.

operator. When this step terminates, U_j holds s_j—that is, the jth element of the sorted sequence.

The algorithm is given next as algorithm BSR SORT:

Algorithm BSR SORT

Step 1: for $j = 1$ **to** n **do in parallel**
    (1.1) $r_j \leftarrow 0$
    (1.2) **for** $i = 1$ **to** n **do in parallel**
$$r_j \leftarrow \sum_{x_i < x_j} 1$$
    end for
  end for
Step 2: for $j = 1$ **to** n **do in parallel**
    (2.1) $r_j \leftarrow r_j + 1$
    (2.2) **for** $i = 1$ **to** n **do in parallel**
$$s_j \leftarrow \bigcap_{r_i \leq j} x_i$$
    end for
  end for. ∎

Example 11.2 Step 1 of algorithm BSR SORT is illustrated in Fig. 11.4 for the sequence $X = \{8, 5, 2, 5\}$. Processors P_1, P_2, P_3, and P_4 broadcast the pairs $(8, 1)$, $(5, 1)$, $(2, 1)$, and $(5, 1)$, respectively, to all four memory locations U_1, U_2, U_3, and U_4, whose *limits* are 8, 5, 2, and 5, respectively. Since $8 \not< 8$, $5 < 8$, $2 < 8$, and $5 < 8$, we have $r_1 = 3$. Similarly, since $8 \not< 5$, $5 \not< 5$, $2 < 5$, and $5 \not< 5$, it follows that $r_2 = 1$. Also, $8 \not< 2$, $5 \not< 2$, $2 \not< 2$, and $5 \not< 2$, giving $r_3 = 0$. Finally, $8 \not< 5$, $5 \not< 5$, $2 < 5$, and $5 \not< 5$, resulting in $r_4 = 1$.

Step 2 of the algorithm is illustrated in Fig. 11.5. Processors P_1, P_2, P_3, and P_4 broadcast the pairs $(4, 8)$, $(2, 5)$, $(1, 2)$, and $(2, 5)$, respectively, to all four memory locations U_1, U_2, U_3, and U_4, whose *limits* are 1, 2, 3, and 4, respectively. This gives the sorted sequence $\{2, 5, 5, 8\}$. □

Note that if it is necessary to distinguish among equal values of the input sequence X, then the *datum* broadcast by P_i is the pair (x_i, i), instead of simply x_i. Now, when two data x_j and x_k are found equal during the reduction phase, x_j is considered smaller than x_k, provided that $j < k$. (See also Problems 11.4, 11.5, 11.6, and 11.7).

Analysis. Algorithm BSR SORT uses $p(n) = n$ processors and runs in $t(n) = O(1)$ time, for a cost of $c(n) = O(n)$. This would appear to violate the $\Omega(n \log n)$ lower bound on the number of operations required to sort a sequence of n numbers in the worst case. However, recall that for BSR, *uniform analysis* was assumed; that is, $\tau_a(N, M)$, the time required for memory access, was taken to be $O(1)$, in keeping with the assumption made for the PRAM. Suppose, alternatively, that *discriminating analysis* is used; that is, $\tau_a(N, M)$ is taken to be equal

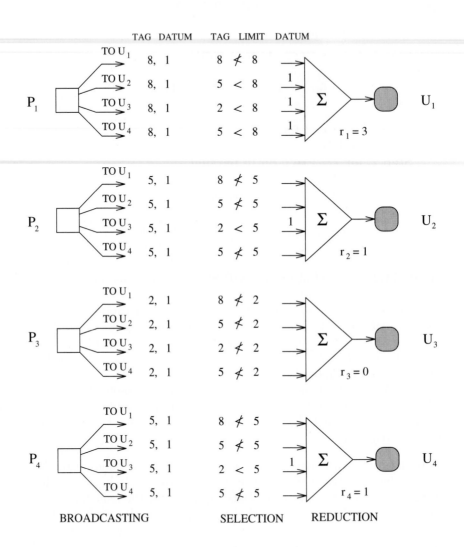

Figure 11.4: Step 1 of the BSR sorting algorithm.

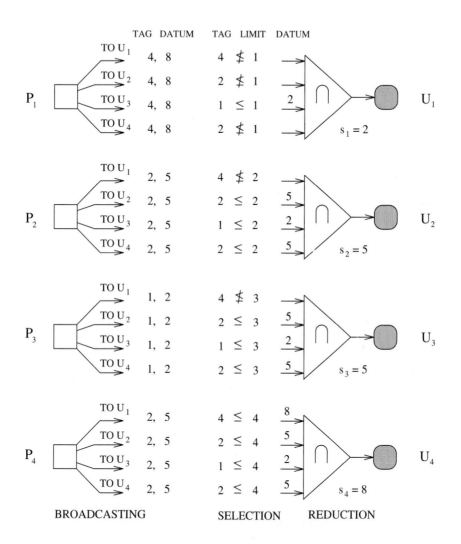

Figure 11.5: Step 2 of the BSR sorting algorithm.

to $O(\log M)$, for both BSR and the PRAM. Let us now examine the effect of this different assumption. (We continue to take $\tau_c(N, M) = O(1)$ for both models.)

In the case of algorithm BSR SORT, $N = M = O(n)$. Thus, $\tau_a(N, M) = O(\log n)$. The algorithm consists of two steps, each executed once and each containing a constant number of computations and memory accesses. Consequently,

$$t(n) = O(1) \times (\tau_a(N, M) + \tau_c(N, M)) = O(\log n),$$

for a cost of

$$c(n) = n \times O(\log n) = O(n \log n),$$

which is optimal.

Now consider algorithm PRAM SORT (of Section 4.9.2) for the sake of comparison. It, too, has $N = M = O(n)$. Thus, $\tau_a(N, M) = O(\log n)$. The algorithm executes $O(\log n)$ computational and memory access steps. Therefore,

$$t(n) = O(\log n) \times (\tau_a(N, M) + \tau_c(N, M)) = O(\log^2 n),$$

and the cost of executing the algorithm is equal to

$$c(n) = p(n) \times t(n) = O(n) \times O(\log^2 n) = O(n \log^2 n).$$

Obviously, this cost is not optimal.

11.2.3   Computing Maximal Points

Two points q_i and q_j in the plane are given by their Cartesian coordinates (x_i, y_i) and (x_j, y_j), respectively. Point q_i is said to *dominate* point q_j if and only if $x_i > x_j$ (i.e., the x-coordinate of q_i is larger than the x-coordinate of q_j) and $y_i > y_j$ (i.e., the y-coordinate of q_i is larger than the y-coordinate of q_j).

Let $S = \{q_1, q_2, \ldots, q_n\}$ be a sequence representing n points in the plane, where $q_i = (x_i, y_i)$ for $1 \le i \le n$. A point of S is said to be *maximal* with respect to S if and only if it is not dominated by any other point of S. Given such a sequence S, the problem of computing maximal points requires that we identify those points of S which are dominated by no others. (See Section 4.10.1.)

A BSR algorithm for this problem uses n processors and n memory locations, and consists of three steps:

1. An auxiliary sequence $\{m_1, m_2, \ldots, m_n\}$ is created, where m_i, associated with point q_i, is set initially to equal y_i, for $1 \le i \le n$.

2. Among all points to the right of q_i, the one with the largest y coordinate is found, and m_j is assigned the value of that coordinate. This is done simultaneously for all points q_j, $1 \le j \le n$, using a **BROADCAST** instruction. Processor P_i broadcasts (x_i, y_i), with x_i as the *tag* and y_i as the *datum*. Memory location U_j uses x_j as its *limit*, the relation $>$ for selection, and $\bigcap$ for reduction, to compute m_j. It accepts the y-coordinate of every point that lies strictly to the right of q_j and assigns the maximum of these to m_j.

3. A decision is made as to whether q_i is a maximal point. Suppose that in Step 2 m_i was assigned the y-coordinate y_k of some point q_k. If q_k lies above q_i, then q_k dominates q_i, since it is also to the right of q_i. In this case, m_i is set to 0. Conversely, if q_k does not lie above q_i, then q_k does not dominate q_i, and neither does any point in S. In this case, m_i is set to 1.

The algorithm is given next as algorithm BSR MAXIMAL POINTS. When the algorithm terminates, point q_i is maximal if and only if $m_i = 1$.

Algorithm BSR MAXIMAL POINTS
    Step 1: for $i = 1$ **to** n **do in parallel**
        $m_i \leftarrow y_i$
    end for
    Step 2: for $j = 1$ **to** n **do in parallel**
        for $i = 1$ **to** n **do in parallel**
            $m_j \leftarrow \bigcap\limits_{x_i > x_j} y_i$
        end for
    end for
    Step 3: for $i = 1$ **to** n **do in parallel**
        if $m_i > y_i$
        then $m_i \leftarrow 0$
        else $m_i \leftarrow 1$
        end if
    end for. ∎

Analysis. Each step of the algorithm uses n processors and runs in constant time. Therefore, $p(n) = n$, $t(n) = O(1)$, and $c(n) = O(n)$. This would seem to violate the $\Omega(n \log n)$ lower bound on the number of basic operations required to compute maximal points in a planar set of size n. However, by taking $\tau_a(N, M) = O(\log n)$, as we did in the previous section, the algorithm's cost becomes $O(n \log n)$, and that is optimal. Note, though, that when $\tau_a(N, M) = O(\log n)$, the PRAM algorithm for computing maximal points (described in Section 4.10.1) would have a running time of $O(\log^2 n)$ and a cost of $O(n \log^2 n)$, which is not optimal.

Example 11.3 Consider the three points in Fig. 11.6. After Step 1 of algorithm BSR MAXIMAL POINTS, we have $m_1 = y_1$, $m_2 = y_2$, and $m_3 = y_3$. After Step 2, $m_1 = y_3$, $m_2 = y_3$, and $m_3 = y_3$. Since $m_1 < y_1$, $m_2 > y_2$, and $m_3 = y_3$, both q_1 and q_3 are maximal. □

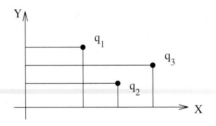

Figure 11.6: Computing maximal points in a planar set.

11.2.4   Maximum Sum Subsequence

Given a sequence of numbers $X = \{x_1, x_2, \ldots, x_n\}$, it is required to find two indices u and v, where $u \leq v$, such that the subsequence $\{x_u, x_{u+1}, \ldots, x_v\}$ has the largest possible sum

$$x_u + x_{u+1} + \cdots + x_v$$

among all such subsequences of X. This problem is studied in Section 4.3, and a PRAM algorithm is given there for its solution that uses $O(n/\log n)$ processors and runs in $O(\log n)$ time (assuming that $\tau_a(N, M) = O(1)$). We now show how the same algorithm can be implemented on the BSR model to run in $O(1)$ time using n processors (again under the assumption that $\tau_a(N, M) = O(1)$). The algorithm is given next as algorithm BSR MAXIMUM SUM SUBSEQUENCE:

Algorithm BSR MAXIMUM SUM SUBSEQUENCE

Step 1: for $j = 1$ **to** n **do in parallel**
 for $i = 1$ **to** n **do in parallel**
  $s_j \leftarrow \displaystyle\sum_{i \leq j} x_i$
 end for
end for

Step 2: (2.1) **for** $j = 1$ **to** n **do in parallel**
 for $i = 1$ **to** n **do in parallel**
  $m_j \leftarrow \displaystyle\bigcap_{i \geq j} s_i$
 end for
end for

(2.2) **for** $j = 1$ **to** n **do in parallel**
 for $i = 1$ **to** n **do in parallel**
  $a_j \leftarrow \displaystyle\bigcap_{s_i = m_j} i$
 end for
end for

Step 3: for $i = 1$ **to** n **do in parallel**
$$b_i \leftarrow m_i - s_i + x_i$$
      end for

Step 4: (4.1) **for** $i = 1$ **to** n **do in parallel**

          (i) $L \xleftarrow{\text{MAX}} b_i$

          (ii) **if** $b_i = L$

               then $u \xleftarrow{\text{ARBITRARY}} i$

               end if

        end for

    (4.2) $v \leftarrow a_u$. ∎

This BSR algorithm consists of four steps:

1. The prefix sums s_1, s_2, ..., s_n of x_1, x_2, ..., x_n are computed. This step uses algorithm BSR PREFIX SUMS.

2. For each j, $1 \le j \le n$, the maximum prefix sum to the right of s_j, beginning with s_j, is found. The value and index of this prefix sum are stored in m_j and a_j, respectively. To compute m_j, a **BROADCAST** instruction is used, where the *tag* and *datum* pair broadcast by P_i is (i, s_i), while U_j uses j as *limit* $\ge$ for selection, and $\bigcap$ for reduction. Similarly, to compute a_j, a **BROADCAST** is used, where P_i broadcasts (s_i, i) as its *tag* and *datum* pair, while U_j uses m_j, =, and $\bigcap$ as *limit*, selection rule, and reduction operator, respectively.

3. For each i, the sum of a maximum sum subsequence, beginning with x_i, is computed as $m_i - s_i + x_i$. This step is implemented using an **EW** instruction.

4. Finally, the sum and starting index u of the overall maximum sum subsequence are found. This requires a **MAX CW** instruction and an **ARBITRARY CW** instruction, respectively. The index at which the maximum sum subsequence ends is computed as $v = a_u$.

Analysis. Each step of algorithm BSR MAXIMUM SUM SUBSEQUENCE runs in $O(1)$ time and uses n processors. Thus, $p(n) = n$, $t(n) = O(1)$, and $c(n) = O(n)$, which is optimal.

Example 11.4 Let $X = \{-1, 1, 2, -2\}$. After Step 1 of algorithm BSR MAXIMUM SUM SUBSEQUENCE, the prefix sums are $s_1 = -1$, $s_2 = 0$, $s_3 = 2$, and $s_4 = 0$. The second **BROADCAST** instruction of the algorithm is illustrated in Fig. 11.7. When executed, it computes $m_1 = 2$, $m_2 = 2$, $m_3 = 2$, and $m_4 = 0$. The third **BROADCAST** instruction is illustrated in Fig. 11.8. Upon execution, it computes $a_1 = 3$, $a_2 = 3$, $a_3 = 3$, and $a_4 = 4$. Step 3 computes $b_1 = 2$, $b_2 = 3$, $b_3 = 2$, and $b_4 = -2$. Finally, in Step 4, $L = 3$, $u = 2$, and $v = a_2 = 3$. □

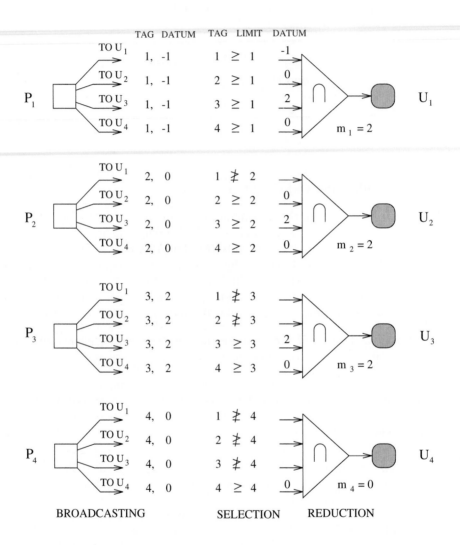

Figure 11.7: Second **BROADCAST** in maximum sum subsequence algorithm.

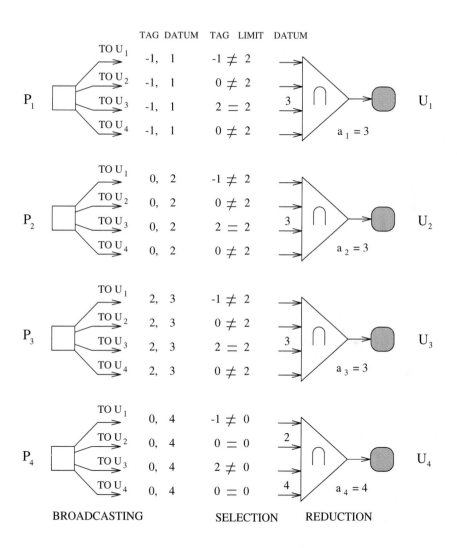

Figure 11.8: Third **BROADCAST** in maximum sum subsequence algorithm.

11.3   IMPLEMENTING MEMORY ACCESS

BSR, like the PRAM, is a shared-memory model of computation, consisting of a number of processors sharing a common memory to which they have access through a memory access unit. We now complete the specification of the BSR model, as we did previously for the RAM and the PRAM, by giving a full description of its MAU. This unit should be able to execute all forms of memory access allowed on the PRAM, plus the **BROADCAST** instruction. The principal conclusion of this section is that BSR, while more powerful than the PRAM, requires asymptotically no more resources than the latter to be implemented.

11.3.1   Building Blocks

We begin by recalling some notions presented in earlier chapters—combinational circuits for merging and sorting described in Chapter 3, the memory access unit designed for the PRAM in Chapter 2, a combinational circuit for computing prefix sums presented in Chapter 1, and the interval broadcasting problem discussed in Chapter 4.

Merging and Sorting Circuits.   Combinational circuits for merging and for sorting are described in Sections 3.1.1 and 3.5, respectively. The odd-even merging circuit of Fig. 3.3 merges two sorted sequences of total length n. The sorting-by-splitting circuit depicted in Fig. 3.24 sorts a sequence of length n. Both circuits have a width of $O(n)$, a depth of $O(\log n)$, and a size of $O(n \log n)$.

A MAU for the PRAM.   In Section 2.4.2, a memory access unit is designed for a PRAM with N processors and M memory locations. It uses a sorting circuit and a merging circuit, as shown in Fig. 2.30. When $N = O(M)$, this MAU has a width of $O(M)$, a depth of $O(\log M)$, and a size of $O(M \log M)$, all of which are optimal in view of the corresponding lower bounds derived in the section. Since BSR is more powerful than the PRAM, a memory access unit for it would be asymptotically optimal if its width, depth, and size matched those of the PRAM's MAU, up to a constant multiplicative factor.

A Circuit for Prefix Sums.   A combinational circuit for computing the prefix sums of a sequence of n numbers is presented in Example 1.3 and illustrated in Fig. 1.4. The circuit has a width of $O(n)$, a depth of $O(\log n)$, and a size of $O(n \log n)$.

Interval Broadcasting.   A PRAM algorithm for interval broadcasting, based on prefix computation, is discussed in Section 4.7. The structure of the algorithm, illustrated in Fig. 4.9, is essentially identical to the circuit of Fig. 1.4 for computing prefix sums.

A Circuit for Two-Way Prefix Computation.   A circuit that implements the PRAM algorithm of Section 4.7 for interval broadcasting is not difficult to obtain. By the last observation in the previous paragraph, the circuit of Fig. 1.4

for computing prefix sums fits the bill. Suppose now that the interval broadcasting problem is generalized as follows: A set of processors $P_1, P_2, \ldots, P_N$ is given, where some processors are marked as *leaders*. Each processor holds a variable. Depending on the context, each leader P_i may wish to assign the value of its variable:

1. Either to the variables of all the processors which follow it—that is, P_{i+1}, $P_{i+2}, \ldots, P_{j-1}$, up to, but not including, the next leader P_j.

2. Or to the variables of all the processors which precede it—that is, P_{i-1}, $P_{i-2}, \ldots, P_{k+1}$, down to, but not including, the previous leader P_k.

We refer to this as the *two-way interval broadcasting* problem. A circuit which solves the problem is obtained from that in Fig. 1.4 by simply adding a link going upward for each link going downward. This is shown in Fig. 11.9 for $N = 8$. The circuit consists of $1 + \log N$ stages (columns), each with N components numbered 1 to N from top to bottom. In each stage, component i is associated with processor P_i. The leftmost stage of components receives the input: Component i receives a variable from processor P_i. If P_i is a leader, then it also delivers to component i in the leftmost stage the direction in which it wishes to broadcast (i.e., up or down). The rightmost stage of components delivers the output, where each variable has been assigned a value appropriately. The circuit in the figure can, of course, be used for prefix and suffix computation, provided that each processor can perform all basic arithmetic and logical (binary associative) operations. Hereafter, we refer to this as *the circuit for two-way prefix computation.*

11.3.2   A Memory Access Unit for BSR

We now describe an implementation of the BSR's memory access unit as a combinational circuit. The MAU consists of three components:

1. A circuit for merging.

2. A circuit for sorting.

3. A circuit for two-way prefix computation.

All three circuits were reviewed in the previous section. We refer to them as the MERGE, SORT, and PREFIX circuits, respectively. The complete MAU is shown in Fig. 11.10; the MERGE circuit appears once, the PREFIX circuit twice, and the SORT circuit three times. In the remainder of the section, we show how the **BROADCAST** instruction is executed by this MAU. Other forms of memory access (i.e., **ER, EW, CR**, and **CW**) are executed by the MAU of Fig. 11.10 in a straightforward way.

Performing a BROADCAST.   When the **BROADCAST** instruction

$$\underset{1 \le j \le M}{U_j} \leftarrow \underset{\substack{g_i \, \sigma \, l_j \\ 1 \le i \le N}}{\mathcal{R}} d_i$$

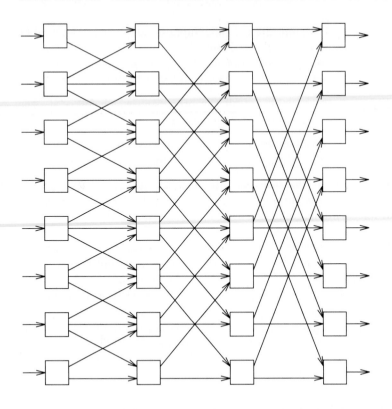

Figure 11.9: A circuit for two-way prefix computation.

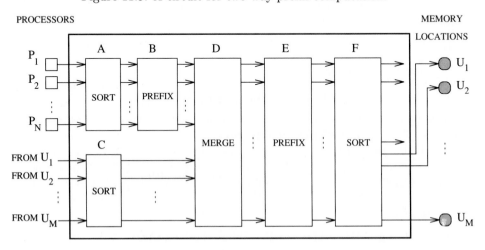

Figure 11.10: A MAU for BSR.

is to be executed, the information contained in the instruction is provided to the MAU as follows:

1. For $1 \leq i \leq N$, processor P_i produces a record (i, g_i, d_i), where i is the processor's index, g_i its *tag*, and d_i its *datum*. These N records are received as input by the MAU. Those processors which are not active at the point of execution of the **BROADCAST** produce records (i, g_i, d_i), with d_i equal to the identity element of the reduction operator $\mathcal{R}$ (e.g., 0 for $\sum$, 1 for $\prod$, and so on).

2. For $1 \leq j \leq M$, memory location U_j produces a record $(j + N, l_j, v_j)$, where j is U_j's *index*, l_j its *limit*, and v_j a *variable* that holds the datum to be stored in U_j. Those M records are also received by the MAU as input.

3. The specific instances of σ and $\mathcal{R}$ used by the **BROADCAST** (for example $\leq$ and $\sum$, respectively) are also received as input by the MAU.

The MAU uses this information to implement the **BROADCAST** instruction as follows:

1. The first SORT circuit (labeled A in Fig. 11.10) receives the processor records and sorts them on the *tag* fields g_i. The *datum* field d_i is used to order records whose *tag* fields are equal.

2. The first PREFIX circuit (labeled B in Fig. 11.10) receives the output of the SORT circuit A and performs a prefix computation on the d_i, as dictated by σ and $\mathcal{R}$. Thus, when the processor records exit this circuit, their d_i fields have been modified.

3. The second SORT circuit (labeled C in Fig. 11.10) receives the memory records and sorts them on the *limit* field l_j.

4. The MERGE circuit (labeled D in Fig. 11.10) receives a list of (modified) processor records sorted on g_i from the PREFIX circuit B and a list of memory records sorted on l_j from the SORT circuit C. It merges the two lists into one sorted list based on the g_i and l_j values.

5. The second PREFIX circuit (labeled E in Fig. 11.10) uses interval broadcasting to pass the values computed in the first PREFIX circuit B from the processor records (the *leaders*) to the memory records. It is here that the v_j's get their values from the (modified) d_i's.

6. The third SORT circuit (labeled F in Fig. 11.10) simply sorts all the records received from the PREFIX circuit E on their first—that is, *index*—fields, in order to separate the processor records from the memory records. Memory records thus emerge on lines $N + 1, N + 2, \ldots, N + M$ of the SORT circuit.

The value v_j thus exits the MAU on the proper line leading to U_j, and execution of the **BROADCAST** instruction is complete.

Example 11.5 Assume for the purpose of this example that $N = M = 4$, and let the **BROADCAST** instruction be

$$v_j \underset{1 \le j \le M}{} \leftarrow \underset{\substack{g_i < l_j \\ 1 \le i \le N}}{\sum} d_i.$$

Suppose that the four processor records (i, g_i, d_i) are

$$(1, 15, 9), \quad (2, -4, -5), \quad (3, 17, -2), \quad (4, 11, 10),$$

while the four memory records $(j + 4, l_j, v_j)$, are

$$(5, 16, v_1), \quad (6, 12, v_2), \quad (7, 18, v_3), \quad (8, -6, v_4).$$

Initially, $v_j = 0$, for $1 \le j \le 4$. When the **BROADCAST** instruction is complete, we want $v_1 = 9 - 5 + 10 = 14$ (since 15, -4, and 11 are less than 16), $v_2 = -5 + 10 = 5$ (since -4 and 11 are less than 12), $v_3 = 9 - 5 - 2 + 10 = 12$ (since all *tags* are less than 18), and $v_4 = 0$ (since no *tag* is less than -6). The progression of the processor and memory records through the BSR's MAU is illustrated in Fig. 11.11. Note that after merging of the records takes place (in circuit D), interval broadcasting is implemented (in circuit E), with the processor records as the *leaders*. Each *leader* assigns the value of its *datum* to the variables in all memory records separating it from the next leader. Thus, $(4, 11, 5)$ assigns the value 5 to v_2 in $(6, 12, v_2)$, while $(1, 15, 14)$ assigns 14 to v_1 in $(5, 16, v_1)$, and $(3, 17, 12)$ assigns 12 to v_3 in $(7, 18, v_3)$. Since no leader precedes $(8, -6, v_4)$, the variable v_4 is not assigned a new value and remains equal to 0. $\square$

Analysis.   Assuming that $N = O(M)$, each of the six circuits used by the MAU is easily seen to have a width of $O(M)$, a depth of $O(\log M)$, and a size of $O(M \log M)$. The MAU takes $O(M)$ inputs and produces M outputs. Therefore, the BSR's MAU has a total width, a total depth, and a total size of $O(M)$, $O(\log M)$, and $O(M \log M)$, respectively, all of which are optimal. An alternative MAU for BSR whose width, depth, and size are also optimal is described in Problem 11.28.

11.4   A GENERALIZATION OF BSR $(\star)$

Suppose that in some computational problem it is necessary for the datum d_i, broadcast by P_i, to satisfy more than one condition before being selected by memory location U_j. In other words, in order for a datum d_i received by U_j to participate in the reduction process leading to the value eventually stored in U_j, it must first pass several tests of the form $g_i \ \sigma \ l_j$.

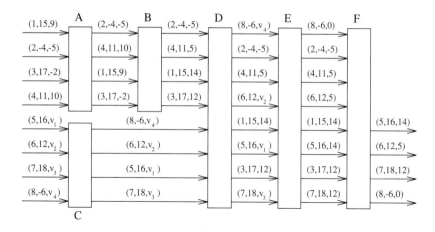

Figure 11.11: Implementing a **BROADCAST** instruction.

Example 11.6 Recall the GPC problem of Section 4.9. In it, we are given two sequences of elements $\{f(1), f(2), \ldots, f(n)\}$ and $\{y(1), y(2), \ldots, y(n)\}$, with a binary associative operator $*$ defined on the f elements and a linear order $\prec$ defined on the y elements. For $m = 1, 2, \ldots, n$, it is desired to compute

$$D(m) = f(j_1) * f(j_2) * \cdots * f(j_k),$$

where $j_1 < j_2 < \cdots < j_k$ and $\{j_1, j_2, \ldots, j_k\}$ is the sequence of indices for which $j_i < m$ and $y(j_i) \prec y(m)$, $1 \leq i \leq k$. In order to solve the GPC problem in constant time in BSR, a double selection is required, the first selection rule being $j_i < m$ and the second $y(j_i) \prec y(m)$. □

11.4.1 The Multiple-Criteria BROADCAST

We now describe a generalization of the BSR model in which each broadcast datum can be tested for its satisfaction of k selection criteria, for some $k \geq 1$. To that end, a new **BROADCAST** instruction is derived that is a natural extension of the one used so far. Let:

1. σ_h be a selection rule, equal to one of $\{<, \leq, =, \geq, >, \neq\}$, for $1 \leq h \leq k$.

2. $g(i, h)$ be a *tag* broadcast by processor P_i, $1 \leq i \leq N$, to be used with σ_h, $1 \leq h \leq k$.

3. $l(j, h)$ be a *limit* value associated with memory location U_j, $1 \leq j \leq M$, to be used with σ_h, $1 \leq h \leq k$.

The k-criteria BROADCAST instruction is thus denoted by

$$U_j \underset{1 \le j \le M}{\leftarrow} \underset{1 \le i \le n}{\mathcal{R}} d_i \mid \underset{1 \le h \le k}{\bigwedge} g(i,h) \; \sigma_h \; l(j,h),$$

where, as before, d_i is the datum broadcast by P_i, $\bigwedge$ stands for AND, and $\mathcal{R}$ is equal to one of

$$\Sigma, \; \Pi, \; \wedge, \; \vee, \; \oplus, \; \cap, \; \cup.$$

This instruction is interpreted as follows: Simultaneously with all other processors, P_i, $1 \le i \le N$, broadcasts the *tags* $g(i,1)$, $g(i,2)$, ..., $g(i,k)$ and the *datum* d_i. Each memory location U_j, $1 \le j \le M$, is associated with the *limits* $l(j,1)$, $l(j,2)$, ..., $l(j,k)$. If $g(i,h) \; \sigma_h \; l(j,h)$ is **true** for each h, $1 \le h \le k$, then d_i, $1 \le i \le N$, is accepted by U_j, $1 \le j \le M$. The set of all *data* accepted by U_j is reduced to a single value using $\mathcal{R}$, and this value is stored in U_j. If only one *datum* is accepted, then U_j is assigned the value of that *datum*. If no *data* are accepted by a given memory location U_j, then no writing in U_j takes place (i.e., the value originally in U_j remains unchanged).

11.4.2 Constructing Adjacency Maps

As an illustration of the generalized BSR model, we describe a problem that can be solved using a **BROADCAST** instruction with three selection criteria. Consider the sequence $V = \{v_1, \, v_2, \, \ldots, \, v_n\}$ representing a set of n vertical straight-line segments in the plane. Such a set is shown with solid lines in Fig. 11.12. Each segment v_i is given by the two coordinates of its top and bottom endpoints, namely, (x_i, a_i) and (x_i, b_i), respectively. Through each endpoint of each segment, we trace two horizontal half lines, one extending to the right and one to the left. These lines are shown dashed in the figure. Each of these half lines either terminates by meeting another vertical segment or continues to infinity. In this manner, the plane is partitioned into several regions. Two of these regions are half planes (denoted with A and B in the figure), some are unbounded rectangles (for example, the rectangles C and D in the figure), and some are bounded rectangles (for example, the rectangles E and F in the figure). Each region consists of those points in the plane which have the same closest segment to the right (if any) and the same closest segment to the left (if any). For example, segments v_3 and v_4 are the closest segments to the points in rectangle F. This partition is called a *horizontal adjacency map*. It can be fully specified by giving, for each endpoint of a segment, its closest segment to the right (if any) and its closest segment to the left (if any).

In order to construct the horizontal adjacency map for a given set V in BSR, we assume that the segments have been sorted by their x-coordinates, using algorithm BSR SORT, such that $x_1 \le x_2 \le \cdots \le x_n$, as shown in Fig. 11.12. Note that if it is required to distinguish between two segments that happen to have the same x-coordinate, then algorithm BSR SORT must first be modified as described in Section 11.2.2.

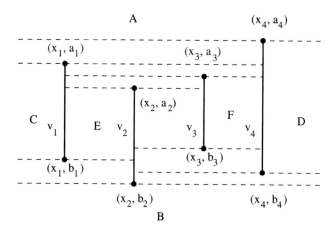

Figure 11.12: Computing the adjacency map for a set of vertical segments.

Let la_j and ra_j be the indices of the closest segments to the left and right, respectively, of the top endpoint of v_j. These indices are computed from

$$\underset{1 \le j \le n}{la_j} \leftarrow \bigcap_{1 \le i \le n} i \mid x_i < x_j \bigwedge a_i \ge a_j \bigwedge b_i \le a_j,$$

$$\underset{1 \le j \le n}{ra_j} \leftarrow \bigcup_{1 \le i \le n} i \mid x_i > x_j \bigwedge a_i \ge a_j \bigwedge b_i \le a_j.$$

Similarly, let lb_j and rb_j be the indices of the closest segment to the left and right, respectively, of the bottom endpoint of v_j. These indices are computed from

$$\underset{1 \le j \le n}{lb_j} \leftarrow \bigcap_{1 \le i \le n} i \mid x_i < x_j \bigwedge a_i \ge b_j \bigwedge b_i \le b_j,$$

$$\underset{1 \le j \le n}{rb_j} \leftarrow \bigcup_{1 \le i \le n} i \mid x_i > x_j \bigwedge a_i \ge b_j \bigwedge b_i \le b_j.$$

The adjacency map is therefore obtained using four **BROADCAST** instructions.

11.5 PROBLEMS

11.1 Given a sequence of n numbers $\{x_1, x_2, \ldots, x_n\}$, it is required to determine whether the numbers are all distinct. This is known as the *element uniqueness problem*. One simple way to solve the problem is to sort the numbers and then check whether any two adjacent numbers in the sorted sequence are equal. Show that the following BSR algorithm solves the element uniqueness problem (without explicitly sorting the input sequence):

Algorithm BSR ELEMENT UNIQUENESS

Step 1: for $i = 1$ **to** $n + 1$ **do in parallel**
$\qquad a_i \leftarrow 1$
end for

Step 2: for $j = 1$ **to** n **do in parallel**
$\qquad$ **for** $i = 1$ **to** n **do in parallel**
$$a_j \leftarrow \sum_{x_i \, = \, x_j} 1$$
$\qquad$ **end for**
end for

Step 3: for $i = 1$ **to** n **do in parallel**
$\qquad$ **if** $a_i > 1$
$\qquad$ **then** $a_{n+1} \xleftarrow{\text{SUM}} a_i$
$\qquad$ **end if**
end for

Step 4: if $a_{n+1} = 1$
$\qquad$ **then** all the elements are distinct
$\qquad$ **else**   at least two elements are equal
$\qquad$ **end if.** ∎

11.2 For two positive integers x and y, let $x \mid y$ denote the fact that x is a divisor of y; that is, $y = ax$ for some integer $a \geq 1$. An integer $m > 1$ is said to be a *prime number* if its only divisors are 1 and itself; otherwise m is *composite*. Given a positive integer n, show that the following BSR algorithm (based on a method known as the *sieve of Eratosthenes*) finds all primes smaller than or equal to n:

Algorithm BSR SIEVE

Step 1: for $i = 2$ **to** n **do in parallel**
$\qquad d_i \leftarrow 1$
end for

Step 2: for $j = 2$ **to** n **do in parallel**
$\qquad$ **for** $i = 2$ **to** n **do in parallel**
$$d_j \leftarrow \sum_{i \mid j} 1$$
$\qquad$ **end for**
end for

Step 3: for $i = 2$ **to** n **do in parallel**
$\qquad$ **if** $d_i = 1$
$\qquad$ **then** i is prime
$\qquad$ **else** i is composite
$\qquad$ **end if**
end for. ∎

11.3 Given an $m \times n$ matrix D, all of whose elements d_{ij} are integers, it is required to find indices q_1, q_2, r_1, and r_2, where $q_1 \leq r_1$ and $q_2 \leq r_2$, such that

$$\sum_{i=q_1}^{r_1} \sum_{j=q_2}^{r_2} d_{ij}$$

is maximal over all choices of q_1, q_2, r_1, and r_2. In other words, a submatrix of D is to be found whose sum is the largest among all submatrices of D. (See Problem 4.22.) Use algorithm BSR MAXIMUM SUM SUBSEQUENCE to obtain a BSR algorithm for solving this problem.

11.4 A sorting algorithm is said to be *stable* if two equal values occupy the same respective positions after the sorting, as they did before the sorting. In other words, if x_i and x_j are input elements, where $x_i = x_j$ and $i < j$, then a stable sorting algorithm places x_i before x_j in the sorted sequence. Show that algorithm BSR SORT is not stable.

11.5 Show that the following BSR algorithm for sorting the sequence of numbers $\{x_1, x_2, \ldots, x_n\}$ is stable. Begin by computing the smallest positive difference δ (if any) between two inputs, as follows:

> **Step 1: for** $j = 1$ **to** n **do in parallel**
>   **(1.1)** $a_j \leftarrow x_j$
>   **(1.2) for** $i = 1$ **to** n **do in parallel**
> $a_j \leftarrow \bigcup_{x_i > x_j} x_i$
>   **end for**
> **end for**
> **Step 2: for** $i = 1$ **to** n **do in parallel**
> $\delta \overset{\text{MIN}}{\longleftarrow} (a_i - x_i)$
> **end for.** ∎

Now each input x_i is mapped to a number y_i, where $y_i = (x_i \times n) + (i \times \delta)$, for $i = 1, 2, \ldots, n$. Algorithm BSR SORT is then applied to the sequence $\{y_1, y_2, \ldots, y_n\}$. Finally, each element of the sorted sequence is mapped back to its original value.

11.6 Show that the following BSR algorithm, which takes the sequence $\{x_1, x_2, \ldots, x_n\}$ as input and sorts it into the sequence $\{s_1, s_2, \ldots, s_n\}$, is stable:

> **Algorithm BSR STABLE SORT**
>   **Step 1: for** $j = 1$ **to** n **do in parallel**
>   **for** $i = 1$ **to** n **do in parallel**

$$r_j \leftarrow \sum_{x_i \leq x_j} 1$$

end for
end for
Step 2: (2.1) **for** $i = 1$ **to** n **do in parallel**
(i) $g_i \leftarrow r_i - (1/i)$
(ii) $l_i \leftarrow g_i$
end for
(2.2) **for** $j = 1$ **to** n **do in parallel**
for $i = 1$ **to** n **do in parallel**

$$q_j \leftarrow \sum_{g_i \leq l_j} 1$$

end for
end for
Step 3: for $i = 1$ **to** n **do in parallel**
(3.1) $k \leftarrow q_i$
(3.2) $s_k \leftarrow x_i$
end for. ■

11.7 A stable sorting algorithm can be obtained by using the following condition when comparing two elements x_i and x_j of the input sequence to be sorted: Element x_i is said to be smaller than element x_j, provided that

$$(x_i < x_j) \quad \text{or} \quad (x_i = x_j \text{ and } i < j).$$

(a) Show that this condition can be expressed as

$$i \times (x_i - x_j + 1) < j \times (x_j - x_i + 1).$$

(b) Design a stable sorting algorithm for BSR that uses the condition in **(a)**.

11.8 Consider the following algorithm for computing the upper hull (as defined in Section 5.4.1) of a set of points in the plane represented by the sequence $S = \{q_1, q_2, \ldots, q_n\}$, where no three points form a straight line:

Algorithm BSR UPPER HULL

Step 1: Sort the points of S by their x-coordinates.
Step 2: for each point q_i of S **do**
(2.1) Among all points to the *right* of q_i, find the point q_j such that the line supporting the segment (q_i, q_j) forms the largest angle with the horizontal
(2.2) Label all the points of S that fall below (q_i, q_j)
end for
Step 3: All unlabeled points form the upper hull. ■

Show how this algorithm can be implemented on the BSR model. In particular, provide the details of the instructions used for memory access in Step 2.

11.9 Let the sequence $S = \{q_1, q_2, \ldots, q_n\}$ represent n points in the plane, no three of which form a straight line. Design a BSR algorithm that computes the convex hull of S using the following approach: Consider a point q_i. Connect q_i to each of the other $n-1$ points in S using straight line segments. Now measure the angle between each pair of adjacent segments (q_i, q_j) and (q_i, q_k). If the largest such angle is smaller than 180 degrees, then q_i is not a corner of the convex hull; otherwise it is.

11.10 Consider an image represented as an $n \times n$ array of elements $a_{ij} = 1$ (called *feature* elements) and elements $a_{ij} = 0$ (called *nonfeature* elements), for $i, j = 1, 2, \ldots, n$. It is required to find, for each point (i, j) of the array, its minimum distance from the set of feature elements (i.e., the set of pairs (x, y) such that $a_{xy} = 1$). In the field of *image processing*, this is known as a *distance transform* (DT). Design a BSR algorithm for computing the DT, using an appropriate definition of *distance*.

11.11 Design a BSR algorithm for solving the parenthesis-matching problem described in Problem 4.31.

11.12 A set of intervals (a_i, b_i) on a straight line is given. Design a BSR algorithm to determine whether any intervals overlap.

11.13 Given a set of intervals on a straight line, design a BSR algorithm that finds the size of the interval resulting from the union of the original intervals.

11.14 Given $n+1$ real numbers $x_1, x_2, \ldots, x_n$ and $\epsilon > 0$, design a BSR algorithm that determines whether any two of the first n numbers (for example, x_i and x_j, where $i \neq j$) are at a distance less than ϵ from each other.

11.15 Design a BSR algorithm for finding the intersection of two polygons.

11.16 Let Q_1 and Q_2 be two convex polygons, and let α be some angle. Design a BSR algorithm that determines, for each edge of Q_1, a vertex of Q_2 closest to it, after Q_2 has been rotated counterclockwise by the angle α.

11.17 Let X_1 be a string of n characters, called the *text*, and X_2 a string of m characters, called the *pattern*, where $m \leq n$. It is required to design an algorithm that finds all occurrences of the pattern in the text. Specifically, the algorithm should determine all i, $1 \leq i \leq n$, such that $X_1(i + j - 1) = X_2(j)$, for all $1 \leq j \leq m$.

11.18 Repeat Problem 11. 17 for the case where the pattern contains a number of "don't care" characters, denoted by '$*$', each of which may match any text character.

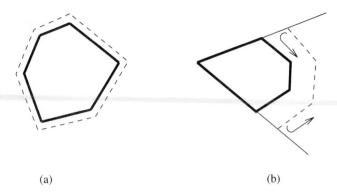

(a)   (b)

Figure 11.13: External watchperson's routes for convex polygons: (a) Wrapping route; (b) Two-leg route.

11.19 Let Q be a convex polygon in the plane. Two points outside Q are *visible* from one another if the straight-line segment connecting them does not intersect the boundary of Q. A closed path C in the plane with the property that each point outside Q is visible from some point on C is called an *external watchperson's route* for Q. There are two kinds of watchperson's routes, namely, a *wrapping route* (as shown in Fig. 11.13(a)) and a *two-leg route* (as shown in Fig. 11.13(b)). Design a BSR algorithm to compute a shortest external watchperson's route for a given convex polygon Q.

11.20 A *matching* in an undirected graph $G = (V, E)$ is a subset $\mathcal{M}$ of E such that no two edges in $\mathcal{M}$ share a vertex. A matching has *maximum cardinality* if no other matching in G contains more edges. Design a BSR algorithm for finding a maximum cardinality matching in a given graph G.

11.21 Repeat Problem 11.20 for the case where G is bipartite.

11.22 A matching of $G = (V, E)$ is said to be *perfect* if it includes all the vertices in V. Assume that G is a graph with $2n$ vertices that is weighted and *complete* (i.e., every two vertices of G are connected by an edge). Design a BSR algorithm for computing a perfect matching of G that has minimum weight.

11.23 Repeat Problem 11.22 for the case where G is bipartite. This instance of the minimum-weight perfect-matching problem is known as the *assignment problem*.

11.24 Repeat Problem 11.22 for the case where the vertices of G are points in the plane and the weight on each edge is the Euclidean distance separating the two endpoints of the edge.

11.25 Repeat Problem 11.24 for the case where the set of points in the plane is bipartite. Specifically, let $2n$ points in the plane be given, of which n are colored red and n are colored blue. It is required to design a BSR algorithm that associates every blue point with exactly one red point and every red point with exactly one blue point, such that the sum of the Euclidean distances between the pairs thus found is the smallest possible. This is a special case of the assignment problem (Problem 11.23) for points in the plane.

11.26 Let T be a given binary tree (which is not necessarily complete). It is sometimes useful to encode such a tree as a sequence of 0's and 1's in the following way: All vertices of T are labeled with a '1', and all *absent* children are replaced by vertices labeled with a '0'. (Any vertex, other than a leaf, with one or no children has one or two absent children, respectively.) The resulting tree is called the *extended tree*. A preorder traversal of the extended tree is a sequence of 0's and 1's representing the encoding $E(T)$ of T. Given $E(T)$, design a BSR algorithm that obtains T from $E(T)$. (In other words, the algorithm reconstructs the tree from the sequence of 0's and 1's.)

11.27 Given a finite family $\mathcal{F}$ of nonempty sets, the *intersection graph $G = (V, E)$* of $\mathcal{F}$ is designed as follows: Each vertex in V corresponds to a set in $\mathcal{F}$, and each edge in E connects two vertices corresponding to two sets in $\mathcal{F}$ that intersect. If $\mathcal{F}$ is a family of arcs on a circle, then G is called a *circular arc graph*. If there exists a family $\mathcal{F}$ of arcs such that G is the intersection graph of $\mathcal{F}$, then G is called a *proper circular arc graph*. Repeat Problem 11.20 for the case where G is a proper circular arc graph.

11.28 It is required to show that the combinational circuit depicted in Fig. 11.14 and described in what follows can serve as a memory access unit for both the PRAM and the BSR model. In the circuit of that figure:

(a) SORT is a sorting circuit (for example, the sorting-by-splitting circuit of Section 3.5).

(b) PREFIX is a circuit for two-way prefix computation (as described in Section 11.3.1), each of whose components can perform all basic arithmetic and logical operations.

On the PRAM, when a memory access instruction (e.g., **ER**, **EW**, **CR**, or **CW**) is to be executed, each processor P_i submits a record (IN-STRUCTION, a_i, d_i, i), and each memory location U_j submits a record (INSTRUCTION, j, h_j), as explained in Section 2.4.2. These records are sorted collectively by their second fields (i.e., the memory addresses) in the SORT circuit. All transfers of information from processor to memory records (including all computations required by a **CW**), and vice versa,

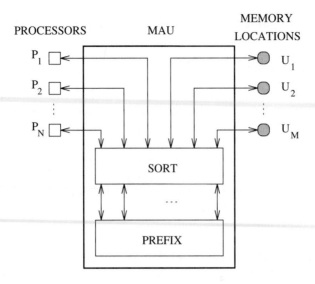

Figure 11.14: An alternative MAU for the PRAM and BSR models.

take place in the **PREFIX** circuit. Each record then returns to its source (processor or memory location) by retracing its own path through the MAU.

On the BSR model, the memory access instructions **ER**, **EW**, **CR**, and **CW** are executed in the same way as just described for the PRAM. When a **BROADCAST** instruction is to be executed, each processor P_i submits a record (i, g_i, d_i), and each memory location U_j submits a record (j, l_j, v_j), as explained in Section 11.3.2 (with the exception that the first field of the memory record here is j, not $j + N$). These records are now sorted by their second fields (i.e., the *tags* and *limits*) in the SORT circuit. Again, all transfers of information among records, including selection and reduction, take place in the **PREFIX** circuit. All records are then routed back to their sources.

11.29 Suggest other selection rules, besides $<, \leq, =, >, \geq, \neq$, and $|$, for BSR.

11.30 Suggest other reduction operators, besides $\sum, \prod, \wedge, \vee, \oplus, \cap$, and $\bigcup$, for BSR.

11.31 The memory access units for BSR, described in Section 11.3.2 and Problem 11.28, are based on sorting the *tags* and *limits*. As such, they are geared for problems whose data obey a linear order. However, if the selection rule is not an order relation, as in Problem 11.2, then these memory access units are not appropriate. Design a MAU for BSR that is capable of handling other relational operators besides $\{<, \leq, =, >, \geq, \neq\}$, and analyze its width, depth, and size.

11.32 Give an algorithm for performing GPC in BSR.

11.33 Design a MAU for the generalized version of BSR described in Section 11.4, and analyze its width, depth, and size.

11.34 Given a set S of n segments in the plane, each of which is either horizontal or vertical, design a BSR algorithm that determines, for each segment, the number of segments in S intersecting it.

11.35 Given a set of n points in the plane, design a BSR algorithm that finds, for each point, the point nearest to it among the $n-1$ remaining points. Use an appropriate definition of distance.

11.36 Let S be a set of n colored points in the plane. Design a BSR algorithm that finds the closest pair of points with different colors. Use an appropriate definition of distance.

11.37 Let the sequence $S = \{q_1, q_2, \ldots, q_n\}$ representing n points in d-dimensional space be given. A point q_i is said to *dominate* a point q_j if and only if $q_i[k] > q_j[k]$ for $k = 1, 2, \ldots, d$, where $q[k]$ denotes the kth coordinate of a point q. Design a BSR algorithm which finds the maximal points in S—that is, those points in S not dominated by any other point.

11.38 Given a set S of n points in d-dimensional space and a set R of r rectangles, also in d-dimensional space, whose sides are parallel to the coordinate axes, design a BSR algorithm that finds the number of points of S lying inside R.

11.39 An $n \times n$ matrix D is given whose elements are real numbers. Each row of D is sorted in nondecreasing order, and so is each column of D. It is required to find the kth smallest element of D for some integer k, where $1 \leq k \leq n^2$. Design a BSR algorithm for this problem.

11.40 Suggest problems that can be solved efficiently in BSR using combinations of the selection rules σ and the reduction operators $\mathcal{R}$ not illustrated in this chapter. For example, suggest a problem that uses $<$ (i.e., less than) for selection and $\oplus$ (i.e., EXCLUSIVE-OR) for reduction.

11.41 The generalized BSR model described in Section 11.4 requires that a datum d_i satisfy *all* k selection criteria of the form $g(i,h) \; \sigma_h \; l(j,h)$ before being accepted for reduction by U_j. An even more general version would allow the algorithm designer to specify other combinations of the selection criteria (to be satisfied before d_i is accepted for reduction). Such combinations include the following rules:

(a) At least m of the k criteria are to be satisfied, where $1 \leq m < k$.

(b) Exactly m of the k criteria are to be satisfied, where $1 \leq m < k$

Suggest problems in which each of (a) and (b) would be useful.

11.42 In Section 11.2.2, discriminating analysis is used to derive the running time of algorithm BSR SORT. Study the effect of using this type of analysis (instead of uniform analysis) on the running times of other algorithms presented in this chapter.

11.6   BIBLIOGRAPHICAL REMARKS

The BSR model of parallel computation was first proposed by Akl and Guenther [38]. Algorithms for solving a variety of computational problems on this model are described in Akl [23], Akl and Chen [28], Akl and Guenther [39], Akl and Lyons [42], Gewali and Stojmenović [257], and Melter and Stojmenović [419]. Different implementations of the MAU for BSR appear in Akl et al. [36], Akl and Guenther [38], and Fava Lindon and Akl [226]. A generalization of BSR to allow for multiple criteria is proposed in Akl and Stojmenović [56]. An implementation of the MAU for this generalization and several algorithms for solving problems on it are described in Akl and Stojmenović [57]. As pointed out in Akl [23], Akl and Guenther [38], Akl and Stojmenović [57], and Fava Lindon and Akl [226], many problems related to the BSR model are still open. One such problem is to find a general characterization of those problems which can be solved efficiently in BSR. This would allow a classification of problems according to whether they are amenable to constant-time solution by BSR. A second problem concerns what happens when the constant-time requirement imposed implicitly on all BSR algorithms is relaxed. An investigation of this possibility may reveal problems for which a BSR algorithm that does not run in constant time is nevertheless faster than all previously known (or even possible) PRAM solutions. Finally, there are many problems that have so far resisted efficient solution in BSR (and hence on the PRAM), including matrix problems (e.g., iterated matrix multiplication), graph-theoretic problems (e.g., computing the minimum-weight spanning tree), list problems (e.g., list ranking), and sequence problems (e.g., finding the longest common subsequence of two sequences). It is not known whether any of these computations can be performed in constant time in BSR using a number of processors that is a polynomial in the size of the problem.

The parallel computational complexity of some problems related to sequences is studied by Akl et al. [40]. An $\Omega(n \log n)$ lower bound on the number of operations required to find the maximal points in a set of n planar points and an optimal sequential algorithm for this problem that runs in $O(n \log n)$ time are derived in Preparata and Shamos [500]. Parallel and sequential algorithms for computing distance transforms of binary images are given in Pavel and Akl [476]. Several problems related to computing matchings on graphs and their parallel solutions are discussed in Osiakwan [456] and Osiakwan and Akl [457, 458, 459, 460, 461].

Other extensions of the PRAM were proposed in the literature. For example, the bulk-synchronous parallel (BSP) model of Valiant [619] is a shared-memory model whose name derives from the composition of a program as a set of supersteps of size H. Synchronization is provided among processors only at the end of each superstep. When $H = O(\log N)$, where N is the number of processors, the model is called an *XPRAM* (see Valiant [620]). The size of a superstep, namely, H, is chosen to hide the time required for global memory access.

In the LOGP model of Culler et al. [191], the memory is distributed among the processors, and PRAM algorithms are simulated by taking into account various parameters, such as the *communication latency L* (i.e., the maximum time taken by a message to travel from any source to any destination), the *communication overhead O* (the time taken by a processor to send or receive a message), the *gap G* (the time between two successive messages sent or received by a processor), and the number of processors P.

Of particular interest is the associative computing (ASC) model described in Potter et al. [497]. ASC consists of an array of processors, each with its own local memory. The processors are connected by a bus to one or several control units that broadcast instruction streams. The model allows the execution of constant-time functions for associative searching and selection, logical operations, and finding the maximum and minimum. Given certain search criteria, constant-time searching allows all active processors to be examined and the ones satisfying the search criteria to be identified. Algorithms for ASC are described in Atwah et al. [76], Esenwein and Baker [220], and Potter et al. [497]. A programming language for ASC is provided in Potter [496].

Several other variations and extensions of the PRAM are reviewed in Akl and Fava Lindon [34].

Chapter 12

Parallel Synergy

The two most often cited and used concepts in parallel computation are the folklore theorems introduced in Chapter 1, namely:

> **Speedup Folklore Theorem:** For a given computational problem, the speedup provided by a parallel algorithm using p processors, over the fastest possible sequential algorithm for the problem, is at most equal to p; that is, $S(1, p) \leq p$. □

> **Slowdown Folklore Theorem:** If a certain computation can be performed with p processors in time t_p and with q processors in time t_q, where $q < p$, then $t_p \leq t_q \leq t_p + p t_p / q$. □

The speedup folklore theorem essentially says that if a computation requires t_1 time units to be solved sequentially, then a parallel algorithm using p processors can perform the same computation in t_p time units, where t_p is *at least* equal to t_1/p. Thus, the maximum speedup that we can hope to achieve is equal to p, the number of processors used by the parallel algorithm. The slowdown folklore theorem, on the other hand, assures us that a computation performed in time t_p with p processors can be performed *at worst* in time $t_p(1 + p/q)$ by the same algorithm running on a computer with only q processors, where $q < p$. This can also be interpreted as saying that the speedup achieved by using p processors instead of q, where $p > q$, is at most $1 + p/q$. Indeed, denoting this speedup by $S(q, p)$, we have

$$S(q, p) = \frac{t_q}{t_p} \leq \frac{t_p + \dfrac{p}{q} t_p}{t_p} = 1 + \frac{p}{q}.$$

The speedup folklore theorem can therefore be viewed as a "bad news" theorem, as it limits to p the speedup that can be expected when performing a task using p processors. By contrast, the slowdown folklore theorem is seen as a "good news"

511

theorem, as it guarantees that the time required to perform a task with p processors will be slowed down at most by a factor of $(1 + p/q)$ when q processors are used instead of p, for $p > q$.

As mentioned in Chapter 1, these two theorems apply to the majority of standard computations, including typical problems in computer science, such as sorting and searching, as well as problems in application areas such as numerical analysis, combinatorics, and computational geometry. However, because they do not apply to a large number of nonconventional computations, we refer to them as folklore theorems. Such nonconventional computations arise, for example, in time-dependent applications in which a computer receives its input in real time and has to produce an output by a certain deadline. In these and many other applications, a parallel algorithm using p processors can perform the required computation:

1. More than p times faster than the best possible sequential algorithm; in this case, the speedup folklore theorem does not hold.

2. More than $1 + p/q$ times faster than a parallel algorithm using q processors, where $q < p$; in this case, the slowdown folklore theorem does not hold.

Instances of such computations were given in Examples 1.17 and 1.19. This chapter is devoted to a further exploration of the theme: We describe a number of computational paradigms in which $S(q, p)$ is asymptotically larger than p/q, for $1 \leq q < p$. We refer to this phenomenon as *parallel synergy*.

Some intuition is helpful initially, in order to better appreciate the general paradigms exhibiting parallel synergy, introduced subsequently. Therefore, we begin by presenting the following two simple examples in which the phenomenon manifests itself:

Example 12.1 Everyday life provides many situations illustrating parallel synergy. They involve people who are required to perform a certain task. These situations relate to our discussion of the folklore theorems in that a person is thought of as a *processor* and a task as a *computational problem*. Consider, for instance, a large piece of furniture that needs to be moved from one place to another. One mover working alone is unable to lift, push, or drag the item and, in order to move it, must take it apart, transport each of the parts individually, and then put them back together at the indicated spot. The job requires one hour. On the other hand, four movers working together can simply lift the piece of furniture and put it in its new location in 15 seconds. This is much faster than the 15 minutes predicted by the speedup folklore theorem! In fact, if fewer than four movers cannot lift, push, or drag the item, the slowdown folklore theorem is also contradicted. □

Example 12.2 There are cases where using fewer than a certain number of processors to solve a computational problem is not an option. Suppose, for example, that on a given day a parallel computer with 2,000 processors takes three minutes to forecast a sudden change in the weather that will occur two hours later and cause a devastating storm (a tornado, for instance). This gives enough time to issue warnings and perhaps save lives. By contrast, a sequential computer requires over four days to process the data and perform the calculations necessary to make the same prediction! In fact, a parallel computer with fewer than 50 processors completes its computation only after the probable disaster. In this case, the time at which the weather changes acts as a *deadline*. The presence of such a deadline gives parallelism a significance well beyond merely speeding up computation. Parallel synergy allows a parallel computer with the right number of processors to succeed in solving a problem in a situation in which any simulation using fewer processors is rendered totally absurd. Placed in this context, both the speedup and the slowdown folklore theorems become devoid of meaning. □

The remainder of this chapter is organized as follows: In Section 12.1, we describe a computation in which the use of discriminating analysis leads to a contradiction with the speedup folklore theorem. The next five sections use uniform analysis. Sections 12.2 and 12.3 illustrate two diametrically opposed instances in which a speedup is achieved that is asymptotically larger than the number of processors used on the parallel computer. In Section 12.2, an example is described in which memory is protected from illegal access, while Section 12.3 introduces a situation wherein memory is totally vulnerable to overwriting by so-called *memory-filling computations*. The paradigms of Sections 12.4, 12.5, and 12.6 are based on computations that capture the essence of tangible processes occurring in real time and space. It is shown how each of these computations contradicts the two folklore theorems through parallel synergy.

The models of computation used throughout the chapter are the RAM and the PRAM. While the same results can be obtained with other models, these idealized machines are chosen for their simplicity. They allow the comparison between sequential and parallel computation to be presented in the clearest way, without being cluttered with unnecessary details. We also assume that the two models use the fastest processors possible. In particular, the RAM's processor is assumed to operate at the speed of light and hence represents the fastest sequential computer that can be obtained. The PRAM uses multiple copies of this same processor.

12.1 USING DISCRIMINATING ANALYSIS

We begin by recalling the notion of discriminating analysis introduced in Chapters 1 and 2.

Memory Access on the RAM. On a RAM with M memory locations, each step of an algorithm consists of a READ phase, a COMPUTE phase, and a WRITE phase. The COMPUTE phase requires $\tau_c(1, M)$ time units, while the READ and WRITE phases each require $\tau_a(1, M)$ time units. Using *uniform analysis*, we have $\tau_c(1, M) = \tau_a(1, M) = O(1)$. By contrast, if we use *discriminating analysis*, then $\tau_c(1, M) = O(1)$, whereas $\tau_a(1, M) = O(\log M)$. However, if k consecutive memory accesses need to be performed and are known ahead of time, then they can be *pipelined* through the MAU, resulting in a total execution time of $O(k + \log M)$.

Memory Access on the PRAM.   The same is true of a PRAM with N processors and M memory locations. Each step of an algorithm consists of a READ phase, a COMPUTE phase, and a WRITE phase. The COMPUTE phase requires $\tau_c(N, M)$ time units, while the READ and WRITE phases each require $\tau_a(N, M)$ time units. Under *uniform analysis*, $\tau_c(N, M) = \tau_a(N, M) = O(1)$. Using *discriminating analysis*, on the other hand, we take $\tau_c(N, M) = O(1)$, and $\tau(N, M) = O(\log M)$. Here also, k memory accesses can be pipelined through the MAU to terminate in $O(k + \log M)$ time.

12.1.1   Computational Problem

Let $\{f_1, f_2, \ldots, f_n\}$ and $\{g_1, g_2, \ldots, g_n\}$ be two sequences of functions defined as follows:

1. Each function f_i, $1 \leq i \leq n$, takes an integer argument and returns an integer value.

2. For some positive integer n, each function g_i, $1 \leq i \leq n$, takes an integer argument k, $1 \leq k \leq n$, and returns an integer value h, $1 \leq h \leq n$.

Each f_i and each g_i can be computed by a RAM, and by any processor on a PRAM, in one time unit. Consider two arrays A and B:

1. Array A is a one-dimensional input array of size n whose elements $A(1)$, $A(2)$, $\ldots$, $A(n)$ each contain a given integer number.

2. Array B is an $n \times n$ two-dimensional output array whose elements $B(1,1)$, $B(1,2)$, $\ldots$, $B(n,n)$ hold some initial values.

The problem to be solved is as follows: For $1 \leq i \leq n$ and $1 \leq j \leq n$, it is required to:

1. Compute $v = f_j(f_{j-1}(\ldots f_2(f_1(A(i)))\ldots))$.

2. Write v in $B(j,l)$, where $l = g_j(g_{j-1}(\ldots g_2(g_1(i))\ldots))$.

The latter is shown in Fig. 12.1 for a pair of indices i and j.

The computation is subject to the following conditions:

1. If two or more integers are to be written into $B(j,l)$, then the latter is to store the smallest of these integers. For example, for two values i_1 and i_2 of i, let l_1 and l_2 be the two indices that result from computing

$$
\begin{aligned}
l_1 &= g_j(g_{j-1}(\ldots g_2(g_1(i_1))\ldots)) \\
\text{and} \quad l_2 &= g_j(g_{j-1}(\ldots g_2(g_1(i_2))\ldots)).
\end{aligned}
$$

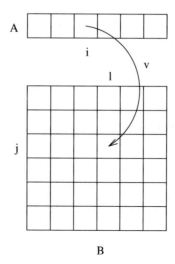

Figure 12.1: Computational problem for discriminating analysis paradigm.

If it so happens that $l_1 = l_2$, then $B(j, l_1)$ is the same as $B(j, l_2)$, and that element of array B is to store the smaller of

$$v_1 = f_j(f_{j-1}(\ldots f_2(f_1(A(i_1)))\ldots))$$
$$\text{and} \quad v_2 = f_j(f_{j-1}(\ldots f_2(f_1(A(i_2)))\ldots)).$$

2. If an element $B(j, h)$ of array B is not the target of a WRITE, then $B(j, h)$ is to keep its initial value. In other words, if $B(j, h)$ holds a value x initially, and $h \neq g_j(g_{j-1}(\ldots g_2(g_1(i))\ldots))$, for $1 \leq i \leq n$, then it is required that $B(j, h) = x$ at the end of the computation.

Example 12.3 Let $n = 2$, and suppose that $A(1) = 5$, $A(2) = 3$, $B(1, 1) = 2$, $B(1, 2) = 17$, $B(2, 1) = 18$, and $B(2, 2) = 10$. Further, assume that $f_1(x) = x + 1$, $f_2(x) = 2x$, $g_1(k) = k$, and $g_2(k) = n - \lceil k/2 \rceil$.
For $i = 1$ and $j = 1$, we compute

$$v = f_1(A(1)) = f_1(5) = 6$$

and write it in $B(1, 1)$, since $l = g_1(1) = 1$. Note that this is the first value to be written in $B(1, 1)$, and hence the initial value of the latter, namely, 2, is simply overwritten. Similarly, for $i = 1$ and $j = 2$, we compute

$$v = f_2(f_1(A(1))) = f_2(6) = 12$$

and write it in $B(2, 1)$, since $l = g_2(g_1(1)) = g_2(1) = 1$. Here also, the initial value of $B(2, 1)$, namely, 18, is overwritten. Now, for $i = 2$ and $j = 1$, we compute

$$v = f_1(A(2)) = f_1(3) = 4$$

and write it in $B(1,2)$, since $l = g_1(2) = 2$, thus overwriting the initial value of $B(1,2)$, namely, 17. Finally, for $i = 2$ and $j = 2$, we compute

$$v = f_2(f_1(A(2))) = f_2(4) = 8$$

and write it in $B(2,1)$, since $l = g_2(g_1(2)) = g_2(2) = 1$ *and* the previous value of $B(2,1)$, namely, 12, is larger than 8. This concludes the required computation. Note that, because $B(2,2)$ is never overwritten, it retains its initial value of 10. $\square$

12.1.2   PRAM Solution

Let a PRAM be available with n processors P_1, P_2, ..., P_n and a shared memory consisting of $M = n^2 + n$ memory locations to store A and B. The foregoing problem can be solved in a straightforward way by the following algorithm:

> **Algorithm PRAM COMPUTATION**
> **for** $i = 1$ **to** n **do in parallel**
>   (1) $v \leftarrow A(i)$
>   (2) $l \leftarrow i$
>   (3) **for** $j = 1$ **to** n **do**
>   (3.1) $v \leftarrow f_j(v)$
>   (3.2) $l \leftarrow g_j(l)$
>   (3.3) $B(j,l) \xleftarrow{\text{MIN}} v$
>   **end for**
> **end for.** ∎

Analysis.   We now use discriminating analysis to derive the running time of algorithm PRAM COMPUTATION. In Step (1), P_i reads $A(i)$ from memory and stores it in register v. This requires $O(\log M) = O(\log n)$ time units. Step (2) takes constant time. Each iteration of Step (3) involves two constant-time computations, in Steps (3.1) and (3.2). Since Step (3) is iterated n times, Steps (3.1) and (3.2) require $O(n)$ time. Step (3) also involves a **MIN CW** in Step (3.3). Because these n memory accesses, performed throughout the n iterations of Step (3), can be pipelined, they require a total of $O(n + \log n) = O(n)$ time units. Step (3) therefore runs in $O(n)$ time. Hence, the overall running time of algorithm PRAM COMPUTATION is $O(n)$.

12.1.3   RAM Solution

In designing a RAM solution to the problem, we are faced with the difficulty of having to distinguish between two kinds of values in the array B during the course of the computation. Indeed, any RAM algorithm, by definition, is sequential. If the minimum of two or more values v is to be stored in location $B(j,l)$, then these values will have to be treated *in sequence*: For each new value, the minimum of that value and the previous one (if any) is stored in $B(j,l)$. Therefore, the RAM algorithm must be able to recognize elements of B that still hold their initial values, as well as elements of B that have had their initial values overwritten. This is important, since, in the statement of the problem, once v is computed, it is to be compared to $B(j,l)$ only if the latter holds the result of a previous computation. Thus, when a RAM algorithm computes a value v to be written in $B(j,l)$, it has to be able to choose correctly between the following two situations:

1. $B(j,l)$ still holds its initial value, in which case this is the first time a value is to be written in it, and the algorithm is to execute

$$B(j,l) \leftarrow v.$$

2. $B(j,l)$ no longer holds its initial value, the latter having been overwritten in a previous step, in which case the algorithm is to execute

$$B(j,l) \leftarrow \min(B(j,l), v).$$

Since each $B(j,l)$ must somehow be examined before being updated, any sequential algorithm must involve n^2 READ requests. However, pipelining is not possible because a READ request cannot be issued for a value that may be updated after it has been read (i.e., the value of $B(j,l)$ may be modified, while its old value is traversing the MAU en route to the processor). Therefore, any RAM algorithm must require $\Omega(n^2 \log n)$ time. We note here that this difficulty is not present in the PRAM solution, since, whenever several values are to be written into $B(j,l)$, they are submitted simultaneously to the MAU, which computes the smallest among them and stores it in $B(j,l)$.

A RAM Algorithm. There are several ways for a RAM to solve this difficulty. One way is to use an auxiliary two-dimensional $n \times n$ array W. Initially, $W(j,l) = 0$, for $1 \le j, l \le n$. If, at any point during the execution of the algorithm, $B(j,l)$ is modified, then the value of $W(j,l)$ is changed to 1. Now whenever $B(j,l)$ is selected for writing v, the value of $W(j,l)$ is first read, and as a result:

1. If $W(j,l) = 0$, then v overwrites the original value of $B(j,l)$.

2. If $W(j,l) = 1$, then v is compared to the existing value of $B(j,l)$, and the smaller of the two is written in $B(j,l)$.

In either case, $W(j,l)$ is assigned the value 1.

The approach is described formally in the following RAM algorithm:

Algorithm RAM COMPUTATION

Step 1: for $i = 1$ **to** n **do**
      for $j = 1$ **to** n **do**
        $W(i,j) \leftarrow 0$
      end for
    end for
Step 2: for $i = 1$ **to** n **do**
        (2.1) $v \leftarrow A(i)$
        (2.2) $l \leftarrow i$
        (2.3) **for** $j = 1$ **to** n **do**
            (i) $v \leftarrow f_j(v)$
            (ii) $l \leftarrow g_j(l)$
            (iii) **if** $W(j,l) = 0$
                then $B(j,l) \leftarrow v$
                else $B(j,l) \leftarrow \min(B(j,l), v)$
                end if
            (iv) $W(j,l) \leftarrow 1$
        end for
    end for. ∎

Analysis. We use discriminating analysis. The RAM's memory has $M = 2n^2 + n$ locations to store arrays A, B, and W. Steps 1 and (2.3)(iv) involve n^2 accesses to memory for the purpose of writing. These can be pipelined and so require a total of $O(n^2 + \log n) = O(n^2)$ time units. Step (2.1) is iterated n times, each iteration involving an access to memory for the purpose of reading $A(i)$. Since these accesses can be pipelined, the overall running time of this step is $O(n + \log n) = O(n)$. In Step (2.2), the value of l is initialized in constant time. Steps (2.3)(i) and (ii) are constant-time computations; they are repeated n^2 times and hence require a total of $O(n^2)$ time units. In Step (2.3)(iii), both $W(j,l)$ and $B(j,l)$ are read, and *then* a new value is written into $B(j,l)$. These three memory accesses are repeated n^2 times each. However, they cannot be pipelined, as the value of $W(j,l)$ must be known before the value of $B(j,l)$ is updated. Therefore, since each memory access takes $O(\log n)$ time units, Step (2.3)(iii) requires $O(n^2 \log n)$ time. The overall running time of algorithm RAM COMPUTATION is therefore $O(n^2 \log n)$. We note here that the RAM algorithm was allowed to use more memory than the PRAM algorithm (in the form of array W). This was done because otherwise, no RAM solution is possible.

12.1.4 Speedup

The speedup achieved by algorithm PRAM COMPUTATION over algorithm RAM COMPUTATION is given by

$$S(1, n) = \frac{O(n^2 \log n)}{O(n)} = O(n \log n).$$

This speedup is asymptotically larger than n, the number of processors used on the PRAM, in direct contradiction to the speedup folklore theorem.

Slowdown. Assume that N processors are available on the PRAM instead of n, where $2 \leq N < n$. By the slowdown folklore theorem, if n processors can solve the problem using algorithm PRAM COMPUTATION in $O(n)$ time, then N processors can solve the same problem in

$$O(n)(1 + \frac{n}{N}) = O(\frac{n^2}{N})$$

time, in the worst case. It is possible to show, however, that N processors require a time that is asymptotically larger than n^2/N, hence contradicting the slowdown folklore theorem. (See Problem 12.1.)

12.2 PROTECTING A DATA STRUCTURE

In most applications of computers, it is necessary to protect the contents of the computer's memory against unauthorized access. The methods used to that end vary significantly and are part of an area of computer science known as *computer security*. One way to restrict access to information stored in a data structure is to dynamically change the locations in which the components of the data structure are stored. We now describe an example of such a protected data structure that, when used on a parallel computer with n processors, leads to a speedup asymptotically larger than n.

12.2.1 Computational Problem

Consider the following data structure DS, depicted in Fig. 12.2. It consists of n linked lists numbered 1 to n, each with k nodes numbered 1 to k. An additional node, called the *root*, is also part of DS. The root has n pointers, each of which points to the *head*—that is, to the first node of one of the linked lists. One can view DS as a tree whose root has n subtrees of k nodes each, and in which each node (other than the root or a leaf) has exactly one child. All nodes at distance l from the root are said to be at *level l*. Thus, the root is at level 0, its children at level 1, and so on. The leaves are at level k. Each node holds a distinct piece of information (i.e., a datum x) to be protected.

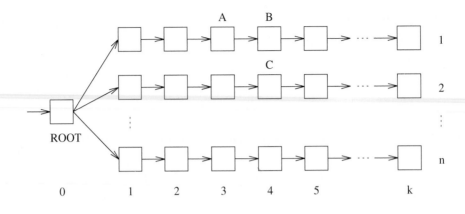

Figure 12.2: A data structure consisting of n linked lists.

The data structure DS is stored in a computer's memory. We are given a pointer to the root; this pointer is essentially the address in memory where the root is stored. Throughout the computation, the address of the root never changes. The address of any one of the remaining nodes, however, cannot be known in advance. In fact, DS is managed in such a way that nodes are moved to new locations by the memory manager during and after the use of the data structure by an algorithm. This prevents a user from saving the address of a node in order to return to that node at a later time. Instead, in order to gain access to a node in DS, a user must begin at the root and traverse the data structure as explained in what follows.

Node Relocation. The rule used by the memory manager to relocate nodes is simple. Suppose that the data structure is being traversed. Whenever a node at level l, $1 \le l \le k$, is reached for the first time during this traversal, the memory manager relocates:

1. All nodes at level l that have not yet been reached during the current traversal.

2. All nodes at levels $1, 2, \ldots, l-1$.

Consequently, all pointers to nodes that have been relocated change. In order to reach a new node at level l, a new traversal must begin at the root. This rule is applied recursively at each level from 1 to l and for every traversal beginning at the root. In other words, whenever a node at level l', $1 \le l' \le l$, is reached, all nodes at levels 1 to $l'-1$ and all nodes not yet reached in level l' are relocated. Of course, if $l' = 1$, then only the nodes at level 1 that have not been reached are relocated, the root never changing its address during the execution of an algorithm. Note that access is denied to a section of DS while that section is being relocated by the memory manager.

Pointer Computation. Pointers to nodes at levels 2, 3, ..., k of DS are not stored explicitly. Suppose that a node A is the parent of a node B. The address of B consists of a *base address* and an *offset*. The offset is stored explicitly in A. Each node at levels 1, 2, ..., $k-1$ of the tree holds an offset as a local value d. For a given level l, $1 \leq l < k$, let D_l be the value obtained by computing a certain function F (e.g., summation) of all local values d held by nodes at level l. This value D_l is the base address for all nodes at level $l+1$. Thus, a node at level $l \geq 1$ computes the address of its child node by adding D_l to its local offset value d. In the special case of the root, the addresses of its n children are stored explicitly. The root holds n pointers d_1, d_2, ..., d_n, where d_i is the address of its ith child.

Note that there is one d value per node, except for the root, which has n such values, and the leaves, which have none. Therefore, the number of d values in DS is $n + n(k-1)$. These are possibly all distinct. Every time a node is moved to a new location, all d values involved in computing its address are modified by the memory manager. Note also that, although the pointer to the root remains valid throughout the execution of an algorithm, the following two properties hold:

1. The pointer d_i held by the root is modified as soon as its ith child is relocated.

2. The pointer *to* the root is itself changed immediately after the termination of an algorithm.

The computational problem defined on DS is as follows: Given a pointer to the root, it is required to visit the n leaves and read the information they contain. In other words, it is required to obtain the n data held by the leaves and denoted by x_1, x_2, ..., x_n.

12.2.2 PRAM Solution

Let the computer that is used be a PRAM with n processors P_1, P_2, ..., P_n whose shared memory holds DS. At the beginning of the computation, all processors receive a pointer to the root. For $1 \leq i \leq n$, processor P_i reads d_i—that is, the pointer from the root to the head of list i. The n linked lists are then traversed synchronously by the n processors, with each processor traversing a distinct list. At each level l, the local d values stored at that level are read and combined using a **CW**, thus giving D_l. In linked list i, the offset value d stored in a node at level l, together with D_l, is used by P_i to compute $D_l + d$—that is, the pointer to the next node (at level $l+1$). Together, all processors then move to the nodes in the next level. The leaves are therefore reached simultaneously, one leaf per processor. Processor P_i now reads x_i. The entire computation requires $O(k)$ time units.

It is important to note here that all n processors reach the nodes at level l at the same time and extract their d values, necessary to proceed to level $l+1$. The subsequent relocation of the nodes at levels 1 to $l-1$, as well as *all* those at level l, by the memory manager has no effect whatsoever on the progress of the processors. Thus, the processors never need to wait for the memory manager to finish relocating nodes, since any node that is relocated must be at a level lower than the one reached by the processors at any step. Similarly, the processors always move forward and never have to revisit a node.

12.2.3 RAM Solution

Suppose now that the computer which is used is a RAM, whose memory holds *DS*. By the definition of the problem, traversing the linked lists to reach the leaves requires knowledge of D_l at each level. Therefore, all the nodes at a given level must be visited before proceeding to the next level. Suppose that the RAM processor has just visited a node at level l (for example, node B in Fig. 12.2) and read its d value. In order to move to another node at the same level (for example, node C), the RAM processor must start a new traversal at the root and visit every node at levels 1 to $l-1$. This is necessary, since the memory manager has moved all unvisited nodes at level l (including node C) and all nodes in levels 1 to $l-1$, immediately after the d value of B has been read. Thus, the time required by a RAM processor to reach all the leaves is $O(n^k)$. The latter is derived under the assumption that the relocation process is executed by the memory manager in constant time. Accounting for the actual time taken by the memory manager to move the nodes between steps would in fact *increase* the running time of the RAM solution, since the algorithm has to wait until all nodes have been relocated before proceeding.

12.2.4 Speedup

The speedup provided by a PRAM with n processors over a RAM is therefore

$$S(1,n) = \frac{O(n^k)}{O(k)}.$$

In other words, the speedup is $O(n^k/k)$, which is asymptotically larger than n for $k > 1$. Note here that k can be arbitrarily large. For example, if $k = n$, then a PRAM with n processors is $O(n^{n-1})$ times faster than the RAM, thus violating the speedup folklore theorem.

Slowdown. If only N processors are available on the PRAM, where $2 \leq N < n$, then, by the slowdown folklore theorem, they should be able to traverse the data structure and reach the leaves in at most

$$O(k)(1 + \frac{n}{N})$$

time—that is, in $O(n^2/N)$ time—when $k = n$. However, it can be shown that the time required in this case is asymptotically larger than $O(n^2/N)$, in direct contradiction to the slowdown folklore theorem. (See Problem 12.6.)

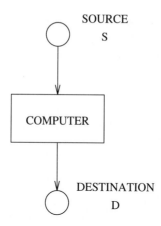

Figure 12.3: A computer receives data from S and delivers results to D.

12.3 MEMORY-FILLING COMPUTATIONS

This paradigm is in some sense symmetrical to the one of Section 12.2 in the way memory is treated. Rather than restricting access to memory, the example that we now describe uses a totally unprotected memory. Any location in memory can be overwritten by an algorithm at any time. The algorithms of interest here are iterative in nature. Each iteration produces a value and an address where this value is to be written. The value produced by an iteration depends on the value and on the address computed during the previous iteration. Similarly, the address where the current value is to be written depends on the previous value and on the previous address. For this reason, we refer to these algorithms as *memory-filling computations*.

12.3.1 Computational Problem

Suppose that a source S delivers a set of data d_1, d_2, ..., d_n to a computer whose memory consists of n locations U_1, U_2, ..., U_n. Datum d_i is stored in U_i, $1 \leq i \leq n$, and the source ceases to exist. A certain computation is to be performed on d_1, d_2, ..., d_n. When the computation is completed, the solution is delivered to a destination D, which is waiting to receive it, as illustrated in Fig. 12.3.

The computation to be performed consists of a number of iterations. During each iteration, three functions f, g, and h are computed in constant time. All three functions receive the contents and address of a certain memory location U_j—that is, d_j and j. Each function returns a value specified as follows:

1. Function f returns the address k, $1 \le k \le n$, of some location U_k.

2. Function g returns a new value d_k to be stored in U_k.

3. Function h returns an address l, $1 \le l \le n$, so that the pair (d_l, l) is used by f, g, and h in the next iteration.

The functions f and h are *permutations* of $\{1, 2, \ldots, n\}$; in other words, $f(d_i, i) \ne f(d_j, j)$ and $h(d_i, i) \ne h(d_j, j)$, for $i \ne j$. The values computed by g converge to a value V that is the result of the computation and that can be recognized in constant time.

Convergence.   Let m be an integer such that $1 \le m \le n$. When the pair (d_m, m) is used by f, g, and h in the first iteration, exactly n iterations are required to converge to V. On the other hand, when the pair (d_i, i), where $1 \le i \le n$, $i \ne m$, is used as a starting point, the number of iterations required to reach V is 2^n. Of course, the index m is not known in advance. However, all d_i are equally likely to be d_m. In what follows, we take $h = f$ for simplicity.

12.3.2   PRAM Solution

Let the computer receiving $d_1, d_2, \ldots, d_n$ from S be a PRAM with n processors $P_1, P_2, \ldots, P_n$ and n shared-memory locations. The PRAM algorithm for finding V proceeds as follows: Processor P_i, $1 \le i \le n$, performs the computation defined in Section 12.3.1, initially using the pair (d_i, i) as input to the functions f, g, and h. At the end of the first iteration, P_i deposits a new value d_k in U_k, as specified by f and g. Since f is a permutation function, all processors write their values in distinct memory locations.

During the second iteration, P_i, $1 \le i \le n$, again uses the pair (d_i, i), where d_i is the new value stored in U_i by one of the n processors at the end of the first iteration. Since h is a permutation function, P_i executes the second iteration of a distinct computation (not necessarily the one started by P_i in the first iteration).

In general, during the jth step of the algorithm, there are n distinct computations in progress, and P_i executes the jth iteration of a distinct computation using (d_i, i).

During the nth step, exactly one processor (for example, P_l) performs the last iteration of the computation that began with (d_m, m) and produces

$$g(d_l, l) = V.$$

The processor delivers V to the destination D by writing V on an output device, where it is read by D. All processors then halt.

Note that the function h, while part of the definition of the problem, is not really needed (and, in fact, is not explicitly used) by the PRAM algorithm. Its effect is obtained by making the processors read from distinct memory locations at each iteration. In this way, there are n independent threads of computation, although no single processor necessarily follows the same thread from beginning to end.

Example 12.4 Consider the case where $n = 5$ and $m = 2$. The five iterations of the algorithm are illustrated in Fig. 12.4 for some (unspecified) hypothetical function f. Since $m = 2$, the computation beginning with d_2 leads to V in five steps. The sequence of values produced from d_2 is $\{d_5, d_4, d_1, d_2, d_5\}$, with the last value in the sequence equal to V. These values are computed by P_2, P_5, P_4, P_1, and P_2, respectively, as shown in the figure. $\square$

Analysis. Since each of d_1, d_2, ..., d_n is used as a starting point of a computation, one of these n computations carried out simultaneously is guaranteed to start with d_m and hence complete in n iterations. The PRAM solution therefore requires $O(n)$ time.

12.3.3   RAM Solution

Suppose now that the computer receiving d_1, d_2, ..., d_n from the source is a RAM whose memory consists of n locations. The RAM processor has no way of "knowing" m, and so it chooses one of the d_i at random as a starting point and performs the computation required to produce V. Since all of the d_i are equally likely to lead to V in n steps, d_m is chosen with a probability of $1/n$. Thus, with a probability of $1 - 1/n$, the RAM solution runs in $O(2^n)$ time units.

Note that once d_i is chosen and the computation is started, there is no way to halt it prematurely and start a new computation afresh from another original datum d_j. This is because, by its definition, the computation causes original data to be overwritten. Thus, even after a single iteration starting with d_i, any of the data d_j, $1 \leq j \leq n, i \neq j$, may be overwritten and lost forever. It is also impossible to predict which values will be overwritten without performing the computation (and hence overwriting the data!), since all addresses where writing occurs are dependent on the data. Similarly, it is possible neither to undo the effect of the computation and return to the original data (since intermediate values have been overwritten) nor to restart by rereading the data (since the source S has ceased to exist). Therefore, if V is not reached after n iterations, the RAM cannot attempt another computation and must proceed to completion with the current one.

What about increasing the size of the RAM memory? That way, perhaps we could use the extra memory locations as a work space for the computation and hence protect d_1, d_2, ..., d_n from being overwritten. This is of no help either, however, since we are executing a memory-filling computation. If the computer's memory consists of M locations, then whatever the value of M, the function f is, by definition, automatically a permutation of $\{1, 2, ..., M\}$, and consequently, any memory location can be overwritten.

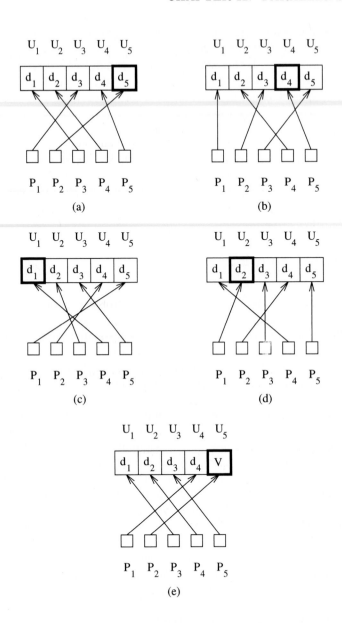

Figure 12.4: Iterative computation with an unprotected memory: (a) In the first iteration, P_2 computes, from d_2, a new value for d_5; (b) In the second iteration, P_5 updates d_4 using d_5; (c) In the third iteration, P_4 uses d_4 to obtain a new value for d_1; (d) In the fourth iteration, P_1 computes a new d_2 from d_1; (e) In the fifth iteration, P_2 obtains $d_5 = V$ from d_2 and the computation terminates.

12.3.4 Speedup

The speedup achieved by a PRAM with n processors over the RAM is equal to

$$S(1, n) = \frac{O(2^n)}{O(n)}$$

—that is, $O(2^n/n)$—with a probability of $1 - (1/n)$. For large n, this probability tends to 1. Therefore, the speedup is asymptotically larger than n, the number of processors used by the PRAM, with a probability close to 1, thus violating the speedup folklore theorem.

Slowdown. According to the slowdown folklore theorem, if N processors, instead of n, are available on the PRAM, where $2 \leq N < n$, then convergence to V should be possible in at most

$$O(n)(1 + \frac{n}{N})$$

time. With a probability approaching 1 for large n, however, the time required by N processors to solve the problem is asymptotically larger than $O(n^2/N)$, which contradicts the slowdown folklore theorem. (See Problem 12.10.)

12.4 TRAVERSING A STATE SPACE

Consider a real-life process, such as a phenomenon occurring in physics, chemistry, or biology. This process manifests itself in real time and space—the way a chemical reaction, for example, takes place. We distinguish such a real-life process from the abstract concepts of mathematics, which may be used to *describe* the process, but are not themselves concrete phenomena.

Suppose now that this real-life process is represented pictorially as a tree T. This tree, shown in Fig. 12.5, has the following characteristics:

1. Its root R has n children A_1, A_2, ..., A_n.

2. For $1 \leq i \leq n$, A_i is the root of a complete binary tree with 2^n leaves. Thus, the distance from A_i to any of its leaves (i.e., the number of tree edges separating them) is n.

3. Each node in T represents a *state* of the process. The root R is the initial state. Beginning with R, each node can create its children (i.e., the states that follow it).

4. Exactly one subtree, whose root is A_m, contains a *goal* node, representing a goal state, at distance $\log n$ from A_m. The subtree rooted at A_i, for all $1 \leq i \leq n$, $i \neq m$, contains a goal node, and that goal node is a leaf (i.e., at distance n from A_i). The value of m is unknown in advance. However, all n subtrees are equally likely to contain the shallow goal node (i.e., the one at distance $\log n$ from the subtree's root).

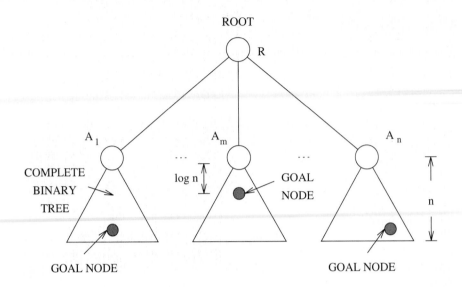

Figure 12.5: A tree-structured state space.

5. By its nature, the process is such that, once it has started, it cannot be reversed. In other words, once the process leaves its initial state R, it has no way of returning to it. For example, R may represent a radioactive material that decays, a chemical sample that oxidizes, or a biological specimen that dies.

6. The process terminates when a goal state is reached.

A real-life process such as this can be related to the notion of computation in a number of ways:

1. When moving from one state to another, the physical, chemical, or biological phenomenon taking place could itself be viewed as a *computation* that occurs spontaneously in nature or that is provoked intentionally to carry out an arithmetic or logical calculation.

2. One or several conventional computers may be in charge of the real-life process, controlling its behavior and interpreting its output.

3. The real-life process may be simulated on one or several conventional computers.

In the remainder of this section, we focus on the third of these alternatives, in which a standard simulation is used to model a real-life process. This is primarily for the purpose of presenting the analysis in a straightforward way using our usual PRAM and RAM models.

12.4.1   Computational Problem

The standard computational counterpart to the real-life process just described takes the form of a *state-space search*. Starting from its root R, the tree T is generated state by state, until a goal node is reached. The unrecoverability of the initial state is modeled by imposing a high penalty on returning to the root R. Thus, to go from R to any one of its children A_i, $1 \leq i \leq n$, requires $O(1)$ time, while returning to R from A_i takes $O(2^n)$ time. All other edges of T are traversed in $O(1)$ time, whether they are traversed from parent to child or vice versa.

12.4.2   PRAM Solution

Let a PRAM with n processors P_1, P_2, ..., P_n be available whose shared memory contains R. Processor P_i, $1 \leq i \leq n$, reads R and uses it to generate A_i. The n processors then proceed independently, with P_i performing a breadth-first traversal of a binary tree rooted at A_i. Since *all* the subtrees are searched simultaneously, one of the processors, namely, P_m, is guaranteed to search the tree rooted at A_m and hence reach the shallow goal node (at distance $\log n$ from A_m). All processors then halt. This requires at worst $O(n)$ time.

Assume now that N processors are available on the PRAM, where $2 \leq N < n/2$. Each of the processors is assigned to search one of the subtrees of R. Thus, only N of the n subtrees of R are searched, and these are selected at random. If none of the trees that are searched contains the shallow goal node, a leaf goal will have to be reached. This requires $O(2^n)$ time in the worst case. The probability that none of the trees selected for searching contains the shallow goal node is

$$\frac{n-1}{n} \times \frac{n-2}{n-1} \times \frac{n-3}{n-2} \times \cdots \times \frac{n-(N-1)}{n-(N-2)} \times \frac{n-N}{n-(N-1)} = 1 - \frac{N}{n} > \frac{1}{2}.$$

Therefore, with probability greater than $1/2$, this solution requires $O(2^n)$ time.

It is important to note here that, if after $O(n)$ steps, the N processors do not find the goal node, they have no reason to return to R to generate new subtrees to be searched, as this would require $O(2^n)$ additional time.

Slowdown.   The slowdown folklore theorem guarantees that, if n processors can solve a problem in $O(n)$ time, then N processors, $N < n$, can solve the same problem in at worst

$$O(n)(1 + \frac{n}{N}) = O(\frac{n^2}{N})$$

time. However, as we have just seen, with probability greater than $1/2$, N processors, $2 \leq N < n/2$, require $O(2^n)$ time to find a goal node in T. Since 2^n is asymptotically larger than n^2/N, the slowdown folklore theorem is violated.

12.4.3   RAM Solution

Suppose that T is to be searched for a goal node on a RAM. The processor reads R from memory and then generates one of R's children A_i at random. Next, breadth-first traversal is used to generate the states of the tree rooted at A_i, until the goal node of that tree is reached. With probability $1/n$, the tree selected for search will be the one rooted at A_m (i.e., the tree with the shallow goal node), and the goal node is found in $O(n)$ time. However, with probability $(n-1)/n$, the tree selected for search will not be the one rooted at A_m. Therefore, with probability approaching 1 for large n, the goal node is a leaf, and the time required to reach it is $O(2^n)$ in the worst case.

12.4.4   Speedup

For the preceding problem, the speedup achieved by the n processors of the PRAM over the single RAM processor is

$$S(1, n) = \frac{O(2^n)}{O(n)}$$

—that is, $O(2^n/n)$—with probability $1 - (1/n)$. This speedup is asymptotically larger than n, the number of PRAM processors, with probability close to 1, thus contradicting the speedup folklore theorem.

12.5   DEALING WITH SEVERAL INPUT STREAMS

One of the main limitations of sequential computation is captured by the notion that a single processor lacks the ability to be "in more than one place at one time." By its definition, the RAM can examine only one datum at any given instant. If several independent steady streams of data arrive simultaneously, the RAM can monitor only *one* of these streams from start to finish. We say that the RAM has *tunnel vision*. A PRAM, by contrast, allows *panoramic vision*. Provided that enough processors are available, *all* incoming streams of data can be monitored at the same time, from start to finish. Depending on the context, this results in either a more efficient computation, a higher probability of successful execution, or a more accurate solution.

Pursuit and Evasion on a Ring.   We begin with a motivational example. Consider the ring in Fig. 12.6, consisting of a number of discrete positions, numbered 1, 2, and so on. Suppose that two people, A and B, play a game, beginning at diametrically opposed positions of the ring, as shown in Fig. 12.6(a). The purpose of player B is to catch player A, by moving from position to position on the ring until A and B occupy the same position. The purpose of A is to not be caught by B. The two players are allowed to move simultaneously, clockwise or counterclockwise as each wishes. However, each player can move, from a given position, only to an

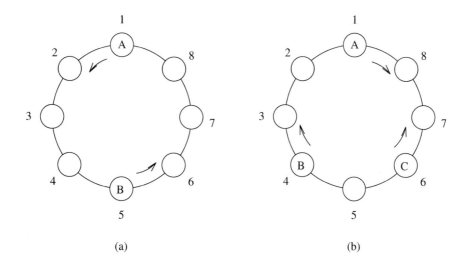

(a) (b)

Figure 12.6: Pursuit and evasion on a ring: (a) Player B can never catch player A; (b) One of the two players, B or C, is guaranteed to catch player A.

adjacent position at a time; in other words, the players are not allowed to jump. (For example, in Fig. 12.6(a), player B can go from position 5 either to position 4 or to position 6, but not to position 2 or 8, in one step.) It is clear that B can never catch A. Suppose now that there are three players, A, B, and C, as shown in Fig. 12.6(b). All the previous rules apply, except that now C also wishes to catch A. This time, it is clear that A will be caught, by either B or C. In computational terms, this pursuit-and-evasion game is expressed as follows: There are two streams of input, represented by A's clockwise and counterclockwise motion on the ring, respectively. A single processor (represented by B) cannot cope with the two input streams and hence always fails to complete the computation. Adding one processor (represented by C) guarantees that the computation will be completed successfully. In other words, using the notation of Section 1.4.4, we have

$$sr(1,2) = \frac{Pr(2)}{Pr(1)} = \frac{1}{0} = \infty;$$

that is, an *infinite* success ratio is achieved by going from one to two processors.

12.5.1 Computational Problem

Consider a problem in which n independent and steady streams, each consisting of n data, are received from n sources in parallel by a computer, as shown in Fig. 12.7. All streams contain data needed to solve a given computational problem. For $1 \leq i \leq n$, the data in the ith stream are necessary and sufficient to solve the

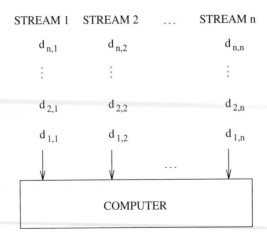

Figure 12.7: A computer receiving several streams of input.

problem. However, for a certain m, $1 \leq m \leq n$, unknown in advance, the data in the mth stream lead to a solution in $O(n)$ time. The data in all other $n-1$ streams lead to a solution in $O(2^n)$ time. All streams are equally likely to be the one stream containing the data leading to a solution in linear time.

The data in the n streams satisfy the following additional conditions:

1. The n data streams are totally disjoint: No two streams contain the same datum, and no subset of one stream can be combined with a subset of another stream to solve the computational problem at hand.

2. A stream continues to exist if and only if its data are being processed by the computer. The reason for this is that, by processing $d_{1,i}$, $d_{2,i}$, $\ldots$, $d_{j,i}$, the computer directs the source of stream i in producing $d_{j+1,i}$, $d_{j+2,i}$, $\ldots$, $d_{n,i}$.

Example 12.5 Suppose that n objects are launched towards n targets simultaneously, one object per target and one target per object, as shown in Fig. 12.8. For instance, the objects may be microscopic robots traversing an organism in search of diseased cells. The trajectories taken by the objects and the positions of the targets when reached by the objects are unknown in advance. The length of a trajectory is measured in a number of discrete steps. One of the objects, m, has a short trajectory—of $O(n)$ steps—to its target. All other objects have long trajectories—of $O(2^n)$ steps— to their targets. It is not known which object has the short trajectory. The problem to be solved requires that the trajectory of any one object to its target be tracked. As a result, the position of that target is located. It is, of course, preferred that the object with the short trajectory be tracked, but this cannot be predicted in advance. One characteristic of this problem is that the time to record

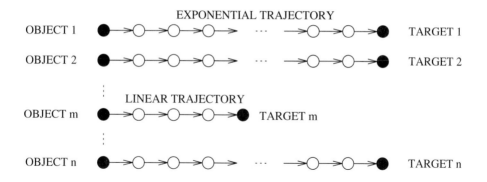

Figure 12.8: Launching n objects towards n targets.

and process the information pertaining to the position of one object is equal to the time taken by the object to move to a new position. Therefore, one processor can track the trajectory of only one object at a time. An object whose trajectory is not tracked is lost. □

Example 12.6 Suppose that a collection of n satellites transmits data to a ground station, as shown in Fig. 12.9. One of the n satellites is best positioned to send data leading to an $O(n)$-time solution to a computational problem back on Earth. All other satellites send data leading to $O(2^n)$-time computations. One processor at the ground station can monitor exactly one satellite. The processor instructs the satellite on which data to collect next. A satellite that is not monitored cannot send data. □

12.5.2 PRAM Solution

On a PRAM with n processors P_1, P_2, ..., P_n, processor P_i, $1 \leq i \leq n$, can monitor the ith stream and attempt to solve the computational problem using $d_{1,i}$, $d_{2,i}$, ..., $d_{n,i}$. Exactly one of the processors, namely, P_m, for some $1 \leq m \leq n$, will use $d_{1,m}$, $d_{2,m}$, ..., $d_{n,m}$ and reach a solution in $O(n)$ time. All processors therefore stop after $O(n)$ time units (since exactly one is guaranteed to have reached a solution).

Suppose now that only N processors are available on the PRAM, where $N < n$. At random, the N processors choose N streams to monitor from among the n streams. With probability

$$\frac{n-1}{n} \times \frac{n-2}{n-1} \times \cdots \times \frac{n-N}{n-N+1} = 1 - \frac{N}{n},$$

none of the processors choose the stream leading to a solution in $O(n)$ time. Therefore, with probability $1 - (N/n)$, the solution will require $O(2^n)$ time.

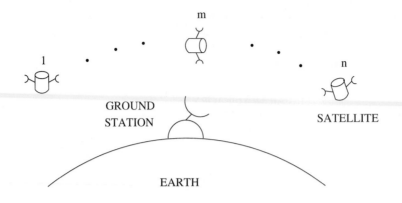

Figure 12.9: Satellites transmitting data to a ground station.

Slowdown.   By the slowdown folklore theorem, if n processors can solve a problem in $O(n)$ time, then N processors, $N < n$, can solve the same problem in at worst

$$O(n)(1 + \frac{n}{N}) = O(\frac{n^2}{N})$$

time. As just shown, however, N processors require $O(2^n)$ time, with probability $1 - (N/n)$. Since 2^n is asymptotically larger than n^2/N, the slowdown folklore theorem does not hold.

12.5.3   RAM Solution

On a RAM, the processor chooses *one* of the streams at random to monitor—for example, stream j. Then it proceeds to compute a solution using $d_{1,j}$, $d_{2,j}$, $\ldots$, $d_{n,j}$. With probability $(n - 1)/n$, the RAM will choose a stream leading to an exponential-time solution. The running time is therefore $O(2^n)$, with probability $1 - (1/n)$, which tends to 1 for large n.

12.5.4   Speedup

The speedup provided by n PRAM processors over the RAM is

$$S(1, n) = \frac{O(2^n)}{O(n)}$$

—that is, $O(2^n/n)$—with probability close to 1. This speedup is asymptotically larger than the number of PRAM processors, namely, n, thus contradicting the speedup folklore theorem.

X

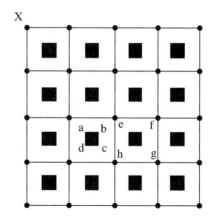

Figure 12.10: An $n \times n$ grid of squares to be traversed.

12.6 ONE-WAY FUNCTIONS

Suppose that in an industrial application, we are given an $n \times n$ grid of squares, as shown in Fig. 12.10 for $n = 4$. Inside each square is an area (also square shaped) shown shaded in the figure. It is required to visit the four sides of each shaded area, in order to perform a certain manufacturing process. For example, the four sides (a,b), (b,c), (c,d), and (d,a) of the shaded area $abcd$ need to be visited. A side is visited by traversing the adjacent grid edge parallel to it. For example, side (a,b) of the shaded area $abcd$ is visited by traversing edge (e,h) of the grid. Note that traversing a horizontal grid edge $((e,f)$, for example) adjacent to the sides of two shaded areas, one above and one below, allows both of these sides to be visited. Similarly, traversing a vertical grid edge $((e,h)$, for example) adjacent to the sides of two shaded areas, one to the right and one to the left, allows both of these sides to be visited. The following properties are satisfied by all grid edges:

1. One time unit is required to traverse a horizontal edge from left to right, whereas traversing the same edge from right to left takes 2^n time units. Thus, going from e to f takes one time unit, while going from f to e takes 2^n time units.

2. One time unit is required to traverse a vertical edge from top to bottom, whereas traversing the same edge from bottom to top takes 2^n time units. Thus, going from e to h takes one time unit, while going from h to e takes 2^n time units.

The difference between the running times (i.e., *one* time unit in one direction and 2^n time units in the opposite direction) may be due to any one of several factors that could make going in one direction easy and going in the opposite direction

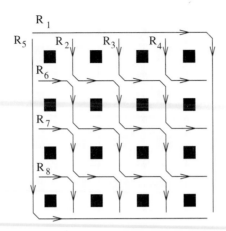

Figure 12.11: An $n \times n$ grid traversed by $2n$ robots.

significantly more difficult. For example, going from left to right and from top to bottom may be downhill (while, obviously, going from right to left and from bottom to top is uphill). Alternatively, the process may require going through some matter (e.g., cutting a metal or penetrating a certain substance) such that one direction is amenable to traversal while the opposite direction resists it.

This manufacturing task is performed by a collection of robots, originally located at the top left corner of the grid—that is, at point X in Fig. 12.10. The robots are confined to the edges of the grid; in other words, in order to go from one point of the grid to another, a robot must traverse a sequence of grid edges and cannot wander outside the grid.

If $2n$ robots R_1, R_2, ..., R_n are available, then they can perform this manufacturing task in $2n$ time units, as shown in Fig. 12.11 for $n = 4$. Note that no grid edge is traversed from right to left or from bottom to top.

If, on the other hand, fewer than $2n$ robots are applied to the task, then some of the grid edges will have to be traversed from right to left or from bottom to top. For example, if only $2n - 1$ robots are used, then $\Omega(2^n)$ time units are necessary. A solution using $2n - 1$ robots is shown in Fig. 12.12 for $n = 4$.

A single robot by itself requires $\Omega(2^n n^2)$ time units. An example of the path taken by one robot is shown in Fig. 12.13 for $n = 4$.

12.6.1 Computational Problem

We now present a computation that captures the essence of the foregoing industrial process. The computation is described by a directed graph G of $(n + 1)^2$ vertices, each representing a state of the computation. The vertices are arranged in $n + 1$ rows and $n + 1$ columns. This is illustrated in Fig. 12.14 for $n = 4$. The vertex

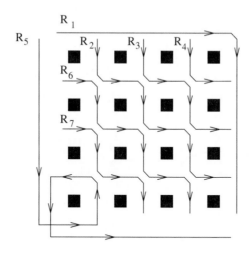

Figure 12.12: An $n \times n$ grid traversed by $2n - 1$ robots.

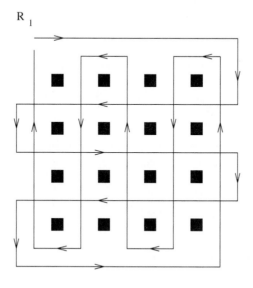

Figure 12.13: An $n \times n$ grid traversed by one robot.

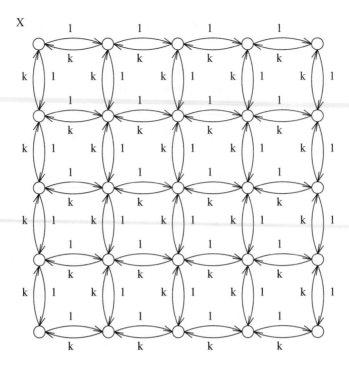

Figure 12.14: An $(n + 1) \times (n + 1)$ directed graph representing a computation.

marked X is the initial state of the computation. Let v_i and v_j be two consecutive
vertices in a row, with v_i to the left of v_j. Then v_i is connected to v_j by an edge
with a weight of 1, and v_j is connected to v_i by an edge with a weight of k, where
$k > 1$. The same is true if v_i and v_j are two consecutive vertices in a column with
v_i above v_j.

Each oriented edge of the graph G represents a sequential computational step
requiring either 1 or k time units, as given by the edge weight of 1 or k. In mathematical terms, the pair of oriented edges (v_i, v_j) and (v_j, v_i) may be thought of
as representing a function that takes a short time to compute, but a long time to
invert. Such a function is sometimes referred to as a *one-way function*. For example, if (v_i, v_j) has a weight of 1, it may represent the simple computational step of
multiplying two given large prime numbers x and y to obtain a number z, while
(v_j, v_i) with a weight of k represents the harder computational step of factoring z
into x and y when only z is given.

Edges of G with a weight equal to 1 correspond to computational steps that
must be performed (at least once). Edges with a weight equal to k correspond to
allowable computational steps, which are not necessarily required. Thus, the state
represented by a vertex is:

1. A precondition to computational steps represented by outgoing edges.

2. A postcondition to computational steps represented by incoming edges.

Only computational steps corresponding to edges in the graph G are permitted (since, in the industrial process being simulated, the robots are confined to the edges of the $n \times n$ grid to be traversed). A successful computation is one that begins at the initial state and terminates when each edge with weight equal to 1 has been traversed (at least once). In what follows, we take $k = 2^n$.

12.6.2 PRAM Solution

A PRAM algorithm using $2n$ processors begins at X and performs the computation in $O(n)$ time. If only $2n - 1$ processors are present, the computation requires $O(2^n)$ time.

Slowdown. According to the slowdown folklore theorem, if $2n$ processors can solve a problem in $O(n)$ time, then $2n - 1$ processors can solve the same problem in at most

$$O(n)(1 + \frac{2n}{2n - 1}) = O(n)$$

time. As already mentioned, however, $2n - 1$ processors require $O(2^n)$ time. Since 2^n is asymptotically larger than n, the slowdown folklore theorem is violated.

12.6.3 RAM Solution

A RAM processor requires $O(2^n n^2)$ time units to perform the computation, and this is optimal.

12.6.4 Speedup

The speedup achieved by $2n$ PRAM processors over the RAM is

$$S(1, 2n) = \frac{O(2^n n^2)}{O(n)} = O(2^n n).$$

This speedup is asymptotically larger than $2n$, the number of PRAM processors, thus violating the speedup folklore theorem.

12.7 CONCLUSION

Computation is undergoing a profound evolution. Its theory and practice are being radically transformed. Over the last 15 years, computers have become indispensable to everything that "works" in our society, from home appliances to manufacturing tools, from vehicles used for transportation to communication media, from education to leisure, from engineering to medicine, and indeed, from business applications on Earth to scientific experiments in outer space. What is more significant, however, is that the meaning of what it is "to compute" is being redefined. Already computers are evolving from their traditional role as *static* engines for calculation that sit atop a desk, inside an apparatus, or in the palm of one's hand. Soon it will be commonplace for computers to be *dynamic*, "perceiving" the physical world around them, traveling within it independently, communicating with it, changing it, and in turn being modified by it, all in real time. In the not too distant future, *parallel computers* consisting of hundreds, thousands, or even millions of processors will be as familiar as today's laptops.

In closing this book on parallel computation, it seems therefore natural to look ahead. We put forward a number of questions, the answers to which will determine whether our discipline is equipped to deal with this new stage in the evolution of computing:

1. The current theory of parallel computation is deeply rooted in concepts inherited from sequential computation. Has the transition from sequential to parallel computational theory been made correctly, and is it still appropriate?

2. Every day computers are being placed in applications never conceived of previously. Does the current theory of parallel computation fit the new tasks that computers will be asked to perform?

3. Traditionally, computing has been regarded strictly as the process of evaluating a function of a certain value stored in memory. How should this narrow and simplistic definition change to accommodate the multitude of cases where input data arrive at the computer in real time or are themselves a function of time, as well as those cases where output data are used to compute the next input or are required to meet a given deadline?

4. Dynamic computers that evolve in a real three-dimensional universe will include a large number of processors to help them process data received from their surroundings. How much of the current theory of parallel computation remains valid in the realm of *dynamic parallel computers*, and how much of it no longer holds?

Current results suggest that a new theory of computation is indeed necessary. Such a theory will have to capture a number of aspects of a radically different computing environment. Some of these aspects were exposed in this chapter. For example, it is now apparent that the speedup achieved by parallel computers can be asymptotically larger than the number of processors used. In fact, in many of the paradigms described, the speedup can be much larger than that obtained here if a different function (other than 2^n, for example) happens to describe the sequential running time. This shakes the putative notion that the maximum speedup possible when employing p instead of q processors, where $p > q$, is $O(p/q)$.

In some cases, a certain number of processors may render possible a computation that is impossible to perform using fewer processors. Therefore, not only are p

processors faster in performing a task than are q processors, where $p > q$, but they can also "do more," by successfully completing computations that are *inherently parallel* and for which any algorithm using fewer than p processors is guaranteed to fail. Thus, the tenet that a smaller machine can do anything a larger machine does, provided that the former is given "enough time" to simulate the algorithm designed for the latter, no longer makes sense in many applications.

The new theory will also have to address other potential consequences of parallel synergy. For example, in numerical analysis, what is the effect of parallel synergy on the accuracy of solutions computed in parallel? And does parallel synergy manifest itself in the quality of approximate solutions to combinatorial problems? These and many other questions are guaranteed to keep the study of parallel computation an engaging and worthwhile endeavor for a long time to come.

12.8 PROBLEMS

12.1 Analyze the slowdown incurred when using fewer than n PRAM processors to solve the computational problem of Section 12.1.1. Specifically, show that a PRAM with N processors requires a time that is asymptotically larger than n^2/N.

12.2 Three arrays A, B, and C are given, each of length n. For $1 \leq i \leq n$, the arrays are initialized such that $1 \leq A(i) \leq n$, $B(i)$ is an arbitrary integer, and $C(i) = 0$. It is required to modify the elements of C such that for $j = 1, 2, \ldots, n$,

$$C(j) \leftarrow \sum_{A(i)=j} B(i).$$

Use discriminating analysis to compare the RAM and PRAM solutions to this problem.

12.3 Suppose that the RAM's repertoire of instructions is expanded to include **COMBINING WRITE** instructions of the form **SUM WRITE, MIN WRITE**, and so on. Thus, when **MIN WRITE** is used to write a value b to a location U containing the value a, the smaller of the two values a and b is stored in U. Use the **MIN WRITE** instruction to obtain a RAM solution to the problem of Section 12.1.1, which runs in $O(n^2)$ time. (*Hint*: The array W is initially filled with the value ∞. Whenever W is written into, **MIN WRITE** is used. Note that if it so happens that a computation yields the result ∞, the latter should be written as $+\infty$ in W, in order to distinguish it from the initial value ∞. When the computation using W is complete, the algorithm should have the following step: **if** $W(i,j) = \infty$ **then** do nothing; **else** $B(i,j) \leftarrow W(i,j)$.)

12.4 Show that even if the RAM's repertoire is expanded as in Problem 12.3, then it is still possible to obtain the same result for the problem of Section 12.1.1 and hence contradict the speedup folklore theorem, through a slight modification to the definition of the problem. (*Hint*: Modify the functions $f_1, f_2, \ldots, f_n$ so that they take an integer argument and return an integer in the range 1 to n, and for $1 \le i, j \le n$, let $f_j(f_{j-1}(\ldots f_2(f_1(A(i)) \ldots))$ be written in $B(x, y)$, where $x = B(i, j)$ and $y = g_j(g_{j-1}(\ldots g_2(g_1(i)) \ldots))$.)

12.5 Two arrays A and B are given, each with n elements. The elements of array A are initialized as follows: $1 \le A(i) \le n$ for $1 \le i \le n$. Array B is initialized arbitrarily. It is required to perform a computation consisting of $\log n$ iterations and defined as follows:

> **for** $j = 1$ **to** $\log n$ **do**
>   **for** $i = (j - 1)(n/\log n) + 1$ **to** $j(n/\log n)$ **do in parallel**
> $B(A(i)) \xleftarrow{\text{MIN}} B(i)$
>   **end for**
> **end for**. ■

Use discriminating analysis to compare the running times of PRAM and RAM algorithms for this computation.

12.6 Repeat Problem 12.1 for the computation of Section 12.2.1.

12.7 In Section 12.2.4, the speedup analysis does not take into account the time required by the memory manager to relocate the nodes of the data structure. Suggest a reasonable function describing this time, and redo the analysis.

12.8 Analyze the speedup achieved by a PRAM with n processors over a RAM in the following variant of the paradigm of Section 12.2.1. Here, once a node at level l has been visited, the memory manager relocates an *arbitrarily selected* subset of the nodes at levels 1 to l.

12.9 Modify the paradigm of Section 12.2.1 as follows: Each node in the data structure holds two values d and b. The d values at each level are used to compute D_l, as in Section 12.2.1. These values are never modified. If a node A at level l is the parent of a node B at level $l + 1$, then the pointer from A to B is equal to A's b value plus D_l. The memory manager relocates nodes as follows: As soon as node A is visited, both A and B are relocated, and the b value of A is updated to reflect B's new address. In order to reach B, the linked list containing B must be traversed from the root. As in Section 12.2.1, it is required to visit all the leaves. Show that in this case, a PRAM with n processors solves the problem in $O(k)$ time, while a RAM requires $O(nk^2)$ time, where n is the number of leaves and k is the distance from root to leaf.

12.10 Repeat Problem 12.1 for the computation of Section 12.3.1. The result obtained in Problem 12.1 should hold here with a probability approaching 1 for large n.

12.11 An array $X(1)$, $X(2)$, ..., $X(n)$ is given that contains n distinct integers I_1, I_2, ..., I_n in the range $(-\infty, n]$ such that $X(i) = I_i$ for $1 \leq i \leq n$. It is required to modify the array X so that for all i, $1 \leq i \leq n$, $X(I_i) = I_i$ if and only if $1 \leq I_i \leq n$; otherwise, $X(i) = I_i$. Show that the PRAM and RAM solutions to this problem lead to a contradiction with the speedup folklore theorem.

12.12 Given an array $X(1)$, $X(2)$, ..., $X(n)$ containing arbitrary data and an integer q that divides n evenly, it is required to shift cyclically the contents of every sequence of q consecutive elements of X by one position to the right. Show how two PRAM solutions to this problem, one with n processors and one with p processors, where $2 \leq p < q$, lead to a contradiction with the slowdown folklore theorem.

12.13 Suppose that the computational problem of Section 12.4.1 is solved by an algorithm running on a PRAM with $n - 1$ processors. Analyze the performance of this algorithm.

12.14 The notion of *success ratio* introduced in Section 1.4.4 can be generalized as follows: For a given computational task, let $Pr(n)$ and $Pr(p)$ be the probability of a successful completion using n and p processors, respectively. For $p < n$, the success ratio is

$$sr(p, n) = \frac{Pr(n)}{Pr(p)}.$$

Now consider the computational problem described in Example 12.5, in which n objects are launched simultaneously towards n targets, one object per target and one target per object. The trajectories of the objects and the positions of the targets are unknown in advance. It is known, however, that all trajectories have the same length n. A sequence of *deadlines* $\{d_1, d_2, ..., d_n\}$ is also given. It is required to track all n (unknown) trajectories of the objects to their (unknown) target positions in real time. In order to meet deadline d_i, it is necessary to know where all the objects are at the ith discrete position of their respective trajectories. As in Example 12.5, the time required to record and process the information about the position of one object is equal to the time taken by the object to move to the next position of its trajectory. Therefore, a single processor can track no more than one object at a time. For this computational task, derive $Pr(n)$, $Pr(p)$, and $sr(p, n)$, where $p < n$.

12.15 Show that $2n - 1$ robots require $\Omega(2^n)$ time units to perform the task described in Section 12.6.

12.16 Show that one robot working by itself requires $\Omega(2^n n^2)$ time units to perform the task described in Section 12.6.

12.17 Consider the following two models of computation involving mobile robots: In the *parallel* model, there are p mobile robots, each of which carries its own processor. These embedded processors implement an algorithm that allows the robots to cooperate in carrying out a task. In the *sequential* model, there are also p mobile robots; however, none of the robots carries a processor. Instead, there is a single processor that issues instructions remotely to the robots. This processor is capable of controlling the motion of one robot at a time. Suppose now that the task to be performed involves moving a mobile object a distance D from one point to another. The object is moved by creating a circle of robots around it and then moving the circle. It is important that the object be kept from moving out of the circle at all times; therefore, the distance separating two adjacent robots on the circle must be smaller than the width w of the object. We assume that $D = aw$ for some constant a, where $a > 1$. Compare the times required by the parallel and sequential models to accomplish this task.

12.18 Consider a parallel model of computation consisting of a number of processors sharing a memory. The model allows several processors to gain access to the memory simultaneously for different purposes. Thus, some processors may be reading, while others may be writing. If two processors gain access to the same location at the same time, one for reading and one for writing, then the reading takes place before the writing. Suppose that an array X of n elements is stored in the shared memory. Each element $X(i)$, $1 \le i \le n$, is associated with a *time stamp*, giving the time when $X(i)$ was last overwritten. This time stamp is modified every time a processor gains access to $X(i)$ for the purpose of writing. Let r be the probability that a given element X is *not* overwritten during a given time unit. The task to be executed is as follows: Select a time D, and return the value of $X(i)$, $1 \le i \le n$, at D.

    (a) Show that n processors can perform the task in constant time.

    (b) Suppose that n/a processors are used, where $a > 1$. Derive the probability that the task is completed successfully (i.e., that all locations of X are read in a time units, without any of them being modified).

    (c) If n/a processors fail to execute the task, they must restart. Derive the expected time required by n/a processors to complete the task successfully.

12.19 For each computational paradigm described in this chapter, a parallel algorithm is derived whose *cost* is asymptotically smaller than the running time of the optimal sequential algorithm for the same problem. It is clear, therefore, that the notion of *cost optimality* of a parallel algorithm, as defined in Chapter 1, needs to be reconsidered. Propose and discuss alternative definitions of cost optimality.

12.20 Suppose that the cost of a RAM or PRAM algorithm is defined as the number of processors the algorithm uses, *including the MAU comparators*, multiplied by the running time of the algorithm, *including the time required to traverse the MAU* for every memory access. Suppose that for a problem of size n, the number of memory access steps dominates all other steps. For this problem, the cost of a RAM algorithm that performs $t_1(n)$ steps is

$$(1 + O(n)) \times (t_1(n) \times O(\log n)) = t_1(n) \times O(n \log n),$$

since the RAM's MAU has a depth of $O(\log n)$ and a size of $O(n)$. Similarly, the cost of an n-processor PRAM algorithm that performs $t_n(n)$ steps is

$$(n + O(n \log n)) \times (t_n(n) \times O(\log n)) = t_n(n) \times O(n \log^2 n),$$

since the PRAM's MAU has a depth of $O(\log n)$ and a size of $O(n \log n)$. Thus, the cost of the RAM algorithm is asymptotically *larger* than that of the PRAM algorithm, provided that $t_1(n)$ is asymptotically larger than $t_n(n) \times O(\log n)$. Give at least two examples of computational problems for which this condition holds.

12.21 In a certain application, a set of n data is received every k time units and stored in a computer's memory. Here $2 < k < n$; for example, let $k = 5$. The ith data set received is stored in the ith row of a two-dimensional array A. In other words, the elements of the ith set occupy locations $A(i, 1), A(i, 2), \ldots, A(i, n)$. At most 2^n such sets may be received. Thus, A has 2^n rows and n columns. Initially, A is empty. The n data forming a set are received and stored simultaneously: One time unit elapses from the moment the data are received from the outside world to the moment they settle in a row of A. Once a datum has been stored in $A(i, j)$, it requires one time unit to be processed; that is, a certain operation must be performed on it which takes one time unit. This operation depends on the application. For example, the operation may simply be

$$A(i, j) \leftarrow (A(i, j))^2.$$

The computation terminates once all data currently in A have been processed, *regardless of whether more data arrive later*. Compare the performance of a PRAM with n processors to that of a RAM in solving this problem, and contrast your result with that predicted by the speedup folklore theorem.

12.22 Suppose that in Problem 12.21 a PRAM with $p < n$ processors is used to perform the computation. Compare this PRAM's performance to that of a PRAM using n processors, and contrast your result with that predicted by the slowdown folklore theorem.

12.23 Suppose that n data on which a certain computation is to be performed are stored in the memory of a computer. For example, it may be required to compute the sum of the n data currently in memory. Every $n/2$ time units, the values of k of the data (not known ahead of time) change. There are at most n such updates (each involving k values). If the result of the computation is reported after D time units, then it must be obtained using the n values in memory at the end of D time units. Compare the performance of a PRAM with n processors to that of a RAM in executing this computation, and contrast your result with that predicted by the speedup folklore theorem.

12.24 Suppose that in Problem 12.23 a PRAM with $p < n$ processors is used to perform the computation. Compare this PRAM's performance to that of a PRAM using n processors, and contrast your result with that predicted by the slowdown folklore theorem.

12.25 Suggest a computational problem that can be solved optimally on a RAM in time t_1 and on a PRAM with p processors in time t_p, where t_1/t_p is asymptotically larger than p.

12.26 Suggest a computational problem that can be solved on a PRAM with p processors in time t_p and with q processors in time t_q, where $q < p$ and t_q/t_p is asymptotically larger than $1 + p/q$.

12.27 The slowdown folklore theorem states that a computation requiring time t_p with p processors can always be executed in time t_q with q processors, $q < p$, where $t_p \leq t_q \leq t_p(1 + p/q)$. Throughout this chapter, we have focused on the second of these two inequalities. Computations were described that contradict the slowdown folklore theorem by exhibiting a slowdown asymptotically larger than $1 + p/q$. Now consider the first inequality, namely, $t_p \leq t_q$. It would seem possible that in some situations an algorithm which tries to keep all of its processors busy as long as possible ends up taking more time to solve a problem with p than with q processors, $p > q$. In this anomalous case, with $t_p > t_q$, the slowdown folklore theorem is again contradicted. An algorithm exhibiting such anomalous behavior is described in Problem 1.26. Give another example of an algorithm of this type for an appropriate computation.

12.28 Modify your algorithm in Problem 12.27 in order to rectify the anomaly described therein.

12.29 Consider the following alternative definition of speedup: For a given computational problem, let t_p be the time required to solve that problem by a certain algorithm using p processors, where $p \geq 1$. Further, let w be the minimum (known) *work* required to solve the same problem (by the same or another algorithm). Then *speedup* is defined as the ratio w/t_p. With this definition of speedup, show that:

    (a) For any computational problem, the maximum speedup achievable by a *parallel* algorithm using p processors, where $p \geq 2$, is p.

    (b) For conventional problems (i.e., those satisfying the folklore theorems), an optimal *sequential* algorithm has a speedup of 1.

    (c) For inherently parallel problems (such as those described in Sections 12.1–12.6), the fastest possible *sequential* algorithm has a speedup smaller than 1.

12.30 Give examples of computational problems to illustrate cases **(a)**, **(b)**, and **(c)** of Problem 12.29.

12.31 Discuss the appropriateness of the definition of speedup given in Problem 12.29 in capturing the phenomenon of parallel synergy.

12.9 BIBLIOGRAPHICAL REMARKS

The two folklore theorems studied in this chapter permeate the literature on parallel computation, and it is generally taken for granted that they are universally true. The speedup folklore theorem is frequently stated, "proved," and used; see, for example, Akl [21], Almasi and Gottlieb [60], Bertsekas and Tsitsiklis [99], Chaudhuri [140], Eager et al. [211], Faber et al. [222, 223], Fischer [230], Fishburn [231], Golub and Ortega [262], JáJá [310], Kumar et al. [343], Leighton [367], Li and Hudak [382], Modi [431], Schneck [552], Smith [575], and Snyder [579]. In fact, it is often said that a p-fold speedup by a parallel algorithm using p processors over a sequential algorithm *cannot* be achieved in practice and that the speedup is usually strictly smaller than p, due to the inevitable overheads involved in starting up parallel computers, in communication among processors, and in synchronization of parallel computations; see, for example, Akl [18], Baer [81], and Hockney and Jesshope [298]. Also cited in this context are "Minsky's conjecture," which states that the speedup achieved by p processors is at most $\log p$ (see Minsky [428]), and "Amdahl's law," which states that speedup is limited by the number of operations that must be performed sequentially (see Amdahl [64]). This idea is actually taken further in the theory of *P-completeness*, where it is argued that some problems are not amenable to efficient parallelization; see, for example, Greenlaw et al. [269]. As evidence in support of this claim, the theory identifies a class of problems (each of size n) satisfying the following properties:

1. Each problem in the class can be solved by a sequential algorithm whose running time is polynomial in n.

2. Suppose that for some problem in the class, a parallel algorithm is found which solves that problem in time polylogarithmic in n using a number of processors polynomial in n (i.e., an algorithm for which $t(n) = O(\log^a n)$ and $p(n) = O(n^b)$, where a and b are constants). This would immediately imply that *all* problems in the class are solvable in polylogarithmic time by a polynomial number of processors.

Alternative definitions of speedup have also been given in the literature; see, for example, Barton and Withers [88], Golub and Ortega [262], Gustafson [277], Gustafson et al. [278], Hatcher and Quinn [289], Moldovan [432], Quinn [514, 515], Sun and Gustafson [601], Sun and Ni [602], and Ware [637]. An analysis and a comparison of these various definitions are provided in Fava Lindon [225].

The myth that a parallel computer can do no more than what a sequential computer is capable of doing (except sometimes faster) has even made its way into the popular science literature; see, for example, Penrose [486]. Furthermore, it is sometimes correctly pointed out that certain computational tasks are (provably) *inherently sequential* and cannot be executed quickly in parallel. (See Problem 6.13.) For example, the following analogy is used: If one ship can cross an ocean in 10 days, then using 10 ships would not lead to a faster crossing. However, it is also true that certain tasks are *inherently parallel* (also as illustrated in Problem 6.13): Again, by analogy, 10 people can lift a heavy scaffold and move it from one place to another in less than one-tenth of the time required by one person working alone, who would have to take the scaffold apart, move the pieces one by one, and then reassemble the scaffold at the new location; see Fischer [230]. In fact, if the scaffold cannot be disassembled, then the problem cannot be solved at all by a single person.

The slowdown folklore theorem is also routinely cited and applied in many different contexts. It appears in various forms in Bertsekas and Tsitsiklis [99], Chaudhuri [140], Cole [166], Cole and Vishkin [173], Cormen et al. [185], Gibbons and Rytter [258], JáJá [310], Karp and Ramachandran [323], Manber [402], Pan and Preparata [464], Reif [533], and Smith [575]. Often, the theorem is formulated with the proviso that processor allocation (i.e., the task of distributing jobs to processors or vice versa) may in some cases limit its practical applicability; see, for example, Gibbons and Rytter [258] and Karp and Ramachandran [323]. Note also that the theorem is usually attributed to Brent [123, 124], although in fairness, Brent's formulation was for a special context, namely, the evaluation of arithmetic expressions.

Despite the widespread use and acceptability of the folklore theorems since the early days of parallel computation, several attempts were made at disproving them, specifically by showing that the speedup folklore theorem is "too pessimistic," whereas the slowdown folklore theorem is "too optimistic." The speedup folklore theorem, in particular, has been the subject of many studies. For example, with p processors, Janssen [313], Mehrotra and Gehringer [414], Parkinson [470], and

Shonkwiler et al. [567] obtain speedups larger than p. However, it would appear that these speedups are due to the fact that *the sequential algorithms* used for the purpose of comparison *are inefficient*. Sometimes a speedup larger than p is obtained using p processors *only in some instances* of the computational problem being solved; see, for example, Barr and Hickman [87], Goerdt and Kamps [260], Grit and McGraw [270], Kornfeld [329], Lai and Sahni [353], Lai and Sprague [354], Leach et al. [361], Li and Wah [376, 377], Li [381], Mahanti and Daniels [401], McBurney and Sleep [410], Patil and Banerjee [472], Preiss and Hamacher [499], Quinn [514], Quinn and Deo [516], Rao and Kumar [528], Rost and Maehle [539], Shonkwiler and van Vleck [568], Speckenmeyer [581], Speckenmeyer et al. [582], Usui et al. [617], Vishkin [628], and Weide [638]. It is also possible to obtain speedups larger than p by *restricting the size of the memory* on the sequential computer; see, for example, Akl et al. [29], Bagheri et al. [83], Cosnard and Philippe [187], Cosnard et al. [188], and Helmbold and McDowell [292]. The first attempt at disproving the slowdown folklore theorem was made in Akl et al. [29], and it is based on *restricting the size of the local memory* of a processor on the sequential and parallel computers. The results in Bilardi and Preparata [106, 107] apply to the linear array and mesh models. It is shown therein that, due to physical limitations on the size of devices and the speed of propagation of messages, parallelism and locality combined may yield speedups that are asymptotically larger than the number of processors used. Finally, suppose that a computer with q processors executes an algorithm designed for p processors, where $q < p$. Each time this computer needs to simulate the actions of a distinct subset of q hypothetical processors, it must update its variables in order to put itself in the right context. This process is called *context switching*. It has been argued that the overhead involved in context switching could be so significant that it may lead to a contradiction of the folklore theorems; see, for example, Faber et al. [222] and Schneck [552].

Recently, several counterexamples to the folklore theorems have been discovered which do not have the aforementioned limitations; that is:

1. They compare a parallel algorithm using p processors to the *best possible sequential algorithm* (in the case of the speedup folklore theorem) and to the *best possible parallel algorithm with q processors*, $q < p$ (in the case of the slowdown folklore theorem).

2. They hold for *all* instances of the computational problem being used to contradict one or the other of the folklore theorems.

3. The *size of the memory* of the sequential computer *is not restricted* in any way.

4. The overhead incurred due to *context switching* is inconsequential asymptotically.

These counterexamples appear in Akl and Fava Lindon [35], Fava Lindon [225], Luccio and Pagli [395, 396], and Luccio et al. [397]. The paradigms described in this chapter are motivated by examples appearing in these works, as well as in Akl [24] and Fava Lindon [224].

Luccio and Pagli [395, 396] use the following intuitive example, called the *p-shovelers problem*: On a winter morning, as the snow falls, a group of p people wish to get their car out of the driveway. Together, they clear their driveway from snow more than p times faster than their neighbor who works alone, hence longer, and therefore allows more snow to accumulate. In fact, before being able to drive away, the single shoveler ends up removing more snow than the p neighbors do. This example is representative of *data-accumulative* tasks, where some initial data are given and additional data continue to arrive while the task is being performed. The computation terminates when all data received have been processed (regardless of whether more data arrive later). It is shown that a speedup larger than the number of processors used can be achieved for such tasks, since a sequential processor accumulates more data during the course of the computation. This contradicts the speedup folklore theorem. Similarly, if fewer than the optimal number of processors are used, the slowdown folklore theorem is violated. A second counterexample to the two folklore theorems is also given in Luccio and Pagli [395, 396]. Here, the values of certain data vary during the course of the computation, and the algorithm must use the new values. Because a single processor is necessarily slower than the optimal number of processors p, it must deal with more data changes than the p processors and hence takes more than p time longer to complete the task. Similarly, using q processors, $q < p$, leads to a slowdown larger than $1 + p/q$. In the paradigm in Luccio et al. [397], processors fail while solving a problem, with a probability that increases with time. A computer with fewer than the optimal number of processors takes longer to solve a problem and hence is likely to experience more failures.

Special cases of the paradigm in which a single stream of data arrives and is processed sequentially in real time are analyzed in Karp [321] and Paul [474] and the references therein. Robot models are described in Debest [196] and Dudek et al. [209]. A review of one-way functions used in cryptography is provided in Patterson [473] and Seberry and Pieprzyk [557]. Sequential simulations of parallel algorithms are used in Cole [165] and Megiddo [413] to speed up inefficient sequential computations. It is shown in Graham [265, 266, 267] that in some cases, using *fewer* processors leads in fact to a *reduction* in the running time. Such anomalies occur typically within the general context of *scheduling* or *sequencing* jobs for execution on a set of processors. For a review of this problem, see, for example, Garey and Johnson [255] and the references therein.

In this chapter, the case was made that our current computational theory is inadequate for capturing any concept beyond the mere evaluation of functions and that our present models cannot appropriately represent a wide variety of computations. In particular, the theory and its models are very limited in their ability to handle stimuli from the outside world or cope with the concept of real time. Related arguments have been advanced elsewhere. For example, Penrose [487] submits that no computational model (present or future!) can lead to a full understanding of the actions of the human brain. Instead, he suggests that the laws of *physics* could be used to explain our conscious mentality. Along the same lines, *quantum computers* are being proposed as (massively parallel) counterparts of our current sequential models; see, for example, Deutsch [201], Jozsa [318], and Shor [569]. A theoretical analysis is provided in Shor [569] whereby a fast parallel solution is obtained, through quantum computation, to the otherwise time-consuming problem of factoring large numbers (of 100 decimal digits or more). Another example is provided by *molecular computing*, wherein living organisms are regarded and *used* as information processing entities; see, for example, Conrad [177, 178, 179]. Of particular interest in this context is the work of Adleman [2], who used a *biological computer* to attack one of the traditionally hard problems in computer science, namely, the Hamiltonian path problem. In this problem, a directed graph is given, and it is required to determine whether a path exists that starts at a vertex and visits every one of the remaining vertices exactly once. (See, for example, Cormen et al. [185] and Garey and Johnson [255].) Adleman's solution is based on using strands of DNA (deoxyribonucleic acid, the genetic molecule) to encode the data. The existence of a Hamiltonian path is then decided by carrying out, in parallel, a large number of biochemical reactions or DNA *ligations* (a process commonly referred to as *gene splicing*). A description of this work can also be found in Devlin [202, 203], while Lipton [390] proposes a number of extensions. Finally, a model of computation based on a particular chaotic dynamical system is described in Siegelmann [572] and Siegelmann and Sontag [573]. This mathematical model is more powerful than the Turing machine, not so much because of its speed, but in terms of the computations it can perform.

These examples fall well within the thesis of this chapter. They can be seen as putting in question our *conventional* models of computation. The alternatives they propose, however, may be interpreted as new, unconventional computational models in a broad, all-encompassing definition of computation. In this definition, the laws governing various branches of knowledge, such as mathematics, physics, biology, and chemistry, may be invoked (at different levels of abstraction) to serve as powerful and versatile models of computation.

Bibliography

[1] K. Abrahamson, N. Dadoun, D. Kirkpatrick, and T. Prztycka. A simple parallel tree contraction algorithm. *Journal of Algorithms*, Vol. 10, 1989, pp. 187–302.

[2] L.A. Adleman. Molecular computation of solutions to combinatorial problems. *Science*, Vol. 266, 1994, pp. 1021–1024.

[3] A. Aggarwal. A comparative study of X-tree, pyramid and related machines. *Proceedings of the IEEE Symposium on Foundations of Computer Science*, 1984, pp. 89–99.

[4] A. Aggarwal. Optimal bounds for finding maximum on array of processors with k global buses. *IEEE Transactions on Computers*. Vol. 35, 1986, pp. 62–64.

[5] A. Aggarwal, B. Chazelle, L.J. Guibas, C. Ó'Dúnlaing, and C.K. Yap. Parallel computational geometry. *Algorithmica*, Vol. 3, 1988, pp. 293–327.

[6] H. Ahmed, J.M. Delosme, and M. Morf. Highly concurrent computing structures for matrix arithmetic and signal processing. *Computer*, Vol. 15, 1982, pp. 65–82.

[7] A.V. Aho, J.E. Hopcroft, and J.D. Ullman. *The Design and Analysis of Computer Algorithms*. Addison-Wesley, Reading, Massachusetts, 1974.

[8] M. Ajtai, J. Komlós, W.L. Steiger, and E. Szemerédi. Optimal parallel selection has complexity $O(\log \log n)$. *Journal of Computer and System Sciences*, Vol. 38, 1989, pp. 125–133.

[9] M. Ajtai, J. Komlós, and E. Szemerédi. Sorting in $c \log n$ parallel steps. *Combinatorica*, Vol. 3, 1983, pp. 1–19.

[10] M. Ajtai, J. Komlós, and E. Szemerédi. An $O(n \log n)$ sorting network. *Proceedings of the ACM Symposium on Theory of Computing*, 1983, pp. 1–9.

[11] S.B. Akers, D. Harel, and B. Krishnamurthy. The star graph: An attractive alternative to the n-cube. *Proceedings of the International Conference on Parallel Processing*, 1987, pp. 393–400.

[12] S.B. Akers and B. Krishnamurthy. The fault tolerance of star graphs. *Proceedings of the International Conference on Supercomputing*, Vol. 3, 1987, pp. 270–276.

[13] S.B. Akers and B. Krishnamurthy. A group theoretic model for symmetric interconnection networks. *IEEE Transactions on Computers*, Vol. 38, 1989, pp. 555–566.

[14] S.G. Akl. A constant-time parallel algorithm for computing convex hulls. *BIT*, Vol. 22, 1982, pp. 130–134.

[15] S.G. Akl. An optimal algorithm for parallel selection. *Information Processing Letters*, Vol. 19, 1984, pp. 47–50.

[16] S.G. Akl. Optimal parallel algorithms for computing convex hulls and for sorting. *Computing*, Vol. 33, 1984, pp. 1–11.

[17] S.G. Akl. Optimal parallel algorithms for selection, sorting and computing convex hulls. In *Computational Geometry*, G.T. Toussaint, ed. Elsevier, Amsterdam, 1985, pp. 1–22.

[18] S.G. Akl. *Parallel Sorting Algorithms*. Academic Press, Orlando, Florida, 1985.

[19] S.G. Akl. An adaptive and cost-optimal parallel algorithm for minimum spanning trees. *Computing*, Vol. 36, 1986, pp. 271–277.

[20] S.G. Akl. Adaptive and optimal parallel algorithms for enumerating permutations and combinations. *The Computer Journal*, Vol. 30, 1987, pp. 433–436.

[21] S.G. Akl. *The Design and Analysis of Parallel Algorithms*. Prentice Hall, Englewood Cliffs, New Jersey, 1989.

[22] S.G. Akl. On the power of concurrent memory access. In *Computing and Information*, R. Janicki, and W.W. Koczkodaj, eds. North-Holland, Amsterdam, 1989, pp. 49–55.

[23] S.G. Akl. Memory access in models of parallel computation: From folklore to synergy and beyond. *Proceedings of the Workshop on Algorithms and Data Structures*, Lecture Notes in Computer Science, No. 519, Springer-Verlag, Berlin, 1991, pp. 92–104.

[24] S.G. Akl. Parallel synergy. *Parallel Algorithms and Applications*, Vol. 1, 1993, pp. 3–9.

[25] S.G. Akl, D.T. Barnard, and R.J. Doran. Design, analysis and implementation of a parallel tree search algorithm. *IEEE Transactions on Machine Analysis and Artificial Intelligence*, Vol. 4, 1982, pp. 192–203.

[26] S.G. Akl, B.K. Bhattacharya, and D. Kaller. Optimal parallel algorithm for the maximum clique problem in a family of proper circular arcs. In *Snapshots of Computational and Discrete Geometry*, Vol. 3, D. Avis and P. Bose, eds. McGill University, Montreal, Quebec, 1994, pp. 134–166.

[27] S.G. Akl, J.M. Calvert, and I. Stojmenović. Systolic generation of derangements. In *Algorithms and Parallel VLSI Architectures*, Vol. 2, P. Quinton and Y. Robert, eds. Elsevier, Amsterdam, 1992, pp. 59–70.

[28] S.G. Akl and L. Chen. Efficient parallel algorithms on proper circular arc graphs. *Proceedings of the International Conference on Parallel and Distributed Processing Techniques and Applications*, 1995, pp. 71–80.

[29] S.G. Akl, M. Cosnard, and A.G. Ferreira. Data-movement-intensive problems: Two folklore theorems in parallel computation revisited. *Theoretical Computer Science*, Vol. 95, 1992, pp. 323–337.

[30] S.G. Akl and F. Dehne. Pipelined search on coarse grained networks. *International Journal of Parallel Programming*, Vol. 18, 1989, pp. 359–364.

[31] S.G. Akl and R.J. Doran. A comparison of parallel implementations of the alpha-beta and Scout tree search algorithms using the game of checkers. In *Computer Game Playing*, M.A. Bramer, ed. Wiley, Chichester, England, 1983, pp. 290–303.

[32] S.G. Akl, T. Duboux, and I. Stojmenović. Constant delay parallel counters. *Parallel Processing Letters*, Vol. 1, 1991, pp. 143–148.

[33] S.G. Akl, J. Duprat, and A.G. Ferreira. Hamiltonian circuits and paths in star graphs. In *Advances in Parallel Algorithms*, I. Dimov and O. Tonev, eds. IOS Press, Sofia, Bulgaria, 1994, pp. 131–143.

[34] S.G. Akl and L. Fava Lindon. Modèles de calcul parallèle à mémoire partagée. In *Algorithmique Parallèle*, M. Cosnard, M. Nivat, and Y. Robert, eds. Masson, Paris, 1992, pp. 15–29.

[35] S.G. Akl and L. Fava Lindon. Paradigms admitting superunitary behavior in parallel computation. *Proceedings of the Joint Conference on Vector and Parallel Processing (CONPAR)*, Lecture Notes in Computer Science, No. 854, Springer-Verlag, Berlin, 1994, pp. 301–312.

[36] S.G. Akl, L. Fava Lindon, and G.R. Guenther. Broadcasting with selective reduction on an optimal PRAM circuit. *Technique et Science Informatiques*, Vol. 10, 1991, pp. 261–268.

[37] S.G. Akl, D. Gries, and I. Stojmenović. An optimal parallel algorithm for generating combinations. *Information Processing Letters*, Vol. 33, 1989, pp. 135–139.

[38] S.G. Akl and G.R. Guenther. Broadcasting with selective reduction. *Proceedings of the IFIP Congress*, 1989, pp. 515–520.

[39] S.G. Akl and G.R. Guenther. Applications of broadcasting with selective reduction to the maximal sum subsegment problem. *International Journal of High Speed Computing*, Vol. 3, 1991, pp. 107–119.

[40] S.G. Akl, G.R. Guenther, and X. Shi. On the parallel complexity of two subsequence problems. *Utilitas Mathematica*, Vol. 41, 1992, pp. 175–180.

[41] S.G. Akl, G. Labonté, M. Leeder, and K. Qiu. On doing Todd-Coxeter enumeration in parallel. *Applied Discrete Mathematics*, Vol. 34, 1991, pp. 27–35.

[42] S.G. Akl and K.A. Lyons. *Parallel Computational Geometry*. Prentice Hall, Englewood Cliffs, New Jersey, 1993.

[43] S.G. Akl and H. Meijer. On the bit complexity of parallel computations. *Integration: The VLSI Journal*, Vol. 6, 1988, pp. 201–212.

[44] S.G. Akl and H. Meijer. Parallel binary search. *IEEE Transactions on Parallel and Distributed Systems*, Vol. 1, 1990, pp. 247–250.

[45] S.G. Akl, H. Meijer, and D. Rappaport. Parallel computational geometry on a grid. *Computers and Artificial Intelligence*, Vol. 9, 1990, pp. 461–470.

[46] S.G. Akl, H. Meijer, and I. Stojmenović. An optimal systolic algorithm for generating permutations in lexicographic order. *Journal of Parallel and Distributed Computing*, Vol. 20, 1994, pp. 84–91.

[47] S.G. Akl and K. Qiu. Les réseaux d'interconnexion star et pancake. In *Algorithmique parallèle*, M. Cosnard, M. Nivat, and Y. Robert, eds. Masson, Paris, 1992, pp. 171–181.

[48] S.G. Akl and K. Qiu. A novel routing scheme on the star and pancake networks and its applications. *Parallel Computing*, Vol. 19, 1993, pp. 95–101.

[49] S.G. Akl, K. Qiu, and I. Stojmenović. Computing the Voronoi diagram on the star and pancake interconnection networks. *Proceedings of the Canadian Conference on Computational Geometry*, 1992, pp. 353–358.

[50] S.G. Akl, K. Qiu, and I. Stojmenović. Fundamental algorithms for the star and pancake interconnection networks with applications to computational geometry. *Networks, Special Issue: Interconnection Networks and Algorithms*, Vol. 23, 1993, pp. 215–226.

[51] S.G. Akl and N. Santoro. Optimal parallel merging and sorting without memory conflicts. *IEEE Transactions on Computers*, Vol. 36, 1987, pp. 1367–1369.

[52] S.G. Akl and H. Schmeck. Systolic sorting in a sequential input/output environment. *Parallel Computing*, Vol. 3, 1986, pp. 11–23.

[53] S.G. Akl and I. Stojmenović. A simple optimal systolic algorithm for generating permutations. *Parallel Processing Letters*, Vol. 2, 1992, pp. 231–239.

[54] S.G. Akl and I. Stojmenović. Generating binary trees in parallel. *Proceedings of the Allerton Conference on Communication, Control, and Computing*, 1992, pp. 225–233.

[55] S.G. Akl and I. Stojmenović. Parallel algorithms for generating integer partitions and compositions. *The Journal of Combinatorial Mathematics and Combinatorial Computing*, Vol. 13, 1993, pp. 107–120.

[56] S.G. Akl and I. Stojmenović. Multiple criteria BSR: An implementation and applications to computational geometry problems. *Proceedings of the Hawaii International Conference on System Sciences*, Vol. 2, 1994, pp. 159–168.

[57] S.G. Akl and I. Stojmenović. Broadcasting with selective reduction: A powerful model of parallel computation. In *Parallel and Distributed Computing Handbook*, A.Y. Zomaya, ed. McGraw-Hill, New York, 1996, pp. 192–222.

[58] S.G. Akl and I. Stojmenović. Generating combinatorial objects on a linear array of processors. In *Parallel Computing: Paradigms and Applications*, A.Y. Zomaya, ed. International Thomson Computer Press, London, 1996, pp. 639–670.

[59] S.G. Akl and I. Stojmenović. Generating t-ary trees in parallel. *Nordic Journal of Computing*, 1996, in press.

[60] G.S. Almasi and G. Gottlieb. *Highly Parallel Computing*. Benjamin-Cummings, Redwood City, California, 1989.

[61] H.M. Alnuweiri. Constant-time parallel algorithm for image labeling on a reconfigurable network of processors. *IEEE Transactions on Parallel and Distributed Systems*, Vol. 5, 1994, pp. 321–326.

[62] H.M. Alnuweiri. A fast reconfigurable network for graph connectivity and transitive closure. *Parallel Processing Letters*, Vol. 4, 1994, pp. 105–115.

[63] N. Alon. Expanders, sorting in rounds and superconcentrators of limited depth. *Proceedings of the ACM Symposium on Theory of Computing*, 1985, pp. 98–102.

[64] G. Amdahl. Validity of the single processor approach to achieving large scale capabilities. *Proceedings of the AFIPS Spring Joint Computer Conference*, Vol. 30, 1967, pp. 483–485.

[65] R. Anderson and G. Miller. A simple randomized parallel algorithm for list ranking. *Information Processing Letters*, Vol. 33, 1990, pp. 269–273.

[66] R. Anderson and G. Miller. Deterministic parallel list ranking. *Algorithmica*, Vol. 6, 1991, pp. 859–868.

[67] APL2 Programming, Language Reference. IBM Corporation, San Jose, California, 1994.

[68] T. Asano and H. Umeo. Systolic algorithms for computing the visibility polygon and triangulation of a polygonal region. *Parallel Computing*, Vol. 6, 1988, pp. 209–216.

[69] M.J. Atallah. Parallel computational geometry. In *Parallel and Distributed Computing Handbook*, A.Y. Zomaya, ed. McGraw-Hill, New York, pp. 404–428.

[70] M.J. Atallah and D.Z. Chen. Parallel computational geometry. In *Parallel Computing: Paradigms and Applications*, A.Y. Zomaya, ed. International Thomson Computer Press, London, 1996, pp. 162–197.

[71] M.J. Atallah, R. Cole, and M.T. Goodrich. Cascading divide-and-conquer: A technique for designing parallel algorithms. *SIAM Journal on Computing*, Vol. 18, 1989, pp. 499–532.

[72] M.J. Atallah and M.T. Goodrich. Efficient parallel solutions to some geometric problems. *Journal of Parallel and Distributed Computing*, Vol. 3, 1986, pp. 492–507.

[73] M.J. Atallah and M.T. Goodrich. Deterministic parallel computational geometry. In *Synthesis of Parallel Algorithms*, J.H. Reif, ed. Morgan Kaufmann, San Mateo, California, 1993, pp. 497–536.

[74] M.J. Atallah and S.R. Kosaraju. A generalized dictionary machine for VLSI. *IEEE Transactions on Computers*, Vol. 34, 1985, pp. 151–155.

[75] M.J. Atallah and J.J. Tsay. On the parallel decomposability of geometric problems. *Proceedings of the ACM Symposium on Computational Geometry*, 1989, pp. 104–113.

[76] M.M. Atwah, J. Baker, and S.G. Akl. An associative implementation of Graham's convex hull algorithm. *Proceedings of the IASTED International Conference on Parallel and Distributed Computing and Systems*, 1995, pp. 273–276.

[77] B. Awerbuch and Y. Shiloach. New connectivity and msf algorithms for ultra-computer and pram. *Proceedings of the International Conference on Parallel Processing*, 1983, pp. 175–179.

[78] B. Awerbuch and Y. Shiloach. New connectivity and msf algorithms for shuffle exchange networks and pram. *IEEE Transactions on Computers*, Vol. 36, 1987, pp. 1258–1263.

[79] R.G. Babb, ed. *Programming Parallel Processors*. Addison-Wesley, Reading, Massachusetts, 1988.

[80] S. Baase. *Computer Algorithms*. Addison-Wesley, Reading, Massachusetts, 1988.

[81] J.L. Baer. *Computer Systems Architecture*. Computer Science Press, Potomac Maryland, 1980.

[82] J.L. Baer, H.C. Du, and R.E. Ladner. Binary search in a multiprocessing environment. *IEEE Transactions on Computers*, Vol. 32, 1983, pp. 667–676.

[83] B. Bagheri, A. Ilin, and L.R. Scott. Parallel 3-D MOSFET simulation. *Proceedings of the Hawaii International Conference on System Sciences*, Vol. 1, 1994, pp. 46–54.

[84] R.H. Barlow, D.J. Evans, and J. Shanehchi. A parallel merging algorithm. *Information Processing Letters*, Vol. 13, 1981, pp. 103–106.

[85] G.H. Barnes, R.M. Brown, M. Kato, D.J. Kuck, D.L. Slotnick, and R.A. Stokes. The Illiac IV computer. *IEEE Transactions on Computers*, Vol. 17, 1968, pp. 746–757.

[86] A. Bar-Noy and D. Peleg. Square meshes are not always optimal. *IEEE Transactions on Computers*, Vol. 40, 1991, pp. 196–204.

[87] R.S. Barr and B.L. Hickman. Parallel simplex for large pure network problems: Computational testing and sources of speedup. *Operations Research*, Vol. 42, 1994, pp. 65–80.

[88] M.L. Barton and G.R. Withers. Computing performance as a function of the speed, quantity, and cost of the processors. *Proceedings of Supercomputing '89*, 1989, pp. 759–764.

[89] K.E. Batcher. Sorting networks and their applications. *Proceedings of the AFIPS Spring Joint Computer Conference*, 1968, pp. 307–314. (Reprinted in *Interconnection Networks for Parallel and Distributed Processing*, C.L. Wu and T.S. Feng, eds. IEEE Computer Society, 1984, pp. 576–583.)

[90] K.E. Batcher. Design of a massively parallel processor. *IEEE Transactions on Computers*, Vol. 29, 1980, pp. 836–840.

[91] K.E. Batcher. On bitonic sorting networks. *Proceedings of the International Conference on Parallel Processing*, Vol. 1, 1990, pp. 376–378.

[92] G. Baudet and D. Stevenson. Optimal sorting algorithms for parallel computers. *IEEE Transactions on Computers*, Vol. 27, 1978, pp. 84–87.

[93] M. Behzad, G. Chartrand, and L. Lesniak-Foster. *Graphs and Digraphs*. Prindle, Weber, and Schmidt, Boston, 1979.

[94] Y. Ben-Asher, D. Peleg, R. Ramaswami, and A. Schuster. The power of reconfiguration. *Journal of Parallel and Distributed Computing*, Vol. 13, 1991, pp. 139–153.

[95] Y. Ben-Asher and A. Shuster. Ranking on reconfigurable networks. *Parallel Processing Letters*, Vol. 1, 1991, pp. 149–156.

[96] V.E. Beneš. *Mathematical Theory of Connecting Networks and Telephone Traffic*. Academic Press, New York, 1965.

[97] M. Ben-Or. Lower bounds for algebraic computation trees. *Proceedings of the ACM Symposium on Theory of Computing*, 1983, pp. 80–86.

[98] J. Bentley. *Programming Pearls*. Addison-Wesley, Reading, Massachusetts, 1986.

[99] D.P. Bertsekas and J.N. Tsitsiklis. *Parallel and Distributed Computation: Numerical Methods*. Prentice Hall, Englewood Cliffs, New Jersey, 1989.

[100] D. Bhagavathi, H. Gurla, S. Olariu, J.L. Schwing, and J. Zhang. Square meshes are not optimal for convex hull computation. *Proceedings of the International Conference on Parallel Processing*, Vol. 3, 1993, pp. 307–311.

[101] D. Bhagavathi, P.J. Looges, S. Olariu, and J.L. Schwing. Selection on rectangular meshes with multiple broadcasting. *BIT*, Vol. 33, 1993, pp. 7–14.

[102] D. Bhagavathi, P.J. Looges, S. Olariu, J.L. Schwing, and J. Zhang. A fast selection algorithm for meshes with multiple broadcasting. *Proceedings of the International Conference on Parallel Processing*, 1992, Vol. 3, pp. 10–17.

[103] D. Bhagavathi, S. Olariu, J.L. Schwing, and J. Zhang. Convex polygon problems on meshes with multiple broadcasting. *Parallel Processing Letters*, Vol. 2, 1992, pp. 249–256.

[104] D. Bhagavathi, S. Olariu, W. Shen, and L. Wilson. A unifying look at semigroup computations on meshes with multiple broadcasting. *Parallel Processing Letters*, Vol. 4, 1994, pp. 73–82.

[105] G. Bilardi and F.P. Preparata. Size-time complexity of Boolean networks for prefix computations. *Proceedings of the ACM Symposium on the Theory of Computing*, 1987, pp. 436–442.

[106] G. Bilardi and F.P. Preparata. Horizons of parallel computation. *Journal of Parallel and Distributed Computing*, Vol. 27, 1995, pp. 172–182.

[107] G. Bilardi and F.P. Preparata. Lower bounds to processor-time tradeoffs under bounded speed message propagation. *Proceedings of the Workshop on Algorithms and Data Structures*, Lecture Notes in Computer Science, No. 955, Springer-Verlag, Berlin, 1995, pp. 1–12.

[108] G. Birkhoff and T.C. Bartee. *Modern Applied Algebra*. McGraw-Hill, New York, 1970.

[109] D. Bitton, D.J. DeWitt, D.K. Hsiao, and J. Menon. A taxonomy of parallel sorting. *Computing Surveys*, Vol. 13, 1984, pp. 287–318.

[110] N. Blais and H. ElGindy. Algorithmic utilization of local memory in mesh connected computers. *Proceedings of the Allerton Conference on Communication, Control, and Computing*, 1989, pp. 1094–1102.

[111] G.E. Blelloch. Scans as primitive parallel operations. *IEEE Transactions on Computers*, Vol. 38, 1989, pp. 1526–1538.

[112] G.E. Blelloch. *Vector Models for Data-Parallel Computing*. MIT Press, Cambridge, Massachusetts, 1990.

[113] G.E. Blelloch and J.J. Little. Parallel solutions to geometric problems on the scan model of computation. *Proceedings of the International Conference on Parallel Processing*, Vol. 3, 1988, pp. 218–222.

[114] S.H. Bokhari. Finding maximum on an array processor with a global bus. *IEEE Transactions on Computers*, Vol. 33, 1984, pp. 133–139.

[115] V. Bokka, H. Gurla, S. Olariu, and J.L. Schwing. Time- and VLSI-optimal convex hull computation on meshes with multiple broadcasting. *Information Processing Letters*, Vol. 56, 1995, pp. 273–280.

[116] R.B. Boppana. Optimal separations between concurrent-write parallel machines. *Proceedings of the ACM Symposium on Theory of Computing*, 1989, pp. 320–326.

[117] R. Boppana and C.S. Raghevandra. On self-routing in Beneš and shuffle-exchange networks. *Proceedings of the International Conference on Parallel Processing*, Vol. 1, 1988, pp. 196–200.

[118] A. Borodin and J.E. Hopcroft. Routing, merging and sorting on parallel models of computation. *Journal of Computer and System Sciences*, Vol. 30, 1985, pp. 130–145.

[119] V.J. Bouknight, S.A. Denenberg, D.E. McIntyre, J.M. Randell, A.M. Sameh, and D.L. Slotnick. The Illiac IV system. *Proceedings of the IEEE*, Vol. 60, 1972, pp. 369–379.

[120] G. Brassard and P. Bratley. *Algorithmics: Theory and Practice*. Prentice Hall, Englewood Cliffs, New Jersey, 1988.

[121] S. Brawer. *Introduction to Parallel Programming*. Academic Press, San Diego, 1989.

[122] R.P. Brent. On the addition of binary numbers. *IEEE Transactions on Computers*, Vol. 19, 1970, pp. 758–759.

[123] R.P. Brent. The parallel evaluation of arithmetic expressions in logarithmic time. In *Complexity of Sequential and Parallel Numerical Algorithms*, J.F. Traub, ed. Academic Press, New York, 1973, pp. 83–102.

[124] R.P. Brent. The parallel evaluation of general arithmetic expressions. *Journal of the ACM*, Vol. 21, 1974, pp. 201–206.

[125] R.P. Brent and H.T. Kung. A regular layout for parallel adders. *IEEE Transactions on Computers*, Vol. 31, 1982, pp. 260–264.

[126] P. Brinch Hansen. *Studies in Computational Science: Parallel Programming Paradigms*. Prentice Hall, Upper Saddle River, New Jersey, 1995.

[127] C.S. Burrus and T.W. Parks. *DFT/FFT and Convolution Algorithms*. Wiley, New York, 1985.

[128] P. Capello and K. Steiglitz. A VLSI layout for a pipelined Dadda multiplier. *ACM Transactions on Computer Systems*, Vol. 1, 1983, pp. 157–174.

[129] M.J. Carey and C.D. Thompson. An efficient implementation of search trees on $\lceil \log N + 1 \rceil$ processors. *IEEE Transactions on Computers*, Vol. 33, 1984, pp. 1038–1041.

[130] D.A. Carlson. Solving linear recurrence systems on mesh-connected computers with multiple global buses. *Journal of Parallel and Distributed Computing*, Vol. 8, 1990, pp. 89–95.

[131] N. Carriero and D. Gelernter. *How to Write Parallel Programs*. MIT Press, Cambridge, Massachusetts, 1990.

[132] B.A. Chalmers and S.G. Akl. Optimal parallel algorithms for a transportation problem. *Proceedings of the Canadian Conference on Electrical and Computing Engineering*, 1991, pp. 36.1.1–36.1.6

[133] B.A. Chalmers and S.G. Akl. Optimal parallel algorithms for computing a vertex of the linear transportation polytope. *Proceedings of the ORSA Conference on Computer Science and Operations Research: New Developments in Their Interfaces*, 1992, pp. 295–306.

[134] B. Chan and S.G. Akl. Generating combinations in parallel. *BIT*, Vol. 26, 1986, pp. 2–6.

[135] I.W. Chan and F. Choi. An optimal systolic dictionary. *Parallel Processing Letters*, Vol. 5, 1995, pp. 451–460.

[136] A. Chandra and R. Melhem. Reconfiguration in fault-tolerant 3D meshes. *Parallel Processing Letters*, Vol. 5, 1995, pp. 387–399.

[137] S. Chandran and A. Rosenfeld. Order statistics on a hypercube. *Information Processing Letters*, Vol. 27, 1988, pp. 129–132.

[138] K.M. Chandy and J. Misra. *Parallel Program Design: A Foundation.* Addison-Wesley, Reading, Massachusetts, 1988.

[139] S.K. Chang. Parallel balancing of binary search trees. *IEEE Transactions on Computers*, Vol. 23, 1974, pp. 441–445.

[140] P. Chaudhuri. *Parallel Algorithms: Design and Analysis.* Prentice Hall, Sydney, Australia, 1992.

[141] B. Chazelle. Computational geometry on a systolic chip. *IEEE Transactions on Computers*, Vol. 33, 1984, pp. 774–785.

[142] C.C.Y. Chen and S.K. Das. Breadth first traversals of trees and integer sorting in parallel. *Information Processing Letters*, Vol. 41, 1992, pp. 39–49.

[143] C.C.Y. Chen, S.K. Das, and S.G. Akl. A unified approach to parallel depth-first traversals of general trees. *Information Processing Letters*, Vol. 38, 1991, pp. 49–55.

[144] G.H. Chen and M.S. Chern. Parallel generation of permutations and combinations. *BIT*, Vol. 26, 1986, pp. 277–283.

[145] G.H. Chen, M.S. Chern, and R.C.T. Lee. A new systolic architecture for convex hull and half-plane intersection problems. *BIT*, Vol. 27, 1987, pp. 141–147.

[146] S. Chen and D.J. Kuck. Time and parallel processor bounds for linear recurrence systems. *IEEE Transactions on Computers*, Vol. 24, 1975, pp. 701–717.

[147] T.C. Chen, K.P Eswaran, V.Y. Lum, and C. Tung. Simplified odd-even sort using multiple shift-register loops. *International Journal of Computer and Information Science*, Vol. 7, 1978, pp. 295–314.

[148] Y.C. Chen and W.T. Chen. Constant time sorting on reconfigurable meshes. *IEEE Transactions on Computers*, Vol. 43, 1994, pp. 749–751.

[149] Y.C. Chen, W.T.Chen, and G.H. Chen. Efficient median finding and its applications to two-variable linear programming on mesh-connected computers with multiple broadcasting. *Journal of Parallel and Distributed Computing*, Vol. 15, 1992, pp. 79–84.

[150] Y.C. Chen, W.T. Chen, G.H. Chen, and J.P. Sheu. Designing efficient parallel algorithms on mesh-connected computers with multiple broadcasting. *IEEE Transactions on Parallel and Distributed Systems*, Vol. 1, 1990, pp. 241–245.

[151] M.Y. Chern and T. Murata. Sorting on gated-bus array processors. *Proceedings of the Allerton Conference on Communication, Control, and Computing*, 1983, pp. 863–865.

[152] W.K. Chiang and R.J. Chen. The (n, k)-star graph: A generalized star graph. *Information Processing Letters*, Vol. 56, 1995, pp. 259–264.

[153] D.M. Chiarulli, R.G. Melhem, and S.P. Levitan. Using coincident optical pulses for parallel memory addressing. *The Computer Journal*, Vol. 30, 1987, pp. 48–57.

[154] B.S. Chlebus, K. Diks, T. Hagerup, and T. Radzik. Efficient simulations between concurrent-read concurrent-write PRAM models. *Proceedings of the Symposium on Mathematical Foundations of Computer Science*, 1988, pp. 231–239.

[155] A.L. Chow. A parallel algorithm for determining convex hulls of sets of points in two dimensions. *Proceedings of the Allerton Conference on Communication, Control, and Computing*, 1981, pp. 214–223.

[156] N. Christofides. *Graph Theory: An Algorithmic Approach*. Academic Press, London, 1975.

[157] F. Chung. On concentrators, superconcentrators, generalizers, and nonblocking networks. *The Bell System Technical Journal*, Vol. 58, 1978, pp. 1765–1777.

[158] K.L. Chung. Sorting on mesh-connected computers with segmented multiple buses. *Journal of Parallel Algorithms and Applications*, Vol. 4, 1994, pp. 71–75.

[159] K.L. Chung. Prefix computations on a generalized mesh-connected computer with multiple buses. *IEEE Transactions on Parallel and Distributed Systems*, Vol. 6, 1995, pp. 196–199.

[160] K.M. Chung, F. Luccio, and C.K. Wong. Magnetic bubble memory structures for efficient sorting and searching. In *Information Processing 80*, S.H. Lavington, ed. North-Holland, Amsterdam, 1980, pp. 439–444.

[161] C. Clos. A study of non-blocking switching networks. *The Bell System Technical Journal*, Vol. 32, 1953, pp. 406–424.

[162] W.T. Cochran, J.W. Cooley, D.L. Favin, H.D. Helms, R.A. Kaenel, W.W. Lang, G.C. Maling, Jr., D.E. Nelson, C.M. Rader, and P.D. Welch. What is the fast Fourier transform? *IEEE Transactions on Audio and Electroacoustics*, Vol. 15, 1967, pp. 45–55.

[163] E.F. Codd. *Cellular Automata*. Academic Press, New York, 1968.

[164] B. Codenotti and M. Leoncini. *Introduction to Parallel Processing*. Addison-Wesley, Reading, Massachusetts, 1993.

[165] R. Cole. Slowing down sorting networks to obtain faster sorting algorithms. *Proceedings of the IEEE Symposium on Foundations of Computer Science*, 1984, pp. 255–260.

[166] R. Cole. Parallel merge sort. *SIAM Journal on Computing*, Vol. 17, 1988, pp. 770–785.

[167] R. Cole and M.T. Goodrich. Optimal parallel algorithms for polygon and point-set problems. *Proceedings of the ACM Symposium on Computational Geometry*, 1988, pp. 201–210.

[168] R. Cole, M.T. Goodrich, and C. Ó'Dúnlaing. Merging free trees in parallel for efficient Voronoi diagram construction. *Proceedings of the International Conference on Automata, Languages, and Programming*, Lecture Notes in Computer Science, No. 443, Springer-Verlag, Berlin, 1990, pp. 432–445.

[169] R. Cole and U. Vishkin. Approximate and exact parallel scheduling with applications to list, tree, and graph problems. *Proceedings of the IEEE Symposium on Foundations of Computer Science*, 1986, pp. 478–491.

[170] R. Cole and U. Vishkin. Deterministic coin tossing and accelerating cascades: Micro and macro techniques for designing parallel algorithms. *Proceedings of the ACM Symposium on Theory of Computing*, 1986, pp. 206–219.

[171] R. Cole and U. Vishkin. Deterministic coin tossing with applications to optimal parallel list ranking. *Information and Control*, Vol. 70, 1986, pp. 32–53.

[172] R. Cole and U. Vishkin. Approximate parallel scheduling. Part 1: The basic technique with applications to optimal list ranking in logarithmic time. *SIAM Journal on Computing*, Vol. 17, 1988, pp. 128–142.

[173] R. Cole and U. Vishkin. Faster optimal parallel prefix sums and list ranking. *Information and Control*, Vol. 81, 1989, pp. 334–352.

[174] R. Cole and C. Yap. A parallel median algorithm. *Information Processing Letters*, Vol. 20, 1985, pp. 137–139.

[175] R. Cole and O. Zajicek. The APRAM: Incorporating asynchrony into the PRAM model. *Proceedings of the ACM Symposium on Parallel Algorithms and Architectures*, 1989, pp. 169–178.

[176] R. Cole and O. Zajicek. The expected advantage of asynchrony. *Proceedings of the ACM Symposium on Parallel Algorithms and Architectures*, 1990, pp. 85–94.

[177] M. Conrad. Molecular computing: The lock-key paradigm. *Computer*, Vol. 25, 1992, pp. 11–20.

[178] M. Conrad. Integrated precursor architecture as a framework for molecular computer design. *Microelectronics Journal*, Vol. 24, 1993, pp. 263–285.

[179] M. Conrad. Multiscale synergy in biological information processing. *Optical Memory and Neural Networks*, Vol. 4, 1995, pp. 89–98.

[180] S.A. Cook, C. Dwork, and R. Reischuk. Upper and lower time bounds for parallel random access machines without simultaneous writes. *SIAM Journal on Computing*, Vol. 15, 1986, pp. 87–97.

[181] J.W. Cooley. How the FFT gained acceptance. In *A History of Scientific Computing*, S.G. Nash, ed. Addison-Wesley, Reading, Massachusetts, 1990, pp. 133–140.

[182] J.W. Cooley, P.A. Lewis, and P.D. Welch. The fast Fourier transform and its application to time series analysis. In *Statistical Methods for Digital Computers*, K. Enslein, A. Ralston, and H.S. Wilf, eds. Wiley, New York, 1977, pp. 377–423.

[183] J. Cooper and S.G. Akl. Efficient selection on a binary tree. *Information Processing Letters*, Vol. 23, 1986, pp. 123–126.

[184] D. Coppersmith and S. Winograd, Matrix multiplication via arithmetic progressions. *Proceedings of the ACM Symposium on Theory of Computing*, 1987, pp. 1–6.

[185] T.H. Cormen, C.E. Leiserson, and R.L. Rivest. *Introduction to Algorithms*. McGraw-Hill, New York, 1990.

[186] M. Cosnard and A.G. Ferreira. Generating permutations on a VLSI suitable linear network. *The Computer Journal*, Vol. 32, 1989, pp. 571–573.

[187] M. Cosnard and J.L. Philippe. Achieving superlinear speedups for the multiple polynomial quadratic sieve factoring algorithm on a distributed memory multiprocessor. *Proceedings of the Joint Conference on Vector and Parallel Processing (CONPAR)*, Lecture Notes in Computer Science, No. 457, Springer-Verlag, Berlin, 1990, pp. 863–874.

[188] M. Cosnard, Y. Robert, and B. Tourancheau. Evaluating speedups on distributed memory architectures. *Parallel Computing*, Vol. 10, 1989, pp. 247–253.

[189] M. Cosnard and D. Trystram. *Parallel Algorithms and Architectures*. International Thomson Computer Press, London, 1995.

[190] L. Csanky. Fast parallel matrix inversion algorithms. *SIAM Journal on Computing*, Vol. 5, 1976, pp. 618–623.

[191] D. Culler, R. Karp, D. Patterson, A. Sahay, K.E. Schauser, E. Santos, R. Subramonian, and T. von Eicken. LogP: Towards a realistic model of parallel computation. *Proceedings of the ACM SIGPLAN Symposium on Principles and Practice of Parallel Programming*, 1993, pp. 235–261.

[192] Z. Cvetanović. The effects of problem partitioning, allocation, and granularity on the performance of multiple-processor systems. *IEEE Transactions on Computers*, Vol. 36, 1987, pp. 421–432.

[193] S.K. Das, N. Deo, and S. Prasad. Parallel graph algorithms for hypercube computers. *Parallel Computing*, Vol. 13, 1990, pp. 143–158.

[194] S.K. Das and R.H. Halverson. Simple deterministic and randomized algorithms for linked list ranking on the EREW PRAM model. *Parallel Processing Letters*, Vol. 4, 1994, pp. 15–27.

[195] M.D. Davis and E.J. Weyuker. *Computability, Complexity, and Languages*. Academic Press, New York, 1983.

[196] X.A. Debest. Remark about self-stabilizing systems. *Communications of the ACM*, Vol. 38, 1995, pp. 115–117.

[197] E. Dekel, D. Nassimi, and S. Sahni. Parallel matrix and graph algorithms. *SIAM Journal on Computing*, Vol. 10, 1981, pp. 657–675.

[198] E. Dekel and S. Sahni. Binary trees and parallel scheduling algorithms. *IEEE Transactions on Computers*, Vol. 32, 1983, pp. 307–315.

[199] N. Deo. *Graph Theory with Applications to Engineering and Computer Science*. Prentice Hall, Englewood Cliffs, New Jersey, 1974.

[200] N. Deo, R. Guha, A. Jain, and M. Medidi. Constant-time list ranking on a reconfigurable processor array. Technical Report No. CS-TR-92-08, Department of Computer Science, University of Central Florida, Orlando, Florida, 1992.

[201] D. Deutsch. Quantum theory, the Church-Turing principle and the universal quantum computer. *Proceedings of the Royal Society*, London, Vol. A400, 1985, pp. 97–117.

[202] K. Devlin. Test tube computing with DNA. *Math Horizons*, April 1995, pp. 14–21.

[203] K. Devlin. What is computation? *Math Horizons*, September 1995, pp. 24–29.

[204] J. Diedrick, N. Morgan, and V. Vemuri, eds. *Artificial Neural Networks*. IEEE Computer Society Press, Los Alamitos, California, 1990.

[205] M. Dietzfelbinger, S. Madhavapeddy, and I.H. Sudborough. Three disjoint path paradigms in star networks. *Proceedings of the IEEE Symposium on Parallel and Distributed Processing*, 1991, pp. 400–406.

[206] B. Djokić, M. Miyakawa, S. Sekiguchi, I. Semba, and I. Stojmenović. Parallel algorithms for generating subsets and set partitions. *Proceedings of the SIGAL International Symposium on Algorithms*, Lecture Notes in Computer Science, No. 450, Springer-Verlag, Berlin, 1990, pp. 76–85.

[207] J.J. Dongarra, ed. *Experimental Parallel Computing Architectures*. North-Holland, Amsterdam, 1987.

[208] M. Dowd, Y. Perl, L. Rudolph, and M. Saks. The balanced sorting network. *Proceedings of the Conference on Principles of Distributed Computing*, 1983, pp. 161–172.

[209] G. Dudek, M. Jenkin, E. Milios, and D. Wilkes. A taxonomy for swarm robots. *Proceedings of the IEEE/RSJ International Conference on Intelligent Robots and Systems*, 1993, pp. 441–447.

[210] C.R. Dyer. Pyramid algorithms and machines. In *Multicomputers and Image Processing: Algorithms and Programs*, K. Preston, Jr., and L. Uhr, eds. Academic Press, New York, 1982, pp. 409–420.

[211] D.L. Eager, J. Zahorjan, and E.D. Lazowska. Speedup versus efficiency in parallel systems. *IEEE Transactions on Computers*, Vol. 38, 1989, pp. 408–423.

[212] Ö. Eğecioğlu, E. Gallopoulos, and Ç.K. Koç. Fast computation of divided differences and parallel Hermite interpolation. *Journal of Complexity*, Vol. 5, 1989, pp. 417–437.

[213] Ö. Eğecioğlu, E. Gallopoulos, and Ç.K. Koç. Parallel Hermite interpolation: An algebraic approach. *Computing*, Vol. 42, 1989, pp. 291–307.

[214] Ö. Eğecioğlu, E. Gallopoulos, and Ç.K. Koç. A parallel method for fast and practical high-order Newton interpolation. *BIT*, Vol. 29, 1990, pp. 268–288.

[215] Ö. Eğecioğlu and Ç.K. Koç. Parallel prefix computation with few processors. *Computers in Mathematics with Applications*, Vol. 24, 1992, pp. 77–84.

[216] H. ElGindy and M.T. Goodrich. Parallel algorithms for shortest path problems in polygons. *The Visual Computer*, Vol. 3, 1988, pp. 371–378.

[217] H. Elhage and I. Stojmenović. Systolic generation of combinations from arbitrary elements. *Parallel Processing Letters*, Vol. 2, 1992, pp. 241–248.

[218] H. El-Rewini, T.G. Lewis, and H.H. Ali. *Task Scheduling in Parallel and Distributed Systems*. Prentice Hall, Englewood Cliffs, New Jersey, 1994.

[219] D. Eppstein and Z. Galil. Parallel algorithmic techniques for combinatorial computation. *Annual Review of Computer Science*, Vol. 3, 1988, pp. 233–283.

[220] M.C. Esenwein and J.W. Baker. String matching using an associative computing model: Exact match and match with don't cares. Manuscript, Department of Mathematics and Computer Science, Kent State University, 1995.

[221] S. Even. *Graph Algorithms*. Computer Science Press, Potomac, Maryland, 1979.

[222] V. Faber, O.M. Lubeck, and A.B. White, Jr. Superlinear speedup of an efficient sequential algorithm is not possible. *Parallel Computing*, Vol. 3, 1986, pp. 259–260.

[223] V. Faber, O.M. Lubeck, and A.B. White, Jr. Comments on the paper: "Parallel efficiency can be greater than unity." *Parallel Computing*, Vol. 4, 1987, pp. 209–210.

[224] L. Fava Lindon. Discriminating analysis and its application to matrix by vector multiplication on the CRCW PRAM. *Parallel Processing Letters*, Vol. 2, 1992, pp. 43–50.

[225] L. Fava Lindon. *Synergy in Parallel Computation*. Ph.D. Thesis, Department of Computing and Information Science, Queen's University, Kingston, Ontario, 1996.

[226] L. Fava Lindon and S.G. Akl. An optimal implementation of broadcasting with selective reduction. *IEEE Transactions on Parallel and Distributed Systems*, Vol. 4, 1993, pp. 256–269.

[227] A. Ferreira. Parallel and communication algorithms on hypercube multiprocessors. In *Parallel and Distributed Computing Handbook*, A.Y. Zomaya, ed. McGraw-Hill, New York, 1996, pp. 568–589.

[228] F.E. Fich. New bounds for parallel prefix circuits. *Proceedings of the ACM Symposium on Theory of Computing*, 1983, pp. 100–109.

[229] F.E. Fich, P. Ragde, and A. Wigderson. Relations between concurrent-write models of parallel computation. *SIAM Journal on Computing*, Vol. 17, 1988, pp. 606–627.

[230] D. Fischer. On superlinear speedups. *Parallel Computing*, Vol. 17, 1991, pp. 695–697.

[231] J.B. Fishburn. *Analysis of Speedup in Distributed Algorithms*. UMI Research Press, Ann Arbor, Michigan, 1981.

[232] P.M. Flanders, D.J. Hunt, D. Parkinson, and S.F. Reddaway. Efficient high speed computing with the Distributed Array Processor. *Proceedings of the Symposium on High Speed Computer and Algorithm Organization*, 1977, pp. 113–128.

[233] P.M. Flanders and S.F. Reddaway. Sorting on DAP. In *Parallel Computing 83*, M. Feilmeier, G. Joubert, and U. Schendel, eds. North-Holland, Amsterdam, 1984, pp. 247–252.

[234] M.J. Flynn. Very high-speed computing systems. *Proceedings of the IEEE*, Vol. 54, 1966, pp. 1901–1909.

[235] M.J. Flynn. *Computer Architecture: Pipelined and Parallel Processor Design*. Jones and Bartlett Publishers, Boston, 1995.

[236] S. Fortune and J. Wyllie. Parallelism in random access machines. *Proceedings of the ACM Symposium on Theory of Computing*, 1978, pp. 114–118.

[237] I. Foster. *Designing and Building Parallel Programs*. Addison-Wesley, Reading, Massachusetts, 1995.

[238] M.J. Foster and H.T. Kung. The design of special purpose VLSI chips. *Computer*, Vol. 13, 1980, pp. 26–40.

[239] T.J. Fountain. *Parallel Computing*. Cambridge University Press, Cambridge, England, 1994.

[240] G.C. Fox, M.A. Johnson, G.A. Lyzenga, S.W. Otto, J.K. Salmon, and D.W. Walker. *Solving Problems on Concurrent Processors*, Vol. 1. Prentice Hall, Englewood Cliffs, New Jersey, 1988.

[241] P. Fragopoulou. On the efficient summation of N numbers on an N-processor reconfigurable mesh. *Parallel Processing Letters*, Vol. 3, 1993, pp. 71–78.

[242] P. Fragopoulou. On the comparative power of the 2D-PARBS and the CRCW-PRAM models. *Parallel Processing Letters*, Vol. 3, 1993, pp. 301–304.

[243] P. Fragopoulou. *Communication and Fault Tolerance Algorithms on a Class of Interconnection Networks*. Ph.D. Thesis, Department of Computing and Information Science, Queen's University, Kingston, Ontario, 1995.

[244] P. Fragopoulou and S.G. Akl. A parallel algorithm for computing Fourier transforms on the star graph. *IEEE Transactions on Parallel and Distributed Systems*, Vol. 5, 1994, pp. 525–531.

[245] P. Fragopoulou and S.G. Akl. Optimal communication algorithms on star graphs using spanning tree constructions. *Journal of Parallel and Distributed Computing*, Vol. 24, 1995, pp. 55–71.

[246] P. Fragopoulou and S.G. Akl. Fault tolerant communication algorithms on the star network using disjoint paths. *Proceedings of the Hawaii International Conference on System Sciences*, Vol. 2, 1995, pp. 5–13.

[247] P. Fragopoulou and S.G. Akl. A framework for optimal communication on a subclass of Cayley graph based networks. *Proceedings of the International Conference on Computers and Communications*, 1995, pp. 241–248.

[248] P. Fragopoulou and S.G. Akl. Efficient algorithms for global data communication on the multidimensional torus network. *Proceedings of the International Parallel Processing Symposium*, 1995, pp. 324–330.

[249] P. Fragopoulou and S.G. Akl. Edge-disjoint spanning trees on the star network with applications to fault tolerance. *IEEE Transactions on Computers*, Vol. 45, 1996, pp. 174–185.

[250] P. Fragopoulou, S.G. Akl, and H. Meijer. Optimal communication primitives on the generalized hypercube network. *Journal of Parallel and Distributed Computing*, Vol. 32, 1996, pp. 173–187.

[251] T.L. Freeman and C. Phillips. *Parallel Numerical Algorithms*. Prentice Hall International, London, 1992.

[252] N. Friedman. Some results on the effect of arithmetics on comparison problems. *Proceedings of the IEEE Symposium on Switching and Automata Theory*, 1972, pp. 139–143.

[253] O. Gabber and Z. Galil. Explicit constructions of linear-sized superconcentrators. *Journal of Computer and System Sciences*, Vol. 22, 1981, pp. 407–420.

[254] G. Gamow. *One Two Three...Infinity.* Bantam Books, New York, 1979.

[255] M.R. Garey and D.S. Johnson. *Computers and Intractability: A Guide to the Theory of NP-Completeness.* Freeman, San Francisco, 1979.

[256] F. Gavril. Merging with parallel processors. *Communications of the ACM,* Vol. 18, 1975, pp. 588–591.

[257] L.P. Gewali and I. Stojmenović. Computing external watchman routes on PRAM, BSR, and interconnection models of parallel computation. *Parallel Processing Letters,* Vol. 4, 1994, pp. 83–93.

[258] A. Gibbons and W. Rytter. *Efficient Parallel Algorithms.* Cambridge University Press, Cambridge, England, 1988.

[259] P.B. Gibbons. A more practical PRAM model. *Proceedings of the ACM Symposium on Parallel Algorithms and Architectures,* 1989, pp. 158–168.

[260] A. Goerdt and U. Kamps. On the reasons for average superlinear speedup in parallel backtrack search. *Proceedings of the Workshop on Computer Science Logic,* Lecture Notes in Computer Science, No. 832, Springer-Verlag, Berlin, 1994, pp. 106–127.

[261] A.V. Goldberg. *Efficient Graph Algorithms for Sequential and Parallel Computers.* Ph.D. Thesis, Department of Electrical Engineering and Computer Science, Massachusetts Institute of Technology, Cambridge, Massachusetts, 1987.

[262] G. Golub and J.M. Ortega. *Scientific Computing: An Introduction with Parallel Computing.* Academic Press, San Diego, 1993.

[263] S.E. Goodman and S.T. Hedetniemi. *Introduction to the Design and Analysis of Algorithms.* McGraw-Hill, New York, 1977.

[264] M.T. Goodrich. Triangulating a polygon in parallel. *Journal of Algorithms,* Vol. 10, 1989, pp. 327–351.

[265] R.L. Graham. Bounds for certain multiprocessing anomalies. *The Bell System Technical Journal,* Vol. 45, 1966, pp. 1563–1581.

[266] R.L. Graham. Bounds on multiprocessing timing anomalies. *SIAM Journal of Applied Mathematics,* Vol. 17, 1969, pp. 416–429.

[267] R.L. Graham. Bounds on multiprocessing anomalies and related packing algorithms. *Proceedings of the AFIPS Spring Joint Computer Conference,* 1972, pp. 205–217.

[268] A.G. Greenberg and U. Manber. A probabilistic pipeline algorithm for *k*-selection on the tree machine. *IEEE Transactions on Computers*, Vol. 36, 1987, pp. 359–362.

[269] R. Greenlaw, H.J. Hoover, and W.L. Ruzzo. *Limits to Parallel Computation: P-Completeness Theory*. Oxford University Press, Oxford, England, 1995.

[270] D.H. Grit and J.R. McGraw. Programming divide and conquer for a MIMD machine. *Software—Practice and Experience*, Vol. 15, 1985, pp. 41–53.

[271] X. Guan and M.A. Langston. Time-space optimal parallel merging and sorting. *IEEE Transactions on Computers*, Vol. 40, 1991, pp. 596–602.

[272] L.J. Guibas, H.T. Kung, and C.D. Thomborson. Direct VLSI implementation of combinatorial algorithms. *Proceedings of the Caltech Conference on VLSI: Architecture, Design, Fabrication*, 1979, pp. 509–525.

[273] Z. Guo. Optically interconnected processor arrays with switching capability. *Journal of Parallel and Distributed Computing*, Vol. 23, 1994, pp. 314–329.

[274] Z. Guo, R.G. Melhem, R.W. Hall, D.M. Chiarulli, and S.P. Levitan. Pipelined communications in optically interconnected arrays. *Journal of Parallel and Distributed Computing*, Vol. 12, 1991, pp. 269–282.

[275] P. Gupta and G.P. Bhattacharjee. A parallel derangement generation algorithm. *BIT*, Vol. 29, 1989, pp. 14–22.

[276] H. Gurla. Leftmost one computation on meshes with row broadcasting. *Information Processing Letters*, Vol. 47, 1993, pp. 261–266.

[277] J.L. Gustafson. Reevaluating Amdahl's law. *Communications of the ACM*, Vol. 31, 1988, pp. 532–533.

[278] J.L. Gustafson, D. Rover, S. Elbert, and M. Carter. The design of a scalable, fixed-time computer benchmark. *Journal of Parallel and Distributed Computing*, Vol. 12, 1991, pp. 388–401.

[279] T. Hagerup. The parallel complexity of integer prefix summation. *Information Processing Letters*, Vol. 56, 1995, pp. 59–64.

[280] T. Hagerup and C. Rüb. Optimal merging and sorting on the EREW PRAM. *Information Processing Letters*, Vol. 33, 1989, pp. 181–185.

[281] R. Häggkvist and P. Hell. Sorting and merging in rounds. *SIAM Journal on Algebraic and Discrete Methods*, Vol. 3, 1982, pp. 465–473.

[282] R. Halverson and S.K. Das. A comprehensive survey of parallel linked list ranking algorithms. Technical Report CRPDC-93-12, Department of Computer Sciences, University of North Texas, Denton, Texas, 1993.

[283] M. Hamdi. Communications in optically interconnected computer systems. In *Interconnection Networks and Mapping and Scheduling Parallel Computations*, D.F. Hsu, A.L. Rosenberg, and D. Sotteau, eds. DIMACS Series in Discrete Mathematics and Theoretical Computer Science, Vol. 21, 1995, pp. 181–200.

[284] M. Hamdi and Y. Pan. Efficient parallel algorithms on optically interconnected arrays of processors. *IEE Proceedings on Computers and Digital Techniques*, Vol. 142, 1995, pp. 87–92.

[285] T. Han, D.A. Carlson, and S.P. Levitan. VLSI Design of high-speed low area addition circuitry. Technical Report, Department of Electrical and Computer Engineering, University of Massachusetts, Amherst, Massachusetts, 1987.

[286] Y. Han. Parallel algorithms for computing linked list prefix. *Journal of Parallel and Distributed Computing*, Vol. 6, 1989, pp. 537–557.

[287] Y. Han. An optimal linked list prefix algorithm on a local memory computer. *IEEE Transactions on Computers*, Vol. 40, 1991, pp. 1149–1153.

[288] T.J. Harris. A survey of PRAM simulation techniques. *ACM Computing Surveys*, Vol. 26, 1994, pp. 187–206.

[289] P.J. Hatcher and M.J. Quinn. *Data-Parallel Programming on MIMD Computers*. MIT Press, Cambridge, Massachusetts, 1991.

[290] F.M. auf der Heide and H.T. Pham. On the performance of networks with multiple buses. *Proceedings of the Symposium on Theoretical Aspects of Computer Science*, 1992, pp. 97–108.

[291] D. Heller. A survey of parallel algorithms in numerical linear algebra. *SIAM Review*, Vol. 20, 1978, pp. 740–777.

[292] D.P. Helmbold and C.E. McDowell. Modeling speedup(n) greater than n. *IEEE Transactions on Parallel and Distributed Systems*, Vol. 1, 1990, pp. 250–256.

[293] F.B. Hildebrand. *Introduction to Numerical Analysis*. McGraw-Hill, New York, 1974.

[294] W.D. Hillis. *The Connection Machine*. MIT Press, Cambridge, Massachusetts, 1985.

[295] W.D. Hillis and G. Steele. Data parallel algorithms. *Communications of the ACM*, Vol. 29, 1986, pp. 1170–1183.

[296] D.S. Hirschberg. Parallel algorithms for the transitive closure and the connected component problems. *Proceedings of the ACM Symposium on Theory of Computing*, 1976, pp. 55–57.

[297] D.S. Hirschberg, A.K. Chandra, and D.V. Sarwate. Computing connected components on parallel computers. *Communications of the ACM*, Vol. 22, 1979, pp. 461–464.

[298] R.W. Hockney and C.R. Jesshope. *Parallel Computers*. Adam Hilger, Bristol, England, 1981.

[299] J.A. Holey and O.H. Ibarra. Iterative algorithms for planar convex hull on mesh-connected arrays. *Proceedings of the International Conference on Parallel Processing*, 1990, pp. 102–109.

[300] Z. Hong and R. Sedgewick. Notes on merging networks. *Proceedings of the ACM Symposium on Theory of Computing*, 1982, pp. 296–302.

[301] J.E. Hopcroft and J.D. Ullman. *Introduction to Automata Theory, Languages, and Computation*. Addison-Wesley, Reading, Massachusetts, 1979.

[302] R.M. Hord. *The Illiac IV: The First Supercomputer*. Computer Science Press, Rockville, Maryland, 1982.

[303] E. Horowitz and S. Sahni. *Fundamentals of Computer Algorithms*. Computer Science Press, Potomac, Maryland, 1978.

[304] E. Horowitz and A. Zorat. Divide-and-conquer for parallel processing. *IEEE Transactions on Computers*, Vol. 32, 1983, pp. 582–585.

[305] C.C. Hsiao and L. Snyder. Omni-sort: A versatile data processing operation for VLSI. *Proceedings of the International Conference on Parallel Processing*, 1983, pp. 222–225.

[306] M.E.C. Hulle, D. Crookes, and P.J. Sweeney. *Parallel Processing: The Transputer and Its Applications*. Addison-Wesley, Reading, Massachusetts, 1994.

[307] K. Hwang and F.A. Briggs. *Computer Architecture and Parallel Processing*. McGraw-Hill, New York, 1984.

[308] L. Hyafil and H.T. Kung. The complexity of parallel evaluation of linear recurrences. *Journal of the ACM*, Vol. 24, 1977, pp. 513–521.

[309] K. Iverson. *A Programming Language*. Wiley, New York, 1962.

[310] J. JáJá. *An Introduction to Parallel Algorithms*. Addison-Wesley, Reading, Massachusetts, 1992.

[311] L.H. Jamieson, D.B. Gannon, and R.J. Douglass, eds. *The Characteristics of Parallel Algorithms*. MIT Press, Cambridge, Massachusetts, 1987.

[312] J. Jang and V.K. Prasanna. An optimal sorting algorithm on reconfigurable meshes. *Proceedings of the International Parallel Processing Symposium*, 1992, pp. 130–137.

[313] R. Janssen. A note on superlinear speedup. *Parallel Computing*, Vol. 4, 1987, pp. 211–213.

[314] J.F. Jenq and S. Sahni. Reconfigurable mesh algorithms for the Hough transform. *Journal of Parallel and Distributed Computing*, Vol. 20, 1994, pp. 60–77.

[315] S. Jimbo and A. Maruoka. Expanders obtained from affine transformations. *Proceedings of the ACM Symposium on Theory of Computing*, 1985, pp. 88–97.

[316] A.E. Joel, Jr. On permutation switching networks. *The Bell System Technical Journal*, Vol. 47, 1968, pp. 813–822.

[317] H.F. Jordan. A special purpose architecture for finite element analysis. *Proceedings of the International Conference on Parallel Processing*, 1978, pp. 263–266.

[318] R. Jozsa. Characterizing classes of functions computable by quantum parallelism. *Proceedings of the Royal Society*, London, Vol. A435, 1991, pp. 563–574.

[319] J.S. Jwo, S. Lakshmivarahan, and S.K. Dhall. Embedding of cycles and grids in star graphs. *Proceedings of the IEEE Symposium on Parallel and Distributed Processing*, 1990, pp. 540–547.

[320] T.W. Kao, S.J. Horng, Y.L. Wang, and K.L. Chung. A constant time algorithm for computing Hough transform. *Pattern Recognition*, Vol. 26, 1993, pp. 277–286.

[321] R.M. Karp. On-line algorithms versus off-line algorithms: How much it is worth to know the future? *Proceedings of the IFIP Congress*, 1992, pp. 416–429.

[322] R.M. Karp, R.E. Miller, and S. Winograd. The organization of computations for uniform recurrence equations. *Journal of the ACM*, Vol. 14, 1967, pp. 563–590.

[323] R.M. Karp and V. Ramachandran. A survey of parallel algorithms for shared memory machines. In *Handbook of Theoretical Computer Science*, Vol. A, J. van Leeuwen, ed. Elsevier, Amsterdam, 1990, pp. 869–941.

[324] M. Klawe. Limitations on explicit constructions of expanding graphs. *SIAM Journal on Computing*, Vol. 13, 1984, pp. 46–56.

[325] D.E. Knuth. *The Art of Computer Programming*, Vol. 3. Addison-Wesley, Reading, Massachusetts, 1973.

[326] P.M. Kogge. Parallel solution of recurrence problems. *IBM Journal of Research and Development*, Vol. 18, 1974, pp. 138–148.

[327] P.M. Kogge and H.S. Stone. A parallel algorithm for the efficient solution of a general class of recurrence equations. *IEEE Transactions on Computers*, Vol. 22, 1973, pp. 786–792.

[328] D.M. Koppelman and A.Y. Oruç. A self-routing permutation network. *Journal of Parallel and Distributed Computing*, Vol. 10, 1990, pp. 140–151.

[329] W.A. Kornfeld. Combinatorially implosive algorithms. *Communications of the ACM*, Vol. 25, 1982, pp. 734–738.

[330] V.M. Krapchenko. Asymptotic estimation of addition time of a parallel adder. *Systems Theory Research*, Vol. 19, 1970, pp. 105–122.

[331] E.V. Krishnamurthy. *Parallel Processing: Principles and Practice*. Addison-Wesley, Reading, Massachusetts, 1989.

[332] C.S.R. Krishnan and C. Siva Ram Murthy. A faster algorithm for sorting on mesh-connected computers with multiple broadcasting using fewer processors. *International Journal of Computer Mathematics*, Vol. 48, 1993, pp. 15–20.

[333] D. Krizanc and L. Narayanan. Zero-one sorting on the mesh. *Parallel Processing Letters*, Vol. 5, 1995, pp. 149–155.

[334] L.A. Kronsjö. *Algorithms: Their Complexity and Efficiency*. Wiley, Chichester, England, 1979.

[335] L.A. Kronsjö. *Computational Complexity of Sequential and Parallel Algorithms*. Wiley, Chichester, England, 1985.

[336] C.P. Kruskal. Searching, merging, and sorting in parallel computation. *IEEE Transactions on Computers*, Vol. 32, 1983, pp. 942–946.

[337] C.P. Kruskal, T. Madej, and L. Rudolph. Parallel prefix on fully connected direct connection machines. *Proceedings of the International Conference on Parallel Processing*, 1986, pp. 278–283.

[338] C.P. Kruskal, L. Rudolph, and M. Snir. The power of parallel prefix. *IEEE Transactions on Computers*, Vol. 34, 1985, pp. 965–968.

[339] C.P. Kruskal, L. Rudolph, and M. Snir. Efficient parallel algorithms for graph problems. *Algorithmica*, Vol. 5, 1990, pp. 43–64.

[340] L. Kučera. Parallel computation and conflicts in memory access. *Information Processing Letters*, Vol. 14, 1982, pp. 93–96.

[341] D.J. Kuck. *The Structure of Computers and Computations*, Vol. 1. Wiley, New York, 1978.

[342] M. Kumar and D.S. Hirschberg. An efficient implementation of Batcher's odd-even merge algorithm and its applications in parallel sorting schemes. *IEEE Transactions on Computers*, Vol. 32, 1983, pp. 254–264.

[343] V. Kumar, A. Grama, A. Gupta, and G. Karypis. *Introduction to Parallel Computing*. Benjamin-Cummings, Menlo Park, California, 1994.

[344] V. Kumar and V.N. Rao. Parallel depth-first search, Part II: Analysis. *International Journal of Parallel Programming*, Vol. 16, 1987, pp. 501–519.

[345] M. Kunde. Optimal sorting on multi-dimensionally mesh-connected computers. *Proceedings of the Symposium on Theoretical Aspects of Computer Science*, 1987, pp. 408–419.

[346] H.T. Kung. Let's design algorithms for VLSI systems. *Proceedings of the Conference on Very Large Scale Integration: Architecture, Design, Fabrication*, 1979, pp. 65–90.

[347] H.T. Kung. Special-purpose devices for signal and image processing: An opportunity in VLSI. *Proceedings of the SPIE: Real-Time Signal Processing*, Vol. 241, 1980, pp. 76–84.

[348] H.T. Kung. The structure of parallel algorithms. In *Advances in Computers*, Vol. 19, M.C. Yovits, ed. Academic Press, New York, 1980, pp. 65–112.

[349] H.T. Kung. Why systolic architectures? *Computer*, Vol. 15, 1982, pp. 37–46.

[350] H.T. Kung and M.S. Lam. Wafer-scale integration and two-level pipelined implementations of systolic arrays. *Journal of Parallel and Distributed Computing*, Vol. 1, 1984, pp. 32–63.

[351] H.T. Kung and C.E. Leiserson. Algorithms for VLSI processor arrays. In *Introduction to VLSI Systems*, C. Mead and L. Conway. Addison-Wesley, Reading, Massachusetts, 1980, pp. 271–294.

[352] R.E. Ladner and M.J. Fischer. Parallel prefix computation. *Journal of the ACM*, Vol. 27, 1980, pp. 831–838.

[353] T.H. Lai and S. Sahni. Anomalies in parallel branch and bound algorithms. *Communications of the ACM*, Vol. 27, 1984, pp. 594–602.

[354] T.H. Lai and A. Sprague. Performance of parallel branch-and-bound algorithms. *Proceedings of the International Conference on Parallel Processing*, 1985, pp. 194–201.

[355] S. Lakshmivarahan and S.K. Dhall. *Analysis and Design of Parallel Algorithms: Arithmetic and Matrix Problems*. McGraw-Hill, New York, 1990.

[356] S. Lakshmivarahan and S.K. Dhall. *Parallel Computing Using the Prefix Problem.* Oxford University Press, New York, 1994.

[357] S. Lakshmivarahan, S.K. Dhall, and L.L. Miller. Parallel sorting algorithms. In *Advances in Computers*, Vol. 23, M.C. Yovits, ed. Academic Press, New York, 1984, pp. 295–354.

[358] S. Lakshmivarahan, C.M. Yang, and S.K. Dhall. Optimal parallel prefix circuits with $(size + depth) = 2n - 2$ and $\lceil \log n \rceil \leq depth \leq \lceil 2 \log n \rceil - 3$. *Proceedings of the International Conference on Parallel Processing*, 1987, pp. 58–65.

[359] H.W. Lang, M. Schimmler, H. Schmeck, and H. Schröder. Systolic sorting on a mesh-connected network. *IEEE Transactions on Computers*, Vol. 34, 1985, pp. 652–658.

[360] D.H. Lawrie. Access and alignment of data in an array computer. *IEEE Transactions on Computers*, Vol. 24, 1975, pp. 1145–1155.

[361] R.J. Leach, M. Atogi, and R.R. Stephen. The actual complexity of parallel evaluation of low-degree polynomials. *Parallel Computing*, Vol. 13, 1990, pp. 73–83.

[362] D.T. Lee, H. Chang, and C.K. Wong. An on-chip compare/steer bubble sorter. *IEEE Transactions on Computers*, Vol. 30, 1981, pp. 396–405.

[363] K.Y. Lee. A new Beneš network control algorithm. *IEEE Transactions on Computers*, Vol. 36, 1987, pp. 768–772.

[364] D.H. Lehmer. Teaching combinatorial tricks to a computer. *Combinatorial Analysis*, Vol. 10, 1960, pp. 179–193.

[365] F.T. Leighton. *Complexity Issues in VLSI.* MIT Press, Cambridge, Massachusetts, 1983.

[366] F.T. Leighton. Tight bounds on the complexity of parallel sorting. *IEEE Transactions on Computers*, Vol. 34, 1985, pp. 344–354.

[367] F.T. Leighton. *Introduction to Parallel Algorithms and Architectures.* Morgan Kaufmann, San Mateo, California, 1992.

[368] C.E. Leiserson. *Area-Efficient VLSI Computation.* MIT Press, Cambridge, Massachusetts, 1983.

[369] E.L. Leiss. *Parallel and Vector Computing.* McGraw-Hill, New York, 1995.

[370] J. Lenfant. Parallel permutations of data: A Beneš network control algorithm for frequently used permutations. *IEEE Transactions on Computers*, Vol. 27, 1978, pp. 637–647.

[371] J. Lenfant and S. Tahé. Permuting data with the omega network. *Acta Informatica*, Vol. 21, 1985, pp. 629–641.

[372] B.P. Lester. *The Art of Parallel Programming*. Prentice Hall, Englewood Cliffs, New Jersey, 1993.

[373] G.F. Lev, N. Pippenger, and L.G. Valiant. A fast parallel algorithm for routing in permutation networks. *IEEE Transactions on Computers*, Vol. 30, 1981, pp. 93–100.

[374] S.P. Levitan, D.M. Chiarulli, and R.G. Melhem. Coincident pulse technique for multiprocessor interconnection structures. *Applied Optics*, Vol. 29, 1990, pp. 2024–2033.

[375] T.G. Lewis and H. El-Rewini. *Introduction to Parallel Computing*. Prentice Hall, Englewood Cliffs, New Jersey, 1992.

[376] G.J. Li and B.W. Wah. Coping with anomalies in parallel branch-and-bound algorithms. *IEEE Transactions on Computers*, Vol. 35, 1986, pp. 568–573.

[377] G.J. Li and B.W. Wah. Computational efficiency of parallel combinatorial OR-tree searches. *IEEE Transactions on Software Engineering*, Vol. 16, 1990, pp. 13–31.

[378] H. Li and M. Maresca. Polymorphic-torus network. *IEEE Transactions on Computers*, Vol. 38, 1988, pp. 1345–1351.

[379] H. Li and M. Maresca. Polymorphic-torus for computer vision. *IEEE Transactions on Pattern Analysis and Machine Intelligence*, Vol. 11, 1989, pp. 233–243.

[380] H. Li and Q.F. Stout, eds. *Reconfigurable Massively Parallel Computers*. Prentice Hall, Englewood Cliffs, New Jersey, 1991.

[381] K. Li. IVY: A shared virtual memory system for parallel computing. *Proceedings of the International Conference on Parallel Processing*, 1988, pp. 94–101.

[382] K. Li and P. Hudak. Memory coherence in shared virtual memory systems. *ACM Transactions on Computer Systems*, Vol. 7, 1989, pp. 321–359.

[383] Y. Liang, S.K. Dhall, and S. Lakshmivarahan. Finding Hamiltonian circuits in circular-arc graphs. *Proceedings of the Allerton Conference on Communication, Control, and Computing*, 1991, pp. 484–485.

[384] C.J. Lin. Parallel generation of permutations on systolic arrays. *Parallel Computing*, Vol. 15, 1990, pp. 267–276.

[385] C.J. Lin and J.C. Tsay. A systolic generation of combinations. *BIT*, Vol. 29, 1989, pp. 23–36.

[386] R. Lin. Fast algorithms for lowest common ancestors on a processor array with reconfigurable buses. *Information Processing Letters*, Vol. 40, 1991, pp. 223–230.

[387] R. Lin and S. Olariu. A simple optimal parallel algorithm to solve the lowest common ancestor problem. *Proceedings of the International Conference on Computing and Information*, Lecture Notes in Computer Science, No. 497, Springer-Verlag, Berlin, 1991, pp. 455–461.

[388] R. Lin, S. Olariu, J.L. Schwing, and J. Zhang. Simulating enhanced meshes, with applications. *Parallel Processing Letters*, Vol. 3, 1993, pp. 59–76.

[389] R. Lin, S. Olariu, J.L. Schwing, J. Zhang. Computing on reconfigurable buses—a new computational paradigm. *Parallel Processing Letters*, Vol. 4, 1994, pp. 465–476.

[390] R.J. Lipton. DNA solution of hard computational problems. *Science*, Vol. 268, 1995, pp. 542–545.

[391] C.L. Liu. *Elements of Discrete Mathematics*. McGraw-Hill, New York, 1977.

[392] V.M. Lo, S. Rajopadhye, S. Gupta, D. Kelsen, M.A. Mohamed, and J. Telle. Mapping divide-and-conquer algorithms to parallel architectures. *Proceedings of the International Conference on Parallel Processing*, Vol. 3, 1990, pp. 128–135.

[393] B.D. Lubachevsky and A.G. Greenberg. Simple efficient asynchronous parallel prefix algorithms. *Proceedings of the International Conference on Parallel Processing*, 1987, pp. 66–69.

[394] A. Lubotzky, R. Phillips, and P. Sarnak. Explicit expanders and the Ramanujan conjectures. *Proceedings of the ACM Symposium on Theory of Computing*, 1986, pp. 240–246.

[395] F. Luccio and L. Pagli. The p-shovelers problem (computing with time-varying data). *SIGACT News*, Vol. 23, 1992, pp. 72–75.

[396] F. Luccio and L. Pagli. The p-shovelers problem (computing with time-varying data). *Proceedings of the IEEE Symposium on Parallel and Distributed Processing*, 1992, pp. 188–193.

[397] F. Luccio, L. Pagli, and G. Pucci. Three non conventional paradigms of parallel computation. *Proceedings of the Heinz Nixdorf Symposium*, Lecture Notes in Computer Science, No. 678, Springer-Verlag, Berlin, 1992, pp. 166–175.

[398] S. Madala and J.B. Sinclair. Performance of synchronous parallel algorithms with regular structures. *IEEE Transactions on Parallel and Distributed Systems*, Vol. 2, 1991, pp. 105–116.

[399] T. Maeba, S. Tatsumi, and M. Sugaya. Algorithms for finding maximum and selecting median on a processor array with separable global buses. *Electronics and Communications in Japan*, Vol. 73, 1990, pp. 39–47.

[400] G.A. Mago. A network of microprocessors to execute reduction languages. *International Journal of Computer and Information Sciences*, Vol. 8, 1979, Part I: pp. 349–385; Part II: pp. 435–471.

[401] A. Mahanti and C.J. Daniels. IDPS: A massively parallel heuristic search algorithm. *Proceedings of the International Parallel Processing Symposium*, 1992, pp. 220–223.

[402] U. Manber. *Introduction to Algorithms: A Creative Approach*. Addison-Wesley, Reading, Massachusetts, 1989.

[403] D. Mandrioli and C. Ghezzi. *Theoretical Foundations of Computer Science*. Wiley, New York, 1987.

[404] J.M. Marberg and E. Gafni. Sorting in constant number of row and column phases on a mesh. *Algorithmica*, Vol. 3, 1988, pp. 561–572.

[405] M. Maresca. Polymorphic processor arrays. *IEEE Transactions on Parallel and Distributed Systems*, Vol. 4, 1993, pp. 490–506.

[406] M. Maresca and H. Li. Connection autonomy and SIMD computers: A VLSI implementation. *Journal of Parallel and Distributed Computing*, Vol. 7, 1989, pp. 302–320.

[407] M. Maresca, H. Li, and P. Baglietto. Hardware support for fast reconfigurability in processor arrays. *Proceedings of the International Conference on Parallel Processing*, Vol. 1, 1993, pp. 282–289.

[408] C. Martel and R. Subramonian. Asynchronous PRAM algorithms for list ranking and transitive closure. *Proceedings of the International Conference on Parallel Processing*, Vol. 3, 1990, pp. 60–63.

[409] C. Martel, R. Subramonian, and A. Park. Asynchronous PRAMs are (almost) as good as synchronous PRAMs. *Proceedings of the IEEE Symposium on Foundations of Computer Science*, Vol. 2, 1990, pp. 590–599.

[410] D.L. McBurney and M.R. Sleep. Transputer-based experiments with the ZAPP architecture. *Proceedings of the Conference on Parallel Architectures and Languages Europe (PARLE)*, Lecture Notes in Computer Science, No. 258, Springer-Verlag, Berlin, 1987, pp. 242–259.

[411] R. McNaughton. *Elementary Computability, Formal Languages, and Automata*. Prentice Hall, Englewood Cliffs, New Jersey, 1982.

[412] C. Mead and L. Conway. *Introduction to VLSI Systems*. Addison-Wesley, Reading, Massachusetts, 1980.

[413] N. Megiddo. Applying parallel computation algorithms in the design of serial algorithms. *Journal of the ACM*, Vol. 30, 1983, pp. 852–865.

[414] R. Mehrotra and E.F. Gehringer. Superlinear speedup through randomized algorithms. *Proceedings of the International Conference on Parallel Processing*, 1985, pp. 291–300.

[415] H. Meijer and S.G. Akl. Optimal computation of prefix sums on a binary tree of processors. *International Journal of Parallel Programming*, Vol. 16, 1987, pp. 127–136.

[416] H. Meijer and S.G. Akl. Bit serial addition trees and their applications. *Computing*, Vol. 40, 1988, pp. 9–17.

[417] H. Meijer and S.G. Akl. Parallel binary search with delayed read conflicts. *International Journal of High Speed Computing*, Vol. 2, 1990, pp. 17–21.

[418] R.G. Melhem, D.M. Chiarulli, and S.P. Levitan. Space multiplexing of waveguides in optically interconnected multiprocessor systems. *The Computer Journal*, Vol. 32, 1989, pp. 362–369.

[419] R.A. Melter and I. Stojmenović. Solving city block metric and digital geometry problems on the BSR model of parallel computation. *Journal of Mathematical Imaging and Vision*, Vol. 5, 1995, pp. 119–127.

[420] A. Menn and A.K. Somani. An efficient sorting algorithm for the star graph interconnection network. *Proceedings of the International Conference on Parallel Processing*, Vol. 3, 1990, pp. 1–8.

[421] M.S. Merry and J.W. Baker. A constant time algorithm for the channel assignment problem using the reconfigurable mesh. *Journal of Parallel Algorithms and Applications*, Vol. 6, 1995, pp. 259–271.

[422] M.S. Merry and J.W. Baker. A constant time sorting algorithm for a three dimensional mesh and reconfigurable network. *Parallel Processing Letters*, Vol 5, 1995, pp. 401–412.

[423] M.S. Merry and J.W. Baker. A constant time algorithm for computing the Hough transform on a reconfigurable mesh. *Image and Vision Computing*, Vol. 14, 1996, pp. 35–37.

[424] J. Mikloško, M. Vajteršic, I. Vrťo, and R. Klette. *Fast Algorithms and Their Implementation on Specialized Parallel Computers*. North-Holland, Amsterdam, 1989.

[425] R. Miller, V.K. Prasanna-Kumar, D.I. Reisis, and Q.F. Stout. Data movement operations and applications on reconfigurable VLSI arrays. *Proceedings of the International Conference on Parallel Processing*, Vol. 1, 1988, pp. 205–208.

[426] R. Miller and A. Shuster, eds. *Parallel Processing Letters, Special Issue on Dynamically Reconfigurable Architectures*, Vol. 5, 1995, pp. 1–124.

[427] R. Miller and Q.F. Stout. Mesh computer algorithms for computational geometry. *IEEE Transactions on Computers*, Vol. 38, 1989, pp. 321–340.

[428] M. Minsky. Form and content in computer science. *Journal of the ACM*, Vol. 17, 1970, pp. 197–215.

[429] M. Minsky and S. Papert. *Perceptrons*. MIT Press, Cambridge, Massachusetts, 1969.

[430] G. Miranker, L. Tang, and C.K. Wong. A "zero-time" VLSI sorter. *IBM Journal of Research and Development*, Vol. 27, 1983, pp. 140–148.

[431] J.J. Modi. *Parallel Algorithms and Matrix Computation*. Clarendon Press, Oxford, 1988.

[432] D.I. Moldovan. *Parallel Processing: From Applications to Systems*. Morgan Kaufmann, San Mateo, California, 1993.

[433] H.S. Morse. *Practical Parallel Computing*. Academic Press, New York, 1994.

[434] D.E. Muller and F.P. Preparata. Bounds to complexities of networks for sorting and for switching. *Journal of the ACM*, Vol. 22, 1975, pp. 195–201.

[435] K. Mulmuley. *Computational Geometry: An Introduction through Randomized Algorithms*. Prentice Hall, Englewood Cliffs, New Jersey, 1993.

[436] K. Nakano, T. Masuzawa, and N. Tokura. A sub-logarithmic time sorting algorithm on a reconfigurable array. *IEICE Transactions*, Vol. 74, 1991, pp. 894–901.

[437] D. Nassimi and S. Sahni. Bitonic sort on a mesh-connected parallel computer. *IEEE Transactions on Computers*, Vol. 28, 1979, pp. 2–7.

[438] D. Nassimi and S. Sahni. Data broadcasting in SIMD computers. *IEEE Transactions on Computers*, Vol. 30, 1981, pp. 101–106.

[439] D. Nassimi and S. Sahni. A self-routing Beneš network and parallel permutation algorithms. *IEEE Transactions on Computers*, Vol. 30, 1981, pp. 332–340.

[440] D. Nassimi and S. Sahni. Parallel algorithms to set up the Beneš permutation network. *IEEE Transactions on Computers*, Vol. 31, 1982, pp. 148–154.

[441] D. Nath, S.N. Maheshwari, and P.C.P. Bhatt. Efficient VLSI networks for parallel processing based on orthogonal trees. *IEEE Transactions on Computers*, Vol. 32, 1983, pp. 569–581.

[442] M. Nigam and S. Sahni. Sorting n numbers on $n \times n$ reconfigurable meshes with buses. *Journal of Parallel and Distributed Computing*, Vol. 23, 1994, pp. 37–48.

[443] M. Nigam, S. Sahni, and B. Krishnamurthy. Embedding Hamiltonians and hypercubes in star interconnection graphs. *Proceedings of the International Conference on Parallel Processing*, Vol. 3, 1990, pp. 340–343.

[444] N. Nishimura. Asynchronous shared memory parallel computation. *Proceedings of the ACM Symposium on Parallel Algorithms and Architectures*, 1990, pp. 76–84.

[445] C. Ó'Dúnlaing. Some parallel geometric algorithms. In *Lectures on Parallel Computation*, Vol. 4, A. Gibbons and P. Spirakis, eds. Cambridge University Press, 1993, pp. 77–108.

[446] Y. Ofman. On the algorithmic complexity of discrete functions. *Soviet Physics Doklady*, Vol. 7, 1963, pp. 589–591.

[447] S. Olariu and J.L. Schwing. A novel deterministic sampling scheme with applications to broadcast-efficient sorting on the reconfigurable mesh. *Journal of Parallel and Distributed Computing*, Vol. 32, 1996, pp. 215–222.

[448] S. Olariu, J.L. Schwing, and J. Zhang. On the power of two-dimensional processor arrays with reconfigurable bus systems. *Parallel Processing Letters*, Vol. 1, 1991, pp. 29–34.

[449] S. Olariu, J.L. Schwing, and J. Zhang. Fundamental algorithms on reconfigurable meshes. *Proceedings of the Allerton Conference on Communication, Control, and Computing*, 1991, pp. 811–820.

[450] S. Olariu, J.L. Schwing, and J. Zhang. A constant-time channel-assignment algorithm on reconfigurable meshes. *BIT*, Vol. 32, 1992, pp. 586–597.

[451] S. Olariu, J.L. Schwing, and J. Zhang. Applications of reconfigurable meshes to constant time computations. *Parallel Computing*, Vol. 19, 1993, pp. 229–237.

[452] S. Olariu, J.L. Schwing, and J. Zhang. Integer problems on reconfigurable meshes, with applications. *Journal of Computer and Software Engineering*, Vol. 1, 1993, pp. 33–45.

[453] A.V. Oppenheim and A.S. Willsky. *Signals and Systems*. Prentice Hall, Englewood Cliffs, New Jersey, 1983.

[454] J. O'Rourke. *Computational Geometry in C*. Cambridge University Press, Cambridge, England, 1994.

[455] G.A. Orton, L.E. Peppard, and S.G. Akl. Bi-way sorter: A two-dimensional systolic array. *IEE Proceedings on Computers and Digital Techniques*, Vol. 139, 1992, pp. 147–155.

[456] C.N.K. Osiakwan. *Parallel Computation of Weighted Matchings in Graphs*. Ph.D. Thesis, Department of Computing and Information Science, Queen's University, Kingston, Ontario, 1991.

[457] C.N.K. Osiakwan and S.G. Akl. A perfect speedup parallel algorithm for the assignment problem on complete weighted bipartite graphs. In *Parallel Architectures*, N. Rishe, S. Navathe, and D. Tal, eds. IEEE Computer Society Press, Los Alamitos, California, 1991, pp. 161–180.

[458] C.N.K. Osiakwan and S.G. Akl. Parallel computation of matchings in trees. *Parallel Computing*, Vol. 17, 1991, pp. 643–656.

[459] C.N.K. Osiakwan and S.G. Akl. An EP algorithm for computing a minimum weight perfect matching for a set of points in the plane. *ORSA Journal on Computing*, Vol. 6, 1994, pp. 436–444.

[460] C.N.K. Osiakwan and S.G. Akl. An efficient parallel algorithm for the assignment problem on the plane. *Journal of Parallel Algorithms and Applications*, Vol. 4, 1994, pp. 193–210.

[461] C.N.K. Osiakwan and S.G. Akl. The maximum weight perfect matching problem for complete weighted graphs is in PC*. *Journal of Parallel Algorithms and Applications*, Vol. 6, 1995, pp. 143–166.

[462] T.A. Ottman, A.L. Rosenberg, and L.J. Stockmeyer. A dictionary machine (for VLSI). *IEEE Transactions on Computers*, Vol. 31, 1982, pp. 892–897.

[463] Y. Pan. A more efficient constant time algorithm for computing the Hough transform. *Parallel Processing Letters*, Vol. 4, 1994, pp. 45–52.

[464] V.Y. Pan and F.P. Preparata. Supereffective slow-down of parallel computations. *Proceedings of the ACM Symposium on Parallel Algorithms and Architectures*, 1992, pp. 402–409.

[465] C.H. Papadimitriou and K. Steiglitz. *Combinatorial Optimization*. Prentice Hall, Englewood Cliffs, New Jersey, 1982.

[466] I. Parberry. *Parallel Complexity Theory*. Research Notes in Theoretical Computer Science, Pitman Publishing, London, 1987.

[467] I. Parberry. Single-exception sorting networks and the computational complexity of optimal sorting network verification. *Mathematical Systems Theory*, Vol. 23, 1990, pp. 81–93.

[468] I. Parberry. *Circuit Complexity and Neural Networks*. MIT Press, Cambridge, Massachusetts, 1994.

[469] B. Parker and I. Parberry. Constructing sorting networks from k-sorters. *Information Processing Letters*, Vol. 33, 1989/90, pp. 157–162.

[470] D. Parkinson. Parallel efficiency can be greater than unity. *Parallel Computing*, Vol. 3, 1986, pp. 261–262.

[471] M.S. Paterson. Improved sorting networks with $O(\log N)$ depth. *Algorithmica*, Vol. 5, 1990, pp. 75–92.

[472] S. Patil and P. Banerjee. A parallel branch and bound algorithm for test generation. *IEEE Transactions on Computer Aided Design*, Vol. 9, 1990, pp. 313–322.

[473] W. Patterson. *Mathematical Cryptology*. Rowman and Littlefield, Totowa, New Jersey, 1987.

[474] W. Paul. On-line simulation of $k+1$ tapes by k tapes requires nonlinear time. *Information and Control*, Vol. 53, 1982, pp. 1–8.

[475] W. Paul. A note on bitonic sorting. *Information Processing Letters*, Vol. 49, 1994, pp. 223–225.

[476] S. Pavel and S.G. Akl. Efficient algorithms for the Euclidean distance transform. *Parallel Processing Letters*, Vol. 5, 1995, pp. 205–212.

[477] S. Pavel and S.G. Akl. Area-time trade-offs in arrays with optical pipelined buses. *Applied Optics*, Vol. 35, 1996, pp. 1827–1835.

[478] S. Pavel and S.G. Akl. Matrix operations using arrays with reconfigurable optical buses. *Journal of Parallel Algorithms and Applications*, Vol. 8, 1996, pp. 223–242.

[479] S. Pavel and S.G. Akl. Efficient algorithms for the Hough transform on arrays with reconfigurable optical buses. *Proceedings of the International Parallel Processing Symposium*, 1996, pp. 697–701.

[480] S. Pavel and S.G. Akl. On the power of arrays with reconfigurable optical buses. *Proceedings of the International Conferenceon Parallel and Distributed Processing Techniques and Applications*, 1996, pp. 1443–1454.

[481] S. Pavel and S.G. Akl. Integer sorting and routing in arrays with reconfigurable optical buses. *Proceedings of the International Conference on Parallel Processing*, Vol. 2, 1996, pp. 90–94.

[482] S. Pavel and S.G. Akl. Algorithmic aspects of meshes enhanced with broadcast buses. In *Advances in Parallel Algorithms*, D. Evans, ed. Gordon and Breach Science Publishers, New York, 1996, in press.

[483] M.C. Pease. Matrix inversion using parallel processing. *Journal of the ACM*, Vol. 14, 1967, pp. 757–764.

[484] M.C. Pease. An adaptation of the fast Fourier transform for parallel processing. *Journal of the ACM*, Vol. 15, 1968, pp. 252–264.

[485] M.C. Pease. The indirect binary n-cube microprocessor array. *IEEE Transactions on Computers*, Vol. 26, 1977, pp. 458–473.

[486] R. Penrose. *The Emperor's New Mind*. Oxford University Press, New York, 1989.

[487] R. Penrose. *Shadows of the Mind*. Oxford University Press, New York, 1994.

[488] Y. Perl. The bitonic and odd-even networks are more than merging. Technical Report No. DCS-TR-123, Department of Computer Science, Rutgers University, New Brunswick, New Jersey, 1983.

[489] R.H. Perrott. *Parallel Programming*. Addison-Wesley, Reading, Massachusetts, 1987.

[490] K. Perumalla and N. Deo. Parallel algorithms for maximum subsequence and maximum subarray. *Parallel Processing Letters*, Vol. 5, 1995, pp. 367–373.

[491] G.F. Pfister. *In Search of Clusters*. Prentice Hall, Upper Saddle River, New Jersey, 1995.

[492] G.C. Plaxton. Load balancing, selection and sorting on the hypercube. *Proceedings of the ACM Symposium on Parallel Algorithms and Architectures*, 1989, pp. 64–73.

[493] G.C. Plaxton. On the network complexity of selection. *Proceedings of the IEEE Symposium on Foundations of Computer Science*, 1989, pp. 396–401.

[494] J.L. Potter. Programming the MPP. In *The Massively Parallel Processor*, J.L. Potter, ed. MIT Press, Cambridge, Massachusetts, 1985, pp. 218–229.

[495] J.L. Potter, ed. *The Massively Parallel Processor*. MIT Press, Cambridge, Massachusetts, 1985.

[496] J.L. Potter. *Associative Computing—A Programming Paradigm for Massively Parallel Computers*. Plenum Publishing, New York, 1992.

[497] J.L. Potter, J.W. Baker, S.L. Scott, A. Bansal, C. Leangsuksun, and C. Asthagiri. ASC: An associative computing paradigm. *Computer*, Vol. 27, 1994, pp. 19–25.

[498] V.K. Prasanna Kumar and C.S. Raghavendra. Array processor with multiple broadcasting. *Journal of Parallel and Distributed Computing*, Vol. 4 1987, pp. 173–190.

[499] B.R. Preiss and V.C. Hamacher. Semi-static dataflow. *Proceedings of the International Conference on Parallel Processing*, 1988, pp. 127–134.

[500] F.P. Preparata and M.I. Shamos. *Computational Geometry: An Introduction*. Springer-Verlag, New York, 1985.

[501] F.P. Preparata and J.E. Vuillemin. Area-time optimal VLSI networks for matrix multiplication. *Proceedings of the Princeton Conference on Information Science and Systems*, 1980, pp. 300–309.

[502] F.P. Preparata and J.E. Vuillemin. The cube-connected cycles: A versatile network for parallel computation. *Communications of the ACM*, Vol. 24, 1981, pp. 300–309.

[503] W.H. Press, B.P. Flannery, S.A. Teukolsky, and W.T. Vetterling. *Numerical Recipes: The Art of Scientific Computing*. Cambridge University Press, Cambridge, England, 1986.

[504] K. Preston, Jr., and L. Uhr, eds. *Multicomputers and Image Processing: Algorithms and Programs*. Academic Press, New York, 1982.

[505] C. Qiao and R.G. Melhem. Time-division optical communications in multiprocessor arrays. *IEEE Transactions on Computers*, Vol. 42, 1993, pp. 577–590.

[506] C. Qiao, R.G. Melhem, D.M. Chiarulli, and S.P. Levitan. Dynamic reconfiguration of optically interconnected networks with time-division multiplexing. *Journal of Parallel and Distributed Computing*, Vol. 22, 1994, pp. 268–278.

[507] K. Qiu. *The Star and Pancake Interconnection Networks: Properties and Algorithms*. Ph.D. Thesis, Department of Computing and Information Science, Queen's University, Kingston, Ontario, 1992.

[508] K. Qiu and S.G. Akl. Load balancing, selection and sorting on the star and pancake interconnection networks. *Journal of Parallel Algorithms and Applications*, Vol. 2, 1994, pp. 27–42.

[509] K. Qiu and S.G. Akl. On some properties of the star graph. *Journal of VLSI Design, Special Issue on Interconnection Networks*, Vol. 2, 1994, pp. 389–396.

[510] K. Qiu, S.G. Akl, and H. Meijer. On some properties and algorithms for the star and pancake interconnection networks. *Journal of Parallel and Distributed Computing*, Vol. 22, 1994, pp. 16–25.

[511] K. Qiu, H. Meijer, and S.G. Akl. Parallel routing and sorting on the pancake network. *Proceedings of the International Conference on Computing and Information*, Lecture Notes in Computer Science, No. 497, Springer-Verlag, Berlin, 1991, pp. 360–371.

[512] K. Qiu, H. Meijer, and S.G. Akl. Decomposing a star graph into disjoint cycles. *Information Processing Letters*, Vol. 39, 1991, pp. 125–129.

[513] K. Qiu, H. Meijer, and S.G. Akl. On the cycle structure of star graphs. *Congressus Numerantium*, Vol. 96, 1993, pp. 123–141.

[514] M.J. Quinn. *Designing Efficient Algorithms for Parallel Computers*. McGraw-Hill, New York, 1987.

[515] M.J. Quinn. *Parallel Computing: Theory and Practice*. McGraw-Hill, New York, 1994.

[516] M.J. Quinn and N. Deo. An upper bound for the speedup of best-bound branch-and-bound algorithms. *BIT*, Vol. 26, 1986, pp. 35–43.

[517] P. Quinton and Y. Robert. *Algorithmiques et Architectures Systoliques*. Masson, Paris, 1989.

[518] P. Quinton and Y. Robert, eds. *Algorithms and Parallel VLSI Architectures*. Elsevier, Amsterdam, 1992.

[519] P. Ragde. Analysis of an asynchronous PRAM algorithm. *Information processing Letters*, Vol. 39, 1991, pp. 253–256.

[520] P. Ragde. The parallel simplicity of compaction and chaining. *Journal of Algorithms*, Vol. 14, 1993, pp. 371–380.

[521] C.S. Raghavendra. HMESH: A VLSI architecture for parallel processing. *Proceedings of the Conference on Algorithms and Hardware for Parallel Processing*, 1986, pp. 76–83.

[522] V. Rajan, R.K. Ghosh, and P. Gupta. An efficient parallel algorithm for random sampling. *Information Processing Letters*, Vol. 30, 1989, pp. 265–268.

[523] S. Rajasekaran. Sorting and selection on interconnection networks. In *Interconnection Networks and Mapping and Scheduling Parallel Computations*, D.F. Hsu, A.L. Rosenberg, and D. Sotteau, eds. DIMACS Series in Discrete Mathematics and Theoretical Computer Science, Vol. 21, 1995, pp. 275–296.

[524] S. Rajasekaran and J.H. Reif. Optimal and sublogarithmic time randomized parallel sorting algorithms. *SIAM Journal on Computing*, Vol. 18, 1989, pp. 594–607.

[525] C.V. Ramamoorthy, J.L. Turner, and B.W. Wah. A design of a fast cellular associative memory for ordered retrieval. *IEEE Transactions on Computers*, Vol. 27, 1978, pp. 800–815.

[526] S. Ranka and S. Sahni. *Hypercube Algorithms*. Springer-Verlag, New York, 1990.

[527] V.N. Rao and V. Kumar. Parallel depth-first search, Part I: Implementation. *International Journal of Parallel Programming*, Vol. 16, 1987, pp. 479–499.

[528] V.N. Rao and V. Kumar. On the efficiency of parallel backtracking. *IEEE Transactions on Parallel and Distributed Systems*, Vol. 4, 1993, pp. 427–437.

[529] G.J.E. Rawlins. *Compared to What?* W.H. Freeman, New York, 1992.

[530] D.A. Reed and R.M. Fujimoto. *Multicomputer Networks*. MIT Press, Cambridge, Massachusetts, 1987.

[531] P.K. Rees and F.W. Sparks. *Calculus with Analytic Geometry*. McGraw-Hill, New York, 1969.

[532] J.H. Reif. Probabilistic parallel prefix computation. *Proceedings of the International Conference on Parallel Processing*, 1984, pp. 291–298.

[533] J.H. Reif, ed. *Synthesis of Parallel Algorithms*. Morgan Kaufmann, San Mateo, California, 1993.

[534] J.H. Reif and L.G. Valiant. A logarithmic time sort for linear size networks. *Proceedings of the ACM Symposium on Theory of Computing*, 1983, pp. 10–16.

[535] E.M. Reingold, J. Nievergelt, and N. Deo. *Combinatorial Algorithms: Theory and Practice*. Prentice Hall, Englewood Cliffs, New Jersey, 1977.

[536] R. Reischuck. A fast probabilistic sorting algorithm. *Proceedings of the IEEE Symposium on Foundations of Computer Science*, 1981, pp. 212–219.

[537] Y. Robert. *The Impact of Vector and Parallel Architectures on the Gaussian Elimination Algorithm*. Manchester University Press, Manchester, England, 1990.

[538] F. Rosenblatt. *Principles of Neurodynamics*. Spartan Books, New York, 1962.

[539] J. Rost and E. Maehle. Implementation of a parallel branch-and-bound algorithm for the traveling salesman problem. *Proceedings of the Conference on Parallel Processing (CONPAR)*, 1988, pp. 152–159.

[540] J. Rothstein. Bus automata, brains, and mental models. *IEEE Transactions on Systems, Man and Cybernetics*, Vol. 18, 1988, pp. 522–531.

[541] L. Rudolph. A robust sorting network. *IEEE Transactions on Computers*, Vol. 34, 1985, pp. 326–335.

[542] K. Ryu and J. JáJá. Efficient algorithms for list ranking and for solving graph problems on the hypercube. *IEEE Transactions on Parallel and Distributed Systems*, Vol. 1, 1990, pp. 83–90.

[543] G.W. Sabot, ed. *High Performance Computing: Problem Solving with Parallel and Vector Architectures*. Addison-Wesley, Reading, Massachusetts, 1995.

[544] K. Sado and Y. Igarashi. Some parallel sorts on a mesh-connected array and their time efficiency. *Journal of Parallel and Distributed Computing*, Vol. 3, 1986, pp. 398–410.

[545] M.R. Samatham and D.K. Pradhan. The de Bruijn multiprocessor network: A versatile parallel processing and sorting network for VLSI. *IEEE Transactions on Computers*, Vol. 38, 1989, pp. 567–581.

[546] M.R. Samatham and D.K. Pradhan. Correction to "The de Bruijn multiprocessor network: A versatile parallel processing and sorting network for VLSI." *IEEE Transactions on Computers*, Vol. 40, 1991, pp. 122–123.

[547] J. Sanz and R. Cypher. Data reduction and fast routing: A strategy for efficient algorithms for message-passing parallel computers. *Algorithmica*, Vol. 7, 1992, pp. 77–89.

[548] C. Savage and J. JáJá. Fast, efficient parallel algorithms for some graph problems. *SIAM Journal on Computing*, Vol. 10, 1981, pp. 682–691.

[549] S. Saxena, P.C.P. Bhatt, and V.C. Prasad. On parallel prefix computation. *Parallel Processing Letters*, Vol. 4, 1994, pp. 429–436.

[550] I.D. Scherson, S. Sen, and A. Shamir. ShearSort: A true two-dimensional sorting technique for VLSI networks. *Proceedings of the International Conference on Parallel Processing*, 1986, pp. 903–908.

[551] H. Schmeck and H. Schröder. Dictionary machines for different models of VLSI. *IEEE Transactions on Computers*, Vol. 34, 1985, pp. 151–155.

[552] P.B. Schneck. Superlinear speed-up and the halting problem. *Software—Practice and Experience*, Vol. 16, 1986, pp. 781–782.

[553] C.P. Schnorr and A. Shamir. An optimal sorting algorithm for mesh connected computers. *Proceedings of the ACM Symposium on Theory of Computing*, 1986, pp. 255–261.

[554] H. Schröder. Partition sorts for VLSI. *Informatik Fachberichte*, Vol. 73, 1983, pp. 101–116.

[555] W. Schröder-Preikschat. *The Logical Design of Parallel Operating Systems*. Prentice Hall, Englewood Cliffs, New Jersey, 1994.

[556] J.T. Schwartz. Ultracomputers. *ACM Transactions on Programming Languages and Systems*, Vol. 2, 1980, pp. 484–521.

[557] J. Seberry and J. Pieprzyk. *Cryptography: An Introduction to Computer Security*. Prentice Hall, Sydney, Australia, 1989.

[558] C.L. Seitz. Concurrent VLSI architectures. *IEEE Transactions on Computers*, Vol. 33, 1984, pp. 1247–1265.

[559] C.L. Seitz. The cosmic cube. *Communications of the ACM*, Vol. 28, 1985, pp. 22–33.

[560] M.J. Serrano and B. Parhami. Optimal architectures and algorithms for mesh-connected parallel computers with separable row/column buses. *IEEE Transactions on Parallel and Distributed Systems*, Vol. 4, 1993, pp. 1073–1079.

[561] C.E. Shannon. Memory requirements in a telephone exchange. *The Bell System Technical Journal*, Vol. 29, 1950, pp. 343–349.

[562] J.A. Sharp. *Data Flow Computing*. Ellis Horwood, Chichester, England, 1985.

[563] H. Shi, G.X. Ritter, and J.N. Wilson. Simulations between two reconfigurable mesh models. *Information Processing Letters*, Vol. 55, 1995, pp. 137–142.

[564] Y. Shiloach and U. Vishkin. Finding the maximum, merging, and sorting in a parallel computation model. *Journal of Algorithms*, Vol. 2, 1981, pp. 88–102.

[565] Y. Shiloach and U. Vishkin. An $O(\log n)$ parallel connectivity algorithm. *Journal of Algorithms*, Vol. 3, 1982, pp. 57–67.

[566] S.G. Shiva. *Pipelined and Parallel Computer Architectures*. HarperCollins, New York, 1996.

[567] R. Shonkwiler, F. Ghannadian, and C.O. Alford. Parallel simulated annealing for the n-queen problem. *Software—Practice and Experience*, Vol. 16, 1986, pp. 781–782.

[568] R. Shonkwiler and E.S. van Vleck. Parallel speed-up of Monte Carlo methods for global optimization. *Journal of Complexity*, Vol. 10, 1994, pp. 64–95.

[569] P.W. Shor. Algorithms for quantum computation: Discrete logarithms and factoring. *Proceedings of the IEEE Symposium on Foundations of Computer Science*, 1994, pp. 124–134.

[570] D.B. Shu and J.G. Nash. The gated interconnection network for dynamic programming. In *Concurrent Computations*, S.K. Tewsburg, B.W. Dickinson, and S.C. Schwartz, eds. Plenum Publishing, New York, 1988, pp. 645–658.

[571] H.J. Siegel. *Interconnection Networks for Large Scale Parallel Processing*. D.C. Heath, Lexington, Massachusetts, 1985.

[572] H.T. Siegelmann. Computation beyond the Turing limit. *Science*, Vol. 268, 1995. pp. 545–548.

[573] H.T. Siegelmann and E.D. Sontag. Analog computation via neural networks. *Theoretical Computer Science*, Vol. 131, 1994, pp. 331–360.

[574] J.D. Smith. *Design and Analysis of Algorithms*. PWS-KENT, Boston, 1989.

[575] J.R. Smith. *The Design and Analysis of Parallel Algorithms*. Oxford University Press, New York, 1993.

[576] M. Snir. On parallel searching. *SIAM Journal on Computing*, Vol. 14, 1985, pp. 688–708.

[577] M. Snir. Depth-size tradeoffs for parallel prefix computation. *Journal of Algorithms*, Vol. 7, 1986, pp. 185–201.

[578] L. Snyder. Introduction to the configurable, highly parallel computer. *Computer*, Vol. 15, 1982, pp. 47–56.

[579] L. Snyder. Type architectures, shared memory, and the corollary of modest potential. *Annual Review of Computer Science*, Vol. 1, 1986, pp. 289–317.

[580] L. Snyder, L.H. Jamieson, D.B. Gannon, and H.J. Siegel, eds. *Algorithmically Specialized Parallel Computers*. Academic Press, Orlando, Florida, 1985.

[581] E. Speckenmeyer. Is average superlinear speedup possible? *Proceedings of the Workshop on Computer Science Logic*, Lecture Notes in Computer Science, No. 329, Springer-Verlag, Berlin, 1988, pp. 301–312.

[582] E. Speckenmeyer, B. Monien, and O. Vornberger. Superlinear speedup for parallel backtracking. *Proceedings of the International Conference on Supercomputing*, Lecture Notes in Computer Science, No. 297, Springer-Verlag, Berlin, 1988, pp. 985–993.

[583] F. Springsteel and I. Stojmenović. Parallel general prefix computations with geometric, algebraic and other applications. *International Journal of Parallel Programming*, Vol. 18, 1989, pp. 485–503.

[584] C. Stanfill and B. Kahle. Parallel free text search on the connection machine system. *Communications of the ACM*, Vol. 29, 1986, pp. 1229–1239.

[585] I. Stojmenović. Computational geometry on a hypercube. *Proceedings of the International Conference on Parallel Processing*, Vol. 3, 1988, pp. 100–103.

[586] I. Stojmenović. An optimal algorithm for generating equivalence relations on a linear array of processors. *BIT*, Vol. 30, 1990, pp. 424–436.

[587] I. Stojmenović. A simple systolic algorithm for generating combinations in lexicographic order. *Computers and Mathematics with Applications*, Vol. 24, 1992, pp. 61–64.

[588] I. Stojmenović. On random and adaptive parallel generation of combinatorial objects. *International Journal of Computer Mathematics*, Vol. 42, 1992, pp. 125–135.

[589] I. Stojmenović. Direct interconnection networks. In *Parallel and Distributed Computing Handbook*, A.Y. Zomaya, ed. McGraw-Hill, New York, 1996, pp. 537–567.

[590] H.S. Stone. Parallel processing with the perfect shuffle. *IEEE Transactions on Computers*, Vol. 20, 1971, pp. 153–161.

[591] H.S. Stone. An efficient parallel algorithm for the solution of a tridiagonal linear system of equations. *Journal of the ACM*, Vol. 20, 1973, pp. 27–38.

[592] H.S. Stone. Parallel tridiagonal equation solvers. *ACM Transactions on Mathematical Software*, Vol. 1, 1975, pp. 289–307.

[593] H.S. Stone, ed. *Introduction to Computer Architecture*. Science Research Associates, Chicago, 1980.

[594] H.S. Stone. *High-Performance Computer Architecture*. Addison-Wesley, Reading, Massachusetts, 1987.

[595] H.S. Stone. Parallel querying of large databases: A case study. *Computer*, Vol. 20, 1987, pp. 11–21.

[596] Q.F. Stout. Sorting, merging, selecting and filtering on tree and pyramid machines. *Proceedings of the International Conference on Parallel Processing*, 1983, pp. 214–221.

[597] Q.F. Stout. Mesh-connected computers with broadcasting. *IEEE Transactions on Computers*, Vol. 32, 1983, pp. 826–830.

[598] Q.F. Stout. Meshes with multiple buses. *Proceedings of the IEEE Symposium on Foundations of Computer Science*, 1986, pp. 264–273.

[599] Q.F. Stout. Supporting divide-and-conquer algorithms for image processing. *Journal of Parallel and Distributed Computing*, Vol. 4, 1987, pp. 95–115.

[600] R. Suaya and G. Birtwistle, eds. *VLSI and Parallel Computation.* Morgan Kaufmann, San Mateo, California, 1990.

[601] X.H. Sun and J.L. Gustafson. Toward a better parallel performance metric. *Parallel Computing*, Vol. 17, 1991, pp. 1093–1109.

[602] X.H. Sun and L.M. Ni. Another view on parallel speedup. *Proceedings of Supercomputing '90*, 1990, pp. 324–333.

[603] S. Sur and P.K. Srimani. A fault tolerant routing algorithm in star graphs. *Proceedings of the International Conference on Parallel Processing*, Vol. 3, 1991, pp. 267–270.

[604] S.L. Tanimoto. Sorting, histogramming, and other statistical operations on a pyramid machine. Technical Report 82-08-02, Department of Computer Science, University of Washington, Seattle, Washington, 1982.

[605] S.L. Tanimoto. Programming techniques for hierarchical parallel image processors. In *Multicomputers and Image Processing: Algorithms and Programs*, K. Preston, Jr., and L. Uhr, eds. Academic Press, New York, 1982, pp. 421–429.

[606] S.L. Tanimoto and T. Pavlidis. A hierarchical data structure for picture processing. *Computer Graphics and Image Processing*, Vol. 4, 1975, pp. 104–119.

[607] R.E. Tarjan and U. Vishkin. An efficient parallel biconnectivity algorithm. *SIAM Journal of Computing*, Vol. 14, 1985, pp. 862–874.

[608] P. Thangavel and V.P. Muthuswamy. Parallel algorithms for addition and multiplication on processor arrays with reconfigurable bus systems. *Information Processing Letters*, Vol. 46, 1993, pp. 89–94.

[609] C. Thompkins. Machine attacks on problems whose variables are permutations. *Numerical Analysis*, Vol. 6, 1956, pp. 195–211.

[610] C.D. Thompson. *A Complexity Theory for VLSI.* Ph.D. thesis, Computer Science Department, Carnegie-Mellon University, Pittsburgh, 1980.

[611] C.D. Thompson. Fourier tansforms in VLSI. *IEEE Transactions on Computers*, Vol. 32, 1983, pp. 1047–1057.

[612] C.D. Thompson and H.T. Kung. Sorting on a mesh-connected parallel computer. *Communications of the ACM*, Vol. 20, 1977, pp. 263–271.

[613] S. Todd. Algorithms and hardware for a merge sort using multiple processors. *IBM Journal of Research and Development*, Vol. 22, 1978, pp. 509–517.

[614] A. Trew and G. Wilson, eds. *Past, Present, Parallel.* Springer-Verlag, Berlin, 1991.

[615] J.D. Ullman. *Computational Aspects of VLSI.* Computer Science Press, Rockville, Maryland, 1984.

[616] D.R. Ulm and J.W. Baker. Solving a two-dimensional knapsack problem on a mesh with multiple buses. *Proceedings of the International Conference on Parallel Processing,* Vol. 3, 1995, pp. 168–171.

[617] H. Usui, M. Yamashita, M. Imai, and T. Ibaraki. Parallel searches of game trees. *Systems and Computers in Japan,* Vol. 18, 1987, pp. 97–109.

[618] L.G. Valiant. Parallelism in comparison problems. *SIAM Journal of Computing,* Vol. 4, 1975, pp. 348–355.

[619] L.G. Valiant. A bridging model for parallel computation. *Communications of the ACM,* Vol. 33, 1990, pp. 103–111.

[620] L.G. Valiant. General purpose parallel architectures. In *Handbook of Theoretical Computer Science,* Vol. A, J. van Leeuwen, ed. Elsevier, Amsterdam, 1990, pp. 943–971.

[621] A. Varma and C.S. Raghavendra, eds. *Interconnection Networks for Multiprocessors and Multicomputers.* IEEE Computer Society Press, Los Alamitos, California, 1994.

[622] U. Vishkin. Implementation of simultaneous memory address access in models that forbid it. *Journal of Algorithms,* Vol. 4, 1983, pp. 45–50.

[623] U. Vishkin. A parallel-design distributed implementation (PDDI) general-purpose computer. *Theoretical Computer Science,* Vol. 32, 1984, pp. 157–172.

[624] U. Vishkin. Randomized speedups in parallel computation. *Proceedings of the ACM Symposium on Theory of Computing,* 1984, pp. 230–239.

[625] U. Vishkin. On efficient parallel strong orientation. *Information Processing Letters,* Vol. 20, 1985, pp. 235–240.

[626] U. Vishkin. Randomized parallel speedups for list ranking. *Journal of Parallel and Distributed Computing,* Vol. 4, 1987, pp. 319–333.

[627] U. Vishkin. An optimal parallel algorithm for selection. *Advances in Computing Research, Special Issue: Parallel and Distributed Computing,* Vol. 4, 1987, pp. 79–86.

[628] U. Vishkin. Can parallel algorithms enhance serial implementation? *SIGACT News,* Vol. 22, 1991, p. 63.

[629] H. Volger. Some results on addition/subtraction chains. *Information Processing Letters,* Vol. 20, 1985, pp. 155–160.

[630] W. Wagner and Y. Han. Parallel algorithms for bucket sorting and data dependent prefix problems. *Proceedings of the International Conference on Parallel Processing*, 1986, pp. 924–930.

[631] B.W. Wah and K.L. Chen. A partitioning approach to the design of selection networks. *IEEE Transactions on Computers*, Vol. 33, 1984, pp. 261–268.

[632] W. Wah and S.G. Akl. Simulating multiple memory accesses in logarithmic time and linear space. *The Computer Journal*, Vol. 35, 1992, pp. 85–88.

[633] A. Waksman. A permutation network. *Journal of the ACM*, Vol. 15, 1968, pp. 159–163.

[634] B.F. Wang and G.H. Chen. Two-dimensional processor array with reconfigurable bus system is at least as powerful as CRCW model. *Information Processing Letters*, Vol. 36, 1990, pp. 31–36.

[635] B.F. Wang and G.H. Chen. Constant time algorithm for transitive closure and some related graph problems on processor arrays with reconfigurable bus systems. *IEEE Transactions on Parallel and Distributed Systems*, Vol. 1, 1990, pp. 500–507.

[636] B.F. Wang, G.H. Chen, and F.C. Lin. Constant time sorting on a processor array with reconfigurable bus system. *Information Processing Letters*, Vol. 34, 1990, pp. 187–192.

[637] W.H. Ware. The ultimate computer. *IEEE Spectrum*, Vol. 9, 1972, pp. 84–91.

[638] B.W. Weide. Modeling unusual behavior of parallel algorithms. *IEEE Transactions on Computers*, Vol. 31, 1989, pp. 1126–1130.

[639] Z. Wen. Parallel multiple search. *Information Processing Letters*, Vol. 37, 1991, pp. 181–186.

[640] B. Wilkinson. *Computer Architecture: Design and Performance*. Prentice Hall, London, 1991.

[641] G.V. Wilson. *Practical Parallel Programming*. MIT Press, Cambridge, Massachusetts, 1996.

[642] S. Winograd. On the parallel evaluation of certain arithmetic expressions. *Journal of the ACM*, Vol. 22, 1975, pp. 477–492.

[643] D. Wood. *Theory of Computation*. Harper & Row, New York, 1987.

[644] C. Wu and T. Feng, eds. *Interconnection Networks for Parallel and Distributed Processing*. IEEE Computer Society Press, Los Alamitos, California, 1984.

[645] J.C. Wyllie. *The Complexity of Parallel Computations.* Ph.D. Thesis, Department of Computer Science, Cornell University, Ithaca, New York, 1979.

[646] A.C.C. Yao and F.F. Yao. Lower bounds on merging networks. *Journal of the ACM*, Vol. 23, 1976, pp. 566–571.

[647] H. Yasuura, N. Tagaki, and S. Yajima. The parallel enumeration sorting scheme for VLSI. *IEEE Transactions on Computers*, Vol. 31, 1982, pp. 1192–1201.

[648] C.N. Zhang and D.Y. Yun. Multidimensional systolic networks for discrete Fourier transform. *Proceedings of the International Symposium on Computer Architecture*, 1984, pp. 215–222.

[649] A.Y. Zomaya, ed. *Parallel and Distributed Computing Handbook.* McGraw-Hill, New York, 1996.

[650] A.Y. Zomaya, ed. *Parallel Computing: Paradigms and Applications.* International Thomson Computer Press, London, 1996.

[651] A. Zorat. *A Divide-and-Conquer Computer.* Ph.D. Thesis, Department of Computer Science, University of Southern California, Los Angeles, California, 1979.

Index